Essential Readings in
Management Learning

Christopher Grey is Reader in Organizational Theory at the Judge Institute of Management at the University of Cambridge and Fellow of Wolfson College, Cambridge. Having been Reviews Editor of *Management Learning*, he became its joint Editor-in-Chief in 1999. He is also a European Co-editor of the *Journal of Management Inquiry* and sits on the editorial boards of several journals. His research expertise includes management education, training and socialization in professional services and organizational theory. Apart from publishing widely in these areas, he is a member of the Executive Committee of the Management Education and Development Division of the American Academy of Management; has been a member of the Department for Education and Skills' National Educational Research Forum and was Chair of its Task Group on educational research quality. He is also Chair of the Management Research Advisory Forum to the National College for School Leadership. He has been a Visiting Fellow at the Stockholm Centre for Organizational Research, Sweden and is a Fellow of the ESRC Centre for Skills, Knowledge and Economic Performance (SKOPE).

Elena Antonacopoulou is Professor of Organizational Behaviour and Director of GNOSIS, a centre of Excellence in Management Research at the School of Management at the University of Liverpool. She is also a Fellow of the Advanced Institute of Management (AIM). Having been Reviews Editor of *Management Learning*, she became its joint Editor-in-Chief in 2000. She serves on the editorial boards of several journals including the Academy of Management Learning and Education Journal. Her research expertise includes organizational learning and knowing, human resource development and organizational change. Apart from publishing widely in these areas, she has served on several executive positions in the Management Education and Development Division of the American Academy of Management leading to her election as Division Chair in 2001. She has also served as a Chair of the Ethics Committee and Representative-at-large of the Board of Governors of the American Academy of Management and is currently serving a second term of office following her re-election on the Board of the European Group for Organization Studies.

Essential Readings in Management Learning

Edited by

Christopher Grey

and

Elena Antonacopoulou

⑤SAGE Publications
London • Thousand Oaks • New Delhi

Introduction and editorial arrangement © Christopher Grey
and Elena Antonacopoulou 2004
Chapters 1–23 © SAGE Publications Ltd 2003

First published 2004

SAGE Publications Ltd
1 Oliver's Yard
55 City Road
London EC1Y 15P

SAGE Publications Inc.
2455 Teller Road
Thousand Oaks, California 91320

SAGE Publications India Pvt Ltd
B-42, Panchsheel Enclave
Post Box 4109
New Delhi 110 017

British Library Cataloguing in Publication data

A catalogue record for this book is available from the British
Library

ISBN 1-4129-0141-3
ISBN 1-4129-0142-1 (pbk)

Library of Congress Control Number: 2004104840

Typeset by Photoprint, Torquay, Devon
Printed in Great Britain by The Cromwell Press Ltd,
Trowbridge, Wiltshire

Contents

Acknowledgements

As this book arises from work published in the journal *Management Learning* since 1994, it is appropriate that we thank all those who have been involved in its editorship and publication in that period. These include a succession of Commissioning Editors at SAGE Publications: Sue Jones, who brought the journal to SAGE in the first place; Rosemary Nixon, who appointed us as its Editors-in-Chief and Kiren Shoman, the current Commissioning Editor of the journal and of this book. Many others have been involved on the production and marketing side of the journal and we thank them all: former editors – David Sims, Laurie McCauley and Yiannis Gabriel, as well as current Associate Editors – Steve Fox and Gordon Dehler, and Emeritus Editors – Joe Raelin and Mark Easterby-Smith, have all played a major part in developing the work we showcase here. The one continuity throughout these changes, whose contribution we gratefully acknowledge, is Linda Birch, Editorial Assistant to the journal. All of the readings reprinted were anonymously peer-reviewed prior to acceptance for the journal. This system, whilst acting as a hallmark of quality, requires considerable effort from reviewers, which often goes un-recognized, so we are particularly pleased to acknowledge it here. Finally, and most importantly, we gratefully acknowledge the authors of each of the readings reproduced in this volume.

Christopher Grey and Elena Antonacopoulou

Introduction

Overview

This reader reprints a selection of contributions to the journal *Management Learning*, which have appeared since its launch a decade ago. Each was originally published after an anonymous peer review process. Taken together, we believe that the readings constitute a selection of some of the best and most innovative writing within the field since the journal's inception in 1994. In fact, *Management Learning* was a re-launch of its predecessor, *Management Education and Development* which, for a quarter of a century, had provided an interface between the latest academic thinking in the field and practitioners of, in particular, organizational development and consulting. The relaunched journal had new publishers and new editors and, in some respects, a new purpose. Yet, both then and now, it continues to offer a bridge between theory and practice and to be concerned with innovative ideas. Perhaps nowadays it has the appearance of being a more 'academic' journal, and this was part of its new purpose. In 2000, *Management Learning* was the highest ranked management journal in the Social Science Citation Index edited from outside the US, and it continues to be one of the top academic journals in the management field.

However, the journal continues to speak of and to the lived experience of people in organizations and in training and educational institutions. It does so in ways that are increasingly sophisticated and that are, and this too was part of the purpose of the re-launch, increasingly international. Nowadays, around two thirds of the published output of the journal originates from outside the UK. More than anything else, the journal has promoted a view of management, learning and 'management learning', which is extremely broad and catholic. Like our editorial predecessors we have tried to envisage management learning as potentially encompassing a range of issues far beyond those of training and development. Almost every, is it too much to say *all*, human activity, and perhaps especially within managerial and organizational contexts, entails processes of formal and informal learning and knowledge, whether conceived of as entity, process, relation, resource or socialization.

Of course, in this respect, *Management Learning* has been no more than a barometer of its times. For all sorts of reasons there has been a huge increase in interest in organizational learning, knowledge-based or knowledge-intensive organizations and human capital. This interest links in with wider shifts, or alleged shifts, not just in organizations but in society, economy and polity. For it is not just organizations that have been re-configured as 'learning organizations', but societies which are seen as 'learning societies'. It is not just organizations that are 'knowledge-intensive', but whole economies. The development of human capital is not just the business of businesses, but is also the key responsibility of politics in a globalized world.

At the same time, *Management Learning* has been both receptive to, and to some degree influential in, the currents of radical change that have swept across the intellectual landscape of the humanities and social sciences and, a little later, the study of management and organizations, which grows out of that landscape. For the years since the journal's inception have seen a flowering of ideas about epistemology, ontology, identity, methodology, politics, ethics and much else besides. The journal has been an outlet for such thinking whilst also being sufficiently pluralistic to provide a home for more traditional approaches to the broad arena of management learning. Yet the more critical edge that many contributions to the journal have taken over the last ten years calls into question many of the tenets of the supposedly definitive shifts in organizations, societies, economies and polities to which we just referred.

So for all these reasons, we believe that now is a good time to bring together some of the best writing in *Management Learning* since 1994. It is not just a matter of celebrating whatever success the journal may have had. It is, much more importantly, a matter of reflecting upon the quite extraordinary attention that has been accorded to subjects with which the journal is concerned. Management learning, in its expanded sense, is not just about individuals in organizations, nor is it about organizations in a narrow sense. It is connected with the broad sweep of social, economic and political thought which characterizes our times. We hope that the contributions to the journal have much of importance to say about these times. In this volume we could not reproduce all of these contributions, but those we have selected do constitute a good selection of the more innovative papers. We believe that they deserve a wider airing, and that as a collection, they will provide a valuable resource for those studying. researching, working in or thinking about management learning.

We have structured this volume around six key themes:

• Organizational Learning and Learning Organizations
• Individual Learning
• Critical Approaches to Management Education and Learning
• Pedagogical Practice
• Globalization and Management Learning
• Beyond Management Learning

In the following pages we will outline the contributions made by the readings to each of these themes.

Part 1: Organizational Learning and Learning Organizations

As the journal of managerial and organizational learning, *Management Learning* has been instrumental in fostering vibrant debate around two themes that lie at the core of its focus and which have captured the attention of many scholars in recent years. As management researchers continue to search for new ways of conceptualizing organization, organizing and organizations, the idea of organizations as learning systems and of 'learning organizations' as a new image of the ideal form of organization have been key themes that have influenced thinking in management learning. Despite the lack of agreement as to whether it is possible to talk of organizations as possessing learning capabilities or indeed identifying 'learning organizations', these ideas present us with very useful possibilities to rethink the way in which we understand learning in the context of organizations.

In one of the earliest pieces of work published on these themes Amy Edmondson and Bertrand Moingeon (1998), present a rich analysis of the literature and put forward a new definition of organizational learning drawing attention to 'individual mental models as a critical source of leverage for creating learning organizations'. In the aptly entitled paper 'From Organizational Learning to the Learning Organization', they show how learning in organizations and organizational learning more specifically, can be better understood as a process that 'requires individual cognition and supports organizational adaptiveness'. That learning can be 'initiated, developed and practiced' lies at the core of the message Edmondson and Moingeon provide. Their 'integrative approach', linking the work of Senge and Argyris, two leading figures in this field, engages both kinds of cognitive models at the same time – cause–effect assumptions and interpersonal strategies – to show that organizational learning can lead to the development of learning organizations if cognitive issues are addressed.

Popper and Lipshitz, on the other hand, extend this discussion by revisiting the relationship between organizational learning and learning organizations, problematizing the relationship between individual and organizational learning, and drawing attention both to their similarities and differences, as well as to the challenges presented in fostering organizational learning. They draw a clearer distinction between '*learning in organizations*' and '*learning by organizations*'. Their concern with reification and hypothetical constructs prompts them to turn their attention to concrete structural and procedural arrangements, which influence the actions taken by organizational members. They call these arrangements 'organizational learning mechanisms' and they metaphorically associate them to the human nervous system. They do emphasize that such mechanisms provide no guarantee that learning can be beneficial to their owners unless they are embedded in 'a normative system of shared values and beliefs that shape how organization members feel think, and behave'. By emphasizing the role of social structures like that of the learning culture, Popper and Lipshitz move the debate of organizational learning beyond behaviourist and cognitivist perspectives. The role of social forces in shaping interpretation mechanisms, transparency and accountability are brought to the fore as forces shaping the feasibility of organizational learning. Their analysis leads them to define learning organizations as 'organizations that embed institutionalized learning mechanisms into a learning culture'.

Anders Örtenblad is not convinced that we have yet fully grasped the idea of the learning organization and presents a 'Typology of the Idea of Learning Organization'. In his 2002 paper, Örtenblad provides the most rigorous analysis yet of the multiple meanings of the learning organization demonstrating the vagueness of the concept and highlighting the need for greater clarity. Unlike previous typologies, which tend to take a deductive mode in presenting the various perspectives on organizational learning, Örtenblad's typology is formulated inductively using not only secondary sources in published books and articles on this topic. Instead he draws on practitioners' understanding of the idea of the learning organization providing further insights into how individuals are very much seen as the agents for organizational learning. A key strength of this analysis is that it presents, not only different meanings of learning organizations as organizational learning, learning at work, learning climate and leaning structure, but more importantly, it challenges the ontology of the idea of the learning organization through these various meanings and problematizes the political aspects of legitimization in the use of the term rather than the application of the idea.

These political forces are further developed in the rich analysis Bente Elkjaer provides through a case study of an organization (ACC) seeking to become a learning organization. In her captivatingly entitled paper 'The Learning Organization: An Undelivered Promise' not only does Elkjaer provide one of the earliest empirical studies of organizations attempting to implement the idea of the learning organization, but she also shows powerfully the socio-political dynamics that underpin both the choice of method and approach to instilling the idea of the learning organization. Perhaps what becomes even more clear through Elkjaer's paper is the restricted understanding of learning in organizations often equated with training. Her work provides many useful insights into the relationship between learning and training, which help explain why indeed the learning organization remains an undelivered promise, particularly, when training interventions are the main method for developing a learning organization. Interestingly, the focus of the training interventions in this study is not collective learning and development. Instead, the focus is on individuals' change and development. There is so much one can learn from this paper about the political dynamics which underpin organizational transformations, such as the process of instilling a learning organization ideal. One of the most central lessons emerging is how very little we know about the nature of individual learning on which much of the thinking on organizational learning and the learning organization is being built. As we delve further to explore the what, how and why of learning in organizations, Elkjaer encourages us to pay more attention to individuals' experiences and, drawing on Dewey's emphasis on inquiry and reflectivity, to explore the relationships between actions in response to problematic situations.

Part 2: Individual Learning

The central focus on individuals' learning to understand organizational learning does not only present us with the problem of reification, it also presents us with methodological challenges in understanding how phenomena, such as learning, find expression across levels of analysis. Multi-level analysis is essential to future research in this field, but future research may not get very far if individual learning, which lies at the core of a multi-level analysis, is not itself carefully studied. Individual learning needs to be explored beyond the dominant psychological perspective that seems to underpin issues of motivation. Instead, as the articles selected for this section strongly argue, to understand individual learning one must understand the social nature of learning with and from others: such inquiry positions at the core of an analysis of individual learning a need for greater understanding of what it means to be individual.[1] If we accept that the individual is an undivided part of the social whole, this provides us with a much wider spectrum for exploring the black box of individual learning, particularly in the context of managing and organizing. Over the years several studies have sought to illuminate the nature of individual/managerial learning resulting in several useful ways of representing different modes of learning by individuals, as well as styles of learning.

Megginson's paper contributes to these long-standing debates by highlighting that learning styles do not provide sufficient insight into individual learning. Instead, individuals' learning strategies may be a better focus. Distinguishing between 'planned' and 'emergent' learning strategies, Megginson proposes a model drawn from empirical research that identifies four types of learners: 'sleepers', 'warriors', 'adventurers' and 'sages'.

These are examined in the context of the changing career patterns managers follow and the shift in responsibility for development. Through this analysis the importance of self-awareness and learning contracts in self-development is clearly articulated, as are the difficulties experienced by some individuals in setting learning contracts. Megginson draws out a number of important implications from his analysis, for both future research in this field, but perhaps more fundamentally, for 'developers' (Mentors, Line Managers, HRD Departments and learners themselves). Megginson's message is clear: 'The framework ... can be of use to developers in examining their own learning preferences and in checking to ensure that they are not recommending to others what they do not practice themselves'.

This strong message is echoed by Spender in his 1994 paper entitled 'Knowing, Managing and Learning: A Dynamic Managerial Epistemology'. Spender examines the nature of the knowledge managers need and the implications for management education in terms of supporting the development of such knowledge. In a sophisticated analysis, typical of Spender's scholarship, the paper provides a valuable platform for understanding the social nature of learning and knowing in organizations. He distinguishes between 'practical knowledge, which shapes particular practice', and 'theoretical knowledge which is the product of reflecting on and abstracting from experience'. Consistent with previous, similar categorizations, such as that of William James ('knowledge about' and 'knowledge of acquaintance'), Spender emphasizes that managers have varying epistemologies depending on the objectives they have. Consequently, 'scientific knowledge' needs to be supplemented by 'social knowledge', 'local knowledge' and 'self-knowledge'. Through this analysis Spender places at the core of individual learning, individual experience as a key element of knowing, which Polanyi also clearly articulated in his distinction between tacit and explicit knowledge. Drawing on Vygotsky, Spender extends the analysis to sensitize us to the socio-political dynamics that underpin and define individual learning, thus showing how learning at the individual level is a social process shaped by inter-subjective forces.

The importance of acknowledging individual learning as a social process, with the individual as an active participant in the co-construction of the meanings and importance of learning, is also central to Ingrid Richter's message in her examination of 'Individual and Organizational Learning at the Executive Level: Towards a Research Agenda'. Richter draws attention to the role of 'learning projects' as useful vehicles for understanding a fundamental aspect of individuals' roles as learning; namely their 'sense-making' (following Karl Weick). Richter is particularly emphatic about the role of 'committed action' in understanding executive learning and in her own commitment to contribute to our understanding of the relationship between individual and collective/organizational learning. She points out that examining the 'actions, commitments and justifications, which follow what individuals identify as learning' is key to uncovering the relationship between micro and macro learning processes. She rightly, therefore, warns that 'both individual and organizational learning may be more collective, dynamic, improvisational and emergent than much of the literature has described to-date'. With this powerful assertion Richter prompts us to embrace, more fully, criticality as a key aspect of understanding the relational nature of learning – a point which is central to the next section of papers selected under the theme of critical approaches to management learning.

Part 3: Critical Approaches to Management Education and Learning

The expansion of interest in and activity around management education and learning has been quite remarkable and a great deal of this expansion has occurred within the institutional context of business schools normally contained within universities. In many ways, these have been one of the major success stories for universities in the last few decades. Fuelled by the demands of organizations and economies, they have also been a beneficiary of a shifting educational culture in which vocationally-oriented study has become increasingly valued.

Business school provision takes a variety of forms but perhaps the flagship has been the expansion of MBA programmes. Certainly, it is these which most obviously connect with wider developments in the corporate world, having become an increasingly mandatory requirement for the development of high level careers in industry, banking, consultancy and many other fields. MBA programmes have a much longer history in the United States than elsewhere, going back to the 1880s. In Germany and Japan they scarcely exist at all. In the UK they did not begin until the 1960s and only became widespread in the 1980s, but the UK now produces more MBAs than the rest of Europe put together. Other European countries, such as Spain, Italy and Sweden, lie somewhere between the UK and Germany in the extent of their provision. Other areas of significant growth have been Australia and South-east Asia, although in the latter case many programmes are partnered or remote operations of, in particular, US, UK and Australian universities.

All of this growth forms the background to the articulation of a great deal of critical thinking and analysis of business schools in general and MBAs in particular. There are many reasons for this but, in outline, there are two obvious causes. One is just that the growing importance of business schools has automatically rendered them more likely to be subject to such analysis. The second has been the remarkable growth, especially in Europe, of so-called 'critical management studies'. Whilst largely research-based and focusing on management practice, this has inevitably informed a movement, located inside the business schools themselves, towards applying the same ideas to the practice of management education.

Management Learning has been in many ways at the forefront in publishing work of this sort, and this is reflected in the articles we have selected. One of the earliest manifestations of a critical approach within the journal was Grey and Mitev's paper entitled 'Management Education: A Polemic', originally published in 1995. This is indeed a polemic that is explicitly informed by the critical management studies literature and uses this to denounce 'managerialist' approaches to management education, which the authors claim constitutes the mainstream of, in particular, MBA programmes. They argue that the managerialist approach is technicist, positivist and instrumental, and, has been so comprehensively challenged, and perhaps even discredited, by critical approaches that those who continue with it have 'abdicated their fundamental intellectual responsibilities'. In the course of their polemic Grey and Mitev also have occasion to criticize the narrowly instrumental orientations of many students on management programmes and the 'bureaucratic totalitarianism', which they claim characterizes quality assurance arrangements in business schools and more widely.

It is fair to say that this paper provoked a certain amount of reaction. The editors at the time commissioned a series of replies (which we have not reproduced here) that took Grey and Mitev to task for, amongst other things, a lack of evidence for their claims and an overgeneralized stereotyping of management education, management students and quality assurance arrangements. These criticisms may have some force (although in a further response to the replies Grey and Mitev gave a fairly uncompromising defence of their original article), yet the piece did have the merit of setting up a clear, even if overly-simplified, position around which an increasingly large and vociferous group of management academics could rally and, in the process, refine.[2]

One area where Grey and Mitev's work clearly needed not just refinement but substantial addition was that of precisely what form management education was to take if and when the mainstream orthodoxy was abandoned. The other articles reprinted in this section do, in different ways, just that. Dehler, Welsh and Lewis's 2001 paper discusses 'Critical Pedagogy in the 'New Paradigm'. Their work is very much located within what, by this time, had become quite an extensive literature on critical management education and learning. However, they also draw upon a wider and more long-standing tradition of critical pedagogy, for example, in the work of Henri Giroux. In this way, they identify a series of principles and tactics for critical management education, which include addressing power relations within and beyond the classroom, questioning and problematizing received knowledge and wisdom, and, overall developing 'complicated understanding'. This latter concept entails a move away from traditional attempts in management education to give neat, simplified and idealized solutions towards opening up the paradoxical, messy and contested nature of management and organizational situations.

In the course of, or more accurately at the outset of, this argument Dehler, Welsh and Lewis make a move which has characterized much of how critical approaches have developed. They state that 'management education needs to become both transformational and emancipatory [i.e. critical] in order adequately to prepare students for the turbulent new century'. In this they somewhat soften those formulations which reject the very linkage of management education and management practice. They are saying, in effect, that critical management education offers a more appropriate 'skill set' than does the mainstream. This is clearly an important development, since it offers a way in which critical management education may legitimately be advanced within business school contexts without necessarily undermining what is usually claimed to be the very basis of such schools. This way the capacity for critical approaches to have influence is very much enhanced.

If Dehler, Welsh and Lewis are largely concerned with the principles which should underlie critical approaches to management education and learning, Michael Cavanaugh, in his 2000 paper 'Head Games: Introducing Tomorrow's Business Elites to Institutionalized Inequality', takes the reader inside his classroom. Informed by the critical management education literature, Cavanaugh shows how it is possible to 'chip away' at assumptions and received wisdom about, in particular, gender and racial inequality. He describes how he uses the case of campus elections as a vehicle for allowing students to explore their pre-conceived assumptions and world-views about gender, ethnicity, sexuality and other issues. In particular, he uses the case to explore how these assumptions and world-views, and their effects, cannot be understood as formed separately from, or having no impact upon, wider structural and institutionalized patterns of inequality. Clearly this is as relevant to the corporate world in which inequalities are enacted as it is to the campus and classroom.

In this way, Cavanaugh's discussion of management education goes well beyond more traditional, liberal humanist concerns with self-awareness and personal tolerance by connecting with the broader social structures of power, a concern which is part of what is distinctive about critical approaches.

Cavanaugh's interweaving of the theoretical literature and concerns of critical approaches to management education with the here-and-now of student experience exemplifies the way these approaches have tackled the classroom. This suggests that, rather than present knowledge as an abstract, remote and established body of facts, concepts and theories, knowledge is rather a contested social practice instantiated in the classroom and therefore, accessible by reflection upon the classroom itself. In other words, critical approaches to management education and learning do not consist of simply changing its content, and still less in engaging in sermonizing, but require a radical reform of educational processes.

Amanda Sinclair is one of the world's leading scholars of the nexus of issues around gender, leadership, change and learning. Her paper, 'Teaching Managers about Masculinities: Are you Kidding?', like Cavanaugh's, shows how critical management educators try to link the here-and-now of the classroom to wider issues of social structure. But, beyond re-illustrating this, her work is important for two reasons. Firstly because, in relation to gender, she shows how the 'problem' of gender can be re-worked, so that it is no longer presented in terms of 'the issues facing women', towards an appreciation of how gender structures the experience of men and the practices of masculinity. In this, Sinclair shows how critical approaches to management education that are informed by seemingly 'theoretically' research scholarship can be brought into the classroom. Secondly, and perhaps more importantly for this volume, she shows how critical approaches differ not just from the traditional mainstream, but even from its apparently more progressive variants. For Sinclair's focus upon masculinity as a problematic differs not just from the gender-blindness of traditionalism but also from the 'women in management' or 'diversity' approaches of progressivism in management education.

How Sinclair approaches this teaching contains many features of interest, but the one we wish to highlight here is that which differentiates it from Cavanaugh's analysis, and certainly from Grey and Mitev as well as Dehler, Welsh and Lewis, who say relatively little about classroom practice. This feature is the embodied and emotionalized experience of the teacher who seeks to practise, and not just espouse to, a critical approach. Teaching is perhaps always an emotionally charged experience, at least potentially, but to raise issues of masculinity is also to raise the dynamics of sexuality within the teacher–student relationship. More generally, by adopting approaches to management education which go beyond the 'neutral' transmission of 'objective' knowledge, the enmeshment of the teacher with the learner and with that which is being taught becomes inescapable. This places particular emotional demands upon management educators, but in doing so, it points

9

up the pedagogical specificity of critical approaches to management education and learning.

Part 4: Pedagogical Practice

A concern with pedagogy and educational process is by no means confined to avowedly critical approaches to management learning. It has a much wider currency across a range of approaches. *Management Learning* has carried a great deal of work on pedagogy over the last ten years from a wide variety of perspectives. Perhaps, too, a particular contribution made by the journal has been to blur the rigidity of the boundaries between approaches so that it is increasingly common to see references made across, otherwise separate, literatures. Although substantive differences remain, as we will indicate.

Whilst pedagogy has long been the subject of attention from educationalists, there can be little doubt that the remarkable upsurge of interest in learning that we alluded to earlier – and, as subsets within that, the growth of formal management education and of organizational learning – has revivified the study of the practice of teaching. Perhaps it has also done something to transform traditional conceptions of the relationship between teaching and learning. The more active accent on the learner as having both responsibilities and rights must perforce recast the role of the teacher. Moreover, increasingly sophisticated understandings of the nature of knowledge move pedagogy ever further from being simply about the effective transmission of discrete bodies of knowledge towards a more engaged and engaging relationship. Put in this way, it is easy to see the continuities between critical approaches and those which, whilst remaining within a more orthodox frame of reference, address, in not entirely dissimilar ways, the changing context of management learning.

Tony Watson is well-known as an ethnographic researcher as well as being, no doubt as a consequence, one of the most acute analysts of managerial work. It has been one of the hallmarks of *Management Learning* to carry contributions from those whose work, whilst going beyond 'learning', has an implication for management learning, as well as from those for whom the latter is a central concern. Watson is one of a rare breed amongst academics who can write stylishly and accessibly, and the title of the paper we reproduce here is highly expressive: 'Motivation: that's Maslow, isn't it?' Watson is reporting upon an encounter with students in which they configure their learning in terms of blocks of knowledge, packaged but not reflected upon. Watson reports on an 'ethnographic experiment' in which such reflection occurs, and gives rise to a considerable scepticism about the value of commonly taught management theories and, even, confusion about what a theory is and how it can be evaluated.

This sceptical reflection he suggests, is normally hidden by a 'contract of cynicism' in which management educators and their students are complicit in an unstated agreement. The students accept that the knowledge they receive in the classroom bears scant relationship to workplace realities and is simply something which must be mastered for assessment purposes. For teachers the encounter is an easy and unchallenged one in which they can preserve an almost 'priestly' status. Watson suggests that this situation is unsatisfactory for both teachers and learners and for the development of forms of management education and learning, which speak meaningfully of and to managerial practice.

The remaining readings in this section could be understood as attempts to construct a more satisfactory and meaningful version of management education and learning through various pedagogical initiatives. The contract of cynicism, as well as less jaundiced versions of learning, configures the teacher or trainer as an expert. In positive versions, the expert has possession of valuable knowledge to be conveyed to the learner. In more negative versions, the learner accepts that the expert has knowledge that must be mastered for credentialist reasons. But Naomi Raab's 1997 article offers quite a different version of teacher/trainer identity and thereby recasts the relationship between 'teacher' and 'learner'. She doesn't deny the expertise of teachers, but reconfigures expertise in terms that stress 'not knowing' rather than knowing.

This conception of learning, in a way that is not dissimilar to some of the critical approaches, makes use of classroom experience, for example, by reflecting upon the tensions generated by (quite small) changes in the conduct of classes in order to better understand reactions to organizational change. Much of what Raab envisages is a removal of the familiar structures of educational experience, not just the teacher as expert, although this is the most important, but the many artefacts such as handouts and visual aids associated with that expertise. In a very radical way this entails that teachers and learners are forced to 'stay in the present' of the here and now of the classroom. This process inevitably generates anxieties. For teachers, it means abandoning the safety net of 'knowing', to which may be added the projection, by students, that their teachers 'should' deliver expert knowledge. For learners, it places a new accent on their involvement in and responsibility for learning. In a sense, by challenging the contract of cynicism, Raab also reveals some of the psychological investments made in it by teachers and learners alike.

Teaching and learning do not, of course, simply take place within the context of educational institutions. One of the failures implicit in the contract of cynicism is the artificiality of formal management education compared with the daily realities of practice. Yet it does not follow that an immersion in that practice will in and of itself yield much in the way of learning. From that point of view Karen Ayas and Nick Zeniuk's analysis of project-based learning in Ford and Fokker Aircraft is illuminating. In their 2001 paper, they point out that learning is not an inevitable or natural result of the increasingly common phenomenon of project-based working and, in particular, that such learning as does occur may not have any wider or longer duration than that of the project itself. They are concerned to explore the circumstances under which more enduring learning does occur and, in particular, when it might form the basis for the development of communities of reflective practitioners. This might be conceived of as analogous to the kind of experiential situation Raab tries to engender, but with the difference that it is not experienced as 'experiential' but simply experienced as 'experience'. Even so, Ayas and Zeniuk point out the need for psychological safety and, in particular, the need for an atmosphere of trust in which errors can be made and openly discussed. Moreover, a key element in successful project-based learning, they suggest, is the involvement of an outsider, perhaps in a hybrid action research/consulting role as a catalyst for reflection and learning. At the heart of their analysis, then, is a 'genuine partnership . . . between academics and project and team leaders'.

In this way, the readings in this section take us full circle. At the heart of pedagogy in management lies the problem of reconstituting the relationship between teachers and learners in ways that are attentive to the anxieties and emotions within that relationship, but which also deal with them not by constructing a mutual cynicism, but by finding new forms of partnership founded on respect for the distinctive capabilities on each side. It bears saying, however (and this is why we have created separate sections in the readings), that this vision is somewhat at odds with at least some versions of the critical approaches, for all that there are some overlaps in terms of pedagogy. For a stress on partnership assumes that there is, or could be, a commonality of interests and purposes between academics and practitioners, a proposition at least questioned within the critical literature.

Part 5: Globalization and Management Learning

We have referred continually to the way in which the last ten years (and more) have seen some quite remarkable shifts in the appeal of and to learning as a significant facet of individual, organizational, economic and social life. We have also pointed to the upsurge in provision of management education in business schools, but part and parcel of these developments has surely been globalization. It is important to recognize that management learning is at one and the same time affected by globalization and is a significant means through which globalization has occurred. Thus, on the one hand, the globalization of trade and of corporations has carried with it, like seeds in the wind, the provision and practice of management learning. It has also necessitated and facilitated the migration of students and organizational members and has required management learning to be attentive to the requirements and effects of globalized capital and globalized corporate reach. But, on the other hand, management learning has a role as an agent of globalization. The global distribution, whether through education and training or through other means, of management ideas, concepts and techniques, is one of the things which makes the global distribution of goods and services possible, if only through the provision of a structure of shared understandings and vocabularies. Indeed, the very growth of concepts and practices of, for example, organizational learning is itself a part of the basis upon which management learning, generally, globalizes. Thus, the globalization of management learning is both a condition and a consequence of globalization more generally. One small part of this, it may be noted, is that, as a journal, *Management Learning* has become increasingly globalized in its authorship, readership and editorship.

All of which begins to point up some rather sharp issues. Globalization is itself, of course, a hotly contested topic. Exactly what it means, the extent to which it is occurring and, in particular, the desirability of its effects has been perhaps the most contentious political issue of the last ten years, and looks set to continue as such. One inescapable aspect of the politics of global-ization, which is equally pertinent to the politics of management learning, is whether it is a process that is bound up with a homogenization in which local and indigenous practices and cultures have been damaged or destroyed by Western and, in particular, North American, priorities. Within such debates, management learning has a particularly important place. For the bulk of management ideas and practices have been developed within the West, and in particular North America, and transported or translated into other contexts. Equally, the agents of this process have in many cases been management developers and trainers, business schools, consultancies and other parts of the institutional apparatus of management learning. This poses complex issues both as to whether management learning can travel in this way and as to whether it should do so.

The articles we have selected to reprint in this section are very much engaged with these kinds of problems. Rajesh Kumar and Jean-Claude Usunier's 2001 study of 'Management Education in a Globalizing World: Lessons from the French Experience' takes the case of French business schools and explores a number of important themes. They recognize that business schools both promote, and are impacted upon by, globalization. In particular, they suggest that globalization produces a need for new kinds of managerial capacities, which can be learned by, amongst other things, business schools. They argue that, at least as far as the French schools are concerned, it is unlikely that they will be successful in developing these new capacities because of a series of cultural, historical, institutional and linguistic barriers.

But, apart from identifying these limits to the capacity of business schools to be agents of globalization, Kumar and Usunier's work also tells us something about the way local practices (in this case, those of French business schools) are embedded in ways which are both threatened by, but resistant to, globalization. In particular, it becomes clear that the spread of the US model of management education causes profound stresses for non-US educational and cultural systems. However, it also offers the possibility of the development of models which are more strongly defined because they exist in contrast to this US model. Globalization, then, emerges as having conflicting, or even paradoxical, effects upon management education that cannot be captured simply through an image of homogeneity.

Something not dissimilar emerges in Yin Fan's analysis of the transfer of Western management to China, originally published in 1998. China is perhaps a particularly interesting site for this kind of study given the very rapid transformations that are taking place there and the extent to which these are informed by Western management ideas. As Fan reports, this is something which post-dates the development of extensive industrialization in China in the 1970s at a time when management know-how 'was branded as "bogus science and bourgeois evils"'. It is, therefore, a feature not of industrialization as such, but of the process of marketization and globalization, recently spurred on by China's membership of the World Trade Organization.

The transfer of Western management ideas to China has been spearheaded by the influence Western multi-nationals and their joint ventures with Chinese partners.

However, it is also increasingly a feature of indigenous state-owned enterprises. Fan's analysis is that many of these ideas, especially those relating to human resource management and marketing, do not readily transfer to Chinese contexts and, when they do, it is in ways which are quite superficial. In the process, these ideas are modified and also are chosen between on the basis of underlying cultural and philosophical values. Whilst Fan admits that it is too early to see what the end-product of this encounter will be, the analysis is again suggestive of the way that management ideas are part of the globalization process, but that that process has a complex dynamic in which global and local are mediated and each is changed.

However, it has to be recognized that another aspect of the complexity of globalization is not just that it lacks homogeneity, but that the *way* in which it lacks homogeneity, itself lacks homogeneity! The Chinese context is one in which there is strong cultural and political bulwarks against the simple, wholesale transfer of Western management. Other contexts, and Eastern Europe is a good example, are rather different because, amongst other things, these countries experience the rapid loss of existing political structures. Monika Kostera, writing mainly about Poland in her 1995 paper on 'The Modern Crusade: The Missionaries of Management come to Eastern Europe', presents a picture in which the influx of management ideas is somewhat less susceptible to local redefinition than in China. Indeed, the modern crusade is a religious metaphor in which the 'missionaries of management' come with proselytizing zeal to Eastern Europe. Kostera describes an influx of management-speak and management technique, and of agencies, educational, consultants and so on, offering these as a route to economic and political 'salvation'. And, she suggests, many have embraced the message and become 'disciples'. But it is a message that is essentially in one direction so that Kostera regards it as being a monologue rather than a conversation or, in the religious metaphor, a 'sermon'.

On Kostera's account, there was, at least at this time, relatively little resistance to what she regards as colonization, and she gives a series of explanations as to why, in the specific context of Polish culture and recent historical experience, this might be so. Her conclusion is an important challenge to management education and learning to develop as dialogue rather than crusade. This is a crucial issue which must be addressed as management education and learning continues to be affected by and to contribute to globalization.

Part 6: Beyond Management Learning

In this last section we capture some of the papers that open the debate in management learning to a much wider set of issues. In many ways these papers pave the way for future research in the field of management learning. They highlight important aspects that could be incorporated and worked with in efforts to support learning in and outside organizational boundaries. We entitled this section 'Beyond Management Learning' in order to emphasize the new directions and possibilities these chosen papers provide in our ongoing efforts to understand the dynamics of managing, organizing and learning. Each of these papers is unique in that it touches a theme that has not previously been sufficiently explored in management learning debates. Moreover, the three papers together share a common theme – an effort to engage the complexity of learning as a key aspect of an interconnected understanding of the multiple forces at play when learning is taking place.

'Learning through Complexity' is Steve McKenna's message. He emphasizes the pressures managers are subjected to arising from the complexity central to environmental turbulence, organizational change and ambiguity, and the need to be in control of this complexity. In a pragmatically illustrated analysis based on empirical research undertaken by the author, the typical concerns and dilemmas experienced by managers are discussed, as are the main strategies for designing and developing mechanisms to address these dilemmas. For example, McKenna shows how developing a 'complexity map' provides a more clear representation of the perceived reality and complexity managers perceive. The illustrative case studies clearly show how the complexity map, when applied, not only highlights the key network of human resources informing individuals' practice and learning agenda, but it also helps to map the interactions between the various learning resources, which reveal the 'chaotic, conflictual and diverse nature of organizations'. More importantly however, McKenna illustrates defensive routines by managers, which he calls 'avoidance' strategies based on 'cover-up' and 'defensiveness'.

Holloway, Skinner and Tagg, in their 2000 paper entitled 'Managers and Research: The Pros and Cons of Qualitative Approaches', place the paradox of stability and change and *re-search* at the core of managerial practice. They show how research is learning and how learning is embedded in research approaches, such as qualitative methods, which support managers to 'think about the unprogrammable complexities which they face'. The empirical findings they present capture the way in which being a research manager provides a greater access to personal subjectivities and the challenges of inter-subjectivity.

This is a point that Taylor and his colleagues return to with their 2002 paper on 'The Aesthetics of Management Storytelling: A Key to Organizational Learning'. They provide a convincing case for the role of storytelling

15

as a meaning–making process and through an aesthetic lens they show how by taking a micro perspective the relationship between storyteller and audience becomes more accessible, as does the process of sense-making and sense-giving. Consistent with the overall focus on interaction and connectivity, this paper encourages us to understand the intuitive leaps that underpin the way learning allows an element of surprise as reasoning is 'abducted'. Applied to the management roles identified in Mintzberg's classic categorizations, the authors leave us with a powerful message about the discursivity that underlies learning in organizations.

Conclusion

We have been honoured to have the opportunity to edit *Management Learning* for five of the ten years of its existence and to have had an involvement in the development, not just of the journal, but of the field it addresses and the community it serves. The journal, the field and the community have both grown and changed since 1994. Partly this has been coincidental with the explosion of interest in management learning, some of the reasons for which we set out earlier.

However, we hope and believe that the contributions we have reprinted in this reader show that something more has occurred than a simple effusion of work in the area – if by that one means a repetitive and unreflective torrent. There has indeed, in general terms, been such an effusion but much of the work in the journal, and certainly that presented here, has sought to extend, probe, refine, problematize and critique management learning across a very broad front. This seems to us to be an important contribution. In the wider arena, too much that has been written on management learning breathlessly reproduces a rather naïve, and certainly optimistic, discourse of learning in general, and in management and organizational learning in particular. Rarely are the basic assumptions and limits of this discourse explored.

The contributions that follow are extremely varied in their focus and orientation, both theoretically and politically. Yet, they do have a common thread in their willingness to question the taken for granted, whether in the form of scepticism about the achievement of learning organizations (Elkjaer): dissatisfaction with static models of learning (Spender); outrage at the narrowness of business schools (Grey and Mitev); concern to re-evaluate the meaning of being a teacher (Raab); discontent with the imposition of Western management thinking in Eastern Europe (Kostera): or fascination with the neglected realm of aesthetics in learning (Taylor, Fisher and Dufresne).

It has become fashionable in some circles to denigrate academic work for being, in a pejorative sense, 'academic'; that is, self-indulgent and disengaged from reality. But there are more positive images of academic work: careful, thoughtful, reflective and illuminating of reality. We believe that the contributions which follow exemplify attributes of the latter sort and will prove useful in the further exploration of the broad field of management learning in the coming years.

Notes

1 Etymologically the word individual means both unique/single and un-divided.

2 Since one of us is also one of the authors of this paper, readers may feel that we have given too generous or alternatively too neutral an account of it.

part one

Organizational Learning and Learning Organizations

1

Amy Edmondson and Bertrand Moingeon

From Organizational Learning to the Learning Organization

Introduction

To remain viable in an environment characterized by uncertainty and change, organizations and individuals alike depend upon an ability to learn. Yesterday's knowledge and skills are vulnerable to obsolescence, and future success requires flexibility, responsiveness and new capabilities. Yet psychological and organizational factors conspire to make organizations and their members resist change and miss opportunities to create preferred futures. These sources of resistance, as well as strategies for overcoming them, have been explored under the broad rubric of organizational learning by a diverse group of researchers, including practicing managers (e.g. de Geuss, 1988; Stata, 1989) and scholars from fields as diverse as organizational behavior (Argyris, 1982; Levitt and March, 1988; Huber, 1991; Schein, 1992), operations management (Hayes et al., 1988), strategy (Redding and Catalenello, 1994; Collis, 1996) and system dynamics (Senge, 1990).

With this growth comes confusion. 'Organizational learning' encompasses considerable territory in the management literature; it is presented as occurring at different levels of analysis – from individuals (Argyris, 1982) to organizations (Levitt and March, 1988) – and as applying to such disparate processes as the diffusion of information within an organization (Huber, 1991), how individuals interpret and thereby create their organization (Weick, 1979; Daft and Weick, 1984), how interpersonal communication precludes detection and correction of error (Argyris and Schön, 1974), and the encoding of organizational routines (Cyert and March, 1963; Nelson and Winter, 1982; Levitt and March, 1988). In some conceptions, organizational learning is prescriptive, that is, viewed as an outcome that can be brought about through intervention (e.g. Hayes et al., 1988; Senge, 1990; Argyris, 1993); elsewhere, organizational learning is the focus of descriptive theories which document factors influencing or impeding organizational adaptation (e.g. Levitt and March, 1988; Huber, 1991). In our view, this confusion limits the accessibility and potential usefulness of this literature for practitioners. Thus, in this article we provide a framework to organize these diverse scholarly contributions into meaningful categories. Our aim is to foster discussion among scholars and practitioners that facilitates future application of these ideas.

This article contributes to the literature in three ways. First, we review existing ideas about organizational learning and present a two-by-two framework for categorizing these diverse contributions; this review is intended to identity and illustrate distinctions we have identified in the literature rather than to be exhaustive. Second, we discuss differences between the terms *organizational learning* and *the learning organization.* The term organizational learning encompasses a broad range of phenomena, including, but not limited to, desired processes of individual development and organizational adaptation, while work discussing the learning organization forms an explicitly normative subset of the literature. Third, we identify substantive relationships between different foci in the literature and show how these relationships together suggest a model in which the leverage for creating a learning organization lies in the cognition of organization members. To illustrate and provide additional support for this model and its implied strategy for creating organizational change, we offer a brief discussion of the work of two of the most visible researchers in this field, Peter Senge and Chris Argyris. The article concludes by showing how integrating these two different approaches may help to overcome shortcomings of each one implemented in isolation, and this discussion suggests specific questions for future research.

Organizing Organizational Learning Research

Dimensions of Organizational Learning

The organizational learning literature is notably fragmented, with multiple constructs and little cross-fertilization among scholars (e.g. Shrivastava, 1983; Fiol and Lyles, 1985; Huber, 1991). Primary unit of analysis – or, the entity seen as 'learning' – provides one distinction in the organizational learning literature; research goal or objective provides another. Some researchers study how *organizations* as whole systems adapt or change (as a function of individual cognitive properties or of organization policies and structures) and label this system-level phenomenon 'learning'. Other researchers focus on how *individuals* embedded in organizations learn – that is, how individuals develop, adapt, or update their cognitive models.[1] At the same time, across both groups, some authors primarily attempt to describe relationships among variables. The intended research product is an accurate description of a phenomenon or a robust model of causality. Others undertake research primarily aimed at creating organizational change. Their research objective is to identify and test managerial actions that improve organizational effectiveness. The distinction between descriptive and intervention research thus provides a second dimension, and the two-by-two matrix shown in Figure 1 depicts the resulting categories of learning phenomena. Each of the four categories is discussed below.

PRIMARY UNIT OF ANALYSIS

	Organization	*Individual*
Descriptive research	**Residues** (1) organizations as residues of past learning (e.g. Levitt and March, 1988)	**Communities** (2) organizations as collections of individuals who can learn and develop (e.g. Pedler et al., 1990)
Intervention research	**Participation** (3) organizational improvement gained through intelligent activity of individual members (e.g. Hayes et al., 1988)	**Accountability** (4) organizational improvement gained through developing individuals' mental models (e.g. Senge, 1990; Argyris, 1993)

RESEARCH GOAL (row label spanning left side)

Figure 1   *A typology of organizational learning research*

Residues: Organizations as Residues of Past Learning

Descriptive research at the organization level of analysis includes approaches stemming from behavioral theories of the firm and from theories of social construction. Organizational learning in this category encompasses phenomena such as how routines shape organizational behavior, how knowledge is acquired, and the role of interpretive processes in precluding rational adaptation.

Several scholars focus on the role and stability of routines in organizations. Levitt and March (1988) distinguish theories of organizational learning from theories of rational choice, resource dependency and population ecology. Rather than treating learning as a way to combat inertial tendencies in organizations, these authors view organizational learning as an alternative mechanism to account for existing organizational behavior – that is, a mechanism that explains how organizations evolve over time and thereby accounts for the status quo. Organizational learning, in their model, describes processes such as imitation and trial-and-error experimentation that explain how organizations behave and evolve over time. In contrast to the normative approaches discussed below, learning is seen as a faulty mechanism. Because behavior in organizations is routine driven (Cyert and March, 1963; Nelson and Winter, 1982), the lessons of the *past* – embodied in current routines – dominate organizational life. Organizational routines, in which 'action stems from a logic of appropriateness or legitimacy, more than from a logic of consequentiality or intention' (Levitt and March, 1988: 320), are thus over-learned, such that actors are more habit driven and imitative than rational. Learning, in this model, is essentially the accumulated residues of past inferences.

Levitt and March (1988) embrace the organization as their primary unit of analysis, and focus on the ecological nature of how organizations select and encode routines. They observe that organizations as entities stop actively seeking alternatives once they have built up experience in known routines; this creates built-in barriers to adaptation at the organizational level, such as 'superstitious learning' (viewing desired outcomes as a result of well-reasoned organizational actions) and 'competency traps (beliefs that current practices are better than potential alternatives, leading to the continuity of inferior work processes). Because of these organizational barriers, only exceptionally inappropriate routines are likely to lead to a perceived need for change (Levitt and March, 1988).

Other scholars define organizational learning as a process through which an organization expands its repertoire of actions, and they focus on how knowledge is acquired and distributed. For example, citing behavioral learning theory, Huber (1991) defines *learning* as a process that enables an entity to increase its range of potential behavior through its processing of information. *Organizational learning* is then defined as occurring when any of an organization's units acquires knowledge that the unit recognizes as potentially useful to the organization (Huber, 1991).

Finally, others examine interpretive processes as a form of organizational learning. Weick (1979) notes that adaptation can preclude adaptability; that is, shared interpretations of reality can inhibit perceiving a need for change. The following quote from Weick (1979: 135) highlights the phenomenon also captured by Levitt and March's competency trap; organizations that acquire an exquisite fit with their current surroundings may be unable to adapt when those surroundings change'. This notion is also similar to that discussed in 'groupthink' research, in which social psychological mechanisms in high-level decision-making groups are thought to foster cohesiveness and inhibit disagreement (Janis, 1982). Social construction processes are at the root of these organizational dilemmas, as shared perceptions of the appropriateness of current practices are seen as precluding effective adaptation by the system. Weick (1979) takes social construction a step further in his descriptions of 'enactment' as a process in which organizations make sense of the chaotic stimuli of experience – sorting chaos into separate events and parts that can be connected and sequenced. In his model, the organizational context is in fact created through a sense-making process.

Communities: Organizations as Collections of Individuals Who Can Learn and Develop

Descriptive research at the individual level of analysis includes descriptions of individual learning in organizations, models that specify conditions that enable employee learning, and models that describe beneficial outcomes of individuals engaging in learning. Brown and Duguid (1991: 48) describe learning as becoming 'an insider' by acquiring tacit or 'noncanonical' knowledge. Ray Stata, CEO of Analog Devices, takes a more normative approach, describing widespread individual learning as a source of competitive advantage for his organization (Stata, 1989). Others show how organizations affect the learning and development of individuals. For example, flatter organizational structures create a tension that elicits personal development by employees, and this individual learning contributes to a process of continual transformation of the organization (Pedler et al., 1990). New interpersonal challenges encountered in less hierarchical, team-based organizations encourage individuals to engage in developing communication and other interpersonal skills, which creates a kind of institutionalized learning or 'organizational capability' (Pettigrew and Whipp, 1991).

Others have shown how individual learning can lead to organizational change. For example, in a study of how a large software firm responded to the implementation of new information technology, Orlikowski (1996) describes the subsequent unplanned, ongoing adjustment and improvisation activities of organizational actors, and proposes that this individual learning transformed the organization.

In sum, when its members learn an organization's capability may be enhanced. This approach can be distinguished from intervention research (discussed in the following two sections) in that it is primarily descriptive and does not prescribe strategies for implementing organization change. In contrast, researchers in the remaining two categories have embraced this objective.

Participation: Organizational Improvement Gained Through Intelligent Activity of Individuals

Intervention research at the organization level of analysis explores questions of what policies can be employed to create flexible and responsive ('learning') organizations. Researchers in this group often advocate human resources or manufacturing policies to improve organizational responsiveness. For example, operations management researchers Hayes et al. (1988) focus on initiating changes in organizations' operating systems to create what they call learning organizations. Making critical information accessible and transparent, such as by increasing the on-line inter-dependencies among workers, is one element of increasing both the probability and importance of problem-solving by individuals. Individual members thereby can contribute to creating more flexible, efficient organizations. This pragmatic research focuses on technical solutions to the problem of sustaining organizational learning, and on the role of people in making these changes. In their model, fostering the participation of all employees and putting their innate ability to think to work for the organization is described as essential for organizational effectiveness. This participation can extend beyond the boundaries of the organization to include learning by customers, whose input can contribute to innovation in the organization (von Hippel, 1988).

In this category, the *organization* learns when its members participate fully, such as by solving problems and communicating about substantive issues with each other. In contrast, in the accountability group discussed below, when *individuals* learn, through explicit interventions designed to foster self-reflection, their organizations become more effective.

Accountability: Organizational Improvement Gained Through Developing Individuals' Mental Models

Intervention research at the individual level of analysis explores strategies for examining and developing the way individuals think about the organization. Organizational learning is portrayed as a phenomenon in which individuals in organizations take action to develop and refine their cognitive maps – for example, their 'theories-in-use' (Argyris and Schön, 1974) or 'mental models' (Senge, 1990) – and thereby become more effective decision makers. The goal of researchers is to develop intervention strategies to facilitate this process. For example, John Seely Brown at Xerox describes the use of laboratories in which employees experiment with computerized simulations designed to help them develop new mental models of how the business operates (Brown, 1991). Research traditions as different as system dynamics (e.g. Sterman, 1989; Senge, 1990) and action science (e.g. Argyris, 1982) exemplify work in this category. The term 'accountability' captures a common theme characterizing much of this work; that individuals' decisions and cognitions shape their organizations and, equally important, that they can learn to change these cognitions in preferred ways. These researchers invite individuals to be accountable for changing their organizations, as seen in the work of Senge in system dynamics and in the work of Argyris in action science.

System dynamics examines ways in which features of human cognition, such as blindness to interconnections among elements of a complex system, produce managerial policies that neglect the long term and ignore the effects of feedback (Forrester, 1961; Sterman, 1989). According to this perspective, in order to reduce the organizational ineffectiveness caused by counter-productive managerial policies individuals must learn how to diagnose organizations as complex dynamic systems. Yet, the behavior of complex systems like corporations is difficult to decipher, in part because human cognition is insensitive to non-linear relationships and to the effects of feedback delays (Sterman, 1989). Learning about the effects of decisions in organizational settings is thus difficult; feedback is either missed altogether or misunderstood, an observation that is similar to Levitt and March's concept of superstitious learning. As a result, managers tend to address symptoms rather than underlying causes of problems, thereby focusing only on the proximal results of robust patterns of behavior, themselves shaped by organization policies and structures. Senge (1990) proposes that organizational actors can learn to think systemically so that they can understand how their own organizational systems work and make changes which offer leverage in influencing results; this is how to create learning organizations. We revisit this approach in the second part of this article.

Although it focuses on the nature of interpersonal competence rather than on the systemic complexity of organizations, action science also maintains that the way individuals think is a critical cause of organizational ineffectiveness (e.g. Argyris et al., 1985). Argyris (1993) shows that individual actors engaged in difficult or face-threatening conversations fail to communicate relevant information clearly and fail to learn from each other. In these conversations, individuals' implicit theories, or 'theories-in-use', lead them to behave in ways that produce outcomes exactly contrary to what they hope to produce in interpersonal interactions (Argyris, 1982). Moreover, these theories-in-use systematically preclude learning about ways to escape their counterproductive effects, and thereby contribute to organizational systems that reinforce anti-learning interpersonal dynamics (Argyris and Schön, 1978). Analogous to the competency trap, theories-in-use constitute built-in impediments to learning at the micro-level of individual reasoning processes. Based on this understanding of how organizational effectiveness is limited, Argyris conducts intervention research designed to help individuals develop new theories-in-use to enhance their ability to learn in interactions with others. This approach is also discussed in the second part of this paper.

Summary

A brief review of the organizational learning literature reveals considerable diversity. Some authors describe how organizations learn whatever it is they learn, while others view learning as something that needs to be created through intervention. Given the variety of phenomena labeled organizational learning, the *learning organization* rubric can be used to separate research aimed at developing strategies to improve organizational adaptiveness from the larger body of work. Within this normative subset, two levels of analysis represent two different – potentially complementary – theoretical views. Those in the *participation* category view organizational effectiveness as an outgrowth of policies that engage individuals in contributing to the organization, while those in the *accountability* category view effectiveness as dependent upon properties of individual cognition.[2]

In the second half of this article, we offer our own definition of organizational learning and argue that engaging individuals in reflecting upon and developing their own thinking processes is an essential component of creating learning organizations. Relationships among the different areas of research described above form the basis of our argument, which is supported further by the work of two well- known intervention researchers, Peter Senge and Chris Argyris. Although the theories of Senge and Argyris at first appear as different as the academic traditions that influenced them, we show that they are similar in a fundamental way.

An Integrative Approach to Addressing Cognitive Barriers to Learning

Although this article notes that the organizational learning literature is fragmented, we also wish to draw attention to benefits of this diversity. First, with its many different foci, this literature represents an encompassing effort to understand a complex phenomenon. Studies of organizational routines, of interpretive processes, or of individual learning and development each offer a part of a complete picture of organizational adaptation. Describing the 'elephant' of an organization's behavior requires more than one observer and more than one lens (Waldo, 1961; Adams, 1994). Second, substantive relationships among these parts point to leverage for intervention, as we will show below. In this section, we first present our own definition of organizational learning, and then examine relationships among parts of the literature and draw some new conclusions.

Organizational Learning (Re)defined

Although we view the diversity of issues covered in the literature as valuable, we propose that the multiplicity of definitions of what 'organizational learning' *is* contributes to confusion for practitioners and limits the usefulness of scholars' contributions. Thus, we propose a new definition, synthesized from the literature, followed by a brief discussion of its merits. We define organizational learning as a process in which an organization's members actively use data to guide behavior in such a way as to promote the ongoing adaptation of the organization. To use data is to seek and attend to task-relevant information, in particular for assessing collective performance and progress against goals. Guiding behavior involves choosing actions based on data-driven observations, including actions designed to test inferences. Adaptation is change by an organization in response to external changes – both problems and opportunities. Ongoing adaptation suggests sustained attention to relevant data, especially regarding results of new actions. Such an iterative cycle of action and reflection has been described by Schön (1983) as integral to the practice of highly effective individual professionals. This definition views organizational learning as a process – one that requires individual cognition and supports organizational adaptiveness. It is a process of acting, assessing, and acting again – an ongoing cycle of reflection and action that cannot be taken for granted in organizations, noted for their adherence to routine. However, as thus defined, organizational learning is a process that can be initiated, developed, and practiced.

Where does this definition fit in to the literature? We note that intervention may be needed for individuals to engage in this learning process in support of their organization's ongoing effectiveness. This framing places us in the accountability category. However, we have drawn upon other approaches in developing our model of change, as shown below. By examining relationships among three of the different foci discussed above – routines, interpretive processes and intervention to develop individual mental models

– we will show that work from other categories can be used to strengthen the argument put forth by accountability researchers.

The Relationship between Organizational Routines and Collective Interpretive Processes

As discussed above, behavioral theories of the firm have depicted organizations as entities made up of routines. Human beings play little or no role in these descriptions; the innumerable routines that transform organizational inputs into outputs are seen as having a life of their own. However, even theories that focus on people recognize the importance of routine, and few scholars of organizational behavior would deny its importance. Standard operating procedures create routines; manufacturing processes are routines, and even work groups fall into habitual routines (Gersick and Hackman, 1990). A high level of agreement exists in the literature that organizational routines endure (e.g. Hannan and Freeman, 1984; Levitt and March, 1988), and that the nature of an organization's routines determines the organization's performance and results (Nelson and Winter, 1982). We maintain that an organization's routines constitute one part of a more complete description of that organization, but a part which offers little leverage for producing organization change.

Routines are created and sustained by the decisions and actions of individual actors. Human beings design their behavior based on their interpretations of their environment (Miller et al., 1960), and behavior in organizations is an emergent product of such interpretations. If interpretive processes in organizations shape routines, they may offer a way to change them. However, first, as these subtle cognitive processes occur without actors' conscious awareness (Daft and Weick, 1984; Goleman, 1985) they cannot be altered easily. Second, as organization members share the same tacit assumptions (Schein, 1992), they are unaware of the extent to which their interpretations are subjective. Third, organizational routines themselves reinforce the validity of shared interpretations, creating a self-reinforcing dynamic, as illustrated in Figure 2. Neither routines nor interpretive processes can be altered by management decision; instead, individual organization members' attention must be called to the nature and effects of the way they see their environment. A critical question is how to help people to reduce the counterproductive consequences of tacit assumptions they are unaware of holding. This question, the focus of those in the accountability category, is explored further below.

Developing Individuals' Mental Models to Alter Collective Interpretive Processes

Interventions designed to explore and change individuals' mental models offer a way to alter organizational interpretive processes, and a way out of the self-reinforcing cycle in the integrative model shown in Figure 2. In this model, leverage for influencing routines lies in engaging organization members in a process of developing their mental models. For this reason, our

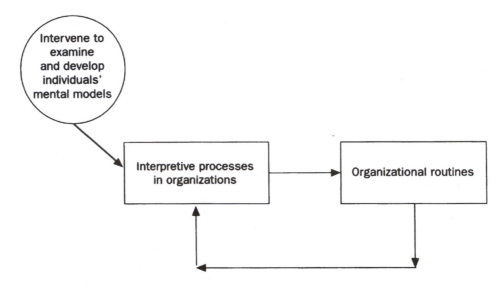

Figure 2   *An integrative model*

definition of organizational learning involves individuals actively using data to test their interpretations and conclusions. This cyclic learning process facilitates exposing erroneous or obsolete inferences. Along similar lines, Peter Senge and Chris Argyris have each advocated working with the cognitive maps of individuals to create learning organizations. In the next sections, we review their intervention strategies and conclude by suggesting that an integration of these two approaches offers a more powerful intervention strategy than either approach alone.

Integrating Intervention Strategies

System Dynamics and Mental Models

Senge's unique contribution to system dynamics, discussed above, lies in his proposal that organization members must engage in a process of learning to understand their own system, rather than relying upon expert consultants (Senge, 1990). To do this, he designs 'learning laboratories' – facilitated computer simulations that enable people to improve their mental models of how parts of their organization interact (Isaacs and Senge, 1992). Senge calls these simulations 'management practice fields', as, with them, managers can develop their thinking through trial and error without being hampered by the real-life consequences of actual decisions. A central objective of such an intervention is to allow organizational members to discover how their own thinking creates some of the problems they face. Thus, Senge combines technical models with the 'softer' concepts of vision and personal growth, as he maintains that technical issues are not easily remedied by technical solutions. This is because of the tendency for people to attribute causality to factors outside themselves – that is, to blame other managers, recessions, customers, or suppliers – and thus to fail to see their own causal role in creating or exacerbating problems. Senge's core message is that without individuals learning to shift their own ways of thinking about systems, organizations will be ineffective. Thus, fostering an experience of account-ability for results is a central component of the intervention.

Senge's approach includes involving people throughout an organization, despite the fact that the system dilemmas uncovered relate to policy issues addressed primarily by top management. His belief that participation in diagnosis should occur organization-wide is driven by his commitment to team learning and shared vision. The support of a team is needed to deal with the 'central threatening message' of systems thinking; that 'our actions have created our reality' (Senge, 1990: 237). He believes that individuals must feel a sense of accountability for current results. This approach is limited in two ways. First, those who participate in learning labs may lack the formal power to change the policy issues that the system dynamics models depict, and, second, they will almost certainly lack the interpersonal skills to communicate their new insights productively, particularly in situations charac-terized by face threat (Argyris, 1993). A theoretical concern is thus how participants' new insights into causal dynamics can be translated productively into action.

Action Science and Interpersonal Skill

Argyris (1982) argues that all human action is a consequence of design; not deliberate design but rather implicit if–then statements analogous to a computer program. Ineffective action in organizations is as much a result of design as is effective action. None the less, it is not possible simply to ask people to change their cognitive 'programs to improve their own effective-ness and the effectiveness of their organizations because these programs are largely tacit. There are two kinds of action programs, the espoused kind (if–then propositions that we think lie behind our actions) and the 'theory-in-use' ('if–then propositions an individual actually uses when he or she acts' (Argyris, l982: 4)). Moreover, people are unaware of the discrepancy between their espoused and their theories-in-use. This unawareness is partly due to learning these theories-in-use early in life. More insidiously, however, such theories-in-use are designed to keep people unaware of the discrepancy; a phenomenon Argyris calls 'designed ignorance'.

Argyris (1982) defines learning as detection and correction of error, and he documents how hard it is for individuals to detect their own errors in difficult interpersonal interactions. This is partly because of their reliance on abstractions and evaluations – inferences made by actors on both sides of a difficult interaction that are not tied to 'directly observable data' but are treated by actors as facts. Most people utilize a dysfunctional theory-in-use called by Argyris and Schön (1974) 'Model I'. Model I is a kind of causal reasoning that reduces sensitivity to feedback and thus inhibits the detection of error, and precludes learning about the real causes of problems. Model I is characterized by a need to control, maximize winning, suppress emotions, and be rational; its strategies involve making untested attributions about others, unshared evaluations, and advocating positions without illustration or openness. Its consequences include miscommunication and escalating error (Argyris, 1982).

Individuals using Model I will create Organizational I (O-I) systems, characterized by 'defensiveness, self-fulfilling prophecies, self-fueling processes, and escalating error' (Argyris, 1982: 8). O-I systems are difficult to change, due to imbedded reinforcing dynamics created by defensive reasoning strategies that individuals are unaware of using. This sets up a 'Catch 22'; individuals' theories-in-use 'cause' social systems to malfunction and at the same time, O-I social systems 'cause' individuals to reason and act as they do (Argyris et al., 1985).

To change these self-reinforcing dynamics, Argyris argues that individuals must learn an alternative cognitive program to Model I – Model II. A Model II theory-in-use, in Argyris's words, is based on directly observable data, and requires that advocacy be supported by illustration, testing and inquiry into others' views (Argyris, 1982). Although it is not difficult to agree with these premises, employing Model II in interpersonal interactions requires profound attentiveness and skill for human beings socialized in a Model I world. A skilled interventionist can demonstrate and use these skills while engaging organization members in a diagnostic process aimed at helping them to understand ways in which their own actions inhibit learning. With considerable commitment and practice, it may be possible for members of an organization to improve their skill and their ability to learn in difficult interpersonal exchanges. For example, Argyris (1993) describes a five-year change project in a single organization, in which significant behavioral changes are observed.

The levels of skill and commitment required to successfully implement such an intervention make this approach extremely vulnerable to neglect in the face of financial or management changes in an organization. Similarly, organizations have shown reluctance to commit to behavioral change programs in the first place (e.g. Beer et al., 1990). Finally, the link between learning Model II theories-in-use and changing organizational strategy is under-specified, and Argyris pays insufficient attention to the complexity of interacting organization systems (Blake and Mouton, 1988). Thus, this approach is limited by its apparent lack of connection to strategic business issues, a gap that can be addressed by integration with a system dynamics approach.

Overcoming Cognitive Barriers to Creating a Learning Organization

Despite their contrasting backgrounds and different theories, both Senge and Argyris view properties of individual cognition as the critical source of leverage for creating more effective organizations. Both document self-sealing dynamics in organizations that require the development of individual cognitive maps to escape their counterproductive effects. Both researchers show that taken-for-granted cognition of organizational actors leads to unintended, counterproductive effects. Furthermore, the taken-for-granted elements – whether erroneous causal models or theories-in-use – contain features that block actors' own awareness of their counterproductive nature. Senge explains that once causality is misattributed (inevitable in complex dynamic systems) decision makers stop seeking a cause for an outcome. Thus, mental models – once formulated – endure, and actors remain unaware that these observed relationships are simply hypotheses rather than facts. Similarly, Argyris describes Model I theories-in-use as learned so early that individuals are unaware of them. Thus, for example, we are able to perceive others as defensive and remain unaware of our own contributing role in producing this outcome. In short, Argyris and Senge agree on the need for a cognitive level for intervention if real change and learning are to occur.

Their intervention strategies, considered in the context of a broad range of organizational development techniques, are also similar in important ways. Both propose that tacit sources of ineffectiveness must be made explicit in order to be changed, and maintain that this blindness is unlikely to correct itself without an outside interventionist. Senge advocates the use of a researcher to facilitate diagnosis about non-obvious causal relationships in the system, and Argyris believes that organization members can learn Model II skills by working with an interventionist.

Discussion

A common focus on cognition   In light of these common premises, we propose that *an integrative approach* can begin to address the core challenges or gaps identified for each of the two researchers. We concur with both Senge and Argyris that programmatic and policy-oriented changes, such as those described in the participation category, will have limited effectiveness if underlying sources of resistance embedded in the mental models of organization members are not addressed. In our integrative approach, the adaptation and enactment perspectives discussed above come together. The work of both Senge and Argyris reflects an understanding that human cognition both interprets and influences the organization – much like Weick's notion of enactment; at the same time, this work includes a prescription for engaging cognitive maps to promote effective organizational adaptation.

We view the contributions of Senge and Argyris as complementary parts of a theory of intervention that focuses on examining and developing mental models. Our analysis of relationships among different foci in the organizational learning literature suggests that this intervention strategy offers critical leverage for reinterpreting organizational situations and changing persistent routines. While Senge's model provides valuable insights to decision makers about the effects of current policies, his approach does not address participants' lack of decision-making authority to act on these diagnoses, and thus risks fostering frustration; it also fails to teach the skills to communicate new insights to others without engendering defensiveness. Argyris, on the other hand, provides a process for learning to change counterproductive interpersonal dynamics, without including a substantive focus for participants to engage while learning these Model II skills. We believe that becoming a learning organization requires engaging in both practices at once. Fostering significant organizational change requires productive interpersonal conversation to collectively diagnose substantive cause–effect relationships.

Integration: filling gaps Both Senge (1990) and Argyris (e.g. Argyris and Kaplan, 1994) have advocated integration in broad terms. Argyris's recent work advocates the need to work simultaneously with *behavioral* and *technical* issues for successful organizational intervention, as technical changes will fail if they threaten those who are to implement them (Argyris, 1996). Similarly, Senge (1990) advocates integrating systems thinking with behavioral disciplines. Thus, we are in agreement with these recent writings; however, we offer two additional contributions. First, we have included a rationale for focusing on the cognitive representations of organization members in the context of the range of issues addressed in the organizational learning literature. Second, we identify specific ways in which system dynamics and action science – as intervention strategies – each present concerns that can be addressed in part by integrating the other. Senge's approach engages participants in substantive strategic issues, while Argyris helps them to develop critical reasoning and communication skills for learning. If an intervention includes an important substantive focus, we believe that organizational commitment to developing interpersonal theories-in-use is less vulnerable. Similarly, if participants are to take action based on new diagnoses of system interrelationships, an action science component provides training in the interpersonal competence and ability to learn in difficult interactions that are needed to communicate these insights and plans to others. Both approaches emphasize a sense of personal accountability for results, thereby mutually reinforcing a message of ownership and self-reflection. Similarly, both strive to turn participants into on-the-job researchers, in the sense of being able to examine data critically and learn from them. Our proposed definition of organizational learning emphasizes this ability, as we view it as a core competence of learning organizations.

Conclusion

The organizational learning literature encompasses a range of phenomena, some of which involve learning as a source of effectiveness. In this article, we propose that the learning organization rubric be used to distinguish these normative approaches from the larger body of work. We address the question of what it means to become a learning organization, and discuss the intervention theories of two prominent researchers in the field, Peter Senge and Chris Argyris. Although trained by very different academic disciplines, Senge and Argyris both advocate a cognitive approach to intervening in organizations to improve their adaptability and effectiveness. In the context of the broader literature on organizational learning, the work of these two researchers shares important similarities; yet each offers only part of the puzzle, and each carries important limitations when implemented separately.

In this article, we propose an equal, critical role for developing interpersonal theories-in-use and the ability to diagnose systemic implications of organizational actions. Our analysis suggests that engaging both kinds of cognitive models at the same time – cause-effect assumptions and interpersonal strategies – has the potential to prove far more effective than either approach to intervention implemented alone. Although our focus is on improving intervention, this article also draws from the descriptive organizational learning literature to find support for its conclusions. Specifically, we note that descriptive research has found that organizations fail to adapt effectively to change, and show that the stabilizing interaction between interpretive processes and routines requires addressing individual mental models to escape this self-reinforcing dynamic. Finally, we propose that empirical research must be undertaken to assess the effects of these complementary processes in producing organizational change.

Notes

1. Although both groups are interested in organizational effectiveness, the entity discussed as *learning* (or not learning) differs. In some treatments, individuals learn and organizational conditions can enhance or inhibit that potential. In other treatments, human learning is used as a metaphor to describe adaptation at the level of the organizational system.

2. These two perspectives can be seen as complementary, rather than mutually exclusive, in that implementation of well-intentioned policies in organizations as advocated by researchers in the participation category often fails due to the psychological and cognitive barriers explored in the accountability category. At the same time, those who focus directly on cognition may be able to incorporate attention to organizational policies and strategies into their approach to intervention (Edmondson, 1996).

References

Adams, G.B. (1994) 'Blindsided by the Elephant', *Public Administration Review* 54(1): 77–83.

Argyris, C. (1982) 'Action Science and Intervention', unpublished manuscript, (Sept) Harvard University.

Argyris, C. (1993) *Actionable Knowledge: Changing the Status Quo.* San Francisco: Jossey-Bass.

Argyris, C. (1996) 'Prologue', in B. Moingeon and A. Edmondson (eds) *Organizational Learning and Competitive Advantage.* London: Sage.

Argyris, C. and Kaplan, R. (1994) 'Implementing New Knowledge: The Case of Activity-based Costing', *Accounting Horizons* 8(3): 83–105.

Argyris, C., Putnam, R. and Smith, D.M. (1985) *Action Science.* San Francisco: Jossey-Bass.

Argyris, C. and Schön, D. (1974) *Theory in Practice.* San Francisco: Jossey-Bass.

Argyris, C. and Schön, D. (1978) *Organizational Learning: A Theory of Action Perspective.* Reading, MA: Addison-Wesley.

Beer, M., Eisenstat, R. and Spector, B. (1990) *The Critical Path to Corporate Renewal.* Boston, MA: Harvard Business School Press.

Blake, R. and Mouton, J. (1988) 'Comparing Strategies for Incremental and Transformational Change', in R. Kilman and T. Covin (eds) *Corporate Transformation.* San Francisco: Jossey-Bass.

Brown, J. S. (1991) 'Research that Reinvents the Corporation', *Harvard Business Review* 69(1): 102–11.

Brown, J.S. and Duguid, P. (1991) 'Organizational Learning and Communities of Practice: Toward a Unified View of Working, Learning, and Innovation', *Organizational Science* 2(1): 40–57.

Collis, D. (1996) 'Organizational Capability as a Source of Profit', in B. Moingeon and A. Edmondson (eds) *Organizational Learning and Competitive Advantage*. London: Sage.

Cyert, R.M. and March, J.G. (1963) *A Behavioral Theory of the Firm*. Englewood Cliffs, NJ: Prentice-Hall.

Daft, R.L. and Weick, K.E. (1984) 'Toward a Model of Organizations as Interpretation Systems', *Academy of Management Review* 9: 284–95.

de Geuss, A.P. (1988) 'Planning as Learning', *Harvard Business Review* 66(2): 70–4.

Edmondson, A. (1996) 'Three Faces of Eden: The Persistence of Multiple Perspectives and Competing Theories in Organizational Intervention Research', *Human Relations* 49(5): 571–95.

Fiol, C.M. and Lyles, M.A. (1985) 'Organizational Learning', *Academy of Management Review* 10: 803–13.

Forrester, J. (1961) *Industrial Dynamics*. Cambridge, MA: Productivity Press.

Gersick, C.J.G. and Hackman, J.R. (1990) 'Habitual Routines in Task-performing Teams', *Organizational Behavior and Human Decision Processes* 47: 65–97.

Goleman, D. (1985) *Vital Lies Simple Truths: The Psychology of Self-Deception*. New York: Simon & Schuster.

Hannan, M.T. and Freeman, J. (1984) 'Structural Inertia and Organizational Change', *American Sociological Review* 49: 149–64.

Hayes, R.H., Wheelwright, S.C. and Clark, K.B. (1988) *Dynamic Manufacturing: Creating the Learning Organization*. London: The Free Press.

Huber, G.P. (1991) 'Organizational Learning: The Contributing Processes and the Literature', *Organizational Science* 2(1): 88–115.

Isaacs, W.N. and Senge, P.M. (1992) 'Overcoming Limits to Learning in Computer-based Learning Environments', *European Journal of Operational Research* 59: 183–96.

Janis, I. (1982) *Groupthink: Psychological Studies of Policy Decisions and Fiascoes*. Boston: Houghton-Mifflin.

Jones, A.M. and Hendry, C. (1992) *The Learning Organization: A Review of Literature and Practice*. University of Warwick: The HRD Partnership.

Levitt, B. and March, J. (1988) 'Organizational Learning', *Annual Review of Sociology* 14: 319–40.

Miller, G., Gallanter, E. and Pribram, K. (1960) *Plans and the Structure of Behavior*. New York: Holt, Rhinehart, and Winston.

Nelson, R. and Winter, S. (1982) *An Evolutionary Theory of Economic Change*. Cambridge: Harvard University Press.

Orlikowski, W. (1996) 'Organizational Transformation Over Time', *Information Systems Research* 7(1): 63–92.

Pedler, M., Burgoyne, J. and Boydell, T. (eds) (1990) *Self-development in Organizations*. London: McGraw-Hill.

Pettigrew, A.M. and Whipp, R. (1991) *Managing Change for Competitive Success*. Oxford: Blackwell.

Redding, J.C. and Catalenello, R.F. (1994) *Strategic Readiness: The Making of the Learning Organization*. San Francisco: Jossey-Bass.

Schein, E.H. (1992) 'How Can Organizations Learn Faster: The Problem of Entering the Green Room', invited address to the World Economic Forum, 6 February.

Schön, D. (1983) *The Reflective Practitioner*. New York: Basic Books.

Senge, P. (1990) *The Fifth Discipline: The Art and Practice of the Learning Organization*. New York: Doubleday.

Shrivastava, P. (1983) 'A Typology of Organizational Learning', *Journal of Management Studies* 20(1): 7–28.

Stata, R. (1989) 'Organizational Learning: The Key to Management Innovation', *Sloan Management Review* 12(1): 63–74.

Sterman, J.D. (1989) 'Modeling Managerial Behavior: Misperceptions of Feedback in Dynamic Decision-making', *Management Science* 35(3): 321–39.

von Hippel, E. (1988) *The Sources of Innovation*. New York: Oxford University Press.

Waldo, D. (1961) 'Organization Theory: An Elephantine Problem', *Public Administration Review* 21 (Autumn): 210–25.

Weick, K. (1979) *The Social Psychology of Organizing*. New York: Random House.

2

Michael Popper and Raanan Lipshitz

Organizational Learning
Mechanisms, Culture, and Feasibility

'Organizational learning' and 'learning organizations' are currently in vogue in the academic and applied discourse on organizations (Levitt and March, 1988; Senge, 1990; Cohen and Sproul, 1991; Howard and Haas, 1993; Argyris and Schön, 1996). The down side of the ensuing outpouring of publications is a confusing proliferation of definitions and conceptualizations that fail to converge into a coherent whole: 'Research in organisational learning suffered from conceptions that were excessively broad, encompassing merely all organisational change ... and from various other maladies that arise from insufficient agreement among those working in the area on its key concepts and problems' (Cohen and Sproul, 1991: 1; see also Daft and Huber, 1987; Dodgson, 1993; Garvin, 1993; Hawkins, 1994; Huber, 1991; Miller, 1996). The present article tries to clarify this confusion by considering four questions: (1) what are the similarities and differences between organizational learning and individual learning? (2) what conditions promote organizational learning? (3) what conditions promote productive organizational learning? and (4) how is organizational learning related to learning organizations? These questions touch four sources of ambiguity and contention in the literature on organizational learning. Clarifying them may help to reduce the conceptual haze surrounding the twin concepts of organizational learning and learning organizations, thus making them more amenable to study and normative intervention.

Individual Learning vs Organizational Learning

The notion of organizational learning proves particularly slippery in the interface between individual and organizational learning. However defined, organizational learning is clearly mediated by the learning of individual organizational members. Where then lies the border between individual and organizational learning, and to what extent can models of individual learning describe organizational learning?

Researchers take different positions on these issues. Some equate organizational learning with individual learning; others see the two as distinct processes. Representing the former position Hedberg suggests that: 'Organisations do not have brains, but they have cognitive systems and memories. As individuals develop their personalities, personal habits and beliefs over time, organisations develop their views and ideologies' (Hedberg, 1981: 6).

Taking the contrary view, Cook and Yanow argue that

> What organisations do when they learn is necessarily different from what individuals do when they learn. Specifically, we believe that organisational learning is not essentially a cognitive activity, because at the very least, organisations lack the typical wherewithal for undertaking cognition ... To understand organizational learning we must look for attributes that organizations can be meaningfully understood to possess and use. (Cook and Yanow, 1993: 378)

Examination of Figures 1 and 2 illustrates the Procrustean bed that appears when models of individual learning are extended to organizational learning. Figure 1 is an adaptation of Kolb's (1984) four-stage model of individual experiential learning, to which we added a fifth phase, retention. This nonessential modification was designed to bring out the similarity between this model and Shaw and Perkins's (1992) six-phase model of organizational learning (Figure 2). Taking 'knowledge and belief systems' in Figure 2 to be

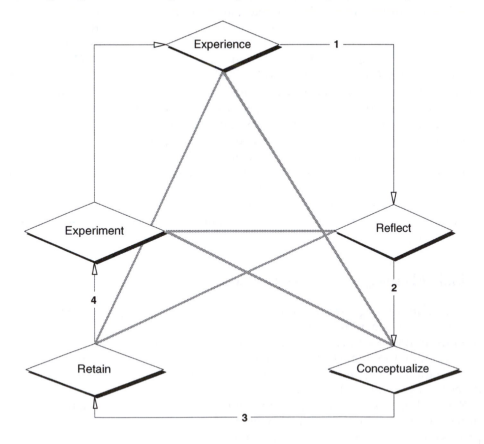

Figure 1   *Experiential learning*

organizational level analogues of 'retention' in Figure 1, the essential identity of the star-shaped configurations in both models shows that models of individual learning can serve, with slight modifications, as models of organizational learning. Note, however, that dissemination is left out of the shared star-shaped configuration in Figure 2, thus showing that some aspects of organizational learning are fundamentally different from individual learning (Weick, 1991).

Elsewhere (Popper and Lipshitz, 1998) we argued that treating organizations *as if* they were human beings blurs the distinction between two very different conceptions of organizational learning, *learning in organizations* and *learning by organizations*. Both conceptions lurk in Simon's assertion that 'All learning takes place inside individual human heads; an organisation learns in only two ways: (a) by the learning of its members, or (b) by ingesting new members who have knowledge the organisation previously did not have' (Simon, 1991: 125). The first part of the assertion represents learning in organizations. Equivalent to the star-shaped configuration in Figures 1 and 2,

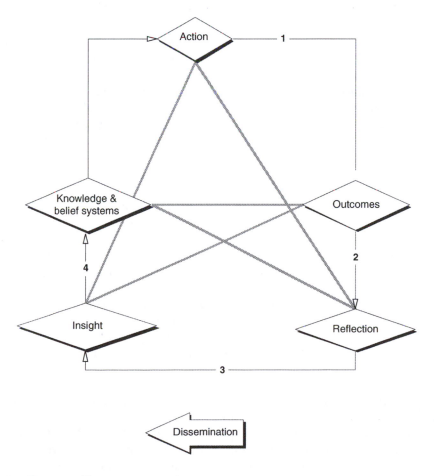

Figure 2 *Organizational learning*

it locates organizational learning in 'individual human heads', reducing organizational learning to individual learning taking place in organizational settings. The second part of the assertion represents learning by organizations. Locating organizational learning in processes (e.g. recruitment and dissemination) that occur outside 'individual human heads', it defies the reduction of organizational to individual learning. Conceiving organizational learning as learning in organizations invites a puzzle as to how the learning of individuals becomes organizational (e.g. how newly acquired insights and skills produce changes in norms and standard operating procedures). Learning by organizations invites a different puzzle: how does learning take place 'outside individual human heads?' These are not mere conceptual niceties. Can we really hope to design effective methods of instituting organizational learning – or 'learning organizations' – without knowing how to go beyond learning by individuals?

Two types of solution to the problem of learning in organizations vs learning by organizations have been proposed in the literature. Argyris and Schön (1978, 1996) fused learning in organizations and learning by organizations by positing organizational theories of action – a hypothetical construct denoting shared (i.e. organizational-level) individual-level theories of action. Following Senge (1990), Kim (1993) uses a somewhat different hypothetical construct – shared mental models. In both cases, organizational learning can be studied – and facilitated – by making individual models explicit and inquiring into their behavioural consequences. Specifically, organizational learning occurs when inventions and evaluations of individual members are embedded in the organization's theory-in-use or shared mental models (Argyris and Schön, 1978).

Positing collective-level hypothetical constructs does bridge the gap between learning in and learning by organizations. A drawback of this strategy is that measuring hypothetical constructs at the individual – let alone collective – level 'involves inferring the existence and nature of entities that cannot be empirically proven to exist' (Rouse and Morris, 1986; Rouse, Cannon-Bowers and Salas, 1992: 1304). An alternative strategy, which does not use hypothetical 'as-if' constructs, relates organizations to the experiences and actions of their members by studying the concrete structural and procedural arrangements through which 'actions by [organizations' individual] members that are understood to entail learning are followed by observable changes in the organisations' pattern of activities' (Cook and Yanow, 1993, p. 375). We call these arrangements organizational learning mechanisms, that is, OLMs.

OLMs are institutionalized structural and procedural arrangements that allow organizations to learn non-vicariously, that is, to collect, analyse, store, disseminate, and use systematically information that is relevant to their and their members' performance (Popper and Lipshitz, 1998). OLMs link learning in organizations to learning by organizations in a concrete, directly observable and malleable fashion. On the one hand they are organizational-level entities and processes. On the other, they are operated by individuals and, at times, dedicated to facilitating learning in organizations or to disseminating what individuals and groups learn throughout the organization. Thus, OLMs concretize Edmondson and Moingeon's (1998:12) definition of organizational learning as 'the process in which an organisation's members actively use data to guide behavior in a way as to promote the ongoing adaptation of the organisation', and permit one to attribute to organizations the capacity to learn and help them build such a capacity, without using metaphorical discourse or positing hypothetical constructs.

OLMs can be classified as *integrated* or *non-integrated* mechanisms, and *designated* or *dual-purpose* mechanisms, depending on *when* and *by whom* they are operated. An OLM is integrated if its 'operators' and 'clients' (i.e. organizational members who are responsible for generating and applying its 'lessons learned', respectively) are identical. An OLM is non-integrated if operators and clients are not identical. Interaction reviews in which fighter pilots in the Israeli Defense Force (IDF) review their own performance (Popper and Lipshitz, 1998) exemplify integrated OLMs. Strategic planning units that prepare their reports for the management of the organization exemplify non-integrated OLMs. After-action reviews additionally exemplify designated OLMs, namely, mechanisms in which learning takes place away from task performance. In dual-purpose mechanisms, learning is carried out in conjunction with task performance. We observed this learning in the weekly patient reviews in a vascular surgery unit in a general hospital. These are principally performed to deliver treatment to the patients. In addition, they are used to assess and improve the effectiveness of treatment in general, in which capacity they result in the adoption of new forms of treatment, establishing new procedures in the work of the medical staff, and other system-level outcomes. Non-integrated and designated OLMs represent the lowest – and easiest to achieve – level of organizational learning. The price of assigning learning to specialists is lower probability of implementation owing to the separation between learning and acting. Integrated and non-designated OLMs represent the highest – and most difficult to achieve – level of organizational learning. The price paid for aiming at this level is greater exposure to numerous threats to validity owing to various cognitive and emotional biases (Argyris, 1982; Brehmer, 1980).

In conclusion, individual learning and organizational learning are similar in that they involve the same phases of information processing; namely, collection, analysis, abstraction and retention. They are dissimilar in two respects: information processing is carried out at different systemic levels by different structures (Roth, 1997), and organizational learning involves an additional phase, dissemination, i.e. the transmission of information and knowledge among different persons and organizational units.

The 'basic equipment' that enables individuals to learn is the nervous system. OLMs constitute the metaphorically equivalent and substantively different system that enables organizations to learn. Neither the nervous system nor OLMs ensure that learning will be productive, that is, beneficial to their owners. This brings the discussion to a second source of confusion in the literature, namely the dispute over the relationship between organizational learning and organizational effectiveness.

When is Organizational Learning Likely to be Productive?

Is organizational learning necessarily beneficial? The controversy among students of organizations over this question has been another source of confusion in regard to organizational learning (Argyris and Schön, 1996). While it is probably fair to say that a majority of these students answers in the affirmative, a significant minority disagrees. In our opinion, this source of confusion is a pseudo-argument that can be resolved by differentiating between descriptive and normative approaches to organizational learning, and by delineating which form of learning is of interest.

The claim that organizational learning is beneficial rests on an analytical argument and a normative argument. According to the analytical argument, survival in dynamic environments entails a capacity to learn: 'To remain viable in an environment characterized by uncertainty and change, organisations and individuals alike depend upon an ability to learn' (Edmondson and Moingeon, 1998: 9). According to the normative argument, organizational learning creates idyllic environments in which 'people continually expand their capacity to create the results they truly desire, where new and expansive patterns of thinking are nurtured, where collective aspiration is set free, and where people are continually learning how to learn together' (Senge, 1990: 2). Arguments that doubt the beneficial nature of organizational learning are grounded in the voluminous literature on the difficulties encountered by individuals, groups and organizations who try to draw valid lessons from experience (Brehmer, 1980; Janis and Mann, 1977; Neustadt and May, 1986). Levitt and March (1988: 335) summarized this argument succinctly as follows: 'Learning does not always lead to intelligent behavior. The same processes that yield experiential wisdom produce superstitious learning, competence traps, and erroneous inferences'. Argyris and Schön (1996: 193) resolved the controversy by proposing that 'organisational learning is a meaningful notion but not always beneficent', implying that the question of interest is not 'is organizational learning beneficial to the organization?' but 'when is organisational learning likely to be productive, namely result in the detection and correction of error?'

We suggest that organizational learning mechanisms are likely to yield productive learning if they are embedded in an appropriate organizational culture, that is, a normative system of shared values and beliefs that shape how organization members feel, think, and behave (Schein, 1990). We posit a hierarchy of five values (Figure 3). Situated at the apex of the hierarchy is continuous learning, which in turn requires valid information, transparency, issue orientation, and accountability. These values are manifested either by compatible rhetoric (espoused values) or (more convincingly) by an actual investment of resources and the willingness to incur losses in order to realize compatible outcomes (values in use).

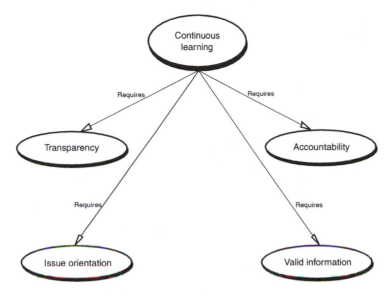

Figure 3   *Values hierarchy of a learning culture*

Continuous Learning

Continuous learning is essential for surviving – let alone prospering – in dynamic and competitive environments (De Geus, 1988; Garvin, 1993; Nonaka, 1991; Schein, 1990; Senge, 1990). As BP's CEO John Browne puts it (Prokesch, 1997: 148):

> Learning is at the heart of a company's ability to adapt to a rapidly changing environment. It is the key to being able both to identify opportunities that others might not see and to exploit those opportunities rapidly and fully ... In order to generate extraordinary value for shareholders, a company has to learn better than its competitors and apply that knowledge throughout its business faster and more widely than they do ... Anyone in the organisation who is not directly accountable for making a profit should be involved in creating and distributing knowledge that the company can use to make profit.

Valid Information

Learning at both individual and organizational levels involves the transformation of data (uninterpreted information) into knowledge (interpreted information). To be productive, learning clearly requires complete, undistorted, and verifiable information. Argyris and Schön (1996) suggest that organization members are often pressured to withhold, distort or fabricate information in order to defend themselves and/or others. Holding valid information as a value acts as a countermeasure to such pressures.

We infer that valid information is a value of the Israeli Air Force's culture from the constant efforts that the Air Force makes to improve the objectivity and scope of the information that is available for after-action reviews, and from the socialization of pilots to surface and rigorously dissect their own and others' performance.

Transparency

Transparency is the willingness to hold oneself (and one's actions) open to inspection in order to receive valid feedback. Transparency serves valid information by reducing the likelihood of self-deception, by countering pressures to distort or suppress threatening information, and by broadening the scope of one's information base and points of view for its interpretation. Transparency is facilitated by technical aids such as VCRs or small-scale organizational designs. Quoting BP's John Browne again:

> We divided the company up [into smaller units] . . . to let everyone see clearly how things are done and understand what each person's role is in getting it done . . . The virtue of [this] organisational structure is that there is a lot of transparency. Not only can the people within the business unit understand more clearly what they have to do, but I and the other senior executives can understand what they are doing. Then we can have an ongoing dialogue with them and with ourselves about how to improve performance and build the future. (Prokesch, 1997: 162–3)

Technical means, such as VCRs and appropriate task and organizational designs cannot in themselves produce valid information if people feel defensive and threatened. The lack of defensiveness that characterizes pilots' behaviour in the after-action reviews that we have observed in the IDF can thus be partly attributed to pilots' willingness to lay themselves open in order to receive the valid feedback required for maximizing the benefits of learning from their experience.

Issue Orientation

Issue orientation is the evaluation of information strictly on its merit without regard to irrelevant attributes such as the social standing of its source or recipient. According to McGill and Slocum (1993), one task of management in learning organizations is to expose failure and constructively promote dissent. This task cannot be accomplished unless information is presented – and received – subject to issue orientation. Issue orientation is related to (but is more focused than) democratization, power equalization, and participation which also open communication channels, thereby enhancing innovation and learning (Kanter, 1991; McGill, Slocum and Lei, 1993). In the Israeli Air Force's after-action reviews the military's rigid hierarchical system is suspended, thus increasing the likelihood that subordinates will express their honest opinions to their superiors. Note that the rigid military hierarchical command structure *is suspended* for the duration of the after-action review, forming a kind of time- and task-bound 'cultural island' in which issue orientation, particularly when modelled by senior officers, promotes learning. Thus this hierarchy is neither cancelled nor undermined in the Air Force's flight units.

Accountability

Accountability is holding oneself responsible for one's actions and their consequences and for learning from these consequences. It facilitates overcoming obstacles to effective learning in the form of action barriers that prevent the implementation of lessons learned (March and Olsen, 1976; Shaw and Perkins, 1992). This value is reflected in the flight instructors' demand that trainees debrief themselves. It also was nicely illustrated to us by the head of the vascular unit of the general hospital that we observed:

> I believe that if a patient dies or fails to heal it is our [i.e. the staff's] fault. This is a healthy attitude, even if factually it may not be true. One can always rationalize that the patient was 80 years old, that his heart was weak, that his wife nagged him to death, and so on and so forth. The list of justifications that one can use to CYA ['cover your ass'] is endless. For me, this attitude is unacceptable. If the basic premise is that we are at fault, it follows that we should find out what went wrong so that next time we will avoid this error. That, in my opinion, is the key to constantly learning and improving.

In conclusion, we suggest that organizational learning is likely to be productive if the organization's learning mechanisms are embedded in a culture of learning. Many, if not most, organizations cannot claim to have this combination. A question that presents itself thus is, what conditions make organizational learning more feasible?

The Feasibility of Organizational Learning

A casual review of the literature on organizational learning reveals that much of the empirical evidence regarding either organizational learning or learning organizations comes from organizational settings characterized by at least some of the following factors: a high level of environmental uncertainty, costly potential errors, a high level of professionalism, and strong leadership commitment to learning. Accordingly, we hypothesize that unless some of these factors are present, efforts to institutionalize organizational learning are most likely to fail. We now review existing support for the posited relationships among these factors and the feasibility of organizational learning.

Environmental Uncertainty

Numerous writers proposed that organizational learning is virtually a sine qua non for surviving in uncertain environments (Daft and Huber, 1987; Dodgson, 1993; Fiol and Lyles, 1985; Freeman and Perez, 1988; Garvin, 1993; Pavitt, 1991; Toffler, 1990). The basic rationale is simple enough: dynamism (rate of change), a basic component of uncertainty (Daft, 1989), requires adaptation, and successful adaptation is contingent on effective learning. Hence, organizations that do not learn will not survive, particularly if the environment is competitive – another basic component of environmental uncertainty (Daft, 1989). The relationship between environmental uncertainty and organizational learning was recently refined by Edmondson and

Moingeon (1996). These researchers posit a contingent relationship between two types of environmental uncertainty and two types of organizational learning. One type of uncertainty is due to competitiveness (characterized by clear criteria of success and failure), and the other is due to ambiguity (characterizing interpersonal 'relationships in which such clarity is typically lacking). The types of learning are learning how (which involves the transfer and improvement of existing skills and routines) and learning why (which involves inquiring into the causes of difficulties and problems). According to Edmondson and Moingeon (1996), engaging in learning how is important in situations of market competitiveness, in which criteria for success are relatively clear, and where response speed, product quality, and consistency of service are crucial determinants of success. Engaging in learning why is important for avoiding the dysfunctional interpersonal relationships and defensive routines thoroughly documented by Argyris (1991, 1993).

A recent study (Ellis and Shpielberg, 1998) provides empirical support for the often claimed – and rarely studied – relationship between environmental uncertainty and organizational learning. These researchers tested the relationship between the intensity of environmental uncertainty and the regularity of organizational learning. Three hundred and ninety-five product managers in industries operating in certain or uncertain environments completed two questionnaires, one measuring perceived environmental uncertainty and the other measuring the operation of OLMs in five areas or facets of learning: formal learning, training, information gathering, information storage and retrieval, and information dissemination (Globerson and Ellis, 1996). There were negative correlations between perceived environmental uncertainty and the intensity of use of all the five measured facets of organizational learning. These correlations were higher in industries operating in uncertain environments than in those operating in certain environments. In addition, when perceived uncertainty was regressed on the five organizational learning facets, the regression weight of information gathering was positive, indicating that without the operation of organizational learning (in the form of training, information storage, retrieval and dissemination), information gathering increases uncertainty.

Costly Potential Errors

A high perceived likelihood of potentially costly but avoidable errors facilitates learning. This proposition is based on research showing that failure stimulates risk seeking (Kahneman and Tversky, 1979) and diagnostic behaviour (Wong and Wiener, 1981), and that perceived moderate-sized threats stimulate vigilant behaviour (Janis and Mann, 1977). Consistent with this proposition, some examples of organizational learning come from organizations under crisis (e.g. a general walk out; Rayner, 1993), or from organizational settings in which people routinely face potentially catastrophic (e.g. life threatening) errors such as nuclear power plants (Carrol, 1995; DiBella, Nevis and Gould, 1996); surgery hospital wards (Lipshitz and Popper, in press); and fighter flight units (Popper and Lipshitz, 1998).

Notwithstanding the latter evidence, the effects of failure on organizational learning are controversial. On the one hand Sitkin (1992: 243), claims that 'failure is an essential prerequisite for learning, as it stimulates the sort of experimentation that Campbell (1968) and others (March, 1978; Staw, 1983; Weick, 1979; Wildavsky, 1988) have advocated as fundamental for sound policy development and organizational management'. In contrast, based on an analysis of an organizational failure Clarke and Perrow (1996: 1040), concluded that 'high-technology, high-risk systems do not foster organisational learning'. Careful analysis resolves this apparent disagreement. Sitkin (1992: 243) conceded that:

> ... not all failures are equally adept at facilitating learning. Those failures that are most effective at fostering learning will be referred to as 'intelligent failures' ... Five key characteristics that contribute to the intelligence of failure are: (1) they result from thoughtfully planned actions that (2) have uncertain outcomes and (3) are of modest scale, (4) are executed and responded to with alacrity, and (5) take place in domains that are familiar enough to permit effective learning.

And Clarke and Perrow's (1996) data and analysis show that their case of the Shoreham Nuclear Power Station illustrates at least three of Sitkin's conditions (items 1, 4, and 5 above).

Finally, Ellis et al. (1998) compared the relationship between perceived cost of potential error and the existence of a learning culture in two populations characterized by relatively high costs of error (air-traffic controllers and managers in high-tech organizations) and two populations characterized by relatively low costs of error (psychiatrists and physicians in a mental hospital, and teachers). Consistent with the proposition that costly potential errors facilitate organizational learning, subjects in the first two populations obtained significantly higher scores on the sub-scales of a learning values questionnaire measuring valid information, transparency, accountability, and issue orientation.

High Level of Members' Professionalism

Professionals are evaluated by the extent to which they master and keep abreast of the knowledge (both 'knowing that' and 'knowing how') pertinent to their field (Hoffman, 1989). Accordingly, we propose that organizational learning is facilitated by a norm, or mindset, of professionalism. This proposition is consistent with two of Sitkin's (1992) conditions that facilitate learning from failure listed above, thoughtful action in a familiar domain, as well as with British Petroleum's CEO John Browne's suggestion that BP is a learning organization partly owing to the insistence that:

> ... every time we do something again, we should do it better than the last time ... One process that we employ to promote learning is not that unusual. It involves understanding the critical measures of operating performance in each business, relentlessly benchmarking those measures and their related activities, setting higher and higher targets, and challenging people to achieve them. (Prokesch, 1997: 147–8)

The example of universities shows that a large proportion of professionals (i.e. people with specialized knowledge, such as PhDs, lawyers, and engineers) among an organization's members does not in itself facilitate organizational learning. Faculty members are professionals of the first order (or, at least, are reputed to be). However, since they are committed more strongly to their profession than to their organization, universities, whose core missions are research and teaching, are prime examples of conservative systems (Weisbord, Lawrence and Charles, 1978). In conclusion, to facilitate organizational learning professionalism must be accompanied by organizational commitment.

Strong Leadership Commitment to Learning

Managers are central figures on a stage watched by all (Carlzon, 1989) and the creators of images that influence organization members' feelings and behaviour (Zaleznik, 1992). It is thus not surprising that management's commitment and support has been found to be crucial for successful change programmes in general (Huber et al., 1993; Rodgers and Hunter, 1991), and for the success of programmes that involve cultural change in particular (Kanter, 1991; Lundberg, 1985; Schein, 1990). BP's CEO Browne aptly summarized the importance of managers' active and visible commitment to learning for instituting organizational learning as follows: 'Leaders have to demonstrate that they are active participants in the learning process. You can't say "Go do it" without participating' (Prokesch, 1997: 160).

Organizational Learning and Learning Organizations

Logically there should be a straightforward relationship between 'organizational learning' and the 'learning organization'. In line with this reasoning, Pedler, Boydell and Burgoyne (cited in Hawkins, 1991) define the learning organization as one which facilitates the learning of all its members and continuously transforms itself. More typically, references to organizational learning and learning organizations reflect yet more controversy, a deep, albeit bridgeable, division between

> ... the practice-oriented, prescriptive literature of 'the learning organization,' promulgated mainly by consultants and practitioners, and the predominantly skeptical scholarly literature of 'organisational learning,' produced by academics. The two literatures have different thrusts, appeal to different audiences, and employ different forms of language. Nevertheless, they intersect at key points: their conceptions of what makes organizational learning 'desirable' or 'productive;' their views of the nature of the threats to productive organizational learning; and their attitudes toward whether – and if so, how – such threats may be overcome. (Argyris and Schön, 1996: 180).
>
> Both branches do concern themselves with the capability of real-world organizations to draw valid and useful inferences from experience and observation and to convert such inferences to effective action. But authors of prescriptive bent tend to

assume, uncritically, that such capabilities can be activated through the appropriate enablers, and learning skeptics tend to treat observed impediments as unalterable facts of organizational life. (Argyris and Schön, 1966: 199; see also Edmondson and Moingeon, 1996).

Pedler et al.'s definition of learning organizations quoted above raises three conceptual questions with serious implications for research and intervention. How can we test whether a particular organization facilitates the learning of its members? Are organizations that transform themselves necessarily learning organizations? Must an organization transform itself in order to qualify as a learning organization? The structural and cultural approach to organizational learning (Popper and Lipshitz, in press), which underlies the present discussion, relates 'organizational learning' to 'learning organization' in a way that avoids these difficulties: learning organizations are organizations that embed institutionalized learning mechanisms into a learning culture. Testing whether a particular organization is a learning organization can be done, therefore, by mapping its organizational learning mechanisms, the culture in which they are embedded, and the contribution of both to improved performance and members' ability to change the organization's mission and values (i.e. single-loop and double-loop learning, respectively). Working within this framework, Popper and Lipshitz (1998) used a standard semi-structured interview and observations to map the OLMs, culture, and leadership styles of two wards of a general hospital. In addition to concrete descriptions of the nature and effectiveness of the organizational learning carried out in the two wards, their findings highlighted general issues attesting to the complexity and contextuality of organizational learning such as what are the relevant organizational boundaries in which organization learning should take place, and what exactly should be learned in particular organizational settings. The structural and cultural approach lends itself equally well to testing general hypotheses on the antecedents and consequences of organizational learning. Ellis and Maidan-Gilad (1997), for example, tested the effect of organizational learning on the success of planned organizational change and found that the intensity of organizational learning (as measured by Globerson and Ellis' (1996) questionnaire described above) was related to various indicators of successful change. For applications of the structural and cultural approach to introduce organizational learning and build learning organizations see Popper and Lipshitz (1998) and Friedman, Lipshitz and Overmeer (in press).

Conclusion

In this article we applied our structural and cultural approach to organizational learning (Lipshitz and Popper, in press) to four controversies on organizational learning: (1) What are the similarities and differences between individual and organizational learning? (2) What are the conditions that promote productive organizational learning? (3) When is organizational learning feasible? and (4) How is organizational learning related to learning organizations? We advance the answers outlined above not as definitive solutions, but as hypotheses for empirical research that will, we hope, generate as many new questions for further research as new answers for old controversies.

References

Argyris, C. (1982) *Reasoning, Learning and Action.* San Francisco, CA: Jossey-Bass.

Argyris, C. (1991) 'Teaching Smart People How to Learn', *Harvard Business Review* 69(3): 99–109.

Argyris, C. (1993) *Knowledge for Action.* San Francisco, CA: Jossey-Bass.

Argyris, C. and Schön, D. A. (1978) *Organizational Learning: A Theory of Action Perspective.* Reading, MA: Addison-Wesley.

Argyris, C. and Schön, D.A. (1996) *Organizational Learning II: Theory Method and Practice.* Reading, MA: Addison-Wesley.

Brehmer, B. (1980) 'In One Word: Not from Experience', *Acta Psychologica* 45: 223–41.

Campbell, D.T. (1968) 'Reforms as Experiments', *American Psychologist* 24: 409–29.

Carlzon, J. (1989) *Moments of Truth.* New York: Harper & Row.

Carrol, J.S. (1995) 'Incident Reviews in High-hazard Industries: Sensemaking and Learning under Ambiguity and Accountability', *Industrial and Environmental Crisis Quarterly* 2: 175–97.

Clarke, L. and Perrow, C. (1996) 'Prosaic Organizational Failure', *American Behavioral Scientist* 39: 1040–55.

Cohen, M.D. and Sproul, L.E. (1991) 'Editors' Introduction', *Organization Science* 2(1): 1–3 (Special issue on Organizational Learning – Papers in honor of [and by] James G. March).

Cook, S.D.N. and Yanow, D. (1993) 'Culture and Organizational Learning', *Journal of Management Inquiry* 2: 373–90.

Daft, R. L. (1989) *Organization Theory and Design,* 3rd edn. St Paul, MN: West.

Daft, R.L. and Huber, G.P. (1987) 'How Organizations Learn: A Communication Framework', *Research in Sociology of Organizations* 5: 1–36.

De Geus, A. (1988) 'Planning as Learning', *Harvard Business Review* 66(4): 70–4.

DiBella, A., Nevis, E.C. and Gould, J. M. (1996) 'Understanding Organizational Learning Capability', *Journal of Management Studies* 33 (May): 361–79.

Dodgson, M. (1993) 'Organizational Learning: A Review of Some Literatures', *Organization Studies* 14: 375–94.

Edmondson, A. and Moingeon, B. (1996) 'Organizational Learning as a Source of Competitive Advantage: When to Learn How and When to Learn Why', in B. Moingeon and A. Edmondson (eds) *Organizational Learning and Competitive Advantage,* pp. 17–37. London: Sage.

Edmondson, A. and Moingeon, B. (1998) 'From Organizational Learning to the Learning Organization', *Management Learning* 29: 5–20.

Ellis, S., Caridi, O., Lipshitz, R. and Popper, M. (1998) *Error Criticality and Organizational Learning: An Empirical Investigation.* Tel Aviv, Israel: Recanati Graduate School of Business Administration, Tel Aviv University.

Ellis, S. and Maidan-Gilad, N. (1997) 'Effects of Organizational Learning Mechanisms on Organizational Performance During Planned Change', paper presented at the 26th conference of the Israeli Psychological Association, Tel Aviv University, 27–29 October.

Ellis, S. and Shpielberg, N. (1998) 'Organizational Learning Mechanisms and Managers' Perceived Uncertainty', paper presented at the conference on Managerial and Organizational Cognition, Stern School of Management, New York University, New York, 7–8 May.

Fiol, M.C. and Lyles, M.A. (1985) 'Organizational Learning', *Academy of Management Review* 10: 803–13.

Freeman, C. and Perez, C. (1988) 'Structural Crises of Adjustment: Business Cycles and Investment Behavior', in G. Dosi et al. (eds) *Technical Change and Economic Theory,* pp. 38–66. London: Pinter.

Friedman, V., Lipshitz, R. and Overmeer, W. (in press) 'Creating Conditions for Organizational Learning', in M. Dierkes, J. Child and I. Nonaka (eds) *Handbook of Organizational Learning*. London: Sage.

Garvin, D.A. (1993) 'Building a Learning Organization', *Harvard Business Review* 73(4): 78–91.

Globerson, S. and Ellis, S. (1996) 'Analysis of Learning Profiles in Project Environments', paper presented at Project Management Institute Conference, Boston, October.

Hawkins, P. (1991) 'The Spiritual Dimension of the Learning Organization', *Management Education and Development* 22: 172–87.

Hawkins, P. (1994) 'Organizational Learning: Taking Stock and Facing the Challenge', *Management Learning* 25(1): 71–82.

Hedberg, B. (1981) 'How Organizations Learn and Unlearn', in C.P. Wystrom and W.T. Starbuck (eds) *Handbook of Organizational Design*, 1. Oxford: Oxford University Press.

Hoffman, L.M. (1989) *The Politics of Knowledge*. Albany: State University of New York Press.

Howard, R. and Haas, R.D. (eds) (1993) *The Learning Imperative: Managing People for Continuous Innovation*. Cambridge, MA: HBS Press.

Huber, G.P. (1991) 'Organizational Learning: The Contributing Processes and the Literature', *Organizational Science* 2: 88–115.

Huber, G.P., Sutcliff, K.M., Miller, C.C. and Glick, W.H. (1993) 'Understanding and Predicting Organizational Change', in G.P. Huber and K.M. Sutcliff (eds) *Organizational Change and Redesign*, pp. 215–65. Oxford: Oxford University Press.

Janis, I.L. and Mann, L. (1977) *Decision Making: A Psychological Analysis of Conflict, Choice and Commitment*. New York: Free Press.

Kahneman, D. and Tversky, A. (1979) 'Prospect Theory: An Analysis of Decision under Risk', *Econometrica* 47: 263–91.

Kanter, R.M. (1991) 'Championing Change: An Interview with Bell Atlantic's CEO Raymond Smith', *Harvard Business Review* 69(1): 119–30.

Kim, D.H. (1993) 'The Link Between Individual and Organizational Learning', *Sloan Management Review* 34(1): 37–50.

Kolb, D.A. (1984) *Experiential Learning*. Englewood Cliffs, NJ: Prentice Hall.

Levitt, B. and March, G. (1988) 'Organizational Learning', *Annual Review of Sociology* 14: 319–40.

Lipshitz, R. and Popper, M. (in press) 'Organizational Learning in a Hospital', *Journal of Applied Behavioral Science*.

Lundberg, C.C. (1985) 'On the Feasibility of Cultural Intervention in Organizations', in R. Pondy, R. Frost, P.G. Morgan and T. Dandridge (eds) *Organizational Symbolism*. Greenwich, CT: JAI Press.

McGill, M.E. and Slocum, J.W. (1993) 'Unlearning the Organization', *Organizational Dynamics* 22: 67–79.

McGill, M.E., Slocum, J.W. and Lei, D. (1993) 'Management Practices in Learning Organizations', *Organizational Dynamics* 22: 5–17.

March, J.G. (1978) 'Bounded Rationality, Ambiguity and the Engineering of Choice', *Bell Journal of Economics* 9: 587–608.

March, J.G. and Olsen, J.P. (1976) 'Organizational Learning and the Ambiguity of the Past', in J.G. March and J.P. Olsen *Ambiguity and Choice in Organizations*, pp. 54–68. Bergen: Universitetsforlaget.

Miller, D. (1996) 'A Preliminary Typology of Organizational Learning: Synthesizing the Literature', *Journal of Management* 22: 485–505.

Neustadt, R.E. and May, E.R. (1986) *Thinking in Time*. London: Collier.

Nonaka, I. (1991) 'The Knowledge-creating Company', *Harvard Business Review* 69(6): 96–104.

Pavitt, K. (1991) 'Key Characteristics of the Large Innovative Firm', *British Journal of Management* 2: 41–50.

Popper, M. and Lipshitz, R. (1998) 'Organizational Learning Mechanisms: A Cultural and Structural Approach to Organizational Learning', *Journal of Applied Behavioral Science* 34: 161–78.

Prokesch, S.E. (1997) 'Unleashing the Power of Learning: An Interview with British Petroleum's John Browne', *Harvard Business Review* 77(5): 147–68.

Rayner, B. (1993) 'Trial-by-fire Transformation: An Interview with Globe Metallurgical's Alden C. Sims', in H.R. Howard and R.D. Haas (eds) *The Learning Imperative*, pp. 277–97. Cambridge, MA: HBS Press.

Rodgers, R. and Hunter, J.E. (1991) 'Impact of Management By Objectives on Organizational Productivity', *Journal of Applied Psychology* 76: 322–36.

Roth, G. (1997) 'From Individual and Team Learning to Systems Learning', in S. Cavaleri and D. Fearn (eds) *Managing in Organizations that Learn*. Cambridge, MA: Blackwell.

Rouse, W.B., Cannon-Bowers, J.A. and Salas, E. (1992) 'The Role of Mental Models in Team Performance in Complex Systems', *IEEE Transactions on Systems, Man and Cybernetics* 22: 1296–1308.

Rouse, W.B. and Morris, N.M. (1986) 'On Looking into the Black Box: Prospects and Limits in the Search for Mental Models', *Psychological Bulletin* 100: 349–63.

Schein, E.H. (1990) 'Organizational Culture', *American Psychologist* 45:109–19.

Senge, P. (1990) *The Fifth Discipline: The Art and Practice of the Learning Organization*. New York: Doubleday.

Shaw, R.B. and Perkins, D.N.T. (1992) 'Teaching Organizations to Learn: The Power of Productive Failures', in D.A. Nadler, M.S. Gerstein and R.B. Shaw (eds) *Organizational Architecture*, pp. 175–91. San Francisco, CA: Jossey-Bass.

Simon, H.A. (1991) 'Bounded Rationality and Organizational Learning', *Organization Science* 2: 125–34.

Sitkin, S.B. (1992) 'Learning Through Failure: The Strategy of Small Losses', *Research in Organizational Behavior* 14: 231–66.

Staw, B.M. (1983) 'The Experimenting Society: Problems and Prospects', in B.M. Staw (ed.) *Psychological Foundations of Organizational Behavior*, pp. 421–37. Glenview, IL: Scott-Foresman.

Toffier, A. (1990) *Power Shift*. New York: Bantam Books.

Weick, K.E. (1979) *The Social Psychology of Organizing*. Reading, MA: Addison-Wesley.

Weick, K.E. (1991) 'The Non-traditional Quality of Organizational Learning', *Organization Science* 2: 116–24.

Weisbord, M.R., Lawrence, D.R. and Charles, M.D. (1978) 'Three Dilemmas of Academic Medical Centers', *Journal of Applied Behavioral Science* 14: 284–304.

Wildavsky, A. (1988) *Searching for Safety*. New Brunswick, NJ: Transaction Publishers.

Wong, P.T.P. and Wiener, B. (1981) 'When People Ask Why Questions and the Heuristics of Attributional Research', *Journal of Personality and Social Psychology* 40: 650–63.

Zaleznik, A. (1992) 'Managers and Leaders: Are they Different?', *Harvard Business Review* 72(2): 126–35.

3

Anders Örtenblad

A Typology of the Idea of Learning Organization

A Need for a Typology

Many authors have tried to define and describe *the* learning organization, as if the idea was homogeneous. However, no one seems to have succeeded with that task. Authors point out that confusion still exists about the concept (e.g. Burgoyne, 1999). Others use the terms 'organizational learning' and 'learning organization' interchangeably (e.g. Fulmer et al., 1998; Klimecki and Lassleben, 1998; Preskill and Torres, 1999). Many authors emphasize the difficulty, or even the impossibility, of describing what a complete learning organization looks like (e.g. Marquardt and Reynolds, 1994: 109; Pedler and Aspinwall, 1998: 2; Swieringa and Wierdsma, 1992: 72; Watkins and Marsick, 1993: xxii). They argue that learning organizations change continually or that each learning organization must be different in order to fit the specific company. However, another explanation may be the difficulty of grasping and defining the concept. Furthermore, many authors present some definitions of 'the learning organization' and make a synthesis (e.g. Garvin, 1993). However, most syntheses and definitions have more differences than similarities. For instance, Watkins and Marsick (1993: 8) define 'the learning organization' as 'one that learns continuously and transforms itself', while, according to Senge (1990: 14), it is 'an organization that is continually expanding its capacity to create its future'. In spite of the heterogeneity, the 'learning organization' is often described as a necessity and is implicitly or explicitly argued to be suitable for any company – irrespective of culture and branch. For instance, both Pedler et al. (1991: ix) and Pedler and Aspinwall (1998: 1) begin their books by citing a speech by Geoffrey Holland, where he declares that:

> If we are to survive – individually or as companies, or as a country – we must create a tradition of 'learning companies'. Every company must be a 'learning company'.

What we need is clarity, not consensus. Although some researchers claim they are happy with the vagueness of the concept (Watkins and Golembiewski, 1995), there is certainly a lot to gain from clarity. Thus it is time to carry out a systematic classification of the idea of 'learning organization', in order to capture the different meanings of the concept.

Many typologies of the idea of 'organizational learning' have been put forward (e.g. Argyris and Schön, 1978; Cook and Yanow, 1993; Daft and Huber, 1987; Easterby-Smith, 1997; Fiol and Lyles, 1985; Shrivastava, 1983). However, there are few overviews of the idea of 'learning organization'. Only in one case is the whole article dedicated to categorizing subfields in the area. DiBella (1995) presents three different orientations as to how learning organizations can be achieved: a normative perspective, a developmental perspective and a capability perspective. Furthermore, I have found three other articles that include typologies. Easterby-Smith and Araujo (1999) describe two approaches to the creation of learning organizations: a technical variant and a social view. They also divide the subject between those who use linear models for enhanced learning capability, and those who use cyclical models. Finger and Bürgin Brand (1999) differentiate between a systemic approach and a psycho-sociological approach. Further, they distinguish between three conceptions of learning on which the approaches build: cognitive, humanist and pragmatic learning. Finally, Argyris (1999) divides the subject of 'learning organization' into seven subfields where the different authors referred to give primary attention to different organizational functions: socio-technical systems, organizational strategy, production, economic development, systems dynamics, human resources and organizational culture.

All typologies mentioned are deductive, in that the authors first define 'the learning organization' or delimit the literature on the 'learning organization', by distinguishing it from 'organizational learning' or the literature on organizational learning. DiBella (1995) claims that the 'learning organization' is a form of organization while 'organizational learning' is the processes of learning in organizations. Finger and Bürgin Brand (1999) see the 'learning organization' as an ideal organization form and 'organizational learning' as an activity and process by which organizations reach this ideal. Easterby-Smith and Araujo (1999) describe the organizational learning literature as dealing with observation and analysis of processes involved in learning in organizations. They describe the learning organization literature as action oriented, focusing on finding tools that can help to increase the quality of the learning processes. Argyris (1999) describes the organizational learning literature as sceptical, scholarly and produced by academics and the learning organization literature as practice-oriented, prescriptive and promulgated by consultants and practitioners.

After having defined 'the learning organization', the authors present typologies of the idea. They classify only literature in the delimited area. The deductive approach entails that literature that does not explicitly deal with the 'learning organization' also has to be categorized. For instance, one book and one article about organizational learning (Dixon, 1994; Shrivastava, 1983) appear in the typologies. In this article, I will instead create an inductive typology, investigating what is meant by the term 'learning organization' (and 'learning company'). Further, this typology is based not only on books and articles, but also on practitioners' understandings of the idea. Accordingly, the aim of this article is to present an inductively created typology of the idea of 'learning organization', i.e. what authors and practitioners mean by the term 'learning organization'. Labels for the different understandings will be suggested. The differentiation of the idea will also be discussed, in order to understand whether it is good or bad for companies. I will also discuss and try to explain how a practitioner comes to have a certain understanding of the idea of 'learning organization'.

Method

The objective was to create a typology consisting of not too many and not too few categories, into which as much as possible of the literature on the subject and of the practitioners' accounts could fit. The process of creating a typology was creative and dialectic. The typology was not out there, waiting to be discovered. I was the creator of the typology in that it made sense to me and others (see Weick, 1995). Even though the aim was to create an inductive typology, I needed a starting point for the development work. I had a specific theoretical dimension in mind when I started to study a small amount of literature on the 'learning organization'. When I realized that that particular dimension was not making sense of the literature, I tried another dimension, and so on. As a starting point for the final typology, I used one of the most common distinctions between 'the learning organization' and 'organizational learning' in the literature. While 'organizational learning' is regarded as processes (of learning) in the organization, 'the learning organization' is a form of organization itself (DiBella, 1995: 287; Elkjaer, 1999: 75; Finger and Bürgin Brand, 1999: 136–7; Lundberg, 1995: 10; Tsang, 1997: 74–5). Before using that distinction, I tried to create a typology using other theories. If the dimension worked on a small amount of literature, I tested it on a larger sample. If the dimension was still working, I tested it on a group of academic reference people, experienced in creating interesting typologies. Some typologies were rejected because they did not appeal to the reference group.

The idea of 'learning organization' was studied both in the literature and empirically. The starting point for choosing literature, as well as practitioners to interview, was the appearance of the term 'learning organization' (and 'learning company'). The literature was chosen from the papers on the 'learning organization' presented at the three conferences in the series of 'organizational learning' and the 'learning organization' ('Symposium on organizational learning and the learning organization: Theoretical developments', Lancaster University, September 1996; 'Conference on organizational learning: Moving from theory to research', George Washington University, March 1998; '3rd international conference on organizational learning', Lancaster University, June 1999). All the papers with the term 'learning organization' in the title and/or as a central theme, were selected. All the works on the 'learning organization' referred to in these papers were studied – in total 12 books and articles. In this way I could get an overview of the researchers' understandings regarding the idea of 'learning organization'. (This despite the fact that at least some of the literature I have studied is certainly popular also among practitioners, as well as intended for practitioners rather than for researchers.)

In order to see whether the same understandings as appear in the literature occur also among practitioners, I interviewed 10 people during the period 1994–5. It was important to make contact with people who had some understanding of the idea of 'learning organization', since the aim was to understand how they were using the term. They were all voluntarily connected to a formal network in Sweden, called 'Forum for learning organizations' (FLOR). They had meetings where they discussed definitions of the concept of 'learning organization' and reported on how they were trying to make their companies into learning organizations. Most of the members worked with personnel matters in their companies. In depth interviews were held with the FLOR members. Every member of the network was interviewed for approximately two hours, concerning their understandings of the idea of 'learning organization' and of their organizations – in case they told me that they were learning organizations. The interviews were open, with very few standardized questions, in accordance with the inductive approach of creating a typology. I simply asked questions like 'What is a "learning organization"?' and 'In what way is your company a "learning organization"?'

The texts – i.e. the books and the transcripts of the interviews – were then studied in detail. In order to 'find' a typology, they were read about five to 10 times each, with time for reflection allocated both during and between readings. The objective was to study the language of the statements and to try to determine what the authors or practitioners meant by 'learning organization'. The texts were carefully studied in order to identify and understand the parts of the texts dealing with the authors' or the practitioners' understandings of 'learning organization', while ignoring the other parts of the texts. For instance, I did not include in the analysis any reviews of literature that the authors disclaimed. Another example concerns Senge's acclaimed book *The Fifth Discipline* (Senge, 1990). Senge's understanding of the 'learning organization' may be interpreted as the five disciplines that are the cornerstones of the book. However, according to Senge (1990: 363) the disciplines are only *conditions* for creating the learning organization – not the learning organization itself. Finally, a typology that was sufficiently satisfactory for my purposes had been created. I could then make quantitative and qualitative interpretations of the texts, in order to decide which one/s of the four understandings that was/were apparent in the texts, as well as the relations between them.

The Typology

First, the four understandings of the idea of 'learning organization' will be presented. The typology implies different perspectives of the ontology of the 'learning organization', i.e. what 'learning organization' is. Such themes as why companies need to become learning organizations are excluded. The first two understandings emphasize processes in organizations, while the other two are forms of organization.

Citations both from the literature and the practitioners will illustrate the understandings, since the same four understandings appear in both groups (my translations of the accounts of the practitioners from Swedish into English). Each of the four perspectives connects, at least to some extent, explicitly or implicitly to current debates in the fields of management and pedagogics in general and, accordingly, to the field of management learning.

Second, I present an overview of the literature on 'the learning organization' as well as of the practitioners, based on the typology of understandings. What, then, would a typology of the idea of 'learning organization' look like that contains the understandings from both the literature and the practitioners?

Organizational Learning

There has been an ongoing debate for a long time in the literature on organizational learning about what the entity of learning is (for an overview of the main arguments in this debate, see e.g. Araujo, 1998; Cook and Yanow, 1993; Jones, 1995; Richter, 1998). Some of the researchers argue that only individuals are capable of learning – not organizations (Leymann, 1989; Simon, 1991). Others argue that organizations, like superpersons (Czarniawska-Joerges, 1994), are able to learn – either as they are or metaphorically (Jones, 1995) – but that we need to understand in what ways organizations are similar to individuals (Argyris and Schön, 1978; Hedberg, 1981; Jones, 1995; Kim, 1993). However, most authors who have written about 'organizational learning' seem to agree that *both* the individuals and the organization learn. The employees learn as agents for the organization (e.g. Argyris and Schön, 1978), and the knowledge is stored in the memory of the organization (e.g. Hedberg, 1981; Huber, 1991). The memory consists of routines, dialogue or symbols – i.e. knowledge is embedded, encultured or encoded (Blackler, 1995).

However, the literature on 'the learning organization' shows, together with the accounts by the practitioners, that what originally was claimed to be 'organizational learning' – i.e. that the individuals learn as agents for the organization and that the knowledge is stored in the organizational memory – can also be called 'learning organization':

Learning organizations, in which learning is accomplished by the organization system as a whole rather than by individual members of the system, have been defined in several ways. (Marquardt and Reynolds, 1994: 20)

Many aspiring learning organizations interpret the idea in terms of individual learning opportunities. Although this is a useful step, no amount of individual development alone will produce an organization able to change itself as a whole. The learning organization is not just the training organization. (Pedler and Aspinwall, 1998: 45)

A further suggestion regarding how organizations learn concerns the systematization of knowledge into practices, procedures and processes – in other words, the routinization of knowledge. (West, 1994: 16)

Each person in our organization works with their separate tasks, and – of course – they learn from it. But the organization as an entity has not learnt anything. The individuals have learnt, but the knowledge doesn't permeate the organization. (Respondent 2)

The focus of this perspective of the 'learning organization' is on the storage of knowledge in the organizational mind. Learning is mostly described as implying different levels, as in, for instance, single- and double-loop learning (Argyris and Schön, 1978). Another important element is that the stored knowledge actually is used in practice. I suggest that those who use the term 'learning organization' in this sense use the label 'organizational learning' instead. Also, I will call this type of understanding of the 'learning organization' *organizational learning*.

Learning at Work

Some authors and practitioners see the idea of 'learning organization' as an organization where the employees learn at work – not on formalized courses:

The 'Total Quality Management' (TQM) concept has also been an important factor in broadening approaches to training and company learning. This means people learn as they do their jobs and this experiential learning seems to be a key issue in understanding how firms can more readily utilize on-the-job learning, a characteristic much admired in Japanese firms. (Jones and Hendry, 1992: 2)

Learning should become a continuous, strategically used process, integrated with and running parallel to work. (Marquardt and Reynolds, 1994: 66)

What is a learning organization? Training plays an important role in the learning organization, but training is not its sole distinguishing feature. Learning is closely intertwined with daily work activities, and as a result, it may not stand out as separate from effective individual or organizational practices. (Watkins and Marsick, 1993: 7)

We say that we are a 'learning organization' – we do not have very many instructors or special courses. Instead, we will try to become what you can call a 'learning organization', i.e. that the local manager is responsible for the competence development of the employees. (Respondent 8)

I suggest that we call this type of understanding of the idea *learning at work*.

This understanding connects to the debate whether learning and knowledge are context-dependent or not. One of the questions in this debate concerns whether learning at formal courses can be applied in practice, i.e. the work situation. An early protest against decontextualized learning was Revans' approach of Action Learning (see e.g. Revans, 1998).

Learning Climate

Another perspective of the 'learning organization' is an organization that facilitates the learning of its individuals:

From the four conditions mentioned above it follows naturally that the key facilitating role of directors is to create the climate by which learning is encouraged, rewarded and allowed to flow freely around the organisation. (Garratt, 1990: 24)

Some organizations create better conditions for this sort of learning than others. They make learning a value at the heart of the enterprise, they encourage people to talk to each other, they simply have a better 'learning climate'. (Pedler and Aspinwall, 1998: 43)

'Learning organization', as I see it, is that the company or the organization believes that competence development is important, that they create opportunities, a positive attitude towards learning. (Respondent 10)

I believe that the best label for this kind of 'learning organization' is *learning climate*. This perspective may also include structural elements, provided that the focus is not on the structure itself but on the facilitative character of the structure.

The perspective of learning climate connects to the debate about whether learning should be tightly controlled or unrestricted. At one end of this dimension are the teaching machines developed by Skinner, where the learner is rewarded with positive feedback by a correct answer and gets a 'remedial' example or question when answering incorrectly (Phillips and Soltis, 1985: 28). At the other end is *freedom to learn* (Rogers, 1969), which is similar to the learning climate perspective. There is space for learning, but the learning per se is not controlled, it is only facilitated.

Learning Structure

Finally, a popular perspective of the 'learning organization' is that it is a flexible organization. Of the various perspectives, the use of the prefixes 'the' or 'a' in front of the label (*the* or *a* learning organization) is perhaps most suitable in this perspective. It connects to a debate that is more about structure than about learning, the debate about whether a bureaucratic or an organic structure is the best one (e.g. Mintzberg, 1983). The authors on the 'learning organization' clearly prefer the organic structure, which I will call *learning structure*.

The result is a flatter organization and movement away from hierarchy and unnecessary bureaucracy. Information flows freely in the learning organization – among people, across boundaries, and through information and data processing systems. (Watkins and Marsick, 1993: 258)

Based on the demands of the customer I learn what I need to learn and organize the company analogously. Thus, the organization has to be very flexible – if one market disappears, we have to change quickly. (Respondent 3)

However, in order for *structure* to be referred to this perspective, it is not enough that it is mentioned. The perspective focuses on the *flexibility* of a specific kind of structure.

The best description of this perspective may actually be found in Morgan (1996), where he describes the holographic perspective of organizations.

Although Morgan does not specifically connect that perspective to the concept of 'learning organization', it represents one way of seeing organizations as learning.

The individuals in the organization learn from the environment – especially from the customers. Further, they must continuously learn in order to solve the problems of the customers. Thus the learning processes are means, not ends. The structure is decentralized – the individuals need to make their own decisions in order to satisfy the customers quickly:

> The whole organization is expected to think and act directly on organizational strategy and planning. All employees are empowered to take part in and develop the strategy. Learning organizations realize that empowered workers can make better decisions than managers because they need and have the best information. (Marquardt and Reynolds, 1994: 56)

> learning organizations will, increasingly, be 'localized' organizations, extending the maximum degree of authority and power as far from the 'top' or corporate center as possible. (Senge, 1990: 287)

There are also other ways of creating flexibility. The work is organized in teams, where everyone can perform the tasks of the other team members, which calls for a considerable amount of learning:

> Employees are expected to learn not only skills related to their own jobs but also the skills of others in their work unit and how their work unit relates to the operation and goals of the business. (Watkins and Marsick, 1993: 26)

In addition, everyone in the organization has a holistic approach:

> In a learning organization, everyone has an idea of what the whole picture looks like, knows how to get something done in the organization, has a budget with which to take action, and has knowledge of how to influence or work with people. Everyone has access to information about how to plan learning and how to assess their needs in relation to the needs of the organization; they also have access to data-based information on their desktop computer. (Watkins and Marsick, 1993: 17)

Thus the members of one team can assist the members of the other teams.

Relations Between the Four Understandings

Although almost all of the literature contains more than one of the perspectives of the 'learning organization' (see Figure 1), the perspectives mostly occur separately in the texts. Furthermore, many of the practitioners show quite homogeneous understandings of the idea (see Figure 2). Some will probably argue that the four perspectives are different aspects of the 'learning organization', that they are all important and that they therefore have to be included in order to create an understanding both of the idea as such and of the learning organization (see e.g. Jones and Hendry, 1994: 157, who consider 'organizational learning' to be an aspect of the 'learning organization'). However, the different views are usually presented too distinctly to be considered parts of a whole.

But mixed understandings do occur. For instance, Pedler et al. sometimes mix the understandings of 'learning structure' and 'learning climate':

> Roles are loosely structured, in line with the established and contracted needs of internal customers and suppliers, and in such a way as to allow for personal growth and experiment. (Pedler et al., 1991: 22)

Further, Watkins and Marsick mix the perspectives of 'organizational learning' and 'learning at work':

> The learning organization is one that learns continuously and transforms itself. Learning takes place in individuals, teams, the organization, and even the communities with which the organization interacts. Learning is a continuous, strategically used process – integrated with, and running parallel to, work. Learning results in changes in knowledge, beliefs, and behaviors. Learning also enhances organizational capacity for innovation and growth. The learning organization has embedded systems to capture and share learning. (Watkins and Marsick, 1993: 8–9)

Thus the understandings can appear one by one – which they mostly do – or as mixed understandings.

What 'Learning Organization' Is Not

Although 'learning organization' can mean many different things, there are subjects that are not included under this label. First, the other ends of the four dimensions that the four perspectives of the 'learning organization' connect to might not logically constitute a 'learning organization'. However, since each of the understandings can stand alone, we cannot claim that any specific opposite to the understandings cannot be considered as 'learning organization'. A 'learning organization' can imply individual learning, learning on courses, the absence of a learning climate, or a bureaucratic structure. However, 'learning organization' cannot imply all of these conditions – at least one of the four understandings must be apparent. Besides, in at least the case of 'learning at work', the other end of the dimension is also needed. Both the literature and the practitioners claim that there is a need for formal education and training also in a learning organization.

Second, in the 1990s a social approach to learning appeared in the organizational literature, which is not included under the label of 'learning organization'. Instead, it is placed under the label of 'organizational learning' (e.g. Brown and Duguid, 1991; Cook and Yanow, 1993). I will borrow the term 'new organizational learning' from Turner (referred to in Gherardi, 1999: 108), for this social approach of learning. Again referring to Turner, I will, from now on, call the perspective of 'organizational learning' '*old* organizational learning'. There are two main differences between 'new organizational learning' and 'old organizational learning' (see e.g. Gherardi et al., 1998: 274). First, the former perspective rejects both cognitive learning by individuals and by the organization as an individual. Instead, the *collective* learns (Cook and Yanow, 1993) or humans as social beings within a *community of practice* learn (Brown and Duguid, 1991; Lave and Wenger, 1991; Richter, 1998; Wenger, 1991). Thus learning means participation, not acquisition of information. Despite the fact that Wenger (1991: 8) suggests that 'those who can understand learning as a social phenomenon and can translate this understanding into learning organizations will be the architects of to-morrow', the label 'learning organization' is not used for this participatory approach of organizational learning (an exception, though, may be Leitch et al., 1996). Thus neither collective learning nor learning within communities of practice is called 'learning organization'.

The other main difference between 'new' and 'old' organizational learning is the contextual dependence of knowledge in the former perspective; learning is *situated* (Lave and Wenger, 1991). The term 'situated learning' does not occur together with the term 'learning organization' in the texts that I have studied. However, the theme connects to the perspective of the 'learning organization' as 'learning at work', since the learning is not seen to take place independently of where the knowledge will be used. Further, a common theme in the literature is apprenticeship (e.g. Lave and Wenger, 1991), which connects to 'learning at work'. The perspective of 'learning at work' implies, however, that the learning can be quite individual. Further, the

Author(s)	Understanding of the idea of learning organization			
	Old Organizational learning	Learning at work	Learning climate	Learning structure
Garratt, 1990		▤	■	
Senge, 1990			▤	■
Lessem, 1991			■	
Pedler, Burgoyne & Boydell, 1991				▤
Jones & Hendry, 1992	▤	■	▤	■
McGill, Slocum & Lei, 1992	■		▤	
Garvin, 1993	■			
Watkins & Marsick, 1993	■	■		
Jones & Hendry 1994	■		■	
Marquardt & Reynolds, 1994		▤	■	▤
West, 1994		▤	■	
Pedler & Aspinwall, 1998	▤		■	

■ Primary focus

▤ Minor focus

Figure 1 *Understandings of the idea of 'learning organization' in the literature*

perspective mostly differentiates between contextualized learning (e.g. learning at work) and decontextualized learning (e.g. formal education). The situated learning approach implies instead that learning is social and that no learning whatsoever is decontextualized – all learning is contextualized (Lave, 1993; Lave and Wenger, 1991).

Thus there seems to be a limit to what is called 'learning organization', since there are subjects in close connection to learning and organizations that are not included. At least some of these subjects are quite radical, which means that the idea of 'learning organization' is not.

A Summary of the Literature and the Practitioners' Statements

Figure 1 shows the understandings of the 'learning organization' found in the literature. Most of the books and articles contain more than one understanding.

Figure 2 shows the understandings of the interviewed practitioners.

The tendency is that the understandings of the practitioners are slightly more homogeneous than in the literature. Further, the practitioners tend to see the 'learning organization' as 'learning at work' or as a 'learning structure'. The other two perspectives – 'old organizational learning' and

Understanding of the idea of learning organization

	Old Organizational learning	Learning at work	Learning climate	Learning structure
Respondent 1		Minor focus		Primary focus
Respondent 2	Minor focus	Primary focus	Minor focus	
Respondent 3				Primary focus
Respondent 4				Primary focus
Respondent 5				Primary focus
Respondent 6		Primary focus		
Respondent 7		Primary focus	Primary focus	
Respondent 8		Primary focus		Primary focus
Respondent 9		Primary focus	Minor focus	Primary focus
Respondent 10		Primary focus	Minor focus	

Primary focus

Minor focus

Figure 2 Practitioners' understandings of the idea of 'learning organization'

63

'learning climate' – seldom occur among the interviewed practitioners, even though they exist.

Discussion

Two main subjects will be discussed. First, I give some suggestions about how the nature of the idea of 'learning organization' can be understood. Next, I discuss the limited variety of understandings of the idea. I also try to explain the relation between the understandings of the literature and the understandings of the practitioners. Finally, I compare the typology developed in this article with other typologies connected to the idea of 'learning organization'.

The Nature of the Idea of 'Learning Organization'

Let us first look at the idea of 'learning organization'. The empirical findings show that for most people – authors as well as practitioners – the idea implies individual learning in an organizational context (see also Confessore and Kops, 1998). Individuals learn in a learning climate, in a learning structure, or at work. Only the 'old organizational learning' perspective explicitly expresses learning of another entity – the organization. It claims that 'learning organization' means storage of knowledge in the organizational memory. The perspective of 'new organizational learning', i.e. a social approach to learning, is not called 'learning organization'.

Since the label of 'learning organization' is used in various ways both by authors and by practitioners, one possibility is to call it a *convenience term*, i.e. a term denoting a conglomerate of things (Kahn, 1974). However, the term is not all-inclusive. As phenomenographic researchers claim, the number of understandings is limited (Marton, 1981, 1986). Thus the term 'learning organization' is a *homonym*, i.e. one word is used with different meanings (Sartori, 1984).

Another popular expression is 'old wine in new bottles' (e.g. Kimberly, 1981; Lammers, 1988), which would explain 'learning organization' as a new label with an old content. This explanation fits if, instead of one bottle and one label, we think of four bottles and – hitherto – only one label. All of the perspectives on the 'learning organization' in the typology are quite familiar, and they are all labelled 'learning organization'. Thus the label of 'learning organization' may be more important than the content.

The Limited Variety of Understandings

The fact that the literature contains different perspectives of the idea of 'learning organization' can be explained by using Kieser (1997; see also Brunsson and Olsen, 1993: 37). He claims that authors have to differentiate the idea, in order to legitimize the books they write. This is perhaps what we can call the more *negative* kind of differentiation, since it might create confusion rather than giving the companies an opportunity to construct their own unique version of a learning organization:

One sees whatever one wants to see. Quality consultants view the learning organization as the next venue of quality efforts. Change agents use the learning metaphor to justify their initiatives. Organizational anthropologists take the concept as an extension of their work on corporate culture. Those interested in strategy implementation use the learning metaphor as the means for making strategy happen. If the metaphor of the learning organization becomes all things to all people, it adds little value to anyone. (Ulrich et al., 1993: 57–8)

The confusion probably lies in the uncertainty regarding which variant of the idea is intended (see Sartori, 1984).

However, the continuous differentiation of ideas that Kieser suggests is not the case with the idea of 'learning organization'. As we have seen, the number of understandings is limited to four. The practitioners use one, or some, of the perspectives. Another way to explain this is that they use the label of 'learning organization' for their already existing understandings, in order to legitimize themselves (e.g. Brunsson and Olsen, 1993). A thorough explanation of the relation between the understandings in the literature and among practitioners is beyond the scope of this article. It might be that the practitioners have studied and obtained their understandings from the literature, that the authors have written about already existing themes used by the practitioners, or that the set of understandings has existed for a long time both in the literature and in the discourse of the practitioners.

However, during the analysis of the texts I noticed something that may be part of an explanation of the relation. All of the practitioners with a homogeneous understanding of the 'learning organization' as a 'learning structure', worked in companies which were formerly under the control of the public sector and had been protected within a monopoly situation in the market (practitioners 3, 4 and 5). The companies had just recently been exposed to competition. A more flexible structure might have been exactly what those companies needed in order to meet the new competition. Those seeing the 'learning organization' as 'learning at work' had either worked with education in their companies (practitioners 2 and 10), had worked in education companies (practitioners 2 and 8), or – in one case – had recently closed down their internal school (practitioner 6). Naturally, those working with education might be more interested in learning (at work) than for instance a specific type of organization (e.g. 'learning structure'). The same goes for the education companies. Whether the closing down of the internal school gave inspiration to the understanding of the 'learning organization' as 'learning at work', or the other way around, is difficult to say.

These findings suggest that factors such as education, affiliation, branch, situation of the company etc., may at least explain in part why a person has a certain understanding of the idea (see also Calvert et al., 1994; Muller and Watts, 1993). However, in three cases (practitioners 1, 7 and 9), no obvious indicators were present – at least none that I have studied.

Accordingly, the existence of the different perspectives does not only create ambiguity – it also gives the companies an opportunity to use a version of the idea of 'learning organization' that suits them. Their perception is selective (see Hambrick and Mason, 1984; Hambrick and Snow, 1977; Starbuck and

Milliken, 1988), but the occurrence of several perspectives probably still confuses them.

A Comparison with Existing Typologies

The typology in this article contains some advantages in comparison with existing typologies of the idea of 'learning organization'. This typology is an inductive one, building on how the term 'learning organization' is actually used by authors and practitioners, in contrast to the existing typologies of the idea, which are deductive. A probable explanation of the difficulty of grasping the idea of 'learning organization', which is described both in the literature and by practitioners, is the use of different perspectives. People probably sense this pluralistic use of the typology without being able to understand or explain it. An inductive typology that builds on the definitions actually being used will certainly be more helpful in creating clarity than a deductive typology would.

An additional difference between the typology developed in this article and existing typologies lies in their focuses. DiBella (1995) as well as Easterby-Smith and Araujo (1999) have created typologies of how the learning organization is developed, while my typology focuses on what a learning organization is. The typology of Finger and Bürgin Brand (1999) is based on different conceptions of learning. Argyris (1999) builds on different organizational functions given primary attention by authors. Some of these functions are similar to learning. The typology in this article focuses on both learning and the organization. While two of the perspectives – the 'learning organization' as 'old organizational learning' and as 'learning at work' – focus on learning, the 'learning structure' perspective focuses on the organization, and the 'learning climate' perspective focuses on both learning and the organization. Also, while more than one of the perspectives presented in this article can often be found in any book on the 'learning organization', the previous typologies assign each book and article to one perspective only.

Furthermore, as we have seen, some authors distinguish between 'organizational learning' and the 'learning organization' by claiming that the former implies processes or activities in organizations while the latter means a form of organization (DiBella, 1995; Elkjaer, 1999; Finger and Bürgin Brand, 1999; Lundberg, 1995; Tsang, 1997). While that may be a normative effort, this study shows that there are also those who use the term 'learning organization' for processes in organizations (i.e. the understandings of the 'learning organization' as 'old organizational learning' and 'learning at work'). Therefore, the understanding of the 'learning organization' as 'old organizational learning' is included in the inductive typology of the idea of 'learning organization'.

Conclusions

I have suggested four different perspectives of the idea of 'learning organization', as well as a specific label for each of them, as a way of simplifying the communication of the idea. First, the term 'learning organization' is used synonymously with 'old organizational learning', i.e. the knowledge that the individuals have learnt as agents for the organization is stored in the organizational memory. Accordingly, I call this perspective *old organizational learning*. Second, the term 'learning organization' can mean an organization where the learning takes place at work and not on courses – *learning at work*. Third, the label can be used to describe an organization that facilitates the learning of all its employees – a *learning climate*. Fourth, a popular perspective today is to consider the 'learning organization' as an organic structure with a high degree of flexibility, in order to satisfy the customers of the company. I suggest that we call this kind of 'learning organization' *learning structure*. Practitioners tend to focus on one of the understandings, while books and articles mostly contain at least two of the understandings. However, the perspectives often appear one at a time, which might imply that they are not very easy to combine in practice.

The aim of creating a typology of the idea of 'learning organization' was to clarify the concept. However, the existence of different perspectives of the 'learning organization' in the literature probably not only gives people a vague picture of the idea but it also creates opportunities for companies to choose a variant of the idea that fits their own interest. In addition, it creates opportunities for more people to take advantage of the popular term 'learning organization' by legitimizing themselves by using it. The differentiation of the idea in the literature can, after all, perhaps not be entirely rejected. The typology will hopefully help managers and others to better understand the variants of the idea, to choose a suitable version of it and to help choose literature in order to develop further understanding. Since most of the literature concerning the 'learning organization' claims that any organization can and should become a learning organization, the typology will certainly reduce the uncertainty in many companies. It will be easier to decide whether a company should become a learning organization or not, in the sense of 'old organizational learning', 'learning at work', 'learning climate' or 'learning structure', than a 'learning organization' in general. Likewise, the process of becoming a learning organization may be simplified with a better understanding of what kind of 'learning organization' is intended. Finally, the literature about the idea of 'learning organization' might be somewhat clearer, when showing explicitly which understanding/s is/are intended.

References

Araujo, L. (1998) 'Knowing and Learning as Networking', *Management Learning* 29(3): 317–36.

Argyris, C. (1999) *On Organizational Learning*. Oxford: Blackwell.

Argyris, C. and Schön, D.A. (1978) *Organizational Learning: A Theory of Action Perspective*. London: Addison-Wesley.

Blackler, F. (1995) 'Knowledge, Knowledge Work and Organizations: An Overview and Interpretation', *Organization Studies* 16(6): 1021–46.

Brown, J.S. and Duguid, P. (1991) 'Organizational Learning and Communities of Practice: Toward a Unified View of Working, Learning, and Innovation', *Organization Science* 2(1): 40–57.

Brunsson, N. and Olsen, J.P. (eds) (1993) *The Reforming Organization.* London: Routledge.

Burgoyne, J. (1999) 'Design of the Times', *People Management* 5(11): 38–44.

Calvert, G., Mobley, S. and Marshall, L. (1994) 'Grasping the Learning Organization', *Training and Development* 48(6): 38–43.

Confessore, S.J. and Kops, W.J. (1998) 'Self-directed Learning and the Learning Organization: Examining the Connection Between the Individual and the Learning Environment', *Human Resource Development Quarterly* 9(4): 365–75.

Cook, S.D.N. and Yanow, D. (1993) 'Culture and Organizational Learning', *Journal of Management Inquiry* 2(4): 373–90.

Czarniawska-Joerges, B. (1994) 'Narratives of Individual and Organizational Identities', in S.A. Deetz (ed.) *Communication Yearbook,* pp. 193–221. Thousand Oaks, CA: Sage.

Daft, R.L. and Huber, G.P. (1987) 'How Organizations Learn: A Communication Framework', *Research in the Sociology of Organizations* 5: 1–36.

DiBella, A.J. (1995) 'Developing Learning Organizations: A Matter of Perspective', *Academy of Management: Best Papers Proceedings* 287–90.

Dixon, N. (1994) *The Organizational Learning Cycle: How We Can Learn Collectively.* London: McGraw-Hill.

Easterby-Smith, M. (1997) 'Disciplines of Organizational Learning: Contributions and Critiques', *Human Relations* 50(9): 1085–113.

Easterby-Smith, M. and Araujo, L. (1999) 'Organizational Learning: Current Debates and Opportunities', in M. Easterby-Smith, J. Burgoyne and L. Araujo (eds) *Organizational Learning and the Learning Organization: Developments in Theory and Practice,* pp. 1–21. London: Sage.

Elkjaer, B. (1999) 'In Search of a Social Learning Theory', in M. Easterby-Smith, J. Burgoyne and L. Araujo (eds) *Organizational Learning and the Learning Organization: Developments in Theory and Practice,* pp. 75–91. London: Sage.

Finger, M. and Bürgin Brand, S. (1999) 'The Concept of the "Learning Organization" Applied to the Transformation of the Public Sector', in M. Easterby-Smith, J. Burgoyne and L. Araujo (eds) *Organizational Learning and the Learning Organization: Developments in Theory and Practice,* pp. 130–56. London: Sage.

Fiol, C.M. and Lyles, M.A. (1985) 'Organizational Learning', *Academy of Management Review* 10(4): 803–13.

Fulmer, R.M., Gibbs, P. and Keys, J.B. (1998) 'The Second Generation Learning Organizations: New Tools for Sustaining Competitive Advantage', *Organizational Dynamics* 27(2): 6–20.

Garratt, B. (1990) *Creating a Learning Organisation: A Guide to Leadership, Learning and Development.* Cambridge: Director Books.

Garvin, D.A. (1993) 'Building a Learning Organization', *Harvard Business Review* 71(4): 78–91.

Gherardi, S. (1999) 'Learning as Problem-driven or Learning in the Face of Mystery', *Organization Studies* 20(1): 101–24.

Gherardi, S., Nicolini, D. and Odella, F. (1998) 'Toward a Social Understanding of How People Learn in Organizations: The Notion of Situated Curriculum', *Management Learning* 29(3): 273–97.

Hambrick, D.C. and Mason, P.A. (1984) 'Upper Echelons: The Organization as a Reflection of its Top Managers', *Academy of Management Review* 9(2): 193–206.

Hambrick, D.C. and Snow, C.C. (1977) 'A Contextual Model of Strategic Decision Making in Organizations', *Academy of Management: Best Papers Proceedings* 109–12.

Hedberg, B. (1981) 'How Organizations Learn and Unlearn', in P.C. Nystrom and W.H. Starbuck (eds) *Handbook of Organizational Design,* pp. 3–27. Oxford: Oxford University Press.

Huber, G.P. (1991) 'Organizational Learning: The Contributing Processes and the Literatures', *Organization Science* 2(1): 88–115.

Jones, A.M. and Hendry, C. (1992) 'The Learning Organization: A Review of Literature and Practice', unpublished report. London: The HRD Partnership.

Jones, A.M. and Hendry, C. (1994) 'The Learning Organization: Adult Learning and Organizational Transformation', *British Journal of Management* 5: 153–62.

Jones, M. (1995) 'Organisational Learning: Collective Mind or Cognitivist Metaphor?', *Accounting, Management & Information Technology* 5(1): 61–77.

Kahn, R.L. (1974) 'Organizational Development: Some Problems and Proposals', *The Journal of Applied Behavioural Science* 10(4): 485–502.

Kieser, A. (1997) 'Myth and Rhetoric in Management Fashion', *Organization* 4(1): 49–74.

Kim, D.H. (1993) 'The Link Between Individual and Organizational Learning', *Sloan Management Review* 35(1): 37–50.

Kimberly, J.R. (1981) 'Managerial Innovation', in P.C. Nystrom and W.H. Starbuck (eds) *Handbook of Organizational Design*, pp. 84–104. London: Oxford University Press.

Klimecki, R. and Lassleben, H. (1998) 'Modes of Organizational Learning: Indications from an Empirical Study', *Management Learning* 29(4): 405–30.

Lammers, C.J. (1988) 'Transience and Persistence of Ideal Types in Organization Theory', *Research in the Sociology of Organizations* 6: 203–24.

Lave, J. (1993) 'The Practice of Learning', in S. Chaiklin and J. Lave (eds) *Understanding Practice: Perspectives on Activity and Context*, pp. 3–32. Cambridge: Cambridge University Press.

Lave, J. and Wenger, E. (1991) *Situated Learning: Legitimate Peripheral Participation*. Cambridge: Cambridge University Press.

Leitch, C., Harrison, R. and Burgoyne, J. (1996) 'Understanding the Learning Company: A Constructivist Approach', paper presented at the Organizational Learning Symposium, University of Lancaster.

Lessem, R. (1991) *Total Quality Learning: Building a Learning Organization*. Oxford: Blackwell.

Leymann, H. (1989) 'Towards a New Paradigm of Learning in Organizations', in H. Leymann and H. Kornbluh (eds) *Socialization and Learning at Work: A New Approach to the Learning Process in the Workplace and Society*, pp. 281–99. Aldershot: Avebury.

Lundberg, C.C. (1995) 'Learning In and By Organizations: Three Conceptual Issues', *The International Journal of Organizational Analysis* 3(1): 10–23.

Marquardt, M. and Reynolds, A. (1994) *Global Learning Organization: Gaining Advantage through Continuous Learning*. New York: Irwin.

Marton, F. (1981) 'Phenomenography: Describing Conceptions of the World Around Us', *Instructional Science* 10: 177–200.

Marton, F. (1986) 'Phenomenography: A Research Approach to Investigating Different Understandings of Reality', *Journal of Thought* 21(3): 28–49.

McGill, M.E., Slocum, Jr J.W., and Lei, D. (1992) 'Management Practices in Learning Organizations', *Organizational Dynamics* 21(1): 5–17.

Mintzberg, H. (1983) *Structure in Fives: Designing Effective Organizations*. Englewood Cliffs, NJ: Prentice Hall.

Morgan, G. (1996) *Images of Organization*. London: Sage.

Muller, J. and Watts, D. (1993) 'Modelling and Muddling: The Long Route to New Organisations', *European Management Journal* 11(3): 361–6.

Pedler, M. and Aspinwall, K. (1998) *A Concise Guide to the Learning Organization*. London: Lemos & Crane.

Pedler, M., Burgoyne, J. and Boydell, T. (1991) *The Learning Company: A Strategy for Sustainable Development*. London: McGraw-Hill.

Phillips, D.C. and Soltis, J.F. (1985) *Perspectives on Learning*. London: Teachers College Press.

Preskill, H. and Torres, R. (1999) 'The Role of Evaluative Enquiry in Creating Learning Organizations', in M. Easterby-Smith, J. Burgoyne and L. Araujo (eds) *Organizational Learning and the Learning Organization: Developments in Theory and Practice*, pp. 92–114. London: Sage.

Revans, R. (1998) *The ABC of Action Learning*. London: Lemos & Crane.

Richter, I. (1998) 'Individual and Organizational Learning at the Executive Level: Towards a Research Agenda', *Management Learning* 29(3): 299–316.

Rogers, C.R. (1969) *Freedom to Learn: A View of what Education Might Become*. Columbus, OH: Merrill.

Sartori, G. (1984) *Social Science Concepts: A Systematic Analysis*. London: Sage.

Senge, P.M. (1990) *The Fifth Discipline: The Art and Practice of the Learning Organization*. London: Century Business.

Shrivastava, P. (1983) 'A Typology of Organizational Learning Systems', *Journal of Management Studies* 20(1): 7–28.

Simon, H.A. (1991) 'Bounded Rationality and Organizational Learning', *Organization Science* 2(1): 125–34.

Starbuck, W.H. and Milliken, F.J. (1988) 'Executives' Perceptual Filters: What They Notice and How They Make Sense', in D.C. Hambrick (ed.) *The Executive Effect: Concepts and Methods for Studying Top Managers*, pp. 35–65. Greenwich, CT: JAI Press.

Swieringa, J. and Wierdsma, A. (1992) *Becoming a Learning Organization: Beyond the Learning Curve.* Wokingham: Addison-Wesley.

Tsang, E.W.K. (1997) 'Organizational Learning and the Learning Organization: A Dichotomy between Descriptive and Prescriptive Research', *Human Relations* 50(1): 73–89.

Ulrich, D., Jick, T. and von Glinow, M.A. (1993) 'High-impact Learning: Building and Diffusing Learning Capability', *Organizational Dynamics* 22(2): 52–66.

Watkins, K.E. and Golembiewski, R.T. (1995) 'Rethinking Organization Development for the Learning Organization', *The International Journal of Organizational Analysis* 3(1): 86–101.

Watkins, K.E. and Marsick, V.J. (1993) *Sculpting the Learning Organization: Lessons in the Art and Science of Systemic Change.* San Francisco, CA: Jossey-Bass.

Weick, K.E. (1995) *Sensemaking in Organizations.* London: Sage.

Wenger, E. (1991) 'Communities of Practice: Where Learning Happens', *Benchmark* (Fall): 6–8.

West, P. (1994) 'The Concept of the Learning Organization', *Journal of European Industrial Training* 18(1): 15–21.

4

Bente Elkjaer

The Learning Organization
An Undelivered Promise

'Any moral theory which is seriously influenced by current psychological theory is bound to emphasize states of consciousness, an inner private life, at the expense of acts which have public meaning and which incorporate and exact social relationships.' (Dewey, 1922, c. 1983: 61)

When the Danish public enterprise, Administrative Case Consideration (ACC),[1] in the mid-1990s launched a project on developing a learning organization, they did not anticipate that one of their professional employees five years later would contend 'it is a long time since the learning organization has been mentioned!' If they had known, they would probably not have spent the time, energy, and money to pursue the development of a learning organization. Now, how can we understand why the development of a lasting learning organization failed in ACC?

ACC's attempt to develop a learning organization appeared to involve letting all employees – office workers and professionals – participate in a training programme that in part took place at a remote course site. Here, the employees were introduced to a course content developed by the course organizers in co-operation with representatives for ACC. The content aimed to change the employees, to make them adopt new ways of thinking and acting that would be more appropriate in a learning organization. At the same time, the organization – its work practices and managerial structures – remained fairly intact.

The idea of developing a learning organization in ACC was sparked off by a threat of privatization in the late 1980s. This led to several rescue activities, the purpose of which was to make work more effective in ACC and to legitimize these efforts to the outside world. The attempt to increase efficiency in ACC was first and foremost related to implementation of new technology, which rendered some of the employees – the office workers – dispensable. However, instead of dismissing these employees they were asked to take over some of the professionals' tasks.

The office workers were prepared for their new tasks by attending a training programme and through a tutorial arrangement where each office worker was paired with a professional. In turn, the reorganization allowed the professionals to take on new tasks for the organization, and therefore they also had to attend a training programme. The objective of the training programme was that the professionals after they had 'almost solely been case-administrators also should become developers' (cited from the ACC evaluation report). In my research, I have focused on the training programme for the professionals in ACC. The question to which I was seeking answers was: how did the training programme prepare the professionals to become active members of a learning organization, which was the ultimate goal of the organizational change processes in ACC? However, as I believe that merely changing individuals cannot develop a learning organization, I also focused on the organizational changes. Did the work practices and managerial structures change in ACC to enable the learning organization to develop?

In the article, I will first present the literature that served as a guideline for ACC's development into a learning organization. I will particularly focus on the learning theory in the literature. Then I will present an alternative learning theory that focuses not only on the development of individuals – e.g. employees – but also on their increased ability to deal with the organizational problems they may encounter in their everyday life and work. After this theoretical exercise, I will turn to my case study, the methodology applied, a more thorough presentation of ACC and, in conclusion, my evaluation of ACC's approach to a learning organization.

Learning as Individual Change and Development

When reading literature on how to develop learning organizations, it strikes one how much focus there is on changing and developing individuals compared with the actual guidelines for changing and developing organizations (Pedler and Aspinwall, 1998; Senge, 1990; van Hauen et al., 1995). The prescriptive literature is also kept in a very abstract language. For example, the results of individuals' learning in organizations are formulated in such general terms as 'personal mastery':

> 'Personal mastery' is the phrase my colleagues and I use for the discipline of personal growth and learning. . . . Personal mastery goes beyond competence and skills, though it is grounded in competence and skills. . . . It means approaching one's life as a creative work, living life from a creative as opposed to reactive viewpoint. (Senge, 1990: 141)

It is hard to disagree with such an aim for human development, but it is not easy to find examples of how this actually might happen in contemporary organizations. Furthermore, we do not get much help on how to create a connection between the unfolding of personal mastery and the organizational development that will let this happen. The reason may be that organizational learning is assumed to be an epi-phenomenon of individual learning:

> The first step in considering the development of a good learning climate is to start with yourself and your own learning. How do you learn best? Which factors in yourself and in your immediate environment help you to learn most effectively? And which factors inhibit your learning? (Pedler and Aspinwall, 1998: 43)

When defining a good organizational learning climate with the point of departure in questions of individual learning, it implies that developing a learning organization *begins* with individual learning and does *not* start with changes in organizational work practices and structures. It also implies that the relation between individual learning and organizational problem solving is regarded as unproblematic, construed simply as a matter of the former meeting the demands of the latter. Thus a method for developing a learning organization may begin with a course on 'personal quality', i.e. 'a course that aims to give the individual participant the opportunity to examine his/her ability to learn, strengthen his/her self-confidence and question his/her assumptions' (van Hauen et al., 1995: 39).

From the literature it is difficult to see how a learning organization can be based on and derive from individual learning. However, 'shared vision' is suggested as the key means to achieve this objective: 'Shared vision is vital for the learning organization because it provides the focus and energy for learning' (Senge, 1990: 206).

There are, however, no real clues as to how personal attitudes can become shared visions, apart from through the individuals. This means that the learning organization comes to rest more on personal adaptation and organizational *socialization* than on learning. Against this background, I will suggest a *learning theory* that is based on employees' attempts to cope with everyday problems that they encounter in organizations.

Learning as Inquiry Resulting in Reflective Experiences

The above mentioned unspecific – and unproblematic – view of how to develop a learning organization has been harshly criticized (Argyris and Schön, 1996; Easterby-Smith, 1997). There have also been several attempts to outline an alternative learning theory to support development of learning in organizations. Thus it has been argued that learning is not solely an epistemological process based upon individual cognition, but learning must also be viewed as social and 'situated' (Brown and Duguid, 1991; Catino, 1999; Cook and Yanow, 1993; Easterby-Smith et al., 1998; Elkjaer, 1999; Gherardi et al., 1998; Østerlund, 1996). This means that learning is related to the institutional and social context in which it takes place and occurs through individuals' participation in communities of practice. The notion of learning as participation in communities of practice was originally coined by Jean Lave and Etienne Wenger (1991) who developed the term to understand learning which did not derive from formal teaching, e.g. learning through an apprenticeship.

I find the work of Lave and Wenger – and others – on situated learning very helpful in trying to understand what learning is when seen as a social process. However, Lave and Wenger operate on a fairly abstract level when it comes to providing an actual guideline for developing organizational learning and learning organizations. They do not seem to address the method of learning: i.e. *how* will learning arise from participation? The question of content also seems to be left in the dark: i.e. *what* can be learned from participating in communities of practice? This is my background for turning to the work of the American pragmatist, John Dewey, who wrote extensively on these matters (Dewey, 1916, c. 1966; 1933; 1938, c. 1963; 1938).[2] It is especially Dewey's notions on *inquiry* and *experience* – that I see as answers to the 'how' of learning (through the use of inquiry) and the 'what' of learning (by developing reflective experiences).

The *method* of learning may be found in Dewey's notion on inquiry, which relates to how knowledge is created – or rather how one gets 'to know' something. Dewey opposed the idea that knowledge is developed by way of abstract propositions as prescribed in the theory of knowledge in formal logic. Instead, he argued that knowledge is constructed by making inquiries into situations of uncertainty. These inquiries are, however, always situated and based upon the present experience of the inquirers.

An inquiry begins with a sense of an uncertain situation. Often, it is not an intellectual sense, but just a hunch that something is wrong. But as soon as the inquirer(s) begin to define and articulate the problem, they will use their experience and the inquiry will enter the sphere of the intellect, of thoughtfulness. One or more suggestions for resolving the problem may be probed and tested until a final solution is reached. To ensure that the problem is solved, the former sense of uncertainty must have gone, with respect to the definition and articulation of the problem.

If we wish our inquiries to turn into new knowledge that can help us act in a more informed way when we encounter new problems, we have to indulge in reflection or thinking. Thus we have to reflect upon the relation between how we defined the problem and how the chosen resolution actually solved the problem. This is how we develop our experiences, i.e. our future ability to sense, define, articulate and solve problems in new situations of uncertainty. The development of new experiences depends upon our ability to reflect – to think – about the relation between our actions when faced with problematic situations and the consequences in addition to the relations we make to our present experiences. However, experiences one 'has' and 'learning experiences' are not the same.[3]

There is a distinction between experiences 'had' and 'reflective' experiences – the latter are what I will call 'learning' experiences. Experiences 'had' are the results of what we do in our daily encounter with 'things'. They reflect how we, as persons, experience these encounters. However, experiences 'had' differ from mere activity.

> It is not experience when a child merely sticks his finger into a flame; it is experience when the movement is connected with the pain which he undergoes in consequence. Henceforth the sticking of the finger into flame *means* a burn. Being burned is a mere physical change, like the burning of a stick of wood, if it is not perceived as a consequence of some other action. (Dewey, 1916, c. 1966: 139–40, his emphasis)

It is our awareness of what our encounters with the world mean that constitutes experiences 'had'. However, if we want to learn from our experiences, we have to apply our ability as humans to reflect on the relations between our acting in and upon situations and the consequences of our actions and, moreover, relate them to our present experiences. Then, experiences 'had' will turn into 'reflective' experiences and become 'learning' experiences.

When we relate the work of Dewey to the work of Lave and Wenger, we may say that Dewey's notion of experience 'had' describes the outcome of our participation in communities of practice, which, therefore, will not automatically result in reflective experiences – or learning. This means that although we are in a situation in which we participate, we do not learn until we actively begin to engage in the situation by making inferences about its meaning and relating it to the experiences that we already have. Thus, learning is an *intentional* effort aimed at discovering relations between our actions and the resulting consequences in addition to our former/present experiences.[4]

My analysis of the development of a learning organization based on a learning theory that stresses inquiry as a method and reflective experiences as an outcome has led me to specify my research question as follows: How did the training programme and the organization as such prepare the professionals to inquire into their encounters with organizational work and daily life? Were the professionals' experiences put to work in the pursuit of developing a learning organization? First, however, I shall present my research methodology.

The Methodology

Towards the end of 1994, when the learning organization had been launched in ACC earlier that year, I had my first meetings with the management of ACC as well as representatives of different groups of employees. The training programme for the office workers had been completed, and the training programme for the professionals was just about to start. According to the plan, the professionals' training programme would be completed within a year. The professionals were divided into four teams, which all completed their training programme over a period of approximately two months. Thus the first team began in January, the second in April, the third in August, and the fourth and last in October.

In the study, I followed the third team of professionals before, during and after their training programme. From May to June 1995, I conducted pre-interviews with the participants in order to form a picture of the professionals in ACC. I was especially interested in their assessment of how the organization was preparing them for the learning organization, and how they viewed this new organizational design, including their readiness to participate in the process.

During the third team's training programme, which ran from the middle of August to the middle of October 1995, I was a participant observer. The purpose of my observations was to observe the method and the content of the training programme and the professionals' reactions to the programme. In January 1996, I returned to carry out post-interviews. In particular, I asked the professionals to assess whether the learning organization had become a more visible organizational form, and if they now felt more prepared to participate in such an organization. In November 1996, I made my report to ACC by giving a speech to all that were interested.

When conducting the interviews, I used the same interview guide for all involved. Normally, an interview would take between 30 and 45 minutes, during which time I took notes. I did not tape and transcribe the interviews because I wanted the research process to be as open and transparent to my informants as possible. From earlier experience with this method of research, I know that reading a transcribed interview often creates a lot of resistance and wishes to change the transcribed text. Thus, when I had typed my notes, they were mailed to the interviewed professionals to allow them to correct mistakes. However, only a few took advantage of my offer to become co-producers of the interview text.

I interpreted the data (including my observation notes) as 'texts', i.e. as descriptions of the part of the person's life that was the object of the study, and I used a phenomenological method of text interpretation (Giorgi, 1975; Kvale, 1996). This meant that I interpreted the texts several times. In the first interpretation, I focused on the actual content of the interviewees' answers and reactions rather than trying to fit these into a pre-defined conceptual scheme or to answer research questions. The aim was, in line with the phenomenological methodology, to reduce the texts to a more manageable size. In the second interpretation, which was based upon the first one, I posed my research questions.

Apart from the interviews and observations, I also used other text documents in the study, such as the annual report and other reports made by and for the organization, newspaper clippings, the training material, the application for financial support to implement the learning organization, evaluation schemes, etc. Informed by this background, I will present the story of the organization.

The Organization and Its Work Practice

ACC is part of the Ministry of Social Affairs, and its primary work consists of processing individuals' claims for economic compensation. At the time I did my research, there were just under 300 employees in the organization, out of which the majority were professionals (mainly law graduates) and office workers. ACC was organized as a traditional, hierarchical public institution with an executive board consisting of a director and a vice-director, in addition to a number of offices managed by a head of department. Besides the offices dealing with administration of individual cases, there were two offices for general case administration and a data processing secretariat. General case administration included interpretation of legal matters, inquiries from the public and the minister, personnel, translation and development of the data processing system.

The third team to go through the programme consisted of 26 professionals who came from all the different departments in ACC. Most of them were individual case administrators, a few were general case administrators and finally there were a couple who did other tasks in ACC. In terms of age, the diversity was great, but with a majority of young employees. For many of the participants, it was their first job as a legal adviser, and half of them had only worked in ACC for one year or less. Largely, the composition of the team corresponded to the composition of professionals in ACC as a whole.

The work practice of individual case administration follows a certain routine but, at the same time, it is highly skilled professional work and requires a degree in law or similar qualifications. However, individual case administration also has features that are similar to industrial mass production. This means that the work is easily measured and counted, and the quantitative aspect of case administration was very pronounced in ACC – from the distribution of cases to the organization's face towards the world. The latter was illustrated in the annual report, which was full of figures and numbers. The annual report showed that there had been a constant increase in cases and that the 'production statistics' had been going up for a number of years.

The number of cases was literally visible when you entered the office of an individual case administrator, as he or she would have piles of cases on shelves and desks. The rhetoric used in connection with individual case administration reflected the quantitative nature of the work. For example, individual case administrators would describe their work as 'piecework', and individual case administration offices were referred to as the 'production line' of ACC.

Despite the applied vocabulary from industry, the professionals also stressed the qualitative aspect of individual case processing. They found their work 'professionally challenging' due to its combination of legal, social and medical matters. Another qualitative aspect was the value and necessity of their work. Although their work was referred to as 'mass production', it was a production that involved human destinies. Each case involved the life of a fellow human being and, as professionals, they felt responsible for securing the economic compensation to which their clients were entitled according to law.

The Learning Organization as a Showcase?

The professionals in ACC had limited expectations with a view to developing a learning organization. Part of their scepticism was due to the amount of work in the organization. But they also doubted the sincerity of management's intentions to develop a learning organization. The essence of the professionals' scepticism can be phrased in the following two questions: 'Would it really be possible to develop a learning organization in ACC, given the amount of work in the organization? And was the whole idea of a learning organization not just a showcase?' A couple of quotations illustrate the issue:

> The problem in ACC is that we have too many cases and not enough employees, and then it is no use letting people attend a training programme.

> Management would like to show ACC off to the outside world. They want to signal that it is an organization where things happen. They want to show that ACC is a modern work place and that the employees have a very positive attitude.

Naturally, not all professionals were equally sceptical, but they were all concerned about whether implementation of the learning organization in ACC would meet the expectations it had created. The following quotation illustrates the point of view:

> It [implementation of the learning organization, BE] is making work more attractive. . . . But it has also raised our expectations in terms of working with matters other than case processing. If these expectations are not met, the professionals will become very disappointed.

In other words, the workload, the feeling that the whole project was just a showcase and doubts about whether they would ever get a chance to work with tasks other than individual case administration made the professionals question the reality of developing a learning organization in ACC. In the following, I will take a closer look at the actual training programme, i.e. its organization and content. Did the training programme make the profession-als more prepared for inquiry and did it utilize the professionals' experience as a prerequisite for developing a learning organization?

A Stressful Training Programme

The training programme designed for the professionals consisted of a range of seminars that ran over a couple of months. Some seminars lasted almost a fortnight and some were organized as 2–3 days of residential courses. Parallel to the seminars, 4–5 days were assigned to problem-oriented project work. The projects were organized in groups of four to seven people, and a supervisor was appointed to each project.

Most of the professionals felt that the training programme was very stressful. The reason was partly that everybody had to complete the pro-gramme within a year, which created a certain tension – especially because most professionals had the same amount of cases to process while attending the programme. Some were also questioning the whole idea of developing a learning organization by way of a training programme, and I quote:

> The process was too exhausting. . . . Is it really necessary to sacrifice so much in a period in order to become a learning organization? The training programme is not the Alpha and Omega if we have to learn a new way of thinking. It may also be done by small everyday steps.

It also created some dissatisfaction that all professionals had to go through exactly the same content regardless of whether they worked with individual or general case administration, or did not work with case administration at all. I quote:

> The social aspects were rewarding, but in terms of my profession I did not benefit from the seminar. It was too tailored for legal advisers [administrators of individual cases, BE]. . . . I think that the benefits would have been greater if the content had been differentiated.

The purpose of the training programme also comprised teaching the participants how to co-operate in problem-oriented projects, which was the background for the concluding project. According to management, the project issues should be related to the work practice in ACC. When the projects were presented (at a residential seminar), several representatives from management were present. They had been selected to comment on the results of the projects and indicate the prospects, if any, to continue working with a project in a cross-organizational group. In principle, the professionals' project work linked their work experiences and the organizational work practice.

For most of the professionals, the project work was a very rewarding process, and some projects were subsequently continued in work groups. However, whether a project was continued in a work group or not depended greatly on how management received the project at the closing seminar, and I quote:

> Quite simply, the group was not united, but the incentive to go on working with the project was not so great because the head of department from office X disagreed with the group's conclusion. It seems that it wasn't well received.

Rather than initiating the development of a learning organization, it appears that learning from the projects had more to do with *socialization* in terms of what was acceptable to present and work with in ACC. In addition, the project work contributed to the stressful atmosphere around the training programme. And the fact that representatives from management were present to comment on and evaluate the projects when they were presented turned the whole thing into an exam-like situation. Furthermore, the atmosphere was affected by the general distrust in management's intention to use the professionals' experiences in practice. This was indicated at the final seminar in a session on 'barriers to develop a learning organization in ACC'. Here, it was commented that 'we (read: management) are not very good at applying the skills that we have in the organization. We will rather procure e.g. teachers from the outside.'

The stressful organization of the training programme, the questioning of whether the same programme was appropriate for all professionals, insufficient time for project work and its nature of socialization rather than learning how to deal actively with everyday organizational problems led me to conclude that the professionals had not been prepared for inquiry into organizational situations of uncertainty, and that their professional experiences would not be applied 'in reality' to develop a learning organization in ACC.

According to Dewey's method of learning – his notion of inquiry – the process of learning requires a preparation of the employees to enable them to sense uncertain situations and act upon them by way of inquiry. The potential of such preparation is the development of active and reflective employees who are capable of developing their own as well as organizational experiences. A training programme in which all employees have to participate regardless of their specific work practice and within a certain time and pace does not provide this preparation. Such a training programme leaves employees with a feeling that whatever their contribution may be, it will be assessed in relation to the organization and the content of the training programme and not in relation to their everyday working life. The content of the training programme where problems and solutions were pre-given knowledge to be acquired by the professionals underlines this conclusion.

The Content of the Training Programme

The content of the training programme for the professionals consisted of the following four modules: 'Total Quality and Personal Quality'; 'Organization and Management Theory'; 'Performance and Negotiation Techniques'; and 'Written Communication'. The modules included two days that focused on legal matters: EU law and administrative law. Examples of project titles were 'Improving the contact to the industrially injured', 'The future of the professionals in ACC', and 'Tutor – thoughts and ideas about the tutorial arrangement'.

The content of the training programme aimed to make the professionals take on a new and more 'responsible' role. No skills and knowledge were taught in depth – primarily due to the stressful organization of the programme. For example, the first module on 'Total Quality and Personal Quality' was a crash course in which the professionals went through the steps in the Total Quality Management (TQM) concept that had been implemented in ACC to make the work routines more efficient. The course had no intention of actually training the professionals to become quality instructors. Some of the general caseworkers had already been assigned to this task and given a much longer course in the techniques of TQM. However, the module on TQM made the professionals consider the time aspect, and I quote:

> Similar to other elements in the course, it is difficult to see to which end quality measures can be used directly. But it [the course in quality measures, BE] increases your awareness of how you perform your work tasks.

The training programme affected the way the professionals thought and acted in connection with their case decisions, i.e. they started to assess the specific steps in the case processing in terms of time and the measures in TQM.

The seminar on 'Organization and Management Theory' conveyed the message that the professionals were going to be in charge of the office workers' training in the tutorial arrangement. But to be told in a training programme to take on managerial responsibilities and to do so in ACC was not the same, and I quote:

> It is not popular from our side to take on the role of management of the office workers. It is only the heads of department who are accepted as management.

The purpose of the two last courses – 'Performance and Negotiation Techniques'; and 'Written Communication' – was to teach the professionals specific skills that would enable them to participate in negotiations, conduct meetings and improve their oral and written presentations on behalf of the organization. In terms of learning actual skills, the outcome was poor, and I quote:

> When we finally were introduced to written communication, everybody was tired. . . . But it was the best part. It was straightforward.

Again, we see evidence that the stressful organization of the training programme hampered learning – even when the content was considered relevant. However, as a result of the training programme, the professionals became better acquainted because the teams had a cross-organizational composition. The projects were also instrumental in creating stronger personal ties between the professionals, but most of the participants did not derive real professional benefits, and I quote:

> We have become acquainted with several colleagues that we would otherwise not have known. So in terms of benefits, it is one up for co-operation and one down for content of programme.

As a result of the training programme, the professionals had a more comprehensive sense of community and viewed the organization as a more unified social whole. But there was no room for voicing issues that related to organizational work practices, which added to the distrust of whether the project would create a learning organization. For example, it was not possible to discuss the concept of quality in the TQM concept, and I quote:

> I cannot use this [quality measures, BE]. We were practically thrown into groups without discussing what quality is. I think that quality equating time is nonsense.

The emphasis on making case processing more efficient through implementation of TQM, and the failure to discuss the implications for the quality of case decisions led some professionals to think that perhaps case processing had become a 'necessary evil' in ACC.

The feeling that the professionals had not really learned any skills or gained any knowledge that they could apply – apart from learning to think more in terms of time and efficiency – the lack of opportunities to practise the postulated managerial responsibilities and the exhaustion that hampered learning have led me to conclude that the professionals' experiences were not really wanted in ACC's project of becoming a learning organization. Furthermore, the sense that the outcome of the seminar was social in nature rather than professional and the professionals' lack of opportunity to publicly discuss their doubt about the postulated benefits of implementing TQM in their work underline the conclusion. The organizational changes – or lack of changes – point in a similar direction.

Organizational Changes in Connection with the Learning Organization

Before attending the training programme, the professionals were looking forward to participating, and most thought that the whole thing was very 'exciting' in spite of their initial scepticism toward the idea of a learning organization. However, the professionals did not have a clear idea of what a learning organization involved. They felt that by introducing the learning organization, management wanted them to become 'more motivated, co-operative, and happy'. They thought that management wanted to introduce a learning organization to improve the employees' contribution to 'efficiency and quality' in the organizational work. In my post-interviews, the profession-als' picture of a learning organization was still rather unclear. Nevertheless, it had a flavour of elaborated democracy attached to it, and I quote:

> In appearance, ACC seems to be very democratic, e.g. in the relationship between the most senior and the youngest professionals. But the failure to renew 25 office worker positions at the turn of the year has shocked the organization. It has upset the organization more than it would have done, had it been a more traditional company. Here, edicts are received with more surprise than in an old-fashioned organization.

The professionals had imagined that a learning organization implied an increase in shared decisions. They did not expect employees to be given the sack by edict. They had believed that implementation of a learning organiza-tion implied more democracy, and therefore it hit hard when it turned out not to be the case. The idea of gathering together to learn something, and to become a learning organization, has positive connotations, and the pro-fessionals' participation in the training programme did leave them with a sense of change and development. They had been told to take charge of the office workers' re-skilling processes and to become more 'responsible' developers of the organization – especially for making the learning organiza-tion a success. However, they did not in any way feel 'empowered' by the development, and I quote:

> The competence has become muddled. On the one hand, certain formal power structures have been blurred because we have to be so equal, learn from each other, etc. But the hierarchies still exist both informally between employees and formally.

The relations between office workers and professionals changed from being rather anonymous to an emphasis on oral and personal communication and co-operation. However, the new relations left some structural problems unsolved as the professionals were not given real powers to make decisions in case of conflicts between them and the office workers. Both groups still worked under the head of department who made the final decisions in case of conflicts. Although the professionals had been promised more responsibility, the basic hierarchy did not change in ACC. The work itself, case processing, did not change either, and I quote:

> I have enjoyed it. I love to attend courses, and I have not felt any pressure. I like my work, but I am still working with cases that are no better and no worse than before.

The work had changed by way of the earlier mentioned TQM project, but it was, nevertheless, experienced as being much the same as always. Case processing continued to be case processing, and the organizational structures were kept intact regardless of the rhetoric used in the training programme. Some even felt that as professionals and employees the control had been tightened although the rhetoric in the training programme indicated the opposite, and I quote:

> In many ways ACC has become a better work place. However, there are also some negative aspects such as more control of our work. We can almost speak of 'Big Brother' conditions. To me it seems contrary to a learning organization. The control derives from an increase in computer control. It seems as if the employees are regarded with suspicion. And that is really unnecessary, as the morale is pretty high. The great focus on quality measures also implies control.

The training programme in addition to the idea and attempt to implement a learning organization may have given the employees a sense of a better work place. But it created tension that changes in the organizational structures were left out of the learning organization and that the means of control over the professionals' efficiency in case processing were increased. It was especially upsetting because the professionals regarded themselves as a committed workforce. In many ways, the organization itself – its managerial structures and work practices – lived its own life within the learning organization, implemented through the training programme and its rhetoric. The learning organization became reduced to a sense of social unity and more coherence, but it was not related to the task organization itself.

Conclusion

I began this article by puzzling over why a lasting learning organization had not been developed in ACC. My eyes were focused on ACC's method for developing a learning organization, namely to make all employees attend a training programme, partly situated at a remote course site. The aim of the programme was to induce the employees to adapt to a learning organization by changing their way of thinking and acting. I have tried to understand the case of ACC in the context of the guidelines for developing learning organizations as presented in literature. The literature on how to develop learning organizations focuses mostly upon the individuals in organizations and views shared vision as the means of connection. The inadequacy of this view led me to suggest a learning theory in which learning is viewed as socially situated. I have developed the contemporary view on social learning further by going back to some of its philosophical roots – namely to John Dewey who introduced the notion of inquiry as a way of gaining learning experiences.

From the outset, the professionals were sceptical about the project of developing a learning organization. Nevertheless, they looked forward to participating in the training programme that would introduce the learning organization. However, as the organization of the training programme turned out to be a very stressful affair, the professionals became even more sceptical as to whether their participation in reality would make ACC into a learning organization. The problem-oriented projects that were intended to link the training programme to the organizational work practices were evaluated in a top-down manner, which also gave the professionals the sense that the process of developing a learning organization was much too stressful to provide a workable outcome. Furthermore, the continuation of the projects in more permanent work groups turned out to depend on the reception of management. Thus I observed that the project work acted more as a means of organizational socialization than as an instrument to prepare the professionals for further inquiries into problematic situations that might lead to learning experiences.

The content of the training programme aimed to induce the professionals to take on new and more responsible roles. No skills and knowledge were taught in any depth, and the professionals' outcome from participating in the training programme was mainly of a social and not a professional nature. There was no real connection between the social outcome and the actual development of the organization itself – its structure and work practices. This development led me to conclude that the experiences gained by the professionals in their work were in fact considered irrelevant in pursuit of developing a learning organization.

The lack of connection between the new feelings of organizational unity and the development of the organization itself was further emphasized by the lack of changes in the organization. The idea of a learning organization created expectations of a more democratic organization, which were not fulfilled. In addition, no changes were implemented in the work that the professionals did before and after the training programme. Finally, implementation of more control measures contributed to kill the expectations for a learning organization in terms of one that would allow the professionals to have a real say regarding the organization and their own work practices.

I have suggested that the main reason why the learning organization did not become a lasting reality in ACC was the reliance on one method of implementation – the training programme – and its sole focus on changing the organization by changing individuals and otherwise leaving the organization alone. I have suggested an alternative way to develop a learning organization – a way that primarily focuses on preparing the employees to act on their perception of problematic situations by creating room for voices and actions based on their direct experiences from their work practices. Such an approach would create a relation between the development of employees and the development of the organization.

The obvious, final question is whether it is at all feasible to create a learning organization by way of a training programme that focuses on changing individuals as opposed to including employees actively in the development of their own work practices and of the organizational structures supporting these. I think that the approach adopted in the case organization neglected the latter possibility, and failed as a result. I believe that my case story shows that there is no such thing as a quick pedagogical fix to a learning organization. Instead, it is a long and winding road in which the notions of inquiry and experience may help members to actualize the wonderful image of a learning organization. However, it requires that management abandons the detailed control that tends to inhibit employees from sensing and inquiring into the uncertainties they meet in their everyday work practices. Such a step might provide the opportunity for developing individual and organizational experiences – and for bringing a continually 'learning learning organization' to light.

Notes

I wish to express my gratitude to Susan Leigh Star, Department of Communication, University of California San Diego, and Janet Dixon Keller, University of Illinois Urbana-Champaign, for having made very useful comments on an earlier version of this article. I also wish to thank Karen Ruhleder, University of Illinois Urbana-Champaign, for having had the patience to read and comment on several versions of the article. Last, but not least, I wish to express my gratitude to two anonymous reviewers from Management Learning for their most helpful and very detailed comments on earlier versions.

1. This is an invented name to secure anonymity.
2. The *Collected Works* by John Dewey and the *Works about John Dewey* (Levine, 1996) are available in book form and as CD-ROMs. For works about Dewey published after 1995, there is a supplementary list on the URL address of the John Dewey Center: http://www.siu.edu/~deweyctr/. The *Collected Works* by Dewey have been published as Early Works (EW), Middle Works (MW), and Later Works (LW). EW cover the period 1882–98 and include five volumes; MW cover the period 1899–1924 and include 15 volumes; and LW cover the period 1925–53 and include 17 volumes. Besides the 37 volumes, an index to the volumes has been published as a separate book. The general editor of the *Collected Works* was Jo Ann Boydston, and Southern Illinois University Press (Carbondale and Edwardsville) published them between 1969 and 1991.
3. Dewey developed his concept of experience throughout his life, and it is not all that clear what he means by the term. For interested readers, I have especially applied his 1905 (c. 1981) essay, 'The Postulate of Immediate Empiricism', and his principal work on education (1916, c. 1966) to discern the distinctions in his concept of experience.
4. When I have presented Dewey's concepts of inquiry and experience, I have sometimes been asked why I do not refer to the later work of David Kolb (1984), as he also talks about 'experience' in relation to his learning cycles and styles, and to Reg Revans (1978, c. 1998) and his concept of action learning. The answer to why I have neglected the work of Kolb is that he

tends to ignore the importance of present experiences of learners in favour of categorizing learners by their different 'learning styles'. The reason why I have not referred to Revans is that he is very focused on measuring the outcome of the learning process. Dewey emphasizes 'learning as growth' (of learning experiences) rather than learning styles, and the process of inquiry leading to growth rather than a measurement of outcomes.

References

Argyris, C. and Schön, D.A. (1996) *Organizational Learning II. Theory, Method, and Practice.* Reading: Addison-Wesley.

Brown, J.S. and Duguid, P. (1991) 'Organizational Learning and Communities-of-Practice: Toward a Unified View of Working, Learning, and Innovation', *Organization Science* 2(1): 40–57.

Catino, M. (1999) 'Learning and Knowledge in Communities of Work Practice: The Case of the Pilot Plants at Cer-Montell', in M. Easterby-Smith, L. Araujo and J. Burgoyne (eds) *Organizational Learning, 3rd International Conference, 1.* Lancaster: Lancaster University.

Cook, S.D.N. and Yanow, D. (1993) 'Culture and Organizational Learning', *Journal of Management Inquiry* 2(4): 373–90.

Dewey, John (1905, c. 1981) 'The Postulate of Immediate Empiricism', in J.J. McDermott (ed.) *The Philosophy of John Dewey. The Structure of Experience (Vol. 1); The Lived Experience (Vol. 2).* Chicago and London: The University of Chicago Press.

Dewey, J. (1916, c. 1966) *Democracy and Education. An Introduction to the Philosophy of Education.* New York: The Free Press.

Dewey, J. (1922, c. 1983) *Human Nature and Conduct: An Introduction to Social Psychology.* New York: Holt.

Dewey, J. (1933) *How We Think: A Restatement of the Relation of Reflective Thinking to the Educative Process.* Boston: D.C. Heath.

Dewey, J. (1938) *Logic. The Theory of Inquiry.* New York: Henry Holt.

Dewey, J. (1938, c. 1963) *Experience and Education.* New York: Collier Books.

Easterby-Smith, M. (1997) 'Disciplines of Organizational Learning: Contributions and Critiques', *Human Relations* 50(9): 1085–113.

Easterby-Smith, M., Snell, R. and Gherardi, S. (1998) 'Organizational Learning: Diverging Communities of Practice?', *Management Learning* 29(3): 259–72.

Elkjaer, B. (1999) 'In Search of a Social Learning Theory', in M. Easterby-Smith, L. Araujo and J. Burgoyne (eds) *Organizational Learning and the Learning Organization. Developments in Theory and Practice.* London: Sage.

Gherardi, S., Nicolini, D. and Odella, F. (1998) 'Toward a Social Understanding of How People Learn in Organizations. The Notion of Situated Curriculum', *Management Learning* 29(3): 273–97.

Giorgi, A. (1975) 'An Application of Phenomenological Method in Psychology', in A. Giorgi, C. Fischer and E. Murray (eds) *Duquesne Studies in Phenomenological Psychology, II.* Pittsburgh: Duquesne University.

Kolb, D.A. (1984) *Experiential Learning.* Englewood Cliffs, NJ: Prentice Hall.

Kvale, S. (1996) *InterViews. An Introduction to Qualitative Research Interviewing.* Thousand Oaks, CA: Sage.

Lave, J. and Wenger, E. (1991) *Situated Learning. Legitimate Peripheral Participation.* Cambridge: Cambridge University Press.

Levine, B. (ed.) (1996) *Works about John Dewey 1886–1995.* Carbondale and Edwardsville: Southern Illinois Press.

Østerlund, C.S. (1996) 'Learning Across Contexts. A Field Study of Salespeople's Learning at Work', in *Psykologisk Skriftserie* (21)1, Aarhus: Aarhus Universitet.

Pedler, M. and Aspinwall, K. (1998) *A Concise Guide to the Learning Organization.* London: Lemos & Crane.

Revans, R. (1978, c. 1998) *ABC of Action Learning.* London: Lemos & Crane.

Senge, P.M. (1990) *The Fifth Discipline. The Art and Practice of the Learning Organization.* New York: Doubleday Currency.

van Hauen, F., Strandgaard, V. and Kastberg, B. (1995) *Den lærende organization – om evnen til at skabe kollektiv forandring* (The Learning Organization – About the Ability to Create Collective Change). København: Industriens Forlag.

part two

Individual Learning

5

David Megginson

Planned and Emergent Learning
Consequences for Development

Assumptions

This paper is about the individual learning of managers and the learning strategies that they adopt. The predominant focus of this paper is individual and psychological, as the learning strategies that managers adopt are not observable and amenable to regulation by others. I also address the impact of the process of programmed self-development on bringing out into the open these previously covert learning strategies. I do not directly address the efficacy of self-development programmes.

The questions at the heart of this paper are whether learners can be assessed as using a planned or an emergent strategy and whether mastery of the two strategies can vary independently among individuals. The models of inquiry which I adopt are mixed. I developed the model which I have tested:

- from grounded experience (Glaser and Strauss, 1967) in the field;
- from noticing the difficulties of learners; and
- from the inconsistencies of developers in considering learning strategies.

I have used a traditional quantitative model to develop an instrument for measuring learning strategies, and to examine what strategies are used by a large sample of managers. This research paradigm has been widely criticized – its limitations have been graphically described, for example, by Gill and Johnson, 1991 – it none the less provides a framework for measuring nomothetically what is amenable to measurement.

My model of individual development is idiographic (a framework I first discovered in Vernon, 1969). So the question of what a manager might do with the frameworks and the data that I can provide is by no means so readily amenable to broad generalization. Instead I assume that what each manager makes of the models and data will be determined mostly by a combination of established routines and conscious choices. These will be mediated to some extent by the managers' circumstances, which can be expressed in terms of organizational culture and learning climate.

Context

Why is an understanding of individuals' learning strategies important to learners, to developers and to those researching development? I will concentrate upon five issues:

• the change in career patterns;
• the shift in responsibility for development;
• the requirement for self-developers to be self-aware;
• the place of learning contracts in self-development;
• the difficulties experienced by some individuals in setting learning contracts.

Changing career patterns

Delayering, the breaking by organizations of their contract with middle managers for guaranteed lifetime employment, portfolio careers, and the need for multiple occupations and skill sets in individuals' working lives, have all led to a sharp decline in the frequency of the incremental managerial career. Much is made of the importance of increasing employability (Bloch and Bates, 1995) rather than the guarantee of employment. However, many managers have responded with a sense of betrayal and powerlessness (Harrison, 1995a).

Recently, a perceptive manager said to me that colleagues in his rich and powerful organization had moved in the last few years from complacency to fear, without spending any time in between being engaged. This intermediate position of engagement is where there is the possibility of confident and exploratory development. By contrast, when I encounter managers who have made the transition from dependence to self-managing, whether they remain in their large organizations or whether they have adopted portfolio careers, I notice their confidence and zest in facing the new employment paradigm.

Responsibility for Development

In the last decade I have detected a progressive move in the locus of responsibility for careers. It can be represented diagrammatically as in Figure 1 (from Megginson and Clutterbuck, 1995; used with permission).

Traditionally, training and development was the job of the training department. With the cutting of staff levels in service functions such as training and development, and the recognition that much off-job training had little impact upon on-job performance, an ideology developed in many organizations that the responsibility for training and development should be

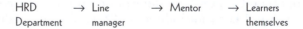

Figure 1 *The evolution of responsibility for development*

Figure 2   *Network of development with the learner at the centre*

vested in the line manager. Unfortunately, just at the time that this new demand was being placed on managers, they were finding that they had a wider span of control as a result of delayering. In addition they often had a dispersed work group, where they seldom saw many of their direct reports. Managers with relatively coercive management styles also found a conflict between the dictates of command and control, and the dynamics of development. Mentors were suggested as an alternative, and in many organizations they are proving a useful adjunct in the development process, but they are often too peripheral to take the central role. Inexorably, the responsibility for development has moved to individuals themselves.

In some organizations this has simply involved dumping the problem in the laps of individuals often too powerless and unskilled in learning to handle it constructively themselves. Sometimes, however, individuals have been supported in using the panoply of resources that are open to them, as represented in Figure 2 (Megginson and Clutterbuck, 1995; reproduced with permission).

The development of programmes of self-development (Megginson and Pedler, 1992), or self-directed (Harrison, 1995b) and self-managed (Cunningham, 1994) learning have provided a process for supporting individuals in taking responsibility for their own learning. Thus the shift of focus from training to development has accompanied and reinforced the shift of responsibility from HRD department to individual learner.

Self-development and Self-awareness

Once learners take a more proactive role in their own development then the requirement for awareness of their own learning strategies and styles grows. While the training department or the line manager dictated the nature of the learning experience that the individual was to submit to, then it did not matter much whether or not the individual knew anything about how they learned best. They just went through what they were sent to do. Once individual managers take responsibility for the *how* and *where* and *what* of learning, however, it matters a great deal that they are aware of their preferred learning style and strategy.

If managers are going to be able effectively to plan their own learning, then they need to know which styles they adopt most readily and which strategy they enjoy using. Learning styles have been well documented and instrumented (Hayes and Allinson, 1994; Honey and Mumford, 1995; Kolb, 1984). This paper outlines the significance of learning strategies and differentiates them from styles.

Learning Contracts in Self-development

Part of the new orthodoxy of development requires each manager to create a learning contract. This specifies the individual's reply to what I call the five Roffey questions (Megginson, 1994):

- where have I been?
- where am I now?
- where do I want to be?
- how will I get there?
- how will I know I have arrived?

I have noticed that, whereas many managers are happy to get on with preparing a learning contract, others seem blocked and unable to commit. I hypothesized that one source of the difficulty may be that some individuals do not like to plan their learning in advance. I wondered whether this was a defect in learning or whether these people possess other abilities or strategies which they use to develop themselves. I felt that I was on to something when I had a conversation with a well-known developer, who has not only written widely about the development of others, but has also served as something of a role model to me in how he developed himself. I asked him first whether he always encouraged people embarking on self-development to prepare learning contracts. He said 'Yes'. I then asked him whether he had ever prepared one for himself, and his reply was a rather rueful 'No'. So, we had a case of a disjunction between espoused theory and theory in use (Argyris and Schön, 1978), but also an example of a highly effective learner who was doing something other than planning.

At about this time I also attended a meeting of a professional association where two speakers were advocating two alternative approaches to learning. One was proposing a formal process of continuous professional development that involved the use of learning contracts; the other was advocating the use of learning logs to capture the essence of experience and extract the learning from it. The difference in the styles of the two presenters (dogged versus dramatic) imprinted the distinction on my memory, and I began to see that there were two strategies at work here. Soon I started calling them 'planned' and 'emergent' strategies. The rest of this paper describes the work that I have done in testing the validity of this distinction and in exploring its implications for learners and developers.

Learning Styles and Strategies: the Literature

David Kolb was one of the first to offer a language for considering learning styles. From the 1960s onward he developed an elegant theory and a powerful practice of experiential learning. This was summarized in his definitive text (Kolb, 1984). In essence he argued that in order to learn deeply and generatively, we need to be able to:

- attend to a palpable and concrete experience – to notice it in a way which engages our full attention;
- be free enough in ourselves and in our time availability to observe reflectively about the phenomenon we have noticed; this involves neither compulsive worrying nor fitting the phenomenon into predetermined categories, but rather it requires us to consider how what we have experienced relates to our mental maps and our presuppositions;
- generalize the reflected-upon experience into an abstract conceptual framework which we own; it may have been invented by someone else, like the framework I am currently discussing was for me, but we make it our own by thinking about it in relation to our own experience and examining how experience and mental model fit, and the implications for both experience and model of the degree of fit;
- test out our evolving sense of the dance of practice and theory by experimenting actively with the world to see how our tentative experience shapes up; the outcomes of this inquiry, if carried out with a degree of energy and rigour, will lead us into another cycle of experience, reflection, and so on.

Kolb's normative position is that we need to be deeply competent in each of the four stages in what he calls his 'learning cycle' in order to learn effectively. His contribution to practice is to advise us to create learning experiences which address each stage. He calls such learning 'experiential' – a word which in the last 10 years has suffered a serious dilution in meaning and power in the hands of educators who have failed to grasp the potent clarity of Kolb's vision.

Kolb has a set of terms for styles which fall within each segment, so experiencer/reflectors are 'divergers'; reflector/conceptualizers are 'assimilators'; conceptualizer/experimenters are 'convergers and experimenter/experiencers are 'accommodators'.

Honey and Mumford (1995) offer an alternative framework based on the same fundamental model. Their terminology for the four points in the cycle is confusingly different – so, whereas reflector and theorist map unmistakably on to Kolb's reflective observation and abstract conceptualization, Kolb's active experimentation is equivalent to their pragmatist, and his concrete experience is equivalent to Honey and Mumford's activist. Honey and Mumford's normative position seems to be somewhat different from Kolb's in that they suggest that it is permissible to develop by strengthening the styles that one already has, and to seek out learning experiences which feed these styles (see for example Mumford, 1993: 52–6). This characteristically prag-matic view has the virtue of permissiveness and acceptance of the learner's position, but it has the disadvantage that it compromises the conceptual and practical insight of Kolb about the cyclical nature of experiential learning.

The learning cycle and learning styles are one of the best-established models in organization psychology, although at the British Academy of Management Annual Conference in 1994 Hayes and Allinson offered a penetrating review which raised questions about the strength of the effects predicted by style theory (Hayes and Allinson, 1994).

So, learning styles seem to be derived from the point or the segment of the learning cycle which is emphasized by the learner. What about learning strategies? I differentiate strategies from styles by recognizing that, while styles reflect an emphasis on a point or segment in the cycle, learning strategies reflect an existential or life position. Other authors have used the term 'learning strategy' differently from the way it is used here (Marsick and Watkins, 1990; Messick, 1976). The essence of my definition is that the learning strategy represents an approach to all experience, which will be constituted of a mixture of deliberation/forethought (planned) and un-premeditated exploration (emergent).

Mumford again is active in considering learning strategies, which he calls 'learning approaches'. He offers four approaches, which I describe below. The terms for the four approaches are Mumford's, but the descriptions are my own, inferred from what he says about them (Mumford, 1993: 19–22):

- intuitive – unconscious reactive responsive learning
- incidental – conscious reactive responsive learning
- retrospective – conscious deliberate responsive learning
- prospective – conscious deliberate proactive learning

I have described Mumford's approaches on three dimensions:

- unconscious to conscious – whether learning is seen as part of un-differentiated experience or whether it is separately codified and named as learning;
- reactive to deliberate – whether the learning is not separated in time from other action, or whether specific time is set aside for attention to learning;
- responsive to proactive – whether the special learning agenda was planned before the event or only allocated afterwards.

Because there seem to me to be three dimensions at work here it is hard to fit these four approaches into the behavioural scientist's beloved two-by-two matrix. Perhaps it is no coincidence that Mumford has not attempted this. Mumford's normative stance on these approaches seems to be that the list is a hierarchy, with intuitive as the least preferable strategy and prospective as the best.

My own notion, that the core strategic distinction is between emergent and planned, is analogous to Mumford's two most developed approaches –

retrospective and prospective. My normative and conceptual position, how-ever, is different. I see both planned and emergent strategies as legitimate and effective, and I would expect come managers to adopt emergent strategy to the relative exclusion of planned *and* vice versa. An advantage of this perspective, as I see it, is that it avoids the trap of placing the establishment of predetermined learning objectives at the pinnacle of a hierarchy of valued approaches to learning. It was this sort of reverence for planning which lay at the heart of the failure of systematic training in the 1970s (Megginson and Pedler, 1992: 2). Acknowledging the equality of status of emergent and planned learning strategies is also congruent with a move towards a parallel process in corporate strategy – led by Mintzberg (1987). Finally, treating emergent and planned strategies with equality of esteem also allows for the use of a two-by-two matrix!

The Model and the Research Questions

My model and the terminology that I use to describe strategies was first outlined by Megginson (1994) and is reproduced in Figure 3, with permission:

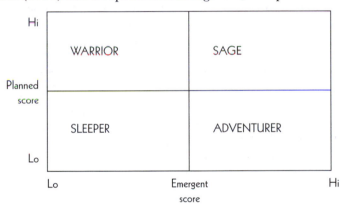

Figure 3 *Types of learner*

The term Sleeper is intended to be non-pejorative, in that it implies no lack of capacity for learning, but simply that the learner has not yet developed it. The Warrior type engages in focused, persistent pursuit of predetermined learning goals. An Adventurer will be open to learning whatever happens, and be keen to make the most sense of events however they turn out. The Sage type uses the ways of both Warrior and Adventurer to a considerable extent, separately or in combination, whenever appropriate.

Earlier, I indicated that the planning Warrior was not superior to the emergent Adventurer; but it is also the case that the Adventurer is not superior to the Warrior. A metaphor for learning frequently used (most memorably by John Cleese in his Video Arts film *The importance of mistakes* with his story of Gordon the guided missile) is that a guided missile is superior to a cannon. It could be argued that Adventurers, with their concern for where they are, can be more like guided missiles than Warriors who have a goal and shoot at it like a cannon, but don't adapt as they go on. I am proposing that the distinction between Warrior and Adventurer is better likened to the difference in foraging strategy between bees and butterflies. Bees seek out a known source of nourishment and return to base, whereas butterflies are blown hither and thither and chance upon all sorts of goodies which might be out of the range of the focused bee. Both strategies have their advantages, and both are clearly successful in terms of allowing the species to perpetuate themselves.

Data and Analysis[1]

In 1994 I had only a draft questionnaire and had not carried out any statistical examination of the scores from the growing sample of managers who had completed it. This paper moves my exploration forwards by examining whether learners can be assessed as using a planned or an emergent strategy and whether mastery of the two strategies can vary independently among individuals. Moving then to my first research question,

Table 1   *Inter-correlations and discrimination index within Planned scale of pilot questionnaire (N = 168)*

Item	Correlation with other items in P	Discrimination index (score 4–6 minus score 0–2)
12 I set targets for my development	0.567	+33
3 For me, learning is a planned process of setting goals, achieving them and setting new goals	0.528	+20
7 I set goals for my own learning	0.487	+45
14 I use learning contracts regularly to focus on my progress in developing	0.441	–99
5 I regularly prepare a learning contract outlining my plans	0.437	–111
1 Writing down appraisals of my work performance is an important basis for my development	0.400	+4
24 Work plans provide a basis for preparing a self-development strategy	0.385	+36
17 It is useful to plan in advance how we want to develop	0.287	+92
22 Most of my development is explicitly directed towards organizational goals	0.259	–4

Mean = 26.667; Standard Deviation = 7.147

Table 2   *Inter-correlations and discrimination index within Emergent scale of pilot questionnaire (N = 168)*

Item	Correlation with other items in E	Discrimination index
11 In order to learn from experience I reflect frequently upon what happens to me	0.483	+96
13 It is important to be open to experience then learning will come	0.482	+150
6 It is important for me to add to/change my learning plans frequently in the light of new information	0.451	+51
21 Most of my new learning emerges unexpectedly from things that happen	0.377	+45
4 In conversation with others I often come to new understandings of what I have learned	0.353	+110
18 Learning is a lifelong adventure	0.335	+167
25 You can't plan significant learning	0.311	−78
9 I write down what happens to me and what I learned from it at least once a week	0.242	−152

Mean = 28.024; Standard Deviation = 5.220

I will outline the content of my pilot questionnaire and specify the results derived from the analysis.

The pilot questionnaire had 25 items. On the basis of assumed content validity I allocated nine of these items to a putative Planned or P scale and eight to a similar Emergent or E scale. I also included in the pilot questionnaire two other short scales of four items each – one about Relying on Others and the other about Finished Development. These yielded some interesting results, but they are not considered further in this paper.

I was interested to see whether the items in the scales intercorrelated with each other, and whether they differed from scores in the other scale. Taking all the items allegedly concerned with P from the pilot questionnaire, Table 1 shows how they inter-correlate within the scale, and also shows an index of how well each item discriminates between the population of 168 respondents. The discrimination index is calculated by assessing how many individuals scored 0, 1 or 2 on the item and subtracting this from the number who scored 4, 5 or 6. A figure of zero would indicate that there was a balanced range of scores rather than all the responses being at one or other end of the scale.

A similar analysis of the putative Emergent items is given in Table 2.

On the basis of these scores, I had confirmation that there were two separate phenomena here and that they varied relatively independently – the inter-correlation between the two scales was 0.336. Some of this was attributable to item 9, which I had placed in the E scale, but which correlated marginally better with the P scale (0.282) than it did with the one where I initially thought it belonged (correlation with E scale 0.242).

Looking at each scale in turn I sought to eliminate items which did not contribute. I started with the E scale. Here I eliminated item 18 where the discrimination index showed that it was an 'easy point' with which everyone can agree. I also decided to cut out item 9 because of its link to the P scale discussed earlier.

For the P scale, which in the pilot had one more item than the E scale, I therefore decided to eliminate the three items which correlated least with the scale score.

Having done this the correlations between the new P and E scale items and their respective scale scores are given in Table 3. The items are identified by their old numbers from the pilot questionnaire.

Table 3   *Inter-correlations between items and scale score for revised P and E scales* (N = 168)

New P item	Correlation	New E item	Correlation
12	0.666	11	0.465
3	0.481	13	0.428
7	0.534	6	0.460
14	0.516	21	0.398
5	0.513	4	0.357
1	0.301	25	0.281

Reducing the items in this way has the effect of reducing the correlation between scores on the new P and the new E scales from 0.336 to 0.287. This can be partly attributed to removal of items which were not discriminating between people and were therefore creating spurious inter-scale correlations, and partly to the omission of item 9 from the E scale because it was contaminated with P.

As one would expect, there is a very high correlation between the new and the old scale scores: 0.925 for P and 0.975 for E. This indicates that there is a streamlining of measurement without any material change in what is being measured.

Table 4 shows the norms for the 168 people who completed the pilot questionnaire, analysed to include just those items in the new P and E scales.

Appendix 1 is a scattergram of the 168 pilot respondents against the new P and E scores. Using roughly the median point on each scale as a dividing line gives a breakdown for the pilot population of 168 as follows:

Sleepers	<17	P	<21	E	N = 41
Warriors	17+	P	<21	E	N = 24
Adventurers	<17	P	21+	E	N = 43
Sages	17+	P	21+	E	N = 60

For the 168 people in the pilot survey I also gathered data about their

Table 4 *Norms for new P and E scales* (N = 168)

Category	Raw score	N	% (N = 168)
NEW P SCALE			
Over 2 SDs below Mean – v. low	0–5	4	2.4
1–2 SDs below Mean – low	6–10	20	11.9
0–1 SDs below Mean – av.–low	11–16	60	35.7
0–1 SDs above Mean – av.–high	17–21	47	28.0
1–2 SDs above Mean – high	22–26	30	17.9
Over 2 SDs above Mean – v. high	27+	7	4.1
NEW E SCALE			
Over 2 SDs below Mean – v. low	0–12	3	1.8
1–2 SDs below Mean – low	13–17	26	15.5
0–1 SDs below Mean – av.–low	18–21	54	32.1
0–1 SDs above Mean – av.–high	22–25	50	29.8
1–2 SDs above Mean – high	26–29	26	15.5
Over 2 SDs above Mean – v. high	30+	9	5.3

gender, age, highest qualification, employment status and, if employed, size of organization. A larger survey will be required to yield significant results, but one tentative finding from the data analysed so far is that males between the ages of 35 and 44 score markedly lower than females of the same age on the P scale, whereas there is no such marked difference on the E scale for people of this age, and indeed no significant differences between women and men of any other age group. Could it be that men facing their mid-life crisis are more susceptible to letting go of a will to plan than are women, or men and women at other ages? Further research is needed.

Discussion

I have been able to generate a scale which measures my two hypothesized learning strategy dimensions which I have labelled planned and emergent. Inter-correlations between items in each scale are higher than the correlation between the two scales. This indicates that the two scales can vary independently, thus allowing for individuals to use the planning or the emergent strategy to a great extent without high use of the other. None the less, there is a low positive correlation between the two scales (0.287) and this is congruent with the notion that as one develops as a learner it is likely that one will develop somewhat in both areas, even though one may be clearly preferred.

Earlier in this paper, I suggested that my position is idiographic, and that I do not prescribe a precedence for either the planned way of the Warrior or emergent Adventuring. It will be clear to the reader that my two by two matrix does have a best box, viz. the approach of the Sage. At this stage of my exploration of these issues, and perhaps this is a value-based position which no amount of further research would shift, I hold the view that how an individual develops from their current strategy is up to them. I do not hold a view as to whether it is better for Adventurers to further strengthen their emergent strategy or whether they would rather be advised to compensate by extending their capacity to plan. It seems to me that this perspective offers developers and individual learners a framework within which they can make informed decisions based on a holistic grasp of their situation.

My personal use of the model has involved both of the possibilities outlined in the previous paragraph. Although I was predominantly an Adventurer, in recent years I have put considerable effort into developing the emergent strategy still further. I have done thin by the use of learning logs, by intensively keeping a journal, and by the use of silent reflection in the midst of what often seems to be a fairly frantic life. I have also developed my capacity to adopt a planning strategy, by the use of a variety of prioritizing techniques, which have highlighted to me how I have avoided doing things which are both urgent and important when I am faced with learning blocks or other challenges that I would prefer to avoid – to-do lists are not just aides memoire, they can challenge in a deep way how we conduct our lives. I have also set goals (a) on a daily basis, (b) intermittently, using the IPD's Continuous Professional Development framework, and (c) annually using the ten goals, four rooms technique, which I have spelt out in some detail in Megginson, 1994.

This source also offers practical advice as to how to develop from each of the four styles in the matrix. The normative position adopted in that paper was that Sleepers should concentrate on increasing their attention to what was going on; that Warriors and Adventurers should learn the opposite strategy to the one they preferred; and that Sages would be pretty good already at developing themselves, and needed little advice from me.

This paper is less prescriptive than my earlier work, but the suggestions that I spelt out there can be chosen by individuals if they wish, and I summarize them below. The scattergram and the norms developed allow users of the scale to invite learners to place themselves on a matrix which offers them options against which they can plan the development of their learning strategy.

My recommendations include the suggestion that Sleepers can start by waking up, and that the awareness exercises from the Gestalt tradition of Perls and his successors provide an excellent framework for this (Stevens, 1993).

Warriors, who have the focus and direction associated with a readiness to set goals, can learn to explore the byways of experience, and in particular can squeeze the learning juice out of what happens around them through the use of reflective tools such as learning logs (Green and Gibbons, 1991).

Adventurers can be encouraged to curb their restless spirits by applying the discipline of goal setting, whether it be for the rest of a lifetime or for the next day, and I describe how I put SPICE in my own life by setting Spiritual, Physical, Intellectual, Career and Emotional goals each day (Megginson, 1994).

Sages are clearly some way forward in the task of developing themselves, and so I make brief suggestions that they can work on four areas: how to help others; how to branch out in new directions; how to renew the self; and how to deepen their direction.

Applications

The framework, methodology and tools outlined in this paper can be of use to developers in examining their own learning preferences, and in checking to ensure that they are not recommending to others what they do not practise themselves. On the other hand this framework can also serve as a reminder that others may adopt learning strategies different from ourselves, and that a learner-centred response would be to recognize these for what they can contribute, before offering alternatives that might point a way forward.

Individuals can use the questionnaire and associated material to point a way forward in their own development. It is perhaps particularly useful to consider learning strategies in the company of others. 1 have encouraged this process at the start of a self-development process, in learning sets, support and challenge groups, or, as they are called in ICL plc (the systems integration company), development network groups.[2]

Perhaps because I am something of an Adventurer myself, I think that this framework can specifically be used to pick up those who may be reluctant to get launched on preparing a learning contract, development agreement or continuous professional development statement. With care it can provide a language for valuing what they have, and it can be used to point the way to what else they may want to develop.

Conclusions

Learning strategies, like learning styles, have a part to play in helping learners, developers and researchers better understand the processes of individual development. In an era when self-development has entered the mainstream (Megginson and Pedler, 1992) employees and managers are frequently asked to take responsibility for their own learning. Typically, the taking of this responsibility involves a requirement for learners to engage in a planning strategy. Competency-based development also demands this approach. In government schemes and in vocational education, the accreditation of prior, so called, experiential learning requires an emergent strategy. The dimensions of the learning company (Pedler, Burgoyne and Boydell, 1991) also require different strategies: in particular, it seems to me that 'Participative policy making' and 'Boundary workers as environmental scanners' invite an emergent strategy, and 'Self development for all', as indicated earlier, evokes a planned one.

Thus many developments in contemporary education, development and training relate clearly to the question of learning strategy, as outlined in this paper, and what I have set out to do is to provide a language, a model and some data within which the debate and practice of learning strategies can be examined.

Further Research

My plan to take forward the issues addressed in this paper includes preparing some idiographic cases of learners who are clearly in one of each of the four quadrants in the model. This will yield dense and living data about the experience of such learners, and provide further information which will enrich the insights available about learning strategies and provide case studies for use in organizations. I will also gather a larger sample of responses to the questionnaire with appropriate biographical data, and this will serve to generate quantitative data about categories of learner, and their learning strategies.

Another fruitful area for inquiry is the relationship of the learning strategies to other measures of people. In particular, it will be interesting to compare learning strategies and learning styles. I am also intrigued to explore whether there is a relationship between individuals' scores on the 'Perceiving–Judging' scale of the Myers-Briggs Type Inventory. My tentative hypothesis is that those who are 'Perceivers' are also likely to be 'Emergers', and those who are at the 'Judging' end of the scale will also be 'Planners'.

This section starts with the words 'My plan ...' As one who is very comfortable with emergent learning I am also open to exploring other lines of inquiry, and any suggestions to that end will receive a warm welcome from me.

Notes

1. I am indebted to my erstwhile colleague, Anne Brackley, for her assistance in coding and analysing the data, using Microsoft EXCEL Version 5.0a.

2. I would like to acknowledge my gratitude to Bianca Kübler, Phil Dickinson and their colleagues in ICL Learning Consultancy, for their involvement in the pilot survey and for the way that they encouraged me to develop this material.

References

Argyris, C. and Schön, D. (1978) *Theory in Practice.* Reading, MA: Addison-Wesley.

Bloch, S. and Bates, T. (1995) *Employability.* London: Kogan Page.

Cunningham, I. (1994) *The Wisdom of Strategic Learning: The Self Managed Learning Solution.* Maidenhead: McGraw-Hill.

Gill, J. and Johnson, P. (1991) *Research Methods for Managers.* London: Paul Chapman.

Glaser, B.G. and Strauss, A.L. (1967) *The Discovery of Grounded Theory: Strategies for Qualitative Research.* Chicago: Aldine.

Green, M. and Gibbons, A. (1991) 'Learning Logs for Self-Development', *Training and Development* 9(2): 30–33.

Harrison, R. (1995a) 'Steps towards the Learning Organization', in R. Harrison (1995) *The Collected Papers of Roger Harrison.* Maidenhead: McGraw-Hill.

Harrison, R. (1995b) 'Self-directed Learning: a Radical Approach to Educational Design', in R. Harrison (1995) *The Collected Papers of Roger Harrison*. Maidenhead: McGraw-Hill.

Hayes, J. and Allinson, C.W. (1994) 'Learning Style: Implications of the Matching Hypothesis for Training and Development', in British Academy of Management, *1994 Annual Conference Proceedings*. Lancaster: BAM/Lancaster University.

Honey, P. and Mumford, A. (1995) *Using your Learning Styles*, 3rd edn. Maidenhead: Peter Honey.

Kolb, D.A. (1984) *Experiential Learning: Experience as the Source of Learning and Development*. Englewood Cliffs, NJ: Prentice-Hall.

Marsick, V.J. and Watkins, K.E. (1990) *Informal and Incidental Learning in the Workplace*. London: Routledge.

Megginson, D. (1994) 'Planned and Emergent Learning: A Framework and a Method', *Executive Development* 7(6): 29–32.

Megginson, D. and Clutterbuck, D. (1995) *Mentoring in Action*. London: Kogan Page.

Megginson, D. and Pedler, M. (1992) *Self-development: A Facilitator's Guide*. Maidenhead: McGraw-Hill.

Messick, S. (1976) *Individuality in Learning*. San Francisco: Jossey-Bass.

Mintzberg, H. (1987) 'Crafting Strategy', *Harvard Business Review* 64: 66–75.

Mumford, A. (1993) *How Managers can Develop Managers*. Aldershot: Gower.

Pedler, M., Burgoyne, J. and Boydell, T. (1991) *The Learning Company: A Strategy for Sustainable Development*. Maidenhead: McGraw-Hill.

Stevens, J.O. (1993) *Awareness: Exploring, Experimenting Experiencing*. New York: Bantam.

Vernon, P.E. (1969) *Personality Assessment: A Critical Survey*. London: Methuen.

Appendix 1: Scattergram of P and E Scores for New P and E Scales (N = 168)

P \ E	Low E 1	3	5	7	9	11	13	15	17	19	21	23	25	27	29	31	33	High E 35
High P 35																		
33																		
31																		
29										1								
27						1				1		1		3	1			
25								1			1	2	1	2	1			
23											2	2	2	1			1	
21							2	4	1	4	6	2	1		1	2		
19						1		2	3	3	4	2						
17								1	6	4	7	2	1	1				
15						1		4	5	4	2	2			2	1		
13						1	3	1	1	4	3		1				1	
11					2	1	3	2	2	3	5	4	1		1			
9								2	4	1	3			3	1	1		
7								1		1	1				2			
5								1								1		
3								1										
Low P 1									1	1								

Appendix 2: Learning Strategies Questionnaire

Version 2. September 1995.

This questionnaire is copyright of David Megginson and may not be reproduced without the express permission of the author.

Score each question in terms of your agreement with the statement:

6   if you think it is always true/you totally agree
5   usually true/you usually agree
4   often true/you often agree
3   sometimes true/you sometimes agree
2   occasionally true/you occasionally agree
1   seldom true/you seldom agree
0   never true/you never agree

1   Writing down appraisals of my work performance is an important basis for my development
2   For me learning is a planned process of setting goals, achieving them and setting new goals
3   In conversation with others I often come to new understandings of what I have learned
4   I regularly prepare a learning contract, development agreement or continuous professional development statement outlining my plans
5   It is important for me to add to/change my learning plans frequently in the light of new information
6   I set goals for my own learning
7   In order to learn from experience I reflect frequently upon what happens to me
8   I set targets for my development
9   It is important to be open to experience; then learning will come
10 I use a learning contract, development agreement or continuous professional development statement regularly to focus on my progress in developing
11 Most of my new learning emerges unexpectedly from things that happen
12 You can't plan significant learning

6

J.-C. Spender

Knowing, Managing and Learning
A Dynamic Managerial Epistemology

Introduction

Global competition, persistent recession and vast social, economic and industrial restructuring remind us that today's managers face new times and need to know new things. Yet management education, ostensibly designed to equip managers to deal with the world, seems to have changed little in recent years. Although there are numerous imaginative initiatives, there is, for the most part, an underlying uniformity among the educational offerings. Indeed most providers seem uninterested in developing their product in any radical way, being more taken up with the problems of continued expansion as management studies remains a major growth area in higher education. This growth continues despite complaints about the content of business education from business people, from students and even from many of those engaged in management research and teaching.

We suggest these paradoxes are not evidence of a massive confidence trick as educators profit from student or employer ignorance. Nor are the paradoxes evidence that nothing fundamental has changed and that management is and always will be simply 'about people'. Rather we argue that the paradox is rooted in the fact that managerial knowledge is of several different types. Mainstream management education is sustained by a rising demand for some types of knowledge, the persistent complaints result from its inability to provide the other types. But the balance between these types is shifting as we move into a 'post-industrial' and information-intensive world. Management education is being challenged to respond.

We step back and reconsider some of the fundamental ideas on which management education is presently based. The most important idea is that about the organization being managed. In the interwar years, the classical theorists saw the organization in qualitative quasi-mechanistic terms, to be managed by planning, organizing, staffing, directing, coordinating, reporting and budgeting (Gulick, 1937: 13). This implied a rich variety of managerial knowledge. In recent years management education has considered other organizational ideas, such as open-systems theory, organizational culture and organic modes of governance. But these have proved analytically elusive and the disciplinary focus has moved onto rigorous decision-making. This has the consequence of separating the analysis of the decision process from that of the decision content. The implication is that the necessary content knowledge is relatively unproblematic. We argue to the contrary, that managers require many types of knowledge, that the relationships between them are highly problematic, and that we need an underlying theory of the firm which embraces this knowledge variety. We also need a correspondingly rich theory of learning.

In the first part of the paper, we consider some of the changes now occurring in management practice and in management education, and some of the implications. We introduce the notion that managers have different types of knowledge. In the second part, we create an analytic framework within which we examine various types of managerial knowledge and their different dynamics. In the final part, we suggest some action implications for management educators.

1 The Changing Worlds of Management and Management Education

It is a common claim that today's managers face unprecedented competition, social diversity, economic turbulence and rapid technological progress. But this claim may be based on a less than complete understanding of our history. Times were also 'turbulent' at the turn of the century when much of what we now take to be the basic managerial techniques were developed (Chandler, 1977; Chandler and Daems, 1980). World economies were also shocked by repeated financial crises (Flamant and Singer-Kerel, 1970) and widespread wars. The motor car, the use of powered production equipment in the factories, the telephone, the electric trolley and commuting to work were all recently arrived (Hershberg, 1981). New methods of cultivating, storing and transporting food had been developed which, along with improved sanitation and declining mortality, resulted in the explosive growth of industrial towns. Indeed, we can look back on the long post-Second World War boom as a period of remarkable economic and social stability and argue that it is stability that is unusual rather than turbulence. But some changes cannot be measured along this dimension of stability–turbulence. There are structural changes which are continuous rather than cyclic. Among the more noted is the transition from an 'industrial' focus on producers to a 'post-industrial' focus on information and service (Bell, 1973; Kumar, 1978). The extent and vitality of today's worldwide markets means that economic activity now depends less on the repeated application of a static body of knowledge, whether manifest in unchanging work practices, the fixed layout of production facilities, or in some specific piece of equipment, and more on the increasingly rapid interplay of the firm's knowledge generation and knowledge application activities. A post-industrial theory redefines the organization as a dynamic action-oriented body of knowledge (Spender, 1992a and b).

The new balance affects both the practice of management and the scope of management's activities. The organization is no longer a production function seeking internal efficiency and monopolistic market power. It is more of a node in a complex network of economic relationships, dependencies and mutual obligations (Brusco, 1982; Miles and Snow, 1986; Powell, 1987). It is also clear that modern society itself is changing. Government is larger and more complex, and intervenes more in organizational affairs. People have diverging expectations of organizations, which therefore have to deal with greater diversity in the workforce. Most obviously, technology is having an increasingly significant impact on every place and type of work, and is changing the methods of administration and of production used in most organizations.

In spite of these developments management education has changed little since the 1960s and the period of swift response following the Ford and Carnegie foundation reports. At that time the business schools eliminated their traditional highly specialized industry-specific courses, such as transportation and banking, which had been a part of the curriculum since their foundation (Heaton, 1968; Sass, 1982). They introduced a core set of subjects designed to equip all students with a common body of knowledge (CBK) which includes business policy, organization theory and behavior, marketing, finance, accounting, operations, statistics and information systems. Yet, as Porter and McKibbin (1988: 54) argue, there have been matching complaints ever since these curriculum reforms: too great an emphasis on quantitative and analytical techniques, and insufficient attention to managing people, communications, ethics, the external and international environment of business, and, overall, an inability to get students to generate a sense of vision or to integrate effectively across functional areas (Bok, 1978).

Recent changes clearly exacerbate these problems. We can also add the further special problems of rapid technological change and that senior managers are now increasingly unlikely to understand the technologies being applied. As a result organizations become increasingly specialized and dependent on others, so demanding managerial skills both broader and deeper than previously. In short, we must look beyond disciplined decision-making and eventually consider the question of what it is that managers really need to know to be able to deal with their organizations, and what management education can do either to get this knowledge to them or to support them as they develop it for themselves.

Knowledge Versus Decision-making

The manager as decision-maker is the model that presently dominates management education (Harrison, 1987; Welsch and Cyert, 1970). The prevalence of analytic methods is simply a facet of this orthodoxy. The model also defines the pedagogical relationship between the teacher and the student: the first provides the theory which the second learns to use as a guide to on-the-job analysis and decision-making.

It is worth considering how this state of affairs arose. The prominence of the work being done at Carnegie-Mellon (Simon, 1958; March and Simon, 1958: 177), and of the faculty and students that were emerging from CMU at the time of the foundation reports (Cyert, March, Simon, Dill, Starbuck, Cohen, Clarkson, etc.), probably contributed significantly to the widespread adoption of the decision-making model. It replaced the earlier 'leadership' model, most obviously the Barnard-based (1938) Harvard model. While it is often said that the new paradigm pushed out faculty who lacked rigorous research methodologies and so merely told war stories (e.g. Rumelt et al., 1991: 8), we may also note that the Barnard-based approach encompassed the politics and ethics of business. In the pursuit of rigor, these areas too were pushed out of the analysis and classroom. At the time, the combination of wartime operational research (OR) successes and the increasing availability of computers had opened up the promise of a formal theory of managerial activity. March and Simon (1958: 179) argue that the basis of this logical decision model lies in the work of Dewey. Simon (1960: 3) reformulates Dewey's model (1910: 72) into three steps – intelligence, design and choice – though on closer inspection this seems a rather restricted interpretation of Dewey's richer five-step model.

While management teachers embraced the decision model, researchers were quick to observe that many managerial decisions were not taken on the objective and logical grounds assumed by the theory. Indeed Simon (1947: 39) earlier argues a compelling case against 'economic man', recognizing the inherent limits of the knowledge, reasoning capacity and values of real human beings. It seemed that there could be a useful distinction between 'programmed' and 'non-programmed' or yet to be programmed decisions (Simon, 1960: 5). Simon and the new decision-based approach to management effectively short-circuited the Harvard experience-based model by arguing that people are always able to bring their generalized problem-solving skills to bear on even the most novel and perplexing of the non-programmed situations (1960: 6). This assertion cleared the way to separating the logical process of the decision-making from that which was being processed. The process could be analyzed without considering the content. Content was to be determined by the rigorous theoretical model considered relevant to the situation.

The 1960s paradigm shift, which separated process and content, is convenient for management teachers as well as for researchers. On the one hand, teachers can focus on training students into the universals of rational decision-making without needing to consider the variety of their backgrounds and interests (Harrison, 1987: 105). On the other, students can be presented with abstract theories and left to make the connection to practice, and so determine the relevance of these theories, by themselves. The students are also left to discover the dynamic and reasoning behind that practice. Under these circumstances it is not surprising that students complain about the excessive attention to analytic methods, or that their employers complain about the students' poor sense of how to apply this 'book' learning to the real world of business.

The Multi-faceted Nature of Managerial Knowledge

The argument above, that many of the complaints about management education can be traced to the abstraction and decontextualization that results from the separation of process and content, is not new. Indeed there has always been an undercurrent of concern about this among management educators. Many accuse academics of re-shaping the research activity and the resulting body of knowledge to suit their own purposes rather than those of their clients (e.g. Behrman and Levin, 1984). Of course, management academics are not alone in this, for it is common among all social-scientists (Diesing, 1991). Many schools are experimenting with methods of creating some synthesis, of closing the gap between the abstractions in the books and the immediacy of business activity, of generating a sense of practical vision (Leavitt, 1987). In this section we focus less on different pedagogical practices than on the argument that there are different types of managerial knowledge and that book learning is simply one type. Instead of attacking the current body of business academic knowledge en bloc, on the grounds that it is inappropriate, we suggest that the decision-based approach needs to be supplemented by other types of knowledge which do not suffer the same defects.

The complaint that business education is too analytic and abstract implies a separation of theory from practice, that there are other more practical types of knowledge. There is a useful distinction to be drawn between practical knowledge, which shapes particular practice, and theoretical knowledge, which is the product of reflecting on and abstracting from experience. This distinction has been noted for many centuries. Within American philosophy, it is part of William James's (1950: 221) pragmatic epistemology. He differentiates 'knowledge about', which is abstract and the product of reflection, from knowedge of acquaintance', which is intimate and the immediate product of experience. He notes that this distinction is clearly present in ancient Greek, and in most of today's European languages with the exception of English, which has to resort to cumbersome neologisms. Ryle (1949) later notes a similar distinction between 'knowing what' and 'knowing how', where the latter adds the capacity for action to the abstract understanding of the situation.

More recently Polanyi (1962) draws a similar distinction between 'objective' knowledge, which is abstract, and 'tacit' knowledge, which is contextualized and reflects the active participation of the knower in a particular domain of activity. While objective knowledge is codified and can be communicated through the proficient manipulation of symbols, tacit knowledge is personal, uncodified and only communicated through activity. Revans (1982) distinguishes between the German *kennen*, knowing what, and *können*, knowing how. At the same time many philosophers argue against multiple types of knowledge. The most celebrated argument concerns the philosophers' persistent failure to identify the criteria demarcating scientific knowledge (Laudan, 1983).

Philosophers such as Polanyi resist the orthodoxy of modern managerial theorizing, cast as it is in a positivist framework which applies the deductive-nomological paradigm of positivist science (Hempel, 1968: 55). Positivism assumes that empirical observation gives us positive evidence of the world 'out there'. Theories which correctly anticipate such evidence are tentative models of that reality, which is assumed to be both knowable and coherent. It follows that there is only one 'type' of knowledge, that which meets these specifications. Hence the notion that there are different types of knowledge denies the epistemology which underpins the bulk of organizational theorizing. The problem is to decide whether the kind of practical knowledge that derives directly from experience is a different kind of knowledge, as Polanyi implies, or whether it is simply 'pre-scientific', as James implies. In the latter case, the methods of science can transform the pre-scientific into scientific knowledge. But managers are not scientists and they have different objectives. Their epistemology may well be different and reflect their different purposes. Thus managers may well use rules of thumb, heuristics and other pre-scientific action-based knowledge at the same time as they use whatever science seems relevant.

Being involved in the pattern of predictable action which is the organization, competent managers clearly have more than a purely abstract understanding of the situations they handle. They are able to abstract from this field of action, to create or apply theoretical models, and to ask and compute the answers to 'what if' questions. They also demonstrate a keen grasp of the action contexts in which these models are to be applied. They know that management is 'getting things done through people', and resolving political and value conflicts and other differences of opinion. They also know that business activity does not take place in a vacuum. Rather it occurs at a particular time and place, within a society with laws and institutions, cultural and religious diversity, and a real and idiosyncratic history. They know, to varying extents, how to take these additional complexities into account as they negotiate their way through the specific difficulties that confront them. In this sense, competent managers know how to complement their manipulation of abstract scientific symbols with a knowledge of the cultural and economic symbols of their wider context, together with the particular psychological perceptions, attitudes and interests of the people they do business with.

In general, then, competent managers must have:

- scientific or objective knowledge about the physical world in which they operate;
- social knowledge about the social, economic and cultural context in which their firms' activities are embedded;
- local knowledge about the particular people and processes embraced by their managerial activities; and
- self-knowledge about their own personal history, attitudes and motives.

The application of scientific knowledge requires the manager to select an abstract theory judged appropriate to the situation. It also requires the manager to bridge back to action, to implement the chosen theory, a matter on which science is silent. Thus scientific knowledge is inherently static because it is decontextualized from both time and context.

On the other hand, the organization's embeddedness requires the manager to negotiate with the social agents and power-holders who make up the organization's environment, whether they are the government, customers or other stakeholders. The knowledge which can be had of this environment is embedded, dynamic and necessarily incomplete. It is descriptive rather than predictive, and calls for continuous involvement rather than decision as the manager protects his/her personal and organizational position against these agents. This knowledge cannot be separated from the process of implementation, it is as much about implementation as it is about explanation.

Local knowledge is similarly embedded and dynamic, but it is also intersubjective in that it synthesizes the different interests of those who have subordinated themselves to the manager as they become involved in the activity, and the different types of knowledge which these actors bring to the activity. Again this knowledge deals with realities beyond the manager's immediate control. Thus it is embedded in action, requiring continuous negotiation with those involved and a continuing awareness of the interplay of events, practice and others' personalities.

Finally, self-knowledge requires the manager to develop insight into the interaction between events, impressions, attitudes and motivations. Far from requiring implementation or attachment to action, the manager's struggle is to achieve some measure of objectivity in understanding his/her impressions of events, to discipline emotion enough to allow some degree of detachment as well as the application of cool reasoning.

These types of knowledge are not, of course, completely divorced from each other. The differences between them reflect our attempts to categorize knowledge which would otherwise appear to be seamless, endlessly interacting and embracing every aspect of human thought. The importance of this kind of typology is that it allows us to generate hypothetical statements about, for instance, ways in which managerial knowledge might develop. For example, James argues that scientific knowledge begins with personal experience. Only by reflecting on experience and extracting the subjective content can objective knowledge be developed. Thus, for pragmatists, objective knowledge is the product of personal discipline focused on a particular domain of activity. For Polanyi, science also begins with tacit knowledge.

But science proceeds by testing the ideas which are grounded in tacit understanding to the canonical methods of science. The positivist convention also externalizes this discipline, arguing that scientific knowledge is the result of the application of the deductive-nomological scientific method. Unlike Polanyi, positivist science has no way of dealing with hypothesizing, for which there are no set procedures (Popper, 1968). The method focuses on testing, and requires careful experimental design and interpretation of the data. Thus while positivist science admits no other type of knowledge, the analyses of James, Ryle and Polanyi are enriched by considering alternatives.

These largely philosophical distinctions have recently been given greater empirical substance by a variety of organizational researchers. Some are psychologists, others are cultural anthropologists, yet others look at technology and the problems of design, work and tools. We consider their particular contributions in the next section. But we can usefully note that these researchers have several interests in common. They all argue that reasoned action, as opposed to abstract thought, requires abstract knowledge to be supplemented with other types of knowledge which are attached to rather than separated from the action context. These other types of knowledge combine thought and action, and go some way to overcoming the dichotomy of process and content. These writers also share an interest in enriching the positivist orthodoxy with insights drawn from the phenomenological and pragmatist positions. The positivist analysis sees action as the unremarkable outcome of reasoning, the thing to be predicted or explained. In this sense action is made secondary to theorizing.

The phenomenological and pragmatic analyses, in contrast, both treat human action as primary. The analysis accords the subjective evidence gained from experience a similar status to that gained from reasoning. The immediacy of action is combined with the power of thought, going some way to overcome the dichotomy that exists between the subjective and objective approaches to knowledge. The objective–subjective distinction is deeply ingrained into western thought and organizational analysis (Burrell and Morgan, 1979). In general, we can say that the researchers considered in the next section try to outflank these distinctions. Instead of denying them, they focus on action as the point where reasoning individuals bring their objective knowledge together with their subjective knowledge, so creating a context-dependent synthesis of the different types of knowledge. Managers need to have several different types of knowledge at their disposal as they think about action. They also need to know how to bridge the gap separating thought and action and generate skilled performance. It seems that management education is strong on the provision of objective knowledge. It is not so strong on helping managers identify their subjectivity. Nor is it strong on helping them develop skilled performance (Leavitt, 1987). Indeed, modern management education was specifically designed to provide a more sophisticated alternative to the performance-oriented vocational business education that was widely available at the turn of the century, whether that was based on the European technical *hochschule* tradition or the US's well-developed commercial school tradition (Sass, 1982).

II Some Different Types of Managerial Knowledge

In the previous section we argued that effective managers have several different types of knowledge at their disposal: scientific, social, local and personal. They synthesize them when they take reasoned action in the social context of their business. In this following section we take these imprecise ideas and force them into a tighter framework. Although it makes for radical oversimplification, its value is that it gives us the basis for thinking about the practical steps that our profession might take to resolve the paradoxes noted at the start of the paper. We are searching for ways of thinking about how management education might deal with its deficiencies while, at the same time, sustaining its successes.

Our first step is to build an analytic structure to identify and isolate the different types of knowledge. As we have seen, the philosophical distinctions between objectivity and subjectivity, and between process and content are controversial and inconclusive. We take a more practical view and adopt two new distinctions: individual–social and explicit–taken-for-granted. These distinctions are drawn from sociology. While they relate to the philosophical distinctions used above, they are not the same. They are grounded in everyday practice, in the ways that managers perceive their world.

A Matrix of Knowledge Types

We can bypass the philosophical debates by going directly to the experimental work of some researchers interested in understanding action, and the limitations of scientific knowledge, in practical organizational contexts. Our purpose here is to suggest two dichotomies to better underpin our typology of managerial knowledge. The conceptual distinctions suggested earlier, between process and content or between objective and subjective, are not intuitively obvious or relevant to managers, so they are impractical. We suggest as alternatives, first, a distinction between the individual and the social types of knowledge, and second, the distinction between the explicit and the taken-for-granted types of knowledge. While these distinctions are not entirely unrelated to those above, we imply, of course, that managers are more sensitive to these distinctions than the abstractions of the philosophers. Experienced managers have difficulty with the process–content distinction because they see the two parts as intertwined and contingent upon each other. They also have difficulty with the subjective–objective distinction since they know all too well how interests shape perception.

With these two distinctions we can set up a 2×2 matrix (Figure 1) we justify this framework in the sections that follow. The social types of knowledge can be explicit, so that they take on a sense of being universal or objective, detached from the individual, or they can be taken-for-granted much as many aspects of a culture are implicit in social behavior. In order to

	Social	Individual
Explicit	Scientific	Conscious
Taken-for-granted	Collective	Nonconscious

Source: Spender (1993)

Figure 1   The different types of managerial knowledge

separate the explicit aspects of culture, a sorely overused term, from its implicit aspects we use the term 'collective' (Weick and Roberts, 1993). By collective we mean knowledge that is embedded in social activity in ways that are relatively hidden from the individual social actors.

The Social Dimension

The positivist paradigm is so familiar from our education that we are scarcely able to imagine an alternative. It denies the distinction between individual and collective knowledge. It presumes knowledge is stored as symbols, whence it can be shared, and brought into action through being understood by individuals. Yet research shows how much of workplace knowledge is collective (e.g. Nelson and Winter, 1982; Brown and Duguid, 1991). Collective types of knowledge smack of a group mind. This goes far beyond the idea of knowledge being shared throughout the organization. We could share some scientific information, such as Ohm's Law relating voltage, resistance and current. The resulting knowledge is not collective, since each individual understands it in ways unaffected by and not contingent upon, their relationships with the other members of the collective. In this sense the knowledge is objective. Collective knowledge is a dynamic concept in that it is not only held collectively but also both generated and applied collectively within a pattern of social relationships.

Orr's (1990) empirical work illustrates this type of knowledge. He researched photocopier technicians whose job it was to repair machines in customers' locations. He notes that the repair practices are not strictly mechanical or technical. The machine is embedded in a social situation or, as Orr puts it (p. 171), the photocopier machines participate in organizational society. Thus fault diagnosis is inherently complex in that the problem may not be technical at all. It may have more to do with the relationship between the machine and the organization. For instance, there may be operator problems which could be solved by changing the print job so that it better fits the work the machine is designed to do, or by training the user to operate the machine as it was designed to be operated. Thus correct diagnosis within a socio-technical complex requires a sophisticated synthesis of several types of knowledge, both explicit and taken-for-granted.

The knowledge required in practice can be contrasted sharply with the canonical notion that the repairers operate as isolated individuals on the basis of knowledge supplied through the company's 'directive documentation'. This literature is relatively abstract because it is prepared by the machine designers and is tightly coupled into the machine's self-diagnostic capabilities. It is also the basis of the repairers' training. But the machine designers cannot have an understanding of the social context in which the machine ultimately becomes embedded, so the directive documentation must fall short in that respect. It is also often inadequate from a technical point of view. As these machines become increasingly complex, so it becomes progressively more difficult for the designers to imagine every possible failure mode. The directive documentation is limited to what has been correctly anticipated. Hence, the knowledge it contains cannot be ideally matched with the experiences to which the repairers are exposed. The repairers are forced to go beyond the documentation, and their training, to develop new knowledge which makes up for the deficiencies.

Orr's principal finding was that the process of generating, distributing and applying this new knowledge is both social and dynamic. While repairers could have been operating individually, building up an independent understanding of how the social and technical aspects interact, and of how the machine in use differs from the machine imagined in the directive documentation, Orr discovered that their process was actually intensely social. The repairers work as a team, though not in the normal sense of this overused and rather vague word. Brown and Duguid (1991), in a re-analysis of Orr's work, use the term 'community of practice' rather than team, so stressing the collective aspects of their knowledge and practice.

The discovery of the impact of collective activity on industrial work comes as no surprise. Since the time of the Hawthorne studies (Roethlisberger and Dickson, 1939), organization theorists have known of the power of the collective interaction in the workplace, of the way it can obstruct (March and Simon, 1958: 37), or energize and direct (Larson and LaFasto, 1989). Orr's analysis is different in that, while most writers on teamwork stress the affective and motivational aspects, he stresses the cognitive. The knowledge itself is collective, as if the repairers are participants in a group mind. Narrative is its integrative mechanism (Hunter, 1991). This applies at the diagnostic and solution-generation stage, as repairers tell stories about past episodes and search for a match to the present situation. It also applies at the knowledge distribution stage, as the repairers share information, leverage their experience, seek help from others, establish norms for dealing with the social context of their work, express their interest in and commitment to their work, and so give meaning to their world and to themselves as its skilled practitioners (Orr, 1990: 175). The field repair technician is here portrayed as if on the frontier, far from the comfortable certainties of the design phase, forced to seek effective context-driven compromises between the divergent interests of company and customers. The ambiguity of the role and the resources leads to a culture with its special themes of the fragility of their understanding of, and their control over, the situation.

Nelson and Winter (1982) also argue for collective knowledge, but for rather different reasons. Organizational performance depends on the effective synthesis of individual specialized skills and knowledge, and this requires coordination in the sense the classical theorists intended. But Nelson and Winter argue (p. 105) that the task of coordinating organizational practice requires more than individuals alone can supply. As a consequence the organization builds up an inventory of 'routines' which are both the cause and effect of the organization's practice under ambiguous circumstances. These routines transcend the sum of the individual organization member's capabilities. Organizations therefore remember by doing, and their doing is not completely understood by any of the members. In this sense the real and active organization comprises both individual knowledge and collective knowledge.

Both Orr, and Nelson and Winter, see collective knowledge as part of a work group's or organization's response to uncertainty. They suggest that the individual might attempt to deal with the uncertainty alone, but characteristically becomes involved in a highly contextualized pattern of social activity. The task of confronting uncertainty is distributed among the social group. The social bonds which hold the group together become channels for this distribution. It is this aspect that leads these writers to posit the development of collective knowledge. There is a strong similarity with Selznick's (1949) earlier analysis of the emergence of social institutions. Selznick (1957: 17) defines institutionalization as the process of 'infusing with value beyond the technical requirements of the task in hand'. We can reverse this idea and argue that it is only under conditions of uncertainty that questions of value, or of norms, identity or meaning, arise. Under conditions of certainty, activity is determined by the facts alone and values are irrelevant. Thus an organization's tendency to institutionalize is simply a facet of its ability, under uncertainty, to generate collective knowledge which supplements that of the participants.

Much of the subsequent debate between institutional theorists has been about the degree to which this collective knowledge can be managed or otherwise brought under the direct control of managers (Scott, 1987). Both Orr, and Nelson and Winter, regard management's control over this type of knowledge as problematic since it is tied up with the work practices of those being managed. However, even if direct control over the organization's collective knowledge is not possible, it is clear that if management familiarize themselves with it, they should achieve better control over the organization.

The Tacit Dimension

Another feature of organizational action under uncertainty is that much of the resulting knowledge is not explicit. Nelson and Winter (1982: 134) argue that organizational routines contain much that is tacit, neither consciously known nor articulatable by anyone in particular. At the same time they point to the shared tacit knowledge which makes effective communication possible. Likewise Orr (1990: 176) argues that narrative draws on the common culture, leveraging the implicit knowledge that the correspondents share and enabling them to focus on the most salient aspects of the situation. Most people are unaware of the degree to which they are shaped by their culture because, as Weber argued, its origins are lost in history. But cultural anthropologists and ethnographers have long been familiar with the task of surfacing the taken-for-granted aspects of social life (Schwartzman, 1993). These research skills can also be applied to surface the taken-for-granted cultures of the workplace (Turner, 1971; Spender, 1989).

The puzzle is how to operationalize the assumption that managerial action involves the taken-for-granted as well as the explicitly known. The question brings the experimental psychologists, especially the cognitive psychologists, into a closer alignment with the cultural anthropologists. For instance, a wider appreciation of the cognitive limits to rationality has made it important to surface the oft-hidden cognition that managers use to make sense of their world and activities (Eden et al., 1979; Huff, 1990). The research depends on these maps being shared by several of the members of the community of practice, so that some measure of intersubjective reliability can be achieved. The relevant community can be the work group or the organization, though the degree of knowledge differs at each respective level. Extending the argument that the taken-for-granted can be at both the individual and organizational level, Spender (1989) argues that knowledge can be associated with higher collective levels, such as at the industry level. Each is involved in many different groups, occupying different roles in different community practice. Some of these communities are very extensive, such as that of culture. Others are close, such as that of the family, or the aircraft cockpit crew.

Aside from the collective taken-for-granted knowledge which shapes action, there is also the question of the individual's own non-conscious reasoning. Recent research (Loftus and Klinger, 1992) has confirmed the importance of non-conscious intellectual activity in contexts beyond the physical activity on which Polanyi focuses. Polanyi (1962: 49) argues that swimmers generally do not know how they keep themselves afloat by regulating their breathing and buoyancy. It follows that they can neither articulate this knowledge nor teach it to others. Polanyi defines tacit knowledge in terms of its incommunicability. All kinetic knowledge, such as ballet dancers or sportspeople possess, is tacit by this definition. Yet it is obvious that one of the many purposes of rigorous physical training is to achieve the kind of discipline over the body that makes it possible to do things in a very conscious fashion. One 'works' consciously on specific moves. Similarly, close observation and visualization is a conscious process of communicating kinetic knowledge. This is not to deny the inevitable non-conscious component of artistic or sporting performance, for we argue that all human action depends on the non-conscious. The point is that performance is not entirely tacit, which is what Polanyi implies with his swimming and bicycle-riding examples. Physical activity encompasses collective knowledge, such as the rules of the game, and both individual conscious activity and unarticulated tacit knowledge about one's own performance.

There are tacit aspects to everyday thinking. It is easier to see this if we think about how we recognize people. Research into the non-conscious processing, and the consequent learning of covariations between the perceived aspects of the world, make it clear that people seldom recognize each other by their specific physical features (Lewicki et al., 1992). It appears they pay more attention to the covariations between a variety of features. Thus one is able to recognize people under very different lighting conditions or situations. The fact that people do not pay attention to specific features often surprises those who have a beard for a time but then shave it off. Colleagues recognize them without difficulty but sense that 'something is different'.

It is not possible for us to tell others how we recognize them, so this kind of knowledge is non-communicable. It is only demonstrated in action, as are

Polanyi's examples, but in this case it is a mental act close to the immediate effect of experience. Lewicki et al. (1992: 798) report the ease with which children acquire these covariation algorithms, even though they are not conscious of learning or knowing them. A similar test conducted of fellow faculty (p. 797) using a computerized position forecasting exercise showed that these experimental subjects (a) acquired covariation algorithms and demonstrated skilled performance without being able to express them, and (b) were not able to identify how they were changed when the researchers later manipulated the algorithms and caused their subjects' performance to deteriorate.

This is not simply a case of reducing conscious analysis to habit, which Simon (1987) argues in the course of denying that intuition is an alternative type of knowledge. In the case of this kind of non-conscious knowledge, the research above indicates that it is not mediated by the conscious. Learning does not entail the development of an abstract model of the phenomenon. The knowledge is the immediate and direct impression, as it were, of events on the awareness. In this way we see that the pattern of events becomes the context of analysis and reasoned action when the non-conscious knowledge is later surfaced and articulated. Reasoned action becomes bounded by and dependent on the non-conscious knowledge. This is the problem which faces those trying to implement analysis in unfamiliar contexts. They are perfectly aware that they confront a profound uncertainty. They often articulate this as an absence of confidence in themselves. We suggest it is better expressed as an absence of the non-conscious knowledge which follows successful action in the particular context. Bruner (1992: 782) expresses this slightly differently, suggesting that the conscious and non-conscious complement each other, and the burden carried by the non-conscious reflects the degree to which the practitioner has mastered and codified a domain of mindful activity.

In this section of the paper we have argued that the notion of managerial knowledge can be organized by the use of the social–individual and explicit–implicit dichotomies. The result is a matrix of knowledge types (Figure 1). We can see these four types as related to our initial suggestion that managers require knowledge which is (a) scientific, (b) social, (c) local and (d) personal. This mapping is relatively straightforward with the scientific and collective types of knowledge. The individual types are trickier, but they enable us to stress the complexity of individual knowledge. The difference between the conscious and the non-conscious is that non-conscious stresses the residual knowledge gained from experience which cannot be made explicit.

The Evolutionary Dynamic Within the Matrix

James (1950) and Polanyi (1962) suggest all types of knowledge begin with the individual's experience. This suggests the flow of learning runs from the bottom right-hand (Box D) of the matrix (see Figure 2) to the upper left (Box A). The priority accorded scientific information in our society is clear for all to see, so James argues that knowledge of acquaintance is inferior or

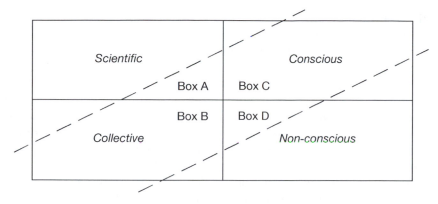

Source: Spender (1993)

Figure 2 *The three different action domains of the knowledge matrix*

'dumb', and awaits the extraction of the subjective element before it can move toward being scientific 'knowledge about'. But, as we have seen, scientific knowledge necessarily leaves the domain of reasoned action behind. Thus, in addition to telling us something about the different types of managerial knowledge, the matrix also tells us about the different types of action. The upper left domain is abstracted from action, while the lower right is wholly submerged within action. We might also argue that action in the upper left region is subordinated to analysis. Action here is consciously selected to test theory. The action in the center region is the given starting point, the result of being in a context to be analyzed.

The center domain comprises reasoned action of two polar types, B and C. In the upper right extreme (Box C), we have the individual's conscious and intentional actions, at the lower left (Box B) we have the group's collective action. Although this collective action is taken-for- granted and not fully conscious, it is reasoned in the sense in which Weber argued the rationality of traditional social action is evident to researchers even though its origins are lost to the social actors. Thus traditional rationality contrasts with an explicit goal-related rationality whose origins can be communicated immediately. In this way the B and C ends of the central diagonal recall Weber's (1970[II]: 186) distinction between the *zweckrational* and *wertrational* types of social rationality.

As soon as we pay proper attention to action, the evolutionary flow from lower right to upper left becomes doubtful. Indeed we see that the conventional story of knowledge growth is only about the generation of scientific knowledge. It is not about the evident human evolution towards more reasoned action at all. The conventional story also leads us directly into confusion about the relationship between science and managerial practice, for the former is about abstract knowledge while the latter is about reasoned action. It leads to confusion about the relationship between management and leadership.

In the central domain there are two types of reasoned action. One type (Box C) is conscious individual action, when an individual is able to construct an appropriate model of the situation. The other type (Box B) is collective action, when the individual becomes part of an established community in practice. At first sight it seems we can ignore both the objective knowledge in Box A, which might inform both individual and collective action, and the contextualized non-conscious knowledge in Box D which, we argue, is the source of the actor's confidence to act. In practice, of course, this does not work satisfactorily. Clearly we need a more sophisticated theory of the interactions within the matrix.

Any theory about these interactions is also a theory of managerial learning. Most theories of learning, such as that of Nelson and Winter, are straightforward and based on naive empiricist notions of trial and error. People do things and observe the consequences. Remembering what they were trying to do, and seeing what transpired, they modify their ideas and behavior and try again. Unfortunately this ignores the social dimension of our matrix, which is not a simple sum of individual knowledge. We need some other kind of process which involves both individual and social activity if our learning theory is to encompass all the different types of knowledge in the matrix.

Learning theorists are paying increasing attention to Vygotsky's activity theory (Vygotsky, 1962; Wertsch, 1985; Moll, 1990). Vygotsky regarded an individual's consciousness as the dynamic outcome of an ongoing interaction between the social and the non-conscious. In one sense the individual is the outcome of a process of internalizing the social situation in which he/she is embedded, such as the culture and language. To a great extent his view is shared by the symbolic interactionists (Blumer, 1969; Blanck, 1990: 47). But this process of internalization is not a slavish deterministic copying, it is an active dialectic between the social and the individual. Nor is the individual's consciousness determined physiologically, as Piaget argues (Vygotsky, 1962: 9) or Simon (1958) later assumes. The individual's consciousness is, instead, the product of learning as the previously internalized becomes a set of tools for new thinking and learning. Thus Vygotsky argues that when learned (internalized), language and culture become tools which the individual can use to learn further from activity.

The Vygotskian approach has two immediate effects. First, it shifts the analytic focus from scientific theory to social and individual practice. 'It is practice that poses the tasks, and is the supreme judge of theory; practice is the criterion of truth; it is practice which dictates how to build concepts and how to formulate laws' (quoted in Rosa and Montero, 1990: 82). Thus Vygotsky reinforces the notion that the objective of knowledge is not to understand the world but rather to transform it. Second, the approach shifts the focus from what has been learned to the learning capability which has been produced. Vygotsky argues that two students who score the same on a test might be considered to be equal in ability, but it is probably more important to know what each was capable of in terms of further learning. The students might be very different in this respect, but, as teachers, most of us recognize that we pay considerable attention to this sense of the student's capability.

To operationalize this notion, which bears some similarity to Cohen and Levinthal's (1990) 'absorptive capacity', Vygotsky introduced the concept of the student's 'zone of proximal development' (ZPD), arguing that the immediate product of learning is the potential to learn more rather than the knowledge already acquired. The teacher's task is to work within the student's ZPD, first by challenging the student, but not so much as to go beyond the ZPD and induce a sense of failure. The ZPD is a product of the interaction between the teacher (or the environment) and the student. Teaching means managing this interaction so that the student teaches him/herself effectively and in context. We can note the interesting contrast between the ZPD and Simon's (1947: 12) 'zone of acceptance'. While the zone of acceptance is passive and defined by a decision, the ZPD is active and constitutes a zone of contextualized and boundedly reasoned mindful activity.

Finally, Vygotsky argues that the process of internalization is not simply mediated by what has been learned before. There is also a genetic or evolutionary change in how this shapes the student's consciousness. At the beginning of the process the individual's mental processes are elementary, more determined by the environmental context. But as more is learned, so there is a shift towards autonomy and, finally, to full self-regulation. It is at this point that the process of individuation becomes complete. In practice, because the learning process continues so long as there is activity and the social context is inevitably dynamic, this process never comes to an end. But the immediate result of self-regulation and autonomy is that the logical link between the collective and the individual is broken. The collective is pushed towards further change as it interacts with the increasingly autonomous individuals who are its members. Expressing these notions into more managerial terms, we can argue that managerial learning is the result of professional activity rather than decontextualized study, and that the learning springs from the contextualized interplay of the current level of consciousness (Box C) and the current patterns of collective identity (Box B).

In Part II above we have sketched a dynamic and evolutionary managerial epistemology which encompasses all four types of managerial knowledge. It also indicates the different relationships between thought and action, and the interplay between the different knowledge types. While most theories of organizational learning struggle with the gap between the organization and its members, without resolving the dichotomy between individual and collective minds, Vygotsky's approach brings the two into a dialectical interaction. While still separate, they are simply different elements of social praxis.

III Some Implications for Management Educators

The first implication is that managerial knowledge is multidimensional in ways that cannot be covered by simple book learning. This is no surprise. But this is not a criticism of the kind of education that most business schools provide. It is important to study theory and to do the research that informs and develops that theory. Objective knowledge can clearly inform awareness, perception, diagnosis and practice, and its quality is vastly improved by following the canonical methods of science. But managerial knowledge comprises more than that. It covers the manager's ability to draw together different views in an inter-subjective compromise that reflects the identities of those involved and that of the organization being managed. It also covers the manager's ability to understand the social processes in which the organizational activity is embedded. Finally the manager requires a multidimensional self-knowledge which can be the basis of self-confidence in action, and the moral fiber to ensure ownership of the activity and responsibility for it with respect to others.

These different types of knowledge call for different kinds of education, where that word is used in its widest sense to mean whatever influences the student's development. The business school and its processes are reasonably well suited to the study of objective knowledge, although this certainly means going beyond the study of business decision-making. It requires coverage of the content of business decision, the particular theories that inform accounting operations, human behavior, economics and so forth, and a study of the temporal and spatial contexts of business activity. It also requires building up a ZPD or capacity for learning through a study of scientific method, the most important part of which is the philosophy of science. From the vantage point of the Vygotskian position, we can see that the real shortcoming of the vocational schools is their failure to build the student's capacity for learning (ZPD) except in the hand crafts. Rote memorization of content cannot achieve this.

But as soon as we consider learning in the central diagonal of the matrix, we see that the educational process cannot be abstracted and separated from the action itself. The ability to envision and create compromise among others with divergent views is not a matter of content. It is a product of experience. It also depends on the actor's confidence that, in spite of appearances, compromise is possible, that it can happen. Students cannot acquire this confidence without interacting with others under carefully constructed settings, such as when they are role playing. However, the manager's intersubjective task goes beyond getting people to compromise; it is also about effecting conceptual, moral and practical compromises between competing objective models. These compromises demand the deep or 'thick' (Geertz, 1983) understanding which only the experience of action can create, since they are bound to the context for which they are made.

The persistence of the case method is a tribute to our profession's collective and poorly articulated understanding that talking through the various ideas, and the context in which they are to be applied, especially with other students (or managers), is a powerful method of both arriving at these compromises and developing the capacity to find compromises in other settings (Christensen, 1987; Christensen et al., 1991). Barnard's (1938) original description of the executive's function, as seeking compromise between the demands of the personal, physical and social sub-systems, while maintaining the dominance of the organization's formal objectives, seems to place this inter-subjective knowledge above all other types. It leads directly to the classic Harvard case tradition in which the task of the executive was to achieve a compromise between what the firm could do, might do, should do, and what the senior executives wanted to do (Learned et al., 1965: 23). The 'pulling it all together' aspect of the MBA's second-year policy case course is specifically designed for the general manager destined for senior office. Bok notes that the Socratic method forces students into an active role in learning for themselves when and how to speak. They thereby discover the action dimensions of inter-subjective managerial knowledge (Bok, 1978: 6). We see that the long dispute between case work and theory is really no contest. The two methods address different components of managerial knowledge. The business school's challenge is to create an experience for the students that makes theory and case work interact in ways that allow and encourage them to develop both types of knowledge.

Bok's (1978) analysis of the Harvard Business School, though narrowly focused on one school, effectively anticipated much of the later criticism of the profession which Porter and McKibbin (1988) report. The strongest words in Bok's critique deal with the school's failure to treat firms as concerned with more than the shareholders' goals. He stresses that modern large-scale enterprise is embedded in an increasingly complex institutional and political matrix, and that faculty do little research to understand this or to help improve the government's process. In addition the school fails to provide students with adequate sense of a business's irreducible social responsibilities, or an effective moral code of conduct, or an understanding of the subtle division of power between the private and public sectors.

Part of understanding how an organization is embedded in an institutionalized context is a matter of study. For instance, those in a multinational corporation can study the local culture, government, family and religious processes of regions in which they are considering operating. But this is abstract knowledge. The notion of collective knowledge goes beyond this since it entails action. The severest test of an understanding of culture is the ability to perform convincingly, so well that one is taken as a native member of that culture. Thus the abstract study of collective knowledge is incomplete until the student demonstrates skilled performance with respect to the external structures in which he or she is embedded. Thus Box B implies the ability to find viable compromises between the many conflicting external pressures. Box C focuses on the internal contradictions and disagreements. The importance of the intersubjective and collective types of managerial knowledge under the uncertain circumstances of business clearly reinforces the call for managers to have social as well as intellectual skills. These are essential resources when searching for compromise, recognizing that, like politics, management in action is the art of the possible.

The central region of the matrix, boxes B and C, is the area where the need for management education is greatest. It is in these areas that Vygotsky's theory of genetic development, through effective management of the ZPD under conditions of activity in uncertain circumstances, gives us insight into the process of management education. It is ironic that most of the research activity in our discipline goes into providing further abstract theory which could, in principle, be placed in Box A. Our critics are telling us that the more pressing problem is to provide a better understanding of what faculty, and the management education process, can do in boxes B and C. Bok, from his vantage point outside the discipline, stresses the power of the activity-based approaches, in the case discussion, in secondment into industry and government, in intimate involvement with managers from other corporations. Indeed it seems that he is closely aligned with Revans's (1971; 1982) action learning methods.

Box D deals with the knowledge managers require to act both mindfully and confidently. If the concept of action is rational decision-making, then schoolroom practice is probably sufficient. But under conditions of un-certainty we are drawn ever more into contextualized action in a social setting, one that bears some relationship to the manager's eventual area of responsibility. For this reason business recruiters look to an applicant's track record, bearing in mind that it is both more productive and more educa-tional to have acted and failed than to have not acted at all. Business educators have struggled with this for years as they have wondered about the wisdom of requiring business experience of students. Clearly if the objective is to train staff members rather than executives, confidence is easier to instill. There may well be unsuspected spill-overs from other areas of competence. Promoters of 'outward bound' and 'wilderness' courses argue that managers exposed to these kinds of challenge acquire confidence in action that can be transported into their organizational contexts, and this clearly warrants further research. It may also be that traditional methods of selection, on the basis of school and class background, where sports and social confidence is taken into account, unknowingly focuses on this aspect of managerial knowledge (Whitley et al., 1981).

Conclusions

In this paper we have sketched a complex and dynamic model of managerial knowledge. We have specifically criticized the notion of the manager as a simple rational decision-maker, one that can, in principle, be replaced by a computer or expert system. Drawing on debates about the nature of practical knowledge within philosophy, and experimental evidence of the contrast between abstract and action-based knowledge, we have created a four-fold typology. Each of the four types of knowledge suggests a different managerial activity. Ultimately the manager must synthesize the four types into a coherent pattern of reasoned activity.

These four types of knowledge stand in varying relationships to action. Abstract knowledge is decontextualized, removed from particular place and time. Managers who wish to apply such knowledge have to transport it back to the particular context of their activity. While business schools strive to provide better theory through their research programs, they are obviously less able to deal with the context-dependent problems of implementation. Non-conscious knowledge is submerged beneath action. The Confucian directive to 'know thyself' is important for managers, but is generally considered as beyond the scope of business education. Yet an increasing number of executives see exposure to wilderness training or other types of extra-organizational challenge as an appropriate way to develop confidence in their ability to act under uncertainty.

We argue that the principal opportunity facing management education today is to deal more effectively with the central domain of our matrix, with developing skills in the intersubjective or cross-functional integration implied by Box C, and with the management of the relationships between external institutions and processes and the activities for which they are responsible implied by Box B.

Another way of expressing this challenge is to see it as a corrective action to the great influence of the 1959 Ford and Carnegie foundation reports. But there will be no progress if the pendulum merely swings back to where it was. The experience of the last 30 years has shown us that we will contribute little to business practice until we develop a solid foundation of insightful theory. This requires business schools to pay continued attention to research and to methodology. In the 1960s this seemed like a sharp break with the previous qualitative and historical tradition. We argue that it was less a break than the development of a second front. Progressive management education recognizes both types of research and knowledge. But we can take this idea further and seek out a richer epistemology. It is sometimes argued that human organizations are the most complex and dynamic of our artifacts. It seems only reasonable that those that manage them must have an appropriately rich epistemology.

Bibliography

Barnard, Chester I. (1938) *The Functions of the Executive.* Cambridge, MA: Harvard University Press.

Behrman, Jack N. and Levin, Richard I. (1984) 'Are Business Schools Doing Their Job?', *Harvard Business Review* (Jan.–Feb.): 140–7.

Bell, Daniel (1973) *The Coming of Post-industrial Society: A Venture in Forecasting.* New York: Basic Books.

Blanck, Guillermo (1990) 'Vygotsky: The Man and His Cause', in Luis C. Moll (ed.) *Vygotsky and Education: Instructional Implications and Applications of Sociohistorical Psychology*, pp. 31–58. Cambridge: Cambridge University Press.

Blumer, Herbert (1969) *Symbolic Interactionism: Perspective and Method.* Englewood Cliffs, NJ: Prentice-Hall.

Bok, Derek (1978) *The President's Report 1977–1978.* Cambridge, MA: Harvard University Press.

Brown, John S. and Duguid, Paul (1991) 'Organizational Learning and Communities-of-practice: Towards a Unified View of Working, Learning, and Innovation', *Organization Science* 2: 40–57.

Bruner, Jerome (1992) 'Another Look at New Look 1', *American Psychologist* 47: 780–3.

Brusco, Sebastiano (1982) 'The Emilian Model: Productive Decentralisation and Social Integration', *Cambridge Journal of Economics* 6: 167–84.

Burrell, Gibson and Morgan, Gareth (1979) *Sociological Paradigms and Organizational Analysis.* London: Heinemann Educational Books.

Chandler, Alfred D., Jr (1977) *The Visible Hand: The Managerial Revolution in American Business.* Cambridge, MA: Belknap Press.

Chandler, Alfred D. and Daems, Herman, eds (1980) *Managerial Hierarchies: Comparative Perspectives on the Rise of the Modern Industrial Enterprise.* Cambridge, MA: Harvard University Press.

Christensen, C. Roland (1987) *Teaching and the Case Method: Text, Cases and Readings.* Boston, MA: Harvard Business School Press.

Christensen, C. Roland, Garvin, David A. and Sweet, Ann, eds (1991) *Education for Judgment: The Artistry of Discussion Leadership.* Boston, MA: Harvard Business School Press.

Cohen, Wesley M. and Levinthal, Daniel A. (1990) 'Absorptive Capacity: A New Perspective on Learning and Innovation', *Administrative Science Quarterly* 35: 128–52.

Dewey, John (1910) *How We Think.* Boston, MA: D.C. Heath.

Diesing, Paul (1991) *How Does Social Science Work? Reflections on Practice.* Pittsburgh, PA: University of Pittsburgh Press.

Eden, Colin, Jones, Sue and Sims, David (1979) *Thinking in Organizations.* London: Macmillan.

Flamant, Maurice and Singer-Kerel, Jeanne (1970) *Modern Economic Crises.* London: Barrie & Jenkins.

Geertz, Clifford (1983) *Local Knowledge: Further Essays in Interpretive Anthropology.* New York: Basic Books.

Gulick, Luther (1937) 'The Theory of Organization', in Luther Gulick and L. Urwick (eds) *Papers on the Science of Administration*, pp. 3–45. New York: Institute of Public Administration.

Harrison, E. Frank (1987) *The Managerial Decision-making Process*, 3rd edn. Boston, MA: Houghton Mifflin.

Heaton, Herbert (1968) *A Scholar in Action: Edwin F. Gay.* New York: Greenwood Press.

Hempel, Carl G. (1968) 'Explanation in Science and History', in P.H. Nidditch (ed.) *The Philosophy of Science*, pp. 54–79. Oxford: Oxford University Press.

Hershberg, Theodore, ed. (1981) *Philadelphia: Work, Space, Family, and Group Experience in the Nineteenth Century.* New York: Oxford University Press.

Huff, Anne S., ed. (1990) *Mapping Strategic Thought.* New York: Wiley.

Hunter, M.K. (1991) *Doctor's Stories: The Narrative Structure of Medical Knowledge.* Princeton, NJ: Princeton University Press.

James, William (1950) *The Principles of Psychology*, Vols I and II. New York: Dover Publications.

Kumar, Krishan (1978) *Prophecy and Progress: The Sociology of Industrial and Post-industrial Society.* Harmondsworth: Penguin Books.

Larson, Carl E. and LaFasto, Frank M.J. (1989) *Teamwork: What Must Go Right/What Can Go Wrong.* Newbury Park, CA: Sage.

Laudan, Larry (1983) 'The Demise of the Demarcation Problem', in R. Cohen and L. Laudan (eds) *Philosophy and Psychoanalysis*, pp. 111–27. Boston, MA: R. Reide.

Learned, Edmund, Christensen, Roland, Andrews, Kenneth and Guth, William (1965) *Business Policy: Text and Cases.* Homewood, IL: Richard D. Irwin.

Leavitt, Harold J. (1987) *Corporate Pathfinders: Building Vision and Values into Organizations.* New York: Penguin.

Lewicki, Pawel, Hill, Thomas and Czyzewska, Maria (1992) 'Nonconscious Acquisition of Information', *American Psychologist* 47: 796–801.

Loftus, Elizabeth F. and Klinger, Mark R. (1992) 'Is the Unconscious Smart or Dumb?', *American Psychologist* 47: 761–5.

March, James G. and Simon, Herbert A. (1958) *Organizations.* New York: Wiley.

Miles, Robert E. and Snow, Charles C. (1986) 'Network Organizations: New Concepts for New Firms', *California Management Review* 28(3): 62–73.

Moll, Luis C., ed. (1990) *Vygotsky and Education: Instructional Implications and Applications of Sociohistorical Psychology.* New York: Cambridge University Press.

Nelson, Richard R. and Winter, Sidney G. (1982) *An Evolutionary Theory of Economic Change.* Cambridge, MA: Belknap Press.

Orr, Julian E. (1990) 'Sharing Knowledge, Celebrating Identity: Community Memory in a Service Culture', in David S. Middleton and Derek Edwards (eds) *Collective Remembering*, pp. 169–89. Newbury Park, CA: Sage.

Polanyi, Michael (1962) *Personal Knowledge: Towards a Post-critical Philosophy*, corrected edn. Chicago, IL: The University of Chicago Press.

Popper, Karl (1968) *The Logic of Scientific Discovery*. London: Hutchinson.

Porter, Lyman W. and McKibbin, L. (1988) *Management Education and Development*. New York: McGraw-Hill.

Powell, Walter W. (1987) 'Hybrid Organizational Arrangements: New Form or Transitional Development?', *California Management Review* 30(1): 67–87.

Revans, Reginald W. (1971) *Developing Effective Managers: A New Approach to Business Education*. New York: Praeger.

Revans, Reginald W. (1982) *The Origins and Growth of Action Learning*. London: Chartwell-Bratt, Bromley & Lund.

Roethlisberger, F.J. and Dickson, William J. (1939) *Management and the Worker: An Account of a Research Program Conducted by the Western Electric Co., Hawthorne Works, Chicago*. Cambridge, MA: Harvard University Press.

Rosa, Alberto and Montero, Ignacio (1990) 'The Historical Context of Vygotsky's Work: A Sociohistorical Approach', in Luis C. Moll (ed.) *Vygotsky and Education: Instructional Implications and Applications of Sociohistorical Psychology*, pp. 59–88. Cambridge: Cambridge University Press.

Rumelt, Richard P., Schendel, Dan and Teece, David J. (1991) 'Strategic Management and Economics', *Strategic Management Journal* 12 (Winter Special Issue): 5–29.

Ryle, Gilbert (1949) *The Concept of Mind*. London: Hutchinson.

Sass, Steven A. (1982) *The Pragmatic Imagination: A History of the Wharton School 1881–1981*. Philadelphia: University of Pennsylvania Press.

Schwartzman, Helen B. (1993) *Ethnography in Organizations*. Newbury Park, CA: Sage.

Scott, W. Richard (1987) 'The Adolescence of Institutional Theory', *Administrative Science Quarterly* 32: 493–511.

Selznick, Philip (1949) *TVA and the Grass Roots*. Berkeley: University of California Press.

Selznick, Philip (1957) *Leadership in Administration: A Sociological Interpretation*. New York: Harper & Row.

Simon, Herbert A. (1947) *Administrative Behavior*. New York: Macmillan.

Simon, Herbert A. (1958) *Administrative Behavior: A Study of Decision-making Processes in Administrative Organizations*, 2nd edn. New York: Macmillan.

Simon, Herbert A. (1960) *The New Science of Management Decision*. New York: Harper & Row.

Simon, Herbert A. (1987) 'Making Management Decisions: The Role of Intuition and Emotion', *Academy of Management Executive* 1: 57–64.

Spender, J.-C. (1989) *Industry Recipes: The Nature and Sources of Managerial Judgement*. Oxford: Basil Blackwell.

Spender, J.-C. (1992a) 'Strategy Theorizing: Expanding the Agenda', in Anne S. Huff (ed.) *Advances in Strategic Management* Vol. 12, pp. 3–32. Greenwich, CT: JAI Press.

Spender, J.-C. (1992b) 'Limits to Learning from the West: How Western Management Advice May Prove Limited in Eastern Europe', *The International Executive* 34: 389–410.

Spender, J.-C. (1993) 'Competitive Advantage from Tacit Knowledge? Unpacking the Concept and its Strategic Implications', *Academy of Management Best Paper Proceedings*, pp. 37–41.

Turner, Barry A. (1971) *Exploring the Industrial Sub-culture*. London: Macmillan.

Vygotsky, Lev S. (1962) *Thought and Language*. Cambridge, MA: MIT Press.

Weber, Max (1970) *From Max Weber: Essays in Sociology*. London: Routledge & Kegan Paul.

Weick, Karl E. and Roberts, Karlene H. (1993) 'Collective Mind in Organizations: Heedful Interrelating on Flight Decks', *Administrative Science Quarterly* 38: 357–81.

Welsch, Lawrence A. and Cyert, Richard M., eds (1970) *Management Decision Making: Selected Readings*. Harmondsworth: Penguin.

Wertsch, James V. (1985) *Vygotsky and the Social Formation of Mind*. Cambridge, MA: Harvard University Press.

Whitley, Richard D., Thomas, Alan and Marceau, Jane (1981) *Masters of Business? Business Schools and Business Graduates in Britain and France*. London: Tavistock.

7

Ingrid Richter

Individual and Organizational Learning at the Executive Level
Towards a Research Agenda

Introduction

Without much prompting, most workers in formalized organizations can describe a set of superstitions, beliefs and maxims about 'how you get ahead around here'. These stories are usually based upon a mixture of fact, conjecture, local myth and archetypal legend (Morgan, 1986). Workers at all levels from a variety of institutions and companies will have within their repertoire at least one tale describing 'the right place, right time'; 'the lucky break'; 'the mistake that turned into an unexpected success', and so on. A common example of these phrases is the maxim about how to get ahead': 'it's not *what* you know, but *who* you know that counts'. As pointed out by Weick (1983), people need heuristics to help them deal with suspicions, doubts, uncertainties (p. 26). The enduring nature of the 'not *what* you know; but *who* you know', epithet suggests that it would not be difficult to find many examples of where it has proven true; and how some careers have profited. It may be somewhat more difficult, however, to answer the question: How does '*who* you know' affect '*what* you know' and consequently, how you 'do', collectively or organizationally?

Miner and Mezias (1996) suggest that there is an urgent need for more systematic empirical learning research in order to develop more precision and practicality in current organizational learning models and their potential applications. Conducting this type of research presents formidable challenges. They state: 'We believe the single most powerful historical reason for the lack of outstanding quantitative empirical research on organizational learning (at any level of analysis, about any mechanism) is that it is excruciatingly hard to do well' (1996: 95). This article takes a modest step towards this challenge by exploring the issues related to researching group or collective learning, particularly among what some would term 'the organizational elite class', or executives. It suggests that one obstacle to research has been the dominance of the philosophy that learning is an individualistic form of activity, and suggests that theories of situated learning, knowledge creation and sensemaking provide more suitable guiding frameworks. It is argued that social constructionist perspectives on learning and communities of practice

(Brown and Duguid, 1991; Lave and Wenger, 1991; Orr, 1990) provide an integrative and encompassing alternative framework for the understanding of learning in organizational contexts. Unlike much of the literature on organizational learning, this perspective gives a central role to the inter-connections and trajectories of participation and practice within the social world in which they take on meaning, and therefore offers rich insights about the more subtle and mutually creating nature of the relationship between individuals, their work practices and their changing environments.

The current literature on organizational learning does not adequately explore the micro-level relationships or linkages between individual and organizational learning and, as a result, may be obscuring some of the most powerful potential value of organizational learning theory. The impact of executives on organizational learning has frequently been noted (Argyris and Schön, 1978; Daft and Weick, 1984; Nonaka and Takeuchi, 1995; Senge, 1990a, 1990b), however, to date, little work has been specifically dedicated to understanding the relationships between executive learning and organiza-tional learning. Inasmuch as executives are considered to be key players in terms of influencing organizational action, it is suggested that the way executives make sense of their own and others' experiences is an important influence on their own learning as individuals (Kouzes and Posner, 1987) and is also a significant contributor to ongoing organizational learning and change.

There have been detailed studies on the characteristics and dimensions of communities-of-practice among various professions; however, there has been little or no examination of whether similar structural characteristics and dynamics exist among managers, specifically senior managers or executives. Do 'communities-of-practice' as described by Brown and Duguid (1991), and as suggested in the work of Lave and Wenger (1991); Lave (1993); Chaiklin and Lave (1993), actually exist among executives? If they do, are their dynamics and properties similar to those of the occupationally and pro-fessionally defined groups examined in studies of flutemakers (Cook and Yanow, 1993), midwives (Jordan, 1989) and service technicians (Orr, 1990)? Could executives be accurately described as 'practitioners' in the same sense? What are the similarities and differences between occupationally defined communities and those defined by levels of responsibility within an organiza-tional structure? Even if similarities exist, to what extent do executive relationships which span organizational boundaries influence actions taken within their 'home' organizations?

It is suggested that micro-level study of executive-level communities of practice could provide valuable illumination of the nature of the relationship and/or transfer processes which influence more macro-level organizational learning. For example, to what extent is inferential learning which occurs in relationships with others, a source of innovation or experimentation in organizations? In addition, this type of study could potentially contribute to an improved understanding of how executives think about their work – do they consider themselves as professionals with a distinct or unique 'discipline?'

Situated Learning vs Individual Learning

Brown and Duguid's (1991) analysis of Orr's study (1990) on how actual collective and informal work practices differ from canonical or formal practices as described in manuals and job descriptions, characterizes the situated and social characteristics of 'learning-in-working' as the activity of 'communities of insiders'.

> The central issue in learning is becoming a practitioner not learning about practice. This approach draws attention away from abstract knowledge and cranial processes and situates it in the practices and communities in which knowledge takes on significance.' (1991: 48)

Descriptions of how the shape and membership of these communities fluctuates and is continually being formed and reformed, and how the central learning issue for participants is about becoming a 'practitioner', move the primary focus of learning away from the individual and dramatically identify the *community* as the centre of 'synergistic collaboration rather than a conflicting separation among workers, learners, and innovators' (Brown and Duguid, 1991: 55).

Within the literature on organizational learning there is a wide variety of opinion about who (or what) is the 'learner' and whether or not the term 'organizational learning' might even be an oxymoron (Weick and Westley, 1995). Views range from the broad and multi-faceted definition of deutero-learning (Argyris and Schön, 1978), to the more extreme views of Simon (1991).[1] Despite variations in terminology, a general consensus has developed that it is *individuals* who learn, not organizations (Miner and Mezias, 1996); and that inasmuch as individuals comprise organizations, the primary entity which learns is the individual, and furthermore, that individuals are repositories of the knowledge thus obtained.

This is not to say that the importance and influence of the social context has been completely overlooked within the literature. Among others, Crossan et al. (1995) give it a central role.

> Indeed, recognizing this role for individuals is critical to avoid reifying organizations; ascribing to organizations' powers of insights, thought and behavior that reside with their members. However, an exclusively individual focus runs the risk of neglecting the social context of learning in which individuals are embedded.' (1995: 7)

In fact this well-established dualistic tradition of separating and abstracting knowledge from action; mind from body, can be traced back to Descartes, and is increasingly being challenged by social constructionist views in the proposition that learning and knowing can also be located within social and mutually creating relations among and between practitioners. The growing literature includes Brown (1992); Brown and Duguid (1991); Chaiklin and Lave (1993); Lave and Wenger (1991); Gherardi et al. (1996); Orr (1990); Smircich (1983); Weick (1983); Weick and Roberts (1993); Weick and Westley

(1995). Contrary to the information-processing view of organizational learning, which is heavily grounded in traditions of cognitive learning theory; this literature suggests that we think about organizations as interpretive systems which are created to make sense of the world, and that products or services get developed and produced as a *byproduct* of the collective sensemaking process. Brown and Duguid (1991) have even argued for a conceptualization of organizations as 'communities of communities' (p. 53), and they express the need for a conceptual reorganization to accommodate learning in working and innovation which can 'stretch from the level of individual communities-of-practice and the technology and practices used there to the level of the overarching organizational architecture, the community-of-communities' (1991: 55). Furthermore, they suggest that 'to understand the way information is constructed and travels within an organization, it is first necessary to understand the different communities that are formed within it and the distribution of power among them' (1991: 55).

From this perspective, the individual's role as a learner is to be engaged in *sensemaking* (Weick, 1995) – acquiring and influencing the development of knowledge within and among his or her trajectory of participation – but it is no longer just the individual who solely retains knowledge, rather knowledge is distributed within and among colleagues. This perspective favors 'a shift away from a theory of situated activity in which learning is reified as one kind of activity, and toward a theory of social practice in which learning is viewed as an aspect of all activity' (Lave and Wenger, 1991: 37).

It also represents a clear shift away from a primarily cognitive epistemology of learning, in which learning processes can be described as *systems* of information acquisition, storage, retrieval and transfer (with knowledge as the substance being transferred), and could be described as a more pragmatic approach in which people co-produce an insight as well as co-producing their own understanding in an environment which fosters conversation and sensemaking. The co-production process, as described by Brown (1992), constitutes part of the 'lived-in level' of organizational life, including how relationships are negotiated, moment to moment improvisation, and shared ways of getting something done.

The importance of improvisation and learning coincident with action is highlighted by Weick and Westley (1995):

> None of these extensions portray some kind of second class rationality practiced by people who read about rational choice and missed the point. Instead, this is the activity of people who are thrown into the middle of things and play their way out by thinking while doing. In other words, this is everyday organizational life. To borrow Thayer's (1988, p. 254) Spanish proverb, *No es lo mismo hablar de toros, que estar en el redondel*,' which translates, 'it is not the same thing to talk of bulls as to be in the bullring.' (1995: 39)

Consistent with Mezirow's (1991) views on adult learning, Weick and Westley (1995) argue that learning is embedded in social interaction mediated by language:

> Language is both the tool and the repository of learning. It is the critical tool for reflection, both at the inter and intra-personal level. And language is a social phenomenon. Stated differently, learning is embedded in relationships or relating ... learning is an inherent property not of an individual or an organization, but rather resides in the quality and the nature of the relationship, between levels of consciousness. (1991:18)

This reference to the 'nature of the relationship between levels of consciousness evokes Polanyi's (1958, 1966) distinction between tacit knowledge and explicit knowledge. According to Polanyi, general, tacit knowledge lies just under the surface of conscious awareness, it is personal and abstract, which makes it hard to communicate. Explicit or 'codified' knowledge refers to knowledge that can be conveyed in language and is more systematic and formal. Socially constructed views of learning or knowledge creation tend to focus on the development of inter-subjective meanings. Similarly, Smircich's (1983) work on organizations as cultures also refers to Polanyi's work in terms of the presence of knowledge in relationships:

> This form of knowledge is not universal in form, but specific to people in particular relationships. It presupposes the uniqueness of persons and recognizes that knowledge is not independent of the knower. It is existential and deals with the quality of *being in relation*.' (1983: 163)

The development of this perspective on learning also has roots in the 1930s with Vygotsky's activity theory (1987) which gives some importance to the socially situated characteristics of learning. Although Vygotsky's theory acknowledges the role and influence of the social context on learning; there is significant variation in the theory's interpretation (Hedegaard, 1988; van der Veer and Valsiner, 1991). According to Lave and Wenger (1991), Vygotsky offers only a narrow place for the social character of learning and still tends to emphasize individualistic internalization or acquisition of concepts, thereby failing to account for 'the place of learning within the broader context of the structure of the social world' (1991: 48).

Situating learning in the context of social practice and human knowing through participation in a social world is also described by Lave and Wenger (1991) as 'part of a long Marxist tradition in the social sciences' (p. 50) and relies, in part, on contemporary theories of the relations or interdependency between human agency, thought and action within a socially and culturally constituted world.[2] The debate about the role and place of individual and collective participation in learning has been expanded by more recent work (Chaiklin and Lave, 1993); however, it is apparent that while more traditionally defined processes of individual learning have contributed greatly to current thinking about organizational learning, social constructionist theories of learning emphasizing informality, improvisation, collective action, conversation and sensemaking are still a somewhat overlooked framework for the exploration of organizational learning process and theory.

In reviewing this line of thinking it is also worth noting that Lave and Wenger's (1991) definition of 'legitimate peripheral participation', could be confused with the ancient teaching technique of apprenticeship; however, this would be an unfair reduction of the concept, since it would again focus on the individual as the somewhat passive object of learning (or change) and development. Lave and Wenger insist that learning is not merely *situated* in practice, rather, 'learning is an integral part of generative social practice in the lived-in world' (p. 35). These informal, emergent and generally un-recognized characteristics, along with the possibility that the insights occur-ring daily are almost completely hidden from the organization as a whole (Brown et al., 1989), would confirm the view that studying it systematically is an extremely difficult undertaking.

Defining and Identifying Communities-of-Practice

Nevertheless, there is a growing list of clues to follow up. Although social constructionist views of learning emphasize its collective and improvisational aspects, there is no indication that it is haphazard or structureless. Lave and Wenger (1991) describe the process as having boundaries which are historic, 'with long-term living relations between persons and their place' (p. 53) and developmental, in the sense that learning is concerned with 'the develop-ment of knowledgeably skilled identities in practice' (p. 55). Brown (1992) also provides a useful list of descriptive characteristics, saying that communities-of-practice are:

- above all, informal – they operate at the 'lived-in' level of organizational life;
- where moment to moment improvisation takes place;
- where real learning goes on;
- where participants co-construct the meaning of the environment. (Brown, 1992: 97)

He also insists that communities of practice are *not* equivalent to:

- formal structures;
- institutions, teams, work groups;
- groups in an instructional context (e.g. groups in training sessions);
- artifacts and documents. (1992: 97)

Most importantly, he insists that a community of practice emerges through *webs of interactions*, it is not designed (1992: 97).

Research leading to the conceptualization of situated learning and on communities of practice has tended to focus on how people from clearly defined occupational groups or professions (e.g. tailors, photocopy repair technicians, or midwives) are interacting about practical and daily issues related to accomplishing their *work*. In contrast to portraying learning as a gradual process of internalization by individuals, these studies provide evidence that learning concerns the whole person in an evolving set of relations focused on achieving full membership in a *community* of practi-tioners. Mirvis gives a valuable set of definitions of *community*, beginning with the view that in this context it is *not* a physical place (neighbourhood, or workplace), nor is it a social space, or affiliation, such as a political party.

> As a starting point, see in the root word 'common' notions of sharing, mutual obligation, and commitment that link people together ... and encompasses the emotive experience of feeling close to others, being connected to them by reciprocity or empathy, and even of living at least some of your life with and through them.' (Mirvis, 1997: 195)

He contrasts these definitions with Peck's (1987) work on community building, in which the idea of community extends to become a 'process', rather than a psychological state or sociological condition. The former definition, in combination with Brown's characteristics cited above, begin to bracket this phenomenon more clearly.

Executive Collectives – Similar or Unique?

The need for further research on the social construction of meaning and how people enact their reality individually or collectively within organizations has been noted for some time in a variety of work, some of which has already been discussed (Brown, 1992; Brown and Duguid, 1991; Crossan et al., 1994; Morgan, 1983; Putnam and Pacanowsky, 1983; Smircich, 1983; Weick, 1983, 1995; Weick and Roberts, 1993). It is a natural human tendency to interpret, to understand, to make meaningful and sensible the events and actions surrounding us. The unrelenting pace of flux and change within many organizations today further fuels our need to continuously understand and make sense of events so that more effective actions and responses can be formulated. When top managers get together informally, they are presumably not much different than the rest of us, and talk about how they perceive their world, what they want from it, and how to solve problems they are encountering within it. But what is the nature of this discourse, and who are the most important participants in it? What is meaningful and, perhaps most importantly, how is this linked to subsequent patterns of decision and action? Clearly, there is also some significant value in tracing the learning pathways, interconnections and inter-dependencies between key decision-makers, and the extent to which their collective learning may influence their organizational contexts.

A critical issue arising from this research agenda is whether executives could be defined as 'practitioners' in the same sense as the occupational groups previously studied. Of course, executives generally have a number of similar roles and responsibilities as senior decision-makers, problem-solvers, planners and leaders, and are generally considered to be key players in the formulation and enabling of strategic interpretations and actions within an organization (Daft and Weick, 1984). But are they practicing a common 'discipline?'

This raises the long-debated question of whether the art or practice of management can be given a coherent definition, apart from the contexts in which it takes place. According to Senge (1990a), a discipline is a body of practice, based in some underlying theory or understanding of the world, which suggests a path of development or 'education' in its true sense of 'drawing out'. Given this definition, one can situate the practice of management (or at least that brand of management which is dedicated to the executive ranks) within certain domains of knowledge. Spender (1994) argues that a competent manager requires different levels or types of knowledge:

- scientific or objective knowledge about the physical world in which they operate;
- social knowledge about the social, economic and cultural context in which their firms' activities are embedded;
- local knowledge about the people and processes embraced by their managerial activities; and
- self-knowledge about their own personal history, attitudes and motives. (Spender, 1994: 393)

At the executive level, there are also unique dynamics which accompany the possession of power in organizational life. This power is disproportionate to other occupational groups or professions (Coopey, 1995; Kotter, 1985) and is linked to an executive's abilities to use it as well as his or her resources within the framework of rules and patterns for resource allocation in the organizational context. Additionally, there are significant personal and corporate gains and losses related to the executive's ability to exercise his or her power. In these terms, becoming a 'fully-fledged' or capable executive practitioner is the central learning issue, just as with other occupational groups. The next level of exploration would then extend to examine the patterns of social engagement in learning (similar or different to other groups?), and how important or valuable is this learning in terms of committed action?

There are also a number of questions about levels of experience. It is possible that for executives who are more junior in their roles, access to 'masters' is central. What is the order or sequence of apprenticeship within the executive ranks; when are you considered to be a 'full' member? Questions may also be asked about the effective use of language and the mastery of meaning (Shotter, 1990). Since skillful use of language is an essential part of executive practice, access to opportunities to talk with 'masters' is important. To what extent are stories and narratives and their accompanying meanings opportunities for learning?

Other lines of inquiry might extend into the genesis of innovation. Nonaka and Takeuchi's (1995) work on knowledge creation highlights the competitive advantages to productively using knowledge existing in the group or collective, and they suggest that the critical task for most organizations is to understand how to create new knowledge through the conversion of tacit knowledge into explicit knowledge (p. 11). These views are also consistent with Weick and Roberts' (1993) assertion that 'connections between behaviors, rather than people, may be the crucial "locus" for mind and that intelligence is to be found in patterns of behavior rather than in individual knowledge' (p. 359). As most executives are aware, informal community 'intelligence' often travels much faster than one might desire. The ways in which this information travels and is made meaningful is an example of one of the less well-documented pathways of organizational learning, and knowledge about the executive's role in it is still rudimentary. In order to track this dynamic pathway it is necessary to begin with a relatively clear picture of the organizational context and how meanings come to life within it.

Key Dimensions to be Explored

Obviously there are many possible dimensions to be explored in order to understand further the linkages between executive-level learning and organizational learning. The following four sets of dimensions are offered as a set of interlocking theoretical platforms, to support further debate and research.

Collective Sensemaking and Participation

In many organizational circles the assumption that work and learning are inseparable is not difficult to accept; however, one of the constraints to conducting research on communities-of-practice at the executive level is the role and distribution of power among and between group participants, and the sensitivity about the content of their discussions, if taken out of context. Naturally, such constraints need to be given serious consideration within the research design; however, this sensitivity also points to the importance of power asymmetries behind the formulation of collective conclusions and interpretations (Coopey, 1995). This is especially difficult to document when relationships are relatively informal, and suggests that the researcher must achieve a significant level of trust in order to obtain accurate data. In terms of categorizing what occurs in these informal relationships, Weick (1995) provides a useful and clearly articulated set of properties which can serve to bracket the cues contained in the collective sensemaking actions and communication patterns of individuals, groups and organizations. These properties are summarized in the text box below:

Seven properties of sensemaking (Weick, 1995: 62)

The recipe 'how can I know what I think until I see what I say?' can be parsed to show how each of the seven properties of sensemaking are built into it.

1. Identity: The recipe is a question about who I am as indicated by discovery of how and what I think.

continued overleaf

---

2. Retrospect: To learn what I think, I look back over what I said earlier.

3. Enactment: I create the object to be seen and inspected when I say or do something.

4. Social: What I say and single out and conclude are determined by who socialized me and how I was socialized, as well as by the audience I anticipate will audit the conclusions I reach.

5. Ongoing: My talking is spread across time, competes for attention with other ongoing projects, and is reflected on after it is finished, which means my interests may already have changed.

6. Extracted cues: The 'what' that I single out and embellish as the content of the thought is only a small portion of the utterance that becomes salient because of context and personal dispositions.

7. Plausibility: I need to know enough about what I think to get on with my projects, but no more, which means sufficiency and plausibility take precedence over accuracy.

As Weick points out (1995: 62) the fit between the recipe and the seven properties still remains if one or more of the pronouns in the recipe is changed to reflect a collective actor (e.g. how can *we* know what we think until we see what we say?). Weick also cites work by Gioia and Cittipeddi (1991); and Ring and Rands (1989) as using the concept of sensemaking as an *individualized* or singular process of developing cognitive maps of the environment (1995: 342), but he also argues that true sensemaking intertwines individual and social processes because when acts of sensemaking are placed into organized contexts, they increasingly display social and mutually creating properties.

Collecting retrospective accounts may reveal a clearer picture of how issues and insights have evolved over time, and how others may have influenced the development or abstraction of what Schutz (1967) calls 'meaningful lived experience'. The importance of retrospective sensemaking is reflected in Weick's (1995) emphasis on synthesis. Given that there are too many possible meanings, the sensemaker's problem is equivocality, not uncertainty (p. 27).

Documenting information about forms of participation and membership patterns in the sensemaking process would also serve to illuminate the question of whether individual executives interact with groups of peers or near-peers, with trusted individuals, both, or neither. In fact, depending on the issue at hand some may prefer to rely on expert advice. Other dimensions to analyze could include:

- structural characteristics of the community of practice (is it interstitial, acknowledged to be legitimate?);
- how is legitimate access achieved? (through friendship, through promotion to a certain level?);
- how is the community-of-practice re-structured or re-constructed after conflicts, or when membership changes?;

- identity of persons (and how this changes from being a newcomer to an old-timer, the role and relations of near-peers);
- power issues and tensions between newcomers and old-timers (issues relating to how it has always been done vs ways in which things could be improved through change);
- forms of communication and language; how conflicts are resolved; changing relations: how, when and about what old-timers to the group (full members) collaborate, collude and collide;
- what they enjoy, dislike, respect and admire;
- relations between peers and near peers (Lave and Wenger (1991: 93) offer some evidence that this is where knowledge spreads most rapidly and effectively).

Executive Learning Projects: Process and Context-Rich Description

Mezirow's (1991) work on the transformative dimensions of adult learning emphasizes how powerfully language and action are intertwined in the learning process. Similarly, Morgan (1983) acknowledges how language can contain inherent paradoxes in the context for action: 'for while humans can in principle be seen as active agents in perceiving, constructing, and acting on their world, they do so in circumstances that are not of their own choosing' (p. 274). Given the complexities of the average executive's set of 'circumstances that are not of their own choosing', in order to develop a deeper understanding of the learning process at the micro-level, It is important to develop a relatively rich description of the business and social contexts they are operating within, and to explore the extent to which they are mutually creating.

Lave and Wenger (1991) also point out the importance of the social and historical perspective:

> Any given attempt to analyze a form of learning through legitimate peripheral participation must involve analysis of the political and social organization of that form, its historical development, and the effects of both of these on sustained possibilities for learning. (1991: 64)

In addition to developing contextually-rich descriptions, another useful layer of data could be obtained by compiling a brief inventory of the executive's current *learning projects*, and then tracing his or her pursuit of them over time. Tough (1971) defined a 'learning project' as a sustained highly deliberate effort to learn, consisting of a series of *episodes*, adding up to at least 7 hours. 'Episodes' were identified by gauging whether more than half of the person's total motivation was to gain and retain certain fairly clear knowledge, skill, or meaningful lasting change in him or herself.[3] Thus defined, in each *episode* more than half of the person's total motivation would be to gain and retain fairly clear knowledge/skill or produce change in himself or herself (or on behalf of his or her company). Tough's research clearly showed that with some definition and prompting, people are easily able to identify their current learning projects (the majority of which had to do with current and contextually-rounded issues and concerns), as well as the strategies they used to pursue them.

An inventory of individual learning projects, and especially of occasions when the accompanying learning strategy involved planned contacts with other individuals and/or with groups, would provide a more detailed map of what is being sought or learned (at least on the explicit level), as well as why someone might choose one learning strategy over another (e.g. why someone might elect to discuss a learning project with a trusted individual, rather than with a group he or she regularly has contact with). It may serve to illuminate questions relating to when and how executives access their communities-of-practice, or even if communities-of-practice exist in the same sense as previous studies have described.

Individual interview accounts of executive learning projects would not necessarily be as powerful as conducting an ethnographic study wherein it might be possible to document significant 'learning' events; unplanned contacts, the use of tacit knowledge, and sensemaking about insights achieved. Orr's work on community memory in a service culture points to the importance of tacit knowledge in helping to differentiate important details from the myriad of unimportant details. He notes that:

> The skilled practice of these operations is informed by tacit knowledge (Polanyi, 1958, 1966), which may be thought of as both the ability to do things without being able to explain them completely and also the inability to learn to do them from a theoretical understanding of the task.' (Orr, 1990: 170)

Managerial Learning and Organizational Action

As noted above, a key aspect of the link between individual and organizational learning is embedded in committed action. The interlocking nature of managerial and organizational action and interpretation was described by Daft and Weick as something more than what occurs by individuals'.

> Managers may not agree fully about their perceptions (Starbuck, 1976), but the thread of coherence among managers is what characterizes organizational interpretations. Reaching convergence among members characterizes the act of organizing (Weick, 1979) and enables the organization to interpret as a system. (Daft and Weick, 1984: 285)

Nicolini and Meznar (1995) emphasize that organizational learning can be a significant influence on the structuring of organizational activity and identity and they also suggest that the periphery of an organization learns faster than the core (p. 742). Depending upon the type and form of organizational context being studied, it is likely that much executive work would tend to be interstitial and/or at the peripheries of the organization. Clearly, executive-level learning has the potential for significant impact on both internal and cross-organizational procedures and practices.

The use of guided reflection with individuals and/or focus groups, aided by reviewing organizational artifacts, such as strategic plans or other documents may be a practical approach to tracking the ways in which specific ideas and insights have infiltrated the organization. However, Nicolini and Meznar (1995) have also argued that the use of reflection and abstraction processes to track organizational learning is slow, over-promoted by academics, and may not be completely effective because these processes are heavily rational: different and unfamiliar territory compared with what people do on a daily basis. By contrast, Weick's work (1995) suggests that this perspective is grounded in the misapprehension that reflection, abstraction or cognition processes are passive in nature. He proposes that if these processes are viewed less as *pondering* and more as acts of *invention*, they come to life as action in the world and significantly affect what the organization then sees and acts upon (p. 163). This is supported by Starbuck (1976):

> Organizations' environments are largely invented by organizations themselves. Organizations select their environments from ranges of alternatives, then they subjectively perceive the environments they inhabit. The processes of both selection and perception are unreflective, disorderly, incremental, and strongly influenced by social norms and customs. (1976: 1069)

Evidence of organization-level learning is typically thought to be embedded or institutionalized in the systems, structures and procedures of an organization, where it is said to become part of organizational *memory* systems and/or part of collective *mind* (Huber, 1991; Walsh and Ungson, 1991; Weick and Roberts, 1993). It has also been suggested that explicit anchors are required in order to document the relationships between organizational learning and individual/collective understanding, communications and assumptions.

Extensive and detailed studies such as those conducted by Orr (1990) and Porac et al. (1989) provide empirical evidence for the influence of learning and sensemaking on organizational decisions and actions. Their work supports cognitive dissonance theorists (Festinger, 1957; Zimbardo, 1969), who would say that true commitment is displayed in explicit behavior or action: 'The basic idea is that people try hardest to build meaning around those actions to which their commitment is strongest (Weick, 1995: 156). Therefore, one approach to uncovering linkages between micro-level individual/community-of-practice learning and macro-level organizational learning processes is to examine the actions, commitments and justifications which follow what individuals identify as learning.[4]

Whether this linkage is traced by reflective methods or through ethnography, more evidence is needed in order to anchor or track the actual results and/or impact of decisions or actions relating to individual insights. At some level, the following characteristics would need to be explored in some detail:

- physical, linguistic and symbolic artifacts tracing decisions made or actions taken;
- evidence of larger social structures which constitute and re-constitute the practice over time.

The Knowledge Conversion Model

In Nonaka and Takeuchi's (1995) work on knowledge creation, they argue that although most modern management theory points to the importance of knowledge creation, it is mainly focused on the acquisition, accumulation and utilization of existing knowledge and there is very little research on how knowledge is created.

> This may be due to the fact that they have not followed modern and contemporary philosophical discussions on how the Cartesian dualism between subject and object or body and mind can be transcended. The subjective, bodily, and tacit aspects of knowledge are still largely neglected. (1995: 49)

As a result of this gap, Nonaka and Takeuchi propose a model of knowledge creation, which is grounded in the idea that organizational knowledge is created in a spiral conversion process which emerges from and between tacit and explicit dimensions. They argue that through four 'modes', known as socialization, externalization, combination and internalization, individual knowledge is 'articulated and amplified into and throughout the organization' (1995: 57). They support Brown and Duguid's (1991) work by suggesting that the process of amplifying knowledge occurs 'within an expanding "community of interaction", which crosses intra- and inter-organizational levels and boundaries' (p. 59); but they place specific emphasis on the social dimensions of knowledge creation and the importance of language and meaning in collective sensemaking.

> Our dynamic model of knowledge creation is anchored to a critical assumption that human knowledge is created and expanded through social interaction between tacit knowledge and explicit knowledge . . . It should be noted that this conversion is a 'social' process *between* individuals and not confined *within* an individual. (Nonaka and Takeuchi, 1995: 61)

Similarly their views are congruent with the notion that, in the knowledge creation process, language is inherently related to action, so that dialogue (Isaacs, 1993) can, for example, be seen as collective action. Their work tends to rely on case study methodology as the means of documenting and further elaborating the knowledge conversion process. It is unclear, but quite possible that they were present as *participants*, and not only as researchers in some of the cases they cite. This participatory research approach has been advocated by Argyris (1982, 1985) for many years, and some of its pitfalls have also been clearly articulated in a recent essay (1996). *Interventionist* research approaches (Miner and Mezias, 1996) need to 'appreciate the potential for unintended outcomes of actions in complex systems' (p. 96), and this is why they argue against this method as the principal vehicle with which to advance understanding of organizational learning.

Nevertheless, Nonaka and Takeuchi have proposed a very powerful model of knowledge creation, and neatly bridge many of the complex epistemological issues which clog the literature on organizational learning. Particularly in their discussion of the 'middle-up down' process for knowledge creation, they describe some of the micro-level aspects of knowledge creation; however, they do not explicitly address the aspect of executive-level learning and participation. It is the specific linkages between executive talk, action, meaning and participation, and organizational talk, action, meaning and participation that are still relatively unexplored and may still hold some further clues about the creation and distribution of knowledge within and between individuals and organizations.

Developing a Systematic Research Agenda

This article began by posing the question: How does '*who* you know' affect '*what* you know' and consequently, how you '*do*', collectively or organization-ally? The question implies that social relationships not only influence the achievement of relative power and status in the hierarchical sense, they also influence *what* is learned, and by extension, what is applied on the job. In organizational life this line of reasoning is so pervasive that it is self-evident; a 'truth'. But in situating this question within current social constructionist thought on learning and on organizational learning, it is suggested that the mechanisms or processes underlying the relational aspects of learning at the individual and organizational level are still far from clear, nor are they obvious.

In order to anchor these issues further, I have explored the fact that little is known about the individual/organizational learning linkages among the relatively powerful elite class within organizations: executives. An in-depth exploration of the nature and dynamics of executive level communities-of-practice requires a relational view of the person and of the learning process. This approach is grounded in the idea that knowledge is not just embedded in the invisible cognitive worlds of individuals, but exists within the multiple relationships and evolving memberships of individuals and groups in society. An individual executive is both defined by and defines these relations, and learns through participation and sensemaking processes across a variety of contexts.

Existing research on communities of practice uses the findings about relations among and between participants to develop a multi-layered view of how learning and knowing are part of social practice in organized settings, and yet, there is still little evidence of the impact of these relations upon more dynamic processes of organizational knowledge creation and transfer. Past research has also focused on more crisply defined occupational groups (flutemakers, midwives and photocopier repair technicians, for example). I have questioned whether the trajectories of relationships with peers, near peers and 'communities-of-practice' in these groups function the same way for executives; or whether, because of their often sensitive and complex web of contexts and responsibilities, a different set of dynamics might exist.

Further study of executive-level relational learning may also shed some new and practical light on questions of how executive competencies are developed, especially on-the-job, and in 'real' time. Lave and Wenger's

(1991) studies have already shown that close examination of communities-of-practice reveal how work issues influence the 'learning curriculum', the structuring of the community's learning resources; what participants enjoy, dislike, respect and admire; and how identities are shaped and changed through participation.

Such research would also contribute to the development of organizational learning theory through the exploration of how micro-level experiences and their meaning structures influence, shape and interact within the varying conditions and contexts. In metaphorical terms, it could be said that much of the literature on organizational learning to date develops theory on the functioning of an organization's perception and thinking, its rational 'brain' or 'memory' systems. More empirical work is needed in order to develop deeper understanding about the organizational 'body's' circulatory system, the veins and capillaries of organizational learning, and how the work of this circulatory system affects the functioning of the 'body' in general.

The second major theme of this article responds, in part, to Miner and Mezias' (1996) challenge that 'learning models are easy to invoke but difficult to study systematically' (p. 95). To this end, a review of some of the current social constructionist thinking on distributed or collective learning is presented, and it is argued that a great deal of the existing literature on organizational learning tends to be dominated by an individualistic and cognitively-oriented philosophy of learning which focuses on macro-level organizational systems of knowledge acquisition, storage and retrieval. The dominance of this perspective influences the idea that effective organizational learning has to do with objectifying individual knowledge and managing it as if it were an organizational commodity, as well as suggesting that to enhance organizational learning this type of knowledge and skill must somehow become embedded within organizational systems, work-group structures, roles and procedures. In contrast, if organizations are viewed as cultures, or 'communities of communities' (Brown and Duguid, 1991), knowledge becomes situated in the social and relational aspects of working life (Lave and Wenger, 1991); and organizational learning processes can be identified by examining actual actions taken and how these are understood or interpreted as meaningful by the actors themselves (Weick, 1995).

The article concludes by suggesting that in order to obtain high-quality findings a combination of research approaches may be necessary. A first step towards this agenda is suggested by describing detailed research questions based on an interlocking platform of theoretical frameworks. Four powerful theoretical frameworks which can serve to structure and guide data collection and analysis are suggested: Tough's (1971) work on the adult's learning projects; Mezirow's (1991) theory of the transformative dimensions of adult learning; Weick's (1995) properties of sensemaking; and the theory of organizational knowledge creation and conversion (Nonaka and Takeuchi, 1995).

Both individual and organizational learning may be more collective, dynamic, improvisational and emergent than much of the literature has described to date. The executive's role in the linkage between individual and organizational learning is a potentially rich area from which to continue this exploration.

Notes

1. 'All learning takes place inside individual heads; an organization learns in only two ways: (a) by the learning of its members; or (b) by ingesting new members who have knowledge the organization didn't previously have' (Simon, 1991: 125).

2. See Giddens, 1979; Bourdieu, 1977 for further elaboration on theories of social practice which put forward a comprehensive theory emphasizing the socially negotiated character of meaning and knowing within a socially and culturally structured world.

3. In this context, it would be useful to expand Tough's definition by asking about motivation to learn for self and/or *on behalf of the company*.

4. Interestingly, in Weick's terminology, 'learning' resembles what he calls 'sensemaking'; however, he has not made the distinction between these terms completely clear, as is evidenced in the followed quotes from Weick (1991):

... the view that knowledge development constitutes learning is compatible with the idea that organizations consist in part of 'shared agreements'. Second, the idea that learning involves the development of knowledge fits better with the proposal of people like Brown and Duguid (this issue) and Duncan and Weiss (1979: 90) that learning resembles sensemaking. (p. 122)

'Bad' definitions can be instrumental to good outcomes, which is why I am personally in no hurry to abandon insights about learning embedded in traditional psychological definitions. Systemic extension of these definitions makes clear the potential uniqueness of organizational learning in ways which link that uniqueness to what we already know about individual learning. (p. 122)

References

Argyris, C. (1982) *Reasoning, Learning and Action*. San Francisco, CA: Jossey-Bass.

Argyris, C. (1985) *Strategy, Change, and Defensive Routines*. Cambridge, MA: Ballinger.

Argyris, C. (1996) 'Unrecognized Defenses of Scholars: Impact on Theory and Research', *Organization Science* 7(1).

Argyris, C. and Schön, D. (1978) *Organizational Learning: A Theory of Action Perspective*. Reading, MA: Addison-Wesley.

Bourdieu, P. (1977) *Outline of a Theory of Practice*. Cambridge: Cambridge University Press.

Brown, J.S. (1992) 'When Change is Constant: Maybe We Need to Change Our Own Eyeglasses', *Learning in Organizations Workshop Transcript June 21–25, 1992*. London, ON: University of Western Ontario.

Brown, J.S., Collins, A. and Duguid, P. (1989) 'Situated Cognition and the Culture of Learning', *Educational Researcher* Jan–Feb: 32–42.

Brown, J.S. and Duguid, P. (1991) 'Organizational Learning and Communities-of-Practice: Toward a Unified View of Working, Learning, and Innovation', *Organization Science* 2(1): 40–57.

Chaiklin, S. and Lave, J. (1993) *Understanding Practice: Perspectives on Activity and Context*. Cambridge, UK: Cambridge University Press.

Cook, S.D.N. and Yanow, D. (1993) 'Culture and Organizational Learning', *Journal of Management Inquiry* 2: 373–90.

Coopey, J. (1995) 'The Learning Organization, Power, Politics and Ideology', *Management Learning* 26(2): 193–213.

Crossan, M.M., Djurfeldt, L., Lane, H.W. and White, R.E. (1994) 'Organization learning – Dimensions for a Theory', *Western Business School Working Paper Series, 94–09R*. London, ON: University of Western Ontario.

Crossan, M.M., Tiemessen, I., Lane, H.W. and White, R.E. (1995) 'Diagnosing Organizational Learning', *Western Business School Working Paper Series, 95–08.* London, ON: University of Western Ontario.

Daft, R.L. and Weick, K (1984) 'Toward a Model of Organizations as Interpretation Systems', *Academy of Management Review* 9(2): 284–95.

Festinger, L. (1957) *A Theory of Cognitive Dissonance.* Stanford, CA: Stanford University Press.

Gherardi, S., Nicolini, D. and Odella, F. (1996) 'Toward a Social Understanding of How People Learn in Organizations: The Notion of Situated Curriculum, from the Symposium on Organizational Learning and the Learning Organization: Theoretical and Research Developments. Lancaster University, UK (in press).

Giddens, A. (1979) *Central Problems in Social Theory: Action, Structure, and Contradiction in Social Analysis.* Berkeley: University of California Press.

Gioia, D.A. and Cittipeddi, K (1991) 'Sensemaking and Sensegiving in Strategic Change Initiation', *Strategic Management Journal* 12: 433–48.

Hedegaard, M. (1988) *The Zone of Proximal Development as a Basis for Instruction.* Aarhus, Denmark: Institute of Psychology.

Huber, G. (1991) 'Organizational Learning: The Contributing Processes and the Literatures', *Organization Science* 2(1): 88–115.

Isaacs, W. (1993) 'Taking Flight: Dialogue, Collective Thinking, and Organizational Learning', *Organizational Dynamics* 22(2): 24–39.

Jordan, B. (1989) 'Cosmopolitical Obstetrics: Some Insights from the Training of Traditional Midwives', *Social Science and Medicine* 28(9): 925–44.

Kotter, J.P. (1985) *Power and Influence.* New York: The Free Press.

Kouzes, J. and Posner, B. (1987) *The Leadership Challenge.* San Francisco: Jossey-Bass.

Lave, J. (1993) 'The Practice of Learning', in S. Chaiklin and J. Lave (eds) *Understanding Practice: Perspectives on Activity and Context.* Cambridge UK: Cambridge University Press.

Lave, J. and Wenger, E. (1991) *Situated Learning: Legitimate Peripheral Participation.* Cambridge, UK: Cambridge University Press.

Mezirow, J. (1991) *Transformative Dimensions of Adult Learning.* San Francisco: Jossey-Bass.

Miner, A. and Mezias, S. (1996) 'Ugly Duckling No More: Pasts and Futures of Organizational Learning Research', *Organization Science* 7(1): 88–99.

Mirvis, P. (1997) ' "Soul work" in organizations', *Organization Science* 8(2): 193–206.

Morgan, G. (1983) 'Toward a More Reflective Social Science', in G. Morgan (ed.) *Beyond Method: Strategies for Social Research*, pp. 368–76. Beverly Hills, CA: Sage

Morgan, G. (1986) *Images of Organization.* Beverly Hills, CA: Sage.

Morgan, G. (1993) *Imaginization: The Art Of Creative Management.* Newbury Park, CA: Sage.

Nicolini, D. and Meznar, M.B. (1995) 'The Social Construction of Organizational Learning: Conceptual and Practical Issues in the Field', *Human Relations* 48(7): 727–46.

Nonaka, I. and Takeuchi, H. (1995) *The Knowledge-Creating Company.* New York: Oxford University Press.

Orr, J.E. (1990) 'Sharing Knowledge, Celebrating Identity: War Stories and Community Memory Among Service Technicians', in D. S. Middleton and D. Edwards (eds) *Collective Remembering: Memory in Society*, pp. 140–69. London: Sage.

Peck, M.S. (1987) *The Different Drum.* New York: Simon & Schuster.

Polanyi, M. (1958) *Personal Knowledge.* Chicago: University of Chicago Press.

Polanyi, M. (1966) *The Tacit Dimension.* London: Routledge & Kegan Paul.

Porac, J.F., Thomas, H. and Baden-Fuller, C. (1989) 'Competitive Groups as Cognitive Communities: The Case of Scottish Knitwear Manufacturers', *Journal of Management Studies* 26: 397–416.

Putnam, L.L. and Pacanowsky, M.E. (1983) *Communication and Organizations: An Interpretive Approach.* London: Sage.

Ring, P.S. and Rands, G.P. (1989) 'Sensemaking, Understanding, and Committing: Emergent Interpersonal Transaction Processes in the Evolution of 3M's Microgravity Research Program', in A.H. Van de Ven, H.L. Angle and M.S. Poole (eds) *Research on the Management of Innovation. The Minnesota Studies*, pp. 337 66. New York. Ballinger.

Schutz, A. (1967) *The Phenomenology of the Social World*. Evanston, IL. Northwestern University Press.

Senge, P. (1990a) *The Fifth Discipline*. New York. Doubleday.

Senge, P. (1990b) The Leader's New Work. Building Learning Organizations', *Sloan Management Review* 7–23.

Shotter, J. (1990) 'The Social Construction of Remembering and Forgetting', in D. Middleton and D. Edwards (eds) *Collective Remembering*, pp. 120–38. London. Sage.

Simon, H.A. (1991) 'Bounded Rationality and Organizational Learning', *Organization Science* 2(1): 125–33.

Smircich, L. (1983) 'Studying Organizations as Cultures', in G. Morgan (ed.) *Beyond Method: Strategies for Social Research*, pp. 160–72. Beverly Hills, CA: Sage.

Spender, J.C. (1994) 'Knowing, Managing and Learning: A Dynamic Managerial Epistemology', *Management Learning* 25(3): 387–412.

Starbuck, W.H. (1976) 'Organizations and Their Environments', in M.D. Dunnette (ed.) *Handbook of Industrial and Organizational Behavior*, pp. 1069–123. Chicago: Rand McNally.

Tough, A. (1971) *The Adult's Learning Projects*. Toronto, Ontario: Ontario Institute for Studies in Education, Research in Education Series, No. 1.

van der Veer, R. and Valsiner, J. (1991) *Understanding Vygotsky: A Quest for Synthesis*. Oxford: Blackwell.

Vygotsky, L.S. (1987) *The Collected Works of L.S. Vygotsky. Vol. 1. Problems of General Psychology*. New York: Plenum Press.

Walsh, J.P., and Ungson, G.R. (1991) 'Organizational Memory', *Academy of Management Review* 16(1): 57–91.

Weick, K.E. (1983) 'Organizational Communication: Toward a Research Agenda', in L.L. Putnam and M.E. Pacanowsky (eds) *Communication and Organizations: An Interpretive Approach*, pp. 7–12. London: Sage.

Weick, K.E. (1991) 'The Nontraditional Quality of Organizational Learning', *Organization Science* 2(1): 116–24.

Weick, K.E. (1995) *Sensemaking in Organizations*. London: Sage.

Weick, K. E. and Roberts, K.H. (1993) 'Collective Mind in Organizations: Heedful Interrelating on Flight Decks', *Administrative Science Quarterly* 38: 357–81.

Weick, K.E. and Westley, F. (1995) 'Organizational Learning: Affirming an Oxymoron'. Unpublished Manuscript, April. [Published 1996 in S. Clegg and C. Hardy (eds) *Handbook of Organizational Studies*. London: Sage.]

Zimbardo, P.G. (1969) *The Cognitive Control of Motivation: The Consequences of Choice And Dissonance*. Glenview, IL: Scott, Foresman.

part three

Critical Approaches to Management Education and Learning

8

Christopher Grey and Nathalie Mitev

Management Education
A Polemic

Introduction

This paper, which is intentionally and unashamedly polemical, is a contribution to the timely, if not overdue, debate on management education to which Willmott (1994) has provided a 'provocation'. Our intention is to provoke critical reflection upon and by management academics. At the present time there is considerable uncertainty in the minds of many management educators as to how they should adapt to the new challenges posed by changing management practice and developments in knowledge. The traditional 'Harvard model' of teaching has now been called into question (Linder and Smith, 1992) whilst management gurus, such as Tom Peters, have begun to articulate visions of chaos (Peters, 1989) which sit uneasily with the old rigidities of traditional management education. It is within this context that we seek to make a case for what we call a 'critical' approach to management education. In making such a case, however, we do not develop the details of an alternative curriculum or pedagogy (see Grey et al., forthcoming). This is partly for reasons of space and occasion, and partly because it is not our intention to lay down, in doctrinaire fashion, a blueprint for what management education should consist of in detailed terms. Nor do we wish to imply that we are somehow in privileged possession of an intellectual or moral advantage over those who hold positions with which we take issue. With these caveats, however, we do wish to suggest that there is something seriously amiss with mainstream management education. In the remainder of this section, we begin to map out the themes which we develop in the paper.

The central argument of the paper is that mainstream management education[1] re-enforces the technicist and commonsensical understandings of many management students. Such students resist learning anything which they perceive as 'theoretical', 'impractical' or irrelevant', preferring to learn specific techniques which they see as useful; and mainstream management education readily serves up a diet of such techniques. This is not to say that mainstream management education is axiomatically devoid of elements of critique. The teaching of management techniques, such as discounted cash flows, organizational design or systems analysis, may present an opportunity for some management students to analyse the deficiencies of current management theory and practice. Equally, much of the mainstream is concerned to produce alternative techniques, for instance soft systems methodologies (Wilson, 1984) in contrast to traditional systems analysis, or 'flat' organizational design which rejects traditional hierarchies. These sorts of development highlight the problematic nature of management techniques and practices, and reflect the diversity of representations of management. However, many of these suggested alternatives can be further analysed, *critically*, as being primarily concerned with providing yet more technical solutions of different (and perhaps higher) levels of sophistication, therefore strengthening, rather than challenging, technicist and instrumental under-standings of management.

We argue that there exists a considerable body of management research, originating in critical social science (e.g. Alvesson and Willmott, 1992), which suggests how and why such views of management could be challenged, but we would contend that this has not been widely translated into management teaching. Admittedly, courses in Business Ethics, Corporate Governance or Women in Management have been attached to many management curricula, adding a 'critical' touch. But although such topics may propose new challenges, a syllabus containing these types of subject will not necessarily be more critical in the sense which we develop shortly, because their emergence is not critically appraised and they are assimilated into mainstream, manage-rialist understandings of management education.[2]

In this context, the term 'managerialist' denotes, broadly speaking, the view that management education stands in a functional relationship to management itself: that the aim of management education is to contribute to and improve organizational effectiveness and the performance of individual managers. Managerialist management academics replicate commonsensical views by treat-ing management as a morally and politically neutral technical activity. Hence, management education becomes primarily concerned with the acquisition of techniques, regardless of the context of their application. Critical management academics, on the other hand, are concerned to analyse management in terms of its social, moral and political significance and, in general terms, to challenge management practice rather than seek to sustain it.

From a critical perspective, the teaching of management techniques is not, in and of itself, a valid model of management education because it aspires (plainly with more or less success) to bolster, rather than debunk, managerial dominance. Consider an example from a textbook, chosen at random from our bookshelves:

> The intention is to help the reader gain a better insight into this complex and multilayered topic [human resource management!] in order ... to be in a better position to shape strategic action in his/her own organisation. (Harrison, 1993: 4)

Here it is plain that the object of management education is to improve the managerial competence of students for instrumental reasons of control ('to shape strategic action'). This may occur because the manager acquires more effective techniques or, perhaps more significantly, because management education bestows a legitimacy upon those managers who possess it. In neither case is the instrumental rationality of control subjected to critical scrutiny. Instead, it is assumed that because practices of control routinely occur in organizations, it is acceptable that management education should contribute to this control.

We go on to argue that this mainstream conception of management education is specifically related to an erroneous distinction of 'academia' and the 'real world', in which the former defers to the latter and is defined by it, with deleterious consequences for the quality of management education. This claim leads directly to a consideration of quality initiatives in higher education, including management education. We argue that these are premised upon the same distinction of academia and the real world, and that they re-enforce the untenable conception of management and management education as neutral, technical activities. But we also argue that, because quality initiatives are managerial in character, management academics have a particular intellectual responsibility to question and analyse their credibility. So on the subject of quality initiatives we make two arguments. First, that they are damaging to education in general: by importing 'real-world' and 'commonsensical' concepts such as customers and markets, they commodify both the teaching relationship and knowledge itself; this has particularly disastrous consequences for management education where the need to satisfy the customer's need for relevance to the real world impoverishes further the teaching/learning experience. Our second argument is that management academics should contribute to exposing the unacceptability of quality management in general, an unacceptability that we claim amounts to a form of managerially based totalitarianism.

From this, it follows that management education is intimately bound up with politics more generally. Although space precludes a proper analysis of the links between the two, we point to some of the connections between management education and the New Right, focusing especially on the link between the concepts of 'commonsense' in both. We conclude by arguing that managerialist management academics, who define the mainstream of management education, avoid the questions of the moral, political, social and philosophical issues which management raises. This is not simply to argue for a more politicized (or even 'politically correct') model of management education. Rather, it is to argue for the recognition of the politicization which is inevitably, albeit implicitly, present whenever management is taught. Unless or until managerialist academics recognize the challenge of critical work, they will be unable to challenge and extend students' existing horizons and unable to do more than defer to managers. In both of these aspects, management education fails in its pedagogical and intellectual responsibilities: to expand students' minds and to 'speak truth to power'.

Critical Research and Technicist Students

In recent years, there has been the development of a substantial, if marginal, tradition of research within management and business disciplines, which may be designated as 'critical'. Such research takes a variety of forms and, for present purposes, may most readily be defined in negative terms, that is in terms of its rejection of managerialism. Managerial research is animated by a desire to describe the activity of management and/or to prescribe ways in which managerial effectiveness may be enhanced, thereby boosting productivity and profitability. Critical research has no such aspirations. Typically, it aims to explore and expose the social, political and moral nature – and, usually, the shortcomings – of management. Managerial research, by contrast, eschews such issues, presenting management as an unproblematic set of techniques and practices.

The perspectives which critical research on management brings to bear are very diverse, and it is not our intention to describe them. Just within the field of organization studies, Reed (1992) identifies at least eight different approaches which could be called critical, and this omits one of the principal critical approaches, namely feminism (e.g. Ferguson, 1984) whilst understating the proliferation of postmodern contributions to organization studies (see Cooper and Burrell, 1988). It is probably true that critical work on management is most developed in the field of work and organization studies, but there also exists a flourishing critical tradition in accounting (e.g. Burchell et al., 1980; Tinker, 1985) and a more limited amount of critical work in other management subjects, such as marketing (Firat et al., 1987). The scope of critical management research is evidenced in the diversity of contributions to Alvesson and Willmott (1992), who amalgamate under the term 'critical' approaches to management those that derive from both Foucault and Post-structuralism as well as those deriving from the Critical theory of the neo-Marxist Frankfurt School. These traditions are used to analyse critically a range of management specialisms. But the invocation of such traditions is a sad contrast to the daily reality of most of the syllabi of management degrees as currently constituted, for the extent to which the critical research tradition has been translated into teaching is extremely limited (cf. Reed and Anthony, 1992; French and Grey, forthcoming).

It is not sufficient to ascribe this to an inadequacy on the part of students, as if they have no need or no ability to engage with or understand the debates which preoccupy at least some of their teachers. Instead, it is necessary to grasp the precise conditions of existence of our students' intellectual worlds. Although the extent to which such precision is possible is limited by the tremendous differences in the interests, abilities and motivations of our students, from our experience,[3] we believe it is possible to identify some recurring themes of tension which arise in teaching management. We conclude this section by offering a characterization of these themes. It is obvious that the tensions that critical academics experience are not felt by managerialist academics, for whom the students' world-view is an approximation to their own.

Many students articulate or imply an attitude to learning management which profoundly contradicts the intellectual projects of critical approaches to management. This attitude consists of a related set of concerns that education should be 'useful', 'practical' and 'relevant to the real world'. Such an attitude places a premium upon learning *techniques*, whose practical relevance should be demonstrable, and these techniques should be backed up by constant reference to real-world examples or case studies.[4] For the purposes of this paper we describe such an attitude as *technicist*. The technicist label relates not only to the focus on techniques but also to the fact that the technicist approach is illuminated by a commitment to instrumental rationality.[5]

Mastering rational and objective techniques preserves the illusion that technical fixes are neutral and universally applicable, and contributes to the building of specialized knowledge which others do not possess, hence justifying management roles and strengthening managerial control. Furthermore, the notion of a management technique is not limited to hard-type techniques, such as accounting or operations management, but includes 'softer' approaches – for instance change management or human resource management techniques. Technicist managerialism also calls upon a range of *commonsense* ideas in order to circumscribe and justify the domain and means of management intervention. But although commonsense is elevated above 'theoretical', 'academic' or 'abstract' thought, it cannot be equated with some kind of basic, pre-theoretical knowledge. On the contrary, commonsense implies a highly complex, albeit unarticulated, set of theoretical commitments. Commonsense is therefore something that is accomplished. Anthony (1986), posing the question as to why management education does not provide intellectually demanding and critical courses, notes that 'The ostensible explanation is that the managers could find such [courses] impractical, unreal, "academic", [but] managers reject critical disciplines and concepts because they have been taught to reject them' (p. 139). So commonsense must be understood not as a 'given' which we have to work within, but as a limiting construct which we must work away from. In the next section we seek to explore the nature and difficulties of notions of commonsense as they impinge upon management education.

The Paradox of Commonsense

The appeal of 'commonsense' appears to be considerable. In this case, the commonsense is, in particular, that management is a necessary and desirable social activity which is morally and politically neutral (cf. MacIntyre, 1981; Roberts, 1984; Anthony, 1986). This supposed neutrality enables the conceptualization of management as a purely technical activity. Therefore, management education is primarily a matter of the acquisition of techniques whose value lies in their potential for practical and effective application. A cursory glance at almost any management textbook will confirm the centrality of all or most of this definition – even in an apparently 'unconventional' text, we find that the exploration of the concept of creativity has an instrumental aim: 'By understanding the creative process and characteristics of a creative environment the creative manager is better placed to remove the barriers to creative action' (Henry, 1991: 11).

Management students, for their part, are commonly more comfortable when learning techniques (such as those of finance, accounting or systems analysis, or 'methodologies' of change management or motivation) which they perceive as practically orientated, useful and immediately applicable. This comfort derives from the fact that insofar as the learning of techniques re-enforces an existing commonsense view, students are not required to reflect critically upon themselves or the world around them.[6] But here a paradox reveals itself because, at the same time, students will often bemoan the lack of stimulation and the tedium associated with the passive receipt of commodified knowledge (Grey et al., 1991) which typically accompanies the technicist curriculum. Although this complaint is articulated, and frequently addressed, through issues of the presentation and style of teaching, such an articulation cannot capture the more fundamental problems of technicist modes of learning and teaching. For these problems are not presentational: rather they derive from the restricted understanding of the world which is entailed by a commitment to commonsense. Commonsense requires the unquestioned delimitation of the terrain of relevance from that of irrelevance.

The paradox of commonsense also becomes apparent when learning about more 'theoretical' topics such as organizational behaviour, organizational culture or change management. Students in the technicist mode will typically react in one of two ways to such topics. One way will be to regard them simply as irrelevant and therefore failing to meet the commonsensical criteria of value: this is implicit when students denigrate such topics as 'the soft, waffly stuff'. 'Soft' concepts are frequently seen as unnecessary academic constructs addressing simple problems which can be more easily solved using, for instance, basic and seemingly unproblematic organizational psychology principles or data-modelling techniques. Students responding in this way will often exhibit considerable hostility when challenged upon the adequacy of their beliefs.

But there is a second response from technicist students to 'soft' topics in management. This response regards such topics as being obvious, and at best codifying what was already known as commonsense: this is implicit in comments such as 'it's just a few diagrams with words and arrows' and explicit in comments such as 'it's obvious' or 'it's just commonsense'. This second type of response is interesting. It may, on occasion, simply indicate a reductionism in which complex ideas are reduced to commonsense and thereby denigrated for having been presented pretentiously. But it may also indicate a legitimate disappointment which reflects the banality of much of what passes as theorizing in management disciplines, involving as it does the simplistic importation of theories from psychology, sociology or economics. At first sight, this might be taken to support a view that there is space for introducing more sophisticated ideas to management students. However, less optimistically, it may suggest simply that technicist students will delight in seizing on simplistic theorizing to prove the validity of their own commonsense prejudice, and that the introduction of greater sophistication would cause students to fall back on the first response of decrying 'theorizing' as irrelevant.

So management education is caught in a vicious circle: what is to be taught has to be practically orientated towards commonsensical understandings of the real world (a term we return to later) otherwise it is 'only' theorizing, but, if it is so orientated, it is 'only' commonsense. In these circumstances, many teachers will fall back upon, or indeed begin with, the presentation of ever more complex 'models' (cf. 'theories') accompanied by very detailed 'real-world' examples which purport to provide generalizable solutions to business problems. This satisfies the technicist students who feel that they are being taught something which is relevant but, because of the level of detail, was previously unknown. It may also provide fresh jargon to impress the uninitiated whilst giving initiates the credentials they need to operate in the contemporary world of management-speak. Teaching is, in this sense, more than commonsense, but never challenges commonsense. Unfortunately, such teaching, whilst perhaps satisfying the short-term desire to get through sessions and courses without confrontation with students, is self-defeating in the long term (Reed and Anthony, 1992).

The long-term problems which arise come from the fact that the solutions to business problems so confidently propounded in the lecture hall can never deliver what they promise because of the inherently uncontrollable nature of social relations, including those in work organizations (MacIntyre, 1981).[7] As this becomes apparent, students may come to look upon their time at university with misgivings,[8] and ascribe these to the 'unrealistic' and 'impractical' approach of academics which they find to be inapplicable in the 'real world'. But because their basic faith in technicist solutions has been pandered to by academics, these ex-students will continue the ever more desperate search for such solutions, perhaps through the services of consultants. At the same time, they can perpetuate their derogatory view of 'academia' as divorced from the commonsense practicality of the real world.

An additional difficulty for teachers of management is that, at least amongst postgraduate and post-experience students, different specialisms, such as HRM, marketing or IT, exhibit different articulations of commonsense and use their set of techniques to assert different professional identities. What this diversity of specialist modes of commonsense should point to is that the notion of the 'real world' as some sort of ultimate ontological court of arbitration is nonsensical. It is commonplace in organizations for functional groups to denigrate each other for their lack of attachment to the real world (for example, production engineers vs personnel managers; accountants vs doctors). This in itself should lead management academics to question the repeated paeans which technicist students and others make to the 'real world'. But beyond this, the acceptance of the dichotomy of real world/academia by many management academics constitutes one of the major obstacles to the provision of an intellectually defensible management education.

The notion of the 'real world' implies a hierarchical pairing of the real and the unreal, academia and not-academia (French, 1993; Grey, 1994a). Yet how is the division between real world and academia to be sustained? It cannot be said that the dividing line is production for profit, since this would render all public-sector work unreal. It is more likely that the dividing line is between 'theory' and 'practice', but again this is problematic since all practice implies some theory even if unstated. Furthermore, academics engage in practice: the practice of teaching, research and administration. Even if, restricting the issue to management, an attempt were made to separate theory and practice, this would still fail since management academics have to practise the management of their teaching, research and administration whilst managers have to reflect upon their practice, and this implies theorizing, even if only in a weak sense.

But, incoherent as it may be, the notion of the real world has a strong hold upon the imaginations of management academics and students. Amongst academics, this seems to be both the condition and consequence of insecurity and fear. The veneration which many management academics display for MBA and post-experience students, in particular, is quite striking. There seems to be a belief, tinged with anxiety, that somehow these students have a privileged key (i.e. 'real-world' experience) which threatens to discredit or undermine their teachers' knowledge. Mainstream management academics elevate the world of the practitioner as 'real' and, conversely, conceptualize their own world as *not* being real. It is small wonder that academics who regard themselves as illusory, false or imaginary experience insecurity when teaching! Insecurity also follows from regarding knowledge as a commodified possession, owned by academics and imparted to students. Such an approach will always be precarious because knowledge is relational (Freire, 1971, 1974): the outcome of an inter-subjective process rather than an object to be distributed. And finally, academics' fear of their students follows from the hollowness of claims to possess solutions to business problems: since such solutions are generally illusory, there is always the possibility that MBA students, and others, will identify the flaws in any specific prescriptions offered by management academics.

Faced with the insecurity which the real world–academia dichotomy produces, management academics often respond by, paradoxically, further entrenching themselves in that dichotomy by seeking to provide ever more 'practical' teaching material, and substituting consultancy for research. In this they seek to distance themselves from 'discredited' academia but, since they remain employed as academics, this attempt is always precarious, and indeed contradictory. These remarks, of course, apply principally to managerialist academics. Critical academics follow a different course. Some, particularly those of sufficient eminence, will be able to establish a legitimate institutional place on their own terms. Others will seek to teach in ways which are congruent with their beliefs, in the process running into the resistance of technicist students, and the disapprobium of managerialist colleagues. Still others will sublimate their intellectual beliefs for the purposes of teaching.

But, in general, all critical academics face a situation where the real-world, commonsense orthodoxy is the dominant force within the institutions where they are employed, and this will be reflected in the prospectuses and PR material of those institutions. There can be very few business schools which tell the world that students will be taught to understand how organizations exploit their workers by the expropriation of surplus value, for example, even though this could plausibly be regarded as just as 'realistic' as, if not more so than, the accounts of the employment relationship to be found in most management textbooks, and might even be more useful to students (Anthony, 1986). Given this official orthodoxy, the attempts of critical academics to introduce more intellectually rigorous teaching on their own initiative must always be marginal and of limited legitimacy.

Our comments so far obviously imply that we are deeply sceptical about the quality of most management education, since we are claiming that it does little more than pander to students' prejudices. But, as most readers of this paper can hardly fail to be aware, the quality of university teaching is currently the subject of considerable attention in UK institutions. How does this relate to what we have been discussing?

Quality and Managerial Totalitarianism

Quality initiatives in higher education are explicitly an attempt to bring academia into the 'real world' under the rhetoric of 'accountability'. Academics, so the argument goes, are in receipt of large quantities of public money and they therefore have an obligation to give an account of how this money is spent, which can then form the basis for decisions as to where money should best be allocated. As part of the general development of performance appraisal in UK universities (Townley, 1993), initiatives on teaching quality have a particular place. In essence, these initiatives are an attempt to introduce bureaucratic management controls into universities, and, within this, student evaluations play a key role. The notion of student evaluation of teaching, whilst superficially a democratic exercise to equalize the relationship of teacher and student, is more profoundly concerned to redefine that relationship in line with a certain conception of the market. Thus universities and university teachers become 'producers' of knowledge and students become 'consumers' or 'customers'. Such a conception, which is becoming widespread in the public sector and in private sector re-organizations (du Gay and Salaman, 1992) is as pernicious as it is absurd.

First, the absurdity. The market conception of the teaching relationship involves the ultimate commodification of both that relationship and know-ledge itself. However, as noted earlier, knowledge is not a commodity (Friere, 1971, 1974) but the outcome of a dialectical relationship between teacher and taught, and any pedagogy worthy of the name needs to engage seriously with the challenges this implies (Grey et al., 1991). On the specific question of students as consumers, it is plain that the market model is inadequate. Whereas the purchase of economic goods requires only that the consumer pay the price in order to enjoy use of the goods, in education, on the other hand, payment of fees is only the condition of entry. It cannot constitute an entitlement, since the benefits of education are only realizable insofar as students, as well as teachers, fulfil mutual obligations in the course of their relationship. Moreover, the value of education is not something which can be known at the time of purchase and, indeed, may not become apparent until well after the point of 'consumption'. One of the central difficulties with the notion of the student as customer in the context of what we have argued so far, is that it legitimates giving technicist students what they 'want', even if this is academically suspect.

But, absurd as it may be, the market conception of education is also pernicious, and especially so in management education, when it is combined with the technicist orientation of students which we have described. For the quality initiatives are predicated upon precisely the same technicist, commonsense assumptions which bedevil management education. Student feedback, particularly on MBA and post-experience courses, typically relates to notions of relevance, applicability and immediate usability of course material. These teaching-quality assessment exercises have an insidious conforming and confirming effect on commonsensical and technicist approaches to teaching management students. Conforming because they encourage academics to pander to students' technicism and confirming because they re-enforce students' belief that relevance and applicability are indeed the criteria by which education is to be judged.

Within the field of quality assessment, management academics have a double responsibility. First, as intellectuals they should assume a general responsibility for questioning underlying values:

> Intellectuals are in a position to expose the lies of governments, to analyse actions according to their causes and motives and other hidden intentions ... [i]t is the responsibility of intellectuals to speak the truth and expose lies. (Chomsky, 1969: 227–8)

Second, as intellectuals who specialize in thinking about management they should engage in a critical analysis of quality initiatives as a dominant part of current management theory and practice.

Our experience suggests that these responsibilities are fulfilled only to a limited extent. Of course, this partly reflects the fact that the political and institutional pressures are such as to make resistance hazardous and largely ineffectual. However, intellectual responsibility is not so easily passed over: in replicating students' assumptions about commonsense and the real world, management academics are not just colluding in the erosion of academic values through quality initiatives, but also abdicating their fundamental responsibility as teachers to expand rather than restrict the ways in which students regard the world. In the present context this amounts to a collaboration with an insidious form of totalitarianism.

For we regard the developing situation, not just in universities but throughout organizations and society, as being akin to totalitarianism and, specifically, totalitarianism based upon management. Marcuse (1964/1986) showed how modern industrial societies exhibited totalitarian and repressive characteristics under the guise of democratic freedom. The principal means of control were seen to be mass consumption and mass media. In contemporary times, management must be added to these controls. As long ago as 1933, Simone Weil suggested that there was 'a new species of oppression, oppression in the name of management' (Weil, 1933/1988: 9).

In claiming that management constitutes a species of oppression or an aspect of totalitarianism, we are not primarily thinking of the traditional functions of control and coordination – or exploitation – which have been carried out by management in work organizations. Instead, we refer to contemporary attempts to forge organizational commitment through 'corporate culturism', excellence prescriptions, quality initiatives and the like. Willmott (1993) argues that corporate culture initiatives have characteristics in common with Orwell's (1949) dystopian vision of totalitarianism in *1984*. Binns (1993), in a brilliant and, regrettably, under-exposed historical and political analysis of quality management, shows very clearly how such management constitutes 'bureaucratic totalitarianism'. This totalitarianism requires not only the acceptance of market relations as natural, just and inevitable but also that individuals give their hearts and minds to the quasi-religious corporate devotions called for by the management gurus. Pursuing this analogy, business schools become the theological colleges of 'managerial evangelism' (Kerfoot and Knights, 1993) or, more straightforwardly, the ideologists of bureaucratic totalitarianism.

But, beyond this, we also see the development of a totalizing discourse of management as a way of organizing social and individual life. Recent work (Rose, 1989; Giddens, 1991) has drawn attention to the ways in which the notion of managing or 'governing' the self have become central to contemporary existence. Individuals increasingly manage their lives as a project, encompassing health, diet, lifestyle (Giddens, 1991), psychic well-being (Rose, 1989) and career (Grey, 1994). At the social level too, every day we are told that 'as a society' we must have a 'strategy' to deal with crime, poverty or energy. The economy must be 'managed' (Miller and Rose, 1990), so too must international relations. So management has become a much wider issue than the control of work organizations. In this sense, management becomes a form of politics beyond the state (Rose and Miller, 1992). Given that our focus here is upon management education, we cannot discuss in depth the argument we have outlined here. Instead, we turn to some specific aspects of the political dimensions of management education.

Management Education and the New Right

Whether the argument about management and totalitarianism is accepted, it is nevertheless plain that there exist a number of connections between what we have been claiming about management education and recent developments in the UK polity. An apocryphal story has it that Margaret Thatcher, when told by a Cambridge undergraduate that she was studying Ancient Norse, commented that this was 'a luxury'. What this underlines is that New Right governments have conceptualized education in terms of its functional utility to the economy. There can be little doubt that the exponential growth of management degree courses in the 1980s reflected the notion that such degrees were desirable because of their usefulness. For individuals this may only have meant that such courses appeared to encourage better job prospects, but for New Right theorists the management student seemed altogether more worthy than the much demonized 'lefty sociology' student, preaching revolution at the taxpayers' expense. More specifically, the growth of MBA programmes in the 1980s was an intrinsic part of the 'yuppie phenomenon'.

The relationship between management and the New Right is complex. Although the rhetoric of the New Right was about the ability of markets to determine resource allocation autonomously, managers were essential to its social vision. The assault on trade unionism vas in part an attempt to create a second managerial revolution in which managers had their hands 'untied', leaving them free to manage. Whilst there is some evidence that the Thatcher governments were dismayed by the failure of management to take full advantage of this new freedom, managers remained an essential part of the New Right programme. Nowhere has this been more obvious than in the public sector where, paradoxically, managerial bureaucracy has been used as the means to create a free market. Equally, in many policy areas, the invocation of the 'businessman' (sic) as the fount of all knowledge has been widespread. Thus businessmen are seen to be able to offer a unique insight into education, social work and healthcare, as well as economic policy. Within this general lionization of managers, management education became an almost uniquely favoured field of academia.

If management subjects became the acceptable face of universities in the 1980s (and there is much more that could be written about that), then, at the same time, the commonsense orientation we have described above became one of the dominant ideologies. Although much of New Right thinking was predicated upon more or less sophisticated versions of laissez-faire economics, its populist appeal was articulated in terms of commonsense (a striking example being Thatcher's 'housewife' analogy for government finances). This trend has become even more heavily emphasized by John Major in his call to get 'back to basics', perhaps because of the lack of even the pretence of a coherent economic and political theory. At the present time, most obviously in recent speeches by Michael Portillo and Prince Charles, commonsense is used as an explicit rallying call against 'so-called experts' in all fields, but especially social policy. Somehow it is believed that if only 'the British' – or even the 'English' – could recover their commonsense from the corrupting effects of 1960s liberals and armchair theorists then, miraculously, traditional values would be restored and, with them, economic success and social harmony.

We do not have space to elaborate on the simultaneously facile and vicious character of these prescriptions. But their banal horror can be seen to be congruent with the commonsensical attitudes displayed by management students and connived in and reproduced by many mainstream managerialist academics. For what management education commonly does is to perpetuate an attitude which leaves inviolate students' prejudices and assumptions about the world. Students demand that their teachers do not disrupt their world-views with complicated theories and critical questions, but instead provide useful facts, models and techniques: most of their teachers slavishly obey. However, it is an abdication of pedagogical responsibility in management education to avoid the moral, political, social and philosophical issues which management raises. It is not intellectually tenable to avoid such issues since they are always *pre-supposed* whenever 'techniques' are taught. Nor is it possible to truncate these issues by subsuming them into a managerialist frame, as with Business Ethics or Women in Management courses. What is necessary in management education is for teachers to assume responsibility for asking serious, critical questions of management, rather than obsequiously adhering to the values of managers and the commonsense prejudices of students.

What is created, in part by the abdication of this responsibility, is the view that the values embodied in management practice are simply 'the way things are', a reality which is unquestioned in terms of its historical and social construction and unchallenged by the spectre of other possibilities. Here again there is a resonance with Marcuse's critique of contemporary modes of totalitarianism:

> The Happy Consciousness – the belief that the real is rational and that the system delivers the goods – reflects the new conformism which is a facet of technological rationalities translated into social behaviour. (Marcuse, 1964/1986: 84)

The conformism induced by the tyranny of commonsense is obviously not confined to, nor simply a product of, management education. But management education occupies a pivotal point between politics, work and intellectual activity. The fact that this is not even recognized by the dominant mainstream of management academics is not simply an indictment of students, managers or politicians (although all of these groups have their own responsibilities) but of management academics themselves.

Concluding Remarks

In this paper we have sought to raise fundamental questions about the nature of management education. In so doing, we join those writers who are beginning to articulate a demand for a management education which takes the intellectual rigour of critical management research and translates it directly into courses on management (Anthony, 1986; Nord and Jermier, 1992; Reed and Anthony, 1992; Willmott, 1994; French and Grey, forthcoming).

We believe that it is indefensible for critical approaches to management to be marginalized as an esoteric research interest. It is also indefensible for management academics to continue working in the managerialist frame, not because they disagree[9] with critical approaches but because they do not even attempt to engage with them. Critical work on management has mounted a serious intellectual challenge to managerialism, but many management academics seem to see it not just as possible but as desirable to act as if no challenge existed, and to pass on to students knowledge which is at best problematic and at worst discredited. What other academic discipline would proceed in such a fashion? It is as if biologists ignored the theory of evolution, or chemists treated the atom as an invisible particle. What would we say if biologists or chemists ignored such developments because to do otherwise would disrupt the commonsense views of their students and employers?

Our answer to this question is that we would say that they had abdicated their fundamental intellectual responsibilities, and this is exactly what the mainstream of management academics has done.

Notes

1. By 'management education' we mean teaching and research on management as practised in universities whether at undergraduate or postgraduate level or as a subsidiary course of study for students of other subjects. This is consistent with Willmott's (1994) distinction between management education and management training. Where relevant, we have drawn distinctions between, in particular, undergraduate and MBA and other postgraduate courses.

2. Thus, for example, Women in Management courses may raise issues of gender discrimination in work organizations by conceptualizing the problem as the fact that women do not share equally in the symbolic and material rewards which male managers enjoy. But this stops short of raising questions about the role of gendered inequality in the maintenance of capitalist social relations, or the problematic masculinity of hierarchical and competitive ways of organizing production.

3. This encompasses our experience as students (of various subjects) at six institutions in two countries and as teachers in seven institutions during 14 years, as well as discussions with colleagues in management education in numerous institutions in several countries.

4. We do not imply that the use of case studies is an inherently managerialist approach to management education. On the contrary, case studies can and are equally used in critical management education to illustrate, develop and clarify arguments. What we are identifying by this remark is the use of case studies as a device to avoid critical reflection by appealing to the practical effectiveness, and therefore desirability, of what is being taught. This has been a traditional mainstay of management pedagogy as defined by the 'Harvard Model' (now abandoned at Harvard).

5. By instrumental rationality we mean a rationality which is concerned only with the adoption of the most appropriate means to achieve a given end, as opposed to reflection upon the rationality and desirability of ends themselves.

6. The opposite, in fact, of the classical meaning of education!

7. The idea that social relations are uncontrollable is one which may be unfamiliar in mainstream management education, where there is an assumption that such control is not only desirable but possible. The issues here are complex, but in essence the argument is that people, unlike physical objects, have the capacity to respond to, resist and reject attempts to control them, and always engage in interpretation, re-interpretation and mis-interpretation of their circumstances. In management, this is perhaps most obvious in the attempt to manage culture. Many writers (e.g. Anthony, 1994) have argued that such attempts will always be limited by the nature of human existence. More generally, we can see that the constant reworking of techniques of management control is evidence that it is not possible to find a formula which unambiguously 'works'.

8. Of course, those managers with academic qualifications will have an interest in claiming the value of those qualifications despite any misgivings. Equally, we recognize that students will often genuinely derive personal benefit from at least some elements within their courses.

9. To underline a point we made in the introduction, it is not our intention to argue that all management educators should take a particular political or intellectual line. But we do believe that, whatever line they take, it should be on the basis of an intellectual engagement with other positions rather than on one of ignoring other positions. This comment applies quite as much to critical as to managerialist academics.

Bibliography

Alvesson, M. and Willmott, H., eds (1992) *Critical Management Studies*. London: Sage.

Anthony, P. (1986) *The Foundations of Management*. London: Tavistock.

Anthony, P. (1994) *Managing Culture*. Milton Keynes: Open University Press.

Binns, D. (1993) 'TQM and the New Right: Towards a Critique of Bureaucratic Totalitarianism', paper presented at the Labour Process Conference, Blackpool, UK.

Burchell, S., Clubb, C., Hopwood, A., Hughes, H. and Naphapiet, J. (1980) 'The Role of Accounting in Organizations and Society', *Accounting, Organizations and Society* 5(1): 5–27.

Chomsky, N. (1969) 'The Responsibility of Intellectuals', in T. Roszack (ed.) *The Dissenting Academy*. Harmondsworth: Penguin.

Cooper, R. and Burrell, G. (1988) 'Modernism, Postmodernism and Organisational Analysis: An Introduction', *Organisation Studies* 9(1): 91–112.

Ferguson, K. (1984) *The Feminist Case Against Bureaucracy*. Philadelphia, PA: Temple University Press.

Firat, A., Dholakia, N. and Bagozzi, R., eds (1987) *Philosophical and Radical Thought in Marketing*. Lexington, MA: D.C. Heath.

French, R. (1993) 'All Work is a Placement: An Analysis of Assumptions about Learning Possibilities Associated with a Work Placement', *MEAD* 24(4): 364–72.

French, R. and Grey, C., eds (forthcoming) *New Perspectives on Management Education*. London: Sage.

Freire, P. (1971) *Pedagogy of the Oppressed*. Harmondsworth: Penguin.

Freire, P. (1974) *Education: The Practice of Freedom*. Harmondsworth: Penguin.

du Gay, P. and Salaman, G. (1992) 'The (Cult)ure of the Customer', *Journal of Management Studies* 29(5): 615–33.

Giddens, A. (1991) *Modernity and Identity. Self and Society in High Modernity*. Cambridge: Polity Press.

Grey, C. (1994) 'Career as a Project of the Self and Labour Process Discipline', *Sociology* 28(2): 479–97.

Grey, C. (1994a) 'Life is Elsewhere: Reflections on the Real World', Working Paper, University of Leeds.

Grey, C., Knights, D., Shaoul, M. and Willmott, H. (1991) 'Beyond Positive Knowledge: Towards a Critical Pedagogy of Management', paper presented at Management Education in an Academic Context, Uppsala, Sweden.

Grey, C., Knights, D., Shaoul, M. and Willmott, H. (forthcoming) 'Towards a Critical Pedagogy of Management' in R. French and C. Grey (eds) *New Perspectives on Management Education*. London: Sage.

Harrison, R. (1993) *Human Resource Management. Issues and Strategies*. Wokingham: Addison-Wesley.

Henry, J., ed. (1991) *Creative Management*. London: Sage.

Kerfoot, D. and Knights, D. (1993) 'Managerial Evangelism: Quality Management in the Financial Services', paper presented at EGOS Conference, Paris, France.

Linder, J. and Smith, H. (1992) The Complex Case of Management Education', *Harvard Business Review* September/October: 16–33.

MacIntyre, A. (1981) *After Virtue*. London: Duckworth.

Marcuse, H. (1964/1986) *One-Dimensional Man*. London: Routledge.

Miller, P. and Rose, N. (1990) 'Governing Economic Life', *Economy and Society* 19(1): 1–31.

Nord, W. and Jermier, J. (1992) 'Critical Social Science for Managers? Promising and Perverse Possibilities', in H. Willmott and M. Alvesson (eds) *Critical Management Studies*. London: Sage.

Orwell, G. (1949) *1984.* London: Secker and Warburg.

Peters, T.J. (1989) *Thriving on Chaos.* London: Pan.

Reed, M. (1992) *The Sociology of Organisations.* Hemel Hempstead: Harvester Wheatsheaf.

Reed, M. and Anthony, P. (1992) 'Professionalising Management and Managing Profession-alisation: British Management in the 1980s', *Journal of Management Studies* 29(5): 591–613.

Roberts, J. (1984) 'The Moral Character of Management Practice', *Journal of Management Studies* 21(4): 287–302.

Rose, N. (1989) *Governing the Soul.* London: Routledge.

Rose, N. and Miller, P. (1992) 'Political Power Beyond the State: Problematics of Government', *British Journal of Sociology* 43(2): 173–205.

Tinker, T. (1985) *Paper Prophets: A Social Critique of Accounting.* New York: Praeger.

Townley, B. (1993) 'Performance Appraisal and the Emergence of Management', *Journal of Management Studies* 30(2): 221–38.

Weil, S. (1933/1988) *Oppression and Liberty.* London: Routledge.

Willmott, H. (1993) 'Strength is Ignorance; Slavery is Freedom: Managing Culture in Modern Organizations', *Journal of Management Studies* 30(4): 515–52.

Willmott, H. (1994) 'Management Education: Provocations to a Debate', *Management Learning* 25(1): 105–36.

Wilson, B. (1984) *Systems: Concepts, Methodologies and Applications.* Chichester: Wiley.

9

Gordon E. Dehler, M. Ann Welsh and Marianne W. Lewis

Critical Pedagogy in the 'New Paradigm'

'the absence of any serious discussion of pedagogy in cultural studies and in the debates about higher education has narrowed significantly the possibilities for redefining the role of educators as public intellectuals and of students as critical citizens capable of governing rather than simply being governed.' (Giroux, 1997: 259)

The reform movement in management education has gained considerable support in the past decade. But transcending the simplification agenda of management orthodoxy has proved troublesome. Grey and French (1996: 9–10) have persuasively critiqued the enduring assumptions underlying traditional conceptions of management education, contending that 'much critical research suggests that management knowledge is not just undesirable but inaccurate. For example, the assumption in much managerialist work of rationality in organizations ... has been widely challenged.' Yet, business curricula persist in privileging rationality and quantitative techniques in direct opposition to calls made by alumni and corporate leaders over a decade ago for greater attention to behaviorally oriented subject matter (Porter and McKibbin, 1988).

Attempts to understand the complexity of management have been approached in a Newtonian attempt to simplify and segment it into separate functional endeavors. Indeed, creating look-alike textbooks and teaching management from a reductionist 'principles' approach have resulted in analogously simplistic and ultimately sterile notions of management as a set of 'content' areas to be 'learned'. Rather than being something that people (including non-managers) in organizations *do*, this fragmented view bounded the domain as a technically grounded content arena in the same vein as operations, finance, or information systems. Students learn management 'content' as separate from – to be added on to rather than *integrated into* – the technically grounded business functions.

These approaches to management as an organizationally based activity have been robustly criticized in the pages of *Management Learning* and elsewhere, of course. With few exceptions, however, elaboration of critical views of management-as-technical-activity has emanated primarily from the UK (e.g. Reed and Anthony, 1992; Willmott, 1984). In the US, scholarly views continue to be constrained by a shoot-the-messenger hegemony. Management scholars who offer thoughtful critiques of business curricula, and their embedded institutionalized pedagogies risk 'cultural suicide' (Brookfield, 1994) by challenging conventional assumptions of managerialist business programs.

This article addresses three topics relevant to the ongoing debate. First, we contribute to the work of an expanding cadre of organizational scholars who constitute the movement toward a more explicit 'new paradigm' of management thought and education. Grounding our fundamental argument in the notion of critical pedagogy (e.g. Barnett, 1997; Giroux, 1997), we posit that management education needs to become both transformational and emancipatory in order to adequately prepare students for the turbulent new century.

Second, we argue that in order for students to comprehend the 'study of management as a socially organized, and not a technically determined, activity' (Willmott, 1994: 106), instructional pedagogies need to overcome longstanding tendencies toward simplification. The complexity of managerial thinking and action needs to be reduced with sufficient clarity that students can comprehend its essence, while simultaneously *raising* their own level of complicatedness in order to grasp that extant complexity. That is, in the teaching of management we face the challenge of creating a learning context whereby students create meaning and personal interpretation with respect to 'managing' while also enhancing their own 'complicated understanding' (Bartunek et al., 1983). We contend that 'effective' instruction is developmental and thereby oriented toward helping students create more sophisticated knowledge structures. This is the starting point for creating a genuinely critical education, however, this is only the starting point.

Third, we extend the notion of complicated understanding into the realm of critical pedagogy and management education by arguing that achieving a complicated understanding is as important for educators as students. We conclude by highlighting the potential for student emancipation and transformational potential unleashed by critical reflection on knowledge, self, and the world (Barnett, 1997). The ultimate aim of this work is to begin transformation of both the outcomes of management education and the instructional pedagogies employed to achieve those outcomes.

The Minefield of Management Orthodoxy

The tenets of command and control grounded in Weberian bureaucracy and Taylorism evolved into a set of taken-for-granted assumptions underlying management orthodoxy. On the education side, preparing managers for the industrial era was a relatively straightforward process, based on the simplification of the management discipline. This simplification imperative manifested itself in many ways – all surrounded in the trappings of rationality. Pressures for accountability from external constituents, adoption of functional and managerialist agendas, relevance concerns raised in the arenas of research and instruction, and resource considerations all contribute to and provide reinforcement for an agenda of simplification.

The first source of pressure stems from the increasing calls for account-ability, exemplified by the increasingly close relationship between universities and external constituents, most notably state legislatures and accreditation associations (Willmott, 1995). Miles (1985: 63) long ago presaged current conditions: 'We clearly are in a period of major change, and questions concerning the quality and direction of business education are, therefore, highly appropriate.' Commentary, emanating primarily from the UK, has confronted some basic, yet thorny and potentially threatening, issues involv-ing fundamental assumptions, topical content, programmatic objectives, and institutional aims. Thomas and Anthony (1996) questioned whether what managers learn in management education programs is worthwhile and if it would really matter if management education was eliminated! In a review of more than 200 articles, Cheit (1985: 50) codified 13 main complaints about MBA programs into four categories: they emphasize the wrong model, ignore important work, fail to meet society's needs, and foster undesirable attitudes. At the institutional level, it has been argued that 'universities are being reconstituted as knowledge factories organized by managers, whose aim is to intensify and commodify the production and distribution of knowledge and skills' to any who desire to purchase them (Prichard and Willmott, 1997: 300).

The impact of the increasing intrusiveness by external constituent groups is paradoxical. Closer linkages between universities and their constituents invite a greater opportunity for management educators to be critical of those constituents' policies and practices. At the same time, however, the internal-ization of constituent agendas limits the application of critical thinking to managerialist concerns such as effectiveness, efficiency, and control. Critique that results in practices aimed at promoting greater effectiveness, efficiency or control is acceptable, but is unfortunately also uncritical.

A second thrust of the simplification movement revolves around the adoption of reductionist agendas. Business schools' (rational) response to the rising demand for accredited programs led to an increased reliance on economics and other rationally based quantitative methodologies. For exam-ple, Grey and French (1996) and Pfeffer (1997) challenged the reliance upon rationality assumptions introduced especially from classical economics. Even noted economist Lester Thurow acknowledged the irony that 'major theoretical foundations of economics survive despite lack of empirical support . . . primarily because they assume sophisticated form devoid of factual content' (Cheit, 1985: 50).

A key assumption of management orthodoxy is that only those who hold 'management' positions engage in 'managerial' activities! Consequently, the dominant focus in educational orthodoxy as played out in business school curricula led to a 'prevailing managerialist and functionalist perspective' (Pfeffer, 1997: 178) with an instrumental orientation grounded in the trappings of technical rationality (e.g. Roberts, 1996). A core artifact of this perspective was the principles of management movement, which thrived into the 1980s before withering (but not disappearing) in the shadow of growing critique (e.g. Carroll and Gillen, 1987; Hales, 1986; Willmott, 1984). These phenomena further impact management education programs by rationalizing business curricula. This occurs through the quantitative technical thrust driven by perceived operational and instrumental needs as well as by the de-legitimization of 'management' as a broad-based context in favor of its presentation as a more narrow set of self-contained 'content' areas virtually disconnected from other business activities.

A couple of examples are illustrative. At the program level, consider this brief discussion between a management faculty member and an MBA program director:

Director: The real 'drivers' of organizations are operations, marketing and finance.

Faculty: Hmmm . . . Don't you think that an equally critical activity is 'management' – the ability to integrate, or coordinate, those functions?

Director: Well . . . no.

Faculty: Oh? What, then, do you think 'management' is?

Director: 'Management' is organizational behavior, organization theory, human resource management, strategy.

At the level of individual courses and topics, Watson (1996) captured an unintentionally humorous (or distressing) example with 'Motivation: that's Maslow, isn't it?' – an actual student response to a query about prior learning on motivation! Students treated motivation as an 'academically-defined topic, as opposed to a task or function to be carried out by a manager' (p. 453). This outcome is readily applicable to other topics. As Watson points out, management knowledge has 'become a series of packages of formalized in-formation' (p. 447). These two examples convey a vital message for manage-ment educators and program directors: business schools persist in emphasizing the wrong model of management education (Porter and McKibbin, 1988). This occurs in large part because 'mainstream approaches to transition are still dominated by concerns for prescription, linearity and the maintenance of order' (Jeffcutt, 1996: 172) and certification (Dore, 1976). Separately, as well as collectively, these changes lead to the establishment of evaluation and control structures disguised under the rubric of strategic planning or operational efficiency.

A third source of simplification emanates from calls for 'relevance', in terms of the research produced by management scholars as well as curricula. Issues pertinent to relevance and practicality in management research have been discussed elsewhere (e.g. Dehler, 1998; Goldberg, 1996). On the instruction side, Grey (1996: 12–13) refers to the 'shibboleth' of relevance, 'Orthodox management education must drop its insistent demand for relevance and utility' and 'recognize the nature of its failures'. Appeals for approaches relevant to the 'real world', driven by contemporary notions of quality and consumerism, are leading to a conformity 'induced by the tyranny of commonsense' (Grey and Mitev, 1995: 87).

The final aspect of simplification can be seen in the arena of resources. Institutionally this is exacerbated by the reduction in traditional resources and the consequent increased dependence on external constituents (especially the business community) for support. In their provocative critique of business schools, Crainer and Dearlove (1999) emphasize the tension between pursuing the demands of an academic institution and managing themselves as businesses. Revenue streams take priority over academic endeavors, leading many business schools to become hotel and restaurant operators, where catering capabilities outweigh academic ones, and 'bedroom occupancy is increasingly a measure of how successful a business school is' (p. 136). This also extends to devoting resources to building alumni relations as a form of 'begging bowl' – MBA graduates represent a 'huge reservoir of alumni waiting to be tapped' for contributions (p. 138). Funding shifts requiring institutions to raise a greater proportion of their own revenues have led to the interpretation of assessment requirements as an opportunity to demonstrate their internalization of the various constituent agendas in an effort to sustain or acquire funding (Barnett, 1997; Giroux, 1997; Willmott, 1995). The boundaries between business organizations and management schools are becoming increasingly permeable as businesses take a heightened interest in curricular matters, e.g. education for jobs and technicist modes of learning and teaching (Grey and Mitev, 1995).

Thus the dilemma posed by the arguments made in this article stems from the reliance on instrumental, rational, positivist approaches that attempt to essentially *remove* (or deny) uncertainty and complexity from the analysis of organizations and managing. Beck (1994: 237) contends that 'the reality of managerial work is much more complex than this [functions] model would suggest'. By stubbornly adhering to the tenets of management orthodoxy, a false simplicity is cast on both organizations and the management of them. But the world has changed and according to one view, there 'is little reliable evidence that management education in general and the MBA in particular contribute to improved managerial performance' (Thomas and Anthony, 1996: 30).

As the precepts of management orthodoxy bear increased scrutiny, it follows that the preparation of students also needs to diverge from traditional approaches. The result is emerging agreement that management educators are in the throes of a paradigm shift as well. In business, Zohar (1997: 32–3) points out that the dominant Newtonian-based serial thinking approach 'does not tolerate nuance or ambiguity'. She explains that associative learning processes construct routine responses to patterns after trial-and-error and sensemaking activities. This includes tacit learning that can handle nuance and ambiguity, but still lacks the ability to articulate protocols to share with others as would Schon's (1983) 'reflective practitioner'. Instead, Zohar favors quantum thinking – holistic, self-organizing, and possessing the capacity to question itself, i.e. double-loop learning. The key point is that this approach moves 'away from certainty, toward an appreciation for pluralism and diversity, toward an acceptance of ambiguity and paradox, of complexity rather than simplicity' (1997: 9).

The challenge management educators face then is to 'prepare managers "for the complexity, uncertainty, uniqueness and value conflicts"' (Beck,

1994: 239, quoting Schon, 1983) found in the emerging new paradigm of business (e.g. Raelin and Schermerhorn, 1994; Ray and Rinzler, 1993). This speaks to raising the level of students' 'complicated understanding'.

Complicating Understanding in Management Education

The notion of 'complicated understanding' is not new, of course. But it does serve management educators well in providing an overarching concept to guide instructional philosophy, to design learning opportunities for students, and to strive for challenging learning outcomes that serve students' needs. Its underlying premise is fairly straightforward. Complicated understanding involves 'increasing the variety of ways [events] can be understood' (Bartunek et al., 1983: 282), i.e. being able to see and interpret organizational phenomena and environmental events from more than one perspective (Weick, 1979). After perceiving a situation from multiple perspectives, people then 'achieve an integration that incorporates the different perspectives' (p. 275).

Fostering more complicated understanding ultimately falls to 'designing management education programs that might increase complexity in managers' (Bartunek et al., 1983: 276). Building on Willmott's (1994: 106–7) argument that in critical management study managerial work should be theorized as 'a social and political practice', the pedagogical challenge is to 'make management education more personally meaningful for students of management'.

A number of critical scholars, have made similar comments. For instance, Caproni and Arias (1997: 301) argued that 'skills in self-reflexivity and cultural critique are designed to *complicate* rather than simplify the manager's life' (emphasis added). Prasad and Cavanaugh (1997: 312) note that 'critical management scholarship's focus on *contradictions* . . . seeks to draw organizational analysis away from the naivete of functionalism'. Grey and Mitev (1995: 84) call for teachers 'to expand rather than restrict the ways in which students regard the world'. Finally, Linstead (1996: 21) describes a pedagogy that develops the manager as anthropologist, enhancing learning and understanding by taking the perspectives of others and testing those views, and engaging in self-critique. The 'key factor in the manufacture of meaning in organizations' ultimately entails 'treating the process as problematic and meaning as an emergent property' (p. 17).

Accepting that understanding 'management' in a new business context requires richer conceptualizations, it follows that teaching and learning necessitate innovative pedagogies that both capture and convey these more complex notions. In the next section we present the fundamentals of a critical pedagogy. Our intent is to link critical pedagogy with management education and learning. Acknowledging calls for bringing a critical perspective to content, Reynolds (1997: 312) argues that 'educational *methodology* should equally reflect a critical position'. Similarly, Barnett (1997) contends that the goal of higher education should be the development of critical beings. Finally, Giroux (1997) offers some specific suggestions on how to engage in critical pedagogy. After outlining the arguments made by these scholars, we then examine the use of a critical pedagogy in educating managers.

The Domain and Practice of Critical Pedagogy

In the 'dawning of a new era' (Beck, 1994: 231), the challenge for management educators is to overcome the hegemony of simplification. The starting point is to adopt the 'premise that the nature of "management" is complex, ambiguous, contradictory and uncertain', where management educators incorporate the '*complexity* of "management" and the social and political dimensions of "managerial practice" in the content and delivery' of their courses (Thompson and McGivern, 1996: 23, emphasis in original). Thus, rather than reducing management knowledge and action to simplistic notions, the aim of educational endeavors would instead seek to resist 'conceptual closure' (Chia and Morgan, 1996).

This calls for 'teachers to assume responsibility for asking serious, critical questions of management, rather than obsequiously adhering to the values of managers' (Grey and Mitev, 1995: 86). This opens the door for critical education and the development of critical beings – individuals in whom critical thinking underscores action, reason, and reflection (Barnett, 1997). Barnett extends critical thinking beyond disciplinary competence (knowledge) to include critical self-reflection and critical action in the world. For students to become critical beings, they need to master the highest levels of critique across all three domains.

Development of critically based education is consistent with Giroux's (1981) and Reynolds' (1997) definitions of critical pedagogy. To produce a critical setting for management education, Barnett, Giroux, and Reynolds concur that both radical content and radical process are required in order to truly complicate student understanding. In order for critical pedagogy to be enacted in the domain of management education, however, at least three aspects must undergo change: the roles and responsibilities of faculty and students, curricular content, and pedagogical methods.

Roles and Responsibilities

Critical pedagogy requires redefining the roles of both faculty and student to embrace a wider conception of their respective critical tasks (Barnett, 1997; Giroux, 1997). At the most fundamental level, this requires an inversion of self-understanding of faculty as educators (Barnett, 1997: 112). Learning is ultimately the responsibility of the student; the educator's task is to create a space in which learning can occur. This raises two questions: What do we mean by this role reversal? And why does it foster critical education?

Teaching should be positioned as part of the research process, not an outcome of it. This suggests that educators can no longer hide behind *conceptual* distinctions between teaching and research. This view presents institutional, pedagogical, and personal implications.

Institutionally, this means a shift in perceptions of and rewards for teaching scholarship. The generation of knowledge speaks as much to teaching as to traditional disciplinary research. Arguments over the value added by each activity (a staple in promotion and tenure discussions) miss the point *and are themselves uncritical.* It is not a matter of demonstrating the equal value of these activities – as this serves the instrumental ends of placating constituencies instead of meeting critical needs. The critical response illustrates that teaching and research are inseparable. It also refutes the conventional belief that faculty are disinterested, that knowledge is unproblematic, and that teaching is simply a means of transmitting information to students (Giroux, 1997; Reynolds, 1997).

Pedagogically, a critical approach means imparting to students the concept of learning as an unfolding process of inquiry to be approached in a genuinely critical way. All agendas (faculty *and student*) must be taken seriously leading to critical assessments across the broadest range of issues. And, if students are to be given the space to form their own critical evaluations, then the educational process cannot just be cognitive, it should also be part of their learning experience. Students must not only engage in substantive learning to develop disciplinary competence, but they need to develop the capacity for critical reflection to evaluate that understanding and its epistemologic underpinnings (Giroux, 1997; Reynolds, 1999). Students may become proficient with material – able to question, reflect on and assess fundamental concepts and categories. But while this demonstrates critical thinking skills, it remains uncritical. Students must move beyond to evaluate the origins and structure of their discipline, its current social functions, and its underlying ideologies – the way it shapes human beings and society (Barnett, 1997; Reynolds, 1997).

Considering the personal implications, faculty 'have their own hidden agenda' (Reynolds, 1999: 181) and must demonstrate that their own favored intellectual frameworks are subject to critique. This explicitly acknowledges the limitations of the frameworks in which their intellectual identity is based (Giroux, 1997), thereby placing faculty and students on the same epistemologic ground. This point is crucial. When the contestability of any and all ideas (even one's own) is recognized, a learning space is created where critical commentary becomes something not to be feared but to be relished and embraced. Barnett (1997: 71) emphasizes this point,

> With understanding of this kind, with a sense that the next book, lecture or experiment is not going to yield all the secrets on even one small topic, a critical stance opens up. All knowledge claims are understood to have an element of openness, they do not close off debate but, on the contrary, their being made serves only to open up debate.

Curricular Content

But debate about what? Both criticalists (e.g. Habermas, 1978) and post-modernists (e.g. Foucault, 1980) focus upon the socially constructed and sustained nature of knowledge as well as its backing by powerful interests. With respect to management learning, an appreciation of the wider context of power relationships impacting curricular content (as well as the potential for change) requires us to examine several aspects of the environment in which management education is occurring.

As Barnett (1997) points out, Schon's (1983) reflective practitioner is really a description of a contemporary professional. In educating our students to be reflective, we ask them to reflect on society and its institutions as they are. Emphasis on skill building is based on the assumption that knowledge for its own sake should take a back seat to knowledge that is immediately useful, i.e. instrumental knowledge. Employing critical thinking as 'a disciplined approach to problem solving' (Reynolds, 1999: 173) presumes that problems are straightforward – easy to diagnose and resolve. Such curricular intent is then typically reinforced by a pedagogy grounded in rational technique. Building a curriculum around these critical thinking skills may develop students with disciplinary competence – yet this is a necessary, but insufficient, condition for critical beings. This point is especially relevant for management educators. Management is neither neutral nor disinterested. Managers, through power and position, affect other people's lives and their future. In a similar sense, management educators affect others via the development and dissemination of knowledge in their disciplines.

So, if our current definition and emphasis on critical thinking falls short, what are we to do? Reynolds (1997: 315) calls for curricula that provide students with the opportunity to question assumptions, understand power relationships, and engage in critical reflection with a collective focus. If students are to learn to question assumptions, they must be not only exposed to a wide variety of topics, but more importantly, they must be exposed to *critical treatments* of those topics. For example, discussions of strategy might explicitly focus upon whose interests are being served; discussions of structure might explicitly consider a range of work designs and who is privileged by autocratic, bureaucratic, or democratic arrangements; discussions of new product development might explicitly incorporate issues of sustainability (Alvesson and Willmott, 1992).

Raising issues critically exposes the relationships between power, knowledge, and their managerial consequences. At the same time, students should be reminded that the educational system of which they are a part is itself based on asymmetries of power, 'Knowledge and professional practice can be constructed in ways which support and maintain those arrangements' (Reynolds, 1997: 315). Understanding the embedded network of power relationships (and their own place within them) helps students develop a strategy for personal inquiry that follows from a view of management as a political, cultural, and ideological phenomenon. Such research is self-consciously motivated by an effort to discredit forms of management that underscore the narrow instrumentality of work-process relationships (Alvesson and Willmott, 1992).

Finally, Reynolds (1998: 183) contends that '*critical reflection* is the corner-stone of emancipatory approaches to education' and speaks to curricular content and pedagogical issues. The aim of management education should be to 'encourage [students] in questioning and confronting the social and political forces which provide the context of their work, and in questioning claims of "common sense" or "the way things should be"' (p. 198). Citing the individualist cast of many pedagogical methods as well as the historical, political, and social nature of management knowledge, Reynolds (1997) suggests that critical reflection is a means for students to overcome the individualism inherent in many experientially-based pedagogies and understand that management is practiced in community. Drawing on an example from Alvesson and Willmott (1992: 7), exposure to material on the historical, political, and social underpinnings of management thought enables the student who is reflecting upon an incompetent manager to move beyond technical and instrumental commentary to consideration of a system in which managers are not held accountable to their subordinates. As critical beings *and* managers, they have the potential to begin to make organizational relationships less exploitative. This is where issues of classroom process become so significant – it is through this experience that students begin to become critically reflective (Barnett, 1997).

Pedagogical Methods

Giroux (1997) presents critical pedagogy as theoretical insights and practices about conditions articulated within a particular context. We extend these ideas to the study of management and power by addressing not only how management is shaped, produced, diffused, and transformed, but also how it is actually taken up within specific organizations. Further, critical pedagogy is deliberately transformational, as it intentionally operates from a perspective in which teaching and learning are committed to expanding rather than restricting the opportunities for students to be social, political, and economic agents (Giroux, 1997).

Among the criticisms of extant treatments of critical pedagogy is that they are long on theory and short on technique, as in, 'how do I implement critical pedagogy in my classroom?' That is, how can management educators create classroom spaces which challenge students to (1) question assumptions, (2) explicitly recognize power relationships in their analysis of managerial situations, and (3) engage with other students in collaborative efforts to critically reflect upon the embedded network of management relationships and to consider alternatives for its transformation (Reynolds, 1997)?

Three themes emerge from the literature on critical pedagogy: de-centering power in the classroom, challenging disciplinary boundaries, and taking up issues in a genuinely problematizing way. We discuss each of these themes briefly and, in the next section, they are examined in the context of curricular choice and classroom activities.

De-centering the classroom is where critical pedagogy enters the debate on the relative virtues of teaching-centered and student-centered classrooms (e.g. Barr and Tagg, 1995). While a student-centered classroom is certainly an improvement over continuation of the dominant teacher tradition, a de-centered classroom is one where faculty and student stand on the same epistemologic ground – recognizing that all issues are contestable (Giroux, 1997) – and engage in a common journey toward what Barnett (1997: 55) calls 'hermaneutical understanding': attempts toward understanding for mutual respect rather than for instrumental ends. Raab (1997) provides a wonderfully rich example of a faculty member's struggle to de-center her classroom. She develops the faculty role as an 'Expert In Not Knowing' where the role becomes one of refusing to tell (i.e. be the 'Expert in Knowing') in an effort to get students to start depending upon their own knowledge and experience as they try to gain more of each. This opens space for students to engage in critical self-reflection.

Giroux (1997) speaks to the issue of challenging disciplinary boundaries at great length through a hybridized space or borderland where these domains overlap and interact. His intent is to expose students to the widest possible array of domains and disciplines. Then, through critique, students become sensitive to the social and political character of thought and of its acquisition by individuals. Working within this space provides a location for discourse that is fundamentally critical. Further, it establishes the foundation for activities (frequently writing) in which students learn to take up issues in a problematic way.

Problematizing means developing a general conceptual scheme organized around a core idea or problem in which the interests and agendas of specific people in specific situations are represented. This, then, provides a range of puzzles for people to identify the values and perspectives which underlie various treatments of the issue (Brookfield, 1995; Dehler and Welsh, 1998; Reed, 1992). When students problematize an issue, they become active knowledge producers instead of passive recipients. Their focus shifts from articulating the meaning in other people's theories to theorizing their *own* experience within the context of the texts, ideological positions, and theories that are introduced as part of the course. In this way, students will come to see how other people's theories serve to position students as a consequence of their institutional and ideological authority. Once understood as a student, it is a short step to understanding how managers are similarly positioned as a consequence of dominant theories about organizations. When this forms the basis for critical reflection, students are demonstrating the best of intentional learning (Dehler, 1996), i.e. they activate prior knowledge, relate old to new in reflective ways, reach conclusions, and assess those conclusions before settling upon them. When this occurs, students have become independent or, in the language of critical pedagogy, 'emancipated' learners.

Summary

By definition, critical pedagogy is context based. This section has discussed critical pedagogy with an emphasis on identifying the necessary structural attributes as well as a deeper discussion of what it means in the context of management education. Context, however, is not limited to discipline, rather it extends outward into the wider community of interests, including student experience. For management education, this means that students occupy a learning space in which the concept of 'educating managers' is just as focal an issue as the traditional content topics in management education. Similarly, curricular content needs to be recast to include not just management texts per se, but also historical, philosophical, social, and political treatments of organizations, business, and society. Emphasis on the so-called critical thinking skills, e.g. skill-building, problem solving, and self-reflection, has to be extended to consider the assumptions underlying these skills and to explicitly consider the extent to which their instrumental benefits may mask their critical potential. Finally, three themes that characterize critical classroom process were identified to serve as levers that enable the potential for critical reason to be transformed into the actuality of critical reflection by students.

Invoking Content Critically

Reynolds (1999) points out that critical pedagogy can be expressed in content and process. Although the topic of the organizational behavior content instructors bring to the classroom has been raised previously (e.g. Boje, 1996; Fineman and Gabriel, 1994), from a critical pedagogy perspective instructional considerations have generally ignored the forms and social practices involved in knowledge transmission (Giroux, 1997). If management learning is to achieve the aims of a 'new paradigm', then pedagogical reform needs to distance itself from instructional orthodoxy – particularly its positivist paradigm (Summers et al., 1997).

Central to this initiative are the textbooks and other resources utilized in the classroom to represent the discipline's body of knowledge. The tenets of management orthodoxy would suggest the field is grounded in what Giroux (1997) calls a 'culture of positivism' that generates 'positive knowledge'. In this view, textbooks treat knowledge as a 'storehouse of artifacts constituted as canon', where 'knowledge appears beyond the reach of critical interrogation except at the level of immediate application' (p. 122).

The instructional challenge is to involve students as active producers of meanings, based in part on their own experiences rather than as passive consumers of information, and proceeds toward overcoming the more instrumental 'reproductive theory of schooling' (Giroux, 1997) – to challenge management practice rather than sustain it (Grey and Mitev, 1995). This view, arguably a growing dilemma in business curricula increasingly dependent upon corporate largesse, posits that programs of study covertly 'reproduce the values, social practices, and skills needed for (perpetuating) the dominant corporate order' (Giroux, 1997: 119). Incorporating student voice creates conditions for de-centering power in the classroom, 'where students can be educated to take their place in society from a position of empowerment rather than a position of ideological and economic subordination' (p. 120). The objective, then, is to involve students in the *construction* of knowledge (rather than *transfer* of knowledge).

With respect to classroom resources, power naturally is most evident in the instructor's choice of text and supporting materials. While it may be more efficient for the instructor to select the text (although there are alternative approaches, e.g. no standardized text), the critical aspect arises in terms of *how* the textbook is utilized in the class. In the de-centered classroom, the text becomes one element in the construction of classroom knowledge and most importantly its interplay with values. Textbooks (and their selection) are not value neutral. Students should treat the text as one social construct produced out of multiple discourses (Giroux, 1997). Questioning underlying assumptions, including the place of the author, whose perspective is adopted, for what purposes, and with what ends, becomes part of the students' role in understanding which voices are privileged and which are silenced. Treating teachers and students as critical agents makes all issues raised in the management classroom contestable.

In challenging disciplinary borders, Willmott (1997: 168–9) posits that management textbooks lack 'a way of making sense of the mundane features of managerial work'. From a critical position, the objective is to expose students to a broader array of understandings than typical of traditional texts. This is in large part an issue of what Steffy and Grimes (1986: 326) term 'descriptive epistemology', which 'requires greater breadth of reflection'. Since a text represents and constructs reality, as well as projecting and negotiating social relationships and identities (Fairclough and Hardy, 1997), exploring different pedagogies to engage content can be constructive. Students are not 'neutral technicians' (Willmott, 1997: 168); their constructions of organizational reality 'involve exercises of power which produce and reproduce inequality' (Grey et al., 1996: 105). For example, using ethnographic studies (Willmott, 1994) and stories can surface under-emphasized emotional aspects of organizations (Vince, 1996), drawing attention to feelings, meaning, and experience. The 'truth' of stories lies not in the facts they communicate but in the meanings they convey (Fineman and Gabriel, 1994). In this sense, then, students derive their own meanings from the context in which they are embedded. Management 'knowledge' then becomes more interpretive than objective (Raelin and Schermerhorn, 1994). Students transcend disciplinary borders by developing their own unique insights on social practices.

Management texts have been criticized for failing to provide depictions of organizations as truly experienced by people. When students become active knowledge producers, they begin to create their own (critical) understandings of managerial work rather than merely accumulating 'facts', i.e. developing their 'quality of thinking, not the quantity of what is thought' (Grey et al., 1996: 104). By approaching topics critically, they incorporate their experience in a manner that organizes knowledge in a compelling way –

one in which they can relate and generate interest. But as a byproduct of constructing their own meanings, students are able to identify the contradictions and gaps in the knowledge base when compared to their experience (Watson, 1996). In essence, experience provides 'a way of problematizing rather than validating that experience' (Grey et al., 1996: 100). Problematizing leads to embracing differences or tensions instead of compromising or privileging one understanding.

When creating alternative understandings by illuminating power considerations, wading into the grayness of pedagogical borders and problematizing the organizational context, content that is produced and legitimated so readily in traditional textbooks now becomes more complex. Students are confronted by issues that are complicated rather than simplified, which can only be critically examined when students raise their own level of complexity. The richness of organizational life can be explored, probed, and challenged in a way that people actually experience it rather than by merely looking at it through a window.

Paradox as a Pedagogical Tool

Shifting from content to process, a critical pedagogy requires application of alternative teaching methods – methods that foster student dialogue, critical reflection, and transformation (Reynolds, 1997). Paradox offers a potentially valuable tool in a critical pedagogy. A paradox denotes the simultaneous, and often seemingly absurd, appearance of contradictions. For example, one 'of the most fundamental and striking paradoxes of contemporary management is the pursuit of "participation," "involvement," and "commitment" on the one hand and the urge for control and exercise of power, familiar themes to managers, on the other' (Koot et al., 1996: 11). Such paradoxes are inherently perceptual. Bateson (1972) explained that actors naturally parse phenomena into distinct and polarized (i.e. either/or) perceptions. Yet, in doing so, actors place themselves in a double-bind in which they use their existing and simplified perceptions to comprehend an increasingly ambiguous and multifaceted world, fueling conflict, frustration, and misunderstanding. In contrast, 'working through paradox' entails learning to explore, critique, and embrace contradictions within a more accommodating and holistic (i.e. both/and) perspective.

'Working through paradox' in the classroom entails encouraging students to define and even exaggerate their polarized perceptions, thereby tapping their natural tendency to stress contrast over connections (Lewis and Dehler, 2000). This process allows students to experience the frustrations of the double-bind. By juxtaposing contradictions, such as participation and control, students may learn to debate opposing perspectives, grapple with their simultaneity, and recognize the biases and limitations of their sensemaking processes. The objective is to develop students' capacities for *paradoxical thinking*: the ability to comprehend the complicated interplay of opposites by picturing a paradox in its more complete surroundings (i.e. recognizing the historical, ideological, political, and social context underlying perceptions). Following our framework, we now discuss the role of paradox in de-centering power in the classroom, helping students question disciplinary borders and problematize fundamental theories of management.

Exploring paradox alters power in the classroom through the introduction of ambiguity. Reminiscent of the participation/control paradox in organizations, using paradox as a pedagogical tool requires that the instructor foster a sense of uncertainty and confusion, while maintaining sufficient order to enable students to feel secure enough to express their frustrations and debate opposing views. The surprising nature of paradox serves as provocation. For example, a class might examine a case of organizational redesign: management in an assembly plant implements self-managing teams and a system of employee involvement, while simultaneously stressing the use of time clocks and adherence to a managerially defined organizational mission. As students *and* instructor struggle with mixed messages of participation and control, discourse equalizes their roles in their learning process. Knowledge becomes the product of interactions among students and between students and teacher (Reynolds, 1997).

Multiple disciplinary or paradigmatic theories may serve as lenses to deepen debates and insights (Bartunek et al., 1983). Juxtaposing conflicting understandings creates a space for learning – an opportunity to recognize how differing perspectives coexist and complicate the learning milieu of organizations. Critical perspectives play a particularly vital role by offering a stark contrast to orthodox management principles. For instance, by viewing this same case from conventional economics (e.g. agency theory) and critical sociology (e.g. radical Weberian theory) perspectives, students may recognize how organizations act as mechanisms for fostering efficient transactions and for subtly tightening the 'iron cage'. Divergent lenses enable students to explore the selective focus and blinkers of alternative theories and question their isolation, while helping them critically self-reflect on their own sense-making processes.

Moving beyond insightful, yet partial perspectives requires paradoxical thinking, as students (and instructor) learn to approach management theory and organizational issues skeptical of one-sided and potentially biased viewpoints. The ability to problematize is vital to gaining an awareness of the intricate underpinnings of perceptions. Again, the case of organizational redesign serves as illustration. In class discussion, students (often with instructor playing the role of 'devil's advocate') may critique the assumptions that underlie each perspective. What is the influence of the historical, ideological, political, and social context? Managerial perceptions may be entrenched in orthodox principles of scientific management and Fordism simultaneous to an awareness of tremendous global competition and demands for continuous production improvements and innovation. Managers may view workers and their labor as a means to an end, desiring to enhance operational efficiency and coordination, as well as foster employee commitment. On the other hand, workers may harbor a strong desire to retain control over their craft and skills, viewing participation as just one in a long line of attempts to increase the power of managers and bolster their exclusive identities as 'decision makers'.

Paradoxical thinking requires recognizing that both perceptions may be equally valid. By polarizing their perspectives, however, managers and workers are incapable of realizing their shared interests in cultivating worker skills and creativity to foster high quality and exceptionally flexible production. Class discussions illustrate the need for organizational actors to engage in 'open communication' (Habermas, 1978) – discourse that surfaces underlying assumptions and sensemaking processes, liberating actors to negotiate more humane and mutually beneficial understandings, practices, and identities.

Conclusion

This article opened with a quote from Giroux concerning the necessity for raising issues of critical pedagogy in debates about education if we are to have any hope of revitalizing management education. The precepts of management orthodoxy continue to influence and cast a false simplicity on present-day conceptualizations of organizations, managing, and management learning. Environmental and competitive changes have made the reality of managerial work much more complex than the orthodoxy schema would suggest. It follows that the preparation of students' needs to diverge from traditional approaches as well – creating the catalyst for a paradigm shift in management education.

Understanding 'management' in a new business context requires updated and richer conceptualizations, which in turn call for teaching and learning through innovative pedagogies that both capture and convey these more complex notions. The challenge management educators face is to prepare future managers for complexity, uncertainty, equivocality, and value conflicts, i.e. raise the level of students' complicated understanding. Doing so opens the learning space to connect a critical perspective to content, as well as to critical methodology. The scope of inquiry expands to include aspects of self and the world in addition to disciplinary knowledge and the process of inquiry practiced in democratic classrooms. This is the domain of critical pedagogy.

Producing a critical pedagogy entails recasting the roles of faculty and students in ways that would enable faculty to turn back the trend toward commodification (e.g. Willmott, 1995) and managerialism currently endemic in higher education, and permit students to achieve an education that sensitizes them to the myriad possibilities for improving human existence. Within the realm of management learning, the aim of a critical pedagogy is 'the empowerment of individuals and an infusion of democratic action into social institutions' (Steffy and Grimes, 1992: 195) – a more explicit focus on social change (Pfeffer, 1997). According to Burgoyne and Jackson (1997: 62), critical management education highlights the continual tension between the emancipatory process of giving divergent views a chance and exposing such deviant thoughts to monitoring and control. This emancipates students as they come to understand the persistence of tension, anxiety, and doubt in the manager's role is a product of the contradictions inherent in current management systems rather than as a statement of their performance potential as managers (Willmott, 1997: 168). Students gain

> the willingness to see one's own world from other perspectives, the willingness to engage with them, the willingness to work things through in a positive spirit, the willingness to risk critique not just from within, but also beyond one's own intellectual and professional world, the willingness to go on giving relentlessly of oneself, and the willingness to go on undercutting one's own social and professional identity as one takes on the conflicting perspectives of one's own frameworks. (Barnett, 1997: 169)

The potential of critical pedagogy is to promote more critical self-reflection on the context and practice of management and to strengthen resistance to its mindless perpetuation (Alvesson and Willmott, 1996).

But these outcomes lurk in the distant future. A more immediate outcome of a critical management education is the development of critical beings (Barnett, 1997). Critical beings apply their critical reflection skills in the knowledge base, the self, and the world. A critical education enables student critique to move from the limited scope provided by simplistic and fragmented critical thinking skills to a metacritique that not only locates management within our traditions, but also offers insights into the unlimited opportunities for refashioning those traditions (Barnett, 1997). In this process students become critically self-reflective. This occurs when self-monitoring relative to established norms gives way to reflection on how the self is developed within prevailing traditions, and then on to critical self-reflection and the reconstruction of the self. Educational projects that were originally viewed as ways of understanding the world (as illustrated in our discussions of text and paradox) become reconstituted as ways of understanding the self.

This process thus moves students beyond the flexibility and adaptability encouraged by Thomas and Anthony (1996) and Schon (1983) to the emancipation of being independent thinkers, able to use educational experience as a source of self-discovery. It also leads to the potential for critical action in the world, enabled by critical reason and critical reflection (Barnett, 1997).

Note

An earlier version of this manuscript was presented at the First International Conference on Critical Management Studies, UMIST, July 1999.

References

Alvesson, M. and Willmott, H. (1992) 'Critical Theory and Management Studies: An Introduction', in M. Alvesson and H. Willmott (eds) *Critical Management Studies*, pp. 1–20. London: Sage.

Alvesson, M. and Willmott, H. (1996) *Making Sense of Management: A Critical Introduction*. London: Sage.

Barnett, R. (1997) *Higher Education: A Critical Business*. Bristol, PA: The Society for Research into Higher Education and Open University Press.

Barr, R.B. and Tagg, J. (1995) 'From Teaching to Learning: A New Paradigm for Undergraduate Education', *Change* (Nov/Dec): 13–25.

Bartunek, J.M., Gordon, J.R. and Weathersby, R.P. (1983) 'Developing "Complicated" Understanding in Administrators', *Academy of Management Review* 8(2): 273–84.

Bateson, G. (1972) *Steps to an Ecology of Mind*. San Francisco: Chandler Publishing.

Beck, J.E. (1994) 'The New Paradigm of Management Education: Revolution and Counterrevolution', *Management Learning* 25(2): 231–47.

Boje, D.M. (1996) 'Management Education as a Panoptic Cage', in R. French and C. Grey (eds) *Rethinking Management Education*, pp. 172–95. London: Sage.

Brookfield, S. (1994) 'Tales From the Dark Side: A Phenomenography of Adult Critical Reflection', *International Journal of Lifelong Education* 13(3): 203–16.

Brookfield, S.D. (1995) *Becoming a Critically Reflective Teacher*. San Francisco: Jossey-Bass.

Burgoyne, J. and Jackson, B. (1997) 'The Arena Thesis: Management Development as a Pluralistic Meeting Point', in J. Burgoyne and M. Reynolds (eds) *Management Learning: Integrating Perspectives in Theory and Practice*, pp. 54–70. London: Sage.

Caproni, P.J. and Arias, M.E. (1997) 'Managerial Skills Training from a Critical Perspective', *Journal of Management Education* 21(3): 292–308.

Carroll, S.J. and Gillen, D.J. (1987) 'Are the Classical Management Functions Useful in Describing Managerial Work?', *Academy of Management Review* 12(1): 38–51.

Cheit, E.F. (1985) 'Business Schools and their Critics', *California Management Review* 27(3): 43–62.

Chia, R. and Morgan, S. (1996) 'Educating the Philosopher-manager: Designing the Times', *Management Learning* 27(1): 37–64.

Crainer, S. and Dearlove, D. (1999) *Gravy Training: Inside the Business of Business Schools*. San Francisco: Jossey-Bass.

Dehler, G.E. (1996) 'Management Education as Intentional Learning: A Knowledge-transforming Approach to Written Composition', *Journal of Management Education* 20(2): 221–35.

Dehler, G.E. (1998) '"Relevance" in Management Research: A Critical Reappraisal', *Management Learning* 29(1): 69–89.

Dehler, G.E. and Welsh, M.A. (1998) 'Problematizing *Deviance* in Contemporary Organizations: A Critical Perspective', in R.W. Griffin, A. O'Leary-Kelly and J.M. Collins (eds) *Dysfunctional Behavior in Organizations: Violent and Deviant Behavior*, Part A, pp. 241–69. Stamford, CT: JAI Press.

Dore, R. (1976) *The Diploma Disease: Education, Qualification and Development*. London: George Allen & Unwin.

Fairclough, N. and Hardy, G. (1997) 'Management Learning as Discourse', in J. Burgoyne and M. Reynolds (eds) *Management Learning: Integrating Perspectives in Theory and Practice*, pp. 144–60. London: Sage.

Fineman, S. and Gabriel, Y. (1994) 'Paradigms of Organizations: An Exploration in Textbook Rhetorics', *Organization* 1(2): 375–99.

Foucault, M. (1980) *Power/Knowledge*. Hemel Hempstead: Harvester Wheatsheaf.

Giroux, H.A. (1981) *Ideology, Culture, and the Process of Schooling*. Philadelphia, PA: Temple University Press.

Giroux, H.A. (1997) *Pedagogy and the Politics of Hope: Theory, Culture, and Schooling*. Boulder, CO: Westview Press.

Goldberg, M.A. (1996) 'The Case against "Practicality" and "Relevance" as Gauges of Business Schools: Responding to Challenges Posed by Criticisms of Business School Research', *Journal of Management Inquiry* 5(4): 336–49.

Grey, C. (1996) 'Introduction: Special Section on Critique and Renewal in Management Education', *Management Learning* 27(1): 7–20.

Grey, C. and French, R. (1996) 'Rethinking Management Education: An Introduction', in R. French and C. Grey (eds) *Rethinking Management Education*, pp. 1–17. London: Sage.

Grey, C., Knights, D. and Willmott, H. (1996) 'Is a Critical Pedagogy of Management Possible?', in R. French and C. Grey (eds) *Rethinking Management Education*, pp. 94–110. London: Sage.

Grey, C. and Mitev, N. (1995) 'Management Education: A Polemic', *Management Learning* 26(1): 73–90.

Habermas, J. (1978) *Knowledge and Human Interests*. London: Heinemann.

Hales, C.P. (1986) 'What Do Managers Do? A Critical Review of the Evidence', *Journal of Management Studies* 23(1): 88–115.

Jeffcutt, P. (1996) 'Between Managers and the Managed: The Processes of Organizational Transition', in S. Linstead, R.G. Small and P. Jeffcutt (eds) *Understanding Management*, pp. 172–93. London: Sage.

Koot, W., Sabelis, I. and Ybema, S. (1996) 'Global Identity–Local Oddity? Paradoxical Processes in Contemporary Organizations', in W. Koot, I. Sabelis and S. Ybema (eds) *Contradictions in Context: Puzzling Over Paradoxes in Contemporary Organizations*, pp. 1–16. Amsterdam: VU University Press.

Lewis, M.W. and Dehler, G.E. (2000) 'Learning through Paradox: A Pedagogical Strategy for Exploring Contradictions and Complexity', *Journal of Management Education* 24(6): 708–25.

Linstead, S. (1996) 'Understanding Management: Culture, Critique and Change', in S. Linstead, R.G. Small and P. Jeffcutt (eds) *Understanding Management*, pp. 11–33. London: Sage.

Miles, R.E. (1985) 'The Future of Business Education', *California Management Review* 27(3): 63–73.

Pfeffer, J. (1997) *New Directions for Organization Theory: Problems and Prospects*. New York: Oxford University Press.

Porter, L.W. and McKibbin, L.E. (1988) *Management Education and Development: Drift or Thrust into the 21st Century?* New York: McGraw-Hill.

Prasad, A. and Cavanaugh, J.M. (1997) 'Ideology and Demystification: Tom Peters and the Managerial (Sub-) Text – An Experiential Exploration of Critique and Empowerment in the Management Classroom', *Journal of Management Education* 21(3): 309–24.

Prichard, C. and Willmott, H. (1997) 'Just How Managed is the McUniversity?', *Organization Studies* 18(2): 287–316.

Raab, N. (1997) 'Becoming an Expert in Not Knowing: Reframing Teacher as Consultant', *Management Learning* 28(2): 161–75.

Raelin, J.A. and Schermerhorn, J. (1994) 'A New Paradigm for Advanced Management Education – How Knowledge Merges with Experience', *Management Learning* 25(2): 195–200.

Ray, M. and Rinzler, A. (1993) *The New Paradigm of Business*. New York: Jeremy P. Tarcher/Perigee Books.

Reed, M. (1992) 'Introduction', in M. Reed and M. Hughes (eds) *Rethinking Organization: New Directions in Organization Theory and Analysis*, pp. 1–16. London: Sage.

Reed, M. and Anthony, P. (1992) 'Professionalizing Management and Managing Professionalization: British Management in the 1980s', *Journal of Management Studies* 29(5): 591–613.

Reynolds, M. (1997) 'Towards a Critical Management Pedagogy', in J. Burgoyne and M. Reynolds (eds) *Management Learning: Integrating Perspectives in Theory and Practice*, pp. 312–28. London: Sage.

Reynolds, M. (1998) 'Reflection and Critical Reflection in Management Learning', *Management Learning* 29(2): 183–200.

Reynolds, M. (1999) 'Grasping the Nettle: Possibilities and Pitfalls of a Critical Management Pedagogy', *British Journal of Management* 9: 171–84.

Roberts, J. (1996) 'Management Education and the Limits of Technical Rationality: The Conditions and Consequences of Management Practice', in R. French and C. Grey (eds) *Rethinking Management Education*, pp. 54–75. London: Sage.

Schon, D.A. (1983) *The Reflective Practitioner: How Professionals Think in Action*. New York: Basic Books.

Steffy, B.D. and Grimes, A.J. (1986) 'A Critical Theory of Organization Science', *Academy of Management Review* 11(2): 322–36.

Steffy, B.D. and Grimes, A.J. (1992) 'Personnel/Organizational Psychology: A Critique of the Discipline', in M. Alvesson and H. Willmott (eds) *Critical Management Studies*, pp. 181–201. London: Sage.

Summers, D.J., Boje, D.M., Dennehy, R.F. and Rosile, G.A. (1997) 'Deconstructing the Organizational Behavior Text', *Journal of Management Education* 21(3): 343–60.

Thomas, A.B. and Anthony, P.D. (1996) 'Can Management Education be Educational?', in R. French and C. Grey (eds) *Rethinking Management Education*, pp. 17–35. London: Sage.

Thompson, J. and McGivern, J. (1996) 'Parody, Process and Practice: Perspectives for Management Education?', *Management Learning* 27(1): 21–35.

Vince, R. (1996) 'Experiential Management Education as the Practice of Change', in R. French and C. Grey (eds) *Rethinking Management Education*, pp. 111–31. London: Sage.

Watson, T.J. (1996) 'Motivation: That's Maslow, Isn't It?', *Management Learning* 27(4): 447–64.

Weick, K. (1979) *The Social Psychology of Organizing*, 2nd edn. Reading, MA: Addison-Wesley.

Willmott, H.C. (1984) 'Images and Ideals of Managerial Work: A Critical Examination of Conceptual and Empirical Accounts', *Journal of Management Studies* 21(3): 349–68.

Willmott, H. (1994) 'Management Education: Provocations to a Debate', *Management Learning* 25(1): 105–36.

Willmott, H. (1995) 'Managing the Academics: Commodification and Control in the Development of University Education in the UK', *Human Relations* 48(9): 993–1027.

Willmott, H. (1997) 'Critical Management Learning', in J. Burgoyne and M. Reynolds (eds) *Management Learning: Integrating Perspectives in Theory and Practice*, pp. 161–76. London: Sage.

Zohar, D. (1997) *Rewiring the Corporate Brain: Using the New Science to Rethink How We Structure and Lead Organizations*. San Francisco: Berrett-Koehler.

10

J. Michael Cavanaugh

Head Games:
Introducing Tomorrow's Business Elites to Institutionalized Inequality

He (Durkheim) accepted the same popular idea that modern man has escaped from the control of institutions, which was shared by most of his contemporaries ... The high triumph of institutional thinking is to make the institutions completely invisible. (Douglas, 1986: 98)

Many, perhaps most, of our white students in the United States think that racism doesn't affect them because they are not people of color; they do not see 'whiteness' as a racial identity. Many men likewise think that Women's Studies does not bear on their own existences because they are not female; they do not see themselves as having gendered identities. Insisting on the universal 'effects' of 'privilege' systems, then, becomes one of our chief tasks, and being more explicit about the *particular* effects in particular contexts is another. Men need to join us in this work. (McIntosh, 1992: 79)

The *optimistic* liberal thinks that though we need to tinker with our political arrangements, we already know pretty well both what it is to be cruel, and who it is that should count as a person. But the *pessimistic* liberal knows that we are always finding out that we have been cruel in ways we never thought about before. And she sees no reason to doubt that the same will happen again. (Law, 1994: 99)

Why Worry? A Case for Pessimism

If the truth be told, as a full-time instructor in an AACSB-accredited institution (the good housekeeping acronym for the American Assembly of Collegiate Schools of Business) I worry that the predominantly white, suburban-bred, genial business majors that fill my classrooms have taken their B-school lessons to heart. What I mean by this is that in countless one-on-one and in-class conversations, not to mention the 'Freudian slips'[1] I regularly encounter in exam books and written reports, I have come to strongly suspect that the vast majority of these students unconditionally buy into the entrepreneurial ethos of free markets and free agency (i.e. every man, woman . . . and child for themselves), meritocracy (i.e. everyone plays by the same, fair rules), level playing fields (i.e. origins aren't supposed to matter), bootstraps (i.e. pluck and merit are everything; or people, in the end, get what they deserve), and that contemporary American society has turned the corner on race, class, and gender (i.e. transcending Otherness with diversity programs [Cavanaugh, 1997]). Freshmen, perhaps not surprisingly, tend to accept these classical liberal aspirations (Lilla, 1994) as articles of faith. But what disturbs me more is that my commencement-bound seniors appear to unblinkingly embrace this trajectory of 'false truisms' (Lawrence and Matsuda, 1997) as well.

So, what's to worry about, you say? In a few words, it's the extravagant inadequacy of this modernist disposition to acknowledge, much less engage, vital end-of-century questions – most particularly the 'deep' (structural) dynamics of racial and sexual inequality (Goldberg, 1993; Van Dijk, 1993; Omi and Winant, 1994; Lemert, 1995; Oliver and Shapiro, 1995). Not only do I fret over the serviceability of these ideas (i.e. whether they are or ever were 'good to think with' [Hall, 1996: 1]), but I am concerned that my manager wannabes will soon join organizations that possess enormous authority over the public good (Deetz, 1992), not to mention the definition of social being itself (Goffman, 1959). And yet they go forward as 'optimistic liberals' armed with a portfolio of self-help theories that, likely as not, do more to recuse 'ourselves as writers of culture' (Battaglia, 1995: 11) than otherwise (Omi and Winant, 1994). If, as some assert, the conservative ideological object of the business school curriculum is to 'fill the mind without altering it' (Cohen, 1997: 46; see Silverman, 1971; Perrow, 1972; Rose, 1975; Greenfield, 1979; Frost, 1980; Denhardt, 1981; Astley, 1984; Steffy and Grimes, 1986; Alvesson and Willmott, 1992; Marsden, 1993; French and Grey, 1996, etc.), as I see it, my mission as an insider (a business school professor) *and* a pessimistic liberal is to work against graduating yet another generation of students without the capacity to engage the refractory politics of inequality. (Whether the focus is economics, marketing, finance, etc., transmitting theories-on-life is the catechistic business of the business school. Perhaps it all boils down to the idea that no one should be set loose in or on the world until they acquire something like a healthy respect for what theory can do.)

Only, considering that this undertow of tacit assumptions 'organizing' my students' everyday thinking will probably seldom, if ever, be redefined via straightforward appeals to ordinary logic and/or data (talking cures) (Gergen, 1978; Elliott, 1992; Stiehm, 1994), I worry also about *my* chances of having much of an impact. Coming from a critical perspective which holds that no one – least of all accounting, marketing, finance, and management majors – should graduate from any university worth its salt without having at least wrestled with the received notions that they entered with, how do I, in one or at most two semesters – against the 18-plus years of around-the-clock, upscale conditioning my students freight to class – slip in a disconcerting idea edgewise (Brown, 1989)? The humbling answer, if we want to be pessimistically liberal about this, is only so often and ever so briefly with many reversals (and, yes, occasional moments of insight and understanding) along the way. That's not what anyone interested in making differences especially wants to hear, of course. But, among other things, this essay makes a pragmatic case for theoretical modesty (Law, 1994), wherein emphasis is placed on gradients, not epiphanies (didactic breakthroughs) as we shall see. Committing Michael Porter's (1980) liturgy of competitive strategies to memory is one thing, persuading college sophomores to abandon 'bred in the bone' mindsets is yet quite another.

But my intent here is not to unnerve those dedicated to rethinking the traditional business classroom. Quite the contrary. Although the odds may seem stacked against you at first, chipping away at a formidable opponent like the reigning disposition is, for me anyway, what makes the against-the-grain classroom worth doing in the first place. Why waste precious time reinforcing what students already know, anyhow? Isn't that the retro-syllabus everyone, some by-the-textbook pedagogues included, swears they are trying to off-load? And who said that this quixotic program has to be carried out alone? (Flying solo is inscribed in the academy's institutional common sense constituting an isolating practice which quietly serves to mainstream critical pedagogy.) Hence, my desire to share a classroom exercise that I have used to admittedly limited effect to contest the inequalities re-inscribed in the gender and racial common sense ritually enacted on my campus. It is my earnest hope that this exercise and any questions it may evoke about the making of everyday social order will become a piece of a broad *and coordinated* critical curriculum that might someday compete with, if not outright upstage, the balmic and essentially politically depotentiating 'amiable stasis' (Cohen, 1997: 47) recreated daily in the contemporary business classroom.[2]

In the narrative that follows I describe the genesis and implementation of a classroom exercise entitled 'Who Gets to Be FUSA (Fairfield University Student Association) President'. The 'FUSA Exercise' addresses a critical conceptual (and political) void – to introduce the spectral construct of inequitable social structure to students who, likely as not, have been 'taught not to see' (McIntosh, 1992: 81) this concept or its debilitating ramifications, and thus are, by and large, 'content to accept the categories of communal affiliation they have inherited' (Kennedy, 1997: 66). Social structure is forever difficult to pin down, because like the economist's 'market' it exists as a virtual reality – a concept of 'unyielding ambiguity' (Bauman, 1973: 1). In Charles Lemert's words, 'neither [structure nor markets] in itself is a particularly concrete thing; both, thereby, work primarily in the imagination' (1995: 16). The concept of 'structure', moreover, doesn't enjoy 'the market's' cachet.

This makes the concept no less real. Here structure is meant to signify our local and intimate familiarity with people, things, and situations 'Fairfield'. A practical consciousness which, when added up, constitutes an overall approach to life, i.e. the informal curriculum casually referred to as the Fairfield University 'Experience'. Think of the university as a more or less semi-permeable, scale-model society where, among other things, everyone knows where he or she fits in or out of the distributions and hierarchies inscribed here. Arguably, for all the changes that have taken place at Fairfield, the university's patrilocal Catholic traditions continue to inform our 'intuitive understanding of the rightness of events' (Evernden, 1993: 106).

Under these circumstances, not only is the instructor starting from conceptual scratch, so to speak, but the issues this exercise is meant to headline generally pull the rug out from under some fundamental (and again, unexamined) beliefs regarding the construction of self-made cultural identities and community attachments. So, I offer no upfront guarantees about programmatic outcomes, except to venture that these are the working conditions that make the critical classroom at times both a gamble and tantalizingly insightful, and to offer the encouragement that by electing to work at the outer (upper?) boundaries of subjectivity (Derrida, 1981; Hall, 1996; Thrift, 1996) you are joined in something quite democratic – making education enabling (hooks, 1994).[3]

While We Were Sleeping

It took place in the dead of night, as a matter of course. While the campus slept on the chilly eve of another round of student council elections (in the fall of 1994), someone or ones furtively scrawled some blatantly racist and sexist graffiti across a dormitory wall. (Actually, two such incidents took place; the second event involved a threatening letter found taped to a dormitory bathroom wall. The perpetrator of the incident was subsequently identified. He no longer attends the university.) When the offense was discovered the next morning, the university to its credit responded swiftly. The president, along with official faculty and student representatives, condemned the incident in no uncertain terms. Many faculty spontaneously transformed their classrooms into impromptu teach-ins. The administration passed out thousands of red buttons declaring the wearer's allegiance to diversity. State and federal police authorities were called in to investigate. The need to beef up efforts to recruit minority students and faculty was visited again. This exceptional week culminated in an outdoor rally where speakers representing a host of campus constituencies pledged their solidarity. And then, just like that, the campus reverted to its everyday routine.[4]

Please don't construe this description as another churlish case of armchair niggling, because my comments are not meant as such. In fact, the university's official rejection of this violent act, I believe, was appropriate and just. The offense deserved unsparing public condemnation. No question, the university community had every right to be offended and angry. But, the nagging question for me was and is – was this enough? Was this all that needed to be done? Had this manicured, church-attending, monochromatic, upper-income campus really arrived at a new consensus on difference? I feared not. Indeed, when you take into account how discursive formations work, I feared the exact opposite. Throughout what amounted to a week of intensifying protest I grew increasingly uneasy because the corrective measures, while no doubt sincere and necessary, seemed – on their face, at least – too easy, too benign.

As with most everyone else touched by this incident, the campus 'aberration' had shaken my self-complacency (something like this only happened at other schools), but, oddly, in the end it was the blink-of-an-eye return to campus normality that really grabbed my attention. During and after the fireworks I grew increasingly concerned that we might actually be missing the point, that we might have unwittingly squandered one of those rare real-time opportunities to teach a lasting lesson about structured discrimination, one leading to a reexamination of the campus's racial and gendered status quo. But, alas, I don't think this happened. The self-reflective window quickly closed and I suspect that most of us walked away from this experience having relearned an old lesson, the reductive formula that racism/sexism/homophobia/ . . . boils down to negative stereotyping (prejudice). *And,* the exculpatory corollary that prejudice and discriminatory acts are practiced by a small minority of damaged individuals (the disturbed few, i.e., 'redneck racism'), not a university community or a society *writ large.* Such is the insidious manner in which racial and gendered structures perpetuate themselves (Omi and Winant, 1994). Tricky stuff this.

Piqued, the insistent teacher in me, however, would not rest until we saw the lesson through. At the same time, the pessimistic liberal in me would not rest until a way was found for my students to *feel* the theoretical *incompleteness* (i.e. minimalism) I believed to be at work on our campus. So, I determined to look around for a way to recapture this lost moment for the classroom. In a previous exercise, I had walked students through the university's telephone directory to help them visualize the gender structuring going on right under their noses. The gendered monopolies of deans and faculty in some departments never failed to set a provocative stage for discussion about skewed dispersions of life opportunities, not to mention the potent lesson set by the gendered curriculum implicit in such arrangements (try it for yourself). But if I was to have any chance of getting through to my innocent students,[5] then something even closer to home was needed, ideally a gender or racial structuring generated by the students themselves. And, as luck would have it, an answer fell into my lap – the annual election of the student council president.

Going Social: Edging Toward Thinking the Unthinkable

We have orders without orders, knowledge without knowing, practice without intention. (Deetz, 1992)

Women gained admission to Fairfield in 1970 (the university was chartered as an all-male institution in 1942). Today, women constitute 53 percent of the university's undergraduate population (1997–1998 *Fact Book,* Fairfield University). Appropriately enough, the university made a point of celebrating women's quarter-century anniversary three years ago. Yet, in the 30 years that women have matriculated at Fairfield no woman has attained the office of Student Council (FUSA) President. Women candidates routinely enter the primaries, but the final ballot count is rarely close.[6] My task was to make this consistent track record into a problem – to turn this unique record back on itself. This transmutation was not as hard as it may sound. It boiled down to formulating a deceptively simple question. So, after a little thought, I proceeded to ask my students: why, how come, year in and year out, our predecessors wrote this history and not some other available to them? And how is it that we alone among Jesuit institutions of higher learning continue to replicate this patrilineal legacy today? (To my knowledge, of the 28 Jesuit universities in the United States, Fairfield is the only school to enjoy this dubious distinction.) Furthermore, why has it taken so long to thematize this situation? My strategy seemed to have worked. No one had anything to say.

Or, more accurately, no one volunteered any credible explanations, anyway. You see, if you work from the position that this unbroken string of outcomes is intentional (intentionally discriminatory, i.e. redneckism) in nature, as my students are inclined to do, you quickly paint yourself into a narrow analytic corner. To wit, you can indulge in the time-honored practice of blaming victims – even after all of this time, there is not one Fairfield woman capable of leading a winning campaign. Or, in a pinch, there's always conspiracy theory to fall back on in the guise of a long-standing, backroom male plot to lock women out of office forever.

Under closer inspection, however, neither of these rationales hold much water with students. No one has any trouble identifying qualified female candidates. And, on its face, a secret 30-year-old conspiracy just didn't seem plausible. Students were quick to agree that no one in their social circles, at least, was smart or plain lucky enough to pull off such a hitchless succession of electoral triumphs, or, for that matter, even harbored a desire to. And no one knew, or was willing to admit they knew, anyone who voted on strictly gender grounds. Besides, you didn't need to be a pre-med major to understand that wooing the female majority was crucial to winning office nowadays. The upshot was that students wasted little time in concluding that, in addition to suffering from near-fatal empirical deficiencies, both answers seemed too facile, suspiciously thin (red herrings). In the parochial parlance of our profession, victim blaming and conspiracy theory were both deemed serious underconceptualizations, if not radical misspecifications. At this point, everyone seemed to agree that the record merited a more *serious* analysis, a second look.

But what *was* the attributing factor? An accident of fate? (the numbers?). Happenstance? Even luck couldn't be that dumb. Stymied, we had, in so many words, reached the perceptual limit of the intentionalist (private prejudice) model. Having taken these familiar rationales as far as they would logically permit and still come up empty-handed, my played-out students were, it appeared to me, on the brink of thinking the unthinkable. Here was a rare (and fleeting) opportunity, as Lemert puts it, 'to show others just how social things are' (Lemert, 1995: 141). In other words, tired of repeatedly hitting their heads against their conceptual walls, would students perhaps be willing to entertain the suggestion that while we could never realistically discount the prejudice factor in Fairfield's peculiar electoral history, the complexity of our patriarchic politics might be *more completely* apprehended if approached as a non-intentional, impersonal phenomenon.

Breaking the Ice: 'White Privilege and Male Privilege'

But how to effect this crossover? What would entice students to think past their familiar intentionalist convictions long enough to, if not come all the way around to, at least to acknowledge, a 'non-intentionalist' dimension? In an effort to soften resistence to the conceptual departure that I am coaxing students to chance at this point, I make Peggy McIntosh's eye-opening essay 'White Privilege and Male Privilege' (1992) a required reading. McIntosh provides a substantive and inspirational example because she too is grappling with the same individualist perception handicapping my students. As she reveals,

> In my class and place, I did not see myself as a racist because I was taught to recognize racism only in individual acts of meanness by members of my group, *never in invisible systems conferring racial dominance on my group from birth*. Likewise, we are taught to think that sexism or heterosexism is carried on only through intentional, individual acts of discrimination, meanness or cruelty, rather than in invisible systems conferring unsought dominance on certain groups. (McIntosh, 1992: 81, my emphasis)

By deliberately and publicly unpacking her own inherited 'knapsack' of culturally prescribed beliefs shoring up her straight, white, female identity, McIntosh sets out to complicate pat definitions of race and gender bias.[7] Rather than the ad hoc, aberrational incidents attributable to individuals operating with warped psychologies, McIntosh sees sexism and racism as preeminently *sociological* phenomena. In other words, prejudice is much more than episodic acts of bigotry, but *pervasive and impersonal* (institutionalized). It is also *systemic* (never rests, operating 24 hours a day). It is also *cultural* in that it is inculcated (socially transmitted surely and effortlessly at our parents' knees, so to speak) and therefore *non-intentional* in nature. And, finally, it is *social, i.e. no one is exempt*. We (the privileged and underprivileged alike) are *all complicit* to some degree in the maintenance and perpetuation of unearned advantage and disadvantage.

It is in this fashion that McIntosh engages the silence surrounding a broader, invisible process of privileging and dominating. At this stage in the students' 'unpacking' process mastery of this concept is not as important as having a preliminary exposure to the ideas that discrimination and prejudice are not strict equivalents and that unequal treatment may actually be a characteristic feature of our society. Lifetimes of egalitarian and free enterprise rhetoric notwithstanding, McIntosh might serve as a conveyance for freeing us from the conceptual bind of our own making, i.e. we can at least begin to discuss the attributes of ingrained discriminatory *orders* that, in contrast to the reigning prejudice model described above, never rest, function (save for their consequences) largely behind our backs and largely unchallenged. Although it's a little early yet, students are in the process of creating an introspective, re-visionary space where it is possible, where it wasn't possible before, to examine the gulf between the 'ought' and the 'is' by specifically asking if our well-meant responses to recent campus events were thorough-going enough.

Note also that the flipside of the defiant genius displayed in 'White Privilege and Male Privilege' is that the author not only unearths the depth and complexity of contemporary racial and gender politics (hooks, 1994) but, through the clarity of her methodological example, equips us to continue the interrogation on our own. That is, by holding a mirror up to her own relatively priviledged position ('I decided to try to work on myself …' [McIntosh, 1992: 73]) rather than pointing a finger at someone else's, McIntosh teaches that if our purpose is to engage the cultural common sense on something approximating our own terms, then above all else we must be pragmatic teachers. Which means that by dint of her personal example (theoretically the best teaching mode) she instructs us to be (1) *inventive*, i.e. conceive ways to make the invisible visible; (2) *non-judgmental*, i.e. sermonizing (naming and blaming) is likely to generate more heat than light (don't forget, in considering the figure-to-ground turnaround we are trying to work here, that learning first consists of unlearning); (3) *mundane*, i.e. discussion of metaphors like 'systems', 'hierarchies', 'structures', etc. won't have much traction unless firmly grounded in the material rhythms of hands-on daily living, otherwise these foreign concepts remain little more than mid-term exam questions; and (4) *transparent*: 'We need more down-to-earth writing' (McIntosh, 1992: 79), i.e. if the agenda of critical scholarship is to impart life-skills in actively thinking about one's relationship with the world, then it's incumbent upon critical scholars to speak plainly (Fraser, 1989; James, 1997).

The 'FUSA Exercise': Out of Sight, But Out of Mind?

It is in the encounter with the specific that important lessons are taught. (Botstein, 1997: 156)

To know how to resist the classifying pressures of our institutions, we would like to start an independent classificatory exercise. Unfortunately, all the classifications that we have for thinking with are provided ready-made, along with our social life. For thinking about society we have at hand the categories we use as members of society speaking to each other about ourselves. (Douglas, 1986: 99)

McIntosh leaves us with a final afterthought in self-overcoming, i.e. seeing may be believing, but only some of the time, which is to say that business students are endowed with a keen respect for 'facts' and figures. In other words, unless social structuring is discussed in empirical terms, don't count on being taken seriously. So, having used the McIntosh reading to soften student cognitive dissonance, I set to the task of making the invisible empirical (viewable), and thereby 'factual', by asking students to help me catalogue the campus's universe of student social categories.

Given the unspoken nature of the subject matter, it's up to the instructor to jump-start this unpacking process. I typically inquire if all students are perceived the same way? Are Asian students interchangeable with Hispanic students, for instance? No? How come? Do women correspond to your image of your run-of-the-mill rugby player? Then who does? Why? Why not women? What social classifications were common in your high school? Did these ascriptions carry any social weight? Explain. Is something comparable at work on this campus, or were such classificatory schemes jettisoned upon admission to the university? Provide me with some local examples. Are these categories the subject of everyday discussion? Why do you suppose that is? What makes one person a preppie and another an athlete? How can you be so certain? Was this a feature of your official freshman (sic) orientation? If not, where were these categories learned? How is it that everyone in this room appears to know these things if they go routinely unmentioned? Why so little disagreement? Indeed, why such unanimity? Do these categories really matter now, today? Fill me in. After only a minute, or at most two, you'll be hard pressed to record the flood of student responses you've unleashed.

Exhibit 1 displays the social universe that sophomores through seniors assemble with remarkable consistency.

Apparently nothing so out of the ordinary here. But recall that one of our goals is to call our brand of student politics into question. So I ask students to complicate *their* homegrown classification scheme with the following instruction: if elections for student council president were held today, rank (along a scale of 1 [low] to 5 [high]) the likelihood of someone from each category being elected. In the process something very McIntoshian happens, i.e. the campus's de facto electoral system comes into focus. The chart at the bottom of this page illustrates the consensus opinion of my student sample.

When students set to analyzing Exhibit 2 two points commonly emerge. Right off, the data suggest that the composite white male preppy category possesses a clear-cut advantage over other student categories *even before the elections are officially held.* The corollary of this, of course, is that the remaining student categories operate at an obvious disadvantage *before* anyone throws their hat into the ring. What isn't registered here, but bears mentioning, is the nature of the discussion driving the ranking process. The relative placement of white women, for example, generates a modicum of debate;

Exhibit 1 Roster of student categories

Student categories ($n = 345$)	Student categories ($n = 345$)
Commuters	Hippies
Black women	Black athletes
Black men	Computer nerds
Hispanic men	Jocks
Hispanic women	Preppies
Native American men	Asian American women
Native American women	Asian American men
White men	Geniuses
White women	(Openly) gay men
(Openly) gay women	

Exhibit 2 De facto politics: the common sense

Chances: 1–5	Student categories	Student categories	Chances: 1–5
1	Commuters	Hippies	1–2
2–3	Black women	Black athletes	2
2–3	Black men	Computer nerds	2
2–3	Hispanic men	Jocks	2
2–3	Hispanic women	Preppies – white male	5
5	White men	Asian American women	3–4
2	Native American women	Asian American men	3
3–4	White women	Geniuses	2–3
2	Native American men	Gay women	1
1	Gay men	White women	3–4

students quibble over whether white women merit a 3 ranking or a 4, or, rarely, even a 5. Although a woman has yet to win an election, the presence of debate (if not the track record) might indicate that compared to other 'also-ran' categories, white women, as possibly representing a category in transition, have something resembling a fighting chance and, it follows, seeming reason to sacrifice the time and effort in a bid for office.

On the other hand, there are categories that appear to be foregone conclusions, noteworthy for their lack of debate. The white male preppy amalgam, as one can readily see, enjoys virtually a legacy applicant status and thus assumed a shoe-in. And gay students, it would appear, are not even eligible to run. It's not possible to show here but both gay categories invariably receive a disenfranchising judgment that is so quick and so final as to be virtually Pavlovian in nature.

One further observation. According to the university's 1997–1998 *Fact Book* 90 percent of the school's 1997 undergraduate population is white. It would appear, then, that at a first glance the 2's and 3's (out of 5) assigned to non-white ethnic categories in Exhibit 2 represent a leap forward when set against the demographic odds (1:10). Likely this token presence operates as a background factor in campus politics. However, caution is warranted. After all, there seems to be a quantum difference between 3's and 4's, not to mention 4's and 5's. Would these perceived rankings change if the student population were made more diverse? No way to tell at this point. The thing to remember is that, base line demographic comparisons notwithstanding, a ranking of 3 or even 4 doesn't get you elected.

This arrangement, I submit, is how we 'hold' elections at Fairfield. 'Electing' the same kinds of people class president is a piece of our social landscape, an acquired habit. And the point to be made here is that we accomplish this patriarchic monopoly without even trying – with our eyes closed. It is a telling symptom of our racial, gendered and class-bound common sense – our de facto curriculum. And no matter how unfair or objectionable on paper, until it is cross-examined, chances are it will remain the only game in town.

Autonomy in Question, or No One Is an Island

At the risk of oversimplifying matters, I would like to suggest that this homespun example of non-intentional politics constitutes a true-to-life example of what Wittgenstein knew as 'background practices' and Bourdieu means by the 'habitus', and what Heidegger referred to as a 'way of being' (Drefus, 1991), concepts united in their concern to ground analysis in what people actually do – their social competencies, rather than on what they say they do (Dreyfus and Hall, 1992). According to Nigel Thrift

> Rather than thinking of action as based on beliefs and desires, Heidegger describes what actually goes on in our everyday skillful coping with things and people and how we are socialized into a shared world. He describes simple skills – hammering, walking into a room, using turn signals, etc. – and shows how these everyday coping skills contain a familiarity with the world that enables us to make sense of things and 'to find (our) way about in (our) public environment'. Thus, like Ludwig Wittgenstein, Heidegger finds that the only ground for the intelligibility of thought and action we have or need is in the everyday practices themselves, not in some hidden process of thinking or of history. (Thrift, 1996: 10)

A Wittgenstein or a Heidegger would, I'll venture, argue that no one knows how to 'get along' in the world from cultural scratch. Contrary to received Western analytic traditions, that is, no one is original or autonomous, but the opposite, culturally saturated. This is because each and every one of us is born into a 'prefabricated' quotidian world of tropes, schemas, templates, discourses, histories, frameworks, paradigms, habitual familiarities, plausibility structures, *Lebenswelts* and *umwelts* passed down from preceding generations (Winch, 1958; Berger and Luckmann, 1966; Schutz, 1962; Kuhn, 1970; White, 1978; Gilkey, 1993). From day one our every waking hour is spent imbibing these tacit 'subuniverses of reality' (Schutz, 1962) until they evolve into 'routine accomplishments' (Garfinkel, 1984). Roy Baumeister, a professor of psychology at Case Western Reserve University, observes, 'Even before a baby is born, it has an identity, a place in the social hierarchy. It may be given a name, a Social Security number, even a bank account, long before it has consciousness' (Angier, 1997: C1). What Professor Baumeister fails to acknowledge is that this same baby is endowed with a class, race, and now (thanks to amniocentesis) a gender as well.

This, of course, is anything but a neutral process. Because culture is a terrain of competing knowledge and practice (Giroux, 1997), some subuniverses are culturally preferred over others. Which is to say that in our long gestation as social beings our youths are not just dedicated to learning how to pound nails, tie shoelaces, build vocabulary, read faces, and master video games, but becoming adroit at the social graces of demarcating, circulating, differentiating and enforcing (Goldberg, 1993; Butler, 1993) as captured at work in our two exhibits above.

In operational terms, structuring entails the intersubjective enactment of centers and fringes (relevance/irrelevance), agencies (causes and effects), histories (memory and forgetting), dualisms (differences/privileges), language (voices and silences) – all impacting and being impacted by the distribution of social resources (i.e. power). Picture structuring as that social space where agency (subjectification) is played out, i.e. where action is produced and what counts for action and actors is decided. As Thrift (1996: 8) and many others note, structures are subjectivities that are derived and played out in the close encounters of everyday relationships. However, and this can't be emphasized enough to students at home with object-lessons, structures are not binding or fixed. Social enactments, that is, are not consecrated by some supra-human agency. No 'puppeteer' is necessary. Given their eminently intersubjective nature, structures are by definition precarious works in progress. Structures tend to reproduce or unravel depending on the circumstances. Unlike Hegel's *Wissenschaft* or Husserl's free-floating phenomenology (Bernstein, 1976), structures have no 'natural tendencies' to stay in place or move in a particular direction (Law, 1994: 103). Any suspected 'materiality' or regularity is just another relational effect.

(Knowledge) structures, then, are backdrops of 'knowing' (Collingwood, 1940) – that automatic, perhaps autonomic, orienting sense of how each of us knows how to 'carry off' a vast repertoire of social settings and relationships. As with so much else few say it better than Richard J. Bernstein:

> Every wide-awake, grown-up individual approaches his world with a *stock of knowledge at hand*. Schutz uses this concept broadly to include not only knowledge but also the beliefs, experiences, rules, and biases by which we interpret the world. This stock of knowledge at hand is formed by both our personal experiences and the socially pre-formed knowledge that we inherit; in the course of our experience, it is constantly being tested, refined, and modified. At any moment in an individual's life, he [sic] finds himself in a *biographically determined situation*. He is not merely a physical being in an objective spatial-temporal world. As a living being who endows his experiences with meaning, he has a *position* in a world that is meaningful to him. (1976: 146) (italics in the original)

In short, our worlds can never be ours alone. There are no solo practitioners, no 'solitary egos' (Bernstein, 1976: 145), no fresh starts. We enter the world encumbered with a biography crafted by others. Knowing is not learned *de novo*, on the spot, or in private, but situated, encultured time and again at our culture's venerable knee (consisting of familial, educational, civic, political, religious, media institutions) until everyday metaphors 'sediment' or congeal into out-of-sight root metaphors. Indeed, our knapsacks of metaphoric lenses are so indelible that we tend to forget that we constantly use them, not to mention, how they were acquired in the first place. In the language of my trade, we are all hopelessly 'theory-laden'. Thus, with an inordinate amount of practice behind us, like kissing or breezing along on a bicycle, 'performing' a college classroom, or washing women out of military flight schools (Boyer, 1996), or growing up in a 'resegregated' suburb (see

Jacobs, 1997), or attending a virtually all-white university, an unbroken string of white male preppy presidents feels 'natural' (uncontestable) somehow.[8]

I'd like to push this line of thinking a little further. Perhaps, contrary to the algorithmic and computational focus of management science, we feel first, act second, and think later (Weick, 1979; Ridley, 1996) and not the other way around. A humbling thought. It may also prove analytically more profitable in that it allows us to think of our off-center campus 'normality' as being as much a product of a practical social intuition as of anyone's ulterior motives. To wit, our electoral process is grounded in an internalized orienting sense whereby each of us knows (by heart) how to carry off a vast array of social settings and relationships – in this particular case the election of student council presidents. This suggests that this ability to engage with others emanates from the gut, not the head. We might say that we are so 'disciplined' at it (Foucault, 1972), we automatically 'know' when a social situation is working (making sense) or not by what we first *feel* about it. Thinking, methodical calculation, is an aftereffect, may even get in the way. Shanon captures the beyond-words, visceral essence of everyday normality-making:

> The body knows whether things are balanced or not, whether they are in equilibrium, or not, whether they fit or not. Agents moving about in the world know how to find their way in it. Social agents appreciate whether the other is kind, honest, or boring, or attractive. Likewise, affectively one knows that things are good or bad (for the given agent), pleasant or not so. And ethically, one appreciates that things are right or wrong, fair or despicable. In all these cases what is being determined is whether things fit, click, or feel right. (1993: 353)

As Shannon seems to be saying, we don't just have political opinions, we embody a politics (Foucault, 1972; Bourdieu, 1990; Thrift, 1996). If anything, just as we 'experience' degrees of intimacy (e.g. friendship, acquaintaince, family ties), a dean's or police officer's authority, when a class is not 'working,' if someone is 'crowding' us, a stranger's stare (someone's eyes 'on' you), the 'right' mate or car, when we have blundered into the wrong bar (feeling class), namebrands, sales records, Nielsen ratings, what constitutes a proper meal, and when to consummate a deal; we also 'divine' the inter-subjective enactment of clubbiness, exclusion, inequity, privilege, staying in place, anonymity, reputation, difference and sameness, misconception and distortion, we and they, familiarity and novelty, norms and extremes, defer-ence and insurrection, civility and disrespect, correctness, race and gender, democracy even. As things presently stand on our campus, at least, if you want to literally feel what it's like to contravene a powerful common sense, try strolling across the Fairfield commons hand-in-hand with a same-sex companion.

In sum, having had nearly three decades to perfect it, our system of primogeniture is second nature to us; an encoded piece of what 'goes on' (Thrift, 1996: 9) on our campus even if this 'going on (and on)' is fundamentally at odds with the university's professed mission of inclusion. The graphic process that we have initiated here makes such matter-of-fact 'going ons' viewable and topical, enabling us to call these overly familiar arrangements into question by 'remembering' (unforgetting) (Chia, 1996) them. But congratulations are not in order just yet. Because we are so accomplished at 'forgetting' (hooks, 1989), it is said that such mirrorwork is notoriously short-lived. But, for the moment at least, a small opening has been created for a few to see that the undeclared affirmative action program advantaging a minority of students while disadvantaging so many others might not be so 'normal' or natural after all.

Anamorphosis:[9] There's More to Exhibit 2 than Meets the Eye

Blame not on eyes the error of the mind. (Lucretius, quoted in Judovitz, 1993: 70)

Let's continue to employ Exhibit 2 as a heuristic device for stepping 'out of place' – a discursive platform for remembering in order that we might acknowledge 'our silences and inarticulateness' (hooks, 1990: 149) in a (pessimistic) bid to formulate 'a different mode of articulation' (hooks, 1990: 147) about who we are and what we are up to. Accordingly, let's proceed to wring Exhibit 2 conceptually dry. For example, try mentally rotating Exhibit 2 (i.e. look around it); view it on anamorphic edge so that its hierarchy of privilege can be seen from another angle.

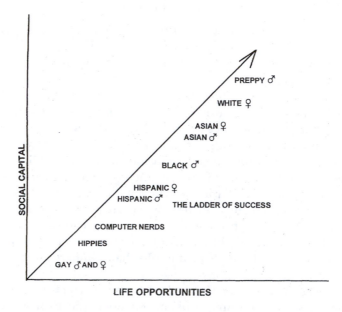

Exhibit 3   *The election behind the election (the structure of opportunity)*

Reproduction: Joint Authorship

From this vantage point the latent data in Exhibit 2 can be reframed into a Foucaultian (1982) lesson in the 'constitution of subjects' or what Ian Hacking calls 'making people up' (Hacking, 1985). Which is to say that broad-brush typecasting of the kind on display in Exhibit 2 really counts for something. Not only does labeling work to 'rig' elections, installing white male preppies at the apex of the political food chain, if you will, but the stock characterizations exhibited here also perform a self-fulfilling, stabilizing function. Henry Giroux observes that we need to understand 'that knowledge does more than distort, it also produces particular forms of life; it has, as Foucault points out, a productive, positive function' (1997: 108). In this regard, Mary Douglas writes that 'labels stabilize the flux of social life and even create to some extent the realities to which they apply' (1986: 100). Under the political circumstances visible in Exhibit 3, it is not unreasonable to assume that gay students as an electable category operate with an altogether different set of expectations and incentives from, say, straight white females. Given the apparent political odds gays face, why would any 'reasonable' person waste time running for office in the first place? Thus, whereas some categories may reasonably opt to slug it out, under the circumstances it is just as 'normal' for others to drop out. In this self-fulfilling dynamic everyone, winners and losers alike, unwittingly 'participates' in the institutionalization (legacy) of an underground politics of location (Foucault, 1982), exclusion (Hall, 1996), and subordination (Scott, 1990).

Real Consequences? Of Head Starts and Multiplier Effects

Some percipient students wonder if the FUSA election matters in the long run. My answer is a probable yes. It stands to reason that the outcome of the FUSA elections is of concern not only to the candidate and his (sic) parents, but to more distant audiences as well, future employers and graduate schools to name two. FUSA presidents probably enjoy a comparative leg up in job and post-grad education markets for the simple reason that class presidents are unique enough to supply their own demand. And we should not overlook the potential career connections (marketable social capital) that regular exposure to the university's inner circle of power (university president and other prominent administrators and faculty) confers. Even if an incumbent does little other than win the election, outside agencies will likely view him (sic) as potential leadership material. Such ticket punching benefits come with the territory. So, although much depends on the individual, there is a cumulative effect attached to winning the FUSA presidency, one extending beyond the campus and into the future. The FUSA president (and likely his children for generations to come) enters the job market with leverage that, for the present, the 'other' categories can't duplicate.

Are we therefore to infer that commuters or black women, say – low and mid-level categories on our social scale – are blocked from launching promising careers or that FUSA presidents always land their dream job? Certainly not. But what it may mean is that in the sociology of opportunity shown in Exhibit 3 differential access to forms of self-actualization are open to some more than others. All else held equal, few 'others' can match the unacknowledged cultural capital (Bourdieu, 1990) that a FUSA president carries into a final job interview. Not all knapsacks are equal.[10]

Generalizable? Fairfield Campus Politics, The Odd 'Man' Out?

Is Fairfield the only institution where such arbitrary 'knowing' plays out? Are the FUSA elections an aberration, an idiosyncratic throwback radically at odds with what is taking place elsewhere? This is not a leap we can make at this point. However, armed with the concept and evidence of local structuring, nothing prevents us from asking hard questions of other institutions. For example, will a woman 'CEO' General Electric, Ford, the Teamsters or the White House anytime soon? Each of these venerable institutions predates Fairfield University. Or, closer to home, what qualifications are needed to be appointed dean of a business, engineering or medical school? *What does the record of our social institutions show?*

On a more encompassing level, does structuring not only influence the selection of FUSA presidents or CEOs at General Electric, but how education,

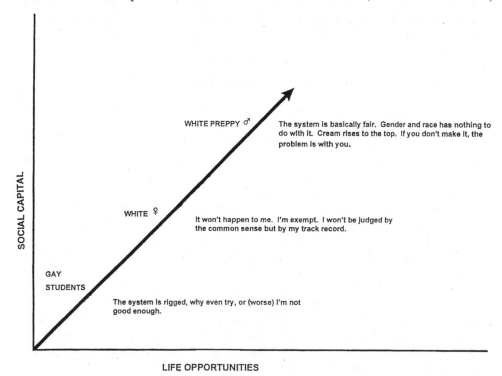

Exhibit 4   *The language of persistence: past repeating itself*

medical insurance, housing, safe neighborhoods, access to orthodontists, infant mortality, immunizations, longevity, home mortgages, earnings, medical research dollars, reading comprehension, poverty, bicycle helmets, personal trainers, and second chances are parceled out in the United States in the year 2000? Does structuring of the kind on display above play a role in the distribution of 'knowledge' jobs (Reich, 1991; Drucker, 1993), blue-collar jobs, and who goes shirtless? Are construction sites, precinct houses, and investment banks teeming with blacks and women? *Let's examine the record.* Or, why, 46 years after *Brown vs Board of Education,* has the Connecticut Supreme Court found it necessary to order the desegregation of the state's public school system? *Let's do the math.*[11]

In sum, is the distribution of our society's life-opportunities and life-expectations (setting your sights) based on just desserts justly 'earned', or is there more at work here than Bell Curves (Fischer et al., 1996) or character (Oliver and Shapiro, 1995)? As we contemplate the end of the 20th century, is it sufficient to go on assuming that inequality is a given of nature, based on the distribution of people's innate talents, and/or a neutral marketplace function, and/or just a matter of good and poor judgments? Yes, extrapolating general cultural meanings from a local context must be pursued gingerly, but methodological caution should not inhibit us from dabbling in a little reality testing. ('Small facts lead to large issues' [Geertz, 1973: 199].) A realization of the *persistent* gap between our rhetoric and the documented 'facts of inequality' separating genders and races in our society (Lawrence and Matsuda, 1997: 13), long after discrimination was officially outlawed (antidiscrimination laws, judicial and executive orders, etc.), may help throw a different light on our cherished notions of merit and level playing fields.

After the Facts: What Makes Race, Gender, and Class so Non-Negotiable? or, Overcoming the Primacy of the First Person Singular

My schooling gave me no training in seeing myself as an oppressor, as an unfairly advantaged person, or as a participant in a damaged culture. I was taught to see myself as an individual whose moral state depended on her individual moral will. At school, we were not taught about slavery in any depth; we were not taught to see slaveholders as damaged people. Slaves were seen as the only group at risk of being dehumanized. My schooling followed the pattern which Elizabeth Minnich has pointed out: whites are taught to think of their lives as morally neutral, normative, and average, and also ideal, so that when we work to benefit others, this is seen as work that will allow 'them' to be more like 'us'. I think many of us know how obnoxious this attitude can be in men. (McIntosh, 1992: 72–3)

To say that current inequality is the result of discrimination against blacks is to state only half the problem. The other half – is discrimination in favor of whites. It follows that merely eliminating discrimination is insufficient. The very direction of bias must be reversed, at least temporarily. If we wish to eliminate substantive inequality we waste effort when we debate whether some form of special treatment for the disadvantaged group is necessary. What we must debate is how it can be accomplished. (Oliver and Shapiro, 1995: 177)

Privatized terms so dominate the public discourse that it is difficult to see or appreciate social evil, communal wrong, states of affairs that implicate us whether we will it or not. (Patricia Williams, quoted in Banks, 1996: 242)

The time-honored notion of social structure is said to lie 'at the heart of social theory and the philosophy of social science' (Thompson, 1989).[12] Yet, apart from the brief appearance of a small body of papers on the subject in the late 1970s and early 1980s (Silverman, 1971; Meyer and Rowan, 1977; Kanter, 1977; Weick, 1979; Van Maanen, 1979; Ranson et al., 1980; Zucker, 1977) the mainstream organizational literature, not to mention business school curricula, remains tonedeaf to the subject of structure except to speak of it in the materialist language of organizational design, i.e. consciously created chains of command, spans of control, functional specializations, degrees of centralization, networks of rules (or what Linda Smircich [1985] has dubbed 'building block' thinking).

For many critical theorists, however, the idea of interpretive structures of subjectivity or consciousness is about as good as it conceptually gets. Structuring or 'non-intellectual intelligibility' (Thrift, 1996) is where all inquiry begins, because it is thought to constitute the operating platform – the conceptual touchstone – for identity, consciousness, and experience (LaCapra, 1983). On the level of the day-to-day, the structure construct represents a robust metaphor for getting in close-up touch with 'the options people have as to how to live' (Thrift, 1996: 8) – a heuristic ploy for actively thinking about our horizon of choices, the problem of interpretation (LaCapra, 1983), and, ultimately, the health of our political imagination (Deetz, 1992).

You see, in the critical tradition your politics is your ontology. That is, the compass of one's political imagination (or one's potential for political 'entanglement' [Ricoeur, 1992]) can be conceived for convenience's sake as composed of a discursive (interpretive) domain and a non-discursive (reified) domain (conventional theory, for example) bisected by a canonical line (C-line) running down the middle (see Exhibit 5).[13] All action takes place at sundry points along the C-line where the discursive sphere deploys critical forms such as irony, contradiction, self-parody (White, 1978), memory (Chia, 1996), in attempts to undo the 'pathos of (unreflective) belief' (LaCapra, 1983: 54) underwriting the non-discursive, 'settled' sphere. One's receptivity to change or, conversely, one's reliance on the status quo, is configured by where one's hypothetical C-line falls on a particular issue. The C-line, in short, demarcates the parameters of one's agency – of consent and dissent. For example, shifting the C-line leftward (expanding the interpretive sphere) constitutes an opportunity to speak to an evaded issue, articulate a silence, to, in a word, broaden the understanding and scope of political reality (Cavanaugh and Prasad, 1996). But this maneuver is never easy nor welcome even. For better or worse, we all grow attached to our C-lines, and expect our environments to conform to them (Weick, 1977). Regardless, critical theorists deem it worth the effort (and risk of marginalization), because by probing the non-discursive dimension one multiplies one's chances for

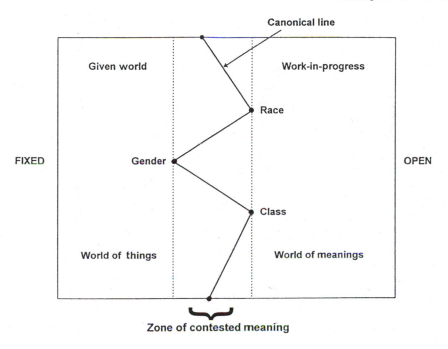

Canonical line

Given world

Work-in-progress

● Race

FIXED

Gender ●

OPEN

● Class

World of things

World of meanings

Zone of contested meaning

Exhibit 5   *The construction of subjectivity*

leading the examined life as opposed to just going along for the ride (political complacency).

In principle, at least, C-lines are moved in the critical (anti-essentialist) classroom by making perspective into an object of reflection and evaluation. Critical instructors in business school settings feel obliged, in other words, to clearcut a space for politics (the practice of dialogic culture) by showing students that 'things' (objectifications) could have turned out otherwise because nothing in a constructed world has to be. If one must resort to virtual 'things' like organizations, free markets, management, gender and race, better that they are understood as effects. At bottom, the critical project – as enacted in *both* research and teaching – is concerned with regaining lost agency by finding ways to loosen the reifying hold objects have over us (Law, 1994) – expanding the domain of the political at the expense of the non-discursive by overcoming the psychic weight of C-lines.

And 'structure' has such a solid ring to it. One way to introduce students to 'the inherent instability of meaning' (Barnes and Duncan, 1992: 7) that the decentering notion of C-lining conveys (meanings as works in progress) is to skill them in re-presenting noun forms ('things') as verbs (Law, 1994). Otherwise, dedicated 'building block' thinkers like many of my students tend to naturalize 'structure' into a monolithic object. In light of this substantiating propensity it's important to keep Dizard's (1991) advice in mind, '. . . social structure is not something that is 'out there', independent of the human beings who happen to be alive at that moment. It is not like gravity, which will work its way whether we like it or not or are even aware of its power' (1991: 148).

Accordingly, the work of critical or anti-essentialist theory is to elucidate how structures, as historical phenomena, 'arise, are sustained, and pass away' (Bernstein, 1976: 159). For example, by 'retracing our steps' (Iris Murdoch, 1970: 1; Murdoch sees the purpose of philosophy as 'a movement of return') or strategically 'retreat[ing] from an object to its conditions of possibility' (Laclau, 1994: 2), fixed-order is reverse-engineered into 'ordering' and organizations into processes of 'organizing' in an effort to reveal their contingency, history, authorships and in the end, their potential for change. The hope is that, by relying on a deconstructive stroke to swim 'upstream' (Chia, 1996), this process of ontological inversion (unpacking; problematizing the essential unity of 'things') will make it easier for students to consider, perhaps for the first time, their everyday interactions as class, gendered, and racial subjects (Deetz, 1992; Giroux, 1997).

Agnosia: Or, Is Going Cold Turkey Conceptually Feasible?

> One can't simply wave a curricular wand and reverse acculturation. (Edmundson, 1997: 49)

> A classroom now is frequently an 'environment', a place highly conducive to the exchange of existing ideas, the students' ideas. Listening to one another, students sometimes change their opinions. But what they generally can't do is acquire a new vocabulary, a new perspective, that will cast issues in a fresh light. (Edmundson, 1997: 45)

But what we see is not always what we 'get'. Which brings us to the question: has this crash course in systemic inequality triggered any C-changes – any discontinuities in thought, an epistemological break or two? After all that we have said about the durability of C-lines, has this (re)introduction to 'structuring' of a qualitative different kind, one (and this is the stumbling block for most students) operating beneath the level of intention, registered with students? In an effort to find out, I routinely pose the following question: 'In light of what we have discussed, define your idea of merit.'

In one manner or another roughly 9 students out of 10 (90%) write that merit is something wholly earned on one's own. Luck may be a factor, but wits, nerve, work, education, and dreaming combine to constitute the critical difference (i.e. good things happen to good people). It would seem, in other words, that for the vast majority of my students their C-lines haven't blinked. Not an enviable record for a neurosurgeon. But perhaps not so surprising when you consider the kind of reconstructive surgery we are attempting to perform here (see James, 1997).

Why such a meager harvest? Shall we attribute this dismal showing to a poor exercise, poor teaching, insufficient exposure, obtuse students, the doldrums of a late afternoon class? Perhaps. But not trying to wiggle off the hook here (I think), we should also recall that the idea of structuring flies in the face of a lifetime of learning. In a sublime piece of writing entitled 'To See and Not See', Oliver Sacks (1995) describes the tragic saga of 51-year-old Virgil, blind from the age of six, who agrees to cataract surgery in a bid to regain his sight. With sympathetic irony, Sacks (1995: 114–15) records that following his 'successful' surgery, 'He [Virgil] saw, but what he saw had no coherence. His retina and optic nerve were active, transmitting impulses, but his brain could make no sense of them; he was, as neurologists say, agnosic.'

Sacks is referring to the refractive nature of perspective, of course. Suppose, for argument's sake, that students share Virgil's predicament – a looking glass-size crisis of thinking regarding the apprehension of social structure. It's not unreasonable to conclude, considering the amount of unlearning involved, that our intervention was doomed from the start. For we are asking students not merely to process yet another piece of confirmatory data along the inductive path to truth (rubber stamping), but to throw a lifetime of self-understanding in doubt. Should we be nonplussed that business-minded students exposed to near-lethal doses of modern human-ism's self-making (Bellah et al., 1985; Lilla, 1994) and B-School 'hyper-factualism' (Ryan, 1972; i.e. what counts is what you can see) can't in a twinkling 'see' the implications of structure: that self-transformation has its limits; that our modes of consciousness are to a large degree second- and third-hand (inherited); and that subjectivity, power, and agency are relational and 'textured' (mediated) effects; and that everyday reality is interdependent and negotiated, thereby resulting at times in our being inadvertently 'cruel in ways we never thought about before' (Law, 1994: 99).

Students, to be fair, are not the only ones with blindspots. The largely psychological and empiricist orientation of organizational theorizing, for example, leaves it conceptually unprepared to acknowledge the existence of an 'invisible' organizational world. Or, perhaps the constrictive 'feel' implicit in the word 'structure' itself threatens to unduly problematize the expansive Enlightenment promises of self-determination (the bootstraps ethos), fair play (meritocracy), and progress (upward mobility) authorizing the work and institutional practices of mainstream theory, not to mention the rhetoric of the competitive marketplace (Blau, 1993).

Structuring might also be said to cross swords with the deep-seated American belief in starting over (Samuels, 1997) as well, i.e. the myth of newness, or that sense of 'perpetual renovation which from the time of the Puritan arrival in the 17th century, stood as the promise of God's contract with a chosen people in the New World' (Boynton, 1997: 44). Westward expansion and technological advances fueled the belief in America's claim to uninterruptable progress and historical exceptionalism. The notion of struc-ture, on the other hand, carries the unpalatable suggestion that perhaps we haven't shaken off the ascriptive legacy of the American antithesis, the 'old' world's (Europe's) alleged fin-de-siècle fatalism. Our forebears didn't leave their old-world knapsacks behind after all. As a consequence, we still have a lot of unpacking to do.

And, lest we forget, for every Yin there exists a counterweight Yang. Structuring, I suspect, also figures prominently, albeit surreptitiously, in the construction of management itself, in making management necessary in the first place (Clegg, 1996). Reincarnated in the decision-paralyzing guise of Iron Cages, red tape, big government (big business?), balky employees, meddlesome unions, dithering committees, deadweight procedures and stultifying hierarchy, structure functions, in effect, as management's identity-conferring 'other' – the specter of institutional entropy that must perforce be bent to managment's will if optimum efficiencies are to be wrung out of organizations. (Apropos, in a recent book review John Kenneth Galbraith quotes Thorstein Veblen as remarking that: 'The heroic role of the captain of industry is that of a deliverer from an excess of business management. It is a casting out of businessmen by the chief of businessmen' (Galbraith, 1997: 13). This calls to mind the payroll-purging rhetoric of the contemporary reengineering discourse, doesn't it?) Management's success as a discourse is predicated on overcoming the institutional inertia subtracting from managerial discretion. In other words, as arch-nemesis and object of management's creative destruction (Schumpeter, 1950), the notion of structure helps to vindicate the mystique of managerial heroism (the manager as indispensible entrepreneurial center-piece, as *auteur*) and managerialism as a transcendent master narrative without historical attachments to time or place. One might say that structure's problem is that it is an ensemble piece, not a star vehicle.

Coda: Double Discoursing

Boys, don't be too hopeful that you only will be president. Women can be president too. (Boris Yeltsin announcing in Moscow that he would not seek a third term as president: *Hartford Courant*, 1997)

As the twentieth century draws to a close the mixed legacy of racial progress and persistent racial disadvantage continues to confront America and shape our political landscape. (Oliver and Shapiro, 1995: 1173)

We professors talk a lot about subversion, which generally means subverting the views of people who never hear us talk or read our work. But to subvert the views of our students, our customers, that would be something else again. (Edmundson, 1997: 49)

As noted early on, this article arose out of a 'pessimistic' concern that the political imagination at work where I teach seriously underestimates the magnitude of the off-radar racial, gender, and class gerrymandering of the politics of student opportunity. Because this campus imagination, if you will, is for the most part constrained to viewing identity, consciousness, and experience as basically characterological phenomena, it has difficulty accounting for the *ritualization* of patriarchy that we unwittingly celebrate each spring. Grounded in the notion that there's always more than meets the eye, this paper attempts to bring the *stamina* of this enactment into prominence so that we might ask questions of it and ourselves, *because there may be some lessons that we do not want our children to unreflexively pass down to their children.*

Connected with this concern is another problem. Democratic tradition depends on an active citizenry, i.e. enough discerning citizens who know how to cut through face values and engage the world on terms other than its own. It's just that B-Schools are by tradition not very good places for acquiring such behind-the-line(s) skills. My fear, therefore, is that we will *persevere* on our present course by graduating students unschooled in breaking the rules. In his feisty yet strongly-researched *When Corporations Rule the World* (1997), David C. Korten complains that business schools leave no room for students to think about commonplace assumptions they may not have thought about before. Moreover, business education generally provides students little opportunity to learn anything critical about corporations. Thus, they operate without perspective on what corporations actually do. The upshot is, that trained to think in strictly functional and functionalist terms, students reenter the world unprepared as social critics and change agents. In effect, they unwittingly become part of the problem. Specifically, our disciplinary emphasis on 'existing ideas' leaves such managers-to-be largely unprepared to deal with the enduring institutionalized practices which exclude 'others' from positions of influence even in 2000. Nor, in their naiveté, will students or their instructors be able to acknowledge their own contributions to the persistence of profoundly racist and sexist organizational designs (Van Dijk, 1993).

And not unlike my university's self-beguiling initiatives, from a structural perspective even the burgeoning corporate diversity movement is similarly handicapped. As a program for tolerance (beyond black and white), diversity, in effect, privatizes race, gender and the causes of and solutions for social inequalities. Thus, though well-intentioned, as ideological mechanisms diversity programs unwittingly serve to freeze the status quo within a 'feel-good [color-blind] racial boosterism' (Boynton, 1995: 67) by forgetting the past. For all its purported faults (the narcissism of ethnic identity, or knuckling under to minority manipulation, for two hackneyed examples), affirmative action (AA), on the other hand, asks much more of us. Specifically, AA asks that we think long and hard about what kind of society we want. In structural terms, AA is about traversing our most intractable fault (C-) lines. Among other things, AA operates as a hard reminder that racial and gender justice can't be bought on the cheap. No doubt it is the remembering that AA tasks us to do that figures in its lightning rod status (see Bergmann, 1997; Burdman, 1997; Eastland, 1997; Gates and West, 1997; Kinder and Sanders, 1997; Holmes, 1997; Lawrence and Matsuda, 1997; Skrentny, 1997). 'Market-driven' or not, corporate diversity projects are unlikely to realize their purported meritocratic goals (i.e. the 'color blind', ecumenical workplace) without squarely facing up to the *obdurate* nature of *impersonal* hierarchic politics. Indeed, if entrenched power is factored in, it is possible to see how these well-meant, yet ultimately benign, efforts unwittingly (and ironically) work to embed the processes of exclusion they ostensibly aim to palliate (Omi and Winant, 1994; Cavanaugh, 1997).

For what it's worth, the much-heralded millennium is upon us, yet the centuries-old consequences of race and gender subordination continue to mock centuries-old commitments to egalitarian values. Is diversity from the neck down really the best we can do? William Calvin sagely reminds us that

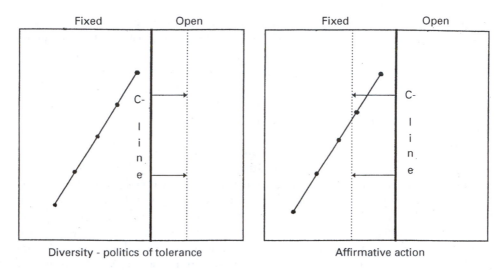

Exhibit6   *Diversity vs AA*

'Without imagination, we have no mechanisms by which to use reflection to mold experience, to bring something new out of the old, or to sympathetically project ourselves into someone else's shoes' (1996: 160). Which, after all is said and done, returns us to the chief concern of this essay: finding ways to dispose the reader to meditate on why we continue to put up with 'things' as they are.

Acknowledgements

My sincere thanks to Paul Caster, Pat Cavanaugh, Lucy Katz, Pushi and Anshu Prasad, David Schmidt, Rob White, and Lisa Yamilkoski for their unstinting support and unstinting comments. An additional salute to Yiannis Gabriel, David Sims, and Chris Grey for shepherding this project to its finish. And, not least, my respects to my anonymous reviewers for their caring and knowledgeable commentary.

Notes

1. By 'Freudian slips' I am referring to those occasional slips of the pen (and tongue) that provide us with telling glimpses of racial boundary-setting at work ('other' vs 'own'). Slips fall in the same category of 'some of my best friends are black' self-toasts, or alleged instances of faculty singling out a class's one black student to serve as unofficial spokesperson for her entire race on some 'racial' issue. Without evident self-awareness, for example, white students routinely refer to their black classmates as 'they'. Such racial peccadilloes did not originate with, nor were ever limited to, the classroom, of course. Recall when the then 1992 presidential candidate, Ross Perot, speaking at the NAACP annual convention, addressed his audience as 'you people' (Kennedy, 1997). Slips are just the tip of the racial *zeitgeist* that one is up against.

2. I realize that *this* aspiration goes against the *critical community's* institutional common sense. On those occasions, for example, when critical colleagues gather to schmooze after long

separations, invariably the first serious question to be asked is 'what are you writing?', *not* 'what are you teaching?' or even 'what are you writing about teaching?' (because even *writing* about teaching doesn't quite figure as respectable intellectual work). (For exceptions to this see hooks, 1994; French and Grey, 1996; and Giroux, 1997.) However, I think an argument can be made that teaching deserves better than the marginalized, Rodney Dangerfield status it currently enjoys. Today, a 'critical' mass of scholar/teachers is at work applying a variety of 'grounds'-breaking approaches in business-oriented classrooms. Why not harness this resource (expanded by scholar/teachers from non-business traditions as well) and set to fashioning the penultimate oxymoronic project, i.e. a collective deconstructive program centered on rewriting the business academy's reductive curriculum (see Mills and Simmons, 1995)? At this point, is there anyone out there who still believes that writing for arcane academic journals has rocked the canonical boat? If the development of new forms of problem-solving subjectivity is what's at stake here, then what better site than that locus of cultural production, the business school classroom (Atkins, 1989; Brick, 1992; Giroux, 1997), to carry this out? Teaching's acceptance as a legitimate form of intellectual labor hinges on the willingness of critical scholars to revisit some of their own pet hierarchies.

3. Allow me to add that while I revert to techspeak now and again, this narrative relies mainly on ordinary language and a certain conversational style so as to make more than academic points with critical and non-critical readers alike. The essay also deviates from the business academy norm with its thicket of endnotes, its attempt to personalize theory, and in that it closes on a cautionary note, i.e. literally centuries of normative inequality won't be displaced in a mere class session or two no matter how potentially 'unsettling' an exercise's design or an instructor's skill in delivering it. Among other things, the critical literature teaches us that canonical texts possess more lives than most cats. (Keep in mind what Goldberg [1993: 41] calls 'the theoretical imperative to closure'. Innately self-referential, peremptory [Morgan, 1986], and self-perpetuating, the sheer vanity of these hidebound conceptual entities leaves them indisposed to sharing the stage with the ideological competition.) Critical pedagogues, therefore, can't afford to indulge in wishful, much less wistful, thinking. However, as I will try to show, something long-term may yet be gleaned from tactical 'disagreements' such as this, including (hopefully), the recognition among critical scholars and educators that the 'rear-ticulation' project of which this is a part is too big and too important to be pursued in academic reclusion. Which is an off-handed way of saying that if critical theorists really mean to blaze progressive inroads, it is imperative, given their numbers and the epistemological resources now at their command (Fraser, 1989), that they commence on a common program rooted in the classroom *and* in the community. This will entail a top-to-bottom rethinking of the divisions separating the academic intellectual from the classroom, and from political activists, unionism (see Berman, 1997) and elected officialdom in general. Otherwise, I fear, the institutional imperatives of academic legitimation and placement will continue to sidetrack critical theory's promise to deliver on its program to broaden our range of commitments to one another (Mouffe, 1996; James, 1997).

4. That is not to say that these incidents have been forgotten, or that the university has stood still in the meantime. For example, the university has since funded two summer faculty workshops on diversity. In addition, a diversity requirement has been added to the under-graduate curriculum requiring all students beginning with the 1995 class to take at least one course giving 'significant treatment' to the subject of diversity and pluralism in the United States. A (non-Western) diversity requirement was installed in the 1999 academic year.

5. It is my experience that, by and large, my privileged business students go about their daily lives oblivious of any concept of social structure, and without any immediate ill-effects. To speak about the question of social structure to an audience of sociologists is not the same as unveiling it to a class of business students or faculty, even. A lesson in structure, in other words, represents the steepest of learning curves for students because it threatens to disconfirm many basic self-understandings. For one, the business discourse is largely empiricist in nature – students and faculty learn early to place their faith in literal facts, i.e. that what you see is what you get, and even 'the social' consists of facts that are unproblematically knowable. When all is said and done, numbers are what really count. This caveat begins to explain why I inserted the sobering 'with some success' disclaimer in my introductory remarks.

6. Remarkably, in 1999 a woman candidate made it to the finals, losing by a mere seven votes. Regressing to the mean, so to speak, this year's pool of candidates is all male.

7. I also regularly assign Omi and Winant's (1994) *Racial Formation in the United States* (2nd edition) for its assiduous analysis of racial genealogy in the United States. While a dense read in places, chapter 4, 'Racial Formation' is a must for white students in particular, who, as someone once observed, are for the most part unaware that they have a racial identity to begin with. Chapter 4 also serves up a useful glossary of terms not customarily found in the mainstream business and (most interestingly) diversity literatures: racism, discourse, resistance, hegemony, the common sense, and essentialism.

8. Social instinct should not be conflated with the mainstream literature's prevailing notion of 'culture'. There are significant differences: for example (1), culture in the conventional literature is largely treated as a noun, an object, a management tool. Among other things, this substantialization tends 'to discourage attention to the worldviews and agency of those who are marginalized or dominated' (Appadurai, 1996: 12); (2), given the management literature's empiricist bent, culture is typically embodied in physical artifacts typified by Rolex watches and executive dining rooms or special events (see Rosen, 1985) designed to get employees to try harder. The idea, for example, that corporate drug testing programs might possess more symbolic than material content is outside the conceptual scope of this literature (see Cavanaugh and Prasad, 1994); (3), the conventional literature treats organizational culture as a prerogative (and independent variable) available only to management – something management makes, owns and shapes at will, i.e. management as puppeteer; and last, (4), as a functionalist discourse, orthodox theory has frequently been faulted for begging 'beginnings' (origins), i.e. covering its tracks. (For more see Mouzellis, 1995.) Fundamentally a language of objects, the mainstream literature is not epistemologically positioned to capture the phenomenology of the world.

9. Anamorphosis refers to the technique of optical illusions first used by an extraordinary group of 16th and 17th century painters to highlight the new laws of visual (and political) perspective. (The skull in Holbein's *The Ambassadors* [1533] is probably the best-known example of this technique.) Consider it the Renaissance equivalent of laser holography where images change shape when viewed from different angles. Dalia Judovitz describes anamorphosis as an early deconstructive technique for redefining vision:

> anamorphosis emerges as a device whose speculative impact lies in the conceptual redefinition of the visible ... Anamorphosis announces a new relation to the visible, one which conceives visual form not as a given but as a conceptual and technical construct ... As a technique that reduces the visible world to a false reality, and ordinary vision to a kind of blindness, anamorphosis announces the emergence of a new concept of vision and a new philosophical outlook. (1993: 69)

10. It is said that Malcolm Forbes Jr was once asked to describe the source of his vast monetary and social standing. His reputed answer: 'I picked the right grandparents.' The link with our story is that the ranking of the designated handicappings depicted in Exhibit 2 are ascribed or, as McIntosh (1992) would say, unearned. As the social nepotism in the Forbes vignette implies, chances are that we inherit not only our parents' blue eyes and flat feet, but their social status as well (Oliver and Shapiro, 1997). In a very real sense, the opportunity game ('the race') is arbitrary from the cradle forward.

11. One can provide a powerful lesson in social calculus by exposing students to the state of Connecticut's Mastery Test Score results, published annually. Used to assess reading, writing, and basic math skills in grades 4, 6, and 8 and tabulated by town and a host of socio-economic indicators, year after year the numbers reveal 'the large *stubborn* [my italics] academic gap between middle class and poor children ...' (Frahm, 1997). For example, 85 percent of the fourth graders in the affluent town of Avon, Connecticut (median family income of $98,495) achieved the state's mathematics goal in 1997. Whereas, in the city of Bridgeport (median family income of $24,349), just over one out of four (26%) children in the fourth grade tested up to standard. This is hard core math.

12. Social structure, for example, operates as the pivotal analytic metaphor for a long honor roll of thinkers including Jean-Jacques Rousseau, Karl Marx, Max Weber, Emile Durkheim, W.

E. B. Du Bois, Alvin Gouldner, C. Wright Mills, Talcott Parsons, Anthony Giddens, Pierre Bourdieu, Michel Foucault, Dorothy Smith, and a host of others.

13. 'Canonical' is derived from the Latin meaning reed. It is used here as a frontier for demarcating settled, orthodox belief (destination) from knowledge still in-the-making (journey).

References

Alvesson, M. and Willmott, H. (eds) (1992) *Critical Management Studies.* London: Sage.

Angier, N. (1997) 'Evolutionary Necessity or Glorious Accident? Biologists Ponder the Self', *The New York Times*, 22 April: C1.

Appadurai, A. (1996) *Modernity at Large: Cultural Dimensions of Globalization.* Minneapolis: University of Minnesota Press.

Astley, G. (1984) 'Subjectivity, Sophistry and Symbolism in Management Science', *Journal of Management Studies* 21(3): 259–72.

Atkins, G.D. (1989) 'Introduction: Literary Theory, Critical Practice, and the Classroom', in G.D. Atkins and L. Morrow (eds) *Contemporary Literary Theory.* Amherst: The University of Massachusetts Press.

Banks, W.M. (1996) *Black Intellectuals: Race and Responsibility in American Life.* New York: W.W. Norton & Co.

Bauman, Z. (1973) *Culture as Praxis.* London: Routledge & Kegan Paul.

Barnes, J.B. and Duncan, J.S. (1992) *Writing Worlds.* New York: Routledge.

Battaglia, D. (ed.) (1995) *Rhetorics of Self-Making.* Berkeley: University of California Press.

Bellah, R., Madsen, R., Sullivan, W.M., Swidler, A. and Tipton, S.M. (1985) *Habits of the Heart.* New York: Harper & Row.

Berger, P. and Luckmann, T. (1966) *The Social Construction of Reality.* Garden City, NY: Doubleday.

Bergmann, B.R. (1997) *In Defense of Affirmative Action.* New York: Basic Books.

Berman, P. (1997) 'Labor and the Intellectuals', *The American Prospect* 34 (Sept.–Oct.): 76–80.

Bernstein, R.J. (1976) *The Restructuring of Social and Political Theory.* Philadelphia: University of Pennsylvania Press.

Blau, J.R. (1993) *Social Contracts and Economic Markets.* New York: Plenum Press.

Botstein, L. (1997) *Jefferson's Children: Education and the Promise of American Culture.* New York: Doubleday.

Bourdieu, P. (1990) *In Other Words: Essays Towards a Reflexive Sociology.* Cambridge: Polity Press.

Boyer, P.J. (1996) 'Admiral Boorda's War', *The New Yorker* 16 September: 68–86.

Boynton, R.S. (1995) 'The New Intellectuals', *The Atlantic Monthly* (March): 53–70.

Boynton, R.S. (1997) 'The Lives of Robert Hughes', *The New Yorker*, 12 May: 44–53.

Brick, M.L. (ed.) (1992) *Ideas and Events: Professing History.* Chicago: The University of Chicago Press.

Brown, R.H. (1989) *Social Science as Civic Discourse: Essays on the Invention, Legitimation, and Uses of Social Theory.* Chicago: The University of Chicago Press.

Burdman, P. (1997) 'The Long Goodbye', *Linguafranca* 7(5): 28–39.

Butler, J. (1993) *Bodies that Matter.* London: Routledge.

Calvin, W.H. (1996) *The Cerebral Code: Thinking a Thought in the Mosaics of the Mind.* Cambridge, MA: MIT Press.

Cavanaugh, J.M. (1997) '(In)corporating the Other? Managing the Politics of Workplace Difference' in P. Prasad, A.J. Mills, M. Elmes, and A. Prasad (eds) *Managing the Organizational Melting Pot: Dilemmas of Workplace Diversity.* Thousand Oaks, CA: Sage.

Cavanaugh, J.M. and Prasad, P. (1994) 'Drug Testing as Symbolic Managerial Action: In Response to "A Case Against Workplace Drug Testing"', *Organizational Science* (May): 2.

Cavanaugh, J.M. and Prasad, A. (1996) 'Critical Theory and Management Education: Some Strategies for the Critical Classroom' in R. French and C. Grey (eds) *Rethinking Management Education.* London: Sage Publications.

Chia, R. (1996) *Organizational Analysis as Deconstructive Practice.* New York: Walter de Gruyter.

Clegg, S.R. (1996) 'Constituting Management', in G. Palmer and S.R. Clegg (eds) *Constituting Management: Markets, Meanings, and Identities*, pp. 1–9. New York: Walter de Gruyter.

Cohen, R. (1997) 'Elegy for the Hobby', *The New York Times Magazine*, 25 May: 46–7.

Collingwood, R.G. (1940) *An Essay on Metaphysics*. Oxford: Oxford University Press.

Deetz, S.A. (1992) *Democracy in an Age of Corporate Colonization: Developments in Communication and the Politics of Everyday Life*. Albany, NY: SUNY.

Denhardt, R.B. (1981) *In the Shadow of Organization*. Lawrence, KA: University Press of Kansas.

Derrida, J. (1981) *Positions*. Chicago: The University of Chicago Press.

Dizard, J.E. (1991) 'Achieving Place: Teaching Social Stratification to Tomorrow's Elite', in *Teaching What We Do: Essays by Amherst College Faculty*. Amherst, MA: Amherst College Press.

Douglas, M. (1986) *How Institutions Think*. Syracuse, NY: Syracuse University Press.

Drefus, H. (1991) *Being in the World: A Commentary on Heidegger's* Being and Time, *Division 1*. Cambridge, MA: MIT Press.

Drefus, H. and Hall, H. (eds) (1992) *Heidegger: A Critical Reader*. Oxford: Blackwell.

Drucker, P.F. (1993) *Post-Capitalist Society*. New York: HarperCollins.

Eastland, T. (1997) *Ending Affirmative Action: The Case for Colorblind Justice*. New York: Basic Books.

Edmundson, M. (1997) 'On the Uses of a Liberal Education: 1. As Lite Entertainment', *Harper's Magazine* 297(1768): 39–49.

Elliott, A. (1992) *Social Theory and Psychoanalysis in Transition. Self and Society from Freud to Kristeva*. Oxford: Blackwell.

Evernden, N. (1993) *The Natural Alien: Humankind and Environment*. Toronto: University of Toronto Press.

Fischer, C.S., Hout, M., Jankowski, M.S., Lucas, S.R., Swidler, A. and Voss, K. (1996) *Inequality by Design: Cracking the Bell Curve Myth*. Princeton, NJ: Princeton University Press.

Foucault, M. (1972) *The Order of Things*. New York: Pantheon.

Foucault, M. (1982) 'The Subject and Power', in H.L. Dreyfus and P. Rabinow (eds) *Michel Foucault: Beyond Structuralism and Hermeneutics*. Chicago: University of Chicago Press.

Frahm, R.A. (1997) 'Mastery Test Scores Up, But Cities Still Lag', *The Hartford Courant*, 18 January: A1.

Fraser, N. (1989) *Unruly Practices: Power, Discourse, and Gender in Contemporary Social Theory*. Minneapolis: University of Minnesota Press.

French, R. and Grey, C. (eds) (1996) *Rethinking Management Education*. London: Sage.

Frost, P. (1980) 'Toward a Radical Framework for Practicing Organizational Science', *Academy of Management Review* 5: 501–7.

Galbraith, J.K. (1997) 'Executive Suite: A Social History of Corporate Man', book review. *The New York Times Book Review*, 29 June: 13.

Garfinkel, H. (1984) *Studies in Ethnomethodology*. Oxford: Blackwell.

Gates, Jr., H.L. and West, C. (1997) *The Future of the Race*. New York: Knopf.

Geertz, C. (1973) *The Interpretation of Cultures*. New York: Basic Books.

Gergen, K. (1978) 'Toward Generative Theory', *Journal of Personality and Social Psychology* 31: 1344–60.

Gilkey, L. (1993) *Nature, Reality, and the Sacred: The Nexus of Science and Religion*. Minneapolis, MN: Fortress Press.

Giroux, H.A. (1997) *Pedagogy and the Politics of Hope: Theory, Culture, and Schooling*. Boulder, CO: Westview Press.

Goffman, E. (1959) *The Presentation of Self in Everyday Life*. Garden City, NJ: Doubleday.

Goldberg, D.T. (1993) *Racist Culture: Philosophy and the Politics of Meaning*. Cambridge, MA: Blackwell.

Greenfield, T.B. (1979) 'Organization Theory as Ideology', *Curriculum Inquiry* 9(2): 97–112.

Hacking, I. (1985) 'Making Up People', in *Reconstructing Individualism*. Stanford, CA: Stanford University Press.

Hall, S. (1996) 'Introduction: Who Needs "Identity"?', in S. Hall and P. du Gay (eds) *Questions of Cultural Identity*. London: Sage.

Hartford Courant (1997) *CLIX* No. 245, 2 Sept.: A1.

Holmes, S.A. (1997) 'U.S. Acts to Open Minority Program to White Bidders', *The New York Times*, 15 August: A1.

hooks, b. (1989) *Talking Back: Thinking Feminist, Thinking Black*. Boston, MA: South End Press.

hooks, b. (1990) *Yearning: Race, Gender, and Cultural Politics*. Toronto: Between the Lines.

hooks, b. (1994) *Teaching to Transgress: Education as the Practice of Freedom*. New York: Routledge.

Jacobs, A. (1997) 'Preserving a Delicate Balance', *The Sunday New York Times*, 18 May (9): 1, 8.

James, J. (1997) *Transcending the Talented Tenth: Black Leaders and American Intellectuals*. New York: Routledge.

Judovitz, D. (1993) 'Vision, Representation, and Technology in Descartes', in D.M. Levin (ed.) *Modernity and the Hegemony of Vision*, pp. 63–86. Berkeley: University of California Press.

Kanter, R.M. (1977) *Men and Women of the Corporation*. New York: Basic Books.

Kennedy, R. (1997) 'My Race Problem – and Ours', *The Atlantic Monthly* May 279(5): 55–66.

Kinder, D.R. and Sanders, L.M. (1997) *Divided by Color: Racial Politics and Democratic Ideals*. Chicago: The University of Chicago Press.

Korten, D.C. (1997) *When Corporations Rule the World*. San Francisco, CA: Berrett-Koehler Publishers, Inc.

Kuhn, T.S. (1970) *The Structure of Scientific Revolutions*, 2nd edn. Chicago: University of Chicago Press.

LaCapra, D. (1983) *Rethinking Intellectual History: Texts, Contexts, Language*. Ithaca, NY: Cornell University Press.

Laclau, E. (1994) *The Making of Political Identities*. London: Verso.

Law, J. (1994) *Organizing Modernity*. Oxford: Blackwell.

Lawrence III, C.R. and Matsuda, M.J. (1997) *We Won't Go Back: Making the Case for Affirmative Action*. Boston, MA: Houghton Mifflin Co.

Lemert, C. (1995) *Sociology After the Crisis*. Boulder, CO: Westview Press.

Lilla, M. (1994) 'The Legitimacy of the Liberal Age', in M. Lilla (ed.) *New French Thought: Political Philosophy*. Princeton, NJ: Princeton University Press.

McIntosh, P. (1992) 'White Privilege and Male Privilege: A Personal Account of Coming to See Correspondences Through Work in Women's Studies', in M.L. Anderson and P.H. Collins (eds) *Race, Class, and Gender*. Belmont, CA: Wadsworth Publishing Co.

Marsden, R. (1993) 'The Politics of Organizational Analysis', *Organization Studies* 14(1): 93–124.

Meyer, J.W. and Rowan, B. (1977) 'Institutionalized Organizations: Formal Structure as Myth and Ceremony', *American Journal of Sociology* 83: 340–63.

Mills, A. and Simmons, T. (1995) *Reading Organizational Theory: A Critical Approach*. Toronto: Garamond Press.

Morgan, G. (1986) *Images of Organizations*, Newbury Park, CA: Sage.

Mouffe, C. (1996) 'Deconstruction, Pragmatism and the Politics of Democracy', in Chantal Mouffe (ed.) *Deconstruction and Pragmatism*. London: Routledge.

Mouzellis, N. (1995) *Sociological Theory: What Went Wrong?* London: Routledge.

Murdoch, I. (1970) *The Sovereignty of Good*. London: Routledge & Kegan Paul.

Oliver, M.L. and Shapiro, T.M. (1995) *Black Wealth/White Wealth: A New Perspective on Racial Inequality*. New York: Routledge.

Omi, M. and Winant, H. (1994) *Racial Formation in the United States from the 1960s to the 1990s*. New York: Routledge.

Perrow, C. (1972) *Complex Organizations: A Critical Essay*. New York: Random House.

Porter, M. (1980) *Competitive Strategy: Techniques for Analyzing Industries and Competitors*. New York: Free Press.

Ranson, S., Hinings, B. and Greenwood, R. (1980) 'The Structuring of Organizational Structures', *Administrative Science Quarterly* 25: 1–17.

Reich, R.B. (1991) *The Work of Nations*. New York: Alfred A. Knopf.

Ricoeur, P. (1992) *Oneself as Another* (translated by Kathleen Blamey). Chicago: The University of Chicago Press.

Ridley, M. (1996) *The Origin of Virtue: Human Instincts and the Evolution of Cooperation*. New York: Penguin.

Rose, M. (1975) *Industrial Behaviour: Theoretical Development Since Taylor*. London: Allen Lane.

Rosen, M. (1985) 'Breakfast at Spiro's: Dramaturgy and Dominance', *Journal of Management* 11(2): 31–48.

Ryan, A. (1972) '"Normal" Science or Political Ideology?', in P. Laslett, W.G. Runciman, and Q. Skinner (eds) *Philosophy, Politics and Society*, 4th edn. Oxford: Blackwell.

Sacks, O. (1995) *An Anthropologist on Mars*. New York: Alfred A. Knopf.

Samuels, D. (1997) 'Bringing Down the House: An Explosion in Las Vegas Plays as Performance Art', *Harper's Magazine* 295(1766): 37–52.

Schumpeter, J. (1950) *Capitalism, Socialism, and Democracy*. New York: Harper & Row.

Schutz, A. (1962) *Collected Papers, Vol. 1: The Problems of Social Reality*. The Hague: D. Reidel.

Scott, J. (1990) *Domination and the Arts of Resistance*. London: Yale University Press.

Shanon, B. (1993) *The Representational and the Presentational: An Essay on Cognition and the Study of Mind*. Hemel Hempstead: Harvester Wheatsheaf.

Silverman, D. (1971) *The Theory of Organizations*. London: Heinemann.

Skrentny, J.D. (1997) *The Ironies of Affirmative Action: Politics, Culture, and Justice in America*. Chicago: The University of Chicago Press.

Smircich, L. (1985) 'Is the Concept of Culture a Paradigm for Understanding Organizations and Ourselves?', in P.J. Frost et al. (eds) *Organizational Culture*. Thousand Oaks, CA: Sage.

Steffy, B.D. and Grimes, A.J. (1986) 'A Critical Theory of Organization Science', *Academy of Management Review* 11(2): 322–36.

Stiehm, J. (1994) 'Diversity's Diversity', in D.T. Goldberg (ed.) *Multiculturalism: A Critical Reader*. Oxford: Blackwell.

Thompson, J.B. (1989) 'The Theory of Structuration', in David Held and John B. Thompson (eds) *Social Theory of Modern Societies: Anthony Giddens and His Critics*. Cambridge: Cambridge University Press.

Thrift, N. (1996) *Spatial Formations*. London: Sage.

Van Dijk, T.A. (1993) 'Introduction: The Reality of Rascism', in T.A. Van Dijk (ed.) *Elite Discourse and Racism*, pp. 1–17. Newbury Park, CA: Sage.

Van Maanen, J. (1979) 'Reclaiming Qualitative Methods for Organizational Research', *Administrative Science Quarterly* 24: 520–6.

Weick, K. (1977) 'Enactment Processes in Organizations', in B.M. Staw and G.R. Salancik (eds) *New Directions in Organizational Behavior*, pp. 267–300. Chicago: St. Clair Press.

Weick, K. (1979) *The Social Psychology of Organizing*, 2nd ed. Reading, MA: Addison-Wesley.

White, H. (1978) *Tropics of Discourse*. Baltimore, MD: Johns Hopkins University Press.

Winch, P. (1958) *The Idea of a Social Science and Its Relation to Philosophy*. London: Routledge and Kegan Paul.

Zucker, L.G. (1977) 'The Role of Institutionalization in Cultural Persistance', *American Sociological Review* 42: 726–43.

11

Amanda Sinclair

Teaching Managers about Masculinities:
Are You Kidding?

It is well accepted that research of gender in organizations needs to encompass analysis of the experiences of men, as well as women. Yet when we turn to teaching managers about gender in organizations there are strong pressures to keep curricula focused on women (Thompson and McGivern, 1995). Masculinities and the way they shape how men manage remain a resisted, if not taboo, subject in teaching. In this article I explore why teaching masculinities is so difficult, particularly for a woman.

Researchers have ably demonstrated the pitfalls of conceptualizing gender within a 'women in management' framework (Riger and Galligan, 1980; Calas and Smircich, 1993; Gray, 1994). From approaches dominated by blanket concerns about women and equity, critical theorizing has illuminated how political and discursive processes construct gender differences and sexual identities and their impacts on organizational life (Linstead, 1995; Brewis, Hampton and Linstead, 1997). Few of us now talk about 'difference' or 'diversity' in managerial parlance, as an untheorized construct or an un-problematized good (Derrida, 1978; Crawford, 1995).

Similarly there is a substantial and growing body of research exploring the relationship between masculinities and management. Kanter was among early management researchers to identify a 'masculine ethic' central to the image of managers (1977: 22) and in his pioneering *The Limits of Masculinity* (1977) Tolson showed how work defined male identity. Hearn and Morgan's 1990 collection entitled *Men, Masculinities and Social Theory* explored the organiza-tion as a critical site in the construction of masculinities. Cockburn followed her earlier work on the masculine cultures of shopfloor workers (1983, 1985), with an investigation of British retail managers (1991). Collinson (1992), Maddock and Parkin (1993), Parkin and Maddock (1995), Roper and Tosh (1991), Roper (1994) and Collinson and Hearn (1994), among others, have documented how masculinities are interwoven into men's organizational and managerial identities.

Theorists are sensibly wary of defining masculinities, yet for reasons elaborated in this article, I argue there is value in helping managers develop an understanding of how the gender identities of men shape organizational experiences. Masculinities are historically and socially constructed categories which define legitimate behaviours and identities for men (Connell, 1987,

1995). This article is titled 'masculinities' in the plural sense to underline the multiplicity of masculine identities, some privileged and others stigmatized and marginalized (Hearn and Morgan, 1990).

Research provides a rich charting of emergent and contesting masculinities – in privileged managerial sites (Kerfoot and Knights, 1993); among entrepreneurs and 'self-made men' (Reed, 1996; Mulholland, 1996); and in the military (Barrett, 1996). Connell provides a powerful analysis of masculinities on the fringe of, or outside, traditionally work-defined maleness: among young unemployed men, feminist-influenced environmentalist men, and men in conventional jobs who are homosexual. This research leaves little doubt that for many men and for most managers, work accomplishes masculinity. In organizational life, the two identities of manager and man have fitted hand in glove (Collinson and Hearn, 1996).

Yet when we turn to teaching managers about gender in organizations there are strong pressures to keep curricula focused on women and to sanitize sex and gender issues, packaging them into more palatable discourses of 'diversity'. There is a hard-to-resist urge to focus on 'the other', on the women or ethnic minority groups and the problems they are seen to bring – and this urge is the enemy of reflection.

This article explores my experiences in introducing masculinities to management education and development. I begin by describing my dissatisfaction with the limitations of teaching gender within traditional frameworks. Discovering the extensive research on masculinities and undertaking my own research, I was inspired to draw these ideas into my teaching and I discuss the difficulties encountered in doing so.

This article is divided into two parts. The first part examines difficulties to do with the subject matter of masculinities which is a resisted topic, I argue, for reasons to do with language and terminology, and because the nature of the phenomenon is so taken for granted that it is invisible (Collinson and Hearn, 1994). The second part of the article focuses on pedagogy. I identify reasons why men who are managers don't want to 'be taught' about masculinities within conventional processes of management education and why they don't want a woman initiating discussion. In practice, of course, the subject matter of masculinities and the means by which it is introduced are interdependent and I conclude underlining the importance of the overarching structure and philosophy within which management learning occurs.

Teaching Gender

My journey in teaching gender began by incorporating material on discrimination and harassment within mainstream organizational theory and organizational change courses. We looked at cases of discrimination and the costs to companies and managers of not being proactive about equal employment opportunity. Much of my efforts were spent dispelling misconceptions about, for example, Affirmative Action, and showing how constructs like 'merit' might not be the refuges of objectivity my students hoped.

Then followed the 'women in management' emphasis which was popular with most of the women, because it helped them explain their experiences as systemic symptoms rather than personal failures. But particularly with pre-dominantly male groups, discussions of the problems women encounter very quickly turned into 'the trouble with women is ...' Experiences were volunteered about no women applying for jobs, about women being unwilling to move interstate, about them wanting to take one day a week off, about them taking a *second* maternity leave (how dare they!). The urge to scapegoat 'the other' as the problem seemed overwhelming.

The only exceptions to this response came from men who had under-standings of the issue anchored to personal experiences. For example, they were more open if they had a female partner or daughter encountering organizational discrimination or if they were struggling to share child-care responsibilities in an unsympathetic corporate environment (see also French, 1995). Sometimes too, if they came from a minority racial or cultural background, there was more interest in the dynamics of discrimination.

It was around this time and driven by the demands of corporate clients that I started talking about gender via diversity. I still utilize the rhetoric and arguments of 'productive diversity' (a term emphasizing cultural differences and given legitimacy by a previous Australian prime minister) on some of my short course teaching and consulting assignments.

The inclusive language of diversity sometimes has more appeal to men than equal employment opportunity, gender or masculinities. Men can see that they are not all the same and an organizational environment that recognizes differences is attractive: 'Everyone is different so let's all develop our communication skills and tolerance to bring out the best of everyone'. At this point someone will have read *Men are from Mars, Women are from Venus* (Gray, 1993) and the discussion can easily degenerate into a 'spot the difference' discussion, with the men resolving to express feelings and the women aiming to be less needy. This kind of discussion is often attractive to participants (and teachers) because it typically diverts attention from power differentials in communication patterns, avoids hostilities and promises simple solutions.

Some Problems with Teaching 'Managing Diversity'

Managers, as well as academics, are suspicious of the term 'diversity' and in my opinion they are right to be. Courses for managers in organizations on 'managing diversity' often stand, or are code, for a more specific issue which is unnamable. The reaction of many managers is that 'this is EEO in another guise' (Hemphill and Haines, 1997).

People involved in equal employment opportunity (EEO) or Affirmative Action are just as sceptical for different reasons. They regard managing diversity as a sellout to management, a management-controlled agenda determined to sanitize a conflict-laden issue and bestow on organizations the appearance of enlightenment without beginning to critique the management framework within which diversity would tidily be subsumed.

There are many problems with the managing diversity model as a vehicle for teaching gender. I will discuss only two of the more fundamental here. The first is that 'diversity' fosters a focus on the 'other' in organizations, on those who are deemed 'different' within the dominant regime. The second problem is that the managing diversity approach ignores power – it takes existing power differentials as granted and it fails to recognize that changing the distribution of power is a prerequisite of any shift in gender relations (Cockburn, 1990). I will briefly discuss these two problems.

When people think about managing diversity, they think of managing those who are different from them, different from the norm. If you look at the course curricula for a great number of Managing Diversity subjects, after dealing with general topics such as prejudice they move through a list like:

Gender dynamics
Sexual preference
Age
Race and ethnicity
Disability
International operation. (Managing Cultural Diversity at Suffolk University, autumn 1992)

Another course has classes on the following: 'African American, Mexican American, Asian American, Native American/Euro American'. Courses on diversity are full of articles on women, racial, cultural and linguistic minorities, gay and lesbian issues.

The best of these courses include time and space to consider the dominant group. Nancy DiTomaso's 'Managing Diversity in Organizations' (1993) at Rutgers Graduate School of Management, includes a session and case on 'US Born, White Men'. But DiTomaso admits: 'The group I still find hardest to address is native-born, white men ... Most of what we think we know about people in organizations, at least at the management level, is about white men', yet this is a curiously difficult session. So she opts to address 'the opportunities and challenges for white men as part of a diverse workforce' (DiTomaso, 1993: 2).

Taylor Cox, a black American who has been a pioneer of diversity research, argues that the solution is more careful specification of the term diversity: 'If the language of diversity encourages people to think of diversity as referring only to members of minority groups, then the definition of the term itself can be used to polarize people and reduce cross-group collaborative effort' (1994: 52–3). My experience is that people will imbue terms with the meaning they want, regardless of how meticulous the definition offered. Diversity is seen by dominant groups to be something to do with other people and it requires considerable ingenuity to redirect this focus.

The best diversity programs teach people about themselves, not others. They help people understand their own power and privilege (Schor, Sims and Dennehy, 1996). They also teach students to tune into their own sense-making structures better, to be aware of the desire for the familiar, their discomfort with ambiguity and 'foreignness' and need for resolution and closure. Good diversity programs show why we stereotype and how prejudice comes about. It puts discrimination in a broader historical context and shows how dismantling discrimination requires much more than watching what one says to, or assumes about, a colleague.

Despite the best efforts of teachers and trainers, however, more frequently diversity education becomes an opportunity to learn about, or worse, exoticize 'the other'. Focusing on gender, the Australian academic, Joan Eveline, argues the need to arrest the drift of discourse emphasizing women's disadvantage. This discourse conveniently obscures to whom the benefits traditionally accrue and makes women answerable for their 'special treatment'. Instead of using 'women's disadvantage' as the pretext for action, Eveline argues, the need is to understand 'men's advantage' (1994).

Critical perspectives advise us that we need to turn our attention from those who are different to exploring how and why that difference is constructed by power relations and discursive practices in organizations and society. Our purpose in seeking to understand difference should be to look at the classification system itself, which casts some as different, and the way in which the label 'difference' is often code for inferior.

The basic justifications for managing diversity seem obvious to the point of being banal. Seeking to accommodate differences in organizations in the interests of organizational health, individual rights and social justice, particularly in a globalizing context, seems like an eminently sensible thing to do. The challenging part is understanding why such good principles have rarely been applied. To answer this question I came to the belief that it was important to shift from advocating how things might be to understanding how they are, why 'managing diversity' is resisted, and bases for attachment to the status quo.

The Incomprehensibility and Invisibility of Masculinities

Having experienced the shortcomings of teaching gender from the perspective of equal employment opportunity, and the weaknesses of the rhetoric of diversity, I began to try to broaden my teaching focus to take in a modest examination of masculinities. I was teaching a new course I had devised called, carefully, *Managing Differences*, in which I hoped to foster critical discussion of 'difference'. I had also realized, in a belated flash of insight, that through my research of documenting the obstacles to women in MBA education and in the Australian executive culture, I was already engaged in research of masculinities (Sinclair, 1994, 1995). I was studying the mechanisms by which particular types of masculine cultures were perpetuated and how they affected others, women and men, who didn't feel part of those cultures.

My 'discovery' of masculinities opened up a whole new chapter of understanding about gender for me. Stivers, among others, has used a particular metaphor to convey the difficulty of 'seeing' the masculinity inherent in leadership for many men. It is, she says, like 'asking the fish to notice the water in which they swim' (Stivers, 1996: 163). For my part, I felt as though I had been seeking to understand the sea by investigating the life of crabs – and missing the fish altogether.

Research focusing on masculinities is one thing, but teaching is another. In this section I explore two sets of related issues which, in my experience, inhibit the discussion of masculinities among managers. The first concerns the difficulty of making masculinities visible and as something that needs to be talked about, and the second is about the undiscussability of masculinities, who uses the term and to what end.

1. The Invisibility of Masculinities

It is my experience that you don't get take-up of a language or term such as masculinities until people *feel* a set of issues or problems that that language helps them explain and come to grips with (Tolson, 1977). Masculinities will remain invisible to managers until two things happen. The first is the recognition that discrimination occurs and is experienced as a problem. The second requirement to make masculinities visible is to move the spectator from a conscious or unconscious belief that women are the problem, to a broader stance of seeing that dimensions of the problem lie in the way things are done, or indeed within an individual's approach to work and life (Jackson, 1990; Hearn, 1992). This recognition opens the way to a discussion in which masculinities are understood as multiple and dynamic, having good and bad effects for men, as well as women.

While these requirements sound relatively straightforward to establish, there are substantial hurdles to doing so. For example, the 'silence' around masculinities in management and the active neglect of gender in analyses of leadership (Collinson and Hearn, 1996) serves the purposes of those who are wedded to and gain from existing understandings. Individual interests in silence and neglect become manifest in complex forms of institutionalized resistance (Agócs, 1997).

Arising from research interviewing eleven Australian chief executives about the challenges facing senior women in their companies, I charted four phases of executive culture's approach to issues of discrimination (Sinclair, 1994). Progress through these four phases marked an increasing recognition of the problem of discrimination against women, particularly at middle and upper levels of their organization, and a changing understanding about who was responsible for the problem and where solutions lay.

Stage 1:   *Denial: No Problem*
            The absence of women from senior levels is not a serious business issue and not a problem.

Stage 2:   *The Problem is Women*
            Women's difference is seen as the problem and the solution lies in women learning how to adapt to (male) norms.

Stage 3:   *Incremental Adjustment*
            A problem is recognized – the organization losing senior women in whom it has invested – but the solution involves improved access to

approved women, who are then expected to solve the broader problem of women in the organization.

Stage 4:   *Commitment to a New Culture*
The exclusion of women is recognized as a symptom of deeper cultural problems meaning the organization resists innovation, is insular and inflexible. Solutions are aimed at changing the existing culture and its leaders. (Sinclair, 1994)

Most large Australian companies are at Stage 1 or 2, even those whose customers and employees consist of a high proportion of women. There are only a few Australian examples of companies making a transition from Stage 3 to 4 and this is often prompted by a crisis such as a high profile legal action or consistently poor financial performance. In these cases it has been CEOs brought in from overseas who, first, 'see' a problem with an overly cosy and discriminatory culture which is not visible to the locals, and who, second, have less to lose and more to gain from radical change. Cockburn's (1990, 1991) in-depth analysis of the machinery of resistance to equal employment opportunity suggests that British organizations, like Australian ones, are more likely to be clustered at Stages 1 and 2, than 3 or 4.

American empirical studies also find evidence that because most men, particularly those in positions of authority, don't experience discrimination, they often believe it doesn't exist and see no need to change existing arrangements in organizations (for an overview of US research see Cox, 1993; and for a recent survey see Ragins, Townsend and Mattis, 1998).

In the next two examples, one with an MBA group and one with a company executive group, I show how masculinities remain invisible and undiscussable unless managers have encountered the experience of discrimination, directly or indirectly. Until and unless they have this experience, the common response is one of denial and disbelief – that there is no problem – followed by the belief that women (including me for identifying gender) are the problem.

My MBA subject *Managing Differences* started out with cultural differences and this was a relatively straightforward undertaking compared with gender and masculinities. Despite having established a good relationship with students, once we moved on to the latter topics, the men grew more and more silent. I was even taken aside after a particularly difficult class and advised by one of my male students that it would be better to drop the gender and masculinities material altogether. The view of some students was that this wasn't an appropriate subject for discussion, even though we had first hand evidence of the discomfort and dysfunctions gender relations could produce in groups. Mostly the view expressed was that there wasn't a problem or that I was the problem by raising it. When I cited research evidence or the 'here and now' evidence of the class, it was often dismissed. Students argued that discrimination was 'not the case now' or 'not relevant in professional organizations' or prevalent only between undergraduates or not something that happens between intelligent, well- educated adults.

Things improved as I tried very different approaches, particularly as 'ways in' to talk about masculinities. For example, men gradually began to volunteer examples of ways they felt imprisoned by traditional corporate masculinities – being pressured back to work after a new baby or not able to talk about the death of a child (Jackson, 1990). However, at least in the first instances, I was perceived as attacking men. My gender contaminated my capacity to establish 'good enough' trust – but more of this later (Winnicott, 1965).

In the second example I was working with other internal and external consultants and an organization's senior management team. Several hours into a workshop framed as 'managing diversity', statistics had been presented about the organization's failure to retain and promote women and men of non-Anglo backgrounds; a commitment to people management had been reaffirmed; and one senior woman had identified a culture of harassment in parts of the organization. Yet it became clear that several managers were unconvinced of any problem. Clearly frustrated, one manager described the organization: 'You work hard, you work long hours and you do battle with everybody else'. This was the way work was. His comment revealed a shared belief that the existing culture was a given, not something deserving of labelling or discussion and certainly not something that should, or could, be changed. In contrast, another manager had experience of dealing with discrimination and harassment among subordinates and recognized that certain norms, such as very long hours and a combative environment, had the effect of discriminating against some employees. For the manager experienced with discriminatory impacts, deconstructing the culture and its intermeshing with particular masculine values helped provide a deeper understanding of why, despite its good efforts, the organization seemed unable to retain women at a senior level.

2. The Undiscussability of Masculinities

Masculinities is a term that seems to leave managers speechless. Is this reaction a matter of simple innocence? Certainly, theorists are wary of the word. In his book entitled *Masculinities* Connell doesn't offer a definition of masculinity until page 44 where he provides the rather strangulated 'config-urations of practice structured by gender relations'. In his later section headed 'Defining Masculinity' he offers no definition that I could find. Beneke similarly agonizes: 'is there a morally legitimate use for the word "masculine"? Can it do anything but oppress us?' (1995: 160).

This theoretical reluctance is well grounded. Post-structuralism reveals the dynamism and multiplicity of meanings attached to words, but also how seeking to define or attach a definitive meaning is a political act which immediately invites subversion. Yet keeping masculinities undefinable and possibly incomprehensible has profound consequences for men and women who are managers. It means that many aspects of organizational life remain opaque, inaccessible, beyond discussion and change. It also means that managers revert to traditional concepts, such as 'the glass ceiling', to understand 'what's going on'. Processes of cognitive sense-making are intrinsically conservative, suggesting explanations which endorse rather than challenge the status quo and solutions which necessitate changes which managers can exact from others rather than consider for themselves. What this means is not that we should avoid discussing masculinities but that we should seek to be clear about why we are doing so and what effects the discussion might have.

Managers share a reluctance to discuss, if not define, masculinities. Identifying what lies behind this reluctance requires research built on thoughtful development work with managers. Here I offer some preliminary observations. There is resistance to what is regarded as an academic term, remote from prized pragmatism. A fair bit of the discomfort is caused by hearing the word used by a woman. In Australia there has been a growing irritation in popular contexts about women discussing men. For example, a recent book, *Secret Men's Business*[1] by John Marsden, a popular fiction writer for young adults, has been promoted as 'written by a man, edited by a man and published by a team of men. It's a book for men only' (*Sunday Age*, 15 March 1998). And researchers have begun to document the forms which a 'backlash' against women's advances has taken in organizations (Burke and Black, 1997).

But there are other reasons why masculinities is a resisted idea, as well as word. I have also listened to men working with ideas around masculinities, but choosing other words – manliness, being a man, mateship or 'being a bloke' . . . In Australia there has been a proliferation of academic (Connell, 1995; Polk, 1994), and popular, books on men. At one estimate in early 1998 one new book a week was being published on the subject of men.

These books have given a wider audience of men ways of talking about being men, including the pressures and problems. However, most of the popular books steer clear of the term 'masculinities'. Steve Biddulph's (1994, 1997) big audiences in suburban school halls come to discuss fathering and raising boys. Don Edgar (1997) comes at masculinities via mateship and the family and Tacey's focus is on the particular issues facing adolescent boys (1997). In general, though not exclusively, these works take an individual perspective, offering useful suggestions about doing things like parenting better and supporting wider choices for men, without examining how masculinities are produced and perpetuated within the broader social structure.

Discourse analysis helps explain why many men might feel uncomfortable not just with the term masculinities, but with a broader pattern, a way of talking about how men are, particularly if that way of talking is initiated by women. Discourses vary in their authority, and how speakers locate themselves in relation to certain discourses reflects the wider dominance of particular ideologies and subjugation of others (Gavey, 1989). Engaging in reflection and discussion of masculinities is a marginalized discourse, accruing little power for the speaker. Managers' traditional rejection of self-disclosure and discussion of what are regarded as 'personal' subjects also helps to explain a silence on masculinities.

Jock Norton argues that one of the reasons men resist change in gender relations is that they have few socially available discursive positions to comfortably take up the subject of masculinities. Men experience themselves through gendered discourses and 'could only be expected to question the usefulness of aspects of their identity when prevailing constructions relating to their sense of identity (and masculinity – *my addition*) begin to fail them' (Norton, 1997: 444). Even if they do experience failure, Norton argues that men will be unlikely to 'solve' that failure through resort to a culturally or discursively sanctioned practice, such as declaring their feelings and seeking intimacy, if they have no history or experience of accessing such a practice. This helps to explain why men's groups have not flourished in the same way as women's and why therapies built around discussion groups of men have had very mixed success.

Similarly, working with managers, masculinities can rarely be tackled directly. Discussion can be prompted by talk of sons and comparisons between sons and daughters. But masculinities as a topic is rarely pursued within the formal structure of training – it will be approached during the breaks, over coffee and as a one-on-one exchange. Reflections on masculine identity are generally regarded as an insight that is incidental to the main business of training or discussion.

An example of managers' reluctance to discuss masculinities comes from a one and a half hour seminar I was leading with a group of middle and senior executives attending a four-week advanced management program. I was asked to present my research on gender issues in organizations but rather than talk at them – which was their experience for most of the rest of the program – I decided to try to engage the participants with ideas about gender which encompassed masculinities, for example, their experience of the pressures to work long hours and subjugate family to work. Although there were a few who enjoyed this discussion, most did not. The subject matter and my discursive approach riled the participants including some of the small number of women, whose strategy on the program to that point had been one of camouflage, with gender issues inadmissable. There was an aggressive silence, a strong resistance to any kind of disclosure which was at odds with the boisterous camaraderie that had developed as the ethos of the group. The feedback I received included the complaints that 'it's her job to present us with the models not ask us questions' and 'she used us as guinea pigs for her research'. This was a confronting experience for me. I cursed the organizer of the program. I cursed myself for naively believing that I could slot in and do some meaningful work on gender given the overarching structure. I vowed that I should have adopted a more didactic (lots of 'models' and overheads) or 'upbeat' approach, which was the style of most other teachers in the program. I searched my motivation, wondering about the attack some perceived me to be launching on them. How much aggression was I feeling? How much unowned? And ultimately, why am I doing this and what do I hope to achieve?

This example reveals, as well as my own naivety, some of the pedagogical issues involved in facilitating a self-disclosing discussion of masculinities among managers. In a program with a strongly didactic ethos, learning by sharing experiences was perceived as an abdication of my responsibility to teach. Participants perceived there to be little 'in it' for them in contrast to the emphasis on the 'takeaways', the armoury of models which they had come to expect as a benchmark of the program's value. I was seen to be abusing my position of authority by offering problems not solutions. In raising not only gender but masculinities, I had mentioned unmentionables and tainted a group ethos.

The use of language, including the ascendancy of particular terms into the status of knowledge, needs to be understood as a political activity (Foucault, 1972). Language and power interact so that which words achieve the status of knowledge is not accidental. In addition, words like diversity resist one set of meanings and take on others which better suit elite interests. The point about terminology and language reveals a deeper point about power and who appropriates language. I will say more about the interaction of the subject matter and the gender of speaker in the next section, but certainly some of the reaction I have encountered when I use the word is because I am a woman.

Introducing masculinities to a discussion allows a richer and deeper exploration of the experiences of men and women in organizations, including the pressures to perform against sex stereotypes. And it helps to take the burden of explanation off women – women as the sole bearers of gender. While masculinities remain implicit and undiscussed, managers remain captive of an untheorized regime – less able to see choices about how they work and lead others. There is also a danger of throwing the baby out with the bathwater – of debasing all aspects of masculine cultures. This is not to underestimate the complexities involved in making masculinities available for understanding, for teachers and students. Yet it is only by rendering masculinities more visible and discussable that managers will be able to identify how work cultures can be shaped to de-couple the links between repressive masculinities and ways of working.

Pedagogy

In the second part of this article I build on some earlier ideas about the gender of management teachers (Sinclair, 1997; also 1996). In this discussion, which should be regarded as reflections from observation and experience rather than theoretical exposition, I argue that the gender of management teachers matters. I also propose that the gender of the teacher and the student group interacts with the subject matter. While women are expected to teach gender issues (which is understood to be about women), they are not expected to teach masculinities.

The idea that leaders and consultants are engaged in seductive exchanges with followers and clients is not new (Calas and Smircich, 1991). Mostly we have been reluctant, perhaps with good reason, to look at the dynamics of attraction, gender and sexuality in the teaching context. American feminist academic, Jane Gallop, has gone furthest in arguing that good teaching can be highly sexualized – involving heightened levels of attraction, desire and playfulness between teachers and their students (Matthews, 1994). Gallop's focus has been attraction between teacher and student of the same sex, though undoubtedly there is much to be said about heterosexual excitement and attraction as a component of teacher–student relations (another paper there!). Reviewing Gallop's recent book *Feminist Accused of Sexual Harassment*, Janet Malcolm concedes, within a class discussion,

> That an erotic current (a transference to use the psychoanalytic term) is the fulcrum of this transformation is unquestionable. The students begin to speak the teacher's language and to ape his thought, like lovers under the illusion that they are alike. (1997)

In 'Sex and the MBA' (1995) and 'The MBA through Women's Eyes' (1997) I began dissecting the transaction I had observed between very good male MBA teachers and their classes. These classes are characterized by a high level of performance – there is strong physical movement (strutting, posturing, leaning confidentially close, sweeping arm movements), there is voice modulation which ranges from oratorial flourish to conspiratorial whisper. Clothes have been carefully chosen, with jackets and ties that are removed or loosened in dramatic flourishes as the pressure builds to a fulsome crescendo. Alternatively there is artful and endearing dishevelment – visually opposing the corporate straitjacket. There is surprise in these performances with dramatic levels of poise and confidence, interposed with intimate admissions about their own vulnerability, and then sudden masterly putdowns to any challengers or doubters in the audience. The context is critical – the lecture room like a stage, the lectern often raised, the seats turned towards the speaker, lighting and sound also designed to magnify and heighten the presence of the speaker. As Luke points out 'these decidedly visceral (pedagogical) moments', for teacher and listener, have received little exploration in the literature (1996: 6).

There is no doubt that these performances leave some students – men and women – infatuated. I know because many earnestly advise me that I should learn how to teach just like them! One of the reasons why this teaching is powerful, I argue, is because of projection – that is, students identify with the masterful and charismatic performance of the teacher. They can see a part of themselves doing this. This strong emotional link mediated by attraction and sexual energy is not incidental to the potential of the situation to inspire learning.

Unconscious processes of transference and countertransference are omnipresent in relations between students and teachers. I have also researched women teaching and interacting with groups of predominantly men, as well as men teaching the same groups. In my early observations I noticed that women in positions of authority in teaching were more readily categorized and stereotyped in pejorative ways. I read evaluation forms from classes taught by women which stated 'she reminded me of my kindergarten teacher'; 'a bit prim and schoolmarm-ish'. Women teachers were judged against a minefield of associations – sexualized, maternalized or, if assertive, dismissed as 'trying to be too like a bloke' (Sinclair, 1998).

Women with power are often viewed more ambivalently than men. One set of explanations attributes this ambivalence to the child's relationship with the mother, the first female authority figure in our lives (Dinnerstein, 1978: Grieve and Perdices, 1981; Kirkman and Grieve, 1984). As adults, a woman with power will often unconsiously evoke these early feelings – a terror at dependence. We deal with this by neutralizing female power – trivializing, marginalizing, sexualizing. For example, investigating reasons for resistance to the ordination of women priests, Kirkman and Grieve conclude that in adult relationships: 'we feel more comfortable when female power is trivial and when female sexuality is controlled ... It is more reassuring when women collude by restricting their (maternal) behaviour to a gratifying, non-judgemental and non-controlling nurturance which applauds male achievement' (1984: 488).

I first became aware of this as a woman teacher of MBA students accustomed to a male faculty. Students often saw in me the worst characteristics of their mothers – the bossiness, intrusiveness, manipulation and orchestrated pathos. More than one student has envisaged me rifling through his bedroom drawers for incriminating secrets. Others have seen me as neglectful until a crisis and then overbearing and controlling. When I realized this I tried lots of strategies to try to prevent these mother images from swamping our relationship. But because they existed independent of my behaviour, the best I could hope for was that we would be able to move past them, that we could eventually develop our own relationship, just the two of us without mum being present as well.

The scarcity of women in authority in society in general increases the likelihood of this negative transference (Bayes and Newton, 1978). Correa et al. (1988) similarly find that the responses of groups to women consultants is more complex because they evoke intense feelings of dependency. With historically created pressures on women to teach with 'selfless, sexless nurturance' (Gallop, 1994: 6), teachers can collude in being over-nurturing while failing to assume appropriate authority. Carmen Luke identifies related pedagogical traps for women teachers who, for sound reasons, align themselves with students and against establishment. Being keen to devolve power and collaborate with students, concerned with questioning absolute truths and wedded to the legitimacy of different 'voices', then the grounds for any authority can give way (1996).

Women teachers are often, then, working with a fundamentally different set of psychodynamics in the classroom. This process is far from gender-neutral and it is not a process from which sexuality is absent (Tanton, 1992). What often distinguishes positive transference in teaching is the shared sex of teacher and students. The process I have termed homosexual identification occurs between groups of predominantly male audiences and male teachers; and more rarely, when women teach groups of predominantly women. In this situation, the audience of students wants to identify with the teacher's mastery of the subject matter.

Good teaching has always been more than an intellectual exchange – it includes elements of drama and physicality, attraction and identification. Instead of pussy-footing around and pretending that effective teaching is simply about being prepared and adept at multi-media, we need to recognize the extra psychodynamics of teaching across gender. Once one adds into this curricula concerned with gender and curricula which ask students to think about their own gender identities, then the exchange becomes particularly complex. Those of us working in management education need to look more deeply at the interactions of gender and sexuality-mediated processes of teaching, and curricula which seek to unpack gender identities and their effects on the way we organize and manage.

Creating a Climate for Teaching Masculinities

In this section I summarize some of the strategies I have drawn from my experience. They include both matters of content and process, of curricula and pedagogy. The best of the management development programs embracing gender or diversity issues that I know of are effectively well-designed personal development programs with experiential opportunities over a sustained period to look at oneself and gain feedback about oneself in a relatively 'safe' though not soporific or solipsistic environment. But these are an exception. Much of management education employs a range of highly effective defences to avoid such self-inspection. Defence mechanisms such as intellectualization, isolation, displacement and splitting and projection (Fenichel, 1946; Kroeber, 1969) are fostered in many analytical techniques and prescriptive methodologies. They encourage a focus on the external managerial environment, not the internal one (Thompson and McGivern, 1995).

Develop a Course Structure which Supports Reflection

Working with executives on short term courses requires teachers to establish authority quickly, often through a reliance on expertise, reputation or bald charisma. For the reasons described above this can be a more complex undertaking for a woman teacher. I rely on the institutional legitimacy in which I am contained and being in command of the subject matter to establish authority. In my experience this works all right – if I am not teaching gender.

In contrast, exploring organizational relationships between men and women with a group is challenging for teacher and participants. Even more than most other management subjects, it is foolish to believe that a teacher or a speaker can 'deliver' the latest expert tips in a one and a half hour slot. It has taken me some years, and many difficult experiences, to accept this. Now, I politely decline most of those invitations that are enthusiastically extended to 'come and give a presentation to our senior managers'. Sometimes these invitations, particularly when they come from female human resource managers, have an edge of desperation – as if their hopes are vested in my magically transforming 'macho' cultures in a lunch time slot. However keen I am to support the efforts of the person inviting me, these sorts of presentations can't possibly achieve very much for attendees, and make me feel a failure.

Rather, reflective discussion of gender requires a structure which includes:

- time and preferably sessions over an extended period (of months rather than hours);
- a teaching environment which is sympathetic to, and models, values of exploration, openness, interaction and expressiveness. This kind of structure is at odds with the big-budget performance extravaganzas that some management gurus favour. It is also difficult to achieve this kind of climate if on either side of sessions is more didactic or one-way teaching;
- support for the teacher. Working in pairs with groups is useful and, particularly on gender issues, a male and female teacher working alongside one another can model behaviours as well as provide space and support;
- opportunities to connect and test out classroom material in other relationships. Much of the work on gender that gets started in class gathers meaning and momentum in outside discussions – with partners, families and friends, in the café, in the pub or at home. I have become aware that with some of my students, partners and whole families become consumers of readings and materials, which are then the subject of lively debate;
- assessment and feedback mechanisms for students and teachers which recognize that a successful program on gender can't be measured in terms of 'customer satisfaction' or knowledge 'topped up'.

Create an Open Environment

Creating an open classroom where students can voice doubts and expose vulnerabilities is hard, time-consuming and anxiety-provoking for students and teachers (Schor, 1994; Schor, Sims and Dennehy, 1996). It is more difficult if the culture of other subjects is intensely competitive.

In a classroom dominated by views like 'discrimination has all but disappeared' and 'discrimination doesn't happen in serious professional organizations', it is invaluable to have minority students describe their experiences of discrimination. Yet such students won't do so unless they have developed confidence in the group to respect that experience. Useful alliances can also develop between people who have had experiences of oppression, although for different reasons. For example, women and gay men will become allies, or women and people of non-English speaking backgrounds. At the same time, it is essential to deconstruct the elements of what is sometimes described as a 'safe' learning environment. There are teaching situations where you don't want students to feel too cosy. The pressures to produce a safe environment, as bell hooks argues, can eliminate the conflict, challenge and intensity which are often requisites of learning (1994). Executive development is particularly vulnerable to trading off learning outcomes in favour of producing good ratings and a contented client.

Working with Stereotypes

Students sometimes enrol in subjects I teach (including those ones which do not include gender) convinced that gender issues will dominate the curricula: in a male dominated faculty, I stand for gender and, narrowly, women. Even among students who are enthusiastic about gender material, preconceptions are strong. One man complained that we spent only two classes on men (the two designated as 'masculinities'), automatically categorizing the classes on gender and work-life issues as about women. I pointed out that a great deal of our discussion in the latter classes was actually about men. It was only because we had built up a relationship and I believe he trusted my motivation, that he could go beyond a critique of my focus (as he saw it) on women and see his own process of categorization.

Once a basis of trust and regard is built, students are more likely to ask me for my views on gender-related matters, even if they are not central or explicit to the course I am teaching. Moving to the topics of gender and masculinities incrementally and woven through discussion of related topics is more successful.

But my observation is that it is often far easier for male teachers and trainers to establish sufficient rapport and elicit the involvement of men in discussions of gender or diversity. Partly this seems to be because they use a language and a set of justifications for their focus with which their male audiences are comfortable. But it is also simply a matter that the teacher's sex doesn't challenge and confront.

Involve Men as Examples and Allies

When I have given presentations of my research on Australian CEOs (Sinclair, 1994), it was miraculous the level of attention I could instantly command when I listed their involvement in the work and the companies they led. I have exploited their power, particularly with predominantly male audiences, to get my message across. One MD, for example, remarked that he could identify with the expectation of 'omnipotency' which one of the CEOs in my book talked about. I doubt he could have said that without reading first that other CEOs had admitted feeling overwhelmed by this expectation.

I also have a file of tapes and articles in which high profile men discuss the regrets they feel, for example, about impaired relations with children. These are invariably valuable catalysts for discussion. Audiences with whom I am working embrace this as evidence of the existence and discussability of masculinities.

Conclusions

Teaching managers about gender faces many obstacles. In the first part of this article I focused on *what* one teaches. The shortcomings of a focus on 'women in management' have been well described elsewhere. I add to this the weaknesses of an unproblematized focus on groups who are deemed to be different within the 'managing diversity' framework.

To move the discussion to a space where reflection is more likely and change is possible, I argue the need to foster discussion among managers about the culture of the dominant group. This encompasses analysis of the forms masculinities take – some elevated and some repressed, about their effects on others, and about resistances. Fostering such discussion is difficult because language and power interact to help masculinities to remain invisible and undiscussable, a marginalized domain of academic theorists rather than a set of ideas to help managers make sense of their work. Despite the range of reasons why masculinities resist definition and discussion, I argue that it is important to find a way for managers to do so as part of management education. Unless we do, our understanding of organizations and leadership will be compromised, as will be our capacity to help managers make sense of and act in their organizations in mindful, constructive ways.

The second part of this article has been concerned with *how* gender might be taught to managers. Much of management education is delivered as if the gender of teacher and student is incidental to the learning. In contrast I argue that pedagogy, and particularly that kind of pedagogy which has come to characterize executive training (one may not wish to call this pedagogy at all), is an interaction in which gender and sexuality are central. Effective teaching of men by male professors has always had a sexual component.

The mechanism that underpins this teaching process is one I have called homosexual identification. As with Kanter's (1977) famous use of the phrase homosexual reproduction, I am not using homosexual in the narrow sense to refer to the sexual act or sexual desire between those of the same sex. I am seeking to capture the powerful learning that can arise when students identify strongly with a teacher of the same sex. I argue that, in these circumstances, learning is mediated by emotion and physical attraction as well as an intellectual identification.

There are both extra hazards and opportunities for learning in a female-led classroom (Stringer, 1995). Precisely because the authority figure is female, more ambivalence and discomfort is likely, among women as well as men. Where there is an opportunity to work with these feelings directly and indirectly over time, the classroom can become a laboratory for mirroring wider organizational dynamics. In this climate one can develop an under-standing of gender that goes beyond women. One can elicit views about gender regimes that oppress men and women in various ways and the subtleties of hierarchically organized masculinities in organizations.

To return to my original topic: teaching managers about masculinities: am I kidding? There is undoubtedly the need to extend curricula on gender issues to include the experiences of men. A program structure and pedagogical philosophy which supports learning from one's experience are crucial ingredients in doing so. Capitalizing on these learning opportunities requires a teacher who is skilled at working with these dynamics and who can withstand and contain the anxieties and transferences that are likely to emerge. For all teachers the task is a challenging one.

Notes

Naomi Raab encouraged me to put 'more juice' and let go of some of my protections and pretensions in this manuscript. Warwick Pattinson and Duncan Smith provided much appreciated insights and their perspectives as men. I would also like to thank the audience when I presented the article at the Emergent Fields in Management Conference and the two anonymous reviewers who provided stimulating and helpful comment.

1. The phrase 'secret women's business' has entered popular usage in Australia following the Hindmarsh Island case where it has been argued to be against aboriginal law to reveal in courts (and to men) the subject of women's spiritual stories.

References

Agócs, C. (1997) 'Institutionalized Resistance to Organizational Change: Denial, Inaction and Repression', *Journal of Business Ethics* 16: 917–31.

Barrett, F. (1996) 'The Organizational Construction of Hegemonic Masculinity: The Case of the U.S. Navy', *Gender, Work and Organization* 3(3): 129–42.

Bayes, M. and Newton, P. (1978) 'Women in Authority: A Sociopsychological Analysis', *Journal of Applied Behavioral Science* 14(1): 7–20.

Beneke, T. (1995) 'Deep Masculinity as Social Control: Foucault, Bly, and Masculinity', in M. Kimmel (ed.) *The Politics of Manhood.* Philadelphia: Temple University Press.

Biddulph, S. (1994) *Manhood.* Sydney: Finch.

Biddulph, S. (1997) *Raising Boys.* Sydney: Finch.

Brewis, J., Hampton, M. and Linstead, S. (1997) 'Unpacking Priscilla: Subjectivity and Identity in the Organization of Gendered Appearance', *Human Relations* 50(10): 1275–1304.

Burke, R. and Black, S. (1997) 'Save the Males: Backlash in Organizations', *Journal of Business Ethics* 16: 933–42.

Calas, M. and Smircich, L. (1991) 'Voicing Seduction to Silence Leadership', *Organization Studies* 12(4): 567–601.

Calas, M. and Smircich, L. (1993) 'Dangerous Liaisons: The "Feminine-in-Management" Meets "Globalization"', *Business Horizons* 36(2): 71–81.

Cockburn, C. (1983) *Brothers: Male Dominance and Technological Change.* London: Pluto Press.

Cockburn, C. (1985) *Machines of Dominance: Women, Men and Technological Know-How.* London: Pluto Press.

Cockburn, C. (1990) 'Men's Power in Organizations: "Equal Opportunities" Intervenes', in J. Hearn and D. Morgan (eds) *Men, Masculinities and Social Theory,* pp. 79–92. London: Unwin Hyman.

Cockburn, C. (1991) *In the Way of Women: Men's Resistance to Sex Equality in Organizations.* London: Macmillan.

Collinson, D. (1992) *Managing the Shopfloor: Subjectivity, Masculinity and Workplace Culture.* Berlin: De Gruyter.

Collinson, D. and Hearn, J. (1994) 'Naming Men as Men: Implications for Work, Organization and Management', *Gender, Work and Organization* 1(1): 2–22.

Collinson, D. and Hearn, J. (1996) *Men as Managers, Managers as Men: Critical Perspectives on Men, Masculinities and Managements.* London: Sage.

Connell, R. (1987) *Gender and Power: Society, the Person and Sexual Politics*. Cambridge: Polity Press.

Connell, R. (1995) *Masculinities*. Sydney: Allen & Unwin.

Correa, M., Klein, E., Stone, W., Astrachan, J., Kossek, E. and Komarraju, M. (1988) 'Reactions to Women in Authority: The Impact of Gender on Learning in Group Relations Conferences', *Journal of Applied Behavioral Science* 24(3): 219–33.

Cox, T. (1993) *Cultural Diversity in Organizations*. San Francisco: Berret-Koehler.

Cox, T. (1994) 'A Comment on the Language of Diversity', *Organization* 1(1): 51–8.

Crawford, M. (1995) *Talking Difference: On Gender and Language*. London: Sage.

Derrida, J. (1978) *Writing and Difference*. London. Routledge and Kegan Paul (translated and introduced by A. Bass).

Dinnerstein, D. (1978) *The Rocking of the Cradle. And the Ruling of the World*. London. Souvenir Press.

DiTomaso, N. (1993) 'Annotations of Syllabus on Managing Diversity in Organizations', in B. Ferdman (1994) *A Resource Guide for Teaching and Research on Diversity in Organizations*. St Louis, MO: American Assembly of Collegiate Schools of Business.

Edgar, D. (1997) *Men, Mateship, Marriage*. Pymble, NSW: HarperCollins.

Eveline, J. (1994) 'The Politics of Advantage', *Australian Feminist Studies* 19 (August): 129–54.

Fenichel, O. (1946) *The Psychoanalytic Theory of Neurosis*. London: Routledge & Kegan Paul.

Foucault, M. (1972) *The Archaeology of Knowledge*. London: Tavistock.

French, K. (1995) 'Men and Locations of Power: Why Move Over?', in C. Itzin and J. Newman *Gender, Culture and Organizational Change: Putting Theory into Practice*. London: Routledge.

Gallop, J. (1994) 'The Teacher's Breasts', in J. Julius Matthews *Jane Gallop Seminar Papers: Proceedings of the Jane Gallop Seminar and Public Lecture 'The Teacher's Breasts'*. Canberra: Humanities Research Centre, Australian National University.

Gavey, N. (1989) 'Feminist Poststructuralism and Discourse Analysis', *Psychology of Women Quarterly* 13(4): 459–75.

Gray, B. (1994) 'Women-only Management Training – A Past and Present', in M. Tanton *Women in Management: A Developing Presence*. London: Routledge.

Gray, J. (1993) *Men are from Mars, Women are from Venus*. New York: Harper.

Grieve, N. and Perdices, M. (1981) 'Patriarchy: A Refuge from Maternal Power?', in N. Grieve and P. Grimshaw (eds) *Australian Women: Feminist Perspectives*. Melbourne: Oxford University Press.

Hearn, J. (1992) 'Changing Men and Changing Managements: A Review of Issues and Actions', *Women in Management Review* 7(1): 3–8.

Hearn, J. and Morgan, D. (eds) (1990) *Men, Masculinities and Social Theory*. London: Unwin Hyman.

Hemphill, H. and Haines, R. (1997) *Discrimination, Harassment and the Failure of Diversity Training*. Westport, CT: Quorum Books.

hooks, b. (1994) *Teaching to Transgress: Education as the Practice of Freedom*. New York: Routledge.

Jackson, D. (1990) *Unmasking Masculinity: A Critical Autobiography*. London: Unwin Hyman.

Kanter, R. (1977) *Men and Women of the Corporation*. New York: Basic Books.

Kerfoot, D. and Knights, D. (1993) 'Management, Masculinity and Manipulation: From Paternalism to Corporate Strategy in Financial Services in Britain', *Journal of Management Studies* 30(4): 659–78.

Kirkman, M. and Grieve, N. (1984) 'Women, Power and Ordination: A Psychological Interpretation of Objections to the Ordination of Women to the Priesthood', *Women's Studies International Forum* 7(6): 487–94.

Kroeber, T. (1969) 'The Coping Functions of the Ego', in R. White (ed.) *The Study of Lives*. New York: Atherton Press.

Linstead, S. (1995) 'Averting the Gaze: Gender and Power on the Perfumed Picket Line', *Gender Work and Organization* 2(4): 192–206.

Luke, C. (1996) 'Feminist Pedagogy Theory: Reflections on Power and Authority', *Educational Theory* 46(3): 283–302.

Maddock, S. and Parkin, S. (1993) 'Gender Cultures: Women's Choices and Strategies at Work', *Women in Management Review* 8(2): 3–9.

Malcolm, J. (1997) 'A Good Teacher but a Bad Girl', *New York Review of Books*, reproduced in *The Australian Higher Education* 10 December 1997. 33–4.

Matthews, J. Julius (1994) *Jane Gallop Seminar Papers. Proceedings of the Jane Gallop Seminar and Public Lecture 'The Teacher's Breasts'*, Canberra. Humanities Research Centre, Australian National University.

Mulholland, K. (1996) 'Entrepreneurialism, Masculinities and the Self-made Man', in D. Collinson and J. Hearn (eds) *Men as Managers, Managers as Men*. London: Sage.

Norton, J. (1997) 'Deconstructing the Fear of Femininity', *Feminism and Psychology* 7(3): 443–9.

Parkin, D. and Maddock, S. (1995) 'A Gender Typology of Organizational Culture', in C. Itzin and J. Newman (eds) *Gender, Culture and Organizational Change: Putting Theory into Practice*, pp. 68–80. London: Routledge.

Polk, K. (1994) *When Men Kill: Scenarios of Masculine Violence*. Melbourne: Cambridge University Press.

Ragins, B., Townsend, B. and Mattis, M. (1998) 'Gender Gap in the Executive Suite: CEOs and Female Executives Report on Breaking the Glass Ceiling', *Academy of Management Executive* 12(1): 28–42.

Reed, R. (1996) 'Entrepreneurialism and Paternalism in Australian Management: A Gender Critique of the "Self-made" Man', in D. Collinson and J. Hearn (eds) *Men as Managers, Managers as Men: Critical Perspectives on Men, Masculinities and Managements*, pp. 99–122. London: Sage.

Riger, S. and Galligan, P. (1980) 'Women in Management: An Explanation of Competing Paradigms', *American Psychologist* 35: 902–10.

Roper, M. (1994) *Masculinity and the British Organization Man Since 1945*. Oxford: Oxford University Press.

Roper, M. and Tosh, J. (eds) (1991) *Manful Assertions: Masculinities in Britain Since 1800*. London: Routledge.

Schor, S. (1994) 'A Framework for Teaching Diversity', in B. Ferdman (ed.) *A Resource Guide on Teaching and Research in Diversity*. St Louis, MO: American Assembly of Collegiate Schools of Business.

Schor, S., Sims, R. and Dennehy, R. (1996) 'Power and Diversity: Sensitizing Yourself and Others through Self-reflection and Storytelling', *Journal of Management Education* 20(2): 242–57.

Sinclair, A. (1994) *Trials at the Top*. Melbourne: The Australian Centre, University of Melbourne.

Sinclair, A. (1995) 'Sex and the MBA', *Organization* 2(2): 295–317.

Sinclair, A. (1996) 'Journey Without Maps: Transforming Management Education', Inaugural Professorial Lecture, Melbourne Business School, University of Melbourne.

Sinclair, A. (1997) 'The MBA Through Women's Eyes: Learning and Pedagogy in Management Education', *Management Learning* 28(3): 313–30.

Sinclair, A. (1998) *Doing Leadership Differently: Gender Power and Sexuality in a Changing Business Culture*. Melbourne: Melbourne University Press.

Stivers, C. (1996) 'Mary Parker Follett and the Question of Gender', *Organization* 3(1): 161–66.

Stringer, D. (1995) 'The Role of Women in Workplace Diversity Consulting', *Journal of Organizational Change Management* 8(1): 44–51.

Tacey, D. (1997) *Remaking Men*. London: Viking.

Tanton, M. (1992) 'Developing Authenticity in Management Development Programmes', *Women in Management Review* 7(4): 20–6.

Thompson, J. and McGivern, J. (1995) 'Sexism in the Seminar: Strategies for Gender Sensitivity in Management Education', *Gender and Education* 5(3): 25–61.

Tolson, A. (1977) *The Limits of Masculinity*. London: Tavistock.

Winnicott, D. (1965) *The Maturational Processes and the Facilitating Environment*. London: Hogarth Press.

part four

Pedagogical Practice

_____

12

Tony J. Watson

Motivation: that's Maslow, isn't it?

Introduction

The words 'Motivation: that's Maslow, isn't it?' were actually used during the course of the research project which is reported here. This utterance captures the essence of the issue which is being investigated: the tendency in education for 'management knowledge' to become a series of packages of formalized information, often seen as the creation of a particular expert with a slightly unusual yet memorable name and having little clear connection to the everyday managerial practice of those who are studying it. We might well in our management teaching experiences all have been asked questions such as: 'Strategy: that's Porter, isn't it?', 'Culture: that's Schein, isn't it?' or even 'Management: that's Drucker, isn't it?'

The intention is not to consider what Maslow, Vroom, or anybody else actually said (as opposed to what students or teachers say that they said) but rather to reflect on aspects of what students themselves appear capable of recognizing to be a rather superficial form of learning. A further intention of the paper is to consider a particular research innovation. Hence, I tell a story about certain substantive issues as well as a story about the shaping of what we might call an *ethnographic experiment*. The piece of research which is examined and reflected upon was inspired by two thoughts (– 'the story starts here'). Both of these thoughts occurred when I was engaged in full-time management participant observation research in industry (Watson, 1994a) and was reflecting on some of the postgraduate evening management teaching I was going to be doing in the business school. I was planning a teaching input one day while sitting in an especially boring meeting in the factory, and was considering the issue of how to relate what I wished to cover to what had been studied before.

While thinking about this and planning my class I remembered a pattern of dialogue in which I had participated on a number of occasions over the years with undergraduates when starting a final year organizational behaviour course. A student would say something like, 'Oh yes, we have *done* Taylorism'. I would then ask, 'So you know all about it then?' to which there would be a reply along the lines, 'Well no, but we don't really want to have to go over that again, do we?' As I sat there half listening to a business planning manager droning on about 'the prospects for the domestic telecommunications market', I found myself reflecting on just what the students' talk of 'doing scientific management' or having 'covered culture in the second year' meant about either the teachers of business and management studies or the expectations of those attending their classes. The notion of 'doing' topics, without their relevance to the vocational area to which they allegedly relate (be that a practical one or a critical one), raises a range of fundamental questions about the rationale and procedures of management and business education. And my experience, at least, suggested to me that the differences between undergraduate and postgraduate education are not as great as some tend to claim. Perhaps this matter could be looked at more formally – and some research carried out on the ways in which teachers and learners in business education *use* the various pieces of 'standard management education content' like 'motivation', 'culture' and 'planning'.

At this point, the second inspiring thought occurred: could the basic participant observation approach that I was currently applying to the managers in ZTC not also be applied to my own practices and those of my students back in the business school? It occurred to me to turn to the literature on developing oneself as a 'reflective practitioner' (Schön, 1983) or to the literature on 'action research' (Susman and Everard, 1978). Instead, however, I decided to frame the investigation in terms of the research style I had reflected on so much in designing and carrying out my ethnographic study of managerial life in ZTC (Watson, 1994b, 1995a). The key issue for me was indeed a *research* one – focusing on the question 'what is actually going on here?' at this stage, rather than the more applied one which might follow later – 'how can management education practice be improved?'

How, then, does one go about applying ethnographic and participant observation principles to one's own *normal* working situation?

Participant Ethnographic Analysis of Business Education Practice

Participant observation as a style of social science research was classically defined by Becker who suggested that participant observers gather data by 'participating in the daily life of the group or organisation' they study. They watch the people they are studying 'to see what situations they ordinarily meet and how they behave in them' and enter into 'conversations with some or all of the participants in these situations' to discover 'their interpretations of the events . . . observed' (Becker, 1958: 652).

The assumption behind this statement, and behind most of those made about this broad style of research, is that the researcher has entered, 'gained access to' or inserted themselves into the research arena; they are an outsider who has become a partial insider in order to learn about the group that they have *joined*. The ethnographer is the 'professional stranger' (Agar, 1980). This is a basic assumption of the whole tradition of ethnographic research, of which participant observation research is a part. Ethnography is traditionally the study of *the other* – of a culture which is initially alien or foreign to the researcher. If a management teacher is going to investigate their own practices they will be examining *self* as well as *other*, where these two elements are much more intertwined than in more normal ethnographic situations in which researchers can more readily 'distance' themselves from those around them and from ongoing events by reminding themselves that they are a 'stranger' and must 'stand back' in order to see more clearly (or 'objectively'). If one is as little a stranger as a teacher must inevitably be in their own classroom, one faces a greater problem than normal of being able to retain the degree of control which is vital if any ethnographer is not to completely 'go native' and hence lose any capacity to see events from the perspective of the investigator as well as from that of the member. To tackle this problem, I decided to introduce an element of the social science research method which traditionally pays great attention to 'control' – the experiment. Hence we have the notion of an *ethnographic experiment*: a compromise between the traditional ethnographic principle of allowing the 'naturally occurring' event (Silverman, 1985; Hammersley, 1992) to unfold with as little interference as possible, and the laboratory principle of attempting to shape and control subjects' behaviour as closely as possible in order for attention to focus on explicitly selected variables.

The Ethnographic Experiment

To maintain the compromise between the openness of research design associated with the ethnographic tradition and the rigour of the experimental method it was decided to design a broad sequence of questions and discussion between the management teacher and groups of students (comparable in terms of age, educational stage, etc.) which would be repeated a sufficient number of times to learn whether or not there was a pattern to be discerned beneath the variety of unique events which each teaching situation represented. Because I found that there were a variety of different modes (day, evening, in-company, etc.) of delivery of the Diploma of Management Studies (in effect, the second stage of a three-stage programme leading to the award of an MBA for many of the students), it would be possible to repeat up to a dozen times over a three-year period a discussion with students of a selected 'management topic' which they would have typically 'covered' in the first year (Certificate in Management). The discussion would be introduced as necessary to 'revising' and evaluating existing knowledge on 'motivation' so that it could be 'built upon' in the ensuing class. A record would be made of the discussion (sometimes using a tape-recorder; sometimes involving an observing colleague; sometimes relying on my own notes – especially those on the 'flip-charts' used in the class) and it was explained to the class that these notes would be used in a research project which was being carried out on management learning processes.

The broad procedure followed in each of the 11 events which constitute the study was as follows:

1. The lecturer, standing at the flip-chart with pen in hand (having introduced the session along the lines explained above), asked the simple

question of the class 'So what do you know about motivation?' Contributions were recorded on the chart. (The fact that entries were bound to be short should be noted as a possible biasing factor in the experiment here – encouraging students to give brief or short-hand responses. This danger, however, was countered by my saying that 'we will expand on each of the points you identify in a moment'.) Only when no further offerings were made from the group was the next stage moved to.

2. Class members were asked 'if you feel able to' and 'in your own words' to expand on these entries.

3. Only after stage two was complete, was stage three introduced – as 'a comparison of your experiences of the usefulness or relevance to your jobs of the material we have just reviewed'.

4. This was the most open-ended of the stages and was simply conceived as an opportunity for class members to 'critically examine', 'reflect upon' and possibly 'theorize about' whatever pattern had emerged in the previous three stages.

I was prepared in this final stage of the experiments, as the 'teacher', to be provocative and challenging. There was a broad and general 'hypothesis' behind this research design to the effect that course members would not readily connect the academic 'motivation' material they had studied to their everyday practices as managers. If this turned out to be so, it would provide an opportunity to provoke discussion by challenging them on why they had not asked harder questions about the material presented to them and its relevance and general validity. The hope was that I might uncover (or provoke the creation of) students' own 'theories' about their course involvement and their management learning, which in turn could help me in my attempts to make sense of the activity that I regularly engage in as a management teacher. These attempts at ethnographically-generated theorizing could then be discussed with other management teachers and, out of such a dialogue, a deeper understanding of the practices, limits and potential of management learning and teaching negotiated. This, indeed, is the logic of the present paper.

The extent to which the 11 events were like each other was remarkable. The pattern which I attempt to represent here was followed in all of the events. Three of the events differed to a limited extent, however, especially in the second stage where students are asked to explain the items identified in the first stage. In two classes there was an unusually 'expert' explanation of key 'theories' as a result of the classes containing individuals who worked, themselves, as management teachers (two in further education colleges, one as a consultant and one as a training officer). In the third class, the proceedings were dominated by a particular individual whose contributions were anything but 'expert' and which were expressed with such force that they tended to discourage other course members from participating in the event ('He knows it all, so why should we speak' said one individual, in a heavily ironic tone).

What do we Know about Motivation?

'Motivation: that's Maslow, isn't it?' captures the flavour and epitomizes the pattern of offerings in the first stage of the experiments, when students were asked what they know about motivation. Here is the sequence of items offered in one group (reported verbatim):

It's helping others to achieve.

It's different things for different people.

It's Maslow's hierarchy of needs.

What about McGregor?

Is that a question or a statement, Helen? Put X and Y on the board, Tony.

It's the Hawthorne studies.

Hertzberg.

And Mintzberg.

Intrinsic satisfaction.

Motivation is what is achievable.

It's basically objective setting.

In two of the groups the offerings were almost entirely in terms of authors' names, with Germanic names predominating – as we might expect from an examination of the standard Organization Behaviour textbook. The name McGregor was the exception to the Germanic sounding names – although, for whatever reason, this author's work was referred to simply as, for example, 'theory x and y' as often as by the writer's name (McGregor, 1960). In contrast to this, however, the term 'hierarchy of needs' was never used without being attached to Maslow's name (Maslow, 1954/1970). Moreover, the term 'expectancy theory' was never used – although Vroom was mentioned – without any additional information by five of the eleven groups, in each case towards the end of this stage of the experiment (Vroom, 1964). The theoretical work referred to was almost exclusively of the 'content theory' type (Watson, 1986). There was little reference to process theories such as 'equity theory' (Adams, 1965) or 'expectancy theory' (Vroom, 1964), let alone any contribution from more recent writings in the culture-excellence tradition (note that one chapter of the allegedly widely-read *In Search of Excellence*, Peters and Waterman, 1982, is entitled 'Man waiting for motivation').

It would be unwise, before looking at how students expanded on these items in the next stage, to reflect too much on this pattern. One comment which can usefully be made at this point, however, is to note the perhaps surprising failure of any student to raise the question of what is meant by the word 'motivation', let alone to offer any kind of definition of it to relate the concept to a practice which occurs in everyday managerial practice. There is almost a Pavlovian response to the word 'motivation' – the sound simply triggers references to what has been presented in a classroom on a previous question. However, this is to move into the kind of interpretation or theorizing that needs to come later. The point will be returned to.

What do we Understand about 'Motivation'?

It is clear that, in the context of these teaching and learning experiments, 'motivation' is being treated by these management students as an academically-defined topic, as opposed to a task or function to be carried out by a manager. This is perhaps not surprising, given that the experiment is happening in an academic context and the questions are being asked by a 'management lecturer' (albeit one with a reputation for being iconoclastic about the standard curriculum – a reputation corroborated for the great majority of these students by the teaching session which they had attended the previous week in which I had emphasized the need for and demonstrated the possibilities of a critical approach to conventional wisdoms). The second stage of the experiment is thus shaped by the first – and the elucidation of the items and 'theories' identified earlier is thus bounded by this 'classroom mentality' (a phrase used by one student in a later stage of one of the sessions). In fact, in all 11 classes, this second stage tended to turn into a comparison between the content theories of motivation (with discussion of Maslow's hierarchy theory dominating here) and the process theories (with expectancy theory dominant).

It was rare to get a clear account of the Maslow theory as anything resembling a theory (in the sense of the way it suggests the connection between different factors). Here is a typical dialogue between the teacher (TJW) and several class members (CM1, CM2, etc.), starting with my question:

TJW	So what is this 'Maslow's hierarchy of needs' that we have on the board?
CM1	It's the way people need food and shelter and so on.
TJW	'And so on'?
CM1	They need other things as well.
TJW	Such as?
CM1	Recognition, self-actualization. Yes, that's it – self-actualization.
TJW	Are these the same thing?
CM1	I think so.
CM2	Yes, they are. [murmurs of agreement from others]
TJW	Is everybody happy with this summary of the theory? [nods of agreement – from about half of the class] So where does the hierarchy come in?

CM3   Some needs are more important than others – and are more difficult to meet.

CM4   Yes, they are higher level needs.

TJW   Is that it then? Is there nothing about the order in which people are said to try to meet their needs. I mean what is the point of the theory?

CM3   The point is that we have to realize that people have a whole range of needs. As managers we must be aware of them if we are going to meet them.

TJW   So that's the whole story? [nods all round] But was not Maslow claiming something much more specific than this – and indeed something we could 'test' by research or even by thinking about our own experience? Was he not arguing that generally people only seek to satisfy higher level needs once they have satisfied lower level ones? And wasn't he and those other writers who followed him making the point that in those societies – like the relatively affluent ones he was addressing – people are not going to be motivated by having their lower level needs satisfied any more. Unlike in the past, they are going to look for more and more esteem, fulfilment, etc. before they will comply with those trying to motivate them. Well?

CM2   Yes, thanks. You cannot blame us for being a bit rusty. We all knew it once.

CM1   We all passed the exam so we must have got it right then.

The typical pattern was for the class then to be asked whether they found the hierarchical claim credible. It was not doubted by any group. The class was consequently asked to reflect on whether, when they thought hard about it, people did in reality only tend to seek, say, the company of others once they had had enough to eat ('don't we often, indeed normally, seek to socially interact at the same time as we eat and drink?'). Once the students accepted the idea of submitting the particular claims of the hierarchy of needs approach to the test of experience and 'common sense' they generally came to demolish it to great effect. 'Wow' said one student, 'We've done a great job; it's bollocks to Maslow from now on'. At this point, suggesting we would return to the issues raised by this, I found myself in almost all the events turning to the rare mentions of 'Vroom' and to the question of expectancy theory' and what this said (whether or not it had been raised at stage one). It was established, sometimes by reference to students' own notes, that this kind of process theory had been given full attention in earlier teaching. Only one student, however, other than two of those who taught management subjects in their 'day jobs' was able to give any explanation of the approach other than broad statements like 'people won't be motivated unless you meet their expectations'. Since the teaching work I wanted to do later in the session (on work orientations, psychological or implicit contracts, etc.) required some knowledge of this particular psychological approach to 'motivational issues', I provided each group with a quick summary of the theory and then got them to submit the approach to critical scrutiny, as with the needs hierarchy model. It was generally felt that here there was a much 'better theory' – something which was very relevant to managerial practice. And this takes us to stage three.

How Useful or Relevant to Managerial Practice do we Find Motivational Theories?

Each class was asked whether, or to what extent, the material they had studied on 'motivation' in the past was, in any sense, 'made use of' in their ordinary managerial practice. Nobody was able to say that they had ever consciously thought about these ideas when they faced issues that might be described as 'motivational'. An argument, developed in only slightly different forms in each of the groups, however, was that having studied the academic material made them more aware of the complexities of human motivation. For example,

> I certainly have never thought consciously about needs hierarchies, or any of the rest of it, when I've been facing people problems at work. But I am much more conscious – I think – than before I started studying that the obvious carrots and sticks are not enough.

Another said,

> I am much more aware that there are a lot of different needs that people bring to work and that I ought to be aware of these.

This kind of rationale was the dominant one expressed in all the groups for course members having fairly uncritically 'swallowed' the material taught. It legitimized for them the pattern that was emerging on this occasion. However, as the session proceeded it became increasingly accepted that this was not enough. My own argument that there were models and theories that could do this to much greater effect ('as you will see later this evening'!) influenced this shift. But in most of the groups, group members themselves developed this more critical line. A student in one of the groups, for example, made the following comment after the group's critical examination of expectancy theories of motivation:

> I am beginning to see this whole subject differently now. I accept that we did expectancy theories before but I admit it did not mean much to me – just another thing to learn up for the exam. But I can now see something to actually follow in my work. I don't just assume that my people want, say, more money or longer holidays. I go out to check what they are actually expect . . . wanting. I then have to set things up so that they only get the thing that they want if they fulfil the requirements which I have of them.

Another student pointed out that this was 'common sense' and that he could not see the point of taking a university course ('and paying you all these exorb. . . – sorry, very modest – fees') just to get taught common sense. The lecturer's work was effectively done for him here by a course member (I think, but cannot be sure, that it was one of the further education lecturers):

> So what's wrong with a theory fitting with common sense? If you can capture common sense in the form of a theory that you can remember, then you are more likely to actually apply common sense.

The generally positive reception which the re-presented expectancy theories received helped most of the groups develop a working concept of what a relevant or useful piece of management knowledge might be. It also enabled me to press the course members on what value they could therefore have found in what at first sight were more popular theories. And these theories – the hierarchy of needs theory and its derivatives – were ones which now, with hindsight, seemed to be somewhat lacking. It was perhaps not surprising that in most groups attempts were now made to point to the value of their having encountered ideas which, they now recognized, fell short. A comment which perhaps epitomizes the arguments presented here was:

> I know that you'll think that I am saying this to try to appear less of a wally than I feel, but Maslow and all that – and I have now had it presented it to me four if not five or more times in my career – has always made me think more about what people at work might be looking for than I think I otherwise would.

Another student followed this up,

> Yes, something might be a crap theory. But if learning a crap theory makes you think, then it's not a bad thing, is it?

But another went on,

> But I think that the question that is arising here tonight is whether any of us have really been thinking at all. I don't know whether to applaud Tony for what he's done tonight or to walk out on him. He's raising some very uncomfortable questions for me.

And yet another,

> Or perhaps he's raising some tough questions for his colleagues. And I don't think that this is just an issue for this business school. I mean, I've had this bloody Maslow triangle on every bloody course I've been on. It was part of my nurse training. And blow me, years later I went on a nutrition course, or something like that, and what came up on the overhead the very first day – the Maslow triangle.

Evidence from various groups suggested that the hierarchy of needs is taught to students on practically every type of vocational course – from health visiting, to teaching, to marketing and tourism management. About half of the course members had met it on more than one previous occasion.

So, What is Going On?

The final stage of each of the ethnographic experiments involved the course members being challenged to explain 'what was going on'. To provoke discussion and, indeed, to reinforce my claim that there really is a research question to be asked – a puzzle to be solved or a mystery to be resolved – something like the following words (recorded on one occasion) were used in each of the eleven events.

> How can we explain all of this? How is it that thousands of thousands of management students – often allegedly hard-headed business practitioners like you – have uncritically swallowed a theory which, upon critical examination, appears to have little scientific or common-sensical credibility, let alone direct relevance to managerial practice? And how do you explain that it is this Maslow model, with all its weaknesses and lack of direct practical relevance, that you remember, whilst you forget the kind of theorizing that, tonight, you have indicated could be very helpful to you in your work? Can anybody offer me an explanation of all of this? Has anybody got a theory? Come on, it's beyond me!

A simple, and rather reductionist, argument often put was that the Maslow work was easy to remember:

> You know when you are studying you like to find things that you will easily remember for the exam. If there is a simple little diagram, then that's really good. It helps you remember the theory. The theories that don't have nice little pictures get forgotten.

It has to be pointed out here, however, that the evidence of the earlier part of the class discussion (as in most of the other groups) was that the *theory*, as such, was not remembered at all – people generally only remembered the point about there being a variety of human needs and that these could be ordered in some way. Few students were able to identify the logic of the hierarchical ordering of needs. This raised the question in several of the classes of just what theories are, and the connections that can be drawn between the predictive potential of theories and the use that could be made of them in guiding managerial practice. The outcome of each discussion of this kind was a recognition that part of the overall problem could be that management students were not being given enough early guidance on such issues as the nature of models and theories and their relevance to practice. One student spoke in especially strong terms,

> I think we could get quite cross here. You are getting us to look closely at how good different theories and things are in management. Well, it's not just that we have not been asked to think in this way before. It is that we have not been equipped with any criteria for making this kind of judgement. I have actually raised this myself and been told that we will get this kind of thing when it comes to the dissertation preparation – research methods is it? This is a bit late, surely.

Criticisms of management teaching staff were the focus of a number of other statements:

All this is dead easy to explain. It's a matter of lazy lecturers who just go through the motions and take stuff out of the textbooks that everybody's been using for years and years.

A lot of the people who teach this stuff haven't got much practical experience of actually having to motivate people at work, so they fall back on what's in the books.

I just don't think that business schools have yet got round to thinking about how you might realistically deal with matters like motivation in the classroom. So they just fall back on 'this American professor said this' and 'this American professor said that'.

One course member was keen to defend teachers,

I think that there is a fair explanation which was given to us back at the beginning of the certificate course. It's not up to the lecturers to tell us what is a good theory and what is a bad one. They simply put the ideas that are on offer in front of us and we choose.

This received a powerful and graphic response from another student,

They might have said that but it's certainly not what they do. Last year it was how Porter's five forces are gospel. This year they say it doesn't go far enough. I've got Porter's model tattooed on my left arm. Now I've got to get it removed. And tonight I find that I've got to get Maslow's triangle removed from the other arm. I'm going to suffer a lot of pain.

Generally, however, in so far as 'theorizing' became a matter of 'blaming', the students were seen as culpable too;

It's just cynical really. The lecturers know that most of us want to pass the course so they serve up undemanding stuff that neither stretches them nor challenges us. It's a sort of contract of cynicism really. The lecturers and the students are equally to blame – let's all go through the motions and everybody will be happy; 'learn this up and spew it out in the exam'. Come on, we all know it don't we.

No other speaker was as negative or as eloquent as this, and none produced a concept as powerful as that of a 'contrast of cynicism', but in each group there was a proportion of members who clearly felt that students were not demanding enough in their expectations of how academic work could inform managerial practice. One discussion went as follows:

CM1   Look, what we should do is not start with textbook headings like 'motivation', 'leadership' and whatever. We should start with a real question – well, it's a real one to me at least – 'how do you go about getting people at work to do things you want them to do?'

CM2   That's motivation, surely?

CM   It is, but it isn't, if you see what I mean. You say 'motivation' and, straight away, you're on to Maslow blah, blah, Misberg [sic] blah, blah.

CM3   OK, motivation is really about why human beings act the way they do. Don't we simply need to examine these theories – if they are worth looking at in the first place (and I am beginning to wonder tonight whether some of them are even worth the time of day) – against whether they throw light on these problems in, in . . .

TJW   In the light of your everyday practice at work? [CM3 nods positively] It seems that you are saying that we should start with commonsense definitions of the questions we want asking – and only then move to the academic material to see what light it throws on these questions.

CM1   Simple, isn't it?

A common theme of all the classes' discussions of these matters was a recognition that, as one student put it, there is a real gap between 'what you do on courses' and 'what you do in real life' and that, in the words of another, 'we all came to learn ages ago that you go to college or university to get qualified; you don't expect teachers and lecturers to tell you that much about things outside their – what shall we say – realm'. This individual went on, instigating some debate in the process:

CM1   You do things in the teaching – the college – realm to get a BA or an MBA. It sort of fills you out as a person, sometimes in a way relevant to your working life and sometimes not. But it's not meant to be too relevant. We just do not expect it to be. If I want something really relevant to my job, I go on a training course. I've come here to, well, like 'pass out' – get my stripes, whatever.

CM2   That's absolute rubbish. As an engineer I cannot relate to what you are saying at all. I agree that one wants the status that goes with a qualification like an MBA, and that you should go on a training course rather than a university course to learn something really specific about your job. But, for goodness sake, we study things called 'motivation' and 'strategic marketing' because, in theory, we want to be better at these things.

CM3   Yes, if coming here was just to develop ourselves or to get badges, we could study something interesting like, well, something interesting.

CM1   [laughing] Not motivation theory anyway.

CM4   OK, but this is serious. There is a real issue here: we are in one sense looking for relevant stuff but we seem to sheepishly accept whatever we get. What's come out here tonight does make us look pretty dumb, doesn't it? We wouldn't buy a new car so easily, would we?

TJW   So why does it all happen as it does?

CM5   Do you really want to know? Do you?

TJW   Yes, I can tell from your tone of voice we are going to get something brilliant.

CM5   It's dead easy. It's just that we are always knackered when we get here at night. We'd take any old crap. We've all been working all day, motivating people and that, and all we are fit to do when we get here is to sleep-walk our way through the course – Maslow and all.

This particular session then ended with an almost frantic bout of joking with students throwing in a variety of quips ranging from ones about 'rude awakenings' to ones about the difficulties of avoiding snoring in finance classes. If there is any truth in the theory of workplace humour which I have developed elsewhere (Watson, 1994a), that we tend to joke about the things which worry us most, this final interlude would suggest that the discussion had touched on matters of deep concern. On the other hand, it might have been that the whole session had come to be seen as 'just a joke'. Subsequent information (in the form of student 'feedback forms') tells me that this was not the case, however.

Conclusions and Implications

The preceding account of aspects of what happened in 11 management classes, organized along the lines of small social experiments, suggests a variety of different explanations of certain features of contemporary management education – explanations and understandings offered by participants to the exercise. This is important to the ethnographic intent of the research. The study is ethnographic in that its logic is one of producing insights into a particular cultural form – the very localized culture of the postgraduate management classroom. The participants' understanding and explanations of what they are engaged in are central to producing such insights. But this is not a culture that has been observed in its 'natural form', as ethnography normally strives to do. The experimental 'intervention' in the shape of the tight structuring of events by the teacher/researcher has forced the processes of social construction – the processes of both individual and group sense-making – into an especially 'high gear'. The degree of artifice on the part of the investigator has not only 'forced the pace' in this way but has made much more visible (or should I say audible?) the variety of norms, values, priorities and 'lay theories' which make up the culture of these miniature learning communities. However, the researcher's role was an intervention of a more substantive kind too. These experiments were 'classes' as well as research events. The fieldworker was a participant in the events. I was the teacher in those classrooms. As a teacher, I was attempting to change the thinking and understanding of these students as much as I was trying to make sense of the ways in which they think and behave.

My own understanding of the culture of the management classroom was directly enhanced – as I hope it has been for the reader of this paper – by the 'lay theorizing', the legitimations and the criticisms put forward by the student participants to the study. Sense has been made in a variety of ways of the tendency in management education for the uncritical teaching and 'learning' of standard content theories of motivation – and Maslow's model in particular – without close attention being paid to its relationship to occupational practice. Notions of certain items of academic material being easy to remember and reproduce are undoubtedly a relevant factor, as course members suggested, and we can usefully pay heed to their comment about lazy and inexperienced tutors and lazy and tired students as we can about their talk of a 'culture of cynicism' and the idea of business school courses being more about 'passing out', 'gaining stripes' or winning badges than about direct vocational learning. Management teachers should perhaps pay close attention to the perception of a separation between what was called the teachers' and lecturers' 'realm' and the students' 'real world', and to the point raised about whether teachers have yet found a way of dealing with matters like 'motivation' in the classroom.

The challenge is one of encouraging management learners to move beyond what Marton and Säljö call *surface-level processing*, where there is a focus on '*the sign* (i.e. the discourse itself or the recall of it)', to learning that involves *deep-level processing* where they concentrate on '*what is signified* (i.e. what the discourse is about)' (Marton and Säljö, 1976: 9). Engagement in surface learning rather than in deep learning has been shown to be widespread in higher education beyond the business school and it is not only described as common but as 'disastrous' (Gibbs, 1992: 3). Ramsden comments that the 'ubiquity of surface approaches in higher education is a very disturbing phenomenon indeed' and takes up observations on university teaching and learning made earlier in the century by Whitehead (1929) to argue that 'surface approaches have nothing to do with wisdom and everything to do with aimless accumulation' and he uses Whitehead's notion of paralysis of thought' to suggest that it 'leads inevitably to the misunderstandings of important principles' and, especially relevant to present concerns, an 'inability to apply academic knowledge to the real world' (Ramsden, 1992: 60).

Although it might be argued that there is something deeply contradictory about the very notion of locating practically-oriented MBA programmes within the tradition of scepticism and rigorous criticism which allegedly epitomizes university education, it can equally be argued that the problems which appear to be arising in the business studies context are part of a wider and more general problem within university education. This is in spite of the fact that a sceptical and critical style of thinking has been central to the European tradition of social science analysis of work and organizations (Watson, 1995c; Thompson and McHugh, 1995), and a situation in which social scientific material is central to the curricula of the business schools (especially in the 'Organizational Behaviour' area where almost invariably 'motivation' theory plays a key role). However, a question arises about the extent to which these business school programmes are in practice influenced by the critical social science tradition and draw students' attention to the basic principles and the relevance to practice of a rigorous and critical social scientific analysis of organizational and managerial work. In connection with this, perhaps the most significant observation made by participants in this study, for those interested in utilizing the social sciences in management education, was the suggestion that, for these students at least, there was too little consideration given early on of how to judge theories and models and too little guidance provided on how academic material might be related to managerial practice. The issues which this raises are major ones. Social science is being taught to management students in our business schools to a considerable extent. Yet, I suspect, we rarely face up to the challenge of including in that curriculum the basic grounding in the philosophy of social science that is perhaps vital to any valid social science learning experience. This is a fundamental challenge facing management education, I suggest.

Switching back, finally, to an anthropological rather than a pedagogical mode of analysis, it could be argued that an attempt more rigorously to utilize social science thinking in management education would miss the point. From the brilliantly entertaining analysis of Cleverley (1971) of management and magic, to the writing of Huczynski (1993a, 1993b) on the roles of 'gurus' in managers' lives and my own ethnographic study of managerial work and experience (Watson, 1995a, 1995b), we are increasingly seeing the need to recognize the insecurities and existential challenges involved in undertaking managerial roles. Many of the myths, rituals and symbols of the managerial world serve to *comfort* managers as they face the confusions, moral uncertainties and ontological insecurities of a type of work which is based on the questionable assumption that they can readily shape, influence and, indeed, *control* the thoughts and activities of other human beings. Once we adopt this perspective, we begin to see the Maslow model (and others like it) in a different light. Perhaps it is to miss the point to ask why so much attention is given in management education to so much highly suspect social science material. For the management teacher unquestioningly to project the Maslow hierarchy diagram on the screen, or the management student to write it down (and reproduce it in countless exam scripts and MBA dissertations) is partly a pragmatic act to 'get by' (in the sense implied by many of the students in my study), but it is also a symbolic act. It is equivalent to the vampire hunter flashing a crucifix in the face of one of Dracula's acolytes or to the Christians who cross themselves when a funeral procession passes by and subliminally reminds them of the potential darkness which lurks beyond the boundaries of their everyday taken-for-grantedness.

Some management educators might be enthusiastic about adopting the kind of priestly role that this analysis suggests. I fear, however, that too many of those who act in this way and engage in the mindless rituals of preaching sermons about the 'founding fathers' [sic] of management; of repeating the great myth of Hawthorne and of demanding readings from the great biblical texts of O.B. or corporate strategy, are probably comforting themselves in the face of their own doubts about fulfilling the terrifying expectation that they might be able actually to teach people to be managers. They are thus comforting themselves in much the same way as the nervous first-year student does when inscribing the triangular representation of Maslow's hierarchy of needs into their examination answer book. I, for one, would prefer to see a much more discomforting and challenging role for the social sciences in management education. It is only by offering challenges to course members, in which social science material itself is treated as critically as the activities to which it is applied, that management education can really become useful and relevant to them.

References

Adams, J.S. (1965) 'Inequity in Social Exchange', in L. Berkovitz (ed.) *Advances in Experimental Social Psychology vol 2*. New York: Academic Press.

Agar, M.H. (1980) *The Professional Stranger: An Informal Introduction to Ethnography.* New York: Academic Press.

Becker, H.S. (1958) 'Problems of Inference and Proof in Participant Observation', *American Sociological Review* 23: 652–60.

Cleverley, G. (1971) *Managers and Magic*. London: Longman.

Gibbs, G. (1992) *Improving the Quality of Student Learning*. London: Technical and Education Services Ltd.

Hammersley, M. (1992) *What's Wrong with Ethnography?* London: Routledge.

Huczynski, A.A. (1993a) *Management Gurus: What Makes Them and How to Become One*. London: Routledge.

Huczynski, A.A. (1993b) 'Explaining the Succession of Management Fads', *International Journal of Human Resource Management* 4(2): 443–63.

McGregor, D.C. (1960) *The Human Side of Enterprise*. New York: McGraw-Hill.

Marton, F. and Säljö, R. (1976) 'On Qualitative Differences in Learning: I – outcome and process', *British Journal of Educational Psychology* 46: 4–11.

Maslow, A. (1954/1970) *Motivation and Personality*. New York: Harper & Row.

Peters, T. J. and Waterman, R.H. Jr (1982) *In Search of Excellence*. New York: Harper & Row.

Ramsden, P. (1992) *Learning to Teach in Higher Education*. London: Routledge.

Schön, D.A. (1983) *The Reflective Practitioner: How Professionals Think in Action*. New York: Basic Books.

Silverman, D. (1985) *Qualitative Methodology and Sociology*. Aldershot: Gower.

Susman, G.I. and Everard, R.D. (1978) 'An Assessment of the Scientific Merits of Action Research', *Administrative Science Quarterly* 23(4): 582–603.

Thompson, P. and McHugh, D. (1995) *Work Organisations*, 2nd edn. London: Macmillan.

Vroom, V.H. (1964) *Work and Motivation*. New York: Wiley.

Watson, T.J. (1986) *Management, Organisation and Employment Strategy*. London: Routledge.

Watson, T.J. (1994a) *In Search of Management: Culture, Chaos and Control in Managerial Work*. London: Routledge.

Watson, T.J. (1994b) 'Managing, Crafting and Researching: Words, Skill and Imagination in Shaping Management Research', *British Journal of Management* 5(special issue): 77–87.

Watson, T.J. (1995a) 'Shaping the Story: Rhetoric, Persuasion and Creative Writing in Organisational Ethnography', *Studies in Cultures, Organisations and Societies* 1: 301–11.

Watson, T.J. (1995b) 'Management "Flavours of the Month": Their Role in Managers' Lives', *International Journal of Human Resource Management* 5(4): 889–905.

Watson, T.J. (1995c) *Sociology, Work and Industry*, 3rd edn. London: Routledge.

Whitehead, (1929) *The Aims of Education and Other Essays*. London: Macmillan.

13

Naomi Raab

Becoming an Expert in Not Knowing
Reframing Teacher as Consultant

He walked into the room, with a pencil in his hand,
He saw a man standing naked and he did not understand
                                    Ballad of a Thin Man, Bob Dylan

This article uses an example of a teaching situation to propose a new understanding of the role of teacher as consultant. The case dramatically illuminates the very real nature of anxiety in teaching and explores the unconscious defences teachers muster to combat it. Structure and control are identified as two critical defences traditionally used by teachers in order to take on the role of Expert in Knowing. Recasting the teacher as consultant permits the teacher to take up a different role, that of Expert in Not Knowing – a more vulnerable yet paradoxically more powerful role. The article presents four strategies for harnessing anxiety productively and taking on the consultant role.

The case itself is a story about what happens when 60 graduate students wanting a lecture do not get one. It is also a story about the discomfort and indeed hatred (Bion, 1961) of having to learn through experience, that is, through not knowing, because of the terrors it unleashes.

When, in the second half of this story, the students were not offered an escape *away* from their experience of not knowing, and *into* their lecturer's knowing, they fought and struggled. They demanded the lecturer's knowing in order to rescue them from their learning experience.

This story, however, is ultimately about belief in a group's and a teacher's capacity to stay with the intolerable tensions of not knowing in order to arrive at totally new insights and learnings. In the story, the lecturer mobilizes the role of *consultant* (Hirschhorn, 1988). The role of consultant is not 'to know' but to help the client confront and explore their not knowing about a particular problem or situation, so as to learn afresh. Some critical features of being an effective consultant in not knowing are discussed in the analysis which follows the story.

The Case: Knowing as a Defence Against Learning

The setting for this case was a tiered lecture theatre in the Science Building of one of the largest of Australia's universities. One hundred and sixteen part-time business students had come to attend a 2-day workshop on 'Managing Change'. The workshop was part of a larger graduate program in management – with details around enrolments, venue, seating arrangements all pre-set. My job was simply to deliver the content. My specific brief was to run a session on two models or ways of working with change loosely titled 'Template Model' and 'Psychoanalytic Approaches'. The same session was presented twice, first in the morning with 60 students and then, after lunch, with another 60 or so students.

The morning session did not go particularly well. I arrived to find students seated and waiting ready for input. I had intended to run the session as 'conversation' around the two models but found myself telling them about the differences between the two styles, about working with groups, about team-building, about black-box consulting and about goodness knows what else. There was so much to tell, to explain – it was an impossible task. I responded to questions which led down paths ever more obscure and fascinating, struggled with choices about which bit of input, which article, which overhead. The long science lab desk drowned in my paperwork.

After an hour or so of this, I decided on a break, followed by a short structured input (I told them I felt I had to give them something concrete) and then a choice: students could go off and spend the remainder of the morning working in small project groups, or continue 'the conversation' with me outside on the lawns.

Ninety percent of the group opted for small group work (which in effect meant a long break for morning tea) and a dedicated band of eight or nine followed me outside to sit in a circle on the grass. What occurred here was the essentially didactic dynamic of guru and followers: students who had been attracted, intrigued by the ideas presented earlier, had now come together to question me further and seek further enlightenment. There is a Zen Buddhist saying, 'If you meet the Buddha on the way slay him.' This Buddha needed slaying, for whilst still alive, real thought and growth was prevented.

The lunchbreak finally arrived and I spent the hour in a turmoil of panic and self-doubt. What on earth was I going to do with the afternoon group? (This second group had spent the morning at another lecture on the systems approach to change.) Unable to come up with a satisfactory answer around the presentation of content, I decided to let go the traditional lecturer role and simply ask the group what they were interested in. I also decided that I didn't want to stand out front and that I wanted the students to talk to each other. This does present a problem in a tiered lecture theatre with all faces turned forward to the fountain of wisdom. I unfolded the desk tops of the front row of seats and sat on one of these, facing the rising rows of seats. As students came in I encouraged them to space their seating so as to form a vertical circle in the auditorium. Students in outer seats were asked to sit on desk tops and so create a sort of amphitheatre. This arrangement was not greeted enthusiastically by all students but with a little humour and gentle persistence a ragged circle formed.

I began with a statement about the morning session not being too successful and in this session searching for another way. I framed the task thus: 'We have a couple of hours in which to explore two models of understanding change in organisations: the Template and Psychoanalytic models, and so I was wondering, what are you curious about?'

There followed a few very long seconds of tension and then one woman began with an interest in developing a point on systems theory (which they had just spent the morning on). Another woman responded eagerly in following up this question. I wondered why it was that we were talking about systems theory when the task for this session was explicitly stated as exploring the other two models. I realized that I had given no 'input' on these other two models. They didn't 'know' anything about them, and I hadn't set out a structure, a process for discussion. In the resultant anxiety, there was a flight into the safety of the 'known' (and the past) of systems theory and away from the uncertainty of the present.

I offered the group this interpretation of what was happening and asked whether they saw any parallels between this and their experiences of change in organizations. At this stage there was somewhat of a ruckus. A number of people expressed their anger and indignation: 'What do you think you're doing?' 'What do you expect? You have the knowledge, we know nothing!' 'You've read the books and we haven't had any articles or handouts on this!' 'We don't know anything about template models or approaches to change!'

I felt I was looking at a huge crowd of helpless angry victims whom I had somehow betrayed. I felt as if I was depriving them of knowledge. At the same time I was shocked to hear a large group of managers telling me that they knew nothing. I told them that I thought I was being made to feel like a bucket of knowledge that could (if only it would) fill them up, them, as empty vessels. There was an angry chorus of 'No, no, it's not like that at all' followed by ever insistent and plaintive cries for 'At least you could give us some definitions!'.

One man complained that no useful guidelines had been given, that the group had no idea of the task. I reiterated the idea of the task as an exploration of the two different approaches to change. He continued, saying: 'Well, if you had asked us, for example, what implications might the idea of a template have for managing change, then we would have had something to discuss.' I answered: 'Well, that's a great question, a question which is worth pursuing and which came from you, not from me. Only a few minutes ago you told me you knew nothing, and now you're coming up with useful questions for exploration. I'm wondering what happened to the critical capacity for thinking earlier, and why you were unable to offer that question. I'm wondering what happened to the experiences and knowledge of 60 managers which for some reason they couldn't access. I'm also wondering if this again bears some resemblance to what happens in organizations when new ideas are required for managing ambiguous and uncertain situations.'

This little speech was greeted with mixed response and a number of things seemed to be happening simultaneously. Amidst grumbles of discontent and statements of feeling sick, feeling nervous and wanting to get up and leave came other interpretations of what was occurring. One woman talked about situations she had seen often in organizations, unstructured situations of uncertainty where people search for definitions and frameworks and labels to hang on to. There was a discussion around the word template and the kinds of templates currently in fashion around organizational change.

Meanwhile, another woman, her voice trembling with anger, said 'Naomi, you've totally destroyed me. Not only have you taken away the structure, but the very foundation of my being here!' At this point I asked the group to listen to the intensity of the language being used and feelings being expressed. Surely I had only changed the seating? Was this not merely a first order, incremental change?

Yet something else was occurring, and people were getting hooked on a much deeper level. 'We're not used to this! Other sessions haven't been like this! This isn't what we did in the morning session!' Again I pushed for a discussion of organizational applications. In the previous day's discussions, members of this group had declared themselves 'change addicts' thriving on the excitement of change, and disappointed with the always present resisters to change. I told them I had been quite excited about the prospect of changing this session yet now where were they? Where was their willingness and openness to new experience?

More interpretations were made by students, more links between what was happening here and in their place of work. One man said he was feeling both scared and excited but that what we needed to do was to let 'order come out of chaos' (the topic of the previous day's input) and trust that it would happen.

Somewhere around this point a couple of people said they felt manipulated, that I'd had it all worked out and that I had some other agenda. I reminded them of my statement made right at the beginning of the session – that the previous session didn't go down too well, and that I didn't know how best to proceed. They insisted on their accusations of manipulation and hidden agendas. My response was along the lines of 'Listen to how hard it is for you to hear that the leader doesn't know, and that there was no agenda, other than that I trusted you. I trusted we could come up with some useful conceptualizations and applications together.' Around this time I talked to the group about my own fear, and the churning in my stomach as a result of the tremendous pressure to go back down behind the desk and give an input. I talked about choosing to resist that pressure, and stay with the anxiety in the belief that more useful insights, links and conceptualizations will emerge from the group.

This prompted discussion of the role of the leader in managing change in situations where directions are unclear and the group seems to be floundering. How do you authorize others to take responsibility and think? Access their intelligence and experience? How, as a leader, do you resist the temptation to offer templates to a group that has 'gone dumb'?

Around this time I perceived huge differences in people's understanding of what was occurring. One man said: 'Haven't we had enough of this soul baring? This sounds like a 60s encounter group! When are we going to get on with the real task?' Others called out in response: 'This is the task! We're learning about change and how it's managed and people's reactions RIGHT

NOW.' At the same time there were angry comments from the sidelines: 'I've had enough of being quiet. Why don't the motor mouths shut up and give the others a go! I'm sick of them always dominating us!' This caused a bit of a stir, some bristling and I asked the group how they had been reacting to this situation of stress and uncertainty. Some spoke of their discomfort, others of their excitement and engagement, and others of various forms of withdrawal.

Somehow at this stage, around an hour or so into the process, it seemed 'safe' for me to introduce some content into the discussion. By safe I mean that the burden of leadership and provision of ideas and applications seemed to be shared more equally. I introduced my 'input' in the context of others doing so and also offered Bion's Basic Assumption groups – dependency, fight/flight and pairing as another way of understanding the behaviour of groups attempting to work on a task. The group worked with this and other 'input' provided by group members. To some extent, the Buddha had been rediscovered within the group. A number of students spoke of changes in their level of understanding and insights they had extracted from our discussions. They began accessing their experience and intelligence to form conceptualizations of the process of managing change. One woman said: 'I feel like I've made a significant second-order change, a deep shift in the way I view not only change, but my assumptions about learning.'

At this time the group began to settle, there was greater interaction between the students and less energy devoted to attacking me. After some further discussion we were ready for a break. Again I offered the group the option of voting with their feet, i.e. working in small groups on projects or returning for further work around exploration of what had occurred with me. Ninety percent of the group returned and we had just under half an hour left before the next session. I offered a description of a group's growth in relation to the parental authority of the leader, closely analogous to the maturing of an individual in relation to parental authority. I did this because it offered a theoretical structure within which we could discuss and make sense of what had just happened, and which students could use to further integrate this experience with work groups in other settings. I was aware of feeling very tired yet also pleased with our progress.

Postscript

A few days after the workshop, I received feedback from two students. One came in the form of a letter of complaint addressed to the Director of the program stressing the student's anger and concern over the session and requesting that no further sessions occur like that one. The student wrote about the negative effect of the experience on her and the resultant discomfort and decline in self-esteem. This alerted me to the leader's role in providing a 'container' for the group's anxiety, some boundary in which to explore new issues. This was not easy to do with 60 individuals, and the container had leaked, the student's anxiety spilling out into the wider system. This also raised the question for me, 'How safe should learning be?'

The second student contacted me by phone to express his thanks for a significant learning experience. He spoke of the effect it had on him, which was largely an affirmation of a less structured more intuitive way of working which he had been trying to squash down or dismiss in his current job in a large technocratic bureaucracy. (He had previously worked in this 'looser' way in his past employment where creativity was more highly valued.) He also sent me a copy of what he had written on his notepad during the session:

> He walked into the room, with a pencil in his hand,
> He saw a man standing naked and he did not understand.

Analysis

The Consultant Role

I work as a lecturer and consultant: both my graduate students and other clients in industry, government and the community sectors are managers and staff consultants working with me around the struggle to implement change in their organizations.

My work with the students, both as a group in the program and individually, is that of teacher as well as consultant. As students, they are also clients. When I frame my students as clients, I do not wish to suggest the kind of knee jerk customer responsiveness often espoused by the customer service literature. My fully taking on the role of consultant to my clients may mean *not* doing what the client wants, as in the previous story.

In viewing the student–teacher relationship as similar to that of client and consultant, I am in no way likening it to relations of consumption and salesmanship. As consultant, be it in the corporate world or as a teacher, my role is to truly *work* with clients not just entertain or please them. My role is to support not supplicate, challenge not discipline them. 'Working' in this sense with clients is risky, because it means risking their disappointment and displeasure.

In fact, it is often mainstream teaching and workshop situations which *are* run on the lines of consumption and salesmanship. Both lecturers and trainers often see their audience as passive consumers of knowledge, ingesting, often without digesting, the information attractively presented to them.[1] The role of the teacher/trainer is to make the information as palatable and easy to swallow as possible. The misguided use of student 'happy sheets' given out after lectures and seminars as 'evaluation and feedback' (often as ritual sacrifices to appease the gods of quality and customer service) further perpetuates the denigration of the role of teacher/consultant to super salesperson.

My use of the terms client and consultant is meant to describe a working relationship of courage and integrity in which difficult often undiscussable issues are brought to the surface and worked through. When teacher and student are present to each other there is a collaboration around both teaching and learning which of itself nourishes the process and makes it a creative endeavour. This kind of client-centred learning should not be confused with notions of customer service in which keeping the customer happy becomes the mantra. Consultants must never abdicate their responsibility in guiding and challenging their students, enhancing their capacity to make wise and courageous choices.

I will be using the words 'teacher' and 'consultant' interchangeably in this article from this point.

Learning as Tolerating Not Knowing

Anxiety is a very real and strong dynamic in both teaching and consulting relationships. In both situations, the 'right path' is not clear. There are many setbacks and quandaries in the work. It is not an easy matter to clearly know what to do. Further, consultants' and teachers' responses to this anxiety, and the kinds of defences utilized will greatly influence both their style of work and its effectiveness. The way they structure their relationships with clients and students, their facilitation style with groups and their operating rules and values will all reflect the responses they have developed in dealing with the anxiety inherent in their professions.

The anxiety present in both teaching and consulting is the anxiety associated with learning; here I am advocating a notion of learning as the struggle of not knowing. The way the anxiety is handled in traditional teaching and consulting is through the collusive taking up of roles which enable the anxiety to be contained but denied. Teachers and consultants take on the role of 'Experts In Knowing'. They do this willingly for two reasons. First, being an expert in knowing is attractive for teachers because it reduces their anxiety about not knowing – not knowing the subject matter and its application exhaustively and definitively in every situation; and not knowing how to transfer this subject matter to the students so that *they* will know it exhaustively and definitively. There may be anxiety and even cynicism and despair as to whether the subject matter is worth knowing anyway or could, or even should, be taught.

The second reason teachers and consultants become experts in knowing is that expertise and knowing is projected on to them by their students or clients. Students and clients split off their own knowing and place it into their teacher or consultant. I am familiar with the powerful, sated feeling this produces. I talk, I make a pronouncement and it is written down and repeated later. Be they guru or snake-oil salesman, many teachers and consultants comment on the passive gullibility of their clients. I have often heard consultants say to each other, 'I don't know why they want me to do this work, they could easily do it themselves'.

The clients and students have their role to play in this dance – that of passive, empty vessels, waiting to be filled with the knowledge that is 'out there'. Anxious themselves about their own not knowing, their role is to deny their own capacity for learning; all intelligence and responsibility is projected on to the teacher or consultant whose *job* it is to know.

This victim stance has its ugly side for there is real anger there too. In this unconscious collusive game that is played out, there is anger on the part of students and clients toward their teacher or consultant: a sense of betrayal is built in: they haven't produced the appropriate amount of handouts or the instant remedy for the client; they have robbed the clients of their intelligence: 'She's treating us like idiots' or 'That consultant was made out to be so smart but what he did was worthless, we could have come up with that or better ourselves!'

The Importance of Unconscious Dynamics

The second insight to emerge from the case is the force of unconscious dynamics and their impact on the learning possible for client and consultant. When students and teacher become follower and guru, something else is happening beyond an attentive audience. And, as in this case, when members of a large group start to feel sick, panicky, angry and betrayed there is a dynamic operating which goes beyond inflexibility or resistance to change.

Working as consultant means acknowledging and working with unconscious processes. At this stage of anxiety, one cannot proceed at the rational problem solving level of 'Let's be reasonable and get this into perspective'. Consulting is not about reassurance. Neither is teaching. It is about helping the client or student face the deeper and seemingly irrational fears not knowing can generate. It may be that this is the very point in which the consultant or teacher feels anxious also – anxiety *is* catching. What happens then is that we, as teachers develop defences against this anxiety, because we are not going to let ourselves get into this pickle again! We call this 'planning and preparation'; the extent to which it serves as a defence against anxiety (both ours and theirs) is not necessarily something of which we are consciously aware.

The anxiety which is so much a part of learning and not knowing is significant for both teachers and students, consultants and clients. Were it not contained in some way, it would overflow and prevent useful work being done. In this sense, some defence against the anxiety is necessary. Defending ourselves against the anxiety inherent in our work is not being condemned as 'bad'. However, what we need to ask ourselves is, are our defences conducive to learning or not? Are they helpful defences, which support learning, or do they suffocate learning? Both consultants and teachers have become adept at marshalling two particular defences against the anxiety associated with not knowing. These are structure and control and are examined in detail later.

Structure and Control as Defences Against Anxiety in the Client–Consultant Relationship

Two very common defences used in consulting are structure and control. Both are important defences because without them no purposeful work would get done. Whilst both can be used productively, they are also often used in ways that deny anxiety and constrain the learning that could take place.

Structure as a Defence Against Anxiety

Structure as a defence against anxiety refers to the various ways a consultant and/or client can structure their work together in order to minimize unexpected and anxiety-engendering occurrences. Thus, a consultant can structure the initial contract with a client so as to specify content, timings, outcomes, resources required, etc. She/he can pre-package the content of interventions (usually based on previous interventions) and deliver these regardless of new questions and issues raised by the client. She/he can present in a manner easily identifiable within a professional role, e.g. 'trainer', 'expert', and keep behaviour strictly within the boundary of that role.

Clients also use structure as a defence against anxiety. In choosing a consultant they may, for example, use people or agencies known for a particularly systematic and structured approach, for example, using specific diagnostic instruments and tests (e.g. Myers Briggs Type Indicator), a particular model of organization effectiveness (e.g. Total Quality Management). In contracting with consultants, they may specify preferred types of intervention and request that the consultant submit objectives, programs and issues to discuss in writing prior to meeting with organization members. They may require written reports, recommendations and detailed implementation plans. Students, too, may gravitate to courses and staff known for their particularly structured or 'prepared' approach.

All these methods aim to increase certainty and predictability, minimize uncertainty, ambiguity and unexpected outcomes. These defences serve the purpose of closing consultants off from the anxiety. Whilst they enable consultants to continue functioning, it is nevertheless at a cost to their capacity for creativity and learning. Denying the anxiety denies the consultant and the client the possibility of working through it to achieve new outcomes. Where structure is used to put the lid on surprises, and on anxiety in dealing with novel situations, it is being used defensively.

My feelings when the morning session failed, and when I nearly had a revolt in the afternoon were certainly those of gut-wrenching panic. I felt quite sick and in danger of losing whatever pretence of competence I had bluffed them with so far. I felt like falling apart.

These thoughts in themselves are enough to send consultants and teachers off in search of the comfort of seemingly similar past consultancies and session notes that 'worked'. The temptation is to allay one's fears about the current situation by making connections with previous work, where what you did then was successful. But the current situation is, by definition, *not* the previous one and therefore unique. Once again it is important to stay with the anxiety and acknowledge what is going on.

Of course it could be argued that the students in the second group were displaying quite legitimate dependency needs and that I should have anticipated their inability to engage with the material and prepared more thoroughly. Perhaps it was I who was so anxious that I abandoned all structure and so minimized my accountability for results? These kinds of arguments suggest some implicit and very important questions around appropriate professional practice:

- Are student or client groups, by definition of being in their role, dependent in the sense of not knowing anything about the problems, and seeking the right answer?
- Is it the teacher's responsibility to provide this expertise?
- Does the provision of this expertise and the 'right answer' prolong or perpetuate students' dependency needs?
- Is it the consultant's responsibility to minimize anxiety around not knowing?
- Is the teacher abdicating her/his responsibility in not meeting students' dependency needs?
- Is the consultant in any way negligent if he/she does not, as an intervention to stimulate learning, provide a structure and fill it with relevant and appropriate content?
- Is a teacher's work best evaluated by the nature of the structures and content she/ he introduces to the students?

Dependency is part of any learning situation, it is a starting point. In an article on the Authority Cycle, Reid (1965) makes the point that dependence is often the starting point of most groups; this is so certainly in educational settings and then subsequently in organizations: the group is assembled around a common purpose and looks to a designated leader to initiate activity. Indeed the most classic example illustrating this state of dependency is the typical classroom situation in which the leader stands before the class with all chairs turned towards her/his elevated position at the front (Reid, 1965: 2). At the level of the human individual, the analogy is the infant–parent relationship in which the infant is clearly dependent upon the leadership and protection of the parent.

The teacher's role is to be aware of this dynamic and contain it. It is a critical responsibility inherent in the teacher role to create a space in which learning can occur. The teacher or consultant must also, through the authoritative taking up of their role and the nature of their interventions, provide a container in which learning and exploration can take place, a container in which learners can access their own knowledge as well as their resilience in the face of not knowing and feeling anxious.

As a teacher and consultant I know the importance of taking up this authority and not abdicating it through either swamping the students with information they cannot access (and further encouraging helplessness over dependency) or abandoning all responsibility and forcing students to go it alone. I think both of these dynamics occurred in the first group with which I worked.

However, with the second group I accessed my authority more strongly. I made a space for *them* to work and access their authority and experience. It is important not to confuse lack of preparation and refusal to take up one's responsibility with a willingness to engage the student/client in a much more complex and dynamic way. My behaviour with the student/client group was an illustration of the authority I took to engage the group in the reality of managing the dynamics of change rather than the fantasy of studying a theoretical solution which they must master.

Certainly the leader (or parent) has clear responsibilities for those dependent upon them, needing their guidance and protection. However, two further points are pertinent here before we draw any conclusion about what, in the context of a learning environment, appropriate leadership behaviour should be. The first concerns the experience level of the group in relation to the task. The second concerns the responsibility of leaders, teachers, consultants and managers to assist and encourage their charges to move beyond dependence and to grow up.

With regard to the first point, the student or client group were all practising managers of some five or more years' experience, working in the private and public sectors, both of which had been experiencing enormous change in recent years. Second, there is a point to be made about how long dependence should be prolonged. In both our educational institutions and then at work in the organizations in which we live, the task of growing up is often difficult. It is hard to be adult and grown up in relation to the authority figures around us. In part, that is to do with those in leadership positions often maintaining a group at the dependence level in order to maintain a pleasurable position as the leader in control. What this does is effectively prevent the growth of the group members. The maintenance of dependence in the group obviously has clear implications for the power relationship between teachers and students.

However, the most important point about the consultant role is that it is mobilized to assist and equip students (clients) to move *beyond* the dependency phase toward a stance of joint exploration and learning. The journey toward this end may be a jolting and painful one. A proper and meaningful evaluation of the consultant's work cannot be made by simply registering and measuring the cries of protest along the way. Rather, it is the learning and growth reached at the end point which needs to be evaluated as well as the structure and processes used to contain and support the endeavour.

Structure then can and should be used to create space for further work. In this sense, structure must be used to create a safe container in which to confront and work through ambiguities, uncertainties and the difficult issues. This is a very different use of structure from that of injecting content into spaces so as to avoid real work and concentrate instead on safer, known topics.

Useful questions for the teacher to ask around structure are:

• Am I making space for the client to explore this?

- Am I clearly allocating sufficient time for exploration?
- Am I explicitly giving permission and support for the client to engage with this material?
- Am I filling up the space with ideas, reassurances and brilliant suggestions?
- Am *I* using the space instead of the client?
- Am I experiencing any of the signals of anxiety – fear, nausea, agitation, going blank?
- Am I acknowledging these feelings?
- Am I using a structure to cover up anxious feelings?
- Am I feeling very cosy, comfortable and 'as one' with the client?
- Have I colluded with the client/student in using an overly protective structure?
- Does this structure feel risky? Challenging?

Control as a Defence against Anxiety

Control in the context of the client–consultant relationship refers to taking control over the agenda of what is to take place and the process of how it is to happen. The term does have a connotation of power in that the individual using control seeks to exert power over the situation and the social actors in that situation. There is little doubt that my actions with the second group of students were powerful.

However, control is usually used to maintain the status quo and prevent any new destabilizing dynamics from occurring. The status quo refers not only to the ranking accorded individuals, but to the status quo of ideas and thoughts. Behaving in a controlling manner is a common defence against anxiety.

Anxiety is not all bad. Increased anxiety occurs when change is imminent. Learning and growth occur more in an acknowledgement of not knowing than knowing. The consultant's role is to create a space where change can happen, where the usual habitual responses are pushed aside and there is room to think differently, to become self-reflective. This is confronting and sometimes uncomfortable. Anxiety surfaces as those unnamed fears emanating from the self are prodded and awakened. To make this space for discomfort and learning, the consultant has to take control. Paradoxically, she/he does this by her/his authority and trusting her/his judgement *so that she/he can relinquish control*. The consultant who is working well can help the client also to desist from control in order to face the issues and master them, that is to *gain control more productively*.

The taking of control (which may entail a process of relinquishing it) and the creation of structure are both central to consulting work. The challenge is to use them adaptively rather than defensively, in such a way that the client is encouraged and supported to confront the demon concealed behind the problem. And the consultant is also stretched, deconstructing the myths she/he has created about the nature of the problem.

Adaptive Strategies in the Client–Consultant Relationship

Thus far in this article I have talked about the anxieties present in the client–consultant relationship and two important defences sometimes misused to contain them.

What is needed instead is the ability to work productively with unconscious dynamics by creating a relatively safe space in which to test out our fears and explore further. We assist clients to do this by not joining them in a collusion against not knowing and learning.

Three strategies, all interrelated are useful in this brave endeavour:

1. Using feelings as data;
2. Tolerating and staying with the anxiety;
3. Going beyond the presenting problem.

Using Feelings as Data

Working with unconscious dynamics means giving validity to feelings as real data which can inform our interventions. As consultants, we need to value feelings as important data about both our own and the client's experience. Feeling can alert us to the nature of our own anxiety, and to the projections of others.

First, with regard to our own feelings when anxious, it is of significance to note that anxiety can also be defined as 'solicitous desire, and eagerness to please' (*Macquarie Dictionary*, 1982). This too gets played out in the consulting/teaching relationship and it can operate both ways, that is, on the part of either client or consultant. The consultant experiencing excessive anxiety can be overly keen to please or placate the client with the effect that it undermines the consultant's ability to work. Instead, she/he performs or dances for the client's pleasure. Overlay gender dynamics on to this situation and you have a wider game being played out. Students and clients can also experience this eagerness to please, to be 'as one' with the teacher or consultant. An unwillingness to risk the teacher's/consultant's displeasure puts the lid on learning.

Consultants can become so sensitive to the client's likes and dislikes, expectations and agendas that they self-censor their thinking and inter-actions. In this sense, they de-skill themselves and both client and consultant lose.

I believe this was one of the risks in the case. If I had censored my feelings and hunches, I would have been unable to risk experimentation and the students' displeasure. The border between wanting to be a good consultant and getting hooked into the dynamic of solicitous desire is a slippery one. For myself, I need to be aware of and alert to the kinds of feelings I have for the client and the fantasies that may flash through my mind. Feelings of wanting to be close to the client, fantasies of us working together on more and more projects, admiration of me as super teacher, guru, 'best' consultant are all warning lights. I believe such fantasies and feelings are commonplace and speak of both the rich potential and rewards of the client–consultant/ student–teacher relationship as well as its pitfalls.

Second, feelings are important because they may not necessarily be our own. Clients, anxious themselves in the struggle around not knowing, can split off their anxious feelings and project them on to the consultant. Remaining open to these allows us to experience the full force of the clients' dynamics. We can then give back these feelings, together with conceptualizations about what is happening for the client in the learning process. Clients need to take back their own projections and deal with them. The consultant's role is to support this process through feedback and assistance in making sense and meaning of it all.

In order to work with these dynamics productively, consultants need to be there, to be present and to be themselves. They need to be open to their own and their clients' feelings and, most importantly, they need to be able to distinguish the difference.

Tolerating and Staying with the Anxiety

In the story, it was only as I began to experience the real pain and panic of my own not knowing that I was able to take the leap into experimentation and learning. I had to hang on to the anxiety and not dissipate it or push it away with packages of pre-thought out comfortable formulae, protocols and solutions. This isn't comfortable: Bion (1961) argues that consultants must suspend both memory and desire – memories of what happened with previous clients and hopes and wishes for what they want to happen this time. In doing this, they are left there, confronting the present, being with what is. Then what happens?

The deal I make with myself is this: if I can stay with it, not fill the silence, not smooth over the discomfort – something will come up. Either the client or myself will gain insight into what is going on and be able to articulate it. We will move forward. We will have worked with what is actually going on.

This is exactly what happened in the story and, as the reader can see, it does not happen smoothly or completely. There is a sense of one step forward and two steps back, and not all the clients move together. Once again there is pressure on the consultant to make it all go smoothly and to finally come up with the answer and relieve the group's and one's own anxiety. The anxiety did not go away throughout the experimentation and learning but was worked with and explored and resolved. Being able to not know, and inviting the students to stay and tolerate a state of not knowing, finally resulted in learning.

Going Beyond the Presenting Problem

As both a consultant and teacher, I have learnt one thing – to go beyond the client's definition of the problem. The space and authority I want as a consultant is to make my own assessment of whether the presenting problem represents the whole problem, end of story or sits on the surface of a whole network of underlying issues. Doing this represents my 'value added' to the client. The presenting problem in the story was initially that the lecture did not go down too well as the majority of the group disbanded and left, under the guise of 'small group work'. Meanwhile the group that stayed with me seemed to be taking on the characteristics of cult followers rather than adult and active learners.

If I were to accept the students' view then I had two relatively easy options: give a more structured and focused lecture; or see the situation as not problematic at all because those who really understood, liked it (and liked me).

However, this would be a simplistic assessment of the problem, and an abdication of my responsibility to my clients. I decided to take up my authority and share the problem with the next group of students and explore and experiment further. In pushing both myself and them to confront the issues, I learnt a lot about their real fears about change and the stress it places them under. In doing this I took control of the process by introducing ambiguity and an absence of predictability. This was not a manipulation – there *was*, in fact, considerable ambiguity as to how best to proceed.

The Courage to Remain Vulnerable

The strategies described here are adaptive with regard to anxiety and seek to work with the anxiety, to harness its energy, rather than to flee from it. What they all have in common is the courage to remain somewhat vulnerable to the anxiety the work will generate.

Vulnerability is the very opposite to feeling in charge and in control. Vulnerability does not feel like problem resolution, it does not invite closure, completion. Rather vulnerability implies susceptibility; weakness in respect to defence. Being vulnerable means not being protected against emotional hurt, and this paradoxically is its great strength in the context of learning and consulting. This kind of vulnerability does not mean to imply an openness in which the consultant is totally unbounded, awash – accompanied usually by feelings of being overwhelmed. Rather, it is a notion of vulnerability taken from Tai Chi and the martial arts in which vulnerability is described as a state of *passive alertness*. This stance is relaxed yet contained; it is not rigid and defensive, but rather flexible and ready for movement.

Both client and consultant, teacher and student need to let themselves feel the pain which connects the problem to them. For clients this means remaining open to the notion of the link between themselves and the problem, acknowledging their role or even stake in the problem. Consultants also need to acknowledge the impact working on the problem has for them, and the questions it may raise for them personally.

This, however, is not done in the role of dispassionate observer or analyst. It is done in the context of an authentic relationship with the client in which the consultant is fully present and *herself (himself)*. This is why the quote given to me at the end of the story spoke of the man's nakedness – it reflected the naked vulnerability of the consultant. Perhaps also, it represented a projection on the part of the student who sent me the quote, for in the process of staying with not knowing, both client and consultant, student and teacher, are naked and vulnerable.

Conclusion

The case presented at the beginning of this article alerts us to the terrible anxiety experienced by both clients and consultant (students and lecturer) when forced to stay in the present and face their own unknowingness. Traditional models of teaching operate without acknowledging the extent of this anxiety and offer little insight into the ways in which teachers unconsciously collude with their students in their attempt to escape from it.

Reframing the teacher role as consultant is one way of confronting and working with that anxiety productively and differently. It means developing a different type of expertise, an expertise in not knowing, and helping the student to stay with it.

Taking on the consultant role in this way, rather than conforming to the expectations of the system which craves consultant or teacher as Expert, is one way of not taking part in this collusion against learning. Mobilizing the consultant role enables one to see and stay in contact with the reality of the work that must be done. Consultants need to develop more adaptive and useful ways of containing anxiety so that a space can be made for real learning.

Note

1. The most successful and highly paid of these performers are the new witch doctors or gurus written about by Clark and Salaman (1996).

References

Bion, W.R. (1961) *Experiences in Groups*. London: Tavistock.
Clark, T. and Salaman, G. (1996) 'The Management Guru as Organisational Witchdoctor', *Organization* 3(I): 85–107.
Hirschhorn, L. (1988) *The Workplace Within: The Psychodynamics of Organisational Life*. Cambridge, MA: MIT Press.
Reid, C.H. (1965) 'The Authority Cycle in Small Groups', *Adult Leadership* (Apr.).

14

Karen Ayas and Nick Zeniuk

Project-based Learning
Building Communities of Reflective Practitioners

Is there a path to sustainable growth of learning capabilities within an organization? Can we meet the challenge of thinking, reasoning, and acting beyond the short term? Can projects enable or facilitate the creation and diffusion of knowledge and innovative practices beyond individuals, specific teams or projects?

These are the questions we set out to explore based on two complementary perspectives: stories from the field by Nick Zeniuk (a former project manager in Ford Motor Company) and findings from action research conducted by Karen Ayas in Fokker Aircraft. Drawing from research findings and practice, we hope to bring in the voice of a practitioner/consultant and a researcher in addressing these questions.

Whether we look into literature or listen to the stories of executives and project leaders engaged in change initiatives in the various SoL (Society for Organizational Learning)[1] member companies, there is an abundance of success stories (e.g. O'Reilly, 1995). Our concern is that the majority of these success stories are associated with a single project or a pilot group in a large organization. To date, there are very few examples of enduring engagement in learning and profound large-scale transformation; not many succeed in diffusing the organizational learning methods and tools throughout the organization (Senge et al., 1999). These dynamics apply to the diffusion of any innovative practice, not just organizational learning, and they have prevailed through the industrial age (Kleiner, 1996). There are numerous examples of 'skunk works' in organizations where project teams produce genuine breakthroughs in product development or process design that do not spread to other parts of the organization.

Senge et al. (1999: 321) explain:

In many ways, zeal and isolation are the most insidious unintended consequences of profound change initiatives. The deeper and more effective the changes that occur in a pilot group, the more easily they can come into conflict with the larger organization. The more people do change, the more different they become, in their thinking and acting, from the mainstream culture. The more they do succeed in producing significant advances in practical results, the more potentially threatening they become to others competing with them for management attention and reward.

Building communities of reflective practitioners may be a way to meet the challenge of diffusion of learning, and projects may serve as practice fields for developing learning capabilities and cultivating effective habits of reflective practice that cross the boundaries of the specific project or project team.

Tolerance for Reflective Practices

Organizational culture entails the shared beliefs, values and norms in the organizational context. Culture may determine individual behavior, but it is also concurrently constituted through human behavior (Swieringa and Wierdsma, 1992). Culture awareness increases the likelihood of learning becoming a natural process in the organization. This requires surfacing the hidden, basic assumptions and beliefs embedded in the organization (Schein, 1997) and developing the capability to engage in 'double-loop learning', using the inquiry processes Argyris and Schön (1978) suggest. A project design effective for learning necessitates a context where project members can question institutional norms. A culture based on commitment to truth and inquiry starts at the individual level as individuals reflect on their personal visions, question their own assumptions, understand what dictates their actions and how they contribute to their problems (rather than outside forces), feel the necessity to change and see their own part in the change process (Senge, 1991).

As Schein (1997) has pointed out and demonstrated with numerous studies, you cannot actually 'create' or 'change' a culture. At best, you can set the stage for the culture to evolve. Over time, through new ways of doing things, an organization may embody a different set of assumptions and ways of looking at things. This in turn requires developing cultural flexibility and tolerance for these new ways of doing, articulating and acting upon new ideas. It calls for allowing the different parts of the organization to operate by different norms than the 'mainstream' culture (de Geus, 1997). Tolerating the use of reflective practices in project work may be a first step in setting the stage for the evolution of a culture that is conducive to learning.

Raelin (see 'Public Reflection as the Basis of Learning', this issue) argues that reflection is fundamental to learning and that it provides a basis for future action. We cannot learn from our actions unless we are aware of the consequences of our behavior. There is a gap between what we think we do – 'espoused theory' – and what our behavior shows – 'theory-in-use' (Argyris and Schön, 1978). Senge (personal conversation, 1999) states that 'our core challenge is to become more reflective on the reasoning that guides our actions and gradually improve our theories-in-use'.

Projects may serve as the ideal setting for developing inquiry skills that enable us to better understand our assumptions and the consequences of our actions. For our purposes, project-based learning is about using projects as vehicles for creating such a context: setting the stage for reflective practices and inquiry at all levels within the organization, to reveal deeper aspiration and construct shared understanding. It is about acquiring habits of reflective practice in the project environment to benefit the individual, the organization and society. The essence, therefore, is the context that projects may or may not provide for double-loop learning and building communities of reflective practitioners. Exploring how to make learning in projects more meaningful, relevant and enduring, our focus here is on reflective practices that increase the 'quality of learning' in projects (Ayas, 1997) and enhance learning capabilities of individuals throughout the organization.

Senge et al. (1999: 45) define 'learning capabilities' as skills and proficiencies that 'enable people to consistently enhance their capacity to produce results that are truly important to them'. The capability to reflect in action (Schön, 1983) or on action (see Raelin, this issue), to question old beliefs and assumptions, to have open and candid conversation, to develop awareness of how our own actions create the systemic structures which produce our problems, to unlearn old ways of doing things and to let go of old habits are all examples of learning capabilities. As Senge et al. (1999) explain, these cannot be 'forced, rushed or imposed on others'.

Developing learning capabilities takes time and practice. They may require us to break from our old habits and acquire new ones. Covey defines habits as 'the intersection of knowledge, skill and desire' (1989: 47) and argues that creating a habit requires work in all three dimensions. 'By working on knowledge, skill, and desire, we can break through to new levels of personal and interpersonal effectiveness as we break old paradigms' (Covey, 1989: 47). Some habits are the result of life-long conditioning. They are deeply embedded and extremely difficult to reverse. It is, therefore, an enormous challenge to change the way we think and the way we act. Acquiring habits of reflective practice in projects and organizations is extremely challenging.

Reflective practices that help develop learning capabilities in projects include the use of various organizational learning tools (e.g. the ladder of inference, left-hand column, system archetypes), dialogue, story-telling, and individual or group exercises for team building, team learning and leadership development. These are all practices that empower project members to reflect on task and team related aspects of project work and help them understand how their own behavior impacts on others. The aim with such practices is to improve project performance and refine learning capabilities of individuals.

Distinguishing Features of Project-based Learning

Project-based learning lays the foundation for communities of reflective practitioners (Schön, 1983; Raelin, this issue). It aims to contribute to the evolution of a culture where project members engage in understanding the underlying system dynamics and unintended consequences of fire fighting that project work may require. As Dewey (1933) notes, reflective practitioners are open-minded and willing to accept responsibility for their decisions and actions. They have enhanced learning capabilities; they can accommodate multiple perspectives and cope with complexity. They have deeper under-standing of the underlying causes of action, and they can discern the discrepancies between theory-in-use and espoused theory (Argyris and Schön, 1978).

We distinguish project-based learning from learning in project-based organizations. Learning is not a natural outcome of projects and a project-based organization is not necessarily conducive to learning. Organizations seek to have flexibility and adapt to the demanding environment through projects. Although an increasing number of organizations manage by projects and through project teams, the vast majority of organizations still underper-form (Hastings, 1993). Adoption of project-based management may indeed offer benefits in the long term (Turner et al., 1996; Lundin and Midler, 1998). It is mostly through projects that knowledge is generated in organiza-tions (e.g. Nonaka and Takeuchi, 1995; Leonard-Barton, 1995). Yet, know-ledge created within a project is not always diffused, and lessons learned may not be shared across projects. In their analysis of 19 project-based organiza-tions, Keegan and Turner (see 'Quantity versus Quality in Project-based Learning Practices', in this issue) conclude that learning continues to evade and that the overwhelming trend is constant deferral of learning to future points in time due to short-term pressures. This trend is especially alarming when projects are increasingly used for organizational change and project teams serve as pilot groups.

Traditional project management is the process of planning, organizing, directing and controlling company resources for a short-term objective or to achieve specific goals. As projects face higher degrees of technical complexity and interdependency across functional boundaries, even the success of a single project becomes increasingly dependent on the organizational cap-ability to generate and share knowledge. The challenge with project-based learning is developing the capability of continually enhancing the collective capacity to reflect, to (un)learn and to 'learn to learn' over time. Developing and cultivating such reflective practices in the project environment and embedding learning into project work on a continual basis requires a fundamental shift from the traditional practice of project management.

We identify the following distinguishing features of project-based learning (see Figure 1):

- there is a *sense of purpose* and clarity of both long- and short-term objectives;
- the project environment offers *psychological safety* and there is a commit-ment to telling the truth;
- there exists a *learning infrastructure* and there is a balance between emerging and formal structures;
- there are *communities of practice* that cross project boundaries;
- *leaders set the tone* for learning and model the reflective behavior;
- there is *systemic and collective reflection*: problems and mistakes are oppor-tunities for learning.

Figure 1 *Project-based learning*

As will be illustrated in the two cases that follow, project-based learning as discussed here applies to large and complex projects where hundreds of people may be involved in a project, and projects may include a large number of teams or groups that need to work together (e.g. new product development projects in the car or aircraft industry). In such large and complex projects learning does not happen naturally, it is a complex process that needs to be initiated and sustained. To be effective and sustainable in the long run, the learning process needs to deliberately cross the boundaries of individual teams or groups that belong to a project.

In each of the cases presented briefly below, the project environment has been conducive to the development of learning capabilities and has nurtured reflective practices. In both cases, each one of the features outlined above has been essential in providing a fertile ground for project-based learning (PBL) and setting the stage for a culture of reflective practices to evolve over time. These cases are intended for providing an account of the practice of PBL in two different contexts.

The Ford Story[2]

The Ford Lincoln Continental project team set company records in multiple measures of cost, quality and timing. The program met all product and business objectives and achieved extraordinary results: it saved US$60 million in launch rework costs (two-thirds of budget); it recovered from starting four months late; and it achieved the most trouble-free production launch in history. This success story has been covered in numerous publications (e.g. O'Reilly, 1995; Roth and Kleiner, 2000) but the focus here is on the transformation that was triggered by project-based learning capturing the reflections of a former project manager. Can we attribute these extraordinary results to the practice of the organizational learning tools that help build learning capabilities, and engaging the project team in reflective practices over the course of four years?

In 1992, the formal structure in product development at Ford was a project-based organization. All new vehicle programs had dedicated project teams with a program manager. The Lincoln Continental program consisted of a cross-functional team of about one thousand members including engineers, planners, manufacturing and finance people. At the beginning of the project, the team's behavior was typical of other Ford teams, with a tendency to advocate and defend individual and functional positions, and to demonstrate little genuine inquiry or communication skill. In addition, team members were trapped by their own assumptions of their job description (an engineer, a controller etc.) and therefore understood the product development process from their own limited perspective. The increasing competitive pressure from Japan was forcing the company to become more productive. Declining budgets, reduced resources, and demand for higher quality were putting a serious strain on team performance.

In 1992, with the program four months behind schedule, a small leadership group at Ford (including Fred Simon, the program manager) decided to collaborate with MIT researchers at the Center for Organizational Learning (now SoL). The Lincoln team was one of the first project teams to practice organizational learning tools. The leadership group encouraged project members to practice and develop learning capabilities of reflective conversation, inquiry skills, dealing with complexity and understanding interdependence. Tools like the 'left-hand column' and 'ladder of inference' (Argyris, 1993) provided the team with the means for inquiry into their assumptions and helped them to understand how they drew their conclusions. Yet, due to time pressures of the project, the use of these innovative practices and other very effective tools like the system archetypes (e.g. 'Fixes that Fail'; 'Shifting the Burden', Kim, 1994) were not so readily tolerated.

The leadership team required seven to eight months of working together to cultivate their reflective practices before they became a cohesive group. Once they realized how their mental models and 'job descriptions' contributed to conflicting problem definitions and solutions, they began to think collectively and differently. They also realized that they were responsible for their own learning and the application of the learning tools to real business issues. MIT researchers assisted the leadership team, providing the knowledge and tools, but the leaders assumed the responsibility for engaging the other team members in the theory and practice of organizational learning.

The leadership team and Daniel Kim from MIT designed a two-day 'learning lab' for introducing the 'five disciplines' of the learning organization (Senge, 1990a) to project members. The reflective learning tools were applied to specific engineering and business issues – the learning lab was designed to integrate the 'on-line' with the 'off-line' work practices. Through a management 'flight simulator', project members discovered the dynamics underlying the product development process and understood how small changes at the beginning of the process could dramatically affect the final outcome. To facilitate reflection, all learning lab participants kept journals.

The Lincoln team did not have the time or the resources to engage every single project member in the learning labs. Although only approximately 150 members (20 percent of the team) participated in 'formal' learning (learning labs), the diffusion of reflective practices was much broader. There was a visible and significant shift in the way project members communicated and related to each other. They were able to conduct reflective conversation without fear and to operate at a level of trust rarely experienced in the organization.

This was most probably attributable to the active involvement of key line managers (including the program manager himself) in the transformation. As the leaders' reflective practices improved and they became 'true believers' (Senge et al., 1999), they were able to successfully engage the team. Their enthusiasm for using these tools and methods grew. Results were immanent. Conversations and relationships improved, meetings became shorter and scarcer, objectives were clarified, innovative processes were developed and new knowledge was created. As a novel learning structure emerged, communities of practice evolved to anchor these creative processes. The project met or exceeded all of its objectives (the first in many years!), yet when asked at the end of the project 'What were you most proud of?', the majority of project members responded: 'the experience' – the experience of working and creating together in an inspiring project environment free from intimidation and mistrust.

In reflecting on this story (Roth and Kleiner, 2000), Kanter concludes that there is no case for organizational learning because it was in fact the 'immune system' of the larger company that won the war; that the learning did not go beyond the team which was disbanded once the project was over. The Lincoln project team did not set out to change the culture, all the learning efforts were focused on the project. Yet, some reflective behavior and innovative processes were diffused beyond the specific project. Project leaders encouraged metaphors that aligned the team as they collectively developed a vision for the launch of the car, contributing to the diffusion of knowledge through 'socialization' (Nonaka and Takeuchi, 1995). This set the stage for use of evocative metaphors that inspired commitment, alignment and passion throughout the supply chain.

The challenge was to improve the collective capacity to collaborate and create new processes for improving product development and facilitate an error-free, on-time launch of the product. As a result, there were seventeen process innovations (e.g. on-line bill of material, interior harmony buck, interposed prove-out program, etc.) which were institutionalized and implemented in all project teams.

In the few years after the successful launch of Lincoln Continental, Ford launched a variety of new products, including two at the same plant. They continued to experience development and assembly launch problems, although there was an improvement relative to prior years. In this period, approximately 20–30 percent of the original Lincoln team members were part of the 1998 Lincoln Continental which was launched successfully – meeting or exceeding all its objectives, similar to the original Lincoln. Another major project, the Lincoln LS, introduced learning initiatives shortly after the Lincoln Continental but with less fanfare and attention. It was successfully launched recently and named 'The luxury car of the year'.

In fact, over the years as team members were reassigned to other projects, their reflective practices did continue to develop. Many were assigned to leadership roles in other project teams and helped their team members engage in reflective practices. 'After initial skepticism, learning initiatives were introduced throughout product development in selected manufacturing facilities and they were no longer perceived as threatening', states Margie Hagene, an internal consultant in product development who continues to work with senior leaders at Ford.

The Fokker Case[3]

The Jetline Avionics project team outperformed all the new product development (NPD) teams at Fokker Aircraft not only in terms of performance indicators such as time, cost and quality but also in 'project maturity assessment' (Ayas, 1997) that included dimensions such as teambuilding, leadership and learning. Comparing project performance before and after the implementation of 'project design for learning' and the practice of project-based learning over a period of two years, the average budget overrun in NPD projects decreased from 17 percent to 6 percent and the time overrun decreased from 11 percent to 7 percent. Additional investment in reflective practices with the pilot project team, Jetline Avionics, made this project achieve what previously was perceived as impossible in the organization.

Project design for learning is an infrastructure conducive to learning that benefits from an alternative way of organizing project teams, the project network structure (PNS). PNS is an organic structure based on the evolution of project work content over the course of the project life cycle. Developed through action research (Ayas, 1997), the project network structure is a modification of the autonomous project team structure designed to compensate for its weaknesses and to deal with the challenge of integrating a large number of people (as in the case of large and complex product development projects). Often, especially with projects of long duration, members of an autonomous project team find it difficult to go back to the organization and tend to leave when the project is complete (Wheelwright and Clark, 1992). The design of PNS, an organic network of self-managing teams, is a dynamic approach to design derived from principles of organizational learning. PNS is constituted by teams within teams, thus enabling teams to stay at their most effective size (Katzenbach and Smith, 1993).

The practice of project-based learning in product development began with the implementation of the new structural arrangement for projects. All ongoing development projects were shifted to project network structures, creating the new product development sector. Setting the stage for the desired cultural evolution required interventions for team building as well as an appropriate leadership model. At the outset, as within any organization, the cultural problems and functional resistance created a major barrier to the desired transformation. It was common that the specialists who were involved in product development projects found working in a team an unnatural and uncomfortable experience. Soon, after shifting the structure, it became evident that it was essential to create the intellectual awareness of the value of project-based learning. Time had to be invested in developing committed, cohesive project teams and cultivating habits of reflective practices.

To cultivate reflective practices, 'team learning' sessions were conducted in the Jetline Avionics project. The content of the sessions evolved as a result of the dynamic interaction with project members, adapting it to the specific project needs and requirements. These sessions provided the means for learning to become an integral part of project work. They were highly interactive and included short lectures, group and individual exercises, brainstorming and dialogue techniques, and simulation games, as well as questionnaires for feedback and assessment. Some of the aspects covered by these sessions were:

- shared vision over project and team objectives
- creative communication for cross-fertilization of individual competencies
- leadership for learning
- assessment for learning (i.e. feedback for continuous improvement).

This pilot study demonstrated that project-based learning might lead to superior performance. A review questionnaire was used to assess present and desired performance (as perceived by project members) after a six-month interval. The initial review indicated an average of 60 percent for the present performance and 75 percent for the desired performance. Six months later the review results were 75 percent for the present performance and 92 percent for the desired performance. These results indicated that while project members had reached their initial desired performance rate of 75 percent, they no longer found this a desirable level of performance: their aspirations now were much higher. This showed the potential for considerable scope of performance improvement and the benefits of investment in project-based learning.

The Jetline Avionics team served the purpose of a demonstration project for other product development projects. It triggered important changes in human resource policies leading to further learning opportunities in projects in the product development sector. It contributed to creating a project environment conducive to building communities of reflective practitioners.

For instance, initially it was not clear to organizational members that project-based learning could be beneficial for long-term career development. Formerly, the career management policies encouraged individuals to set their career goals to excel only within a given functional specialty, rather than to develop the required competencies to become successful project leaders or reflective practitioners. With project-based learning, mobility between functional and project organizations became a prerequisite in order to climb the professional ladder.

Changes in the reward systems also supported project-based learning. At the outset, the existing reward systems acted as barriers: meeting specific short-term goals, rather than the long-term investment in project-based learning, was recognized and rewarded. Project leaders were rewarded for the project's success rather than their contribution to the learning and development of team members. Rewards were based on individual performance. As a consequence of changes that were triggered by PBL, leaders' evaluations were no longer solely based on the contribution to the specific project but also on the contribution to developing team members' learning capabilities. Furthermore, use of self and peer review, rather than solely subordinate review, allowed individuals' contributions in reaching both project and team related goals to be recognized and evaluated.

At Fokker Aircraft, increased emphasis on project-based learning and reflective practices did not remain restricted to the product development sector. Although PBL was intended and proposed for product development, the underlying principles were adopted for different purposes in other parts of the organization, such as the large-scale change program consisting of over 40 different company-wide process improvement projects.

Implications for Theory and Practice

Drawing further examples from these cases and literature we look into the distinguishing features of PBL and identify implications for theory and practice.

Sense of Purpose

Projects such as new product development (NPD) projects offer a clear sense of purpose and urgency. This was the case at both Ford and Fokker. When project members work to create something new, the task at hand is clear, and there is pride and passion around what they create. This may be stronger in NPD projects but may be applicable to many other types of projects.

The paradox of project-based learning is that while individual projects with shared vision and passion may offer an environment conducive to learning, they might also create strong barriers to the continuity of learning beyond the project boundaries. Project-based learning relates to both short- and long-term corporate goals. Unless there is an explicit sense of purpose for the long run, project-based learning cannot be sustained.

In the context of project-based learning, the explicit emphasis is not only on the specific task at hand but also on long-term investment in people. For continuous improvement in project performance and building communities of reflective practitioners, the delicate balance between task and people needs to be maintained. Most project leaders are naturally focused on the short-term results and the task at hand. As the Fokker case illustrated, if they are solely evaluated on their short-term performance, i.e. performing within time and budget constraints, this naturally makes the investment required for learning and reflection a very low priority for them in the first place.

Learning Infrastructure

Senge et al. (1999: 425) define learning infrastructures as 'ways of organizing resources and opportunities to promote regular reflection and sharing'. Leonard-Barton (1995) mentions the 'fractal' of human behavior that gives the organization its character and permeates its daily activities. The behavior of individuals and small groups reflects the attitudes toward knowledge creation and sharing in the organizations. Although individuals are responsible for the behavior patterns in the organizations, the nature of knowledge creating activities – the atmosphere of functional or dysfunctional attitudes – is dependent on the particular setting. At the individual level, the immediate surrounding (whether it is a department, a task group, or a team) affects learning. At the group level, the larger setting within which the groups function influences learning.

The organizational design influences the inter-group relations or to what extent informal networks grow. Galbraith (1994) argues that although informal networks within organizations occur naturally and randomly, organizations can be designed in a way that eliminates the randomness in their creation. As illustrated by the Fokker case, paying deliberate attention to the design of large and complex projects can play a significant role in accomplishing this task (Ayas, 1997). The tendency in the majority of the organizations is to assign projects to the existing structures and thus create formal, rigid structures for large and complex projects. Yet, along the course of a project the needs and requirements may change and the project may benefit from different emerging structures.

We posit that the challenge of the formal system is to allow the informal structures that facilitate project work to evolve and provide the learning infrastructure. As Senge et al. (1999) explain, there needs to be an understanding of the need for formal design (the intentional architecture, strategy and structure) and emergent design (the ways that people naturally redesign the organization as they live in it).

Communities of Practice

To carry on their project work effectively, project members need to develop the capability of managing across boundaries, using the existing governance structures. Project managers have to expand their sphere of influence and build credibility beyond the project. If we assume that learning is social, learning is engagement in practice and dealing with boundaries (Wenger, 1998). Project-based organizations offer an excellent opportunity to engage in learning and to acquire reflective habits that transcend the boundaries of projects. It is not only the nature of single projects that supports learning but also the web of relationships that are created in organizations that manage by projects.

Membership in projects is temporary and thus offers individuals the opportunity to belong to multiple communities. In project-based organizations there are a large number of weak ties that help diffuse knowledge and practices (Granovetter, 1973). In the majority of organizations, project members maintain their links with their functional departments (where they will return upon the completion of the project if they are fully assigned to it). Membership in multiple existing communities contributes to creating informal webs of people who act as knowledge brokers (Wenger, 1998). Project-based organizations thus enable continuous building and cultivation of relationships, nurturing the development of 'communities of practice' (Brown and Duguid, 1999).

Communities of practice are natural internal mechanisms where ideas and practices spread in work settings, although they tend to exist outside the boundaries of the formal hierarchy. Project-based organizations may grow into constellations of interrelated communities of practice, offering a web of mutual support for cultivating reflective practices. When projects share members, they are bound together and become embedded in the same social network (Granovetter, 1973). The recursive interaction among projects creates social networks of mutual assistance. Project-based learning looks to augment the natural workings of such social networks and communities of practice that already exist.

Psychological Safety

With project-based learning the intent is to create a practice field, to provide the playing room – a space where people feel comfortable practicing learning without the fear of failure, a space where they can raise difficult issues; a place where they do not resort to defensive behavior. Creating 'psychological safety' (Schein, 1999) is a considerable challenge. It is not just a matter of intent; it requires very skillful behavior that is developed over time as people learn to trust one another.

The Ford case illustrates this very clearly. As William Isaacs, one of the lead researchers from MIT involved in the Lincoln project explains:

> Many factors contributed to these successes. But a central one that Fred and many others often commented on was the freedom of communication and the capacity to reflect directly on previously undiscussable issues. For perhaps the first time, managers were prepared to listen to engineers in a way that led engineers to feel safe to raise problems early. (Isaacs, 1999: 353)

As Fred Simon, former Ford Lincoln Continental program manager puts it:

> you cannot create trust directly. You can only create conditions conducive to trusting. (Senge et al., 1999: 248)

Isaacs further explains:

> Simon gave his team leaders tools and an atmosphere in which it was possible to share meaning – to reflect on what was working and not working – without being punished . . . People learned. And they found a way to detect and reduce errors much more quickly than before. (Isaacs, 1999: 213)

Project members learned a set of basic tools and skills for conversation, and through a climate of psychological safety they began to talk openly about difficult issues and the problems they were facing.

> Fred and his team developed a method and infrastructure for listening – in particular, for the kind of interpersonal learning that could enable people to conduct difficult conversations more effectively, remaining open to the possibility that they could accommodate and learn from their differences. (Isaacs, 1999: 349)

Leadership for Learning

It is commonly agreed that leaders have great influence on the performance of their team. Senge (1990b) argues that leaders must be capable of building shared vision, inspiring commitment, translating emerging ideas into workable goals, and empowering people. This requires leaders who have the ability to reflect on their view, expose their reasoning and encourage others to be inquisitive.

The leadership model in project-based learning is therefore very different from the management model. It reflects the emergent structure and the evolving culture. Leaders may evolve where and when necessary. Leadership is not equated with position in the project hierarchy.

The safety net that was created in the Ford case was continually reinforced by the project and team leadership. Says Zeniuk: 'Fred Simon, the program manager, . . . became very active in the team transformation. Fred's involvement was necessary to legitimize the process and provide leadership support' (O'Reilly, 1995: 11).

The leader as a reflective practitioner sets the tone for learning. Leaders should ideally also take a significant role in the change process by engaging in personal transformation, and become coaches and facilitators serving others. Sustainability and continuity of learning initiatives seem to be much more prevalent in organizations where leaders 'lead by learning' and are fully engaged in the process, assuming a leadership role in the transformation.

Leaders may be unaware that their behavior is inconsistent with what they espouse. They cannot see themselves and they need others to help them to do this. As the late Dr Deming put it for the Lincoln team, 'The eye cannot see itself'. Drawing from his own experience, Zeniuk states:

> If you are in a senior leadership position, you are alone and you will be the last one to know what really is going on. My greatest challenge was to have people around me who could tell the truth and consequently see myself. But it takes a great deal

of trust before someone can really tell the truth. It can only start by the leaders' commitment to truth.

Shell Oil CEO Phil Carroll puts it even more firmly: 'if you don't have a fundamental commitment to the truth and telling the truth, you can't lead. And telling the truth is so much more difficult than just "not lying"' (Senge et al., 1999: 248).

Systemic, Collective Reflection

Reflective practices and continuous engagement in learning require the use of reflective learning tools. A learning tool is an artefact that will lead to new ways of thinking through its use (Senge et al., 1994). It may be perceived as a supportive mechanism, necessary and useful for developing skills and capabilities to confront new and different issues in future projects. After action reviews, project and team audits, and lessons learned databases are some examples of such supportive tools for project-based learning.

For example, the US Army has institutionalized collective reflection through 'After Action Reviews' (AAR). The AARs help to discover what happened, why it happened, and how it might take place differently next time. As Roth recounts (Senge et al., 1999), the AAR is not a sufficient learning tool by itself, but it is part of an integrated self-reinforcing system established to develop the learning capabilities of organizational members. The Shell group also uses the AAR process for systemic reflection and has a technology infrastructure to enable people to reflect together across projects (Isaacs, 1999).

Project audit is a procedure that can be used for systematically developing data on the project's characteristics and performance, and conducting an analysis of the underlying sources of the performance one observes (Wheelwright and Clark, 1992). The project audit can provide the guidelines for areas of attention, and can focus on specific questions to be addressed at both the team and project levels.

In the case of Fokker, since phasing was used for complex development projects, the project audits were coupled with project reviews that took place at the completion of each phase, i.e. at fixed milestones during the projects. Due to the size and complexity of the majority of product development projects, project audits were performed within every team that constituted the project network, not just at project level or core team. The systematic use of project audits ensured that crucial information was not lost. Causes of failure and underlying sources were identified at the level of teams and 'lessons learned' were accurately recorded. These entailed a set of recommendations to safeguard that the same mistakes were not repeated in future projects and by other teams. Some of the 'lessons learned' were also shared verbally across projects through initiatives of the project or team leaders. In addition, a project history library was set up with all the documents containing concluding reports and lessons learned.

Concluding Remarks: Balancing Action and Reflection

In the typical, task-centered project where short-term pressures prevail, it is not an easy task to shift the focus from action to reflection. Cultivating habits of reflective practice in the fast-paced project environment requires deliberate attention to learning and seeing beyond the task at hand. We posit that this may be facilitated or accelerated through insider/outsider collaboration.

The insider/outsider collaboration creates new ways for people to reflect on what is happening. The outsider brings a broader perspective and thus may help the practitioner see the systemic aspects of the problem, shifting the attention away from blaming and individual preferences.

In many of the current projects ongoing within the SoL companies, it is the collaboration between researchers and practicing managers that leads to theory relevant to practice and to action that stems from reflective practices rather than defensive reasoning. In the case of Fokker, the insider/outsider collaboration provided an environment that fostered reflective practices. At Ford, the partnership between MIT researchers and project leaders enabled the development of learning capabilities. Fred Simon, looking back on his experience with MIT, admits that he had been very much a skeptic about 'having a bunch of academics come in and mess around with his business'. Yet, he soon realized the significance of changing the way people behaved (Isaacs, 1999).

Effective collaboration between academics and managers benefits both practice and theory, enhancing the significance and relevance of research, informing both practitioners' and academics' views and actions. Bartunek and Louis (1996) explain that 'true' insider/outsider research typically includes both taking appropriate action and making a scholarly contribution. It is also not unusual that action research be chosen as the methodology. Action research provides a link between scientific understanding and social action. It helps practitioners articulate their tacit theories and thus incorporates local knowledge.

In the Fokker case, action research played a significant role in building an infrastructure which could support and sustain reflective practices. The inquiry into processes, which the practitioners knew at action level but had not actually thought about conceptually or reflected upon, contributed to the externalization of tacit knowledge. Similarly on the Lincoln Continental team, the new knowledge for developing the innovative product development processes and designs was constituted in action, in the 'doing' – enabled by enhanced reflective practices and 'evocative' leadership style.

In both Ford and Fokker a genuine partnership existed between academics and project and team leaders. There was a commitment among the researchers to contribute to practice by developing effective tools and methods, and the practitioners were willing to invest time and energy in reflection and learning to reach a better understanding in light of new conceptual models and better theories and tools. They worked together to build a community of reflective practitioners who were capable of using the learning tools and helped the organizational members to develop learning capabilities that transcended the boundaries of specific projects.

Notes

1. SoL, formerly the Organizational Learning Center at MIT, is a global learning community dedicated to building knowledge for fundamental institutional change. SoL has corporate, consultant and research members. Both authors of this article are affiliated with the Society for Organizational Learning.

2. This is the Ford story as told by Nick Zeniuk, a project manager at the time, based on his personal experience and observations.

3. This case is based on action research conducted by Karen Ayas at Fokker Aircraft over the course of three years. See Ayas (1997) for a discussion of the methodology and the framework 'Project Design for Learning' which was developed and implemented in the new product development sector.

References

Argyris, C. (1993) *Knowledge for Action: A Guide for Overcoming Barriers to Organizational Change.* San Francisco: Jossey-Bass.

Argyris, C. and Schön, D.A. (1978) *Organizational Learning: A Theory of Action Perspective.* Reading, MA: Addison-Wesley.

Ayas, K. (1997) *Design for Learning for Innovation.* Delft: Eburon.

Bartunek, J.M. and Louis, M.R. (1996) *Insider/Outsider Team Research.* Thousand Oaks, CA: Sage.

Brown, S.J. and Duguid, P. (1999) 'Organizing Knowledge', *Reflections: The SoL Journal* 1(2): 28–42.

Covey, S.R. (1989) *The Seven Habits of Highly Effective People.* New York: Simon & Schuster.

Dewey, J. (1933) *How We Think.* Chicago: Henry Regnery.

Galbraith, J. (1994) *Competing with Flexible Lateral Organizations.* Reading, MA: Addison-Wesley Publishing.

Geus, A.P. de (1997) *The Living Company.* Cambridge, MA: Harvard University Press.

Granovetter, M.S. (1973) 'The Strength of Weak Ties', *American Journal of Sociology* 78: 1360–80.

Hastings, C. (1993) *New Organizational Forms.* London: Heinemann.

Isaacs, W. (1999) *Dialogue: The Art of Thinking Together.* New York: Doubleday.

Katzenbach, J.R. and Smith, D.K. (1993) *The Wisdom of Teams: Creating the High-performance Organization.* Cambridge, MA: Harvard Business School Press.

Kim, D. (1994) *System Archetypes II: Using System Archetypes to Take Effective Action.* Waltham: Pegasus Communications.

Kleiner, A. (1996) *The Age of Heretics.* New York: Doubleday.

Leonard-Barton, D. (1995) *Wellsprings of Knowledge.* Cambridge, MA: Harvard Business School Press.

Lundin, R.A. and Midler, C. (1998) *Projects as Arenas for Renewal and Learning Processes.* Boston: Kluwer Academic Publishers.

Nonaka, I. and Takeuchi, H. (1995) *The Knowledge Creating Company.* New York: Oxford University Press.

O'Reilly, K.W. (1995) *Managing the Rapids: Stories From the Forefront of the Learning Organization.* Waltham, MA: Pegasus Communications.

Roth, G. and Kleiner, A. (2000) *Car Launch: The Human Side of Managing Change.* New York: Oxford University Press.

Schein, E.H. (1997) *Organizational Culture and Leadership,* 2nd edn. San Francisco: Jossey-Bass.

Schein, E.H. (1999) 'Kurt Lewin's Change Theory in the Field and in the Classroom: Notes Toward a Model of Managed Learning', *Reflections: The SoL Journal* 1(1): 59–72.

Schön, D. (1983) *The Reflective Practitioner: How Professionals Think in Action.* New York: Basic Books.

Senge, P.M. (1990a) *The Fifth Discipline: The Art and Practice of the Learning Organization*. New York: Doubleday.

Senge, P.M. (1990b) 'The Leader's New Work: Building Learning Organizations,' *Sloan Management Review* (Fall): 7–23.

Senge, P.M. (1991) 'Transforming the Practice of Management', paper presented at the Systems Thinking in Action Conference, Boston.

Senge, P.M., Kleiner, A., Roberts, C., Ross, R., Roth, G. and Smith, B. (1999) *The Dance of Change*. New York: Doubleday.

Senge, P.M., Roberts, C., Ross, R.B., Smith, B.J. and Kleiner, A. (1994) *The Fifth Discipline Fieldbook: Strategies and Tools for Building a Learning Organization*. New York: Doubleday/ Currency.

Swieringa, J. and Wierdsma, A. (1992) *Becoming a Learning Organization*. Wokingham: Addison-Wesley Publishing.

Turner, J.R., Grude, K.V. and Thurloway, L. (1996) *The Project Manager as Change Agent: Leadership, Influence and Negotiation*. London: McGraw-Hill.

Wenger, E. (1998) *Communities of Practice: Learning, Meaning, and Identity*. Cambridge: Cambridge University Press.

Wheelwright, S. and Clark, K. (1992) *Revolutionizing New Product Development*. Dorset House. New York: Free Press.

part five

Globalization and Management Learning

15

Rajesh Kumar and Jean-Claude Usunier

Management Education in a Globalizing World
Lessons from the French Experience

'Globalization has arrived in the world, but not in most of the world's organizations' (Rhinesmith, 1993: 2). This statement reflects the increasing incongruity between the rapidly evolving global environment and organizational characteristics. Organizations are often locked in to function according to certain standard operating procedures that are shaped by their location, their history, and their identity. Needless to say, globalization has changed the rules of the game. Past success is no guarantee of future success. A widely accepted axiom among strategy theorists is that organizations must achieve strategic flexibility if they are going to survive and prosper over the longer term (Hitt et al., 1998). Strategic flexibility requires strategic leadership (Finkelstein and Hambrick, 1996); strategic intent (Hamel and Prahalad, 1989); the ability to think in non-linear terms (Hitt et al., 1998); and a high degree of creative judgement (Kumar and Weggemann, 1998). This is by no means an exhaustive list of what strategic flexibility might entail (see Volberda, 1998) but it does capture the essence of what organizations need to do to enhance and maintain their competitiveness in a globalizing world. In this new paradigm of organizational functioning, the development and enhancement of managerial skills are seen as critical in determining how firms cope with threats and opportunities in the global market place.

This article will discuss and critically evaluate the trends in management education in France with a specific focus on whether or not these schools are developing the critical competencies required for operating globally. We will analyse in some detail the attempted transformation in business schools in France, highlighting the successes and failures of the transformational attempt. The focus on France is useful for a number of different reasons. First and foremost, France is a major European power and has been the driver behind European integration. Second, the French intellectual tradition has been very Cartesian, in which logical thinking is highly valued. Although a global mindset does value rational analysis, it more broadly stresses the integration of the rational with the intuitive (Rhinesmith, 1993). It would appear that for the French there might be an inherent contradiction between conforming to the demands of local rationality versus conforming to the demands of global rationality. It is also worth keeping in mind the natural ambivalence that the French feel towards the importation of American ideas. There is a desire to acquire the latest techniques but at the same time there is a reluctance to accept American hegemony. Finally, the traditional managerial style in France is an authoritarian one reflective of the high power distance character of the society (Hofstede, 1980). This particular cultural trait is also at variance with the norms associated with developing a culture conducive to maximizing global learning. For all of these reasons the French case is a particularly interesting one and it should highlight lessons valuable to educational organizations seeking to develop global managerial skills in their students.

The first part of this article presents the critical challenges faced by educational institutions when reshaping management education in confronting the challenges of globalization and it highlights the difference between institutional environments and organizational choices in Europe and in the United States. The second part analyses how French higher education in management is organized and embedded in French society. Our case study of French *Grandes Ecoles* (business schools) is discussed in the third part, which analyses the internal dynamics of the *Ecole de Commerce*. In the fourth part, we discuss the strategic posture of French *Grandes Ecoles de Commerce* in relation to the globalization of management education. In the fifth part, we draw the lessons of our case study and examine how management education institutions want to legitimate themselves within the local environment in which they are institutionally embedded, rather than within the global environment. As a consequence, they have difficulty in managing internal change that might be consistent with the imperatives of globalization and tend to use global management education as a rhetorical device for improving their status in the local scene.

Educational Institutions and the Development of Global Management Competencies

Organizations are exhorted to develop global managers (Bartlett and Ghoshal, 1992) who can help an organization to manage competitiveness, complexity, adaptability, cross national teams, uncertainty and learning (Rhinesmith, 1993). Educators, consultants and trainers are grappling with identifying a set of critical skills that global managers need to possess. Rhinesmith (1993) notes, for example, that global managers need to possess a high degree of knowledge; must be good conceptualizers; should demonstrate flexibility and sensitivity; ought to possess good judgement; and must be self-reflective. Vaill (1996) suggests that managers are functioning in an environment that may be best described as a 'permanent white water' and for that reason need to recognize 'learning as a way of being'. This entails that managers should be engaged in self-directed learning, creative learning, expressive learning, feeling learning, on-line learning, continual learning, and reflexive learning. Kumar and Weggeman (1998) suggest that managers need to possess a high degree of creative judgement. Creative judgement has three components,

namely (a) imaginative competence which reflects on the insightful awareness of managers; (b) critical competence which demonstrates their reflective
capability; and (c) commitment generating competence which reflects on
their ability to sustain a high level of organizational commitment within the
organization.

Although the acquisition of these skills is undoubtedly a life-long process
and has a strong experiential component to it, the knowledge and the
training that students receive in business management programmes are
important in shaping the ease and effectiveness with which extant students
can be transformed into managers who make 'learning as a way of being' a
permanent part of their mental repertoire. It is perhaps for this reason that
Porter and McKibbin (1988) in a review of business education suggested that
business schools needed to (a) improve the interpersonal skills of students;
(b) internationalize the course content; (c) engage in cross functional
integration; (d) broaden the exposure of students to electives in non-business
domains; (e) focus on the external organizational environment; and (f)
create an information orientation which would permeate all of the curriculum. This report was written within the context of the American business
education programmes.

A caveat is in order, however. Although in this article we focus on the role
played by business schools in promoting globalization, it is by no means the
case that business schools are the sole repository for fostering globalization.
The competencies necessary for global management may be developed
through in-company training programmes, executive education programmes,
on the job training, and other related activities. In recent years, a number of
firms have sought to develop tailor-made training programmes either
through the establishment of their own in-house educational activities or
through linkages with business schools like IMD, Insead, and London
Business School. In Germany, as Locke (1998) points out, there are very few
MBA programmes similar to the ones prevalent in the United States. The
expectation is that many of the management competencies will be acquired
by the employees either through on the job training or through collaboration
with other academic institutions specializing in management education. That
this is not a problem is noted by Kipping (1998) who cites a 1995 survey of
European managers in which the German managers were rated as the
strongest in their leadership qualities relative to their counterparts in France,
Britain and the Netherlands.

Although it is abundantly clear that business schools are by no means the
only or, for that matter, the most effective means for developing management
competencies, they do possess a high degree of visibility and salience in the
United States. Their popularity has also begun to emerge in Europe with
these programmes gaining particular prominence in the UK, the Nordic
countries and, more recently, France (see Engwall and Zamagni, 1998, for an
overview of trends in management education). Given the rapid development
and expansion of these programmes, it is useful to assess the contribution
that they can make in fostering global management competencies. As
outlined earlier, this article focuses on business schools in France.

Management Education in Europe and the United States

Management education in Europe has traditionally not been associated with the kind of prestige and jazz that characterizes management education in the United States. Indeed, as an article in *Business Week* (1998: 76) notes,

> For decades, European managers disdained American MBAs. They believed US universities churned out arrogant, inexperienced 25 year olds who demanded big salaries and understood little about building consensus, teamwork, or social values.

Historically most managers in Europe had a degree either in engineering or in economics from a local institution. As the article in *Business Week* notes, this is beginning to change. MBA programmes have increased in popularity as indexed by a growing enrolment and accreditation of some European programmes by the AACSB. The enhanced legitimacy of business education in Europe is attributed to pressures stemming from the intensification of global competition.

Although there is now a widespread global recognition for the necessity of global management education and a quiet consensus on the kind of skills that global managers must possess, it is as yet unclear as to whether the process of imparting critical managerial skills to business students will become institutionalized in a manner which will be both effective and efficient. There are several reasons for suspending judgement on the effectiveness of the changes that appear to be sweeping through business schools. To begin with, these changes (be they in the US, Europe or Asia) are only of recent origin. Thus it is by no means clear that organizations will be able to institutionalize these changes in a desired manner. Only time will tell.

Furthermore, as institutional theorists point out, organizations operating in a particular area feel compelled to adopt certain forms of behaviour to acquire legitimacy (Di Maggio and Powell, 1991). The behaviours may or may not be necessary for effective performance. Conformity is fostered by mimetic, normative, and/or coercive processes operating within the environment of the organization. Mimetic processes impel an organization to imitate other organizations; normative processes impel organizations to conform to institutional expectations; while coercive processes impose costs on the organizations for non-compliance. With the theme of globalization becoming a larger than life reality, educational organizations are compelled to talk the language of globalization irrespective of their ability and/or their motivation to become a truly global institution. This means that their commitment and their ability in making their institutions global might be less than what is assumed from their rhetoric.

Even in the event that organizations are sincerely committed to developing global management competencies, they may be prevented from realizing their objectives to the fullest extent by the nature of the institutional environments within which they are operating. It is widely recognized that the business schools in Europe, the United States and Asia are embedded in different institutional environments, with each institutional environment conferring its own advantages and disadvantages in promoting global thinking. Linder (1999: 15) points out that the European university system is not conducive to developing new ideas. The appointment of rectors is more often than not a political process, which leads them to be 'accommodating' rather than 'entrepreneurial'. The university does not have much autonomy in creating new fields of study. Perhaps most significantly he notes (1999: 15) 'Faculty salaries are determined through government decree, and longevity matters more than merit'. This is in sharp contrast with the situation in the United States where the universities are exposed to a much greater degree of competitive pressure. Run as private institutions the universities in the United States are striving to be at the top of their pack.

The American and the European educational systems, for example, also differ in terms of the implicit values/expectations concerning the purposes of education and the mechanisms by which it is to be imparted. This difference may also have implications for their ability to impart skills that are crucial in developing a global mindset. For example, in the United States it is widely accepted that students must pay for their education whereas in much of Europe that is not the norm. Similarly, in the United States students are often obliged to attend classes whereas attendance is not compulsory for European students. Likewise, a participatory style with extensive dialogue is often the norm in an American classroom whereas a more didactic and a top down approach prevails in European universities. Given these differences it is by no means clear that European institutions can move towards a more interactive and a participative style of learning.

The transformation of an education system that has been traditionally rooted in formalism to one rooted in informalism, spontaneity, multi-culturalism and continuous learning is also resource intensive and especially so at the initiation of the change process. Whether or not the institutions possess the relevant resources emerges as a significant factor in facilitating the transition. Resources may be either internally generated (as is the case with students paying fees in the US) and/or may be externally generated through corporate sponsorship, alumni donations, and/or state support. Transformative change also requires strong leadership, with the leader being able to articulate the vision and the values of the emergent organization. This is particularly important as the educational institutions have all the trappings of a 'loosely coupled system' (Orton and Weick, 1990). This means, for example, that the organizational actors within such a system operate auto-nomously with very little responsiveness between them. In varying degrees this state is likely to exist in interactions among individuals; between different departmental units; and across varying hierarchical levels in the educational organization. Hence, synergies are not the natural outcome; on the contrary, they have to be deliberately moulded and shaped by the leadership in the organization.

In the contrast that we draw between the European and the American educational systems we do not wish to imply that the US business schools are necessarily *par excellence* examples of globalization. Indeed, Locke (1998) suggests that the US business schools by creating a managerial elite have undermined the organizational cohesion so critical to achieving success at the operational level. Other scholars have noted that while the North American business schools preach the need for internationalization, they fail to incorporate this dimension in the business school curriculum (Francis and Globerman, 1992). Perhaps the contrast between the European and the American models might become most clear if we were to draw a distinction between the process and the content aspects of globalization. That is to say, it might very well be the case that on the content side the American business schools are not that well globalized, but on the process side they may very well be in so far as they promote an achievement oriented rather than an ascriptive oriented meritocracy. In other words, the mere fact that you have been accepted in a business school does not automatically guarantee you a diploma no matter how good you may have been prior to entering the school – you have to earn it through appropriate work. Furthermore, it is also worth bearing in mind that the North American style business school does not have any pre-eminent challenger. North Americans have been prominent in research activities, and the publication of management textbooks. Most of the publications in top level management journals are written by North American scholars (Engwall and Zamagni, 1998). Similarly, the accreditation of MBA programmes based on AACSB standards represents the only dominant system for accrediting MBA programmes (the EFMD Equis has by no means a brand recognition similar to the AACSB). In sum, while the North American model is by no means flawless, it is a model that has a global reach in spite of its ethnocentricity.

Reshaping Management Education: The Critical Challenges

(a) Curriculum content   Changes in the curriculum content and in the methods by which the content is presented are indeed the primary mechanisms for reshaping management education. The advent of globalization has increased calls for internationalizing the curricula. Historically, the US-based business schools were on an average more deficient in internationalizing the curricula than their European counterparts although that is beginning to change. However, even as educators are agreed that curriculum content must be internationalized there is little consensus as to specific means of accomplishing this. For example, does internationalization mean the introduction of new international courses or does it mean that the existing courses need to become more international in orientation? If new courses are to be introduced then what is the optimal number of such courses? What is the optimal balance between depth and breadth of coverage? How critical are language related courses in promoting internationalization? There is obviously no one right solution to designing the curriculum content. Different schools are likely to make different choices based on their history, their resource endowment, the composition of the student body, and most fundamentally the mission that has been assigned to them by their stakeholders. Most US-based business schools have integrated the international component within their core courses while allowing for some electives with an international component. The underlying premise is that the international component (emic) can be incorporated within an underlying model which is essentially etic. Consistent with this, many US-based business schools have sought to eliminate the international business department as a separate entity. Internationally oriented faculty have either been absorbed within the functional departments or have been let go. How effective this model is in promoting global thinking is still very much an open question. Indeed, a study by Reiss and Orne (1995) suggested that an attempt to internationalize courses in a US business school by introducing information about the global environment and cultural differences increased the ethnocentricity of the students.

European schools have followed a different tradition (the UK being an exception). Internationally oriented courses are a norm in many schools. Many of these courses are offered in conjunction with language courses which are compulsory in European schools. Given the diversity in Europe, acceptance of courses focusing on differences is only natural within this environment. The premise underlying this model is that diversity necessitates emic oriented courses. The problem with this model is that a strong focus on the emic without a corresponding emphasis on the etic will tend to reinforce stereotypes and may make cross national generalizations difficult. This poses a problem opposite to the one that can be discerned in the American model. It is apparent that schools on either side are struggling with the imperatives of developing a curriculum conducive to promoting global thinking. There are merits in each approach but there is as yet no model that can even pretend to have global applicability.

(b) Corporate culture   Educational organizations have been described as having a fragmented corporate culture (Goffee and Jones, 1996). A fragmented corporate culture is characterized by low levels of sociability and low levels of solidarity. Sociability refers to the level of friendliness among organizational members while solidarity refers to the ability to pursue shared objectives effectively and efficiently (Goffee and Jones, 1996). What kind of a corporate culture does an educational institution need to promote global thinking? First, it is imperative that the faculty members work co-operatively for it is only under these conditions that they will be able to develop courses that are cross functional and integrative in character. Second, the faculty members must be viewed as important strategic assets for the school. The administration must follow what Pfeffer (1994) describes as a 'high commitment model' in which they make concerted efforts to retain the loyalty of the faculty for it is only under these conditions that the faculty will be motivated to maximize their effort in developing an organization that promotes global thinking. The leadership of the educational institution must be strongly committed to the goal that they are trying to achieve. They must have a vision, buttressed by appropriate reward systems. All too often, the leaders say one thing but act in contradiction to their espoused values. This is surely not the way of creating or developing an internal learning capability. Just as in business organizations, the administrators must seek to articulate a 'strategic intent' (Hamel and Prahalad, 1996) for their institution.

The corporate culture must also enable the educational organization to achieve legitimacy in relation to its key constituents, be they internal or external. Suchman (1995: 574) defines legitimacy as 'a generalised perception or assumption that the actions of an entity are desirable, proper, appropriate, within some socially constructed system of norms, values, beliefs, and definition'. He distinguishes three alternative forms of legitimacy, namely the pragmatic, the moral, and the cognitive. Pragmatic legitimacy is dependent on an organization meeting the needs of its constituents; moral legitimacy is dependent on the organization doing the right thing; while cognitive legitimacy is dependent on the constituents' understanding of the logic of the organizational strategy. The educational organization has three major constituencies: (a) students; (b) the faculty; and (c) the external market. Although all constituents are likely to be concerned with all forms of legitimacy the relative importance that they accord to the different forms is likely to be variable. One could surmise that students and the employers (as representatives of the external market place) are likely to be the most concerned with achieving pragmatic legitimacy, while the faculty members are likely to place a higher premium on the moral and cognitive dimensions of legitimacy, although they will not be oblivious to the pragmatic dimension.

This is likely to pose a major challenge for the administrators of the educational organizations. First, attaining different forms of legitimacy requires different strategies. For example, pragmatic legitimacy is attained by being responsive to constituent needs, while moral legitimacy is attained by adhering to the basic values of the educational organization in both a symbolic as well as a substantive sense. This means that the administrators are confronted with the need to undertake a wide range of managerial actions leading to a heavy managerial burden. Second, it may well be the case that attaining legitimacy with one group of constituents makes the attainment of legitimacy with another group more problematical. Students, for example, may want to do as little work as possible and/or may resist the notion of compulsory attendance in classes. The faculty, on the other hand, may wish to make the students work harder, and/or penalize them for not attending classes. There is a fundamental conflict here – a conflict that may be particularly hard to resolve given the past history of the educational systems in Europe. It is also worth bearing in mind that educational organizations cannot simply rest once they feel that they have achieved legitimacy. In a dynamic environment, pressures for delegitimation are ever present (see, for example, the annual ranking system of business schools in the United States – it is not unusual for organizations to slip in these rankings). The ability to cope with what Vaill (1996) describes as 'permanent whitewater' is an indispensable quality not just for business organizations but for educational organizations as well.

The French *Grandes Ecoles de Commerce*

Our discussion of the French *Grandes Ecoles de Commerce* begins with an overview of the two-tier French educational system. An understanding of this system is crucial in evaluating the role played by the *Grandes Ecoles* in France. Subsequently, we provide a summary of the evolution of the French *Grandes Ecoles* as concerns management education. Our discussion primarily focuses on the *Ecoles de Commerce*, although we do recognize and comment upon the role played by the *Ecole Polytechnique, Ecoles des Mines,* and *Ecole Nationale d'Administration* in the formation of French managers.

The Two-tier French Higher Education System

Higher education in France offers a unique structure to be found virtually nowhere else in the world with the system of *Grandes Ecoles* which runs parallel to the traditional university system. The 90 universities are centrally managed by the French Ministry of Education, which has more than 1.1 million employees and controls almost all types of education in France from kindergarten to doctoral programmes. The *Grandes Ecoles* fall under the direction of the ministry concerned with their respective field of study (agriculture, telecommunications, industry, etc.) or depend on semi-public bodies such as the *Chambres de Commerce.* After the baccalaureate, a comprehensive examination at the end of secondary school, students who want to enter a *Grande Ecole* must follow two or three years of preparatory studies (*classes préparatoires*) which are integrated to the secondary schools (*lycées*). There are basically two types of *classes préparatoires*, those for engineering schools (*math-sup* and *math-spê*) and those for business schools (*prépas HEC*). After two years of intensive preparation, with heavy emphasis on formal training and general knowledge, students seeking admission to a *Grande Ecole* must pass a series of nation-wide competitive examinations (*concours*) based on both written and oral performances. Ranking is the only criterion for entry; those who have not succeeded must either re-enter the *classe préparatoire* for another year or, alternatively, enter a university where they will either be required to start at entry level or receive a one or two year waiver depending on their performance in the *concours*.

The French higher education system is in fact oddly regulated. On the one hand, universities follow the international model of higher education and use research as input for teaching. The university system has been traditionally viewed by the business community as rather irresponsive to its needs, in contrast to the *Grandes Ecoles*.[1] Universities have the right to run doctoral programmes and award doctoral degrees to successful PhD candidates. Many of them have long traditions, such as the University of Montpellier or the University of Grenoble, which are seven centuries old. Easterby-Smith and Tanton (1988: 44) describe the French universities in the following terms:

> management education in French universities has had to accept the rules and control of the State system. This includes minimal student selection at undergraduate levels and hence extremely large classes, and high drop-out rates. Under

those circumstances didactic teaching methods are inevitable and it is only at the relatively privileged postgraduate levels that more active teaching methods (such as case method) become possible. Within the French system, research is an activity separated from teaching and takes place in research institutes.

On the other hand, the *Grandes Ecoles'* reputation is based on their severe screening procedures but not on the content of teaching. For instance, engineering schools, until recently, turned out future managers who had no idea of what management techniques were. They learnt 'on the job', providing French companies with generations of self-made business leaders, who were clever but unskilled in management techniques. Up to recent years, the *Grandes Ecoles*, with a few exceptions, had no research undertakings. This division of labour resulted in the *Grandes Ecoles* having most of the best students and universities doing research and conferring doctoral degrees.

The divide between universities and *Grandes Ecoles* is deeply rooted in both the French social class system and in the way French elite are recruited. In 1993, among the top managers of the 200 most important French companies, 50% had graduated from either *Polytechnique* (27%) or *Ecole Nationale d'Administration* (ENA; 23%). Interestingly enough, the *Ecole Polytechnique* and *Ecoles des Mines* are primarily engineering schools where general management education was introduced only in the 1970s and 1980s. The students spend only a fraction of their time in studying management. While accounting and basic organization theory are well covered, there are no courses in the area of marketing, finance, and/or human resource management. ENA, on the other hand, is the route for entering the civil service. Most of the students entering the ENA have studied politics and administrative law. Like the other *Grandes Ecoles* alluded to earlier, some management education has been introduced in the curriculum. This education concentrates on strategic and financial management of public organizations. In contrast with the *Grandes Ecoles de Commerce* and the faculties of management in French Universities, the *Ecole Polytechnique*, *Ecole des Mines*, and *Ecole Nationale d'Administration* are not schools of management. Nevertheless, since the mid-1960s the *Ecole des Mines* has established a Centre for Scientific Management Research (the CGS). Although the centre originally dealt with management science it has progressively expanded to study processes of organizational change in public organizations. *Ecole Polytechnique* has also established a similar centre, which is referred to as the *Centre de Recherche en Gestion* (CRG). It has a similar orientation. (See Berry, 1995, for a detailed overview of the CRG and CGS.) While the alumni from *Ecole Polytechnique* and ENA account for about 50% of the top executives of the 200 largest French companies (Bauer and Bertin-Mourot, 1995), all the *Ecoles de Commerce* account for only 10% of them. This in itself is a dramatic illustration of the proposition that management education per se does not lead an individual to become a part of the top managerial elite. Ironically enough, this tendency has increased notwithstanding the imperatives of global competition (Bauer and Bertin-Mourot, 1995). The *Ecoles de Commerce* are the source of middle level managers but not much more.

Grandes Ecoles have historically played a key role in the building of French business elite with only a very minor place left to university graduates. The *esprit de corps* (sense of belonging to a specific in-group) leads certain *Grandes Ecoles* to engage in 'closed shop' recruitment practices in companies and departments where a good number of alumni can control hiring decisions. Alumni are well organized and the *annuaire des anciens* (alumni directory: an institution) helps place young graduates in companies where the *mafia de Grandes Ecoles* (i.e. a relational network) facilitates access to jobs. University education is traditionally seen as open and free education for everybody with no access constraints, directly but poorly financed by the state. The image of university education is that of being more research directed, with less emphasis on the selection of the students. Universities are forbidden by law to select students; however, they have gradually introduced a lot of selection procedures at different stages of the educational process.

The *Grandes Ecoles* have a more elitist, bourgeois and professional image. The upper social classes have a tradition of pushing their children towards the *Grandes Ecole* system: for instance 46% of *Ecole des Hautes Etudes Commerciales* (HEC) graduates came from upper class families involved in small business or managing positions (see Bourdieu, 1989). The selection is based objectively on intellectual qualities and the *Grandes Ecoles'* selection system provides them with a large proportion of the best students. But the number of schools claiming to be a *Grande Ecole* has considerably increased over the years, largely reducing the gap between the *Grandes Ecoles* and the universities.

History of the Grandes Ecoles de Commerce in France

The first *Grandes Ecoles* were the product of the French revolution and they were almost exclusively engineering schools, such as the *Ecole Polytechnique* founded in 1795. The *Ecole Spéciale de Commerce et d'Industrie*, created in Paris in 1819, was the first attempt to create a sort of business school in France. The new institution had great difficulty in defining a model different from that of the engineering schools. Accordingly it was finally taken over by the Paris Chamber of Commerce in 1869. The period 1870–1914 proved very favourable to the creation of the *Ecoles de Commerce* – in Rouen (1871), in Lyons and Marseilles (1872), and in Bordeaux (1874). The *Ecoles de Commerce* were subject to influences from the local Chamber of Commerce, public authorities and the business community (Grelon, 1997). Torn between engineering content and a university style of teaching (with emphasis on law), the *Ecoles de Commerce* experienced difficulties in attracting students and had limited enrolment. Some of them, like the one in Rouen, closed within one year of their inception. That is why the Chambers of Commerce were interested in creating schools which would clearly belong to the higher rather than to the secondary education system. Finally, in 1881 the Paris Chamber of Commerce created the *Ecole des Hautes Etudes Commerciales* (HEC), which was later recognized by the state. In 1890, HEC, in association with the main *Ecoles Supérieures de Commerce* agreed to recruit students by *concours* with similar preparatory programmes and examination schemes for all schools (Grelon, 1997). Later, the *Ecoles Supérieures de Commerce* flourished, some of which were joint ventures between the local Chamber of Commerce and faculty of law (ICN in Nancy, 1896; IEC in Grenoble, 1906).

A typical work schedule at HEC in 1881 included 39 hours of classroom teaching, of which 12 hours were dedicated to accounting, 10 to foreign languages, and $\frac{1}{2}$ to 3 hours to commercial geography, history of commerce, law and political economy. Most students came from the upper middle class with families often involved in trade and industry. The style was that of a '*super-lycée*' (Nouschi, 1997), that is, a vocational school that follows secondary education, rather than a full-fledged higher education institution. During the period from World War I to World War II, there was constant pressure to introduce modern teaching content and instruments, such as case studies, under Rockefeller and Ford Foundation's initiative, and with the inter-mediation of Georges Doriot and André Siegfied (Gemelli, 1997). However, their introduction was to be limited to a management education institution (CPA, opened in 1931) and not introduced in the *Ecoles de Commerce*. Continuity and lack of adaptation to modern teaching contents were the rule: the same director, Maxime Perrin, managed HEC from 1937 to 1958, with growing dissatisfaction among the graduates who could observe the discrepancy between what was taught to them in the classroom (accounting, law, and some presentations of 'personal experiences' by business people) and what would be useful to them in their managerial career (Nouschi, 1997).

Changes were introduced in the French *Grandes Ecoles de Commerce* during the 1960s: the case method was progressively introduced, as well as new content areas (e.g. marketing, finance, strategy, human resource management). While the top *Grandes Ecoles de Commerce*, HEC and ESSEC were leaders in this move, the whole system experienced vast changes in the teaching content. The French Foundation for Management Education (FNEGE) was established in the mid-1960s with the aim of bridging the gap between management education in France and other countries. One of its early achievements was to send young French academics to the United States for their PhD; this was shortly followed by the creation of PhD programmes in management (1970s) and the establishment of academic associations for the main disciplines in the mid-1980s (AFFI, finance, AFM, marketing, AGRH, human resources management, AIM, information systems). However, the fundamentals in the system remained unchanged.

In the last 30 years, a move towards some deregulation has been initiated and the universities have finally come to challenge the *Grandes Ecoles* concerning business education. In the mid-1950s, universities, under the guidance of Pierre Tabatoni, Georges Doriot and Gaston Berger, created the *Institut d'Administration des Entreprises* (IAE), a sort of one-year MBA programme. That proved to be a real success and about 30 programmes were established in France over 20 years. In 1968, the University Paris-Dauphine, a new university entirely dedicated to management and economics was created, and postgraduate programmes (DEA and DESS) were actively developed. In

1977, the position of university professor in the field of management was created through the *Agrégation de Sciences de Gestion*, a *concours* giving access to top academic positions in the field.

Concurrently, some *Grandes Ecoles* like HEC and *Polytechnique* were granted permission to run doctoral programmes and award doctorates, while most universities, though forbidden to select students at the entry level, prudently began to select students at each step of the educational process. Universities also began to raise outside funds in order to supplement the thrifty higher education budget of the French government. Links were then established between the two systems through joint research projects and scientific associations under the guidance of the French foundation for management education (FNEGE). At the end of the 1980s, 20 years of limited university budgets had resulted in ageing buildings, while rising student numbers led to overcrowded facilities. Small research budgets and insufficient non-teaching support staff were the rule (Usunier, 1990). The 1990s witnessed a clear improvement in the welfare of the French universities with increased state involvement in improving faculty compensation and regional authorities' commitment to finance new facilities.

Internal functioning of the French *Grandes Ecoles de Commerce*

What are some of the typical characteristics of French *Grandes Ecoles de Commerce*? What are the internal dynamics of their functioning? What impact do these dynamics have on the ability of these institutions to accomplish their objectives? These, and other closely related issues, will be the focus of our discussion here. Our analysis is derived from:

(a)   an analysis of archival materials detailing the evolution of the French *Grandes Ecoles*;
(b)   existing literature on the functioning of the French *Grandes Ecoles*;
(c)   personal observations of an author who has been a student and a faculty member at one of the *Ecoles de Commerce* for nine years, and is now teaching at a French University;
(d)   experiences of a North American trained scholar who was a visiting professor at two different *Ecoles de Commerce* for a period of one year. The French and the North American trained scholars constructed a joint understanding of their experiences with this joint construction being tested against existing findings. It is this shared construction which is being articulated and elaborated on in this article.

What is the basis for the evaluation that is being attempted in this article? As has been argued earlier, globalization has both a process and a content dimension. We have also noted earlier on that globalization is necessitating the development of global management competencies. Here we are focusing primarily on the processual dimension of globalization. This is important primarily for two reasons. First, process is critical to learning, whatever be the content of learning. In other words, if the right process for learning is not in place, content becomes irrelevant. Second, many of the skills crucial for developing a globally competent manager are essentially process based skills. In other words, in the absence of the right process, many of these skills will only be imperfectly developed, if they are developed at all. We focus on those dimensions of the *Ecoles de Commerce* that shape directly or indirectly the processes that are in place in these *Ecoles de Commerce*.

Students and Programmes in the French *Grandes Ecoles de Commerce*

The main characteristics of the *Grandes Ecoles* are their long teaching schedules (frequently in the range of 30 hours classroom teaching per week, sometimes more), limited choice concerning course topics, and a relative lack of student involvement in the learning task.[2] Admission to a *Grande Ecole* is not easy. The French educational system is highly elitist and lays a lot of emphasis on the innate qualities of students who are accepted for higher education. One implication of this is that the students who gain entry into such schools are intellectually very capable. But, and this needs to be stressed, once they enter, they are virtually assured of a diploma. This implies that there is little motivation to work hard. Compounding this problem is the fact that the administration makes little effort to ensure compliance in the nature of imposing penalties on students, nor does it make any effort to lighten students' workloads so as to render individual accountability more meaningful. Villette (1997: 147), for instance, cites professors of the ESCP commenting about grades in a faculty meeting:

> Students [*les élèves*][3] do what they like with us. A student who has failed eight or nine credits negotiated with each of us in order to get a 10 [passing grade] ... Finally, everybody awards 10 and there is no longer anybody daring to refuse a credit. [Another professor]: A student failed her credit. She was allowed to pass the exam again, and she failed again. Exceptionally, she was allowed to attend the lecture again; finally, she failed the exam again, then she threw a tantrum in the offices of the chairman, the dean, and the department head. I said that I would not change the grade, and that the student should make a fourth year. The jury disavowed me and awarded the diploma. I am sorry but I don't know why I grade exams.

This lack of concern may reflect the administration's greater concern with external image than with substantive content. The two need not conflict as a matter of course, but one's impression is that the former is given greater weight than the latter. The policies pursued by the French *Grande Ecoles* are reinforced by the way companies select graduates for employment. Barsoux and Lawrence (1990: 40) observe:

> Companies are apt to look upon the *Grandes Ecoles* as elaborate sifting systems rather than purveyors of knowledge and some make no secret of the fact that they are primarily purchasing the *concours*, that is, the entrance exam and initial selection rather than the training itself.

The companies' policies can be best explained by the widely held belief in France that managerial qualities are innate and cannot be developed in a formal way through education (e.g. Barsoux and Lawrence, 1990). Whatever the motivation is for the policies pursued by companies and the school administrators, their effects are far reaching and raise fundamental issues about teaching in the *Grandes Ecoles*. The nature of the system makes it often virtually impossible to engage in meaningful teaching activity (Kumar and Usunier, 1994a). Being submitted to an extensive classroom obligation, students tend to skip lectures, especially those who are deeply involved in clubs and associations. This results in low attendance of students and failure to read the assigned articles and/or complete work on time.[4] In a typical situation, half of the attending audience would have prepared the assigned materials and the other half would have not. Two other consequences of the lack of involvement of students in lectures are that there is little classroom participation and, quite often, there is constant chattering in class (Kumar and Usunier, 1994a; Davoine, 1997). An aggravating factor is the high level of involvement of many students in clubs and associations related to the *Ecole de Commerce*, sometimes 20 to 30 associations, ranging from the *Bureau des Elèves* (student association) to the junior enterprise, Amnesty International, or ski club. While there is obviously much to learn from these self-managed activities, which are seen very favourably by the *direction* of the school (Usunier, 1985), they conflict in terms of time allocation with the heavily loaded class schedule.

For instructors used to teaching in an Anglo-Saxon culture, this is bewildering and raises a number of questions as to what is really happening and how can it be controlled. At one level, the explanation seems simple: too many hours of courses per week. This is the explanation routinely put forward by the students. While there may be something to it, it hardly provides the full story. For the most part, students dish out the same story to all the teachers, thereby lessening the importance of individual accountability (Kumar and Usunier, 1994a). Much of the teaching seems to be a waste of money as well as a waste of faculty and students' time. The first in-depth explanation for this over-teaching orientation is based on reasons related to the French cultural background. There is a reluctance in the French, and more generally Latin, mentality to encourage autonomy and self-reliance in the students. Autonomy is achieved by relying on responsible outside work with a proper balance between classroom and homework: MBA students generally take four classes of 2 hours 40 minutes per week, that is, about 11 hours a week. The French *Ecoles de Commerce* seem to believe that more classroom work means a better curriculum, a naive belief in the saying: 'the more, the better'.

If we rely on Hofstede's description (1980, 1991), the score of power distance is fairly high in France while individualism is also high, a rare case which isolates France (and Belgium) in the south-west quadrant of the figure which combines individualism and power distance. Individualism is generally associated with low power distance and collectivism with high power distance. This portrait must be completed by a relatively high score of uncertainty avoidance whereby both subordinates and superiors prefer a strong hierarchical structure (pyramid). As Hall and Hall (1989: 106) observe, 'As managers, the French have the reputation of being autocratic, demanding, hard on subordinates, and thoughtless of their needs'.

In an authoritarian society, people view their authority as *personal authority* rather than *role authority*; superiors who accept debate and are open-minded even on issues which they have to decide, are often considered, in a French context, as weak or dithering. Future superiors primarily will need to show status, to inspire a sense of direction to subordinates, and to exercise authority and power. The acquisition of these 'talents' is perceived as unrelated to any content or task-related learning, that is, to most of formal and even practical management teaching (e.g. case method). The underlying belief here is that managers are mostly machiavellian, cynical types of leaders who consider academic knowledge as slightly naïve compared with organizational and political abilities. The working of French and, more generally, Latin organizations is basically based on power, political influence and power struggles (Lessem and Neubauer, 1994). As the society is power oriented, people have to learn to make their way in the system; it works by sometimes following the rules, sometimes not. There is no equivalent to the phrase *fair play* in French, which is used most often with implicit reference to an Anglo-Saxon type of behaviour. Since a diploma is virtually guaranteed to the students regardless of what they do, the students tend to be very demanding vis-à-vis their teachers (a way to exercise their sense of power) and very undemanding towards themselves. Most often course syllabi are not read and students will feign not to know the rules of the game; and finally discuss and negotiate not only the rules of the game but also their grades. Even though this behaviour may be found among students of many other nationalities, the proportion of French *Grande Ecole* students who are difficult to control is very high (40–50%), which unfortunately makes the whole group difficult to control, although there may be a small minority of manageable students (Kumar and Usunier, 1994a).

A second track for explanation of the teaching content and style is based on institutional reasons. The strategic orientation of the *Grandes Ecoles de Commerce* has always been stuck in the middle of three models and institutional influences,[5] that is, engineering schools (*Grandes Ecoles d'ingénieurs*), universities and the Chambers of Commerce. From the engineering schools, the *Grandes Ecoles de Commerce* have essentially borrowed the *concours* recruitment system. At first, they were deeply influenced by the technical character of the engineering education (Grelon, 1997) and it was only in the mid-1960s that the *Ecole Supérieure de Commerce de Paris* (ESCP; which has in fact succeeded the *Ecole Spéciale de Commerce et d'Industrie*), stopped teaching physics and chemistry to future business graduates.

The second rival model is that of the university, that is, research-driven and favouring a scientific and systematic approach towards the pursuit of knowledge. As shown by the presence of academics in their jury and the recruitment of university professors on well-paid part-time positions in the *Grandes Ecoles de Commerce*, the people who have led these institutions have been constantly both impressed and scared by the university model. For instance, Nouschi (1997) explains that, as early as 1892, the jury at HEC was chaired by a university professor. This model has a clear international dimension, since management education and research was mostly developed in the US in academic institutions such as Harvard, MIT, Wharton or Stanford.

The third rival model is that given by the parent institution, the *Chambre de Commerce*, whose functioning is explained in more detail later. Members of the board of the *Chambre de Commerce* are elected by the business community, ranging from the grocery shopkeeper or the butcher to big industrialists. The general orientation of the governing boards of the *Chambre de Commerce* has been to emphasize vocational training. They have been distrustful of the university style education because it is viewed as being too far from practice. Accounting, for instance, was taught at HEC up to the mid-1960s in the 'bookkeeping' style (*comptabilité générale*), excluding the teaching of cost accounting and management control (Nouschi, 1988).

The strategic approach to teaching contents and style in the *Grandes Ecoles de Commerce* has always been based on an unstable mix of these three rival models. This inconsistent compromise partly explains the lack of internal credibility of the learning process itself.

Faculties in the Grandes Ecoles de Commerce: An Uncomfortable Position

Faculties in *Grandes Ecoles de Commerce* do in fact perfectly reflect this threefold influence. They are recruited under the supervision of a *directeur* who is not elected by the faculty members, but chosen by the Chamber of Commerce. Faculty members are typically asked to be all at the same time: 'good' researchers, managerially relevant, talented teachers, programme organizers, etc. Villette (1997: 150) explains how the dean of the faculty[6] at ESCP described in 1992 the deteriorating situation of the faculty members over the last 10 years:

> In ten years, teaching activity at ESCP has been multiplied by 2.6. There is a quantitative production issue, a worsening of the working conditions of the *corps professoral* and a true quality problem which is growing. Sixty-eight full time faculty are notoriously insufficient to respond to the needs in terms of teaching hours.

The *directeur* has much authority over the faculty members as he has the right to 'hire and fire' as long as they are under short-term contracts. At times he may choose to 'make an example', generally by firing a lecturer whose teaching abilities are openly criticized by the students, in order to let everyone in the faculty be afraid of losing his or her job. Maintaining a high level of anxiety among their subordinates, and dividing them (*divide ut impera*) are two basic rules for superiors who want to maintain their power. That is why the director will often see people in individual meetings. Kumar (in Kumar and Usunier, 1994b) recounts his experience where in fact spying, misinformation and manipulations were the rule in the *Ecole de Commerce* where he was a visiting faculty member. While not completely typical of most

Ecoles de Commerce, where the general atmosphere is more fair, it is clear that, in this case, the personality of the director, his total inexperience of academic life (a frequent case when business-people are hired as directors), and his unquestioned backing by the *Chambre de Commerce* had led him to highly *Florentine* manipulations.

One of the interesting things about *Grandes Ecoles* is that while they do attract very capable students, the corresponding faculty is not equally qualified, at least in terms of faculty members possessing a PhD, who are relatively few in a standard *Grande Ecole de Commerce*. There are exceptions, of course (ESSEC/ESCP/HEC/EAP/EM Lyon), but they prove the rule. Some observers have suggested that this reflects the shortage of management teachers in France. Barsoux and Lawrence (1990) suggest that management education has had trouble in gaining legitimacy. Reasons for this are probably many and may include attitude towards business; the reluctance of universities to teach vocational disciplines; and the strong emphasis given to intellect as opposed to interpersonal qualities in business. In these circumstances, it is not unusual that few people have gravitated towards this profession. In addition, there is a lot of suspicion on the part of the French business community towards PhDs and academics in general. The situation is quite different from that prevailing in Germany, where half of the members of company boards and managing teams hold PhD titles (*Doktor*). There is an avowed misperception of academics for the following reasons: (1) they are supposed to be far from real-world situations; with little concern for the professional education of students, and (2) a PhD is considered, at best, as a proof of persistence, not of expertise or professional capability.

As noted earlier, the French university system remained fairly contemptuous of business education up to the mid-1950s. Many people in the business community, who backed *Ecoles de Commerce* and participated in their strategic management, were convinced that a few faculty, not necessarily holding PhD titles, were enough to run the school. In their view, most courses were better taught by business people, chartered accountants, etc. hired on a per hour basis. The lack of qualified faculty has had a number of consequences for the system. First, there is the issue of the nature of instruction. Although there may be little correlation between the possession of a PhD and teaching quality, there is no doubt that the lack of such credentials raises doubt as to the expertise of teaching staff. The lack of expertise, in turn, raises issues about the content of instruction. Second, the lack of superior qualifications makes most of these institutions give more attention to teaching as opposed to research. And, finally, the lack of such qualifications erodes the bargaining power of the faculty vis-à-vis the administrators. This reinforces their weak position within the system as a whole, given that the administrators are only concerned about the external image and students care only about the diploma.

Indeed, the faculty position is extremely weak (see Kumar and Usunier, 1994b, and Villette, 1997). Their implicit function, especially during conflicts, is to serve as potential victims when the administration of the school lets the students play their power game (as an *exercice d'école*). There is much discontent on all sides with this system; as a consequence, changes (*réforme*) are constantly discussed (but never introduced) within many 'ritual' meetings designed to discuss the *réforme pédagogique*. Students' behaviour in such meetings is inspired by the following: (a) they are very much aware that they could be expelled if they attack the *direction* by raising the real issues; (b) because of the high teaching load, the lack of control, the lack of professionalism in the curriculum and instruction methods, they know that they have good reasons for being discontented; (c) the weakest members of the faculty are favourite scapegoats and easy victims.

How Have the *Grandes Ecoles* Responded to the Imperatives of Globalization?

As explained in the first part of the article, a broad objective of any higher education institution confronting the challenges of globalization is to develop global managers, which necessitates the internationalization of the curriculum and the faculty (Rugman and Stanbury, 1992). A clear sign that an institution has successfully reached such a target is when its excellence, in terms of graduates, faculty and research, is recognized in a large number of countries. Therefore, the *Ecoles de Commerce* have been eager to develop internationalization practices, sometimes as a form of organizational discourse rather than as a full-fledged commitment (Usunier, 1988; Wagner, 1997). We will first analyse the strategic posture of the *Ecoles de Commerce*, then subsequently assess whether the posture is consistent with their corporate culture. We conclude by evaluating their implementation strategies.

What Is Their Strategic Posture?

The strategic posture of the *Grandes Ecoles de Commerce* is a difficult one. There are at least five major structural issues that render their strategic posture fairly weak as far as the challenges of global business education are concerned: (1) the ethnocentric nature of the legitimacy of French managerial elite; (2) the central role given to French language which becomes more and more an impediment in fostering a global strategic posture; (3) the low international recognition of French *Grandes Ecoles de Commerce*; (4) the criteria for excellence which do not follow international standards; and (5) the growing number of *Grandes Ecoles de Commerce* and consequently the dilution of their reputation.

The first problem is that of the international differences in the importance of academic legitimacy for the managerial elite. It differs widely across France, Germany and Great Britain, making the development of 'Euro-managers' a difficult task (Davoine, 1997). As noted above, the French model for recruiting and developing managerial elite is significantly different from the international model. Moreover, any change constitutes a potential 'threat' for the existing elite who pay only lip service to the supposed necessity of internationalizing business curricula. Among the 200 largest French companies, 112 top managers out of the 144 French-owned companies had never worked in a foreign country (Bauer and Bertin-Mourot, 1987).

The second factor which influences the strategic posture is the central role given to the French language. This role is central to French public organizations in their daily working, even though it is a clear obstacle to internationalization in the field of business education (Usunier, 1990). While French is one of the official languages of the United Nations, its influence has been steadily declining against English over the past 30 years. None the less, there are still strong defenders of French as a business language, organized in rather powerful lobbies which influence the adoption of an official vocabulary for marketing, finance, stock exchange operations, etc. However, it appears rather as a *combat d'arrière garde*: one is supposed to say *mercatique* instead of marketing, *publipostage* instead of mailing, etc. French students and business people actually use the words marketing and mailing. The official creed remains, however, that French has number one place as a multipurpose language, in full competition with English. This creed restricts the full acceptance of English as the chosen language for the internationalization of business education in France. This choice has major consequences in terms of standardizing the curriculum and admission procedures on international standards such as those of AACSB. Courses taught in English are exceptions rather than standard practice; the invitation of foreign visiting faculty may partly depend on their language proficiency in French; international textbooks published in English are not used; and the teaching format used in most business schools, based on readings and case assignments, is virtually unknown. A model of internationalization of business education such as that prevailing in Northern Europe (e.g. the Netherlands, Denmark or Sweden), where the local language is downplayed in favour of English, is not even discussed in France.

The third issue, that is the relatively low international recognition of French *Grandes Ecoles de Commerce*, is tightly linked to the preceding one. This low recognition has been noted by many authors and is considered a problem by some of the schools (e.g. Nouschi, 1997, in the case of HEC, the most famous one). By international standards the terminology used for describing French engineering as well as business schools is often confusing: the *Ecole Polytechnique* is often assimilated with 'polytechnics', while the *Ecoles de Commerce* are associated with *Fachhochschulen* in Germany. The very terms '*école*' (school) and '*élève*' (pupil) are positively valued in French, while in Northern European languages they connote generally primary or secondary education, or higher education only when used in conjunction with *graduate*, as in graduate school.

The fourth problem is the criterion for excellence concerning the students, faculty and schools as a whole. The very strong emphasis on the excellence of students based almost exclusively on the entry examination rather than achievements during the courses is reflected in the rigid ranking of schools at the top: HEC in first place, ESSEC in second, ESCP in third, EAP and EM Lyon in fourth place. It is not easily understood outside France that performance during a three-day examination at age 18 to 20 determines your ranking as a future French manager.

The criteria for faculty excellence are necessarily shaky: a strong emphasis on teaching in an environment where teaching excellence is particularly difficult to achieve – and often achieved by *showmen* without many academic credentials – results in an undervaluation of excellence based on research achievements (Villette, 1997), which is, however, more or less the global standard. Furthermore, the highly segmented labour market for faculty in the *Ecoles de Commerce* prevents mobility and consequently the demonstration of excellence by faculty market value. Each *Ecole de Commerce* has its own employment system and few attempts are made to integrate the labour market for business faculty. The criteria (library, research facilities, publications records, etc.) for excellence concerning institutions as a whole are very different from those of AACSB. Directors in *Ecoles de Commerce* and their constituencies in the local Chamber of Commerce have mainly two criteria for excellence which are unrelated to either research, learning facilities or teaching excellence: (1) how their school is ranked via the choices of applicants after the *concours*, and (2) the score of their schools in rankings published in French business magazines on the basis of questionable surveys.

The number of students in the *Ecoles de Commerce* (all of them, not *Grandes!*) has been dramatically rising, from 8410 in 1970–71 to 57,208 in 1993–94 (source: Ministère de l'Education Nationale, DEP/MEN). Simultaneously, tuition fees have considerably increased, often reaching FRF 40,000 to 50,000, that is, about US$7000, which is expensive for France where higher education has traditionally been free. The young *Ecoles de Commerce* graduates have been hit by unemployment which is especially bad in France for younger people. Consequently, the number of baccalaureate graduates willing to enter the preparatory classes has sharply fallen over the last five years. At the end of 1996, an audit by Ernst and Young concerning the 31 top *Grandes Ecoles de Commerce* all of them managed by the *Chambres de Commerce*, highlighted major difficulties in recruiting enough good students to maintain a fair level. It recommended alliances between schools and more international orientation. The report was quite clear about the fact that the increase in student enrolment had been too fast and had largely diluted the image of the *Grandes Ecoles de Commerce* even within France. It went as far as to suggest closing down some recently established *Ecoles de Commerce*.

Is Their Posture Consistent With Their Corporate Culture?

The answer here is clearly no. Corporate cultures in higher education institutions cannot stray too far away from the prevalent international model; that is, a university model partly built on Von Humboldt's model of *Universität*, with independent and autonomous faculties. The *Grandes Ecoles de Commerce* belong to public bodies, the *Chambres de Commerce*, whose corporate culture does not favour an emphasis on faculty development; at best some faculty autonomy is accepted as a necessary evil. The *Grandes Ecoles de Commerce* are relatively resource rich, but their resource endowment is very strongly linked to the traditional centralized French system. These elite institutions and their graduates cannot see internationalization without a strong French ethnocentric bias, whereas the stereotype concerning universities is that they are legitimately poor in resources because they are professionally irrelevant and uselessly emphasize research. Faculty independence is not acceptable in the corporate culture of the *Chambre de Commerce*.

A *Chambre de Commerce* has little to do with a Chamber of Commerce as it is conceived of in the Anglo-Saxon countries where membership is optional. The Chamber of Commerce of London has an annual budget which is a very small fraction of that of the *Chambre de Commerce de Paris*. In France a law of 1898 established the statute of the *Chambres de Commerce* (Magliulo, 1980) as half-private, half-public bodies. Their boards are elected by the business community, but their resources are largely derived from compulsory taxes based on turnover, personnel and assets, which provide them with large and stable resources. They deal with common business undertakings (i.e. exhibition halls, ports, airports, general warehouses, etc.). Part of their service to the business community has traditionally been vocational education, including most of the French business schools. There is a high degree of ambiguity in the corporate culture of the *Chambres de Commerce* when it relates to higher education. The absence of choice between the conflicting educational models mentioned above (engineering schools, university/business school, vocational education) results in constant compromises, and blurs the basic design of any serious strategic guidelines. However, it would be wrong to assume that *Chambres de Commerce* board members and managing teams are totally unaware of the situation. Why then, is it so difficult for them to make clear strategic choices among these conflicting models?

Conflict avoidance and village mentality, which constitute a key aspect of corporate culture in French organizations, are a major obstacle in implementing the internationalization strategy. One of the major differences between French and Anglo-Saxon organizations is in their attitude towards and management of conflict. On the one hand, the French seem to be more aware of the potentiality of conflict in an organization. From their standpoint there is a fundamental contradiction between the individual and the organization as there is also between different units of an organization. Moreover, the contradiction does not arise out of misperceptions or poor communications; it is critically rooted in the context governing the interaction. This assumptive difference is reinforced by the village mentality that dominates French social life. As Barsoux and Lawrence observe (1990: 87):

> The principles that indiscriminate friendship exposes one to manipulation, that property should be enclosed, that outsiders are not to be trusted – these defensive solidarities are all legacies of the village mentality which still has a strong hold over French social relations.

Americans, on the other hand, begin from the assumption that organizational members have a commonality of interests and whatever conflicts arise or exist are fundamentally psychological in origin (Amado et al., 1991). Structural factors are viewed as either being irrelevant or, alternatively, marginal to the issue under discussion. Americans seek to manage conflicts in a very pragmatic way: differences can be split; contentious issues can be handled later; stubborn and inflexible negotiators may be changed. One of the most popular books in this area, *Getting to Yes* (Fisher and Ury, 1981), adopts an explicitly 'contractual/pragmatic' approach to negotiations, where actors within organizations are viewed as independent agents engaged in a contractual relationship with the organization. The dominant calculus is that of 'cost/benefit'. The difference would suggest that the French are more cognizant than the Americans of the potential for conflict among actors. The difference in attitude, however, leads to very different ways of managing conflict. The French, for the most part, avoid overt confrontation, which probably reflects high uncertainty avoidance and the fear that overt conflict resolution may create a crisis-like atmosphere. The attention given to avoiding the resolution of conflicts in an informal way shows how seriously they view conflicts.

How Are They Implementing This Posture? How Successful Have They Been and/or Are Likely To Be in Maximizing Learning?

The implementation is partly window dressing, and it is multi-local rather than global implementation. It is true that a real internationalization process has partly taken place, but it remains deeply constrained by the French environment. Consciously or not, the *Chambres de Commerce* do not want to internationalize the curriculum according to Anglo-Saxon criteria, for instance by using AACSB accreditation procedures or simply by imitating organizational arrangements that can be observed at the London Business School or the Stockholm School of Economics. In most cases, they do not even know what the AACSB is. Their project generally aims to internationalize the curriculum *within a French framework*, that is, change neither the admission procedures nor the curriculum. The main items are: (1) the development of foreign language teaching; (2) hiring foreign, English-speaking faculty, who have to adapt to the French teaching system and organizational life (sometimes in the 'love it or leave it' style); (3) students' exchanges take place mostly with other European business schools; (4) participation in European networks such as HEC participating in the CEMS (Community of European Management Schools); and (5) last, but not least, the *Chambres de Commerce* advertise these efforts in France so as to improve their ranking in the whole *Ecoles de Commerce* system and consequently increase the number of applicants. There is not much more: in particular, no project of adopting an international format for management learning based on three to four three-hour courses per week, lectures related to textbooks, reading and case assignments, suitable library facilities, etc.

Foreign languages are one of the key achievements of the *Ecoles de Commerce* in terms of internationalization: the range of languages offered is very broad; however, a challenge remains to integrate business education and foreign languages. As far as student exchanges are concerned, there has been a considerable development, mostly built on the Erasmus programme. In 1995, business students were the largest group (1290, that is, 28%) among all the French students receiving an Erasmus Grant (Wagner, 1997). In 1993, according to a FNEGE study, 10% of French business students had studied in another country as a part of their programme, with a higher percentage from *Ecoles* (12%) than from universities (6%). However, the French *Ecoles de Commerce* remain far from the international model developed by INSEAD with a highly internationalized student body and only 16% French students (Wagner, 1997) and a truly multinational faculty. While INSEAD's internationalization pattern is largely based on the transposition of the HBS model in Europe, it has a better potential than any 'Frenchocentric' model, given the obvious dominance of American thought in management research and training.

Lessons from the French Experience: Globalization as a Major Strategic Challenge for Management Education Institutions

Our case study of French business schools has clearly demonstrated that globalization is a major strategic challenge for educational organizations. Globalization as a rhetorical device for improving an organization's status with respect to other *Grandes Ecoles* is clearly acceptable; however, genuinely developing a global organization is problematical for it would undermine the raison d'être of the French business school. The problems faced by French *Grandes Ecoles* are not necessarily unique to them; however, due to the unique characteristics of the French educational system, coupled with the authoritarian character of French society, the problems that the French institutions experience are not amenable to any easy resolution. Our case study demonstrates the fundamental proposition that the French managers choose to ignore problems until the time when the problems reach such a magnitude that only a drastic solution is possible.

Globalization poses a fundamental challenge to all educational organizations, no matter where these organizations are located. The challenge is this: will globalization allow us to maintain or enhance our distinctive identity and image? Organizational identity answers the question 'What kind of an organization is this?' (Albert and Whetten, 1985), while image focuses on the perceptions held by others about the organization (Dutton et al., 1994). Organizational identity and image are crucial in shaping how decision makers interpret strategic issues (Gioia and Thomas, 1996). Although organizational identity and image are important everywhere, the content of the image and the identity vary across different societies. This means that the specific challenges posed by globalization for educational institutions are likely to be different in different societies. As we have argued in our case study, the identity of a typical French *Grande Ecole* is particularistic rather than universalistic in substance. That is to say, a French *Grande Ecole* wants to legitimate itself in the local environment within which it is institutionally embedded rather than within the global environment. Only a very few French *Grandes Ecoles* like ESSEC or HEC aspire to have global ambitions.

The rest of the *Ecoles* have very limited ambitions. They may talk the language of globalization but are either incapable of or are reluctant to manage the ambiguities inherent in initiating the process of globalization.

This has a number of implications. First and foremost, it suggests that decision makers in these organizations are likely to perceive any recommendations for making the organization genuinely global as a threat rather than an opportunity (Dutton and Jackson, 1987). Form will be encouraged while content will take a back seat in this process. Second, in the event that decision makers are forced to make changes to conform even to the 'form' of globalization, the changes will be minimal and/or will be accompanied by other actions that may negate the impact of the former. In the case that we recounted earlier (Kumar and Usunier 1994a, b), the decision makers did hire foreign faculty to give a foreign flavour to the school, but the recommendations of the foreign faculty to change or improve the system were all but ignored. Indeed, one foreign faculty member who was considered to be advocating radical changes was promptly fired. It also suggests that changes that either do not threaten the legitimacy of the existing organizational order or enhance the status of the top level decision makers are likely to be more easily accepted vis-à-vis changes that threaten such legitimacy. For example, French institutions have sought to develop a large number of exchange agreements with foreign universities. This is undoubtedly an important facet of the globalization process; however, it does more to enhance the prestige of the director and the institution (especially so if the management team has managed to secure agreements with well known institutions in North America). In sum, identity preservation is the motif of such an institution. If the choice is between becoming more global or preserving one's identity, it is the latter which will take precedence. In this respect, the French *Grandes Ecoles* take on the character of a defender as opposed to a prospector organization (Miles and Snow, 1978). They may espouse the virtues of entrepreneurial behaviour and yet end up behaving in ways that are distinctly non entrepreneurial.

Our case study also suggests that French *Grandes Ecoles* have difficulty in managing internal change that might be consistent with the imperatives of globalization. As we point out, the French *Grandes Ecoles* want to internationalize their curriculum within a French framework. In doing so, the need for making internal changes is minimized. Why should the French institutions seek to minimize changes? In our view, there are several factors that might account for this reluctance. Part of the answer lies in their self-image, which has indeed been a positive one. Traditionally, the French *Grandes Ecoles* have enjoyed a superior status in French society vis-à-vis the universities, and this status is unlikely to change in the foreseeable future. The French elite have been moulded by the *Grandes Ecoles* and they continue to patronize these institutions to reaffirm their unique French identity. If the image is so positive then what is the necessity for change?

Second, as D'Iribarne (1994) has argued, the French organizational model rests on the 'honour principle' as developed by Montesquieu. This means, for example, that every position in a given organization has associated with it a certain set of obligations and privileges which distinguish it from other positions. The derivative implication is that different positions in an organization have different status and this differential needs to be maintained. D'Iribarne (1994) points out that a decline in status is simply out of the question. If the organization is forced to undergo changes to correspond with the requirements of becoming a genuinely global organization, the status hierarchy is unlikely to remain unchanged and this negative outcome is clearly unacceptable within the French tradition.

Finally, as our case study suggests, French organizations have difficulty in coping with internal diversity. Although the French institutions hired a number of foreign faculty members with the objective of developing a global organization, they were unable to cope with the expectations and the needs of these faculty members. Consequently, a large number of these faculty members left the organization. Diversity management requires openness, flexibility, the development of a common working language, and sustained commitment to making the experiment work. These are in short supply for a number of different reasons. First, the directors of these institutions are recruited internally. Many of them may not have had much international experience. This also holds for the directors of *Chambres of Commerce* who control these institutions. Second, the expectation is that the outsiders will adjust to the local requirements and that this adjustment will be non problematical. This is again reflective of ethnocentric assumptions stemming from a lack of exposure to how the French system is viewed by outsiders.

Conclusion

Our article suggests that there are a number of structural obstacles that prevent the French *Grandes Ecoles de Commerce* from imparting management education most effectively. The processual dimension of globalization is particularly problematic. In other words, the *Ecoles de Commerce* are unable and/or unwilling to develop an internal culture conducive to maximizing learning. Several factors are responsible for this, most notably (a) ethnocentric wishful thinking concerning the role of French as an international business language; (b) overvaluation of the traditional French *concours* system for selecting the *élites de la nation*; and (c) a lack of strategic vision of the main actors. This results in suboptimal learning for French business students in the *Grandes Ecoles de Commerce* who remain relatively ethnocentric actors in the world of international business.

A major implication of our study is that French educational organizations are unlikely to cope with the demands of globalization in an efficient and an effective way. Although this proposition holds true for all educational organizations, our study demonstrates that organizations situated in 'tight' cultures (Triandis, 1995) as opposed to 'loose' cultures are likely to face greater difficulty in responding to the imperatives of globalization. In a tight culture deviations from existing norms are punished severely, whereas in a loose culture deviant behaviour is not so severely sanctioned. In other words, process or how things are done comes to occupy centre stage in a tight culture; deviations are not permitted, with the result that flexibility is low. Given the concerns with saving face and maintaining honour, the French organizational system possesses many of the attributes that we might associate with a 'tight culture'. Internal flexibility is constrained by the overriding imperative to maintain honour and avoid explicit conflict. This also means that incremental and, for that matter, radical change cannot be introduced into the system in a controlled fashion. Status quo governs and it is only in cases where the French elite are genuinely supportive of change that true transformation occurs.

Globalization will not go away. Indeed, if anything, the pressures stemming from the globalization of the world economy are likely to continue to intensify. Although the educational organizations may not at first bear the brunt of these changes, sooner or later pressures will be exerted on them to create managers who are comfortable functioning in a global economy. It is critical that the *Grandes Ecoles* come to realize the imperatives of developing an organization that is conducive to maximizing learning.

Notes

1. To a certain extent this is true: French universities have lagged behind considerably in introducing management education, which is still considered by many French universities as being relatively low in scientific legitimacy.

2. These statements are supported by a number of studies (e.g. Usunier, 1985, 1988; Villette, 1997; Kumar and Usunier 1994a, b; Davoine, 1997; Nouschi, 1997).

3. As in English, French makes a distinction between *les élèves* (pupils) and *les étudiants* (students). However, in a *Grande Ecole* setting, the students are generally referred to as *les élèves* (pupils).

4. One of the authors was a student at HEC for three years (1969–72), and taught there from 1979 to 1980 part time, and as a faculty member at ESCP from 1980 to 1989. His experience is that teaching-hours overload is a systemic problem in French business schools; in some *Ecoles de Commerce*, the teaching load can reach almost 40 hours a week on peak weeks (not all year round). At ESCP, an administrative decision limits the weekly class enrolment per student (compulsory courses + elective courses) to 33 hours!

5. There is, in France, a relative lack of imitation of foreign models, such as those contained by the acronyms MBA, HBS, AACSB, although many people in the French academic and business community were aware of these models. However, the French have been much more influenced by American business education than the Italians (Locke, 1996; Gemelli, 1997).

6. In fact, not a *dean* in the international acceptance of the term, rather a representative of the *corps professoral* (the word faculty – *faculté* – is never used).

References

Albert, S. and Whetten, D.A. (1985) 'Organizational Identity', in L.L. Cummings and B.M. Staw (eds) *Research in Organizational Behavior*, 7, pp. 263–95, Greenwich, CT: JAI Press.

Amado, G., Faucheux, C. and Laurent, A. (1991) 'Organizational Change and Cultural Realities: Franco American Contrasts', *International Studies of Management and Organization* 21(3): 62–95.

Barsoux, Jean Louis and Lawrence, Peter (1990) *Management in France*. London: Cassel Education Ltd.

Bartlett, C. and Ghoshal, S. (1992) 'What is a Global Manager?', *Harvard Business Review* (September–October): 124–32.

Bauer, M. and Bertin-Mourot, B. (1987) *Les 200. Comment devient-on grand patron?* Paris: Seuil.

Bauer, M. and Bertin-Mourot, B. (1995) *L'accès au Sommet des Grandes Entreprises Françaises 1985–1994: Caractéristiques Structurelles du Capitalisme Français et Evolution de ses Elites.* Paris: CNRS/Boyden.

Berry, M. (1995) 'From American Standard to Cross Cultural Dialogues', in B.J. Punnett and O. Shenkar (eds) *Handbook for International Management Research*, pp. 463–82. Cambridge, MA: Blackwell.

Bourdieu, P. (1989) *La Noblesse d'Etat. Grandes Ecoles et Esprit de Corps.* Paris: Editions de Minuit.

Business Week (1998) 'The Best B-Schools' (19 October) 65–76.

Davoine, E. (1997) 'Formation "d'Euromanagers" et Formation au Management en France, en Allemagne, et en Grande-Bretagne. L'expérience d'une Promotion de l'Ecole des Affaires de Paris', in M. de Saint Martin and M. Dinu Gheorghiu (eds) *Actes du Colloque 'Les Ecoles de Gestion et La Formation des Elites'*, pp. 170–86. Paris: Maison des Sciences de l'Homme.

Di Maggio, P.J. and Powell, W.W. (1991) 'Introduction', in W.W. Powell and P.J. DiMaggio (eds) *The New Institutionalism in Organizational Analysis.* Chicago: University of Chicago Press.

D'Iribarne, P. (1994) 'The Honor Principle in the Bureaucratic Phenomenon', *Organization Studies* 15: 81–97.

Dutton, J.E., Dukerich, J.M. and Harquail, C.V. (1994) 'Organizational Images and Member Identification', *Administrative Science Quarterly* 39: 239–63.

Dutton, J.E. and Jackson, S.E. (1987) 'Categorizing Strategic Issues: Links to Organizational Action', *Academy of Management Review* 12: 76–90.

Easterby-Smith, M. and Tanton, M. (1988) 'Strategies and Faculty Development in Business Schools and Management Development Institutions: An International Study', Centre for the Study of Management Learning, University of Lancaster, *EFMD*, Brussels, March.

Easterby-Smith, M., Thorpe, R. and Lowe, A. (1991) *Management Research.* London: Sage.

Engwall, L. and Zamagni, V. (1998) *Management Education in a Historical Perspective.* Manchester: Manchester University Press.

Finkelstein, S. and Hambrick, D. (1996) *Strategic Leadership.* St Paul: West Educational Publishing.

Fisher, R. and Ury, W. (1981) *Getting to Yes: Negotiating Agreement Without Giving In.* New York: Houghton Mifflin.

Francis, J.N.P. and Globerman, S. (1992) 'The Internationalization of Management Textbooks: A Survey of the International Components of North American Management Textbooks and Support Materials', in A. Rugman and W.T. Stanbury (eds) *Global Perspective: Internationalizing Management Education*, pp 139–54. Vancouver: Centre for International Business Studies.

Gemelli, G. (1997) 'Un modèle d'Appropriation Collective et ses Tournants Historiques: Les Ecoles de Gestion en France et les Fondations Américaines', in M. de Saint Martin and M. Dinu Gheorghiu (eds) *Actes du Colloque 'Les Ecoles de Gestion et la Formation des Elites'*, pp. 34–55. Paris: Maison des Sciences de l'Homme.

Gioia, D.A. and Thomas, J. (1996) 'Identity, Image, and Issue Interpretation: Sense Making During Strategic Change in Academia', *Administrative Science Quarterly* 41: 370–400.

Goffee, R. and Jones, G. (1996) 'What Holds the Modern Company Together?', *Harvard Business Review* (November–December): 133–48.

Grelon, A. (1997) 'Le Développement des Ecoles de Commerce en France (1800–1914) et les Relations avec les Formations d'Ingénieurs', in M. de Saint Martin and M. Dinu Gheorghiu (eds) *Actes du Colloque 'Les Ecoles de Gestion et la Formation des Elites'*, pp. 15–33. Paris: Maison des Sciences de l'Homme.

Hall, E.T. and Hall, M.R. (1989) *Understanding Cultural Differences: Germans, French, and Americans.* Yarmouth, ME: Intercultural Press.

Hamel, G. and Prahalad, C.K. (1989) 'Strategic Intent', *Harvard Business Review* (May–June): 63–76.

Hamel, G. and Prahalad, C.K. (1996) *Competing for the Future.* Harvard: Harvard Business School Press.

Hitt, M.A., Keats, B.W. and DeMarie, S.M. (1998) 'Navigating in the New Competitive Landscape: Building Strategic Flexibility and Competitive Advantage in the 21st Century', *Academy of Management Executive* 12: 22–42.

Hofstede, G. (1980) *Culture's Consequences: International Differences in Work Related Values*. Beverly-Hills, CA: Sage.

Hofstede, G. (1991) *Culture and Organizations: Software of the Mind*. Maidenhead: McGraw-Hill.

Kipping, M. (1998) 'The Hidden Business Schools: Management Training in Germany Since 1945', in L. Engwall and V. Zamagni (eds) *Management Education in Historical Perspective*, pp. 95–110. Manchester: Manchester University Press.

Kumar, R. and Usunier, J.C. (1994a) 'Internationalizing Business Curricula: Myths and Contradictions in the French Grandes Ecoles', Research Paper, CERAG-ESA, No. 94-03.

Kumar, R. and Usunier, J.C. (1994b) 'The Management of Conflict in a French Grande Ecole: Conflict Avoidance or Conflict Resolution?', Research Paper, CERAG-ESA, No. 94-04.

Kumar, R. and Weggeman, M. (1998) 'Strategic Thinking in a Globalizing World: Understanding Strategy as Creative Judgment', paper presented at the Annual Meeting of the Strategic Management Society, Orlando, Florida, 1–4 November.

Lessem, R. and Neubauer, F. (1994) *European Management Systems*. Maidenhead: McGraw-Hill.

Linder, S.B. (1999) 'Europe's Universities Need to Get Competitive', *International Herald Tribune* (15 January): 7.

Locke, R.R. (1996) *The Collapse of the American Management Mystique*. New York: Oxford University Press.

Locke, R.R. (1998) 'Mistaking a Historical Phenomenon for a Functional One: Postwar Management Education Reconsidered', in L. Engwall and V. Zamagni (eds) *Management Education in a Historical Perspective*, pp. 145–56. Manchester: Manchester University Press.

Magliulo, B. (1980) *Les Chambres de Commerce et d'Industrie*. Paris: Presses Universitaires de France.

Miles, R.E. and Snow, C. (1978) *Organizational Strategy: Structure and Process*. New York: McGraw Hill.

Nouschi, M. (1988) *Histoire et Pouvoir d'une Grande Ecole*. Paris: Robert Laffont.

Nouschi, M. (1997) 'HEC, un Miroir des Evolutions de la Société Française de 1881 à nos Jours', in M. de Saint Martin and M. Dinu Gheorghiu (eds) *Actes du Colloque 'Les Ecoles de Gestion et la Formation des Elites'*, pp. 59–71. Paris: Maison des Sciences de l'Homme.

Orton, J.D. and Weick, K.E. (1990) 'Loosely Coupled Systems: A Reconceptualization', *Academy of Management Review* 15: 203–23.

Pfeffer, J. (1994) 'Competitive Advantage Through People', *California Management Review* 36: 9–28.

Porter, L.W. and McKibbin, L.E. (1988) *Management Education and Development: Drift or Thrust into the 21st Century*. New York: McGraw-Hill.

Reiss, A.D. and Orne, D.S. (1995) 'Does International Management Education Work? Reduction in Ethnocentrism and Negative Stereotyping', paper presented at the Annual Meeting of the Academy of Management, Vancouver, Canada.

Rhinesmith, S. (1993) *A Manager's Guide to Globalization*. Homewood, IL: Irwin.

Rugman, A. and Stanbury, W.T. (eds) (1992) *Global Perspective: Internationalizing Management Education*. Vancouver, BC: Centre for International Business Studies, UBC.

Suchman, M.C. (1995) 'Managing Legitimacy: Strategic and Institutional Approaches', *Academy of Management Review* 20: 571–610.

Triandis, H.C. (1995) *Culture and Social Behavior*. New York: McGraw-Hill.

Usunier, J.C. (1985) 'La Pédagogie Implicite en Gestion', *Enseignement et Gestion* 33(Spring): 19–28.

Usunier, J.C. (1988) 'Les Ambiguïtés de la Formation à l'International', *La Revue du Financier* 60(March): 46–56.

Usunier, J.C. (1990) 'French International Business Education: A Pessimistic View', *European Management Journal* 8(3): 388–93.

Vaill, P.B. (1996) *Learning as a Way of Being: Strategies for Survival in a World of Permanent Whitewater*. San Francisco: Jossey-Bass.

Villette, M. (1997) 'Formation "Ecole de l'Elite" et Savoirs Ordinaires', in M. de Saint Martin and M. Dinu Gheorghiu (eds) *Actes du Colloque 'Les Ecoles de Gestion et la Formation des Elites'*, pp. 140–58. Paris: Maison des Sciences de l'Homme.

Volberda, H.W. (1998) *Building the Flexible Firm: How to Remain Competitive*. Oxford: Oxford University Press.

Wagner, A.C. (1997) 'Les Ecoles de Gestion et la Gestion d'une Culture Internationale', in M. de Saint Martin and M. Dinu Gheorghiu (eds) *Actes du Colloque 'Les Ecoles de Gestion et la Formation des Elites'*, pp. 223–36. Paris: Maison des Sciences de l'Homme.

16

Ying Fan

The Transfer of Western Management to China
Context, Content and Constraints

Introduction and Previous Research

A turning point in contemporary Chinese history occurred in 1979 when China embarked on a long journey of transforming its economy from a centrally-planned system to a market-oriented one. Following this economic reform has been the introduction and transfer of management knowhow from foreign countries, mainly the West. What changes have taken place in China after 19 years of economic reform? Can western management theory and practice be transferred to and applied in China's Socialist Market Economy? And if they can, how? This paper intends to address these questions by examining the context, content and constraints of the transfer of management knowhow to China. It starts with a brief review of existing literature on management transfer. Following a historical introduction on changes in the market and marketing in China, a model of the management transfer is developed and key factors which influence the transfer are identified and discussed.[1]

The debate around whether management knowhow is universal or culture-bounded is not a new one (Negandhi and Estafen, 1965). Research attention on the issue of cross-cultural transfer of management knowhow has been growing steadily since the 1960s. Research in the field can be classified into two types of study: the applicability and transferability of western (mainly American) management knowhow to the developing countries since the 1960s (Gonzalez and McMillan, 1961, in Gennaro, 1969; Cranch, 1974; Cavusgil and Yavas, 1984; Akaah and Riordan, 1988; Kinsey, 1988; Jaeger, 1990); and the transfer of Japanese management knowhow to both developed and developing countries since the 1980s (Fukuda, 1983; Ishida, 1986; Ho, 1993).

Gonzalez and McMillan (1961) are perhaps the first authors to question the universalism. They find that the management knowhow is culture-bound and 'American philosophy of management is not universally applicable' (in Gennaro, 1969). Oberg (1963) emphasizes the importance of cultural differences in the transfer. From his empirical research he concludes that 'Cultural differences from one country to another are more significant than many writers [on management theory] now appear to recognize ... If management principles are to be truly universal ... they must face up to the challenge of other cultures and other business climates'. Farmer and Richman (1964, quoted in Gennaro, 1969) also stress the importance of external environmental factors on the managerial efficiency. According to their model, four types of external constraints have impact on the transfer of management knowhow:

- educational characteristics
- sociological characteristics
- political and legal characteristics
- economic characteristics.

Cavusgil and Yavas (1984), in their study of transferring management knowhow to Turkey, observe that a shortage of qualified local managers who understand modern management concepts and knowhow impedes the developing countries in utilizing foreign investment and technology. Consequently the transfer of management knowhow is seen as necessary and complementary to the transfer of technology. They identify 13 variables which appear to impede the transfer of management knowhow. The major variables are:

- political instability
- economic instability
- educational background of colleagues
- social background of colleagues
- negative attitudes toward modern techniques
- resistance to new ideas.

Jaeger (1990) states that the uncritical use of western management theories and techniques in developing countries could contribute not only to organizational inefficiency and ineffectiveness but also to resentment and other negative feelings associated with the perception of being subject to 'cultural imperialism', i.e. being forced to adopt and accept practices which run counter to deeply held values and assumptions of the local culture. He then compares the characteristics of developing country cultures with those of developed country cultures. However, nations in the developing country category themselves are so diversified that each national culture warrants separate research attention.

Studies on the transfer of management knowhow to China are few and far between. From their experiences in training Chinese managers to use American management techniques, Lindsay and Dempsey (1985) find that traditional Chinese culture and modern socialist development have merged to produce unique forms of management behaviour which do not match western models. Livingstone (1987) warns of the facile application of western marketing techniques to China. He emphasizes that in any non-western developing country, 'marketing techniques are not textbook formulae or cookbook recipes which could be applied indiscriminately to conditions anywhere'. In their discussion of transfer of human resource management (HRM) in Sino-US cooperative ventures, Von Glinow and Teagarden (1988) identify four major impediments:

- a closed versus an open society
- HRM legitimacy
- the technology acquisition versus absorption issue
- the need for management infrastructure creation.

They view the transfer of HRM technology as an integral part of the import of technology and the former could contribute to absorbing transferred technology. From his survey of a group of Chinese executives, Chan (1989) lists five critical barriers against applying marketing concept: 'bureaucratic settling, management's lack of familiarity with marketing, socialist orientation, centrally planned economy and inadequate market information'. Zhuang and Whitehill (1989) note that the fast growth of international joint ventures in China requires Chinese managers to be able to understand western business practices and behaviour, thus promoting the transfer of management knowhow. However, they conclude that China would not completely adopt western management practices, and solutions to Chinese management problems would be uniquely Chinese in nature. While these previous studies discussed the transfer of management knowhow, they did not address the cultural issue to any extent. A welcome exception is a recent article by Easterby-Smith et al. (1995) which describes a comparative study that was carried out in matched Chinese and UK companies to investigate the sensitivity of HRM to culture. The observed differences were then analysed as a product of either *cultural* factors or *contextual* factors. They concluded that HRM is dependent on the cultural assumptions underpinning it. Those areas of HRM most affected by cultural differences are the least likely to be transferred as cultural factors are far less mutable. These strong cultural factors will limit the adoption of western HRM in China. In the following sections, both contextual and cultural factors will be discussed.

Context: Market and Marketing in China

The past 19 years have seen great changes in the Chinese economy and market. Since 1979, China has been undergoing a fundamental transformation from a central-command to a market-led economy. At its 14th congress in October 1992, the Chinese Communist Party approved the 'Socialist Market Economy', thereby signalling that the Chinese government had finally abandoned orthodox Marxist economic theory in favour of the western style free market economy. With the development of this new market system, 400,000 state-owned enterprises (SOEs) will be transformed from 'government production units' to independent economic entities and millions of cadres will become, for the first time, managers and businessmen with real decision-making power.

The development of the market system in China has undergone three stages. From 1949 to 1979, China practised a rigid central-command economy (Richman, 1970; Joy, 1990). The decisions concerning products, prices and distribution were all made centrally by government bureaux. The state set production targets for each enterprise, distributed its products, allocated supplies and equipment, assigned personnel, took over profits and covered losses. Under such state planning, an SOE was no more than a plan-unit or production workshop with the sole objective of fulfilling state output quotas. Problems with the system have been well documented (Mun, 1984; Holton, 1985; Lockett, 1988) and since the market was virtually nonexistent in the planned economy, the concept of marketing, as understood by western scholars, was regarded politically as 'bourgeois decadence' or economically as unnecessary and useless'.

The second stage started in 1980 when urban industrial reform was initiated. The state began to recognize the problems with the planning system and to loosen its control over the economy by reducing mandatory plans and replacing them with guidance plans. SOEs were granted more, though still limited, autonomy over market-mix decision-making (Joy, 1990). An important factor contributing to such reform was the emerging force of non-state sector (rural township and village enterprises as well as private enterprises) and foreign-funded enterprises. Reform during this period was incomplete, however, as the whole central-planning system still remained untouched. The official views on marketing swung from 'almost blank condemnation to enthusiasm tempered by nervousness' (Livingstone, 1987).

In 1992 China adopted the 'Socialist Market Economy' which heralded the third stage. A series of major reforms have been put on the agenda. First, the separation of government bureaux from the control of enterprises, thus SOEs could become independent economic entities; second, the development of new markets, including those dealing in commodities, finance and capital, labour and technology, and pricing regulation (*Beijing Review*, 8 March 1993). Although the Chinese economy is still dominated by SOEs, a great change in the economic structure has taken place since 1992 when, for the first time, the output from non-state sectors accounted for more than half (52%) of GNP. During the economic transition, SOEs appear to be slowly transforming themselves from production-oriented to production/sales-oriented, and becoming more responsive to markets. Changes that have taken place during the reform are summed up by three tables: Table 1 depicts the changes in the macro environment; Table 2 shows the changes in the management system of SOEs; and Table 3 focuses on the changes in marketing. Although major dimensions of the reform have been covered in the three tables, they are not exhaustive. It should also be noted: (a) the demarcation of three stages is for analytical purposes, and there are no clear cut boundaries in reality; (b) the market economy in China is still in the very early stage of evolution and the transition may take many years to complete, therefore the changes for the third period are far from fully realized but based partly on the forward projection; and (c) there exist great variations between different regions and industrial sectors.

Table 1   *Changes in the macro economic environment during the reform*

	Centrally-planned economy (1949–78)	Planned-commodity economy (1979–92)	Socialist market economy (1993–)
Ownership structure	State ownership; collective ownership	State ownership; collective ownership; emergence of private and foreign ownership	State ownership still dominant; high growth in private and foreign ownership; pilot privatization
Government intervention	Direct administrative control	Diminished direct control, more by economic levers	Indirect
State planning	Mandatory plan	Mandatory and guidance plan	? Vary in different sectors
Economic legal system	None	Tentative	Enforcement problems
Competition within industry	Quasi-monopoly; no competition	Limited competition	Intensifying in FMCG sectors, more foreign competition if joining WTO
Relationship between demand and supply	Co-existence of unwanted overstock and serious shortage	Basically a supplier's market	Towards a buyer's market in most consumer goods
Consumer rights	None	Emerged	More attention
Inflation	Unnoticeable	Moderate	High
Urban unemployment	Unheard of until 1970s	Moderate	Increasing rapidly
Regional protectionism	Strong	Moderate	Reduced?
Foreign trade policy	Self-reliance, import for large capital projects only	From import-substitution to export-led	Encourage large scale import and export
Income discrepancy between city and rural areas	Moderate	Reduced	Enlarging
Popular values and concerns	Political correctness; collectivism	Shifts from four modernizations and democracy to personal material life	Rise of consumerism and individualism
Attitude towards western knowhow	Capitalist evils	Transfer of technical knowhow, wary of 'spiritual pollution'	Learn from West; and guard against decadent influences

Table 2   *Changes in the management of stateowned enterprises during the reform*

	Centrally-planned economy (1949–78)	Planned-commodity economy (1979–92)	Socialist market economy (1993–)
Status in the economy	Production/plan unit; cost centre	Business unit; profit centre	Independent entity? investment centre
Relationship with the environment	Closed system	Half-pen system	More open
Relationship with the state	State-owned and state-run	State-owned and semi-controlled	State-owned? independently-run
Decision-making authority	Centralized, almost none at enterprise level	Limited autonomy, 'one foot' in the market	Full autonomy?
Control and leadership	Under the ministry or bureau, enterprise party committee	Director assuming responsibility under the party committee	Inherent conflicts between party and management
Management team	State cadres, loyalty to the party	4 criteria,* most with technical background	Better qualified, with management training
Economic responsibility	Almost none	Very limited	Full?
Economic relationship with the state	Surplus handed-over, losses covered	After-tax profit	Bankruptcy allowed only to small firms
Capital finance	State allocation	Bank loans	Issue of internal shares; bank loans
Business orientation	Production-oriented	Operation- oriented	Market/sales oriented
Performance assessment	Plan-fulfilment; growth in production	Profitability, sales	Profitability; market share
Strategic planning	None	Limited	Formalizing process
Diversification	Single business	Limited diversification	Increasing
R&D	Only state-initiated and financed	Little change	Self-initiated and financed; market-driven
Personnel management	Life-time employment, recruitment assigned and wages fixed by state	Piece-rate and bonus. The break up of 'iron rice bowl'	Emergence of labour market, job contracts, performance linked pay
Supply	From the state allocation system	Half from the state, half from market	More from market

*Four criteria: revolutionary, younger age, educated and specialized.

Table 3 *Changes in the marketing system in the state-owned enterprises*

	Centrally-planned economy (1949–78)	Planned-commodity economy (1979–92)	Socialist market economy (1993–)
Marketing organization	'Supply and sale section', sales function only	Mainly sales, and some marketing	Marketing, shortage of qualified personnel
Attitude towards marketing knowhow	Antithetical to socialism, useless	Sceptical, concern for 'political correctness'	Enthusiastic, sometimes naive learner
Marketing strategy	None	Little, ad hoc	Formalizing process?
Market segmentation	None	Limited differentiation	Increasingly refined
Market research	Non-existent	Primitive	Improving, but lack of reliable data base
Product policy	State plan determining what and how many to produce	Two types of plan: mandatory and guidance	Autonomy, start to diversify
Product design	Out-dated, changes rarely, local standard	Little change	Still at copying stage, Adopt int'l standard
Quality	Very poor	Little attention paid	Improving but unstable
Price	Fixed by the state	State-fixed price, self and black market price	Mainly free market price, pricing strategy
Advertising and sales promotion	Advertising prohibited; no promotion	Rapid growth, but primitive	Greater use, but still lack sophistication
Consumer rights	None	Emerged	More attention
Distribution: – Industrial goods	Central allocation system	Half by allocation, half by direct sales	Shorter channels; still seller's market
Distribution: – Consumer goods	State wholesale-retail system (three levels)	Break up of state monopoly	Multiple channels
Exports & imports	Through the agents of ministries	Limited decentralization	Some allowed to deal with foreign firms direct
Int'l marketing	None	Little	Limited
Market competition	Non-existent	Mainly seller's market; focusing on price	Intensifying, emerging buyer's market
Market education	None	Just started	In great demand

Holton (1985) predicts that 'a market-oriented socialist system is conceptually possible'. After years of exploration, China has finally adopted the market economy. However, it is still not clear what is exactly meant by *The Socialist Market Economy*. What are the characteristics of such a system? There is no ready model in the world to copy, so the Chinese government is left with only one solution; groping for stones to cross the river. The basic contradiction remains that a market economy is based on private ownership while socialism insists on public ownership: how is this to be reconciled? It is not known at this stage what kind of role, or to what degree, state planning will play in the new system. It can be argued that state planning may still be needed in some key industries which have a dominant influence on the national economy until the market mechanism is fully established, otherwise it could collapse and reform could fail. The pace of transformation to the market economy has varied greatly from different regions and industrial sectors. Special Economic Zones and open coast areas are in the bandwagon of reform, while inland provinces lag far behind. Among the state-controlled sectors, consumer goods industries such as food and domestic appliances are well ahead of heavy industries such as steel and petro-chemical, where large SOEs concentrate and the transition will be much more complicated.

Needs for New Management Knowhow

These rapid changes have woken up Chinese managers from their comfortable dreams of yesterday's planned economy, and made them face the great uncertainty in today's environment about how to use the newly-gained autonomy and cope with competition. Like a non-swimmer being suddenly plunged into the 'sea of market' by the force of reform, Chinese managers have become bewildered and rushed in a desperate search for new management concepts and techniques as their previous knowhow has become increasingly obsolete and inadequate in the new marketplace. They are very keen to learn management knowhow from the West, and interest in experimenting with new management approaches has greatly increased during the past decade or so. However, the old system and diehard habits will not be easily changed in a short time. The problems observed by Bentley (1994) in another transitional economy exist also in China:

> The entire economic system of Hungary suffers under the marketing gap, namely the lack of market orientation. Most companies are still product oriented, ... There is still a complete lack of attention towards the presentation of the product, the quality of packaging, of the service, of the promotion, or simply the basic effort to attract the interest of a potential customer. This results in the high level of success of many imported products and in the difficulties of placing Hungarian products on Western markets.

Strategic management and marketing are the subjects that are particularly needed but perhaps least understood in China as the government acknowledged that the majority of Chinese managers lacked marketing knowledge and had no experience of operating in a real competitive marketplace

(Chen, 1993). To make the situation even worse, there is an acute shortage of qualified marketing educators and inadequate training programmes (Zhou, 1991; Sin, 1994). It will be an arduous task to re-educate and retrain Chinese managers (*Marketing Herald*, January 1994: 26) as they have to learn from the basics. When asked by the author about his recent experience of teaching marketing to a group of MBA students in China, an English professor could not hide his disappointment: 'it was too difficult. They simply could not understand some basic concepts and showed little enthusiasm in discussion'. However, these MBA students are an elite class in China. In learning new concepts and methods from the West, Chinese managers have to re-examine their whole value system and practise which they have followed for the past 40 years. Of primary importance is the applicability and transferability of western management knowhow in China, and this will now be examined.

Content and Process: A Model of the Transfer

Management knowhow is defined here in three levels, as shown in Figure 1.

1. Management thoughts and philosophy (the 'core').
2. Concepts, theories and models ('middle layer').
3. Analytical methods, techniques and practice ('outer layer').

A model of the transfer is presented in Figure 2, which consists of five closely-linked stages: selection, adaptation, application, evaluation and integration. The first two stages relate to the *content* to be transferred while the next three stages relate to the application of the content: the transfer *process*. Management transfer is a process of learning, and also a process of 'knowledge

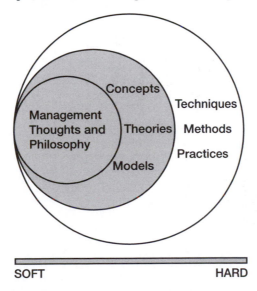

Figure 1   *A model of management knowhow*

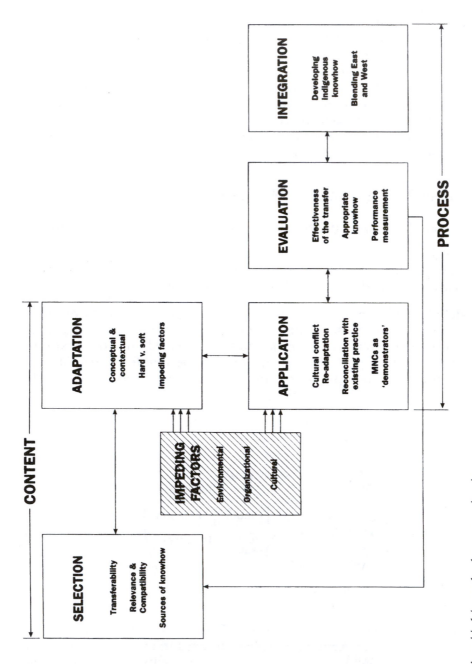

Figure 2   *A model of the transfer of management knowhow*

formation' (Hedlund and Nonaka, 1993) or 'reformation', through which knowhow is reinterpreted, re-contextualized, reconceptualized, refined, adapted and advanced. Integration as the final stage of the transfer has the ultimate objective: developing indigenous management knowhow which combines the best of both western and eastern systems. The transfer of management knowhow is not complete until the received and learned knowledge of the fundamentals of management are actually applied in the way that will lead to effective managerial behaviour consistent with a given environmental-cum-cultural setting (Gennaro, 1969). The remainder of the paper focuses on major elements in the content part of the model as elucidation on the process requires empirical evidence. It is believed that this model will be useful in analysing the transfer of any management discipline, but discussion here will mainly refer to marketing rather than management knowhow in general.

Transferability

The first question to be asked is whether western management knowhow can be transferred to the Chinese context. Transferability should be distinguished from applicability', which is associated with the former but different. Applicability may refer to multinational corporations (MNCs) which apply their management practice in a foreign environment without actually transferring it to local recipients. On the other hand, applicability may be used to describe the degree of usefulness of western knowhow after transferring it to the foreign recipients. Except for the unpleasant experience of transplanting economic systems and management from the Soviet Union in the early 1950s, management transfer from foreign countries is a relatively new experience for Chinese managers compared with technology transfer. When China first announced the modernization (industrialization) programme at the end of the Cultural Revolution in the middle of the 1970s, it intended to import only advanced technology from the West, excluding management knowhow which was then branded as 'bogus science and bourgeois evils'. More than a decade of reform and economic development have gradually created a relatively relaxed political climate in China, despite several setbacks, and an acceptive attitude towards western knowhow. This makes the introduction of western management knowhow to China now politically possible. On the other hand, the emerging market economy and increasing foreign-invested enterprises created a mass demand for western management knowhow and the pre-condition in which this knowhow can be applied.

Suitability/Appropriateness

The first stage of selection decides which elements of western knowhow are transferable and which are not, or at least not at the moment. This has not been widely recognized. Transferability depends on the relevance and compatibility of western concepts to the Chinese context. As western management knowhow is deeply rooted in its own socio-cultural soil, wholesale import of western knowhow is impractical since the content must be suitable to the new environment and local circumstances. There exist huge gaps between western industrial countries and China: western economy is in the post-industrial stage, with well-developed infrastructure, a complete market mechanism and a buyer's market; whereas China is in the early stage of industrialization, with an under-developed infrastructure, embryo market systems and very low personal income. It is obvious that post-industrial models are not suitable to the Chinese context. This may explain why an English professor failed to draw any conclusion from his research in China in the early 1980s when he conducted a survey on job enrichment and job enlargement in SOEs. Chinese employees stated they were interested in nothing but more bonus and better housing since their basic material needs had not been fully satisfied. It can be hypothesized that there may exist an *international management knowhow life cycle*, corresponding to international economic development stages and product life cycles. For example, while western companies have evolved to the fourth stage of planning: integrative strategic management, most Chinese SOEs are still at the first stage of financial planning, or do not have any planning at all. The transition to a real market economy in China may take a very long time. During this period, the Chinese economic system may be characterized as a mixed one: planned state sector mingled with a free private sector. Even at the completion of the transition, the final shape of the system would look more like the economy in Singapore than those in the West. In short, what Chinese managers need is 'appropriate' knowhow: 'useful, acceptable and affordable' (Terpstra, 1991), which can be used to solve their problems.

Sources of Knowhow

In their search for management knowhow, Chinese managers have three different sources to choose from, each having distinctive characteristics:

- western (i.e. western European and North American),
- Japanese, and
- overseas Chinese.

Which is more compatible with the socio-cultural settings in China and easier to be transferred remains an open question. Overseas Chinese management practice has found its way in the open coast areas where investment from Hong Kong and Taiwan is concentrated. Arguably, overseas Chinese have more to offer because they have the same cultural roots and language. Chinese leaders' admiration for the Singaporean model and calls to catch up with the Four Little Dragons (Taiwan, Korea, Hong Kong and Singapore) are very excessive. While there is no doubt that managers in SOEs could learn from overseas Chinese, more research is needed to find out whether overseas Chinese could offer substantial management knowhow and what they could offer. First, overseas Chinese enterprises 'lack almost all characteristics of modern management themselves' (Redding, 1990; Hofstede, 1993). Second, most overseas Chinese businesses operate in a totally different way from SOEs on the mainland. The majority of overseas Chinese firms are still small-scale family businesses, good at production but weak at marketing, and facing the challenge in a new international environment. In addition, both tangible and intangible cultural differences exist between overseas Chinese and mainland Chinese, and most western studies on Chinese culture have so far been confined to overseas Chinese (Hofstede, 1980; Yau, 1988).

Is Japanese management knowhow more relevant to China? It all depends. Japanese management knowhow has been very popular in China since the early 1980s due partly to cultural similarity and partly to its economic influence. The Japanese model seems to offer the Chinese government a different and preferable path to modernization than the western model by stressing economic growth and de-emphasizing political democracy (Lewis and Sun, 1994). Some characteristics observed in Chinese SOEs may appear to be similar to those of Japanese companies, for example, 'iron rice bowl' or life-time employment, but in fact they differ in all important aspects. Contrary to the common belief, Redding and Pugh (1986) found that the differences in organization between Chinese and Japanese firms were even greater than between either of them and the West. Furthermore, although some concepts originated in Japan, most were borrowed and adapted from the West. So why shouldn't Chinese managers learn from the West directly? Comparing the Chinese perception of American and Japanese management models, Wang (1986) observed that many Chinese managers were dissatisfied with the current management system which bore some analogy to the Japanese one, and viewed the American approach as 'ideal'. However, this is in contradiction with the more common phenomenon of 'learning from Japan' (Lewis and Sun, 1994), and needs to be further tested empirically. In addition to the three external sources, the traditional Chinese management knowhow is widely regarded as a treasure and should be explored systematically to serve the present times (Ye et al., 1987). In a nutshell, no matter which source Chinese managers borrow from, adaptation holds the key to the success of the transfer.

Constraints: Factors Influencing the Transfer

Learning consists of absorbing, digesting, adapting and applying. Adaptation and application are the most important stages in the transfer of management knowhow. Adaptation has to be made both conceptually and contextually because (a) western management knowhow is defined on the basis of western assumptions and norms which are fundamentally different from their Chinese counterparts, and (b) Chinese SOEs operate in an environment that differs from the western one in almost every aspect. The purpose of adaptation is to identify those factors which would be inappropriate in the Chinese environmental/cultural setting and modify them to fit into the Chinese context. Factors which influence adaptation and application as well as the whole management transfer process can be divided into three categories:

- environmental factors
- organizational factors
- cultural and behavioural factors.

Environmental factors include political instability, economic uncertainty (Cavusgil and Yavas, 1984), openness of the society and management infrastructure (Von Glinow and Teagarden, 1988). Organizational factors refer to incompatible organization structure or management systems, availability of reliable data and information, and shortage of qualified managers.

Modern Chinese culture is influenced by three sources in descending order: Confucianism, communism ideology and, only recently, western values. Confucianism is basically a non-competitive culture, emphasizing harmony, tolerance and moderation (Waley, 1988). This is in sharp contrast with western management philosophy in the cut-throat competitive market economy. Communist ideology, on the other hand, has long negated the role of market and marketing in the centrally-planned economic system. All these influences, in spite of their profound impact on management practice and the transfer of management knowhow, have so far not been well understood. Some major cultural factors are discussed below.

Ideological and Political Constraints

Although China today is much more open and politically relaxed compared with the dark ages of the Cultural Revolution in the middle 1960s–70s, the rise of consumerism and worship of western commercial culture cannot disguise the fact that China, under communist one-party rule, remains politically a totalitarian state and still, by and large, a closed society. Political ideologies which run counter to many western values still prevail. There were, in the middle of the 1980s, heated debates in China on whether western management disciplines, such as organization behaviour, were bourgeois pseudo-sciences and should be boycotted. Culture-bound knowhow such as marketing faces more ideological obstacles, as marketing has no place in the orthodox Marxist theory which emphasizes production and disdains distribution based on the notion that the creation of economic utilities is largely confined to the production sector. It will not be easy, and will certainly take a long time for Chinese managers to change their old thinking. As long as the Chinese government continues to pursue two contradictory goals: to experiment with capitalism economically and to maintain communism politically, there are always going to be inherent conflicts between the free market practice and hard-line communist ideology. This causes enormous confusion and anxiety among Chinese managers. They still regard 'political correctness as having higher importance than organizational effectiveness or efficiency (Lindsay and Dempsey, 1983). Misgivings of being persecuted in the next political campaign make playing safe a major concern ideologically. On the other hand, the painful memory of the past one hundred years when China was humiliated in wars with, and subsequently suffered from, western powers, will make Chinese managers take extra caution in borrowing western ideas.

Language

Language presents the first barrier to the transfer of western management knowhow to China as the majority of Chinese managers cannot speak a foreign language. It is difficult to translate foreign concepts and theories into Chinese because different meanings exist in the two cultures for the same words such as 'market', 'enterprise' and 'profit'. An SOE in China is traditionally regarded as an administrative unit, or a subordinate unit of the bureau, with the main function of fulfilling production quotas and providing employment and welfare; showing no analogy to the western concept of an economic or legal entity for the conduct of business. Even if the Chinese equivalent of an English term can be found from the dictionary, the actual connotation and extension of the translated term could be very different from the original. For instance, the key term 'marketing' itself cannot be adequately translated into Chinese. Without universally accepted translation in Chinese, the three most commonly used terms are:

- discipline of market;
- discipline of selling;
- discipline of operating and selling.

Moreover, 'marketing research' is translated as 'sales investigation' or 'market survey' in Chinese. There are other more difficult cases in which western terms are almost untranslatable.

Socio-cultural Factors

Social and cultural factors have to be taken into account before any adaptation is made. Culture generally refers to some commonly held beliefs, values and perceptions, and behaviour patterns. In contrast with the western tradition of mercantilism, Chinese culture under the influence of Confucianism has belittled the importance of commercial activities as well as 'businessman' as a profession. Placed on the bottom rung in the Confucian social hierarchy after workers, peasants, soldiers and students, merchants were taxed arbitrarily, treated with suspicion and as inferiors by mandarins, and suppressed by the imperial bureaucrats, who frequently banned foreign trade by merchants as a corrupting influence. This national mentality has been further strengthened under the communist regime since the propaganda machine spared no efforts to revile capitalists and the market economy, and by the centrally-planned economy in which production, not marketing, was regarded as of the utmost importance. The legacy of the past is so immense that its impeding effect on marketing cannot be underestimated. There are other popular beliefs which may hinder the application of marketing, for example:

- Nine out of ten businessmen are unscrupulous.
- Firms only advertise the products they could not sell.
- A good product needs no advertising.
- Advertising tells all lies.

An article in the *People's Daily* (13 December 1992) stresses the need to preserve the Chinese cultural tradition under the market economy. It criticizes the practice of discount and bargaining as being dishonest and running counter to the socialist moral codes. This shows that the transfer of western management knowhow has to overcome resistance from both traditional values and ideological propaganda.

Marketing is new not only to Chinese managers, but also to Chinese consumers. Consumers have an important role to play in the transfer process. They have been exposed to the western-style marketing approach only recently, and need time to get used to it. The key index of the effectiveness of any new marketing technique adopted would be the response from the consumers, because they are the target receivers of marketing; the ultimate judges of success. As consumer goods in China become increasingly a buyer's market and consumers more sophisticated, it would put greater pressure on companies to learn and adopt a new marketing approach.

Hard and Soft

Marketing, like other management disciplines or functions, connotes technical (hard) and social or behavioural (soft) elements. This is in line with the distinction made by Hedlund and Nonaka (1993) between *tacit* and *explicit* knowledge. Soft elements are normally tacit while hard elements are more explicit. Functions like production, R&D, innovation, finance and accounting, have more hard elements, while other functions such as organization, marketing and HRM have more soft elements. Hard elements are less subject to the influence of cultural and environmental variations and can be applied immediately with little or no adaptation; soft elements are more culture-bound and context-specific, and require more adaptation during the transfer. Empirical evidence can be found in a recent study by Easterby-Smith et al. (1995). Unfortunately it might be difficult to distinguish the hard from the soft in practical cases as there is no clear-cut boundary between them like the one shown in Figure 1, and they could be intertwined, particularly at the application stage. It should also be noted that the definition of hard and soft elements may be different under different cultural backgrounds (Jaeger, 1990). In terms of priority it would be easier to start the transfer with those subjects which have more hard elements. As most Chinese managers in SOEs come from a technical or engineering background, they in general tend to be quick learners of hard elements but rather slow, indifferent or even resistant to soft elements. They have never worked or lived in a real market situation until very recent years, and have little knowledge about marketing. Livingstone (1987) describes marketing in China as a 'fuzzier concept' in an alien culture', initially causing more anxiety to the students than more overtly quantitative (hard) disciplines. There may be far greater value for Chinese managers first to learn and apply some 'tools and techniques' of marketing rather than the total body of marketing knowledge as it exists in developed countries (Cavusgil and Yavas, 1984).

Conceptual Barriers

There are two opposite types of preoccupation among Chinese managers, both of which present barriers to the transfer of western management knowhow. The first view rejects the need to learn from the West. It argues that China has had good theories of management since ancient times. For example, 'The Art of War' by Sun Tze is more than two thousand years old and has been said to be a foundation for the Japanese business and marketing strategy. A senior research fellow from the Chinese Academy of Social Sciences is an advocate of the view. He told the author recently that Chinese are born with marketing genius and do not need to learn marketing from the West. The second view favours total and indiscriminate transplanting of western practice regardless of the apparent differences in socio-cultural environment and local circumstances. It believes that anything that is foreign (western) is good; even the moon shines brighter in the West. Both views are one-sided and harmful to the transfer. In his book *The East–West Pendulum,* George (1992) provides interesting accounts of the differences between Chinese and Japanese attitudes towards learning from the West in the last century. Japanese people, managers in particular, were very good at learning from the West while preserving their own tradition. This may offer a partial explanation why, in the past one and a half centuries, reform/modernization programmes were successful in Japan while several similar attempts failed in China. Such an ambivalent mentality to foreign cultures is still deeply imbued among Chinese people. A slogan in the last doomed modernization drive of the late 19th century said:

> To keep Chinese learning for fundamentals, to take Western learning for practical needs.

Interestingly, this was echoed more than one hundred years later by a western scholar. Casting his doubt over the validity of western management theories in a non-western environment, Hofstede (1993) proposes a dialogue between equals in which

> the Western partner acts as the expert in Western technology and the local partner as the expert in local culture, habits and feeling.

However, his view has not been shared by some western academics who still believe that western theory and practice are superior in all aspects and universally applicable. They toured China, Eastern Europe and other developing countries to preach western management without adequate knowledge of local culture and society. This arrogant and ignorant attitude would benefit nobody. Developing countries and countries in economic transition cannot depend on western management in the long term but need to develop their own management systems which combine the best of East and West. To this end, the transfer of management knowhow from the West should be selective and cautious.

The Role of MNCs

The move towards a free market in China is of significance to foreign firms, particularly to multinational corporations (MNCs). By the end of 1994, there were in China 220,000 foreign equity or contractual joint ventures, and wholly foreign-owned enterprises (MOFTEC, 1995). By investing in China, MNCs have brought not only capital and technology, but much-needed management knowhow. With more and more MNCs operating in China, they could contribute to the transfer of management knowhow by acting as a role model to Chinese managers. Many authors highlighted the role of MNCs in the international transfer of technology and the impact of investment upon economic development in the developing countries; more specifically, referring to MNCs as 'change agents' and 'development agents (Thorelli, 1966; Quinn, 1969; Johnson, 1970). In addition to these two roles, MNCs can play a more important role as the *teaching agents*, or *tutors*. Since most Chinese partners in large and medium-sized joint ventures are SOEs, MNCs can demonstrate to their Chinese managers how western management practices work in a first-hand experience. The Chinese government has also called on SOEs to learn management practices from exemplary international joint ventures (Li, 1992). The applicability and adaptation of western management knowhow is the crucial element in the successful operation of these joint ventures, as there exists between Chinese and foreign management practices a wide gap which may cause potential conflicts in joint ventures (Fan, 1996). There are three different approaches to tackling the issue (Child, 1991):

1. wholesale application of foreign practice without any reconciliation with the existing Chinese one;
2. accept and work with Chinese practice with little change;
3. reconcile and incorporate foreign practice with a Chinese perspective.

The second approach adopted in most joint ventures with overseas Chinese partners seems to work well in the short term. However, it is the integrative approach that is likely to be the most successful in the long run. For those MNCs which do not have joint ventures but market their products in China, the applicability of western management knowhow is still relevant. The profound cultural differences that exist between China and the West may translate into distinctive differences in marketing approach. MNCs have to ask to what extent the marketing strategies and practices that have proven successful in their home country can be applied to the Chinese context, and subsequently to make necessary adaptations in terms of marketing mix.

Conclusions

This paper set out to examine the transferability of western management knowhow to China's SOEs. It is concerned mainly with the content of the transfer but not the process, which will be another major area for research. Owing to its exploratory nature, the paper raises more questions than it has answered. Future research is needed along a number of dimensions:

1. Updating our knowledge of the current status of management in SOEs and management education in China is the first step. Tables 2 and 3 provide some guidance for which areas to look at. There is an urgent need to study what changes have taken place and what has not changed; and to identify the similarities and differences in management practice between China and the West. Only on the basis of this understanding can one decide which management concepts are compatible/applicable to the Chinese context.

2. Empirical investigations are needed to study the transfer process in different types of organizations such as SOEs, township and private enterprises, and foreign- invested enterprises. For instance, a foreign joint venture may have far fewer political and organizational constraints than an SOE, but still face problems of coping with clashes between the two cultures and management styles. It is also interesting to know what kind of role is played by three different impeding factors and the links between them.

3. Further studies need to address the practical problems which may arise during the adaptation and application stages (see Figure 2): how to overcome conceptual barriers, how to reduce the resistance to change, how to reconcile new practice with the existing system, and how to assess the effectiveness and measure performance after the transfer process, to name just a few.

4. Last but not least, basic research is needed to examine the differences between Chinese and western management thoughts and philosophies (see Figure 1), and how the differences at the core influence the other two layers as well as the transfer process. The hypothesis that it is more difficult to transfer soft elements across cultures than hard elements needs to be further tested.

The transition to a market economy and relatively relaxed political climate in China have produced the demand for western management knowhow, marketing in particular. However, the transfer of western management to China is a complex and long-term task which is subject to the influence of many factors, among which the cultural factor is the most important. This is crucially important not only to Chinese SOEs, but also to MNCs which are already operating within China or planning to enter the market. As mentioned above, MNCs will be involved either directly or indirectly with management transfer. Understanding of the context, content and cultural constraints of the transfer process holds the key to the success of cross-culture management transfer.

There is little doubt that western management knowhow is useful, and some of it can be applied in China. However, this does not imply a total westernization. Rather, on the contrary, it would be the 'Chinesenization' of western management knowhow, or 'management with Chinese characteristics' as the Chinese jargon goes. It would be naive to believe that by learning western management knowhow China will fully adopt capitalism, or solve all her problems. 'What is transferred from the West is likely to be carefully selected, then redesigned and developed to suit specific Chinese needs rather than adopted wholesale to please Westerners and make them rich' (Garratt, 1981). Ultimately China has to develop her own indigenous theory and practice by blending the best of both East and West. How China can realize this goal has to be answered by future research which would benefit practitioners with insights and advice. This line of research should also address the issue of interaction between different management systems, as the cross-cultural transfer is never one-way.

Notes

1. The author wishes to acknowledge the valuable comments made by two anonymous referees of *Management Learning*.

References

Akaah, I.P. and Riordan, E.A. (1988) 'Applicability of Marketing Knowhow in the Third World', *International Marketing Review* (Spring): 41–55.

Bentley, D. (1994) 'Plugging West Central Gaps', *Forum (EFMD Magazine)* 1: 46–7.

Cavusgil, S.T. and Yavas, U. (1984) 'Transfer of Management Knowhow to Developing Countries: An Empirical Investigation', *Journal of Business Research* 12: 35–50.

Chan, T.S. (1989) 'Teaching Marketing in China: Implications for Effective Marketing Education', *Journal of Teaching in International Business* 1(1): 33–46.

Chen, Q. (1993) 'Enterprise Management in China has Entered a New Stage', *International Business Administration* 3: 4–8 (in Chinese).

Child, J. (1991) 'A Foreign Perspective on the Management of People in China', *The International Journal of Human Resource Management* 2: 1.

Cranch, G. (1974) 'Modern Marketing Techniques Applied to Developing Countries', in R.J. Holloway and R.S. Harcock (eds) *The Environment for Marketing Management*, 3rd edn., pp. 412–16. New York: John Wiley.

Easterby-Smith, M. et al. (1995) 'How Culture-sensitive is HRM? A Comparative Analysis of Practice in Chinese and UK Companies', *The International Journal of Human Resource Management* 6(1): 31–59.

Fan, Y. (1996) 'Research on Joint Ventures in China: Progress and Prognosis', *Journal of Euro marketing* 4(3/4): 71–88.

Fukuda, K.J. (1983) 'Transfer of Management: Japanese Practice for the Orientals?', *Management Development* 21(4): 17–26.

Garrett, B. (1981) 'Contrasts in Chinese and Western Management Thinking', *Leadership and Organisation Development Journal* 2 (1): 17–22.

George, R. L. (1992) *The East–West Pendulum*. Cambridge: Woodhead-Faulkner.

Gennaro, F.D. (1969) 'International Transfer of Management Skills: The Behavioural Patterns – A Preliminary Study', *The Quarterly Journal of AIESEC International* 5: 30–48.

Hedlund, G. and Nonaka, I. (1993) 'Models of Knowledge Management in the West and Japan', in P. Lorange (ed.) *Implementing Strategic Processes*, pp. 117–44. Oxford: Blackwell.

Ho, S. (1993) 'Transplanting Japanese Management Techniques', *Long Range Planning* 26(4): 81–9.

Hofstede, G. (1980) 'Motivation, Leadership, and Organisation: Do American Theories Apply Abroad?', *Organisation Dynamics* (Summer): 42–63.

Hofstede, G. (1993) 'Cultural Constraints in Management Theories', *Academy of Management Executive* 7(1): 81–94.

Holton, R.H. (1985) 'Marketing and the Modernisation of China', *California Management Review* 4 (Summer).

Ishida, H. (1986) 'Transferability of Japanese Human Resource Management Abroad', *Human Resource Management* 25(1): 103–20.

Jaeger, A.M. (1990) 'The Applicability of Western Management Techniques in Developing Countries: A Cultural Perspective', in A.M. Jaeger and R.N. Kanungo (eds) *Management in Developing Countries*. London & New York: Routledge.

Johnson, H.G. (1970) 'The Multinational Corporation as a Development Agent', *Columbia Journal of World Business* (May–June): 25–30.

Joy, A. (1990) 'Marketing in Modern China: An Evolutionary Perspective', *Canadian Journal of Administrative Sciences* (June): 55–67.

Kinsey, J. (1988) *Marketing in Developing Countries*. Basingstoke: Macmillan.

Lewis, G. and Sun, W. (1994) 'Discourses about "Learning from Japan" in Post-1979 Mainland Chinese Management Journals', *Issues and Studies* 63–76.

Li, Z. (1992) 'The Vigour in Exemplary Sino-foreign Joint Ventures and Lessons to be Learned', *The World Economy* (June) (in Chinese).

Lindsay, C.P. and Dempsey, B.L. (1983) 'Ten Painful Learned Lessons About Working in China: The Insights of Two American Behavioural Scientists', *The Journal of Applied Behavioural Science*, 19(3): 265–76.

Lindsay, C.P. and Dempsey, B.L. (1985) 'Experiences in Training Chinese Business People To Use U.S. Management Techniques', *Journal of Applied Behavioural Science* 21(1): 65–78.

Livingstone, J.M. (1987) 'The Marketing Concept in China – A Qualified Acceptance', in M. Warner (ed.) *Management Reforms in China*. London: Frances Pinter.

Lockett, M. (1988) 'Chinese Culture and the Problems of Chinese Management', *Organization Studies* 9(4): 475–96.

MOFTEC (1995) Ministry of Foreign Trade and Economic Cooperation, Beijing.

Mun, K. (1984) 'Marketing in the PRC', in E. Kaynak and R. Savitt (eds) *Competitive Marketing Systems*, pp. 247–60. New York: Praeger.

Negandhi, A.R. and Estafen, B.D. (1965) 'A Research Model to Determine the Applicability of American Management Knowhow in Different Cultures and/or Environment', *Academy of Management Journal* 8: 309–18.

Oberg, W. (1963) 'Cross-cultural Perspectives on Management Principles', *Journal of the Academy of Management* 6(2): 129–43.

Quinn, J.B. (1969) 'Technology Transfer by Multinational Companies', *Harvard Business Review* 47: 147–61.

Redding, S.G. (1990) *The Spirit of Chinese Capitalism*. Berlin: de Gruyter.

Redding, S.G. and Pugh, D.S. (1986) 'The Formal and the Informal: Japanese and Chinese Organisation Structure', in S.R. Clegg, D.C. Dunphy and S.G. Redding (eds) *The Enterprise and Management in East Asia*. Hong Kong: University of Hong Kong.

Richman, B.M. (1970) 'A Firsthand Study of Marketing in Communist China', *Journal of Retailing* 46(2): 27–47.

Siu, W. (1994) 'Marketing Education in China: A Status Report', *Journal of Teaching in International Business* 5(4): 35–50.

Terpstra, V. (1991) 'On Marketing Appropriate Products in Developing Countries', *The International Marketing Digest*: 177–92.

Thorelli, H.B. (1966) 'The Multinational Corporation as a Change Agent', *Southern Journal of Business* 1(3): 1–9.

Von Glinow, M.A. and Teagarden, M.B. (1988) 'The Transfer of Human Resource Management Technology in Sino–US Cooperative Ventures: Problems and Solutions', *Human Resource Management* 27(2): 201–29.

Waley, A. (1988) *The Analects of Confucius*. London: Unwin Hyman.

Wang, R.L. (1986) 'Transferring American Management Knowhow to the People's Republic of China', *SAM Advanced Management Journal* (Summer): 4–8.

Yau, O.H.M. (1988) 'Chinese Cultural Values: Their Dimensions and Marketing Implications', *European Journal of Marketing* 22(5): 44–57.

Ye, X. et al. (1987) 'Developing the Socialist Marketing Discipline with Chinese Characteristics', *Economics Weekly* (20 September) :4 (in Chinese).

Zhou, N. (1991) 'The Revival and Growth of Marketing Education in China', *Journal of Marketing Education* (Summer): 18–24.

Zhuang, S.C. and Whitehill, A.M. (1989), 'Will China Adopt Western Management Practice?', *Business Horizons* 32(2): 58–64.

17

Monika Kostera

The Modern Crusade
The Missionaries of Management Come to Eastern Europe

The connections between religion and society have continued to be explored since Weber's fundamental work on capitalism and Protestant ethics. The influences of religion and theology on philosophy (e.g. Kołakowski, 1989a: 166); on social structure (Kołakowski, 1984); on economy (Boulding, 1989a, 1989b; Stein, 1989) and on organization of industrial society (Fromm, 1989) have long been topics for research and insight. The links between organization and religion also deserve some consideration. Organizations offer their participants rewards not only of a material kind, but increasingly also of an existential and perhaps even spiritual nature. They give people an identity and perform an ontological function, providing a sense of Being to the participants (Schwartz, 1987). Finally, they are *a way of life* (Czarniawska-Joerges 1993), cultures providing *networks of meaning* (Smircich, 1987). Participants are being socialized into organizations (Czarniawska-Joerges, 1993; Czarniawska-Joerges and Kunda, 1992) and culture is used as a means of control (Van Maanen and Kunda, 1989). Thus the cultural perspective (cf. Smircich, 1983) offers us a means of understanding the vital – or, in Schwartz's terms, ontological – role of organizations, and also what I would call the religious significance of organizing.

Metaphors play an increasingly important role in social sciences and organizational analysis (cf. Morgan, 1986; Smircich, 1983). In this paper, the business organization is seen as a religious organization and business administration as religion. The metaphor, besides pointing to an important dimension of organizing, also helps us to see the current transition taking place in Eastern and Central Europe from a new and slightly unorthodox perspective. What is happening is not 'only' an economic and political shift, not 'just' the liberation of repressed peoples, but can also be seen as a religious mission: the capitalist West transmitting its managerial religion to the eastern 'heathens'.

Culture, Symbols and Myths

Culture I understand as the *medium of life* (Czarniawska-Joerges, 1991), through which we make sense of our lives, and that enables us to communicate with the world, with the extensive use of symbols (cf. Schütz, 1982).

It is through symbols that we give meaning to an originally intransparent reality (Schütz, 1966, 1982). Symbols are, according to Schütz, the outcome of choice between multiple options in the sense-making of human perception, making experiences persistent and continuous. The symbols, present in our memory, are open for interpretation and reinterpretation (1982). Symbols can constitute important elements of the social and cultural context we live in, an intersubjective world of our common experience (Schütz and Luckmann, 1973).

Myths are, according to Kołakowski, a specific kind of symbol, containing not words but occurrences and persons. The myth is accounted through, or translated into, words. Myths enable people to participate in those events, ontologically important to them, through a symbolical 'immobilizing' of time (1967). Myth is seldom considered as a serious tool of understanding in management literature: myth is seen as something antithetical to fact; myth is opposed to reality, an implicit assumption being that our set of beliefs is true and not as primitive or arbitrary as those of other cultures or epochs' (Ingersoll and Adams, 1986 as quoted in Bowles, 1989: 406). Mythology elicits and supports a sense of awe before mystery of Being, provides a set of ideas which enable humans to answer the most vital questions, socializes the individual, and guides him or her towards maturation (Bowles, 1989, after Campbell, 1976). Bowles (1992b) also notifies the role of myth in social life, one beyond the 'ego psychology', enabling understanding insights offered by the collective unconscious.

Religion

Religion as the Medium of Spiritual Life

Religion is a kind of culture (Geertz, 1973), constructed as a medium of spiritual life. According to Kołakowski, 'religion is the [s]ocially established cult of infinite reality' (1989: 9). After Kołakowski (1989b) I distinguish between two approaches to religion: the functionalist and the idiogenetic and holistic. The first approach is grounded on the assumption that religion, through participation in ceremonies, rituals, institutions, etc. offers the individual a substitute for other values (or meanings). Religious life is thus a form of communication that offers stability of social structures and institutions. The second approach implies that religion is rooted in human needs, not related genealogically or functionally to other more 'primary' roots. Humans are seeking transcendental values through religion understood in this way.

According to Kołakowski, major religions had the ability to satisfy all the non-religious needs of past societies: the political, societal and those of learning about reality. To achieve this, *sacrum* could not be instrumentally understood and had to have autonomous authority (1988). This point of view is analogous with Fromm's: the 'to have' versus 'to be' approach to faith:

> In religious, political or personalistic understanding, the concept of faith can have two entirely different meanings, depending on if we use it in the sense of 'to have' or 'to be'. In the attitude 'to have' faith is the possessing of answers not needing rational verification. (Fromm, 1989: 44)

These answers are offered by others to whom we adhere. These 'others' are usually bureaucracies that offer us a sense of certainty. Faith is the price we pay for this sense of security that comes from belonging to a big social group that deprives us of the demanding responsibility of autonomous thinking and decision-making. Believers possess this certitude. Faith claims to have the ultimate, absolute knowledge that is valid, because the people protecting and preserving it think it to be undisputed. Faith in the sense 'to be' is not connected to beliefs in certain ideas in the first place, but 'inner orientation, *route*. It would be a better way to express it to say that one is in faith, rather that one *has* faith' (Fromm, 1989: 45, emphasis original).

In this paper the religious metaphor is based on the idiogenetic, 'to be' view on religion. Thus I assume that people engage in the religious discourse because of a relatively autonomous need to do so. The religious construct nevertheless becomes highly institutionalized and entails what Fromm would have labelled the 'to have' dimension of religion.

What is Religion? Proposed Framework

For the purpose of this paper, I would like to propose a definition of religion that will serve as a theoretical framework for presentation of the argument. It is not an ostensive definition, saying what 'religion really is', but a performative definition, aimed at facilitating narration of the phenomenon that interests me here (on ostensive and performative definitions in sociology, see Latour, 1986; in organization theory, see Czarniawska-Joerges 1991, 1993). The elements of my framework are based primarily on Kołakowski's (1967, 1994) view on religion, but in my own interpretation and with my emphases. Further, Kołakowski is not a constructivist, whereas my picture of religion is constructivist.

Religion is an ordering of symbols that carry spiritual meaning to people. By 'ordering' I mean a process whereby certain symbols continuously acquire meaning, the avoidance of chaos. Certain types of participant are important religious actors, among them the believers (followers), the elites and of course the priests. They take part in making religion, a construct, containing several types of symbol, of which the following are central: symbolic language, physical artefacts, norms and values, and myths, including stories about saints and the Grand Myth of the god (see Table 1).

In the case of mission, the actors are respectively followers, or converted pagans, emerging native elites and missionaries. The symbols are exported to a different culture, so there is a need to educate the pagans in the symbolic

Table 1   *Religion as a symbolic construct*

RELIGION	
Actors	*Symbols*
Followers	Symbolic language
Elites	Physical artefacts
Priests	Norms and values
	Myths

language, for example Latin, but as missions are often accompanied by colonization, an official language may also be introduced, such as Spanish in Latin America. Physical artefacts, such as relics, icons or pictures of saints are more or less abundant in different religions. However, missions typically carry other artefacts associated with the culture of origin of the missionaries. So the white colonists brought cheap but seductive jewellery to Africa, and contemporary missionaries bring western clothes and technology to Papua. These artefacts are intended to attract converts. The aim is socialization to imprint the new norms and values in people's mindsets. Those who succeed are rewarded with the opportunity of participation in myths, especially in the Grand Myth – of the god him or (more rarely) herself. Myths play a central role in all religious systems. In missions, stories about saints have an important role in providing the people with examples, at the same time human and superhuman, of successful following.

Substitutes for Religion in Late Modernity

In late modernity (Giddens, 1991) religion tends to be replaced by science (Czarniawska-Joerges, 1993; Kołakowski, 1989a). Fromm perceives yet another substitute for traditional religion, more widespread and powerful: work. Work has become the only way to secure love and respect and thus the new post-Christian religion has emerged, that of the industrial society (Fromm, 1989). The lost meanings (of work and life) are replaced by a surrogate – motivation (Sievers, 1986). So economic organizations keep humans going, in a fragmented and shallow way, yet offering people the only meaning, albeit a surrogate one, generally available in modern society.

Organization and Religion

The religious metaphor (and related experiential ones), has been used (fractionally or in-depth) in management and organization literature, to achieve a literary emphasis, or to demonstrate certain aspects of organization and organizing. For example, eminent management theoreticians have been called 'management gurus' (Clutterbuck and Bickerstaffe, 1982). Expressions such as 'evangelism' have also been used (Bowles, 1992b: 20). A lot has been said and written on charismatic leadership, especially in the corporate culture mainstream (e.g. Deal and Kennedy, 1982; McCormack, 1986; Pascale and

Athos, 1982; Peters and Waterman, 1986). Höpfl (1994) explicitly speaks of the religious significance of leadership in modern organizations. Management literature has been likened to mythological biographies of late antiquity and the middle ages and labelled *edifying literature* (Furusten, 1992).

Bowles has been using religious metaphors to explore organizational myths (1989, 1992b), unconscious (or religious, in my perspective here) needs and symbols (1992a, 1992b) and their consequences for organizational action, human relations (1992c), life in organizations (1992b) and individual maturation (1992a). Bowles (1992a) concludes that modern organizations do have a significant impact on the individual's potential for maturation or individuation such as Jung (1968) has defined it. Organizations model a mass mind, proceed with collectivization and objectivization, and offer ontologic rewards but without deeper religious sense (Bowles, 1992a).

Sievers asserts that 'organizations and enterprises tend to become surrogates for the churches' (1988: 36). Further, he maintains that these organizations are based on 'the assumption that there is evidently no evidence and, therefore, no further understanding beyond what obviously is obvious: the company's and its members' welfare' (1988: 36–7). The metaphor – business administration as religion and business organization as religious institution – is not only an interesting way of depicting the phenomenon but, in modern society, also a useful tool to achieve a greater understanding of the organizational world. In Alvesson's (1993) terms, the religious metaphor is thus a 'second-level', while the cultural symbolist (see e.g. Turner, 1986, 1990) – a 'first-level' metaphor.

In my opinion the cultural perspective is fundamental to understanding the ontological role that organizations play in human life. Looking through cultural glasses helps people to realize that organizations are not only 'tools' or 'instruments' (or machines) for the achievement of goals, invented by the constructor, but a way of life. Organizations are, furthermore, a way of *spiritual life*, offering to their participants a set of meanings, together with proper interpretations; they are also a mental escape from the inevitability of death, as organizations are a substitute for immortality (Sievers, 1986). They offer myths and other important symbols, helping people to deal with the irrational and non-rational, and they become a moral frame of reference, through the shared norms and values.

The shepherds of this kind of religious institution are managers and organizational leaders. They know how to interpret symbols; they, together with the 'experts', the management consultants, offer meanings to the (organizational) people. Leaders perform a vital societal role – that of priests; namely, in Czarniawska-Joerges' words,

> ... to provide the rest of the cast and the audience with the illusion of controllability ... The arbitrariness of life – especially organizational life – is too frightful to envisage. A leader who fails to provide the illusion ... by showing us the illusion for what it is, cannot be applauded. The illusion must be supported at whatever cost. (Czarniawska-Joerges, 1993: 42)

Management educators and consultants teach managers how to perform this role.

The Religion of Business Administration Comes to Eastern Europe – The Mission

A Remark on the Method and the Metaphor

Adopting the interpretive approach, I do not claim the conclusions to be universal or generally applicable. I see them as an insight that can be shared and discussed. The empirical material is founded on my various experiences. From these experiences I chose a few windows (Czarniawska-Joerges, 1992) that I consider 'typical'. I do not claim them to be statistically representative, but they are substantially representative, i.e. they represent the context described in the paper. I contrast the windows with quotations from historical sources (on religious mission among various 'pagan' peoples), marked with a small square (□). The quotations come from the library research on the topic.

I see the modern business organization of the western type as a religious institution, providing the fulfilment of religious needs (as defined above) of the participants. Business administration as the modern religion has its priests: the managers and leaders of business, its missionaries: management consultants, management educators, and its prophets: the authors of management books. While the priests look to their congregations, the missionaries are busy with transmitting the symbols and myths of their religion to the heathens, and supporting the priests. After the fall of the Berlin Wall a thriving field for missionary quest was opened. The as-yet unredeemed peoples are a thrilling opportunity to strengthen the faith of existing believers – to convert the idolatrous has perhaps always been a means of strengthening the faith of those already saved.

The New Latin to Learn

It is widely believed that the East should 'learn' from the West (this is particularly visible to the reader of the East European press, such as myself) and that it has a long way to go before it 'catches up' (this point is often stressed in the Polish mass media). The desire to 'catch up' (or, as Orgogozo put it, 'East European aspirations towards Eldorado now' [1992: 596]) is reflected in the flood of western models, publications, visiting professors and consultants coming to Eastern and Central Europe. First of all, the Polish language was enriched immediately after 1989 with such terms as: *management* (or *menedzment* – instead of or simultaneously with the Polish term *zarządzanie*), *manager* (or *menedzer* – instead of *kierownik*), *cash-flow, controlling, businessman* and *businesswoman, business* or *biznes*, etc. *Marketing* had already existed for a long time, as had *dywizjonalizacja* and *holding*. Similar things happened to the languages of other ex-Eastern Bloc countries.

Some of my postgraduate students of business administration, most of them in their late forties, complained that some of the lecturers used foreign words. One commented: 'I feel like I am listening to a Turkish sermon' (this common Polish expression, meaning that you listen to something you do not understand). They expressed their anger with this kind of treatment: 'Why can't they speak Polish?', but at the same time they refused to talk about it with the lecturers in question. They probably felt ashamed of not being 'adequate', not *au courant*.

□

The white missionaries showed a greater or lesser sensitivity to the native languages of the pagans they sought to convert to Christian faith. Some, like the Jesuits of Missiones in Latin America, used the native language, while communicating with the Indians. Others failed to do so. It is however true that missions spread the original language of the missionaries, which ultimately became the national – as Spanish in Latin America – or the official language – as English in the colonial India and French in Algeria.

Sometimes the Catholic missionaries, who sometimes used Latin, especially to write more important letters and documents, could be met with adversity from suspicious natives. The following conversation took place between a Chinese dignitary and a Catholic missionary, whose letter the former had confiscated:

'In which language is [this letter] written?'

'In Latin.'

'This is very suspect indeed! Why don't you write in Chinese?' (Hunermann, 1961: 273)

Desirable Things: Artefacts

Being 'international', 'American' or 'British' became a virtue *per se*, reflected in the way other products are marketed. Says a private entrepreneur leading a marketing agency:

I often have to put English text and names on the labels of my clients' products, the clients insist. Sometimes the description of the product is in English, I think it is weird, the consumer often does not understand the text. Somewhere on the label, in a corner, with a small font, they add 'Made in Poland'. But this is how products sell nowadays in our country.

Genuine western-made products also invade our markets. They are marketed and advertised on TV; sometimes, in the case of Polish TV, direct translations (often in incorrect and hardly understandable Polish) are accepted and broadcasted. The same entrepreneur remarks:

Many of the advertised western products have already run their life cycle out in the West. They advertise for the 'old version' in Poland and for a 'new, improved one' on Sky or MTV.

□

The white missionaries brought with them glass pearls and mirrors to attract the 'pagans'. The Africans and the Indians would do almost anything to get the 'precious' goods of the white people. Having learned that the [Indians] willingly sell their women for European 'glitter', such as beads, hair-pins, metal buckles, they [the white settlers] fell over themselves to initiate contacts with the Indians. A ... Brazilian historian, Varnhagen, found through studies of Jesuit chronicles from the 15th century that in that epoch it was possible to buy a young Indian girl for a ... hair-pin. (Wójcik, 1974: 23)

The most important feature of the 'new era' of transition is, however, the focus on management and the western-type business organization. In business administration, iconic artefacts such as titles (MBA), advertisements, brands, etc. are now flooding in.

Schooling in Norms and Values

Existing management education institutions (they were not many: Poland had, first, the School of Management of Warsaw University and the Central School of Planning and Statistics, now the Warsaw School of Economics) have been supplemented by new institutions mushrooming throughout the ex-Eastern Bloc. They often have 'international' in their names, or include an English word such as 'management' or 'business'. Management education is increasingly popular in Poland and is viewed as one of, if not *the* most reliable path to a professional career (before studies in foreign languages, law and international trading), as a pilot study presented in the popular weekly *Polityka* indicates (Nowakowska, 1993).

The interest in management is enormous. An employee of a Polish publishing company said: 'Say "management" and people will come running to buy it, whatever it is'. It is also easy to observe: the bookstores are full of publications on management, of varying quality. According to the vendors the clients ask for these books and they sell very well (my interviews, Warsaw and Karpacz, 1993).

Throughout the country numerous seminars, courses and complete studies are arranged by western institutions. These programmes are sometimes of high and sometimes of poor quality. Some are organized jointly with Polish institutions, private or public. They have one thing in common: they teach not only 'new methods, techniques and concepts', but also (or is it: in the first place?) *a new set of norms and values.*[1]

In 1989 I participated in a seminar organized by an eminent western institution, aimed at training in management and management consulting. The participants were seated in a classroom, reminding one of school. A group of people from industry sat in the front half of the class. The back was occupied by university people, among them one tenured professor and two assistants. Into the class came the visiting lecturer and his young assistant. They introduced themselves as professional consultants with academic backgrounds and the lecture started.

First, the senior lecturer explained that communism had a very demoralizing impact on society and in order to achieve wealth and success the Eastern and Central Europeans would have to work hard. It was no longer acceptable to wait for the state to 'give' the citizens all they demanded. Market economy meant competition, hard work and problem-solving. Communism was not a sustainable economic system, anyone could see that.

□

The Indians were not used to hard work, they lived a life in harmony with nature and they had to be 'persuaded' to work by the Jesuits in a special way – work was associated with religious ceremonies so that the natives understood its importance . . . The natives do not cultivate the soil, nor do they keep any domesticated animals. Here there are no cows, horses, goats, sheep or chicken. The natives do not eat anything except for maniok roots, fish, and fruit growing abundantly in the forests. In spite of this they are of remarkably high stature and good health. (Wójcik, 1974: 18)

The Poles were, however, a very dynamic nation, the lecturer went on. He himself, as well as his assistant, was of Polish origin. It was here in Poland that democracy was born in the Eastern Bloc. *Solidarność*, the great social movement of 1980, was an event that shook the world. Now, after the fall of communism, the Poles would easily adapt to the new environment. They had 'economic minds', they would learn fast and outstrip their teachers. Here the lecturer smiled with benevolence.

□

If our colonists who settle in these territories learn the language of these natives, with facility they will convert them to the true religion, in which with God's help they may succeed! It should be noted that these natives seem to be honest people. God gave them human faces and postures, to become like us, and the Lord, Jesus Christ, did not direct us here by accident, knowing that Your Highness wants to multiply His honor through the redemption of new souls to the sacred Catholic faith! (Wójcik, 1974: 17–18)

The lecturer told us a few anecdotes, acquainted us briefly with his job and explained that his assistant would now introduce some basic western managerial concepts and theories we would certainly be needing. He left the room and the assistant, in heart-breakingly poor Polish, explained the concepts of costs, fixed and variable. Then he went on to price-setting and the relationship between demand and supply in a market economy. To the academics and many of the industrialists these issues were trivial, but made almost unrecognizable by the poor language. The assistant emphasized strongly what he was saying: this was certainly the 'good news' of the market economy.

□

The Augustins admitted the pagans to the Holy Mass before their baptism. After the Gospels, a minister explained to them the meaning of the ceremonies . . . Finally, he held a short lesson in catechism. The Indians were not admitted to baptism before they knew the *Pater*, the *Credo*, the commandments of God and the Church and before they had sufficient comprehension of the sacraments. (Ricard, 1933: 105)

Now the senior lecturer returned. He was carrying a video. He explained that we were to see a lecture by the 'big economic guru', Michael Porter. He told a few anecdotes from Porter's life, and then we watched the film. The video was attractive to watch, and included many suggestions about 'how to succeed in business', both recipes and insights. The video offered the participants an opportunity to review what they already knew or believed in, in a splendid 'package'.

□

The more modern Catholic missionaries educate the pagans in the new faith not so much by making them learn the catechism by heart, but by teaching them about what being a good Christian means in practice. They often recount the stories of the saints and other pious Catholics.[2]

Students or Followers?

After acquainting us with the new 'religion', the lecturers conducted a computer game. The participants filled in questionnaires, after having discussed matters in small groups. Then the lecturer collected the papers and left the room to 'process the data in his computer', which we did not see. It was located somewhere else, in the lecturer's individual room. Then he came back with the results. The winning team was honoured and celebrated. Other teams were also praised – they had 'done a good job'. Everybody felt satisfied, and this was perhaps the most gratifying moment of the course, judging from 'break gossip'. None of the gossip, either critical or complimentary, was given voice in class.

The course participants reacted in a way that Jankowicz (1994) describes as common among Polish managers, hindering creative learning. Jankowicz, involved in management education in Poland, observed a passive attitude among Polish managers, waiting for the lecturer 'to teach them'. On explicit request from the lecturer that they participate in a more active way, people tended to react with embarrassment or even started to protest.

The participants were more loquacious in between classes, commenting and forming networks. They formed a lobby with the ultimate aim of grouping influential people within industry and management consulting. 'This was the main benefit from the course', a participant commented. The redeemed souls would now carry the mission further.

Educating the Elites

This kind of brief course is not, of course, the only way of communicating the Good News of Market Economy and Business Administration to the post-communist heathens. An elite must be formed, competent natives who will further the faith in practice and theory.

□

A modern Church cannot live without leaders. The humble mass of peasants, craftsmen, all who live off the work of their hands and to whom, in the New Spain, the missionaries brought the security of tomorrow, this humble mass should be directed, schooled and educated by an elite. A laity, a clerical and an elite of religious orders. The indispensability of [such elites] is not to be disregarded, it is, to put it this way, of theological importance. (Ricard, 1933: 160)

Thus several high-standard, prestigious institutions have been established, based on cooperation between eminent Polish and western educational institutions. One of them is offering fully fledged MBA studies. Some of the lectures and probably most of the course materials are in English. The students, selected from many candidates, are highly motivated and hard working.

☐

Knowing about the importance of formation of such elites, the white missionaries established colleges for the education of future priests and civil leaders. The most successful schools educated natives. (Ricard, 1933)

The workload is immense, compared to other management education curricula I know of in Poland. The students receive regular, bulky reading matter and sit demanding exams, even though they are busy with their work elsewhere – most of them are executives for various enterprises, some of which are of considerable size and importance. The course includes sophisticated financial management techniques, modern accounting, computer science, all in detail and demanding memorization of long and complicated texts and procedures.

☐

If the preliminary education of Motoliníe represented a minimum, it seems certain that the Pláticas des Douze[3] represented, on the contrary, the maximum. Certain indications about the different categories of angels, Seraphins Cherubins, Thrones, Dominions seem excessive for a preliminary education and extremely complicated. (Ricard, 1933: 108)

The courses, of varying prestige and difficulty, all result in a diploma or degree, from MBA to a simple certificate of completing the course. This document is highly valued by the students and candidates – it gives them a good position on the labour market. In the terms of my metaphor they acquire a baptismal certificate: they are members of the 'new church'.

☐

The administration of baptism was . . . always preceded by a schooling which could be more or less abbreviated, more or less rapid, depending on the case and the circumstances. (Ricard, 1933: 105)

The Missionaries: Ethos and Practice

It has to be remembered that before 1989, Eastern and Central Europe were ruled in an undemocratic and totalitarian way (Staniszkis, 1989; Wesołowski and Wnuk-Lipiński, 1992). Totalitarian rule is, according to Wesołowski and Wnuk-Lipiński, 'the rule of an uncontrolled elite, supported by a mass political party, and executed by bureaucratic institutions that pervade public life' (1992: 85). The people were suffering from more or less overt oppression and their human rights were frequently and notoriously violated. Market economy and western-type democracy seemed to them after 1989 almost as the 'coming of the Messiah'; my American interlocutor (private communication, Winter 1991; young American participating in assistance programme) alluded to this, while describing his task:

> I think my job is very important. The Polish people have fought for their freedom, now they are trying to create a democratic society, for the first time since the beginning of World War II. They really had a tough time under communism.

☐

It seems indubitable that among pre-cortesian Indians morality did not reach their level of intelligence. Their religion, indeed, does not appear as anything but an ensemble of mere rituals: human sacrifices, ritual drunkenness and anthropophagy; they were all too often bloody and immoral. (Ricard, 1933: 43)

The West is supporting the ex-communist countries financially, through the activity of many foundations, offering important loans, grants, programmes, etc. This help is more than welcome to the often underinvested and poor countries. It is, however, often difficult for the East and Central Europeans to acquire credit or financial support, as the formal requirements are viewed as complicated and far from what the ex-communist societies are used to. 'It is impossible and infuriating; they make me paranoid and I start thinking they do it on purpose', commented a young researcher (private communication, Spring 1993) on the difficulties of filling in application forms and taking care of the formalities when applying for western grants. Many of the Polish loans wait' unused (J. Kostera, 1992). What is more, they are often connected to specific western services and products which have to be bought if the credit is granted, or so at least my interviewees affirmed (pilot study: interviews with academics and businesspeople, Spring 1993).

☐

It should be remembered that white missionaries often offered genuine valuable help to the natives they were (and still are) working with. The best known example is, perhaps, the one of the Missiones mission in Latin America. But there are others as well (e.g. Si-ing, 1940; Ricard, 1933). However, with this help went the new faith as an 'additional' offering.

There are of course different western 'helpers' and different guest lecturers. I see two broad categories of 'the management missionaries': the 'free-marketeers' and the 'culture sensitive'. While the former tend to concentrate on free market values and classic economics, often explicitly suggesting that the Polish students are to learn the 'universally accepted' rules of the game and typically address an intellectual elite, the latter show concern for the Polish 'common man and woman', gathering information on the culture and students before the lecture and adapting the style and language as much as possible to the listeners. The latter also show interest in the material situation of their listeners, while the former stress the importance of holding onto crucial values (such as competition, individualism, pragmatism, etc.), usually performing in front of middle and upper-class students. However, the message taught is typically very much the same: 'if you work really hard and economize, you will enjoy the fruits of your labour when the time comes.'

☐

The Catholic and Protestant missionaries resembled each other in their way of thinking. The same sentiment of superiority of Christians, having the knowledge about the revealed truth toward the Chinese: 'these ignorant pagans' and the same combination of religious zeal and imperialist ambition ... So, the religious practices could be different among the Catholics and Protestants ... [but] before their eyes the Chinese pagans appeared in the same condition of ignorance and misery. (Si-ing, 1940: 105)

The method of recruitment of the Catholic missionaries was typically one of protection of the peasants or of the poor. Because the Chinese used to group themselves in clienteles they could not have found better protectors against the abuse of local authorities or better supporters than the Catholic missionaries. (Si-ing, 1940: 106)

Simultaneously, the method of recruitment of the Protestant missionaries was based on humanitarian works. Because they were rich in personnel and money, thanks to the American element, they occupied themselves much more often with the citizens than with the peasants. They devoted much money to works having to do with hygiene and assistance. (Si-ing, 1940: 107)

I would like to point out that according to my experiences the role of the 'culture-sensitive' missionaries is more advantageous and helpful than that of the 'free marketeers'. The former often stay at Polish hotels, accept invitations to people's homes and thus learn about the culture and the people's needs and expectations. The 'free marketeers' usually stay at the Marriott in Warsaw (thus their nickname: 'the Marriott brigades'), and are said never to leave the hotel except in one of the hotel's taxis. The 'culturally sensitive' often ultimately develop reciprocal relationships with the students.

Myths and the God

Eastern societies also received a set of myths in which they can now participate to experience the fundamental truths of the new religion. The most important myths are: the myth of *hard work*, the myth of the *free market* and the myth of *economizing*.

An example of the myth of hard work is the well-known story of the shoeshiner who became a millionaire ('rags to riches'), also known as the American Dream. This story is being repeated now to the Poles, and the lecturers emphasize the moral lesson: all you have to do is to work hard, and believe in your product. Success will inevitably follow. There is a Protestant ethic moral in the story, a belief in predestination. Similar myths about the free market are being communicated: the Market as a just judge and fair allocator. If you rely 100 percent on the Market, prosperity and justice will follow. These myths (often the British example) are told especially during lectures in privatization. The third Grand Myth, that of economizing, is told in its various versions, but perhaps most often about the Japanese, who do not consume what they produce but invest and save. This is offered to Polish students as the recipe for success and virtue in itself.

The central value of the religion of business administration is that of *rationality*. It has been pointed out before (Czarniawska-Joerges, 1993; Kostera and Wicha, 1994) that modern organizations are primarily rationality-producing constructs. It is true of both communist and capitalist enterprises. However, their rationality criteria are different, as Kostera and Wicha (1994) show. The communist enterprise was based on political rationality, the capitalist on economic rationality. By economic rationality I mean maximization of material utility. By political rationality I understand maximization of influence and power 'utility' (Kostera and Wicha, 1994). Rationality is socially constructed (cf. Berger and Luckmann, 1966/1983), and the rules for this construction are contingent upon, among other factors, the basic kind of 'utility' the society wishes to achieve. Thus, the eastern peoples are not only unbelievers, they are idolators and this is exactly what the western missionaries are trying to demonstrate to them: that their way of perceiving the organizational world is 'irrational' and that there are 'more effective' alternatives (i.e. better suited to reach the desired ends, salvation or well-being). Economic rationality is such an important and self-justifying value that I would claim it is the god of the new religion. In the name of rationality we prepare our accounts, just as Christians do in order to face God at the day of judgment. This does not apply only to purely economic accounts (such as the Annual Report), but to everyday life in modern society. In organizations, rationality is produced by the introduction of specialized rationalization actions into the system and through preparing rational accounts for external use – the two methods are interrelated (Czarniawska-Joerges, 1993). In modern society this rationality production process is taken for granted; it is regarded as the unquestioned (most often unconscious) ultimate end and meaning of (organizational) life.

Salvation, as communicated by the missionaries, is not only economic well-being and prosperity (measured in GNP per capita), but also the modern society itself, seen as a value in itself. To be 'well-organized' and 'hard-working' on the societal level is an aim as laudible as prosperity. In the 'good news' there is a hidden message: 'You don't have to be as wealthy as we are, as long as you are tidy, hygienic, hard-working and frugal.' Wealth is not a value of the new religion; in western societies people often live modestly and are very careful about how they spend their money, not at all how the Easterners imagine life in the wealthy ('prosperous') West.

Communication between West and East: Sermoning the Idolatrous

As the above windows show, East–West communication seems to be pretty uni-directional. That is exactly what I would like to point out in this paper: the general direction for the transfer of symbols and meanings in the world after 1989 is from West to East. It is not a process of *conversation*, it is a monologue, or, in the terms of my metaphor, a *sermon*. The West is teaching the East to adopt its religion. The missionaries are sometimes cynical, sometimes genuinely devoted and pious, wishing sincerely to see their eastern brothers and sisters saved through the adoption of the 'right' faith. They communicate to them the 'right' symbols, norms, values and myths – with the assumption that *if* they only be espoused and used properly, salvation (prosperity and modernity) will be possible for these peoples.

The most important thing to me is not so much that missionaries from the West are trying to convert Easterners to their religion. What I see as crucial is the fact that the communication is uni-directional. And yet, as Orgogozo (1992) points out, we have so much to learn *from each other* and *together.* Orgogozo notes:

> [T]he discoveries being made by those fleeing to Western Europe regarding relations of mutual aid and cooperation, the coolness and indifference of wealthy Europeans towards each other, can help us become aware of our most serious deficiencies. (Orgogozo, 1992: 598)

She explains that capitalist society has disregarded the cost-free relations, such as family and education, and is replacing them with saleable goods or services. Easterners have experienced life in a differently constructed society, with other goals and rationalities. In the case of Poland many valuable societal meanings and symbols derive from a powerful experience people have had: the *Solidarność* era of 1980–1981, and to a certain degree the years of popular dissent and scepticism under martial law. Furthermore, under communism it was quite normal for working-class people to go to the cinema, the theatre, to read books. During the 1980s in particular, there were many 'people's flying universities' active in Poland, among them that led by Jerzy Popiełuszko, a Catholic priest, who organized high-quality cultural activities in his church, including lectures by eminent professors, concerts and theatre performances, directed primarily at blue-collar workers of Huta Warszawa (Warsaw Steel Mill). Another typical example: an article in the Polish daily *Zycie Warszawy* of 7 May 1993 about the yearly film festival. The western partners were surprised, according to the article, that such a 'post-communist festival of ambitious films' should be arranged in Poland, but since it promised to be profitable, they accepted the idea. The festival lasted for two weeks and was a feast for those interested in non-commercial, ambitious films. According to the media, the overall interest in such events, the tendency to read books other than *Harlequin,* see films other than Hollywood productions and videotapes, is in decline in Poland. What people from Eastern Europe so light heartedly give up today seems very substantial. It is, by the way, not what the conservative-nationalist parties in today's Poland mean by 'safeguarding traditional values'. What they mean is reviving pre-Second World War values and decreasing certain human rights (for example those of women and sexual minorities) (Kostera et al., 1994).

Moreover, the adoption of the new religion in itself might not bring the desired ends. What Western Europe achieved had a high price, and furthermore it was due largely to the Marshall plan, not just 'hard work and economizing'. Are East Europeans willing (and able) to pay the price? Would it lead them in the desired direction, considering the role of the Marshall plan in the development of the economy of Western Europe? And then, would it really be worthwhile? These questions will probably stay unanswered, but they are certainly worth asking by both Easterners and Westerners.

To summarize: it is time that we acknowledged that the East has a culture of its own, its own religion. Eastern Europe was long supposed to suffer a kind of 'non-culture', negligible or even simply negative, undeserving of the label 'culture', designated instead as a 'system'.

Heathens Waiting to be Sermoned

There is another side to the management crusade in Eastern Europe. People reacted with solidarity and irony to administered symbols during martial law in Poland in the 1980s, and there is a treasured myth about Polish society as being particularly unsubmissive and ironic in the face of attempts at colonization. People pride themselves in the Polish history of contradiction and sarcasm: how the Poles made jokes during Nazi occupation, then during communism. This attitude seems to have been lost in recent developments. How has this come about?

One of the answers may be that the colonized somehow allow colonization though their passivity or even active expectations. A western academic told me a story about an aid project in which he was engaged. Before 1989 the Polish were eager to act as partners and he thought of that period as cooperation, even if the material support went in just one direction. The Poles offered other kinds of support and advice that the Westerners appreciated. After 1989 attitudes changed: the very same people began to expect to *be helped*, to be offered material support no longer as a link in cooperation but as a 'gift'. The story suggests a mysterious metamorphosis in the minds of people. The Westerners coming as missionaries are often not the same people who came in the 1980s to participate in the Polish experience of *Solidarność* and then martial law. These Westerners were remarkable people, coming to Poland to give and to take, to participate and to experience. Contemporary 'missionaries' are usually consultants, profit-minded and economically oriented. The 'disciples' are typically not the same people who cooperated with the Westerners during the 1980s. Those were dissidents, workers, academics, people dissatisfied with the regime. Today's disciples are managers, Polish consultants, also economically oriented. However, the metamorphosis of societal attitudes at large remains a reality.

The phenomenon certainly has complex roots, which can be traced to feelings of helplessness revealed by public polls (CBOS, 1993–July 1994), Polish myths about 'rich western society', attitudes that the communist era has successfully developed in people: that the 'rich' should give to the 'poor' who just have to take and nothing more. However, the picture again reminds one of the proud Native American cultures, that nevertheless gave up their dignity when western missionaries came to preach to them about the white man's conditions. The Polish people have long believed that the western god is more powerful: his or her disciples are rich, happy and young. When the Wall fell down (who knows? maybe it was the western god who performed this miracle?), the Easterners resolved to acquiesce, 'open their minds', and this is precisely a question of faith, to which I shall return in my conclusion. According to the framework presented in this paper they do this also because of their autonomous need of a religion. They want not only all the goods, but the whole symbolic sphere that is associated with them. Who would care so much for a Rolex watch if it were not part of a highly developed and attractive symbolic lifestyle?

Conclusions: Toward Syncretic-polyphonic Management Learning

In modern society, religious needs are being fulfilled in a superficial way by organization and especially the business organization. The modern religion of business administration with economic rationality as god has long served as a surrogate for deeper spiritual experiences. It is now being transferred to Eastern Europe, trying to find a model for organization of social life after the fall of communism. I have described this process as mission. The uni-directional communication is not only an imperfection and a relative loss of values that the East Europeans could offer their western neighbours. West-erners probably need these values as much as the Easterners need western experiences. The fact that the communication is so intense (as the metaphor of 'mission' suggests) and uni-directional also means that we all are likely to lose some important values forever. If the East Europeans convert, there will be nowhere to look for the values given up and nobody to learn from.

Another important conclusion concerns attitudes to democracy. People in Poland associate the free market with democracy. When they finally recognize the current situation as colonization and start to resist it, they may refuse to believe in democracy as well. The attitudes toward free market and democ-racy are already worsening, as public opinion surveys show (CBOS, 1993–July 1994). In a recent survey a majority declared that Polish democracy was faulty. While 62 percent said that in principle they were for democracy, as many as 37 percent considered dictatorship as necessary 'in certain cases'. The same percentage claimed that they would welcome a 'strong person' as Poland's leader (CBOS, 1993–July 1994: 5–18). This parallels people's growing disillusion with the free market, as a source of injustice rather than justice, oppression rather than freedom and poverty rather than wealth. The western god can be rejected just as easily as he or she was accepted. Together with the 'new rationality' all other values can be refused, among them democracy. The religious metaphor helps to identify this dimension of social reality, and perhaps provides a perspective to understand the dynamics that pervade it. Democracy and the culture of organization of a society are also about faith, and lost faith is not only a consequence of the deteriorating material situation. There is a need to believe common to humans, thus a readiness to trust and to distrust, beyond the obvious. These needs deserve to be taken more seriously.

It is of critical importance to rethink the management education project in Eastern Europe. The mission need not, and should not, continue as a crusade. The actors should be reconsidered for future participation: from the

West's side less profit oriented, more inclined to 'learn from the East' and from the East's side more oriented to active cooperation. The teaching programmes should also be re-evaluated and directed more toward joint learning, toward common construction of a religion including the values of East and West that can be shared in the future. This is what I call a 'syncretic-polyphonic' religion of business administration, a living construction based on mutual learning. Crusades and colonialism, even if based on strong faith in the 'one best way', are hardly seen as advantageous projects by contemporary western (and eastern) societies. It is my strong conviction that management learning in Eastern Europe should be urgently re-examined.

Acknowledgements

Thank you, Waldemar Wrzesiński, for your help with the historical queries I faced while working on this paper. And thanks, the participants of the Seminar *Sozialanthropologie von Europa im Wandel: Arbeit und Geschäft* organized by *Centre Marc Bloch* in Berlin on 2 Nov. 1994 for your insights, remarks and suggestions that helped me to revise a former draft of the paper.

Notes

1. Speaking of missionaries here, I mean only the lecturers and consultants who come to Poland on behalf of institutions and firms, pursuing well-defined and material interests, earning very good money, and coming with ready-made 'packages' of knowledge and know-how. There are lecturers who come for entirely different reasons and work with Polish partners, often in answer to their explicit questions and problems. I do not include them in my category of 'missionaries'.

2. Modern mission activity is familiar to me mainly through correspondence with a Catholic missionary working in New Guinea.

3. The Pláticas of Br. Bernardino de Sahagún, found by K. P. Pascual Saura and published in 1924 by P. Póu y Martí.

References

Alvesson, M. (1993) 'The Play of Metaphors', in J. Hassard and M. Parker (eds) *Postmodernism and Organizations*, pp. 114–31. London: Sage.

Berger, P. L. and Luckman, T. (1966/1983) *Społeczne tworzenie rzeczywistośI* (The social construction of reality). Warsaw: PIW.

Boulding, K. E. (1989a) 'Religijne perspektywy ekonomii' (Religious perspectives of economics), in J. Grosfeld (ed.) *Religia i ekonomia* (Religion and economy) pp. 48–62. Warsaw: PAX.

Boulding, K. E. (1989b) 'Religijne podstawy postepu ekonomicznego' (Religious foundations of economic development), in J. Grosfeld (ed.) *Religia i ekonomia* (Religion and economy), pp. 63–76. Warsaw: PAX.

Bowles, M. L. (1989) 'Myth, Meaning and Work Organization', *Organization Studies* 10(3): 405–21.

Bowles, M. L. (1992a) 'Maturation and Life in Organizations', working paper, Birmingham Polytechnic.

Bowles, M. L. (1992b) 'The Gods and Goddesses: Personifying Social Life in the Age of Organization', working paper, Birmingham Polytechnic.

Bowles, M. L. (1992c) 'Logos and Eros: The Vital Syzygy for Understanding Human Relations and Organizational Action', working paper, Birmingham Polytechnic.

CBOS (Center for Public Opinion Surveys) (1993–July 1994) *Servis informacyjny* (Information service). Warsaw: CBOS.

Clutterbuck, D. and Bickerstaffe, G. (1982) 'Where Have All the Management Gurus Gone?' *International Management* No. 1: 5–8.

Czarniawska-Joerges, B. (1991) 'Culture is the Medium of Life', in P. J. Frost, L. F. Moore, M. Reis Lois, C. C. Lundberg and J. Martin (eds) *Reframing Organizational Culture*, pp. 285–97. Beverly Hills, CA: Sage.

Czarniawska-Joerges, B. (1992) 'Doing Interpretive Studies of Organizations', working paper (8), Lund University, Institute of Economic Research.

Czarniawska-Joerges, B. (1993) *The Three-dimensional Organization: A Constructionist View.* Lund: Studentlitteratur.

Czarniawska-Joerges, B. and Kunda, G. (1992) 'Socialization Into Modernity; On Organizational Acculturation in Infantocracies', working paper (1), Lund University, Institute of Economic Research.

Deal, T. E. and Kennedy, A. A. (1982) *Corporate Culture.* Reading, MA: Addison-Wesley.

Fromm, E. (1989) *Mieć czy być: Duchowe podstawy nowego społeczeństwa* (To have or to be: the spiritual foundations of the new society). Warsaw: Klub Otrycki.

Furusten, S. (1992) 'Management Books: Guardians of the Myth of Leadership', dissertation, Uppsala University, Department of Business Studies.

Geertz, C. (1973) *The Interpretation of Cultures.* New York: Basic Books.

Giddens, A. (1991) *Modernity and Self-identity: Self and Society in the Late Modern Age.* Cambridge: Polity Press.

Hunermann, G. (1961) *Histoire des Missions: Grandes figures missionaires. Vol. 2 Tempête de feu sur l'Asie.* Casterman/Paris/Tournai: Editions Dalvator-Mulhouse.

Höpfl, H. (1994) 'The Paradoxical Gravity of Planned Organizational Change', paper presented at SCOS Conference, Calgary, June.

Jankowicz, A. D. (1994) 'Parcels From Abroad: The Transfer of Meaning to Eastern Europe', *Journal of European Business Education* 3(2): 1–19.

Jung, C. G. (1968) *The Archetypes and the Collective Unconscious*, Vol. 9/1. London: Routledge & Kegan Paul.

Kołakowski, L. (1967) *Kultura i fetysze* (Culture and fetishes). Warsaw: PWN.

Kołakowski, L. (1984) *Czy diabeł może być zbawiony i 27 innych kazań* (Can the devil be saved? and 27 other sermons). London: Aneks.

Kołakowski, L. (1988) *Jeśli Boga nie ma . . .* (Religion: If there is no God . . .). Kraków: Znak.

Kołakowski, L. (1989a) *Pochwała niekonsekwencji: Pisma rozproszone z lat 1955–1968* (The praise of inconsequence: Dispersed works from 1955–1968), Vol. 2. London: Puls.

Kołakowski, L. (1989b) *Pochwała niekonsekwencji: Pisma rozproszone z lat 1955–1968* (The praise of inconsequence: Dispersed works from 1955–1968), Vol. 3. London: Puls.

Kołakowski, L. (1994) *Obecność mitu* (Presence of myth). Wrocław: Wydawnictwo Dolnośląkie.

Kostera, J. (1992) *Report: The Polish Economy 2nd Quarter 1992.* Warsaw.

Kostera, M., Proppé M. and Szatkowski, M. (1994) 'Beyond the Social Role: The Case of Polish Professional Women', *Scandinavian Journal of Management* 10(2): 99–116.

Kostera, M. and Wicha, M. (1994) 'Ponad blokami: Organizacja i otoczenie', *Przegląd Organizacji* 2: 7–10.

Latour, B. (1986) 'The Powers of Association', in J. Law (ed.) *Power, Action and Belief. A New Sociology of Power?* London: Routledge & Kegan Paul.

McCormack, M. (1986) *What They Don't Teach You at Harvard Business School.* Glasgow: William Collins.

Morgan, G. (1986) *Images of Organization.* London: Sage.

Nowakowska, E. (1993) 'Rynek mózgów' (The brains-market), *Polityka* 18/1878: 12–13.

Orgogozo, I. (1992) 'European Management: Steering the Future Towards the Present', *Futures* (July/August): 593–603.

Pascale, R. T. and Athos, A. G. (1982) *The Art of Japanese Management.* Reading, MA: Cox & Wyman.

Peters, T. and Waterman, R. (1986) *In Search of Excellence: Lessons From America's Best-run Companies*. Sydney: Harper & Row.

Ricard, R. (1933) 'La "conquête spirituelle" du Mexique: missionaires des ordres Mendiants en Nouvelle-Espagne de 1523–24 à 1572', thesis, Paris: Institut d'Ethnologie.

Schütz, A. (1966) 'Studies in phenomenological philosophy I', in A. Schütz (ed.) *Collected papers*, Vol. 3. The Hague: Nijhoff.

Schütz, A. (1982) *Life Forms and Meaning Structure*. London: Routledge & Kegan Paul.

Schütz, A. and Luckmann, T. (1973) *The Structures of the Life-world*. Evanston, IL: Northwestern University Press.

Schwartz, H. S. (1987) 'Anti-social Actions of Committed Organizational Participants: An Existential Psychoanalytic Perspective', *Organization Studies* 8(4): 327–40.

Sievers, B. (1986) 'Beyond the Surrogate of Motivation', *Organization Studies* 7(4): 335–51.

Sievers, B. (1988) 'I Will Not Let Thee Go, Except You Bless Me! Some Considerations About the Constitution of Authority, Inheritance and Succession', working paper, Gesamthochschule Wuppertal.

Si-ing, Liang (1940) 'La rencontre et le conflit entre les idées missionaires chrétiens et les idées des Chinois en Chine depuis la fin de la dynastie des Ming', thesis, Paris: Les Editions Domat-Monchrestien.

Smircich, L. (1983) 'Concepts of Culture and Organizational Analysis', *Administrative Science Quarterly* 28(3): 339–58.

Smircich, L. (1987) 'Studying Organizations as Cultures', in G. Morgan (ed.) *Beyond Method: Strategies for Social Research*. Beverly Hills, CA/London/New Delhi: Sage.

Staniszkis, J. (1989) *Ontologia socjalizmu* (The ontology of socialism). Warsaw: In Plus.

Stein, P. (1989) 'O niektórych związkach religii z gospodarką', (On some connections between religion and economy), in J. Grosfeld (ed.) *Religia i ekonomia* (Religion and economy), pp. 157–91. Warsaw: PAX.

Turner, B. A. (1986) 'Sociological Aspects of Organizational Symbolism', *Organization Studies* 7(2): 101–15.

Turner, B. A., ed. (1990) *Organizational Symbolism*. Berlin/New York: Walter de Gruyter.

Van Maanen, J. and Kunda, G. (1989) 'Real Feelings: Emotional Expression and Organizational Culture', *Research in Organizational Behavior* 11: 43–103.

Wesołowski, W. and Wnuk-Lipiński, E. (1992) 'Transformation of Social Order and Legitimization of Power', in W. Connor and P. Płoszajski (eds) *Escape from Socialism. The Polish Route*. Warsaw: IFiS.

Wójcik, W. (1974) *Nie zabijaj Indianina – czyli rzecz o dwóch kulturach* (Don't kill an Indian, or the story of two cultures). Warsaw: LSW.

part six

Beyond Management Learning

18

Steve McKenna

Learning through Complexity

Over the last 15 years or so it has become common currency that the days of the middle manager are numbered as organizations downsize, retrench, restructure, de-specialize and become process driven. In this context, middle management redundancy has indeed increased and what is expected of those who remain has changed when compared with the previously unidimensional and hierarchical model of such managers (Peters and Waterman, 1982; Peters, 1987, 1992). Despite this, middle managers remain vital to many organizations while an ongoing debate about their role in global corporations and smaller organizations continues as we head towards the 21st century. These issues are captured in the ongoing debate about management itself (Boyatsis, 1982; Dopson and Stewart, 1991; Earl, 1983; Hales, 1986; Handy, 1987; Mangham and Pye, 1991; Reed, 1989; Scase and Goffee, 1989; Silver, 1991; Stewart, 1989, 1991; Westley, 1990; Whitley, 1989). In addition, some writers argue that to distinguish 'middle' management from other levels of management is artificial and they prefer to treat 'management' in a holistic, undifferentiated activity (Watson, 1994).

Watson (1994) also helpfully identifies three ways in which the word management is often used. First, *management as a function.* This refers to the overall 'steering or directing of an organization'. Second, *management as activities*; 'carried out in order to bring about the overall steering or directing of the organization'. Third, *management as a team of people,* 'a group of people responsible for steering or directing the organization through carrying out the various activities which makes this possible'. This is a useful distinction which helps to identify how 'management' is being referred to in this article. A point to which we shall return.

Watson's (1994 and 1996) work with managers is particularly helpful in its use of ethnographic methodology in the study of management. This approach emphasizes the importance of 'getting underneath' management and discovering by working closely with them, how managers think and how they *develop* their thoughts. The dilemma for many managers, Watson argues, arises from having 'to cope with the imposition of strategic and operating decisions by what was sometimes called the "top table"'. He goes on to argue that managers are subjected to pressures arising from complexity and the need to be in control of this complexity that leads to '*paradoxes of consequences*' perhaps more familiar as 'negative feedback loops' – the idea that a chosen decision may undermine the desired end rather than assist in its achievement

(Senge, 1990; Stacey, 1996). In short, managers are continuously confronted with the need to control situations and to control or attempt to exert control over others, not only physically but also psychologically. Indeed, the issue of 'control' is itself an important subject of debate in management and organizational thinking. In particular it could be argued that the obsession with control actually limits the extent to which order emerges from apparently disorderly, chaotic circumstances (see Stacey, 1996; Morgan, 1997). It is this 'complexity', and the attempts of managers and their advisers to make sense of it, that is discussed in this article.

Environmental Turbulence, Organizational Change and Complexity

The extent to which environmental turbulence is impacting on organizational structures and cultures and creating complexity is generally well argued, although it is not without its critics. Whether it is the transformation of the public sector to a more customer-focused, efficiency driven machine; or through the re-engineering of processes and customer-supply chain Total Quality Management in the private sector to meet an increasingly globally competitive environment, the implications of change seem to be clear.

First, organizational structures need to become more flexible and adaptable, changing constantly to reflect the array of new interrelationships, patterns and ambiguities that form, re-form, and emerge from a rapidly changing environment. Second, the globalization of business is bringing together distinct national and organizational cultures through strategic alliances and joint ventures as companies seek to share risks and costs of R&D and gain access to markets. Third, an increasingly turbulent environment requires increasingly proactive organizations. This requires a more 'middle-up' approach to strategy development and planning and/or *strategic thinking* rather than developing plans in the formal sense (Stacey, 1990, 1992, 1993, 1996). Fourth, the development of people in the future will be concerned with 'empowerment'; that is, developing the abilities of people and their willingness and opportunities to contribute innovatively and creatively to the organization. In particular managers at all levels will need to be aware of how to create the organization's future, which will involve an increasingly sophisticated awareness of stakeholders and their needs (Block, 1987, 1993; Greenley and Foxhall, 1996; Hamilton and Clarke, 1996; McDermott and Chan, 1996; Mitchell, Agle and Wood, 1997; Rowley, 1997). Furthermore, it is important to note that organizations exist within a system of 'mutual causality' and can proactively effect change in their environments. They are not simply passive reactors adapting to change, but actively shape environmental conditions in which decisions are made.

The complexity that is embodied in the four implications of change outlined above will impact directly on middle managers. To understand how this increasing uncertainty affects middle managers, three hi-tech communications based businesses decided to initiate a joint project with the objective of:

1. Determining middle managers perception of 'what was going on' in a situation of uncertainty.
2. Identifying the specific needs of and issues that concerned middle managers and assisting them in coping with 'what was going on' and helping them to make sense of it.
3. Designing and building an approach to help middle managers not only cope with and make sense of complexity, but which also had the objective of producing *generative learning*. It was felt that in the future this would enable them to cope with complexity themselves through a better understanding of the issues and problems within their 'reality'.

Of the three companies one is a major North American telecommunications company involved in the research and development, design and manufacture of software and hardware for the telecommunications industry. This includes international gateway switches, underwater cables and telephones and satellite communications. The second company is a British provider of communication services. The third company is also British and is involved in multimedia applications and computer design and manufacture. The companies have a great deal of synergy in the context of the developing telecommunications industry. They are well established in the industry and are regarded as major international players. Together they represent a worldwide employee strength of over 140,000 and combined revenues of US$40 billion.

Determining Middle Managers' Perceptions of 'What Was Going On'

The initial part of the project was an extensive needs analysis in the three organizations. A questionnaire was designed which 350 middle managers were asked to complete. Of these 159 were interviewed. A number of areas of concern were identified as important in an increasingly uncertain environmental and organizational situation. The author was Development Advisor to Senior Management, reporting to the President, Europe of the North American corporation when this project was carried out. His associates were in similar positions in the cooperating companies. The objectives of the project focused very clearly on adding value to the businesses in the fast changing environments in which they operated, primarily through an attempt to develop new 'mental models'. Selling this idea to senior management in all three organizations was difficult. It involved a variety of political manoeuvrings, coalition building and stakeholder 'buy in'. Indeed, the process of design implementation took place only after a complex and complicated web of organizational dynamics and interaction. It was an enormously difficult challenge.

The areas of concern that emerged from the needs analysis can be classified under four headings.

1. Complexity

A key focus of managerial activity is 'getting things done'. However, the problem with greater complexity in the organizational and business environment, as it is perceived by managers, is that it becomes difficult to 'get things done', or to think that things are 'getting done'. This was a key discovery in the needs analysis. In our discussions with managers they referred to the problems of managing in an ambiguous environment, with constant change and 'multiple mandates' in the 'spaghetti organization' (matrix). Getting 'things done', they argued, was becoming increasingly difficult.

Moreover, managers were concerned with how to exert 'power and influence'. They felt that making 'things happen' was becoming more difficult in a situation where 'straightline' directing and reporting were less important. Furthermore, the matrix structure augmented the need to worry about multi-site working which had implications for team building, communication and networking.

2. Strategy Concerns

The interviews highlighted how managers felt as if they were 'dangling in mid air'. They reported a lack of clarity in overall corporate strategy and divisional and product/market strategies. They felt that the connection between corporate, divisional and competitive strategies was vague and that they had problems establishing operational objectives for their operational managers. In particular, they indicated a desire to set objectives that were integrated with higher level strategies, but felt this was impossible because of the vacuum that existed in their knowledge of 'bigger issues'.

3. Structural and Cultural Concerns

Structural attempts to introduce matrix operations may cause 'cultural clashes' both organizationally and nationally in a global company. Middle managers reported being very anxious about the issues involved in establishing cross-functional understanding and building more effective and productive working relationships. It was generally considered to be a time-consuming exercise, made worse by global operations and joint venture and strategic alliance developments.

4. People Concerns

Concerns about people cut through the concerns about complexity, strategy and structure/culture. Generally, managers were concerned about the development of their subordinates. They wanted to be respected by their staff and to create an environment of 'empowerment', even though many of them were unclear about what this meant in practice, and how it may differ from 'delegation'.

In the highly competitive, fast changing world of the telecommunications/multimedia industry, these concerns are perceived as real with no readily available solutions. This is an issue of particular concern when we consider that a good deal of evidence shows that *lack of control* over work can cause anxiety, depression, mental illness and heart problems (Argyle, 1989; Warr, 1987). As Watson (1994: 16) summarizes, 'the world is an essentially ambiguous place in which we cannot realistically make detailed plans'. Complexity, ambiguity, uncertainty and discontinuity are features of organizational life compounded by the constant changes which are a necessary part of ongoing adjustments.

The problems that Watson's (1994: 131) ZTC managers had with strategy formulation and their role in it, mirror the findings from the needs analysis undertaken in the three companies reported here. Indeed, managers were sceptical about the extent to which senior executives understood the companies' strategies. At one joint management development programme operated by the companies involved, a Senior Vice President for Marketing had stated that the *strategy formulation process* needed to be more 'bottom up'; what Stacey (1990, 1992, 1993, 1996) among others has referred to as the process of 'self-organization'. Furthermore, the debate engaged by Watson's ZTC managers over 'loose–tight' structure closely resembles comments and issues raised among the managers in the three companies (1994: 145–9).

Finally, discussions with managers in the three companies were also similar to the discussions reported by Watson in other ways (pp. 118–20). There was tension, or 'discourse' in the minds of managers between believing that 'personal development', 'empowerment' and so on were important, and the extent to which *they* were 'empowered'. They also questioned whether, in fact, they had *any* control over what was going on. This, I believe, reflects a classic dilemma of the difficulty involved in distinguishing *empowerment* from *delegation*. If a clear strategy is established by the organization and its implementation is systematically outlined through plans and goals and passed down, *specific responsibilities can* be *delegated*. When *empowerment* is confused with *delegation* there is a search for an *order* that does not exist, which compounds feelings of lack of control. The need for *empowerment* to be clearly defined reflects the essence of the problem. This is represented in Figure 1.

Organizations that are subject to constant change and a complex environment will need to deal with this complexity. However, in order to do this managers must be able to make sense of it and to create ways of working within it. Managers can only *manage meanings and create learning contexts*, if they can make sense of the reality within which they operate. This presents a particularly challenging management development and learning problem, particularly when there are many possible meanings that can be attached to the circumstances in which managers find themselves.

Identifying Specific Needs that Should be Met to Assist Middle Managers with Coping

The nature of the identified management development and learning issues outlined above, required an approach that goes beyond the traditional menu

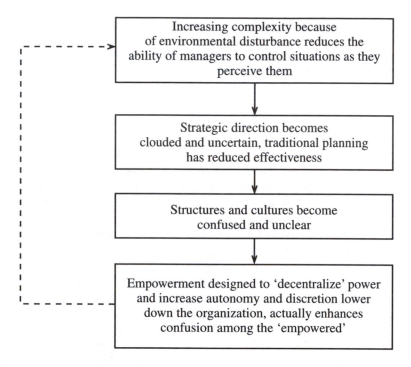

Figure 1   *The negative feedback loop of complexity*

driven approach to management 'training'. Indeed, traditional management development and 'training' is only of use for 'traditional management' (see below). The extraordinary circumstances in which managers now find themselves require new approaches to management learning that supersede those that have previously been used. In particular, three objectives were established for the design of 'events' to meet the needs of the managers and organizations reviewed in this article.

1.   To challenge assumptions and paradigms.
2.   To stretch managers beyond their comfort zone.
3.   To enlighten managers rather than refresh.

1. Challenging Paradigms and Assumptions

It is a given that all management development and learning should be based on an analysis of the business/organization and the managers' needs. However, a problem of turning these needs into the reality of a designed 'event' is that it often becomes an attempt to be all things to all managers or, in the long term, becoming an 'off-the-shelf' delivery. Consequently, the relevance of the programme *for the individual manager* becomes diluted. Ideally an event is required which satisfies generic development and business issues and the immediate reality of a particular manager's situation.

For example, managers in the three organizations were acutely aware of the 'new' and threatening nature of the business environment in which they were operating. They were also acutely aware of the fact that it required cross-functional and cross-global working. However, the tangibility of this message is limited unless it can be specifically related to the participants' circumstances. Questions that managers will be asking are:

- What issues arise from my own reality that prevent me from operating in a more effective way?
- How can I use an understanding of my reality to increase my effectiveness?
- What issues within my reality do I need to concern myself with to be more effective?
- Are these issues psychological, behavioural, interpersonal, structural?
- Where can I focus my attention to make sense of the complexity I'm in?
- Where can I manage and think strategically in my reality?
- What prevents my empowerment? Can I become less dependent and, if so, how?

Confronting these and many other questions will necessarily lead to challenging assumptions and paradigms, both personal and organizational. In addition, and more vitally, dealing with these questions 'at the coalface' brings the issues very much into focus. First, for example, if managers do not recognize that their perception of others is a barrier to cross-functional working, they need to be confronted with it, preferably by coming to the conclusion themselves through analysis of their perceived reality. Second, a view may develop over time in marketing and sales that R&D can never deliver on time. If this view has become institutionalized it will negatively influence relationships between these two functions, with the customer being squeezed in the middle. Third, to what extent might managers be driven by entirely human, yet often unproductive conflict with one another that leads to a permanent state of argumentative readiness, or avoidance?

A good deal of managers' time is spent in these psychological states and organizational impasses. Dealing with them requires a reality based and personally specific approach that questions assumptions and paradigms.

2. Stretch Managers Beyond their Comfort Zone

There are many insights into the learning processes of people that have come from psychological research and study (for a summary see Mullins, 1994). The work of Kolb (1985) and Kolb et al. (1984) has had an important influence on approaches to learning, particularly the learning cycle model of the relationship between *concrete experiences, observations and reflections, the development of conceptualizations and generalizations, and testing the implications of concepts in new situations.* The Kolb model was an important influence on the project team. However, the team also recognized the need to move management from their present 'comfort zone' and into a 'stretch zone'. Going beyond assumptions and paradigms required 'stretching'. Our definition of a 'stretch zone' was related to *learning that was insightful and meaningful for the manager, but may have also been uncomfortable.* Such insights might occur, in the complexity of the manager's world, at a number of levels:

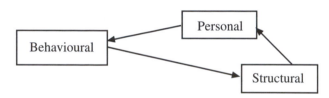

In order to gain meaningful data on the complexity of the manager's world a *mechanism* needed to be created to assist in the clear identification of issues and problems that managers faced. In addition, surfacing issues or diagnosing problems only to avoid treating them would have been worse than ignoring the problems altogether. In short, the diagnosis may be difficult, the patient may be in a lot of trouble, but terminal decline is not an option; this makes for difficult and uncomfortable treatments. Neurotic, unhealthy organizations avoid such traumas, learning organizations do not.

3. Enlightenment Not Refreshment

A remarkable feature of the factors that threatened American industry during the 1970s and 1980s was the extent to which the threats came from where they were least expected. For example, the Japanese selling small motorbikes to Americans; Americans buying small cars; Canon producing photocopiers cheaper than Xerox could produce them; innovative technologies in photography and in personal computing, and so on. The case study literature is replete with examples of management mistakes that were made during this period and which were related to complacency, conceit, etc.

In this respect *enlightenment* is far more useful to management than refreshment. Refreshment reflects an image that all the old messages were correct; that we need to get 'back to basics' and start again. Enlightenment, however, concerns quite literally, freedom from superstition; the superstition that somewhere in the past the 'truth' existed in the 'outside' world. This is, of course, very different from the European philosophical and social movement of the same name. Indeed, our approach to management development represents a reaction against the 'Age of Reason' and scientific rationalism and enlightenment, toward the idea that organizations and people in them are essentially irrational. This enlightenment may occur in a number of ways, or not at all. The search for it, however, is extremely important.

Designing and Developing a Mechanism to Meet these Needs

The mechanism developed in order to achieve the objectives outlined above was the *complexity map*. The concept of the map and its use as a tool had a number of purposes.

1. The map would be a clear representation of the perceived reality and complexity of managers who were participating in the developmental event. It was a snapshot of how a manager's needs and concerns were intimately connected with the map and how they could be deduced from it.

2. The map was a diagnostic tool for identifying personal, behavioural and interpersonal, and structural issues that a particular manager faced.

3. The map was a source of developmental insights that could be used as a foundation for personal growth and development and for making sense of complexity. In short, the interplay of personal, interpersonal and structural forces as they influenced the job of management and 'getting things done' could be investigated in the events/forums where the complexity map was used. In addition, the group of managers in any particular forum could offer insights to others on the best way to manage and make sense of their complexity.

The *complexity map* was the central feature of countless learning events/forums that were facilitated by the author and others with the three companies around the world. Many hundreds of maps have now been constructed. The mechanism designed for developmental activities treated management as primarily a set of *activities and interactions*. These activities are aimed at 'getting things done' and adding value to the business. However to add value, sense needs to be made of complexity, which cannot be controlled in a traditional management sense but it does need to be understood. This requires *extraordinary management* within organizations. Such management is concerned with change and creating the new, 'to provoke and confront the ambiguities and the conflicting forces that are its nature' (Stacey, 1993: 378). The complexity map also emphasizes, following Ackoff (1994), that 'the performance of systems, including corporations, is not the sum of the performance of its parts taken separately, but the product of their inter-actions'.

Stacey goes on to outline how innovation, ideas and action occur, not in the formal but in the *informal* organization. The informal organization is a labyrinth of webs or maps which form the relationships and interrelationships that managers and their teams have with others in the organization and other external stakeholders. These relationships though not formally charted are powerful and important. It is within this network that people will create and destroy, will act and innovate, will excite and neglect. Furthermore, the failure to recognize the importance of this network and its creative potential, will perpetuate dominance of the formal organization and the continuing pre-eminence of outmoded ways of managing. In a later work Stacey (1996) identifies creativity lying *at the edge of personal disintegration* in a psychoanalytic sense, while organizational creativity lies *between the legitimate and shadow systems* in organizations.

The *complexity map* is a representation of the informal or shadow organization. It brings it to life for those for whom it is a reality. If creativity, innovation and ideas are indeed generated through this network, then it is important for managers to understand it better. Moreover, it is important for managers to attempt to make sense of this complexity – for their own well-being, as well as for sound organizational and business reasons.

The Complexity Map in Action: Case Histories

The more advanced the illness the more bitter the pill. Many complexity maps have been constructed as part of the treatment of middle managers in the respective organizations and in many others. From these the following case histories have been selected for explication. It will become clear that although they are unique cases, they are built around the four generic needs identified in the needs analysis; *complexity, strategy, structure and culture,* and *people.* They are real attempts to help managers deal with complex and ambiguous situations and as such reflect both success and failure. The causes of any individual manager's complexity may indeed, be too systemic to rectify without recognition that the problem is much deeper – such is the case in Melvin's complex world.

The two case histories outlined below represent unique sets of circumstances. The problems and issues reflected in each were also reflected in many other cases. It would be possible to build models based on the many cases observed up to this point. This may indeed prove to be an important theoretical contribution however it would not capture the emotional and psychic significance of the situations for Mike and Melvin. Other people, transplanted to the centre of the following 'complexities' may perceive each complexity entirely differently. Thus adopt *relativism* as the modus operandi and can, therefore, find no way of validating the relativistic perceptions of Mike or Melvin beyond their own 'standard of truth'.

Mike

Figure 2 represents Mike's organizational reality as he identified it.

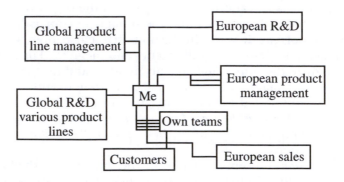

Figure 2   *Mike's complexity map*

Complexity

It is clear that Mike's organizational reality was complex. He had a variety of direct and indirect relationships and reporting structures which caused him anxiety and stress. He was particularly concerned that problems could arise that he would have to deal with in all of the elements of his complexity, as represented by the boxes. Furthermore, he felt that while he was trying to resolve the problems in one box, others would arise elsewhere that he would be unaware of. His complexity was often too much for him to *control* and he often experienced feelings of being overwhelmed.

Strategy

Mike felt that he would be able to manage the competing demands on his time and complexity better if he had help and guidance from the 'top' of the organization, particularly regarding how his energies and efforts were focused. He wanted to understand how he fitted into the 'bigger picture', and to spend less time on the exhausting and time consuming activities associated with others' needs and wants. In short, he believed he had to be too *operational*, rather than thinking strategically about his complexity. It was apparent from discussions with Mike that he felt a sense of hopelessness and powerlessness. He also felt quite strongly that this was the fault of someone 'out there'.

Structure and Culture

The operation of organizational structure was very confusing for Mike. He was never sure of the *formal hierarchy* that affected his situation, or indeed if one existed. He was wary of attempting to operate cross-functionally because he was never sure if he was transgressing protocols about who to inform and so on.

People Concerns

As well as the problems and issues Mike had with his inter-corporate networks, he was also responsible for four teams and had four managers reporting directly to him. This caused him considerable anxiety. He was only able to meet with them once a month; he had to establish priorities and discuss problems, make decisions and push on. He had 'no time to work on their development, and in any case, I need development myself'. It was a potentially vicious cycle of low performing management and teams.

Dealing with Mike's Complexity

Traditional approaches to help Mike deal with his complexity would emphasize the following:

- Network more effectively to build relationships that can help in dealing with difficulties.

- Find out where the company is planning to go and identify how you and your complexity fit in.
- Identify important actors and keep them apprised of your actions.
- Find quality time to spend with your staff.

Such advice might lead to action – attending courses on networking and communication; managing time more effectively and so on. However, Mike had tried some of these approaches but they had not helped to reduce his complexity.

Working with Mike at one of the management forums, it became clear that he had problems identifying how important the *informal/shadow organization* was and the part it played in his complexity and 'getting things done'. In addition he expected somebody else to put his problems right. However, when Mike was asked if the organization had ever helped him to solve problems he said it had not. When further asked why he should expect this now, he answered that he shouldn't, but he said that he had always had this expectation.

Helping Mike required a deeper appreciation of 'Mike' and how he influenced the way his complexity operated. During discussions about his complexity Mike admitted that he was introverted. He was extremely un-comfortable having to develop and build relationships, a key prerequisite of success in the corporation he was working for. In addition he had no means of working out how to empower himself to change this. To use Peter Block's (1993: 33) words 'we choose dependency when we avoid ownership and responsibility by never confronting our own wish for safety and the import-ance we give our own self-interest'. Mike avoided interaction whenever possible. This led to the creation of justifications and rationalizations as to why things were not happening; apportioning of blame to other parts of the business and people; constant demand for direction from above; fear of treading on the toes of others; and blaming his inability to get things done on insufficient time. In assessing Mike's reality we might suggest that his problems derived from a personal strategy of *avoidance*. The chain of events and unintended consequences are modelled in Figure 3.

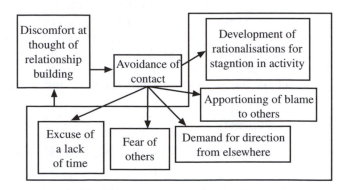

Figure 3   *The unintended consequences of Mike's strategy of interpersonal avoidance*

Helping Mike to deal with his complexity more effectively required recognition of the part he played in his problems. This meant making him aware of the avoidance strategy and confronting it. There would be no rapid solution to this problem. Mike would need help and support to overcome his tendency to withdraw and avoid people and situations. However, recognizing the problem is crucial in dealing with it.

2. Melvin

Figure 4 represents Melvin's complexity. In outlining this map a somewhat different approach will be taken than for Mike's. The emphasis here is on identifying the problems Melvin perceived he had with each of his constituents. His complexity and the problems within it were different from Mike's, but what is of particular interest is the *variety* of problems. As a customer services director Melvin had a wide range of interactions, all of which contributed to the effectiveness with which he dealt with customers. His complexity indicates how difficult it is to focus solely on *external customers* in customer services when servicing external customers effectively depends on satisfactory *internal customer* relationships and boundaries. Each element of Melvin's complexity will be examined in turn.

The Customer

A major problem in hi-tech organizations where primary R&D is conducted in North America and the products based on this technology are 'tweaked' for European markets, is that it creates a number of serious issues for local customer services. In a sense, this is a classic global–local issue. First, at source, (the R&D end) the customer is distanced from the product and the processes of product development. In localities other than where the primary R&D takes place this makes the product somewhat removed from the market

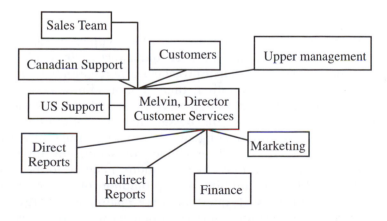

Figure 4   *Melvin's complexity map*

in which it is sold and, consequently, creates difficulties in fitting the two – market and product – neatly together around customer requirements.

Second, the gap between the apparently 'global' product and 'local' market widens as the company does not understand local and new markets. The need for economies of scale in R&D expenditure, which leads to the centralization of R&D activity on the assumption that the 'technology' and therefore the product is 'universal', is actually negatively offset by complex problems it creates for customer services and other functional areas at the local level. At the local level people are re-educating the customer to a 'universal' product, rather than meeting customer requirements. This was a key element of Melvin's complexity and made his role as Director of Customer Services extremely difficult. This fundamental problem was compounded in the rest of Melvin's complexity. The key issue for him was the mindset that assumed a 'universal' product would fit 'local' markets in Europe (see discussion of Melvin's complexity using a metaphorical analysis).

Sales Team and Marketing

Assumptions about global product uniformity were bound to affect the sales team. They had real difficulties understanding the product and its feasibility in the markets that they were selling to. Melvin felt that his situation was made much more difficult by sales and marketing promising a product that was simply unable to live up to established expectations. Once it had been marketed and sold, all the problems of feasibility would fall on customer services, who ultimately had to deal with incompatibilities and oversold expectations. This led to severe problems of *communication* between customer services and marketing and sales which in turn led to a significant 'head in the sand' mentality. Instead of dealing with the problems collectively, each function decided to do its bit and pass the 'hot potato' on. Melvin believed the problem would ultimately rest on him.

Upper Management

Melvin's view of upper management's role in his complexity was interesting. In this particular product area they were ultimately accountable to North American senior management. They projected a perception of the problem as inept marketing and sales rather than a more fundamental issue of product–market incongruity – although Melvin believed that this was political expedience. In discussions with his bosses they had admitted significant problems with product–market incongruity, but that the situation was unlikely to improve because there was little chance of significant investment in primary R&D activity in Europe. Key questions needed to be addressed relating to the viability of continuing with promotion of the product under these conditions. However, such questions were *undiscussable* (Argyris, 1982). This meant that costly customer service problems were inevitable in both tangible financial terms and in company prestige and image.

Canadian and US Support

As one would expect, the problems outlined above made for very difficult relations with North American technical support. Relaying messages of product incompatibility and seeking support from R&D and North American customer services that did not have the European markets as a priority, created enormous problems. Taking *responsibility* became an issue. The fact that the product was not a 'runner', and was recognized as such by North American R&D support and European product line management, sales and marketing, and customer services would make taking responsibility particularly unattractive. In short, nobody wanted to accept ownership and discussion of the *assignment of responsibilities* became another source of conflict, tension and *undiscussability.*

Indirect Reports

The major problems outlined above were reflected in the minutiae of day to day management for Melvin, especially with his indirect reports. Melvin had project management responsibility cross-nationally and cross-functionally but was managing an unmanageable situation, and managing those who realized this to be the case. This exacerbated the already difficult problems of managing to the extent of making it impossible. Melvin felt impotent to manage indirect reports within the context of the key *undiscussability* that pervaded his complexity. This left him feeling that a good deal of his time was completely wasted and left him with a sense of hopelessness.

Dealing with Melvin's Complexity

Raising the issues involved in Melvin's complexity solves few problems, but identifies many (Figure 5). Not least of these is the crucially *undiscussable* problem of 'product–market synergy'. The challenge for Melvin is to find a way of raising this issue in circles where the relevant decisions will ultimately

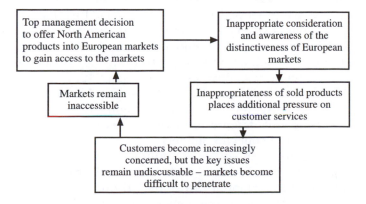

Figure 5   *The negative feedback loop that exists in Melvin's complexity*

be made. This has been difficult for Melvin. The irony is that while the organization continues to have customer service problems because of the introduction of products that do not fit markets, the end result is likely to be the same as if appropriate decisions were made about the problems. That is, either further R&D investment in appropriate market oriented technologies (an unlikely occurrence), or pulling out of the costly market. The current situation of operating in markets with an apparently inappropriate product represents a decision based on a 'reality' other than Melvin's and on something other than *rationality*. It could be an example of a sequence of *skilled incompetence, cover-ups and defensive routines*, which are manifested in the activities of much of Melvin's complexity.

The Usefulness of the Complexity Map

Complexity maps constructed in 'learning events do not provide easy answers to complex issues. However, they do clarify, qualify, support, re-orientate and sometimes amaze the *constructor*. Indeed, the maps may often highlight how an individual's complexity is part of a history of *cover-up and defensiveness*. At other times, the maps offer insights and ways forward, sometimes at a personal level. They present participants with an opportunity to assess their reality and think differently about it in the metaphorical style highlighted by Morgan (1997) and others (Oswick and Grant, 1996). In this sense it is therapeutic. Organizations need to give their management and other staff a regular opportunity to investigate and assess their complexity and experiences. Creating anything approaching a 'learning organization' requires no less than the opportunity to *reflect* and to be involved in *learning laboratories*. These reflections and laboratories need to be facilitated and mediated with the help of competent specialists. By working with the reality of middle managers, as they see it, 'real' insights can be gleaned by the managers themselves and more fundamental questions might be asked about why people, groups and organizations do the things that they do.

For example, let us look at the complexity of Mike and Melvin using the metaphorical analysis developed by Morgan (1997). In relation to Mike we suggest that his complexity can be understood through the *psychic prisons* metaphor; and in particular the Freudian defences of *denial, rationalization, projection* and so on, in such a way as to protect him against the discomfort he feels at having to build relationships. As Morgan (1997: 231) notes in his review of the work of Melanie Klein, 'it is possible to understand the structure, process, culture, and even the environment of an organization in terms of the unconscious defense mechanisms developed by its members to cope with individual and collective anxiety'.

However, as Figure 4 shows, the unintended consequences of Mike's *unconscious defence mechanisms* can be understood in terms of a *negative feedback loop* which connects the metaphor of psychic prisons to the metaphor of flux and transformations. Mike's unconscious is the cause of a negative feedback loop as it impacts on the management of his complexity. Furthermore, the degree to which Mike is able to *rationalize stagnation in activity, apportion blame on to others and use the excuse of a lack of time* (see Figure 4) indicates how the *culture* of the organization may be supporting such a strategy. In addition, here is an organization that has a weak 'DNA' structure (Morgan, 1997), without the capability to learn, and presently without individuals who know how to learn. This suggests a weakly performing organizational 'brain'.

In turn, we would expect that Mike's segment of the organization, his complexity, will increasingly 'drift out of alignment with the challenges of the external environment' (Morgan, 1997: 360). Increasingly, Mike's way of operating is likely to be driven by the politics of 'cover-up' and political manoeuvring, and thus a politicized set of circumstances develops within his complexity, which is related to the rationalization for stagnation of activity, apportioning of blame and so on. Figure 6 represents this dynamic interplay of metaphors.

The interplay of metaphors is itself a metaphor of flux and transformation – a negative feedback loop. Furthermore, the root metaphor used to critically evaluate Mike's complexity, that of psychic prisons, is only a beginning. A change in Mike's behaviour, for example, will elicit a reaction from those with whom he interacts, starting a whole new cycle of events that may be of benefit to him and his complexity, or may not. Here we have suggested that a positive change in Mike's complexity management and his ability to make sense of his 'world' might be possible through building awareness of the unconscious mechanisms that drive his behaviour. However, there are dangers in such a behavioural adjustment. For example, how would others now view the 'new' Mike; would they see his inability to 'socialize' as a weakness? Would we

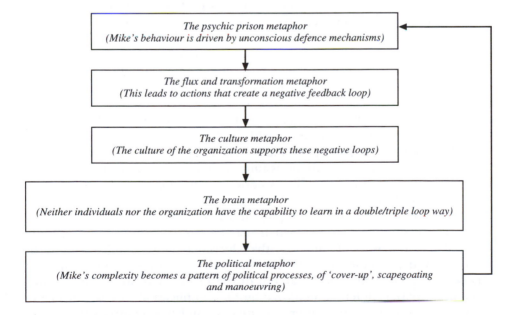

Figure 6   *The interplay of metaphors in Mike's complexity*

require all of those who are important to Mike's complexity to be undergoing the same programme as Mike? These are important questions that require further investigation.

Melvin's complexity (Figure 5) has a different root metaphor. His 'world' is an equally complex 'world', but a somewhat different metaphorical application is appropriate. We have to assume that the essence of his complexity, as he sees it, rests in decisions that have been made to introduce an inappropriate product into markets with which it lacks synergy. To Melvin this decision makes no sense; to those who have made it, however, it may make considerable sense. Let us consider a possibility, with the need to stress that this is a hypothetical development of the case.

The telecommunications environment is a rapidly changing one, with many new market opportunities opening up. In addition, the North American market is mature, offering few opportunities for product or market development. In this context and in an increasingly competitive global environment, it is important to realize market potential as quickly as possible and to at least be visible in the market place. Therefore the decision to be in the European market place may be best understood in the context of the *organism metaphor*. Unless the organization aligns itself with environmental changes, simply by being present in the market place, it will fall behind competitors.

While top management in North America may have been driven by the organism metaphor in decision making there seems to have been an inadequate consideration of other issues better understood using other metaphors. The decision to be in the market place created a *negative loop* that is represented in Figure 5. The flux and transformation metaphor helps us to identify the severe limitations of a decision based on *market presence rather than product–market synergy*. Indeed, the presence in the market place of inappropriate products and the fact that they are bought and require considerable customer service negates the initial decision. Here we have another example of the workings of a poor organizational brain (the brain metaphor) and possibly a view of the 'world' driven by a universalist *cultural* perspective. This, in turn, could be a reflection of a 'favored way of thinking ... which ... act as traps that confine individuals within socially constructed worlds and prevent the emergence of other worlds' (Morgan, 1997: 219). As Morgan recognizes, culture *is a form of* psychic prison, trapping us in ways of seeing. If North American top management assumes Britain is like Europe and Britain is like America, ergo Europe is like America. Technologies merely need to be 'tweaked' to fit different markets.

Overly simplistic though this argument seems, it has considerable hidden power. The prison is so strong (which may be constructed of cultural walls) that it shapes our ways of thinking, that decisions about doing business are often simplistically based on our culturally shaped 'ways of thinking' that imprison us. Our inability to break out of the prison reinforces the weakness of the brain power/potential deployed and the implications it has concerning learning; thus reinforcing other metaphors. Melvin's complexity as seen through a metaphorical analysis is represented in Figure 7.

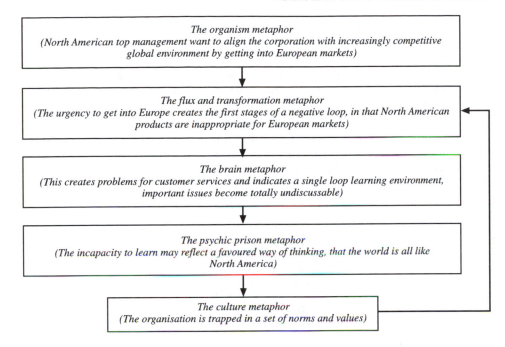

The organism metaphor
(North American top management want to align the corporation with increasingly competitive global environment by getting into European markets)

The flux and transformation metaphor
(The urgency to get into Europe creates the first stages of a negative loop, in that North American products are inappropriate for European markets)

The brain metaphor
(This creates problems for customer services and indicates a single loop learning environment, important issues become totally undiscussable)

The psychic prison metaphor
(The incapacity to learn may reflect a favoured way of thinking, that the world is all like North America)

The culture metaphor
(The organisation is trapped in a set of norms and values)

Figure 7   *The interplay of metaphors in Melvin's complexity*

Summary

The complexity map reflects a *postmodernist* approach to the development of managers and organizations in a broad sense. The use of a range of metaphors to understand the complexity of individuals and organizations is an attempt to move away from a purely objectivist, functionalist and managerialist approach towards an approach that recognizes the essentially chaotic, conflictual and diverse nature of organizations. Indeed, it is possible to go very much further in understanding human life in organizations in a postmodern way than I have chosen to do here. Burrell (1997: 25) in *Pandemonium* argues that to understand human life in organizations it is necessary to appreciate 'networks, markets, gift relationships and straightforward affection'. He further notes that: 'Human life is shaped by emotions such as hatred, fear, loathing, disgust and passion'.

What is important here is the 'logic of difference', which 'denies the belief that any single purpose can determine an organization's order' (Nodoushani, 1996). It is the network of relationships within which people find themselves that both restricts and liberates organizational activity. However, it should be stated that by imposing an explanation for the complexity of Mike and Melvin we may, in fact, be acting in a positivistic way. Perhaps from a *practical postmodernist* position, it is important to address organizational and management issues as socially fabricated, not through rationalist, linear approaches, but through the micro-political processes that form the chaos of organizations. Such an approach requires a considerable transformation in *ways of thinking* in organizations and is a mighty challenge for organizations in the future.

It is also a challenge for organization theory and behaviour and for those involved in the preparation and development of managers in modern organizations. To understand the non-rational shaping of organizations we need to encourage the participants to speak for themselves, but beyond mere description. They need to articulate the feeling, passion and emotion that does indeed influence the behaviour, interaction and experience of organizational life. This is several levels beneath the 'complexity map' and it is an important piece of 'work in progress'.

References

Ackoff, R.L. (1994) *The Democratic Corporation*. New York: Oxford University Press.
Argyle, M. (1989) *The Social Psychology of Work*. Harmondsworth: Penguin.
Argyris, C. (1982) *Reasoning, Learning and Action*. San Francisco: Jossey-Bass.
Block, P. (1987) *The Empowered Manager*. San Francisco: Jossey-Bass.
Block, P. (1993) *Stewardship*. San Francisco: Berrett-Koehler.
Boyatsis, R. (1982) *The Competent Manager*. New York: Wiley.
Burrell, G. (1997) *Pandemonium*. London: Sage.
Dopson, S. and Stewart, R. (1991) 'What is Happening to Middle Management? A Description of the Middle Managers' Situation', *British Journal of Management* 1: 3–16.
Earl, M.J. (ed.) (1983) *Perspectives on Management*. Oxford: Oxford University Press.
Greenley, G.E. and Foxhall, G.R. (1996) 'Consumer and Nonconsumer Stakeholder Orientation in UK companies', *Journal of Business Research* 35(2): 106–15.
Hales, C.P. (1986) 'What Do Managers Do? A Critical Review of the Evidence', *Journal of Management Studies* 23: 88–115.
Hamilton, L. and Clarke, T. (1996) 'The Stakeholder Approach to the Firm: A Practical Way Forward or a Rhetorical Flourish', *Career Development International* 1(2): 39–91.
Handy, C. (1987) *The Making of Managers*. London: NEDO.
Kolb, D. A. (1985) *Experiential Learning: Experience as a Source of Learning and Development*. New Jersey: Prentice-Hall.
Kolb, D.A., Rubin, I.M. and McIntyre, J.M. (1984) *Organizational Psychology: An Experiential Approach to Organizational Behaviour*. New Jersey: Prentice-Hall.
McDermott, M.C. and Chan, K.C. (1996) 'Flexible Intelligent Relationship Management: The Business Success Paradigm in a Stakeholder Society', *The Learning Organization* 3(3): 5–17.
Mangham, I.L. and Pye, A. (1991) *The Doing of Management*. Oxford: Blackwell.
Mitchell, R.K., Agle, B.R. and Wood, D.J. (1997) 'Toward a Theory of Stakeholder Identification and Salience: Defining the Principle of Who and What Really Counts', *Academy of Management Review* 22(4): 853–86.
Morgan, G. (1997) *Images of Organization*. London: Sage.
Mullins, L. (1994) *Management and Organizational Behaviour*. London: Pitman.
Nodoushani, O. (1996) 'The Problems and Prospects of Postmodern Management Discourse', *Management Learning* 27(3): 359–81.
Oswick, C. and Grant, D. (1996) *Organization Development*. London: Pitman.
Peters, T. (1987) *Thriving on Chaos*. New York: Pan.
Peters, T. (1992) *Liberation Management*. New York: Pan.
Peters, T. and Waterman, R. (1982) *In Search of Excellence*. New York: Harper & Row.
Reed, M.I. (1989) *The Sociology of Management*. Brighton: Harvester Wheatsheaf.
Rowley, T.J. 'Moving Beyond Dyadic Ties: A Network Theory of Stakeholder Influences', *Academy of Management Review* 22(4): 887–910.
Scase, R. and Goffee, R. (1989) *Reluctant Managers: Their Work and Lifestyles*. London: Unwin Hyman.

Senge, P. (1990) *The Fifth Discipline.* New York: Doubleday Currency.

Silver, M. (ed.) (1991) *Competent to Manage.* London: Routledge.

Stacey, R. (1990) *Dynamic Strategic Management for the 1990s.* London: Kogan Page.

Stacey, R. (1992) *Managing Chaos.* London: Kogan Page.

Stacey, R. (1993) *Strategic Management and Organizational Dynamics.* London: Pitman.

Stacey, R. (1996) *Complexity and Creativity in Organizations.* San Francisco: Berrett-Koehler.

Stewart, R. (1989) 'Studies of Managerial Jobs and Behaviour: the Way Forward', *Journal of Management Studies* 26(1): 1–10.

Stewart, R. (1991) *Managing Today and Tomorrow.* London: Macmillan.

Warr, P. (1987) 'Job Characteristics and Mental Health', in P. Warr (ed.) *Psychology at Work.* Harmondsworth: Penguin.

Watson, T.J. (1994) *In Search of Management.* London: Routledge.

Watson, T.J. (1996) 'How Do Managers Think? Identity, Morality and Pragmatism in Managerial Theory and Practice', *Management Learning* 27(3): 323–41.

Westley, F.R. (1990) 'Middle Managers and Strategy: Microdynamics of Inclusion', *Strategic Management Journal* 11: 337–51.

Whitley, R. (1989) 'On the Nature of Management Tasks and Skills', *Journal of Management Studies* 26(3): 209–24.

19

Denise Skinner, Clare Tagg and Jacky Holloway

Managers and Research
The Pros and Cons of Qualitative Approaches

Introduction

As academics based in three different institutions, teaching, researching and consulting in the field of management, we talk to hundreds of managers each year and read numerous reports that they have produced. Our collective observations and experience suggest that, while management researchers increasingly make use of qualitative techniques for eliciting and analysing data, practising managers (in Britain at least) tend to restrict themselves to quantitative approaches. Many managers undertake 'research' in the course of their work: in planning, problem solving, market research and decision-support, for example, they have to gather information in order to decide upon a course of action. The outcome of these choices frequently impacts not only upon the people within the organization, but outside in the wider community. Balancing the concerns of a number of different stakeholders requires a deep understanding of what may be a complex and ill-defined problem. Yet, when asked about their choices of tools for investigating and ameliorating work-based problems, managers often expressed concern that quantitative techniques were inadequate, but they were unaware of alternatives.

This paper reports on the first stage of research undertaken to explore the feasibility of managers using qualitative approaches within their normal work. It considers the experiences, including some of the frustrations, of practising managers in diverse organizations. The potential to use qualitative techniques in each of their current activities is explored and the pros and cons as perceived by the managers described. Within the paper 'The Context' draws on the literature to define our terms and to set the project in context. 'Methodology outlines the methodology adopted and 'Case Studies' describes the case studies and the managers' experiences of applying qualitative techniques. In 'Conclusion' we reflect on the cases to consider the practicalities of using qualitative approaches and the issues which need to be resolved if such approaches are to become widely used by managers.

The Context

In this research project our concern is primarily with those management tasks which managers themselves see as involving 'research' and which they feel require richer approaches than standard survey methods. Examples we have met include organizational change projects, evaluation of training schemes, organizational self-assessment and implementation of total quality management, consultation with stakeholders before a major capital development. Such projects are far from unusual: for example, in a survey of factors driving training programmes, over 80 percent of a sample of 500+ sites across most industrial sectors planned to implement significant organizational changes (Benchmark Research, 1994).

Managers as Researchers

Schön (1983) reminds us of the parallels between the experience of the research process and the reflection-in-action of managers trying to make sense of the unique phenomena before them, testing their intuitive understandings and reformulating their questions. Similarities also exist between the practical tasks of research and the 10 roles of managers identified by Mintzberg (1973). Most, if not all, of the roles require an ability to gather, interpret and then make appropriate use of the resultant data. The primary difference between managers and researchers is likely to be the purpose for which the investigation is carried out. Handy's (1985) analogy of manager as general practitioner recognizes the manager as the person who has to take local responsibility for recognizing that a problem exists, initiating diagnosis and prescribing treatment. He also reminds us of the ever present risk that the symptoms may be treated rather than the underlying condition; the same managerial prescription may be given, whatever the organizational disease, owing to a lack of awareness of, or commitment to, alternatives. Yet if today's managers need to undertake research and evaluation projects as part of their routine work, to what extent do they possess the necessary skills and understanding? How well does management education and training equip those who will be driving such projects to handle the 'softer' aspects, the perceptions of stakeholders and the need to assess their 'success' from a range of viewpoints?

In their critique of trends in management education, with its emphasis on rationality and technical competence, Reed and Anthony (1992) identify a fundamental disjunction between what is currently provided and the emerging 'reality of management, the prototype organizational profession.

A necessary competence in analytic skills and techniques does nothing to encourage a reflective understanding of the complexities and nuances of organizational relationships and distributed power, nor does it do much to develop a critical response to the vagaries of organizational and personal authority. (p. 603)

Reed and Anthony propose a fundamental re-orientation of management education (p. 608): 'They [managers] must be encouraged to think about the unprogrammable complexities which face them.'

This has particular significance for the development of the manager as researcher. Sources of guidance to managers embarking on general management studies (for example Cameron, 1991; Cameron and Pearce, 1995) rightly stress the importance of the development of confidence in using numbers and diagramming techniques. However, they do not place equivalent weight on skills for qualitative data collection, analysis or dissemination. This also appears to be true of many of the frameworks underpinning the formal development which today's middle and senior managers may have undergone. For example, those with a marketing or accountancy background, or those who have followed the NVQ routes based on the Management Charter Initiative (MCI) standards, will at least have been exposed to basic quantitative methods. However, the frameworks we have reviewed do not encourage qualitative investigation in any depth (ACCA, 1994; CIMA, 1995; IHSM, 1988; MCI, 1992). MBA programmes, which are increasingly popular as a generalist qualification to complement first degree or professional specialisms, appear rarely to cover qualitative methods in any depth in their syllabi.

What is Qualitative Research and What Can it Offer?

Quantitative techniques focus on the measuring of things that can be counted 'using predetermined categories that can be treated as interval or ordinal data and subjected to statistical analysis' (Patton, 1997: 273). Typically within organizations such data are gathered through surveys, questionnaires and tests. Results are precise and easily comparable.

Qualitative research focuses on people's experiences and the meanings they place on the events, processes and structures of their normal social setting. Such research may involve prolonged or intense contact with people and groups in their everyday situations. This provides an holistic view, through the participants' own words and perceptions, of how they understand, account for and act within these situations (Miles and Huberman, 1994). The data collected may be in the form of spoken or written words, unconstrained by predetermined standardized categories. Thus qualitative data 'focuses on *naturally occurring, ordinary events in natural settings*, so that we have a strong handle on what "real life" is like' (p. 10, emphasis in original).

Marshall and Rossman (1995) describe qualitative research as being particularly valuable for research that seeks to explore real organizational goals, linkages and processes in organizations; to understand the failure of policies and practices. Finally, Miles and Huberman (1994: 10) note that 'qualitative data are useful when one needs to supplement, validate, explain, illuminate, or reinterpret quantitative data gathered from the same setting.'

Within the qualitative field the inquirer's belief system or world view is recognized as an important influence upon the research, intrinsically linked to ontological, epistemological and methodological assumptions. Guba and

Lincoln (1994) identify four inquiry paradigms: positivism, post-positivism, critical theory and constructivism. The paradigms reflect different perceptions about the nature of reality, the means by which it can be explored and the extent to which it can be understood. Of the four, positivism represents the scientific, predominantly quantitative approach. The remaining three, moving from post-positivism through to constructivism, increasingly recognize the need to undertake qualitative research.

We found this system of classification useful when thinking about the implications of the current 'world view' managers were likely to have and the aims of our research. We decided it would be most appropriate to work within the scope of the post-positivist paradigm. Our experience and background research led us to believe that managers who need to undertake research have primarily been influenced by the positivist 'received view', with its emphasis on quantitative approaches (Guba and Lincoln, 1994). As an

Table 1   *Basic beliefs (metaphysics) of alternative inquiry paradigms*

Item	Positivism	Post-positivism	Critical theory	Constructivism
Ontology	naive realism: 'real' reality but apprehendable	critical realism: 'real' reality but only imperfectly and probabilistically apprehendable	historical realism: virtual reality shaped by social, political, cultural, economic, ethnic, and gender values; crystallized over time	relativism: local and specific constructed realities
Epistemology	dualist/ objectivist: findings true	modified dualist/ objectivist: critical tradition/ community; findings probably true	transactional/ subjectivist: value-mediated findings	transactional/ subjectivist: findings created through interaction of researcher and researched
Methodology	experimental/ manipulative: verification of hypotheses; chiefly quantitative methods	modified experimental/ manipulative: critical multiplism; falsification of hypotheses; can include qualitative methods	dialogic/ dialectical	hermeneutical/ dialectical

Source. Guba and Lincoln (1994: 109)

incremental progression the post-positivist approach was likely to be more readily accessible, and acceptable, to our manager/researchers than an introduction to the methodologies and assumptions of critical theorists and constructivists. In line with Guba and Lincoln's argument that qualitative methods can be appropriately used within any of the four paradigms (p. 105), we did not feel that working within this paradigm would seriously limit the adoption of approaches that could prove useful.

Thus within the literature we find similarities being identified between the roles of manager and researcher and a general recognition that qualitative methods have much to offer in an organizational context. On this basis it would seem reasonable to expect that managers should have access to the full range of research methods available. However, evidence from management education and development sources suggest this is unlikely to be the case, as little is offered or expected in terms of expertise and understanding of qualitative methods. Nor does there appear to have been much empirical exploration of either the opportunities for managers to use qualitative techniques or the barriers that deter them in their everyday work.

Methodology

The aim of exploring both the potential for managers to use qualitative approaches and the hurdles that need to be overcome in real situations, together with our desire to understand the complexity of the issues, meant a qualitative approach to the research was most appropriate. As a first stage in identifying and understanding these issues we undertook exploratory case studies (Yin, 1994) working with three managers on research that they were undertaking in the 'real world' as part of their normal duties. The exploratory nature of the cases led us to limit the number, owing to the amount of input and support we suspected might be required in each case. These managers were chosen because collectively they represented large and small organizations, public and private sector, and they each performed a different type of management role. Individually they each had complex projects for which they felt quantitative research methods were insufficient and they were receptive to the possibilities of using a different approach. Our role as researchers was that of participant observers as described by Waddington (1994) in that a relationship developed with the informants. To varying extents we participated in the activities which took place and were completely open about our purpose in doing so. The advantage of this role was that it enabled us to offer support to managers who might not otherwise have had the confidence or knowledge to try qualitative approaches.

An initial semi-structured interview took place with each manager in which we explored their previous experience (both educational and work-based) of research methods and their understanding of qualitative approaches. Their individual projects were discussed in order to gain understanding of the data requirements and the manager's perceptions of the shortcomings of methods they had considered so far.

It was clear from our conversations that the managers were using some aspects of qualitative methods, such as interviews and observation, but not in a structured or rigorous manner. There are a number of useful typologies which can assist the researcher to develop a coherent and internally consistent research proposal. In a management context they offer a means of clarifying the nature and requirements of a project so that appropriate skills can be applied, training obtained, techniques selected and organizational approval negotiated. In our case studies we decided to use an approach that we developed from Morse's (1994) comparison of qualitative strategies. The intention was to provide a framework that would encourage the managers to consider the use of qualitative approaches in a more consciously planned and systematic way.

Morse (p. 224) distinguishes between:

- Meaning questions: eliciting the essence of experiences
- Descriptive questions: of values, beliefs, practices of cultural group
- 'Process' questions: experience over time or change, may have stages and phases
- Questions regarding verbal interaction and dialogue
- Behavioral questions: macro, micro.

Using Morse's categorization of question types, we considered the needs of each project and, in consultation with the managers, formulated a series of questions from which potential qualitative data collection methods and likely outputs were identified. Details of the frameworks appear in the next section. The data collection methods we suggested were deliberately chosen to build on ideas with which managers were familiar and so increase their acceptability to the individuals concerned.

Each framework was then used as a vehicle for discussion with the manager concerned. The practicalities of using these approaches were discussed, including the way in which the data could be captured, and the managers chose whether to adopt any part of the framework. Support and advice were offered while they put the ideas into practice. Contact was maintained, usually through telephone conversations, during the implementation period so that we were aware of their successes and difficulties. Each manager was also interviewed at the point where they decided, for whatever reason, that they had finished the project.

In analysing our data, which took the form of written transcripts of the interviews, informal conversations and observational notes, we believed it important to adopt an approach that would be transparent to the managers. In this way we hoped we could both demonstrate the practical application of techniques and build their confidence in using qualitative methods in real situations. Our approach to analysing our data was a manual descriptive/ interpretative process as outlined by Tesch (1990). We began working with each individual case using themes stemming from the literature and our original research interest, but added to these as new themes emerged from the data. The themes which had emerged from the individual cases were then tested against the rest of the data. In this way themes common across the cases, and those which were not, were identified and considered.

Case Studies

In each case we outline the background of each manager in terms of education and research experience, describe the projects that the managers wanted to research and the limitations of quantitative data in their perception. Details of the frameworks, based on Morse's (1994) categorization of questions, are then given with the managers' reactions to these suggestions and their subsequent experiences in the use of the techniques.

Case (i) Ann – community health care manager

Ann is a manager in an NHS Trust in an urban area, and has operational responsibility for 10 health care professionals working in the community. Ann is also responsible for the development, implementation and evaluation of a pilot project which aims to meet the health needs of elderly people in the community through a team approach. The main purpose of the project is to enable the elderly to remain in their own homes for as long as possible and to retain a degree of choice about their own care.

Ann has had some training in statistical techniques but this has mainly been quantitative methods. Her Diploma in Professional Studies in Nursing did include some discussion of qualitative techniques such as repertory grids, observation and action research. However, unlike the teaching of quantitative methods, these discussions did not incorporate practical exercises or consider the analysis of the data. 'The impression given was that qualitative research was Utopia – it would be useful but takes too long to do.' Consequently Ann's training had left her without any clear understanding of the methods involved and with the belief that, despite the likely benefits, qualitative approaches were too resource-intensive to be practical.

Ann told us that within the Health Service the focus has traditionally been on quantitative measurements. The majority of the statistics currently collected are in the form of quantitative tick lists which are collated and aggregated by a central department: 'Everything is based on amounts, figures and numbers because it's easier to measure and the way it's always been done . . . quantity not quality is important.'

However, in Ann's experience, not only is it 'easy to prove lies with statistics', but quantitative measures can lead to meaningless comparisons when judgements are made about the provision of a service, or the quality of care, because they can only offer a limited understanding of what is involved.

> At a recent meeting a GP made the observation that a Health Visitor's visit was three times more expensive than a District Nurse's visit; but a District Nurse could be putting eye drops in while the Health Visitor might be discussing child abuse.

You could do one visit and say 'You haven't had your child immunized', or you could spend two hours assessing a child. The implication was that the Health Visitor was an expensive luxury and not as effective because they cost three times more. It is difficult to measure the effect of Health Visiting because it is long-term and proactive. How can you measure how effective proactive action is? At the moment we can't.

Concerns about the difficulty of assessing proactive intervention relate directly to the project for which Ann is responsible. The project is an integrated multidisciplinary provision of services to elderly people which involves multiple stakeholders who require different outcomes. For example the Health Department's main concern is achievement of financial savings; however, Ann's primary interests are the effectiveness of the team approach, the impact it has had on the service given, the quality of care and the team's ability to keep elderly people in their own homes. Equally Ann felt it important to identify the benefits and drawbacks perceived by those working in the team, as one intended outcome was an increase in the job satisfaction of the team members.

Ann believed that the nature of the elderly client group meant that purely quantitative surveys were unlikely to be effective. In her experience questionnaires were often completed by relatives rather than the actual client. Many elderly people perceived questionnaires as official forms which were either worrying or had to be answered 'correctly'. They were reluctant to say anything on these forms which in their perception might reflect badly on the nurses or care workers.

Based on the discussion with Ann, the framework in Table 2 was drawn up. Ann felt that the framework usefully clarified issues and focused thinking about approaches. Her initial reaction was that the suggestions could all be useful; however, Ann felt it would be inappropriate to use team members in participant observation and interviews. She believed it was likely to result in biased responses as the client group 'wouldn't want to hurt the nurses' feelings' and were worried 'about being thrown off the list, so the pressure is on them to give a positive viewpoint'.

In the original table we had also identified the recording of dialogue as a possible approach. However, on reflection, Ann had concerns about the effect of the recording process on those involved and decided not to pursue this. The nature of the client group meant that, for most, being recorded was likely to be a new and worrying experience. In the context of an interview with an 'official' from an organization on which they were dependent, Ann believed that this was likely to cause stress leading to a reluctance either to participate or to express their true opinion. There were also cost implications in terms of time to train staff to use equipment (and to build their confidence) and to transcribe the data, in addition to the need to purchase suitable equipment, all of which Ann felt were prohibitive. However, a number of the approaches we had originally identified were used. In-depth interviews with a selection of users were undertaken by a third party, observations have also taken place and focus groups were still planned at the time of writing this paper.

Using technology to analyse qualitative data was unrealistic in Ann's opinion, as there was limited computer availability and managers had 'very little computer experience'. The data collected was analysed manually, identifying themes within each case and comparing across cases to identify common and unique issues, and then using these findings to supplement the quantitative data analysis. The result of the qualitative work undertaken was the identification of issues which could not have been reflected by figures alone. For example, carers misunderstood the purpose of the new approach and had drawn negative inferences; this had resulted from the need on the

Table 2   *Qualitative research framework: pilot project*

Examples of qualitative questions and suggested types	Approaches to data collection	Outputs (From data collection and analysis)
How do elderly people (users) feel about the new service? [meaning]	Recording of in-depth interviews	User perceptions of the way the service has affected their quality of life – a measure of the perceived improvement in service
What are users expectations of the service? [descriptive]	In-depth interviews Observation during visits Focus groups Participant observation	Identification of user expectations including expectation mis-match – unrealistic expectations may explain any negative comments
What are the differences in the service that the users have noticed pre- and post-project implementation and over the life of the project? [process]	Interviews Focus groups	Identification of the changes in performance as perceived by those receiving the service – the extent to which relationships are better, whether the service is prompt, relevant and coherent
How do members of the team interact with the client? [descriptive, process]	Observation Recording dialogue	Assessment of how far all team members are providing an equal quality of care and appropriate level of service – the effect of the different working practices of the professions represented on the service given, and whether it is beneficial The aspects of the process which offer job satisfaction to the team members and why

part of the health service professionals to act quickly in crisis situations when there was little time for explanation. This will now be addressed through early provision of leaflets and information.

Ann was relatively pleased with the report which they had produced, but had concerns about the representative nature of the sample: 'Is it a big enough sample statistically?' We discussed the difference between qualitative and quantitative approaches in this sense, particularly the concept of saturation, i.e. 'the diminishing marginal contribution of each additional case' (Gummeson, 1988: 85). Ann's reaction – 'it puts a whole new slant on it ... I'm not worried now' – reflected the conflict between her belief that the work done was representative and sound, and the lack of knowledge which would enable her to defend this. Ann's perception was still that at regional level management are

> ... only interested in cost ... they don't care about the qualitative stuff, therefore it doesn't get done. But staff actually providing the service don't care about percentages. They are interested in quality: are people getting the care they want, need?

Thus in this case qualitative and quantitative measures were serving two distinct audiences.

Case (ii) Alan – marketing manager

At the time of the interviews Alan was a marketing manager for a small company which specializes in providing electronic information services but he had worked in various marketing positions in the business-to-business sector. He regarded himself as pretty typical of many managers when it comes to qualitative research. He did a lot of fairly unstructured research, much of it qualitative in nature, but his approach was ad hoc and he did not know a great deal about specific tools or techniques for handling qualitative data. Alan had gained Institute of Marketing professional qualifications, and, although this study had included some theory on qualitative techniques, there was no supporting practical work. An illustration of the kind of areas where he had already used some qualitative data was a large piece of work undertaken for the Commission for New Towns, which was concerned with understanding why firms relocate, in order to market new towns effectively to relocating companies. This involved the collection of quantitative data via questionnaires and qualitative data from four focus groups. A separate focus group was held for each kind of decision maker with the objective of finding out what influenced them in relocation decisions. Each group was also asked to comment on a series of advertisement designs and in this way the focus groups were used to get feedback from real people to possible marketing campaigns. Alan thought the groups were very subjective and could easily be tainted by strong or dominant personalities and, in a sense, 'they knew what the answer was before they asked the question'. The focus groups were not recorded (because recording is a 'nightmare') and themes relating to specific questions were just picked out of the discussion.

In his current role as marketing manager in a small company, time and money for research was limited and the activities had been much more ad hoc. In Alan's view, 'research is the cornerstone of all marketing – it's about finding out what people really think rather than what you think they think'. He was interested in qualitative approaches and would welcome a toolkit containing a few established methods. He would have liked both a generic toolkit and specialized toolkits for particular tasks such as investigating new product concepts or testing new products. However, he was concerned about the subjectivity of qualitative work and the impact the researcher's background has on the results.

An upcoming project involved the evaluation of a trial of one of their new products – an interactive teletext service called Swan. Previous evaluations of such products have been based on gathering quantitative data automatically on the number of screens of particular types that are accessed. Alan was particularly concerned that the evaluation should be appropriate for a new product such as this. Table 3 illustrates possible ways of approaching the Swan evaluation.

Alan agreed that the questions we had suggested for Swan were relevant and was keen to actually try a qualitative approach to product development. When we interviewed him he was in the middle of deciding exactly which features a mobile information unit (infomobile) should have. He had already sent out a postal questionnaire but realized that it hadn't given him all the answers he needed. This was illustrated by questionnaires he had completed by phone on which there were copious notes, representing additional information, scribbled in the margins.

Following discussions with us Alan decided to use a lightly structured telephone interview with a small number of potential customers concentrat-

Table 3 *Approaches to the evaluation of Swan*

Examples of qualitative questions and suggested types	Approaches to data collection	Outputs (from data collection and analysis)
How do customers use the product? [process]	Observation and/or in-depth interview	Assessment of interface Evaluation of features
What information services do people like and why? [descriptive, behavioural]	In-depth interview	Information to guide the development of information services (could be used to provide categories for a questionnaire)
Why do people use an interactive service such as Swan? [behavioural]	Diary and/or in-depth interview	Potential product development and marketing information

ing on the question 'How would you like your infomobile?' Alan did have reservations about the lack of a well-defined structure in the interview even though the customers were people known to him: 'Rather than a blank sheet of paper, I, having unfortunately worked in a telephone marketing agency, I'd probably feel it would be nice to have some questions or at least a tree system, you know, yes–no.' As a result of this concern we spent some time drawing up a list of key topics to discuss and explored how these would be used in actual interviews.

Alan intended to speak to five people and had no apparent concerns about presentation or generalizability: 'The company needs a decision on these design issues yesterday and this is informed gut.'

Alan conducted two interviews, during which he took notes as the necessary technology for recording the telephone conversations was not available. Although the notes were brief, when we reviewed them shortly after the conversations they were sufficient to prompt fuller recall and a significant amount of information had been collected. Rather than attempting to open-code his notes they were used to identify key points in the design of the infomobile. The result was that after only two interviews Alan was beginning to get a useful design brief. Unfortunately a change in company priorities meant that the work did not progress further, but the experience demonstrated that the main barrier for Alan had been his lack of confidence in using qualitative approaches.

Case (iii) Jane – internal consultant in a government agency

Jane acts as an internal consultant within a high-profile government agency which has a national network of offices dealing directly with the public. Her role is to assist managers to achieve their performance targets, identifying the causes of problems especially in relation to marketing, suggesting possible remedies and assisting in their implementation. She has been with this organization for 11 years in a variety of roles including field management. Jane has a scientific background and has an MBA which included coverage of quantitative statistics but not qualitative approaches.

Currently the organization makes frequent use of statistics, usually expressed as percentages, particularly to identify areas of weakness. However, Jane believed that most operational managers don't fully understand the figures and tend to take them at face value. 'They fail to link them with the underlying processes, they are not used to build performance or to improve quality.' Jane also observed that 'figures were easy to fiddle'. Senior managers don't pay a lot of attention to the figures unless targets are not being met. Normally there is no exception reporting nor explanation of the figures asked for; consequently there is no detail, and senior managers, who often don't have field experience, don't understand the processes nor the way that individuals impact on statistics.

Surveys are used with clients and staff to measure the performance of the organization, staff satisfaction, etc., but even where open-ended questions are asked, the results given are in a quantitative form and little appears to be done with opinions that have been asked for. In some cases this can produce misleading results. For example, the percentage of clients expressing dissatisfaction with the service may include those genuinely receiving a poor level of service. However, there may also be those who were refused a service to which they were not entitled or who resented restrictions with which they have to comply in order to benefit from the service. Jane believed that this was largely because people don't know how to analyse qualitative information or how to present it.

As an internal consultant Jane's work involved talking to people, both individually and at meetings, in order to explore the problems and issues in a team or office. These conversations and observations were recorded in an ad hoc fashion either in private notes or simply in her memory. Any analysis that was done was either quantitative, e.g. picking out the phrases used most frequently, or based on her 'gut-reaction' analysis of a conversation. 'I did find patterns but didn't know whether I'd gone far enough; it was not done in a reproducible way, it wasn't scientific, it wasn't cross-checked with anyone else.' Jane believed that qualitative information was necessary to identify the 'real' issues, without which it is difficult to solve problems. 'You have to be able to get at the real issues, and if you don't know how to do that scientifically you can't use the information to motivate or get things right.'

Jane felt that much more could be done with qualitative data to explore what lies under the quantitative figures, but in her organization qualitative data were not part of the 'norm'. Statistics were viewed as objective, and as such generalizable, while qualitative data were seen as subjective: people were much more likely to take them as a personal criticism or to reject them as not referring to their team. On occasions where she presented information as people's views she found that managers took it very personally, whereas if it was presented in quantitative format managers would accept it and ask for help. 'With quantitative stats they felt they could shield themselves from any direct blame but with qualitative information they felt failures.'

A typical situation in which Jane would need to undertake some research was that of an office which was not meeting its performance targets. We took this scenario and discussed qualitative approaches which might be useful to her in this situation. Table 4 provides a summary of the discussion.

Jane felt that formulating questions in this way helped to clarify the direction of her research, and would improve the relevance of the data she collected as she would be more focused from the beginning. Currently Jane tended to rely on unrecorded conversations and interviews to provide her data, and had not previously considered some of the techniques included in the table. She had reservations about the use of diaries in terms of people being willing or able to complete them, particularly if circumstances changed, and felt that the already heavily loaded staff would resist an additional burden.

Although she could see benefits, Jane also had concerns about tape recording of conversations. She feared that staff would be less willing to be open and honest and that the fact of recording would cause the conversation

Table 4 *Qualitative approaches to underperformance*

Examples of qualitative questions and suggested types	Approaches to data collection	Outputs (from data collection and analysis)
With whom do these individuals interact, what form does it take and is it effective? [descriptive]	Observation of the 'normal' day Recording of dialogue	Understanding of the communication links Understanding of the work relationships which would allow consideration of how these impact on performance
What does it feel like to do this job? [meaning]	In-depth conversations	Identify positive and negative attitudes and possible causes which could then be addressed Identify the existence of sub-cultures
How is this job done in this particular office? [process]	Observation In-depth conversations Manuals Diaries	Obtain a rich picture
How is this office performing and why? [descriptive, behavioural]	Interviews Diaries Observation	An understanding of the reasons for current performance – connections could be made between results and processes

to be 'unnatural and uncomfortable'. In terms of analysis of the qualitative data collected, Jane was completely unaware of the existence of computer packages that might help. She also had concerns about the amount of training that would be necessary to learn to use them. Jane had had no training or even exposure to possible approaches to analysis and, based on her scientific background, she was extremely concerned about general-izability, validity and being 'scientific'. At the time of writing Jane continues to use the methods with which she is familiar and has not yet adopted any of the approaches we discussed.

The Issues, Driving forces and Restraining Influences

Each of the managers in the scenarios above was initially receptive to the idea of using qualitative techniques and believed that qualitative data were more likely to hold clues about people's real feelings, views and likely behaviour. Indeed our discussions identified that they were all using some aspects of qualitative research, e.g. interviews and observations, but in an ad hoc unstructured way, and with little attempt at systematic analysis of the results. All felt that the nature of their work demanded greater use of qualitative data. They wanted to understand why things were as they were, often because their job meant implementing change, and they perceived a value in holistic approaches within the complexity of their organization.

A number of similar benefits were identified by Jane and Ann; both believed that qualitative research enabled connections to be made between processes, relationships and performance that were not possible through quantitative work. In practice Ann's qualitative data were successful in identifying important process issues to be addressed and enabled some meaningful assessment of service quality to be made. Both Ann and Jane also identified the potential of rich, contextualized data for motivating staff 'on the front line'. Context was important in order to understand the expectations users had of their services and perceptions about its delivery. In Alan's case qualitative data helped him to focus his questioning and with relatively little input begin to gather rich and complex information.

Our conversations with the three managers revealed the need for some education about the theoretical underpinnings of qualitative research. Further research and reflection will be necessary to identify the most effective way of achieving this. While we had expected our managers to have a post-positivist outlook, and thus be able to take on board some qualitative concepts without difficulty, this was not entirely the case. From the reactions of the three managers and their observations about their organizations it is clear that there is a deep-seated unease about data that is seen as subjective. This appears to be the legacy of a culture and education system that accords the objective, scientific approach the highest status. Although enthusiastic about qualitative data, both Alan and Jane had concerns and reservations that revealed that a shift in attitude would be necessary if they were not to assess all qualitative approaches against quantitative criteria. Indeed Jane, who has the educational background most firmly rooted in the scientific tradition, has not yet adopted any of the qualitative approaches suggested. In principle Jane accepts the potential of qualitative methods, but is still wary of progressing beyond the ad hoc approaches she has always used. Ann took a quantitative view of replicability and of sample sizes, but largely because she was unaware of other perspectives rather than because she was uncomfortable with them. All the managers needed to understand the arguments about qualitative research validity in order to convince themselves and their organizations of its potential contribution.

Both Ann and Jane worked in large organizations with a strong bureaucratic, hierarchical tradition in which the validity of quantitative data was accepted. This was despite such data being poorly understood or being perceived as having limited relevance to the decisions being made. Their senior managers believed quantitative data to be inherently more reliable and credible, not least because this was the way things had always been done. Yet in both cases the managers were aware that statistics and the ways they were represented were not always accurate or impartial, nor did they tell the whole story. We suspect this apparent contradiction is further evidence of the strength of the positivist paradigm, in which most Western management has been educated, and which upholds the unique ability of quantitative data to reflect objective reality. It is certainly an area which would benefit from further research.

The perception reported in Jane's organization that quantitative data were somehow less threatening, even when they indicated poor performance, than qualitative data (which would have been more relevant to the service issues under consideration) offers another interesting area for further research. It is not clear whether this is a reflection of the current organizational culture, of prevailing power structures, or the climate of career uncertainty.

Unlike Ann and Jane, Alan worked for a smaller organization where qualitative data was more commonly collected and accepted, and he had more autonomy as an individual manager. Yet despite their different backgrounds they shared some common concerns:

- whether data could stand up to scrutiny; issues such as researcher bias having an undue influence on the interpretation of data, the effect of the bias of those being researched (although it was common knowledge that figures collected by staff were 'fiddled') and the generalizability of findings were raised
- the time and resources involved in collecting and analysing qualitative data (although in Alan's case practice proved this was not a problem), and the need to rely on others in the case of diaries and logs; there was also a great deal of unease about the idea of recording dialogues even if it was practically possible
- the absence of the appropriate knowledge and skills and the difficulty of acquiring them in an environment where the value of qualitative approaches was not widely recognized or understood.

In our discussions with the managers about the practicalities of analysing qualitative data it became clear that they were unaware of the variety of approaches which were possible and the grounds on which choices should be made. Nor were they aware that computer packages existed which could support the approach chosen. We found we were having to explain concepts and techniques in a totally jargon-free way, which suggests that the majority of current qualitative literature would not be easily accessible for these busy managers. while computers can remove some of the laborious tasks of the qualitative researcher, the current generation of qualitative data analysis software does nothing to demystify or simplify the process. All our managers were interested in computer support for qualitative research, but there were serious practical issues which would need to be addressed; it would need to be simple to use, user friendly and obviously relevant to their circumstances if they were to make the effort to become familiar with it. Time, whether for understanding or for using such a system, was a key issue.

Conclusion

Our aim in the first stage of this research has been to identify practical implications of observations we had made about the use of qualitative research by managers. It is clear that qualitative methods can provide ways to explore work-related puzzles, problems and challenges. They may provide new insights at the least, and can lead to powerful explanations for causes that can be a guide to action, moving far beyond the description of symptoms. However, there are a number of significant obstacles that need to be overcome before use of qualitative data is as acceptable and commonplace in everyday organizational contexts as is quantitative data.

We had begun with the belief that the previous education and experience of most managers would enable them to acquire a range of new qualitative research skills, which could lead to internally consistent research, even though they had little or no knowledge of theoretical underpinnings. However, we discovered that the reality was more complex. Two of our three managers persisted in applying positivist criteria to judge qualitative approaches and data; they found it extremely difficult to judge validity in other terms. This suggests that it is more important than we had anticipated to increase managers' awareness and understanding of ontological and epistemological concerns. Based on this, plus Ann's reaction to the discussion on samples, we would also suggest that an understanding of the fundamental principles underpinning qualitative work might also encourage more widespread use and acceptance.

The opportunity to *use* qualitative approaches as a means of developing understanding is crucial; our managers found the ideas and possibilities became much clearer when applied to real projects and issues. While our managers were receptive to our suggestions for action, they did need support when putting them into action, particularly at the analysis stage. Yet it is clear, from our review of both literature and the courses widely on offer, that the opportunity for the average manager to learn about these approaches and to test them in a 'safe' environment is limited. Nor is there a substantial amount of easily comprehensible written work on this subject. We must draw the conclusion that the growing expertise in qualitative research amongst management researchers has yet to filter through to managers themselves. It seems unlikely to do so until those responsible for management development and education recognize and address this gap.

References

ACCA (1994) *Studying And The Examinations*. London: Chartered Association Of Certified Accountants.
Benchmark Research (1994) *Training For Industry And Commerce, Summary Report*, November. London: Benchmark Research.
Cameron, S. (1991) *The MBA Handbook*. London: Pitman.
Cameron, S. and Pearce, S.L. (1995) *The Management Studies Handbook*. London: Pitman.
CIMA (Chartered Institute of Management Accountants) (1995) *CIMA Student* 13 (August).

Guba, E.G. and Lincoln, Y.S. (1994) 'Competing Paradigms in Qualitative Research', in N.V. Denzin, and Y.S. Lincoln (eds) *Handbook Of Qualitative Research*. Thousand Oaks, CA: Sage.

Gummesson, E. (1988) *Qualitative Methods In Management Research*. Bromley: Chartwell-Bratt.

Handy, C. (1985) *Understanding Organizations*. London: Penguin.

IHSM (1988) *AHSM And CHSM: Examination Regulations And Syllabus*. London: The Institute Of Health Services Management.

Management Charter Initiative (MCI) (1992) *Management Standards II*. London: MCI.

Marshall, C. and Rossman, G.B. (1995) *Designing Qualitative Research*. Thousand Oaks, CA: Sage.

Miles, M.B. and Huberman, A.M. (1994) *Qualitative Data Analysis*. Thousand Oaks, CA: Sage.

Mintzberg, H. (1973) *The Nature Of Managerial Work*. New York: Harper & Row.

Morse, J.M. (1994) 'Designing Funded Qualitative Research', chapter 13 in N.V. Denzin and Y.S. Lincoln (eds) *Handbook Of Qualitative Research*. Thousand Oaks, CA: Sage.

Patton, M.Q. (1997) *Utilization-Focused Evaluation: The New Century Text*. Thousand Oaks, CA: Sage.

Reed, M. and Anthony, P. (1992) 'Professionalizing Management And Managing Professionalization: British Management In The 1980s', *Journal of Management Studies* 29(5) September: 591–613.

Schön, D. A. (1983) *The Reflective Practitioner: How Professionals Think In Action*. London: Temple Smith.

Tesch, R. (1990) *Qualitative Research: Analysis Types and Software Tools*. New York: Falmer.

Waddington, D. (1994) 'Participant Observation', in C. Cassell and G. Symon (eds) *Qualitative Methods In Organizational Research*. London: Sage.

Yin, R.K (1994) *Case Study Research: Design And Methods*. Thousand Oaks, CA: Sage.

20

Steven S. Taylor, Dalmar Fisher and Ronald L. Dufresne

The Aesthetics of Management Storytelling
A Key to Organizational Learning

Stories play a prominent part in the practice of management and, correspondingly, in organizational research. Some research is written like a story; some is about organizational stories; some conceptualizes organizational life as storymaking (Czarniawska, 1998). Management practice has long been viewed as 'a matter of art rather than science' (Barnard, 1938: 325), and more recently as 'a performing art' (Vaill, 1989). Recently, there have been a variety of calls for an aesthetic perspective in organizational research (e.g. Dean et al., 1997; Ebers, 1985; Ottensmeyer, 1996; Ramirez, 1996). Because storytelling is recognized as a folk art, and because stories and storytelling are so pervasive in management, organizational storytelling is a useful place to bring an aesthetic perspective to organizational research, management practice, and organizational learning.

We use Boje's definition of story, 'an oral or written performance involving two or more people interpreting past or anticipated experience' (1991b: 111). We take this definition because our interest is in the meaning-making aspect of stories. That is to say, our focus is not with whether the 'facts' of the story are true or what the stories tell us about some underlying objective reality (e.g. Stevenson and Greenberg, 1998), but with the ways in which storytelling is used to socially construct meaning in organizations. We begin with an aesthetic perspective on storytelling to suggest how and why some stories work better than others. Aesthetics supplies a mechanism for understanding how organizational stories work and begins to show how to make stories more effective. We then use Mintzberg's taxonomy of the 10 roles of the manager, in conjunction with the storytelling and organizational learning literature, to show that (a) stories and storytelling play an important part in the full spectrum of management practice, (b) the aesthetic perspective adds to the existing understanding of management storytelling, and (c) artful stories are an effective vehicle for managers to contribute to organizational learning. While there is a well-established link in the literature between stories and learning (Vance, 1991), we aim to use the comprehensiveness of Mintzberg's taxonomy to show how an understanding of aesthetics can contribute to a manager's ability to facilitate organizational learning. We then conclude with implications for theory, research, and practice.

The Aesthetics of Storytelling

We start with a question: what makes a good story?[1] Not all stories are effective (Boje, 1991a; Gabriel, 1995; Martin, 1982; Martin and Powers, 1983), but several writers provide suggestions on what makes the difference. Weick (1995: 61) offers that 'a good story holds disparate elements together long enough to allow people to make retrospective sense of whatever happens, and engagingly enough that others will contribute their own inputs in the interest of sensemaking'. Others are more specific – naming such factors as chronological sequence, a link between the exceptional and the ordinary, dramatic quality, poetic quality, imagery, exuberance, the use of tropes or figures of speech, concrete language, an interesting setting, central characters, and terseness (Boje, 1991b; Bruner, 1990: Chapter 2; Martin, 1982; Wills, 1992: 255–305). These elements point to the literary and dramatic qualities of stories, confirming the value of taking an artistic view of managerial work. While they identify several specific ingredients contributing to good stories, they do not reflect a theory. Given the power of storytelling in organizations, we believe it is important to establish a basis in theory for our understanding of it. Further, since storytelling engages the realm of art, we believe aesthetic theory, although not providing the only explanation, should contribute importantly to explaining story quality.

Storytelling as folk art and performance has been around since the dawn of time. If we look at storytelling as art – that is, if we take an explicitly aesthetic perspective – we start to get an explanation of why one story is more effective than another, why one story works better than another, or in Boje's terms, why one story might win out over another (Boje, 1991b, 1994, 1995).

Boje takes a postmodern stance, discussing a group's power to control discourse as an explanation of why one story becomes dominant. To examine storytelling from an aesthetic perspective means taking a more micro perspective and looking at the individual aesthetic transaction (Berleant, 1970; Fine, 1984), which consists of the storyteller and the audience in a particular aesthetic field or environment. It is by looking at what happens in the aesthetic transaction that we start to understand why and how stories can be such a powerful and important part of management and why and how some stories work better than others.

Aesthetics is seen by Baumgarten as 'one of two components of the theory of knowledge, or gnoseology: on the one hand, logic, which investigates intellectual knowledge; on the other hand, aesthetics, which investigates sense knowledge' (quoted in Strati, 1996: 216). The word *aesthetics* is from Greek. Its root meaning, very broadly, is any kind of sensory experience (White, 1996: 195). So to take an aesthetic perspective is to be concerned with a particular type of knowledge, a knowledge of sensation and feeling. Aesthetic experience produces *felt meaning* (Courtney, 1995) or understanding that is not mediated by inductive or deductive reason (Csikszentmihalyi and Robinson, 1990), but rather is characterized by abductive reasoning (Peirce, 1957).

Two characteristics of aesthetic experience are of particular importance for our explanation of how and why some stories work better than others. The first is that the human element is central to aesthetic experience (Csikszentmihalyi and Robinson, 1990). That is to say, an artful story tells us something about what it is to be human. This human element may be better understood in terms of Ramirez's (1991) concept of the beauty of social organization. Ramirez starts by developing a systems theory of organizational beauty. Being 'a part of' a system simultaneously means 'belonging to' and 'distinct from'. The aesthetic experience of beauty comes from the feeling of 'belonging to'. As Bateson puts it, 'by aesthetic, I mean responsive to the pattern that connects' mind and nature (quoted in Ramirez, 1991: 38). If we, as audience, think of the rest of humanity as part of nature, then the human element that Csikszentmihalyi and Robinson found in their empirical study of aesthetic experience can be understood as resonance with the pattern that connects us with the rest of humanity and with the natural world, which we shall call simply, a feeling of *connectedness*. The second particularly important characteristic of aesthetic experience is 'an intense involvement of attention . . . for no other reason than to sustain the interaction' (Csikszentmihalyi and Robinson, 1990: 78). Or in other words, *enjoyment of the story for its own sake*, independent of any outcomes.

These three ideas about the nature of aesthetic experience – that it is (1) felt meaning from abductive reasoning, (2) characterized by feelings of connectedness, and (3) enjoyed for its own sake – are our starting point in our explanation of how and why stories work.

Felt Meaning

Let us start with the idea of felt meaning that comes from abductive reasoning. Peirce (1957) coined the term abductive reasoning in contrast to deductive and inductive reasoning. Deductive reasoning is conscious movement from a general law to a specific case, while inductive reasoning is the conscious movement from a specific case to a general law. Peirce noted that most great advances in science were neither of those, but instead based on a reasoning that was not a conscious logical process, but was rather an intuitive leap that came forth as a whole, which he called abductive reasoning. It is this intuitive grasping of the whole meaning of something without a conscious logical thought process that is the essential nature of aesthetic experience. This aesthetic felt meaning bypasses conscious critical filters that individuals may apply to information as they try to make sense of events for themselves. Although some individuals may reflect on the felt meaning and question it over time, there is a tendency to trust the intuitively grasped felt meaning because it is based in feelings – it feels right.

Connectedness

The content of aesthetic experience is subjective (Csikszentmihalyi and Robinson, 1990), which means that different people may have very different aesthetic experiences of the same story. This happens through the way the feeling of connectedness works. We connect with the story because it resonates with some part of our own lived experience – to include our experience with similar stories or story fragments we have heard before (Kristeva, 1986). The intertextual reverberation of a story across time and experience provides a resonance with our own experience that provides the anchor to make the story feel right (Plottel and Charney, 1978). The connectedness also makes the story personally meaningful by resonating with our own experience. Different individuals may resonate with very different aspects of the story but the result may still be the same. The resonance provides a strong 'truth' claim for the story and makes the story personally relevant.

Enjoyed For Its Own Sake

The third idea is that the aesthetic experience of the story is enjoyed for its own sake, independent of any instrumental outcomes. Enjoyment produces two effects. The first is engagement. The more the audience enjoy the story, the more they are drawn into the moment and the more the aesthetic experience dominates the instrumental concerns of the moment. As the aesthetic experience dominates the individual's critical functions and filters become less active, the felt meaning of the story is allowed to be accepted uncritically and unquestioned. The second effect is repetition. A story that is enjoyed for its own sake is more memorable and gets repeated. All else being equal, an enjoyable story is more likely to be retold than an unenjoyable story.

Strength of Aesthetic Experience

We know from experience that not all stories have a strong felt meaning, a feeling of connection, or are enjoyable. Imagine a story that produces a very weak aesthetic experience, one that gives virtually no felt meaning. If the audience are to get the meaning of the story, they must intellectually figure out what the story is about based on their own frames and filters, if they are willing to expend the effort. If the story provides no sense of connection, the audience do not resonate with the story and have no reason to believe it and care about it. And if the story is not enjoyable they will not spend time thinking about it or repeating it. The story will fail. It will be a bad story. At the opposite end of the continuum is a story with a very strong aesthetic experience that gives a very strong felt meaning, a strong feeling of connection, and is enjoyable for its own sake. That story will work. The audience will believe it and repeat it. It will be a good, artful story.

Thus the aesthetic perspective provides a definition of what good and bad means for storytelling. Good stories involve a strong aesthetic experience that provides felt meaning, a feeling of connectedness, and enjoyment. Bad stories provide a weak aesthetic experience and leave the audience to make sense of the story intellectually, without a holistic felt meaning and sense of personal connection to guide them. It is important to remember that 'there are several aesthetic categories. The number of aesthetic categories ranges from 6 to 64 in the aesthetics literature, e.g., the ugly, the sublime, the graceful, the sacred, the comic, the picturesque' (Strati, 1992: 568). A good story is not necessarily beautiful or funny. It could be grotesque or sublime or even ugly and have a strong aesthetic experience and be a very good story. A bad story is not one that produces a negative aesthetic experience; it is a story that has no aesthetic experience.

This idea of good and bad stories has implications for every aspect of management practice. To support this point, we will show how the multiple functions of stories and storytelling are recognized in the organizational storytelling literature. We will then show that storytelling contributes to the whole range of management functions identified by Mintzberg (1973) in his taxonomy of the roles of the manager, and can do so more effectively where the storytelling is 'good' from an aesthetic point of view. It is through Mintzberg's taxonomy of managerial roles that we will make explicit a bridge between aesthetic storytelling and organizational learning. While we focus in the following section on the impact of aesthetically good *management* storytelling on organizational learning, we wish to highlight the fact that all organization members can – and do – contribute to organizational learning through the use of artful stories. We use the stories told by managers solely as a means to develop the insights the aesthetic perspective offers concerning the many ways that good stories can affect organizational learning.

Management Storytelling

Stories have yielded many new insights – from the observation that the unique quality of an organization is revealed in 'epic myths' (Mitroff and Kilmann, 1975) to the discovery that an organization's success or failure may reside not in the events themselves but in how the story is told (Rhodes, 1997). Hearing the stories told in an organization can enable the listener to learn the organization's strategy (Barry and Elmes, 1997), its patterns of power and succession (Fletcher, 1996; Gephart, 1991; Hansen and Kahnweiler, 1993), how successful the organization is (Browning, 1991), its norms (Czarniawska, 1997), expectations of new employees (Vance, 1991), and the quality of fantasy that exists within it (Gabriel, 1995).

Boyce (1995) notes further that research shows storytelling contributes to problem solving, action research, socialization of new employees, collective centering, sense making, motivation, and new product development. She lists the following functions of storytelling and calls them to the attention of managers (Boyce, 1996: 19):

- expressing the organizational experience of members and clients;
- confirming the shared experiences and shared meaning of organizational members and groups within the organization;
- orienting and socializing new members;
- developing, sharpening, and renewing the sense of purpose held by organization members;

- preparing a group (or groups) for planning, implementing plans, and decision making in line with shared purposes; and
- co-creating vision and strategy.

But stories are more than just sources of information *about* an organization, they are a central part of the action *of* the organization. Boje (1991b) sees organizations as occurring in and through stories. 'Think of an organization', he says, 'as a big conversation . . . an on-going storytelling event' (quoted in Greco, 1996: 46). Boje (1995, 1998) argues that stories should not be understood as 'objects' playing discrete functions and having static meanings, but rather that story*telling* should be understood as performances within organizational contexts. Boje (1995) uses the Walt Disney Company to illustrate storytelling as a medium of interpretive exchange over time. He observes patterns in which 'official' stories about and within the company compete with more marginal 'local' stories through an evolutionary process across historic eras. The stories were affected by the organizational context and vice versa.

Every event that occurs in an organization gives rise to interpretations by members and these interpretations shape subsequent events. The vice president says, 'We must pursue new opportunities'. What does that mean? How should I interpret that? Interpretations of events are recorded and transmitted in stories (Boyce, 1995). When we discuss an event, we are really telling the story of that event. The story provides the meaning for specific cultural events and artifacts (Boje et al., 1982; Hansen and Kahnweiler, 1993). The meanings of stories are more or less ambiguous (Gabriel, 1991a), and they change over time (Boje, 1991a, 1995). As the stories change, the culture changes. As the culture changes, so do the stories (Pacanowsky and O'Donnell-Trujillo, 1983). Storytelling is micro behavior within the macro context of culture. It is constrained by the existing culture and it also modifies the culture.

Through its interpretive power, storytelling performs a broad array of active functions within organizations, sometimes to sustain and sometimes to modify the culture. Martin and Powers (1983: 97) cite research evidence that

> organizational stories legitimate the power relations within the organization, they rationalize existing practices, traditions, and rituals; and they arbitrate through exemplars the philosophy of management and the policies which make organizations distinctive. In short, this research suggests the proposition that there is an association between stories and organizational commitment.

Considerable research has also shown the place stories and storytelling have in organizational learning. Levitt and March (1988) write that experiences are 'translated into, and developed through, story lines that come to be broadly, but not universally shared. This structure of meaning is normally suppressed as a conscious concern, but learning occurs within it' (p. 324). Stories can also be seen in Huber's (1991) discussion of the information distribution and interpretation aspects of organizational learning. Brown and Duguid (1991) found that organizational learning occurs in communities of practice, where stories are created, exchanged, and added to the community's store of accumulated wisdom. More recently, Crossan et al. (1999) proposed a framework for organizational learning where stories play a vital role in the interpretation of insights and the integration of those insights into action. These authors write:

> Storytelling is a significant part of the learning process. Stories reflect the complexity of actual practice rather than the abstractions taught in the classrooms. As stories evolve, richer understanding of the phenomenon is developed, and new integrated approaches to solving problems are created. Stories themselves become the repository of wisdom. (Crossan et al., 1999: 329)

The pervasive functions of stories and storytelling clearly warrant the attention of organizational leaders. In fact, the literature shows that stories and storytelling perform functions within each of the areas generally recognized as the roles of the manager. But as we have noted before, not all stories are equal. Good stories – those with a strong aesthetic experience – perform these functions better than bad stories.

Mintzberg (1973) draws on his own field observations of managers as well as the managerial behavior literature to identify 10 managerial roles, recognized as describing the activity common to most managerial positions (Yukl, 1998). While we see leadership and management as processes engaged in throughout organizations, including by persons who do not have the formal title of 'manager' (Torbert, 1991), Mintzberg's roles are convenient for showing the importance of the aesthetics of storytelling to all aspects of management. Mintzberg's roles also offer an invaluable link to form a connection between the stories told daily by managers and the organizational learning that might result. While storytelling has been referred to in the organizational learning literature (e.g. Aram and Noble, 1999; Brown and Duguid, 1991; Crossan et al., 1999; Levitt and March, 1988; Rhodes, 1997; Vance, 1991), our intent is to show how artful stories can be used throughout a manager's responsibilities to facilitate organizational learning.

Mintzberg identifies three major clusters of managerial roles: *interpersonal* roles, *informational* roles, and *decisional* roles. The interpersonal cluster includes the roles of figurehead, leader, and liaison. Informational roles are those of monitor, disseminator, and spokesperson. Decisional roles involve the functions of entrepreneur, resource allocator, disturbance handler, and negotiator. A selective review of the literature confirms that stories and storytelling function in all of the areas addressed by Mintzberg's 10 roles, and that artful storytelling by managers in each role can facilitate organizational learning.

Interpersonal Functions

In the role of *figurehead*, according to Mintzberg, the manager acts to symbolize the organization. It is through 'spoken narrative' (including stories) that the identity of an organization is formed (Boje, 1991a, 1995; Czarniawska, 1997; Gabriel, 1999; Glynn, 2000; Harrison, 2000; Stutts and Barker, 1999; Tracy, 2000). Stories serve as symbols, conveying a central theme that typifies the organization (Wilkins, 1984). This articulating of identity was heard repeatedly by Peters and Waterman (1982) in companies they visited where stories of the past, including the heroic deeds of founding fathers or exemplary employees, were told. The 'Bill and Dave' stories at Hewlett Packard recounted the achievements, humor, and inspirational qualities of the company's founders, and expressed the history and identity of the business in a memorable, symbolic way. Such stories portray the organization to outsiders – Mintzberg's *liaison* role – as well as to members. In aesthetic terms, these identity-portraying stories work because they evoke a 'whole' felt meaning of the organization. Since they are often retold, it appears they are enjoyed for their own sake.

An organization's identity story may be read differently by different recipients of the story. Stutts and Barker (1999) studied audience reactions to Exxon's Driver Human advertising campaign, using a 90-second spot presenting a series of 17 drivers and passengers, with printed captions such as, 'I'm late', 'I could use some coffee', or simply, 'Oh'. The advertisement served as a projective stimulus. Audience members differed as to the values they saw depicted in the advertisement and also whether those values were relevant to Exxon. From a postmodern perspective, the organization's identity is formed in the mind of each story recipient. For every story of organizational identity there is a counter story (Boje, 1995; Gardner, 1995). As Exxon battled to repair its image after the Valdez oil spill, all storytelling managers engaged in a constant battle against the counter stories of organizational identity. We suggest that good stories will dominate bad stories as people connect to and enjoy the good story. Thus a good counter story might come to dominate a bad story by having a stronger aesthetic experience. For managers exercising the figurehead and liaison roles, stories about organizational identity become important mechanisms for sharing meaning among members of the community, both within the organization and without. By making the stories artful, they can help ensure that their stories are the ones that are retold – extending their shared meaning and reaching beyond the original founders. The diffusion and extension of meaning that accompanies aesthetically strong stories is vital for an organization to learn (Levitt and March, 1988).

Mintzberg's *leader* role includes guiding, encouraging, criticizing, and motivating individuals as well as giving purpose, vision, and energy to the organization. Storytelling can focus members on a purpose (Bowles, 1989). In her study of a basketball team and a dance company, Boyce (1995: 111) reports,

> Shared storytelling centered these athletes and dancers on essence and purpose. It reminded them of what they had chosen, of what was important. From this centered place, they consciously engaged in collective sensemaking and determined and chose organizational actions that expressed purpose.

From an aesthetics standpoint, Boyce is describing storytelling that achieved connectedness; it resonated with individuals' personal choices. This connectedness is akin to Aram and Noble's (1999) characterization of organizational learning as a 'participative, social experience' (p. 323). Leaders are thus able to share their interpretations and understandings of the organization through artful, connecting stories to which others in the organization will listen and through which the organization can learn (Crossan et al., 1999).

Further attesting to the power of stories in developing shared purpose, an experimental study found that an organizational policy statement was more likely to be believed if accompanied by a story than by statistical information (Martin and Powers, 1983). Stories have helped leaders transform the fundamental ideologies of institutions. The ancient Greek politician Kleisthenes used story along with other artifacts to move Athens toward unity and democracy (Cummings and Brocklesby, 1997). Lincoln's Gettysburg Address is a story that had a profound impact in unifying a divided nation and gaining acceptance for the principle of equality (Wills, 1992). We have to wonder if the Gettysburg Address would have had such a profound impact if it had not become part of such a strong aesthetic experience. Wills (1992) suggests that by crafting his speech to stay away from the specifics of the moment, Lincoln allowed various audiences to connect to the ideas in the Gettysburg Address in their own way. This variety of connectedness and interpretation can furthermore effect more elaborate organizational learning since, according to Huber (1991: 90), 'more organizational learning occurs when more and more varied interpretations are developed'.

Management ideologies are not necessarily accepted by members. Free spirited European employees at the Disney theme park in France resisted the corporate story that 'we are entertainers in costume', not liking having their actions scripted and their clothing prescribed (Boje, 1995). Indeed, stories can criticize the organization (Martin, 1988), and a critical story that is enjoyable is much more likely to be listened to, remembered and repeated than unartful, mean-spirited criticism, even if the stories carry the same message. Watson's (2001) description of 'low stories' that repeatedly vilified senior management shows the power of artful critical stories. But stories also often encourage organization members, conveying motivating themes such as empowerment, collaboration, helpfulness, professionalism, and organizational equity (Hansen and Kahnweiler, 1993). And, again, it is the stories we remember because we enjoyed them, because we connected to them, which are most effective in providing ongoing motivation and empowerment. It is a movie cliché to see a character in crisis remember an inspirational story and draw the needed strength from it. In that cliché is an illustration of the importance of the aesthetics of storytelling in organizational learning.

Informational Functions

The informational roles include seeking and receiving information that enables the manager to understand what is taking place in and outside the organization (*monitor*), and sending information to the organization (*disseminator*), and to the outside environment (*spokesperson*). We suggest that more effective stories produce a strong felt meaning that serves to anchor the information in the story.

Stories perform the *monitor* function by plotting the organization's progress in terms of trend lines. Browning identifies three story types, the 'ascent' story, telling of success; the 'decline' story, telling of a downward spiral; and the 'plateau', telling of steady performance (Browning, 1991). Such stories sometimes gain exposure outside the organization (the *spokesperson* function). Browning tells of a plateau story posted on a sign the size of a billboard outside a Wal-Mart distribution center in San Antonio, Texas, stating that employees at the site have gone '328 days without an accident'. Taken simply as information, this fact might not mean a lot to those who read it, but aesthetically, the reader of the sign intuitively feels right about a company that displays how much it cares about its employees' safety.

Managers can be both *monitors* and *disseminators* by using stories to help employees be aware of and make sense of changes, to allow an opportunity to reflect on and reassemble information to make it actionable, and to reveal unspoken or unconscious norms of the organization (Barry, 1997; Boje, 1991a; Gabriel, 1995). Stories can raise organizational consciousness. Segal (1997) describes a feminist activist group in an organization where stories about issues relating to diversity helped members re-form their identities and made persons outside the group more aware. Aesthetically, these stories, in order to be good stories, must have 'connected' solidly to the members' subjective experience. As Boje puts it, 'Storytelling is the preferred sense-making currency of human relationships among internal and external stakeholders' (1991b: 106).

Taken together, the informational functions of stories suggest that management can engage in ongoing storytelling dialogs with constituents inside and outside the organization from which all can learn, form new shared meanings, and change. Since learning depends on the effective exchange of knowledge and information, the informational functions represent the primary lever managers can use to facilitate organizational learning. When *monitoring*, managers attend to stories in circulation inside and outside the organization, allowing them to acquire knowledge experientially and vicariously (Huber, 1991). Managers also need to monitor how their stories have been interpreted and to use that information as feedback when retelling a story or preparing their next story (Crossan et al., 1999). Effective stories are vital in making implicit knowledge explicit and understandable to audiences inside the organization (*disseminator*) and outside the organization (*spokesperson*). Stories with a strong felt meaning, connectedness and enjoyment are likely to be listened to, retold, and remembered. As these stories with a strong aesthetic experience are spread throughout an organization, more organizational learning occurs (Huber, 1991).

Decisional Roles

To the extent that decision making is viewed as occurring in the manager's internal thought process, stories may not overtly play a part. However, storytelling is important to other elements in the decision process such as fact-gathering, consensus-building, and implementation. Mintzberg defines the decisional roles in an active mode: the entrepreneur as initiator of change, and the resource allocator as one who hears ideas about resources expressed by others and who mediates collaborative decisions (1973: 77–94). In the *entrepreneur* role, the manager is the designer and initiator of change. Stories can be central in the change process (Barry and Elmes, 1997; Boje, 1991a; Gephart, 1991; Rosile, 1998), and, as noted earlier, can increase commitment to policies (Martin and Powers, 1983). Barry (1997) used 'narrative therapy' (White and Epston, 1990) with the co-owners of an osteopathic clinic that had serious business and organizational problems. Their stories, and Barry's reflections on them, served as 'problem externalizations', allowing the co-owners to put problems outside themselves where they could begin to act on them. Barry (1997: 34) comments, 'As long as storytellers characterize themselves as the problem, they have little room to maneuver – wherever they go, the problem goes too, preventing other views from arising.' Aesthetically, these externalized stories helped the co-owners develop new 'whole meanings' of problems that felt better to them.

Boje (1991a: 16) tells of a consulting intervention where he defined his role as

> facilitating the telling of relevant tales and helping managers, vendors, and customers reach some consensus on their stories. . . . [W]e had to get some of these people to tell their stories directly to one another so that their key relationships would be strengthened with customers and vendors. If not, a significant competitive advantage would be lost.

Gephart (1991) conducted interviews with managers about their experiences with changes involving leadership succession. He concluded that 'organizational change is embedded in and constituted through storytelling' (p. 42). This echoes Boje's (1991a: 8) view that 'stories are the blood vessels through which change pulsates in the heart of organizational life'. From an aesthetics standpoint, good stories help achieve consensus because everyone feels connected to the story and, through the story, more connected to each other.

As managers tell change-oriented, entrepreneurial stories, the range of the organization's potential behaviors is expanded, and organizations learn (Huber, 1991). Stories allow managers to verbalize their individual-level intuitions and novel insights, and can facilitate their enactment in the organization (Crossan et al., 1999). In their entrepreneurial capacity, managers can capitalize on unintentional or unsystematic learning as a source of knowledge. An aesthetically strong story allows this knowledge to be related to the organization through a medium to which organization members are likely to attend.

Mintzberg conceives of *resource allocation* 'in the broadest context', including functions relating to reduction of complexity and developing human resources. Organizational stories may be seen as 'maps' (Wilkins and Thompson, 1991) that reduce complexity by leaving out all but the essentials. Aesthetically, such stories would enable people to grasp a 'whole meaning', enhancing memorableness and thus enjoyment. In human resources development, stories have been used to aid teaching, management development, and team building (Greco, 1996). With their ability to reduce complexity, effective stories have been used in a planned way to enhance learning in orientation programs for new employees (Vance, 1991). Viewing managerial stories from the resource allocation frame also gives us insight into the concept of organizational memory. When stories with a strong felt meaning are told, they can reduce information overload and effect better storing and retrieving of information applicable to future action (Huber, 1991).

Mintzberg's *disturbance handler* role includes dealing with crises and conflicts. Martin (1988) observed stories being used in a software firm to symbolize a layoff in a way that made it seem less painful. One vice president's story was, 'They were good people. We were terminating positions, not people. It had nothing to do with the people. They were all good guys. It was just business necessity' (p. 219). The story that 'positions, not people' were being terminated gained general acceptance throughout the company. It was a story that had a felt meaning that was less painful in this particular setting than the counter story of terminating people. In another context, of course, the counter story might well have held sway. Mitroff and Kilmann's (1975) early contribution to the organizational storytelling literature shows stories used to help resolve conflict. The researchers brought persons with conflicting views of an organizational problem together in a group storytelling event to increase the parties' understanding and improve problem-solving quality. The aesthetic quality of connectedness would be essential in such storytelling in order to provide a resonating 'truth' claim in the persons rather than a basis for conflict.

In the *negotiator* role, stories play a part by helping mediate between parties who see different realities, by strengthening persuasive attempts, and by simulating newly proposed futures. Hawes (1991) mediated between pairs from competing subcultures within a large health information firm, helping each individual tell his or her story and achieve better understanding of the other's role. Greco (1996) gives several examples of storytelling as an aid to negotiation, among them how stakeholders in a community health care organization used stories to ' "tinker" with their current reality and to collectivize the vision of an anticipated or desired future' (p. 70). In both the Hawes and Greco cases, connectedness would clearly be essential to story quality. Boje (1991a) describes how a new CEO negotiated with his executives to gain adoption of his strategies. Boje notes that persuasive ability depends on knowledge of the stories of what has gone on leading up to the persuasive attempt, and the use of these stories to argue points. Here again, in terms of the aesthetic experience, the sense of connectedness between individuals' personal past experiences and the present would make a story powerful.

Both the disturbance handling and the negotiating manager aid organizational learning by telling stories that view learning as a social experience, occurring in communities of practice (Aram and Noble, 1999; Brown and Duguid, 1991; Crossan et al., 1999; Schein, 1996). These stories seek to connect people. Brown and Duguid (1991) characterized the practice of service technicians as creating and exchanging stories to diagnose problems and to add to the accumulated wisdom. Aesthetically strong stories would be more effective in facilitating these collaborative efforts since these stories would be more likely to be remembered and repeated. Through the shaping of artful stories, managers can assist in the exchange of knowledge, transport knowledge into new contexts, and consolidate knowledge from disparate points in the organization (Tsoukas, 1996).

Throughout this discussion, we have emphasized one or more of the three elements of the aesthetic experience – felt meaning, connectedness, and enjoyment for its own sake – as we have discussed how aesthetics informs the concepts of management storytelling. Of course, the three elements of aesthetic experience are not independent. Enjoyment may come from the feeling of connectedness, and the feeling of connectedness may be the result of the strength of the felt meaning. The three elements combine into the aesthetic whole of the story and it is the strength of that aesthetic whole that determines how good or bad a story is, and how that story might or might not contribute to the organization's learning.

Implications for Theory and Research

The research that we have cited shows that storytelling contributes across a broad spectrum of management functions. Adding the ideas about the aesthetic experience contributes to theory in two ways. The first is to add aesthetics as a moderating variable for the effectiveness of the story in performing the function. The second is to use aesthetics as a way to compare stories with one another. We shall illustrate by discussing the relationship between power and artfulness in management storytelling theory.

Many researchers explicitly consider power in their discussion of organizational stories. For example, Boje suggests that power is the explanation for why one story wins out over competing stories and becomes foregrounded (Boje, 1995; Boje et al., 1982). In contrast to this, Gabriel (1991b, 1995) finds that storytelling is used by the powerless in opposition to the power practices of the organization to gain power. We suggest that the artfulness of the storytelling moderates how well it is received and how effective the story is at creating an understanding of events that is accepted by members of the organization. Thus the artful, but otherwise powerless, organization member can use storytelling in opposition to other power practices as Gabriel suggests. Then the quality of storytelling is a source of power. The artful storyteller has successfully managed the meaning of events for some portion of the organization and this success is a source of power. If, as Boje suggests, it is the stories of the powerful that win out, the causality is not a simple case of power leading to winning stories. Storytelling quality also leads to power. Throughout this article we have shown artfulness, or a strong aesthetic quality, as a moderating variable in the oft-cited relationship between storytelling and organizational learning (e.g. Aram and Noble, 1999; Brown and Duguid, 1991; Crossan et al., 1999; Levitt and March, 1988; Rhodes, 1997; Vance, 1991).

Further research is needed on what constitutes storytelling quality. We suggest more studies of organizational stories as literature. Wills (1992) argues that Lincoln's Gettysburg Address was not only a revolution in ideas, it was a revolution in style. There are indications that much can be learned about organizational stories by applying hermeneutics, literary theory, and criticism to help identify the differences between more and less effective stories (White, 1992). We believe the same may be said for theories of drama and dramatic criticism.

We recommend efforts to learn more about the storytelling characteristics that distinguish 'healthy' from 'unhealthy' organizations (Boje, 1991a). Under what conditions and by what processes does organizational discourse become more plurivocal or more univocal (Boje, 1995), more spontaneous and creative or more controlled (Gabriel, 1995), more fantasy- and emotion-generating or more rational (Gabriel, 1991a)? Can storytelling increase the pleasure of organizational membership? More studies of organizational stories as literature are needed.

Our interest in management storytelling makes us want to know more about how storytelling can be used consciously to improve organizational effectiveness. By elaborating the role of managers' artful stories in organizational learning, we have aimed to take at least one step in the direction of beginning to understand how storytelling might relate to the conscious improvement of effectiveness. However, many questions remain. How, for example, can storytelling aid in the construction of shared meaning by a total organization? Boyce (1995) terms this knowledge 'a long way off'. How are audiences gained and how do storytelling networks form? We need to know more about how managers can most effectively and responsibly play a part in the diverse mix of stories evolving in the organization. How can managers influence the organizational storytelling that is always occurring?

Implications for Practice

The storytelling literature shows the broad array of leadership functions facilitated by stories. We have shown that all 10 of Mintzberg's managerial roles may be served by storytelling, and that artful stories told in each of these roles can facilitate learning. We have suggested that an aesthetic perspective promises to contribute new understanding of organizational storytelling and to help show how leaders and others can improve the effectiveness of their stories.

Given the broad applicability of storytelling to management, practitioners should be alert to the potential value of storytelling across the full spectrum of their activities. In situations where purely factual/rational information is being presented or exchanged, leaders should realize the value of stories for introducing human quality, emotion, and the creative energies that derive from fantasy, metaphor, and idealization (Gabriel, 1991a; Weick, 1985). In their storytelling, leaders should 'walk the talk', behaving consistently with the goals and ideals expressed in their stories (Martin and Powers, 1983;

Wilkins, 1984). Leaders should encourage others to tell stories as an aid to reflection and learning, to improve understanding across specialties and subcultures, and for cathartic release. The listening orientation toward others' stories adopted by the leader should be that of an 'enthusiastic audience' (Barry, 1997), attending to stories as valuable sources of information, not as arguments to be rebutted (Wilkins, 1984). The leader should be an active participant in the storytelling organization, helping collaboratively in the forming of stories that embody important meanings to stakeholders. The literature makes clear that leadership stories are not told exclusively by formal leaders. The diversity of stories present in organizations shows that nobody 'has the whole story'. As Wilkins and Thompson (1991: 25) suggest, all can learn by alternating 'between doubt and complexity on the one hand and passion and certainty on the other'. The artful story helps capture and communicate the effective manager's multi-layered meanings and thereby helps the organization learn.

Note

1. We recognize that we are equating 'good' with effective here in what may be an overly simplistic and managerialist way. We recognize that there are many possible criteria for what constitutes good (from critical, political, and ethical perspectives for example), but feel that 'effective' is a good place to start and illustrates the value of taking an aesthetic perspective.

References

Aram, E. and Noble, D. (1999) 'Educating Prospective Managers in the Complexity of Organizational Life', *Management Learning* 30: 321–42.

Barnard, C.I. (1938) *The Functions of the Executive*. Cambridge, MA: Harvard University Press.

Barry, D. (1997) 'Telling Changes: From Narrative Family Therapy to Organizational Change and Development', *Journal of Organizational Change Management* 10(1): 30–46.

Barry, D. and Elmes, M. (1997) 'Strategy Retold: Toward a Narrative View of Strategic Discourse', *Academy of Management Review* 22(2): 429–52.

Berleant, A. (1970) *The Aesthetic Field: A Phenomenology of Aesthetic Experience*. Springfield, IL: Charles C. Thomas.

Boje, D.M. (1991a) 'Consulting and Change in the Storytelling Organization', *Journal of Organizational Change Management* 4(3): 7–17.

Boje, D.M. (1991b) 'The Storytelling Organization: A Study of Story Performance in an Office-supply Firm', *Administrative Science Quarterly* 36(1): 106–26.

Boje, D.M. (1994) 'Organizational Storytelling: The Struggles of Premodern, Modern, and Postmodern Organizational Learning Discourses', *Management Learning* 25: 433–61.

Boje, D.M. (1995) 'Stories of the Storytelling Organization: A Postmodern Analysis of Disney as Tamara-Land', *Academy of Management Journal* 38(4): 997–1035.

Boje, D.M. (1998) 'The Postmodern Turn from Stories-as-Objects to Stories-in-Context Methods', Academy of Management 1998, Research Methods Forum No. 3. http://www.aom.pace.edu/rmd/1998_forum_postmodern_srories.html

Boje, D.M., Fedor, D.B. and Rowland, K.M. (1982) 'Myth Making: A Qualitative Step in OD Interventions', *Journal of Applied Behavioral Science* 18(1): 17–28.

Bowles, M.E. (1989) 'Myth, Meaning and Work Organization', *Organization Studies* 10(3): 405–21.

Boyce, M.E. (1995) 'Collective Centering and Collective Sense-making in the Stories of One Organization', *Organization Studies* 16(1): 107–37.

Boyce, M.E. (1996) 'Organizational Story and Storytelling: A Critical Review', *Journal of Organizational Change Management* 9(5): 5–26.

Brown, J.S. and Duguid, P. (1991) 'Organizational Learning and Communities-of-Practice: Toward a Unified View of Working, Learning, and Innovation', *Organization Science* 2: 40–57.

Browning, L.D. (1991) 'Organizational Narratives and Organizational Structure', *Journal of Organizational Change Management* 4(3): 59–67.

Bruner, J.S. (1990) *Acts of Meaning*. Cambridge, MA: Harvard University Press.

Courtney, R. (1995) *Drama and Feeling: An Aesthetic Theory*. Montreal: McGill-Queen's University Press.

Crossan, M.M., Lane, H.W. and White, R.E. (1999) 'An Organizational Learning Framework: From Intuition to Institution', *Academy of Management Review* 24: 522–37.

Csikszentmihalyi, M. and Robinson, R. (1990) *The Art of Seeing: An Interpretation of the Aesthetic*. Malibu, CA: Getty.

Cummings, S. and Brocklesby, J. (1997) 'Towards *Democratia*: Myth and the Management of Organizational Change in Ancient Athens', *Journal of Organizational Change Management* 10(1): 71–95.

Czarniawska, B. (1997) *Narrating the Organization*. Chicago: University of Chicago Press.

Czarniawska, B. (1998) *A Narrative Approach to Organization Studies*. Thousand Oaks, CA: Sage.

Dean, J.W. Jr, Ottensmeyer, E. and Ramirez, R. (1997) 'An Aesthetic Perspective on Organizations', in G.L. Cooper and S.E. Jackson (eds) *Creating Tomorrow's Organizations: A Handbook for Future Research in Organizational Behavior*, pp. 419–37. New York: Wiley.

Ebers, M. (1985) 'Understanding Organizations: The Poetic Mode', *Journal of Management* 11(2): 51–62.

Fletcher, C. (1996) '"The 250 lb man in the alley": Police storytelling', *Journal of Organizational Change Management* 9(5): 36–42.

Fine, E.C. (1984) *The Folklore Text: From Performance to Print*. Bloomington: Indiana University Press.

Gabriel, Y. (1991a) 'On Organizational Stories and Myths: Why It Is Easier to Slay a Dragon Than to Kill a Myth', *International Sociology* 6(4): 427–42.

Gabriel, Y. (1991b) 'Turning Facts into Stories and Stories into Facts: A Hermeneutic Exploration of Organizational Folklore', *Human Relations* 44: 857–75.

Gabriel, Y. (1995) 'The Unmanaged Organization: Stories, Fantasies and Subjectivity', *Organization Studies* 16(3): 477–501.

Gabriel, Y. (1999) 'Beyond Happy Families: A Critical Reevaluation of the Control–Resistance–Identity triangle', *Human Relations* 52(2): 179–203.

Gardner, H. (1995) *Leading Minds: An Anatomy of Leadership*. New York: Basic Books.

Gephart, R.P. Jr (1991) 'Succession Sensemaking and Organizational Change: A Story of a Deviant College President', *Journal of Organizational Change Management* 4(3): 35–44.

Glynn, M.A. (2000) 'When Cymbals Become Symbols', *Organization Science* 11: 285–98.

Greco, J. (1996) 'Stories for Executive Development: An Isometric Solution', *Journal of Organizational Change Management* 9(5): 43–74.

Hansen, C.D. and Kahnweiler, W.M. (1993) 'Storytelling: An Instrument for Understanding the Dynamics of Corporate Relationships', *Human Relations* 46(12): 1391–409.

Harrison, J.D. (2000) 'Multiple Imagings of Institutional Identity', *Journal of Applied Behavioral Science* 36(4): 425–55.

Hawes, L.C. (1991) 'Organizing Narratives/Codes/Poetics', *Journal of Organizational Change Management* 4(3): 45–51.

Huber, G.P. (1991) 'Organizational Learning: The Contributing Processes and the Literatures', *Organization Science* 2: 88–115.

Kristeva, J. (1986) 'Word, Dialogue and Novel', in T. Moi (ed.) *The Kristeva Reader*, pp. 34–61. New York: Columbia University Press.

Levitt, B. and March, J.G. (1988) 'Organizational Learning', *Annual Review of Sociology* 14: 319–40.

Martin, J. (1982) 'Stories and Scripts in Organizational Settings', in A. Hasdorf and A. Isen (eds) *Cognitive Social Psychology*, pp. 255–305. New York: Elsevier-North Holland.

Martin, J. (1988) 'Symbolic Responses to Layoffs in a Software Manufacturing Firm: Managing the Meaning of an Event', in M.O. James, M.D. Snyder and R.C. Snyder (eds) *Inside Organizations: Understanding the Human Dimension*, pp. 209–25. Newbury Park, CA: Sage.

Martin, J. and Powers, M.E. (1983) 'Truth or Corporate Propaganda: The Value of a Good War Story', in L.R. Pondy (ed.) *Organizational Symbolism*, pp. 93–107. Greenwich, CT: JAI Press.

Mintzberg, H. (1973) *The Nature of Managerial Work*. New York: Harper & Row.

Mitroff, I.I. and Kilmann, R.H. (1975) 'Stories Managers Tell: A New Tool for Organizational Problem Solving', *Management Review* (July): 18–28.

Ottensmeyer, E.J. (1996) 'Too Strong to Stop, Too Sweet to Lose: Aesthetics as a Way to Know Organizations', *Organization* 3(2): 189–94.

Pacanowsky, M.E. and O'Donnell-Trujillo, N. (1983) 'Organizational Communication as Cultural Performance', *Communication Monographs* 50(June): 126–47.

Peirce, C.S. (1957) *Essays in the Philosophy of Science*. New York: The Liberal Arts Press.

Peters, T.J. and Waterman, R.H. (1982) *In Search of Excellence*. New York: Harper & Row.

Plottel, J.P. and Charney, H. (1978) *Intertextuality: New Perspectives in Criticism*. New York: New York Literary Forum.

Ramirez, R. (1991) *The Beauty of Social Organization*. Munich: Accedo.

Ramirez, R. (1996) 'Wrapping Form and Organizational Beauty', *Organization* 3(2): 233–42.

Rhodes, C. (1997) 'The Legitimation of Learning in Organizational Settings', *Journal of Organizational Change Management* 10(1): 10–20.

Rosile, G.A. (1998) 'Restorying and the Case of the Sci-Fi Organization', paper presented at the Academy of Management annual meeting, San Diego, CA.

Schein, E.H. (1996) 'Organizational Learning: What Is New?', Society for Organizational Learning, working paper no. 10.012, website: http://www.solonline.org/res/wp/10012. html

Segal, A. (1997) 'Flowering Feminism: Consciousness Raising at Work', *Journal of Organizational Change Management* 9(5): 75–90.

Stevenson, W.B. and Greenberg, D.N. (1998) 'The Formal Analysis of Narratives of Organizational Change', *Journal of Management* 24(6): 741–62.

Strati, A. (1992) 'Aesthetic Understanding of Organizational Life', *Academy of Management Review* 17(3): 568–81.

Strati, A. (1996) 'Organizations Viewed through the Lens of Aesthetics', *Organization* 3(2): 209–18.

Stutts, N.B. and Barker, R.J. (1999) 'The Use of Normative Paradigm Theory in Assessing Audience Value Conflict in Image Advertising', *Management Communication Quarterly* 13(2): 209–44.

Torbert, W.R. (1991) *The Power of Balance: Transforming Self, Society, and Scientific Inquiry*. Newbury Park, CA: Sage.

Tracy, S.J. (2000) 'Becoming a Character for Commerce', *Management Communication Quarterly* 14(1): 90–128.

Tsoukas, H. (1996) 'The Firm as a Distributed Knowledge System: A Constructionist Approach', *Strategic Management Journal* 17: 11–25.

Vaill, P.B. (1989) *Managing as a Performing Art*. San Francisco: Jossey-Bass.

Vance, C.M. (1991) 'Formalizing Storytelling in Organizations: A Key Agenda for the Design of Training', *Journal of Organizational Change Management* 4(3): 52–8.

Watson, T J. (2001) *In Search of Management: Culture, Chaos and Control in Managerial Work*. London: Thomson Learning.

Weick, K.E. (1985) 'Cosmos v. Chaos: Sense and Nonsense in Electronic Contexts', *Organizational Dynamics* 14(2), 51–64.

Weick, K.E. (1995) *Sensemaking in Organizations*. Thousand Oaks, CA: Sage.

White, D.A. (1996) ' "It's Working Beautifully!" Philosophical Reflections on Aesthetics and Organization Theory', *Organization* 3(2): 195–208.

White, J.D. (1992) 'Taking Language Seriously: Toward a Narrative Theory of Knowledge for Administrative Research', *American Review of Public Administration* 22(2): 75–88.

White, M. and Epston, D. (1990) *Narrative Means to Therapeutic Ends*. New York: W.W. Norton.

Wilkins, A.L. (1984) 'The Creation of Company Cultures: The Role of Stories and Human Resource Systems', *Human Resource Management* 23(1): 41–60.

Wilkins, A.L. and Thompson, M.P. (1991) 'On Getting the Story Crooked and Straight', *Journal of Organizational Change Management* 4(3): 18–26.

Wills, G. (1992) *Lincoln at Gettysburg: Words that Remade America.* New York: Simon & Schuster.

Yukl, G. (1998) *Leadership in Organizations,* 4th edn. Upper Saddle River, NJ: Prentice Hall.

Index